CRETE

Eberhard Fohrer

The Traveller's Guide

SPR
BO

Crete: the Traveller's Guide
First English edition 1990
Translated from the fifth German edition

Published by Springfield Books Limited, Norman Road, Denby Dale, Huddersfield HD8 8TH, West Yorkshire, England.
© **Copyright 1990 Michael Müller Verlag**, Erlangen, West-Germany.

TRANSLATION	Jill Pittinger
COVER DESIGN	Brian Ledgard
MAPS	Petra Rost
PHOTOGRAPHY	Eberhard Fohrer
TYPE SETTING	Michael Müller Verlag

British Library Cataloguing in Publication Data
Crete: the Travoller's guide.
   1. Greece. Crete - Visitors's guide
   I. Title II. Kreta. English
   914.9980446
   ISBN 0-947655-86-7

© This book ist copyright under the Berne Convention. All rights are reserved. Apart from any fair dealing for the purposes of private study, research, criticizm or review, as permitted under the Copyright Act, 1956, no part of this publication may be reproduced, stored in a retrieval system, or transmitted in any form or by any means, electronic, electrical, chemical, mechanical, optical, photocopying, recording or otherwise, without the prior permission of the copyright owner. Enquiries should be adressed to the publishers.
The Authors and publishers accept no responsibility for accuracy of information contained in this book.
Printed and bound in West-Germany by Alfa Druck Ltd. Göttingen.

CONTENTS

Crete 63

Traditions 83

History 97

Central Crete 121

Iraklion 124

As might be expected, a large island like Crete has its own dialect and variations in the pronounciation of Greek. The letter γ, which we have transliterated as g in "Agios, Agia, Agii, Sougia and Anogia" is pronounced y as in "yes" on the mainland, but a more approximate transliteration of the Cretan pronounciation would be a softened j, approaching the sound "sh". Cretans themselves transliterate as "gh", as for example "Aghios Nikolaos", on their road signs.

Help us update
We've done our best to make this book as accurate and up-to-date as possible but travel developments are swift and things are always changing. We would greatly appreciate any contributions, suggestions, corrections, improvements or additions you may have for future editions.
Please write us:
Springfield Books Limited c/o Eberhard Fohrer, Norman Road, Denby Dale, Huddersfield HD8 8TH, West Yorkshire, England

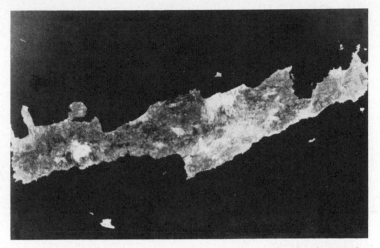

Crete from a height of 620 miles

A trip to Crete . . .

You have chosen well. Crete offers you the most stable weather conditions in the Mediterranean; the sun shines down from a mostly cloudless sky from March until well into October. When the leaves are turning brown at home, you can still enjoy carefree bathing on the southern coast of Crete. There is no industry on the island. Thus there is hardly any air pollution. The waters, too, especially along the western and southern coasts, are among the cleanest in the whole of the Mediterranean.

The Cretans are a hospitable people, even when their patience is sorely tried at times by the overwhelming onslaught of tourists. Prices are still within reason on the island; for example, a complete meal for two people, including wine, will cost c. £7-9 in a taverna. You can hire a car in practically every bathing resort and make excursions into the wonderful mountain scenery. Organised tours by bus, jeep etc. are also frequently offered. There is accommodation everywhere along the coast, and in every price range; you will probably find a bed even in the remotest mountain village.

From the remains of the great Minoan civilisation right down to the Turkish minarets above the old city of Rethymnon, the rich island past has left a great number of places of interest to the visitor. Crete is the cradle of European civilisation. When we were still puffing and grunting our way with wooden clubs and stone axes through the dark forests of central and northern Europe, Minoan craftsmen were already hammering out wafer-thin gold jewellery and producing colourful frescoes that attest to a full *enjoyment of life*. This is exactly what I would like to wish you during your stay on one of the most beautiful islands of the Mediterranean.

At a glance

Crete is a mountain range in the sea and a continent in miniature. The highest peaks rise to eight thousand feet. However, the landscape is also characterised by fertile plains, broad hills, superb vines, millions of silvery-green olive trees, and countless little churches and monasteries. You will find beautiful beaches everywhere on the island, from the palm beach of Vai in the east to the south-sea island beach of Elafonisi in the extreme south-west.

Iraklion. The capital city; a point of arrival and departure for nearly every traveller to Crete. Visit the Archaeological Museum and the world-famous excavations at Knossos.

Rethymnon and Chania. The two most beautiful cities on Crete. Relics of the Venetian and Turkish periods give them their unique character.

Samaria Gorge. One of the most impressive gorges in Europe, deep in the White Mountains in the west of the island. The 10-mile trek down to the Sea of Libya is almost a must.

Lassithi High Plateau. Birthplace of Zeus, father of the gods. This almost circular high plateau is famous for the white sails of its windmills, and for the dark cave of Psychro.

Agios Nikolaos. One of the most favourite of all the holiday resorts, with its countless hotels, tavernas, discos and bustling atmosphere. Very near to it is the well-known Church of Panagia Kera, containing fantastic wall paintings from the 13th/14th centuries.

Spinalonga. A trip to this former leper colony makes a fascinating excursion from Agios Nikolaos. Converted fishing boats also go over there from Elounda.

Matala. Cave dwellings in soft sandstone cliffs, inhabited by Hippies in the seventies; today Matala is a superbly beautiful sandy bay, with tavernas built almost on the sand.

Monastery of Arkadi. The island's national monument. 964 beleaguered Cretans blew themselves up here on 9th November, 1866, to avoid surrender to the Turkish overlords.

Psiloritis. The roof of Crete. The ascent from the Nida High Plateau takes from 4 to 5 hours. At the top, you are greeted by a stillness that can hardly be described.

Plakias. If you have your surfboard with you, come to this dream of a beach on the south coast. Even if you haven't got a surfboard, you should still come . . .

How to get to there

By air

Daedalos did it first. He flew from Crete straight across the Mediterranean to Sicily. Certainly 90% of all modern tourists choose this method of getting to the island; the flight is comfortable, quick, and mostly inexpensive. However, book as early as you can. Direct flights to Crete are quickly sold out.

It is possible to take a charter flight direct to *Iraklion* (seldom to Chania) from the United Kingdom or Ireland. One variation is to take a charter or scheduled flight to Athens and then go on to Crete either by boat or on an internal flight of Olympic Airways.

You can book a *package holiday* to Crete at every travel agency, and not a few agencies nowadays specialise in Greece and even Crete; these offer especially reasonable packages. Collect your information early and compare the prices.

• **Charter flights**: Direct flights to Crete cost around £130-190, and limit you to a stay of four weeks. They are only sold with what is usually a "pro forma" accommodation voucher, to keep the price of the flight low. This means that you cannot avail yourself of the accommodation mentioned on the voucher, but you are also not paying for it. The Greek authorities have been trying to stop this practice since 1988. According to official sources there, travellers can be sent back to where they came from, if they are in possession of a voucher for unlicensed accommodation in Greece. Up till now, however, this rule only exists on paper. Ask your travel agent. Flights are offered in all the large daily newspapers, and also in the magazine **Time Out**/London.

Charter flights to Athens are quite a bit cheaper and because of the large number on offer, they are by no means as quickly booked out as those to Crete. Naturally, however, you should be prepared for delays because of the need to change onto boats or flights to Crete. You can only make a minimal saving with a flight to Athens. Probably bookings made through bucket shops (last minute vacancies) are of interest, and there are sometimes considerable savings to be made in this way.

• **Scheduled airlines**: These do not fly directly to Crete, only to Athens. An advantage is that you can usually book at quite a late date and can stay in the country longer. **APEX flights** are the most reasonable and cost c. £240-280 from London. Olympic Airways usually have interesting offers, especially for students (see next paragraph).

• **Student flights**: These cost c. £120-190, according to season. You must have an international ISIC card, or be under 26 years of age. **USIT** (London Student Travel, 52, Grosvenor Gardens, London SW1 0AG, tel. 01/7303402 and **USIT** (7, Anglesea Street, Dublin 2, Ireland, tel. 0001/778117) have some good offers, and so do **Olympic Airways** (164/5, Piccadilly, London W1V 9DE, tel. 01/4933965). The latter offer a reduction on inland flights if you buy an international ticket. You can also buy one-way tickets in student travel bureaux. These are ideal if you want to stay longer.

• **Flights from the USA**: The range of these on offer is bewildering and extremely varied. Normal scheduled flights are very expensive, but it is possible to make a saving. If you fly in the low season, the prices fall considerably. Even a **one-way flight** to London can save you quite a bit, and you will easily find a cheap return flight in Athens, which is one of the biggest markets for cheap flights in Europe. Otherwise, you should make use of the **APEX tariff** (with a stay of up to 6 months) or **standby**; although the latter affords you the greatest freedom of movement (you can fly out and back whenever you wish), the number of places available is greatly reduced during the high season and can lead to nerve-racking periods of waiting. Olympic Airways offer especially reasonable flights to Athens.

Charter flights are the cheapest means. With these, you can stay up to one year. Once you have booked, however, the dates are fixed and you can only change them on payment of high cancellation fees. There are some interesting special offers towards the end of the season, when the planes are no longer full. Check in the large daily newspapers. One large agency for flights worldwide is **CIEE** (Council on International Education Exchange), 205 E. 42nd St., New York, N.Y. 10017, tel. 212/6611450. Book as early as possible.

By car

Very few people will want to get to Crete by car. The journey of a good 1900 miles from London to Athens is hardly a trifle. For those who want to make the journey across Europe, here are a few observations.

Generally speaking, there are two possibilities. You can either take the longer overland route via Yugoslavia, or the shorter one via Italy and then take the ferry across to Greece. There is a section on ferry connections in a separate chapter further on. Bear in mind that there are tolls payable on the Italian motorways. An interesting stop on the way is *Verona* in northern Italy. Saunter across the Piazza del Erbe with its fine fruit and vegetable market, and visit the huge Roman amphitheatre and Juliet's balcony. You can obtain petrol coupons for Italy from your automobile club (AA).

The way down through Yugoslavia seems endless and is not very exciting, apart from the Alps and some areas in Greece. However the infamous *Autoput*, the long-distance through road which extends from northern Yugoslavia almost to the Greek border, certainly is exciting, since it is not yet entirely built to take four-lane traffic. This means that you and your vehicle will move along in a column of smelly lorries, caravans, and saloon cars filled to bursting with Turks who have been working abroad and are returning home. You need the greatest concentration, as again and again drivers who have been on the road for a long time attempt adventurous overtaking. The burnt-out wrecks on the sides of the road indicate what can happen. Drive carefully and not too fast; the Yugoslavian police like to collect on-the-spot fines (maximum speed permitted on the motorway is 120 km/h (75 m.p.h.), on main roads 100 km/h (62.5 m.p.h.), on all other roads 80 km/h (50 m.p.h.) and in villages 60 km/h (37.5 m.p.h.). Overnight accommodation is available at numerous camping sites connected to expensive motels (private rooms away from the through road are cheaper, c. £9-10 for a double room (DR). You can save quite a bit with petrol coupons, which can be obtained at the Austrian/Yugoslavian border. The motorway runs through the capital *Belgrade;* an interesting place to see, but not worth a stay. In Greece, the main through road to Athens runs near the east coast, and in places you drive directly along beside the sea; you also pass close by the Olympus mountain range, which is well-known from mythology. Motorway tolls (in contrast to those in Italy) are minimal in both Greece and Yugoslavia.

Tip: Before departure, obtain information on speed limits, particular traffic restrictions, and prices of petrol in the countries you will be passing through. The **Green Card** (insurance) is necessary.

By train

You can either go via France and Italy and cross to Greece by ship from there (information in the next chapter), or choose the long railway line through Yugoslavia to Athens.

You will need incredible powers of perseverance if you choose the latter. The journey lasts 50-60 hours. Much more pleasant, even though it does entail changing several times, is the trip via Italy.

The exercise is only worth it from a financial point of view if you take an Interrail ticket. For £139, provided you are under 26 years of age, you can travel over all the state railway networks of most European countries for a period of four weeks (in Britain, however, will you have to pay half the cost of the journey). You should reckon on paying c. £200 return on the *Transalpino* or *Eurotrain* (including the ferry). A normal train ticket will cost you a good £240 return.

In summer, the trains are hopelessly crowded, so reserve your seat early and also your place in a sleeping car, if you want one! Take enough food with you, as the dining cars are not cheap.

By coach

This is the cheapest way to get there. You will have to pay around £100 for the trip from London to Athens. Be prepared for a three-day journey with very short breaks on the way, and take adequate supplies of food and drink with you. You will be more than thankful when you finally get there!

• COACH COMPANIES: There are more and more of these every year, and not all of them are serious enterprises. **USIT London Student Travel**, 52, Grosvenor Gardens, London SW1W 0AU, tel. 017303402) and **Miracle Bus** (408, The Strand, London WC2, tel. 01/3796055) are recommended.

Thumbing your way down

Ostend in Belgium is a good point of departure. Long distance lorries travel half-way across Europe every day. Perhaps you will even get a lift to Greece? Otherwise, try your luck through Italy; the route is more varied, there are interesting cities to see and the trains are reasonable in price, if you can't get a lift.

Connections by ferry from Italy to Greece

There are ferries to Greece from Trieste, Venice, Ancona, Bari, Brindisi and Otranto on the east coast of Italy.

The most important port of arrival is *Patras*, and from there you proceed to Athens along a well-constructed fast road (or on a stopping train which leaves several times daily and takes about 5 hours) to *Athens/Piraeus*, the port from which several ferries depart daily for Crete.

British Ferries operate a service once a week from *Venice* to Piraeus (39 hours), while Adriatica Lines even go directly to Iraklion on Crete, 3-4 times every month, from April to December. This crossing is by far the longest and most expensive, but Venice is the northernmost ferry port and thus the nearest for you (c. 1,100 miles from London).

Most convenient is undoubtedly the crossing from *Ancona* - ships operated by Marlines sail once a week from June to September directly to *Iraklion* on Crete! There is no better way to get to Crete; although the crossing takes 55 hours, the ships are relatively comfortable and you can make friends gradually with the hot Mediterranean sun on the way. There are also frequent boats to Patras from Ancona, just in case you are planning a little tour of the Peloponnese before your stay on Crete.

You would be well advised to book your passage through a travel agency at home, before setting off. Many ferries are booked out in summer; to arrive exhausted at a harbour, only to find that the ship is full when you come to buy your ticket, is more than annoying. Take note of the fact that most ferry companies require you to be at the harbour at least two hours before departure time. Otherwise you may lose your reservation!

• PRICES (high season): **Venice - Iraklion** (Adriatica Lines), berth in a cabin £139-262. Students and young people get a slight reduction. Cars £115-172.
Venice - Piraeus (British Ferries), berth in a cabin with all meals £167-434, cars £77-110.

Ancona - Iraklion (Marlines), berth in a cabin £86-166, pullman-type seats £54, deck class £46.00, cars £91-107.
Ancona - Patras (various shipping lines), berth in a cabin £47-120, pullman-type seats £37, deck class £30, cars £57-67.

▶ **From the Greek mainland to Crete** (by ship): *Athens/Piraeus* is the most important harbour for the ferries to Crete. There are two ferries direct to *Iraklion* and one to *Chania* every evening at about 7.00 p.m., operated by ANEK and Minoan Lines. In addition, there are two ferries nearly every morning (at about 8.00 a.m.), one to Iraklion and one to Chania. Tickets can be obtained from the agencies in the harbour at Piraeus, it is cheaper to buy them there than through your travel agency at home. As the ferries are seldom completely booked up, there is little risk involved.

There are other possibilities. You can make the crossing from Githion in the Peloponnese to Kastelli in western Crete twice a week, and there is also a ferry once weekly from Thessaloniki in northern Greece to both Chania and Iraklion. Some ferries from Piraeus also stop at some of the smaller Greek islands on their way to Agios Nikolaos or Sitia in eastern Crete.

• PRICES: **Piraeus** to **Iraklion** - berth in a cabin £19-27, pullman-type seats (tourist class) £14, deck class £11, cars £30-40.

▶ **From Athens to Crete** (by air): Greek domestic flights are among the cheapest in Europe. The flight from *Athens/West Terminal* to *Iraklion* costs around £30 (night flights £25); the flight from Athens to *Chania* costs £27 (night flight £22). There are several flights daily, and the journey takes 45-50 minutes. Tickets for these flights are also considerably more expensive if you purchase them outside Greece. If you travel to Athens on a foreign airline and wish to change onto a Greek plane, you will have to go to another air terminal (details in the chapter Athens/Arrivals and Departures). The same also applies to your return journey.

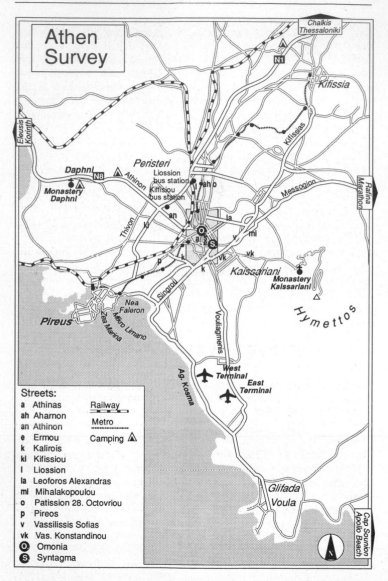

Athen Survey

Chalkis
Thessaloniki

N1

Kifissia

Kifissias

Messogion

Rafina
Marathon

Eleusis
Korinth

Daphni   N8
Monastery
Daphni

Athinon

Peristeri

Liossion
bus station

Kifisiou
bus station

ah   o

Thivon

ki

an

la

ml

O
a   e
S

v

p   k

vk

vk

Kaissariani

Monastery
Kaissariani

Hymettos

Nea
Faleron

Sigrou

Pireus

Mikro Limano

Zea Marina

Vouliagmenis

Ag. Kosma

West
Terminal

East
Terminal

Glifada

Voula

Cap Sounion
Apollo Beach

N

Streets:

a	Athinas
ah	Aharnon
an	Athinon
e	Ermou
k	Kalirois
ki	Kifissiou
l	Liossion
la	Leoforos Alexandras
ml	Mihalakopoulou
o	Patission 28. Octovriou
p	Pireos
v	Vassilissis Sofias
vk	Vas. Konstandinou
O	Omonia
S	Syntagma

Railway

Metro

Camping △

The changing of the guard at 35° C in the shade

A Stop-over in Athens

The Greek capital does not have the very best of reputations among European cities. A high degree of air pollution, endless traffic jams, noise and indiscriminate building activities permit only a glimpse of the spirit of Classical Antiquity.

However, do not let yourself be frightened off. Athens is the Greek city *par excellence*! This bubbling mixture of oriental-type bazaars and the elegant atmosphere of a great city, seasoned with the numerous ruins from its great history and the business-like atmosphere of Piraeus, one of the world's great harbours, will provide an exciting contrast to the peaceful landscape of Crete. Two or three days in Athens are just as much part of the Greek "experience" as the braying of a solitary donkey and the friendly "*kalimera*" of a Cretan vine-grower. Every Greek knows Athens. If you want to get to know and understand Greece, you should also have seen Athens. *Zorba the Greek* and his English friend waited in Piraeus for their ship to Crete, too, while the salty spray from the sea made patterns on the windows of the kafenion.

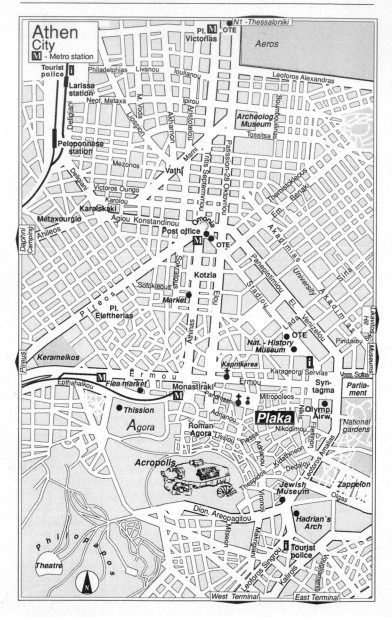

• ARRIVALS AND DEPARTURES (by air): All planes belonging to foreign airlines take off and land at the **East Terminal**. Planes operated by Olympic Airways (both domestic and international flights) use the **West Terminal**. The terminals are situated at opposite ends of the large airport in Athens. If you have to change onto an Olympic Airways flight to Crete, you will have to change terminals. **Express Bus no.19** runs every 30 minutes between the East and West terminals. It continues on to **Piraeus** and stops there at Karaiskaki Square, directly on the quay. Thus you can go directly from the airport to the harbour and vice versa.

You can get from the East Terminal to the centre of the city (Syntagma or Omonia Square) on **Express bus A** or B; if you are going to the station, only take bus B. These double-deckers run about every 20 minutes directly from the terminal exit. **Express Buses A̶ or B̶** run from the West Terminal (if you are going to the station, only take bus B̶).

If you want to go from the centre to the airport, the bus stop for the express buses is situated on the upper side of Syntagma, opposite the National Gardens and in front of the office of Japan Airlines.

• ARRIVALS AND DEPARTURES (by train): The incredibly small main railway station of Athens (**Larissis Station**) is a little outside the centre. The yellow trolley bus no. 1 stops on the right before the station (when you come out of it) and brings you to the centre (Omonia or Syntagma Square), and so do Express buses B and B̶. You can also walk straight on from the station to the nearest underground station at **Victoria Square** (about 7 minutes away).

• TRANSPORT IN ATHENS: There is one single **underground line**, which runs from the suburb of Kifisia, through the centre, and on to Piraeus. Important stations in the city are Omonia, Monastiraki and Thission. The station at the end of the line in Piraeus is directly at the place where the ferries leave for Crete. Note: Travel is free on the Metro before 8.00 a.m.

In addition, there are numerous **bus connections**. The easiest buses to use are the double-decker **express buses** mentioned above. These were only introduced in 1988, and run from the airport through the centre of the city to the railway station and the large bus stations.

• LEFT LUGGAGE: A left luggage facility is available in a small building in front of the departure hall at the **East Terminal**, at **Larissis Station**, and at **Pacific Travel**, 24, Nikis Street, near Syntagma. (In Pacific Travel it costs around 70p per piece; Mon-Sat 7.00 a.m.-8.00 p.m., Sun. 7.00 a.m.-2.00p.m, tel. 3241007.)

• INFORMATION: You can acquire a lot of information (including bus and boat timetables), and in particular, a good **free map of the city** - you really must have one in Athens! - from the **National Bank** in Syntagma Square (Mon-Fri 8.00 a.m.-8.00 p.m., Sat 9.00 a.m.-3.00 p.m., Sun 9.00 a.m.-1.00 p.m.) Another such office has been established in the **General Bank** on the same square, on the corner of Ermou St.

• ACCOMMODATION: Athens is full of visitors, thus you will not find a room right away in every hotel. A place where you can nearly always get a room for a reasonable price is at the large **Attalos Hotel**, in a central position at 29, Athinas St. The rooms are simple but clean, sheets are changed every day, the management is friendly not to mention the attractive roof garden with a view out over the floodlit Acropolis. Cost c. £19 for a DR (double room) with bath (without bath, c. £14). Single room with a bath £14, without a bath £10. Tel. 01/3212801. The attractive **Acropolis House** is also a pleasant place to stay. It is in a quiet but very central location on the edge of Plaka, at 6-8, Kodrou St. There are some fine historic rooms here, but also some modern ones of average quality, at £19 for a DR with bath. Tel. 01/3222344. A simple but friendly hotel is the **Ermiou** on noisy Ermou St. (no. 66) Tel. 3212753. A DR costs c.£13, single room £9. The owners's son lived in the USA for many years and speaks perfect English.

For those with modest means there are numerous hostels, where you can either have a double room (c. £10) or sleep in a dormitory (c. £5). Such accommodation does not offer all the home comforts, of course. You should take your own sleeping bag. Recommended addresses are **Diethnes** (52, Peoniou St, directly by the railway station, tel. 01/8832878), **Thisseos Inn** (10, Thisseos St., near Plaka, tel. 01/3245960) and **Festos**

Guest House (18, Filellinon St., near Plaka/Syntagma, tel. 01/3232455).
For those with more demanding tastes the newly-established and comfortable **Hotel Oscar** (by the railway station) is worth a visit. A DR costs c. £27-32 without breakfast. Tel. 01/8834215-19.
Camping Dafni is situated 6.25 miles to the west of the city centre, directly on the motorway (buses go there from Eleftherias Square).

— ★ —

• FOOD: Of paramount importance in Athens. The tavernas in Plaka impart a lot of atmosphere, as long as you keep away from the places which cater completely for what they consider to be tourists' wishes.
One of the best tavernas in Athens, and always full down the last available chair, is **Xinos** (4, Angelou Geronta St., a side alley off Kidathineon St.). You should definitely arrive there early. A little away from the main route through Plaka is the **Tsegoura** Taverna; efficient service here, a fig tree is growing through the roof and the whole place has a very original atmosphere (Tripodon St.). Equally recommended is the friendly **Gerani Ouzeri**, opposite Tsegoura. A lot of Athenian students congregate here.
The food at the cellar taverna of **Damigos** (41, Kidathineon St.) is nothing out of the ordinary, but you can try the best retsina in the whole city here. The proprietor comes from an old family of

wine producers and still makes his retsina the traditional way in resinated barrels.
Not in Plaka, but thoroughly worth a visit, is **Socrates Prison**, south of the Acropolis (20, Mitseon). The proprietor, Socrates, is tied to the kitchen for 16 hours every day, and this is his "prison". What he conjures up there is, however, interesting and tasty. Some of his dishes are to be found nowhere else in Greece.
If you want to see Athens by candlelight from up above, take the cable car up to the slightly more expensive **Dionysos** Restaurant on Lycavettos Hill.
Those who wish to eat very reasonably can have a couple of souvlaki from the souvlaki "factory" **Thanasis** (Mitropoleos St., near Monastiraki). If you want to spend rather more money, then go out to the little yacht harbour of **Mikrolimano**, in Piraeus. The best and most expensive fish restaurants in the whole city are grouped around the harbour there.

Sightseeing

Let me select a few highlights which you should not miss during a short stay in Athens.

Acropolis: The Acropolis is not the only sight to have seen in Athens, but it is certainly a "must". At present, it is undergoing the restoration of the century; this is so thorough that not a few of the temples are covered in scaffolding and inaccessible. The most impressive buildings are the massive *Parthenon* (bombarded by Venetian cannon in 1687, when it was used as a munitions dump by the Turks), and the *Erechtheion*, with the famous caryatids (all of them copies, but you can admire one of the original statues in the British Museum in London, home of the Elgin Marbles).

Some fine pieces, statues and groups of figures from the ancient temples, are in the *Acropolis Museum*; the remaining original figures from the Erechtheion are also here. There is, of course, a wonderful view from up here over the city (Mon-Fri 8.00 a.m.-7.00 p.m., Sat/Sun 8.30 a.m.-3.00 p.m. Admission c. £3, students half price). The opening times of the Acropolis Museum are the same, except that on Mondays it is only open from 12.00-6.30 p.m. Be careful, these opening times change frequently!

Museums: Naturally, the *National Museum* in Patission/Tositsa St. has the largest collection of antiquities of all the Greek museums. You will need a good 2-3 hours to go round it. A highlight is the exhibition of frescoes, which are over three thousand years old, from the island of Santorini; these are on the upper floor. (Tues-Fri 8.00 a.m.-7.00 p.m., Sat/Sun 8.30 a.m.-3.00 p.m., Mon 12.30 p.m.-7.00 p.m. Admission c. £3. Students half price.)

Brand new and well worth a visit is the very modern *Museum of Cycladic Art* (4, Neofitou Douka, near Syntagma), which contains a large number of beautiful figurines from the islands between Athens and Crete. This area developed a culture of its own, which was vastly independent of the Cretan-Minoan civilisation. The presentation and documentation of the exhibits is exemplary. (Closed on Sundays and Tuesdays, otherwise 10.00 a.m.-4.00 p.m., Sat only until 3.00 p.m. Admission c. £1.)

You can delve into a more recent chapter of Greek history at the *Jewish Museum* (36, Amalias, opposite Hadrian's Arch). This houses a small but very interesting collection of religious objects from the rich Jewish culture of Greece. The staff belong to the little Jewish community of Athens; they are very attentive and interested in visitors to their museum. (Sun-Fri 9.00 a.m.-1.00 p.m. Donations are requested.)

Athens today: probably the most important part of your sightseeing in the city. The "highlight" is literally a visit to *Lycavettos Hill*, the highest point in the city. There is a cable car from Ploutarchou St. to the summit. There is a superb view of Athens and even a passable restaurant up here.

If high places are not for you, and you prefer to keep your feet firmly on the ground, make a visit to the fantastic *market* on Athinas St. The butchers' stalls are an experience by themselves, as is the hectic activity going on there. You can find steamy little market tavernas in the middle of the hall, where you really can eat in very authentic surroundings. Tourists are hardly ever seen here.

Only a little way away, next to the Metro station on Monastiraki Square, there is the entrance to the Athens *Flea Market*. This is huge, and there is great fun to be had sauntering through it. Of course, everything is no longer very cheap here.

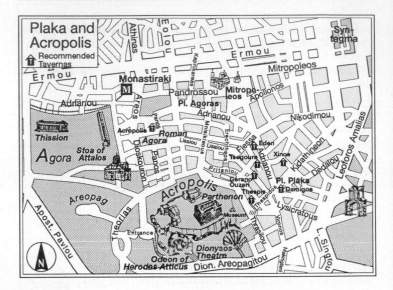

Plaka begins on the other side of Monastiraki; this is the famous old quarter of Athens, where you will probably spend your evenings. Most of the nightlife of Athens takes place here, and there is one taverna next to the other. Higher up on the attractive stepped alleyways are the bouzouki establishments. Some of the shops offer interesting leather goods, but there is also a lot of superfluous stuff for tourists. I have already recommended a couple of tavernas to you; when you are sitting here after your second (or third?) retsina, listening to the bouzoukis and watching the people streaming by, then you really are in Greece!

Practical Information

▶ **Personal Documents**: A valid *passport* is necessary for entry into Greece, and for a stay of up to three months.

▶ **Currency**: The Greek *drachma* is not a stable currency. Its value is constantly falling against the pound sterling and the dollar. Thus, for northern European visitors, prices have happily remained constant over recent years; but this is not the case for the Greeks themselves, who have had to endure horrendous rises in prices since their entry into the EC. However, Greece is no longer a cheap place for a holiday. The prices are lower here than they are in Britain, but not as low as for example in Morocco or Turkey.

Current Exchange Rate in Greece: £1 sterling = 270 Drs.

As of recently, you are only allowed to bring in 100,000 Drs to Greece (there is no limit on foreign currency, but amounts of more than 1,000 US$ have to be declared at the border). The exchange rate in Greece, and of course Crete, is much more favourable than that in Britain. Therefore, only change what is absolutely necessary into drachmas before you leave home. *Eurocheques* (maximum sum of 25,000 Drs.) can be changed without problems at all the banks on Crete (also in hotels and shops, but at unfavourable rates). From 1988 there has been no commission payable and the rate of exchange has been a little more favourable than that for cash. However, your bank at home will levy a charge for the transaction. An advantage is that the amount will only be debited to your account at home several weeks after the transaction. The exchange rates for *currency* and *travellers' cheques* here are about the same, but the charges for the transaction vary between the banks. In addition, many hotels, restaurants and shops accept *credit cards*, but you cannot obtain money through a post office giro account in Greece.

Banks are open throughout Greece Mon-Thur 8.00 a.m.-2.00 p.m., Fri 8.00 a.m.-1.30 p.m. As of late, it is now possible to change money (cash, travellers' and Eurocheques) at all *post offices*, at a slightly less favourable rate. There are centrally-situated *post office kiosks* in the larger cities, such as Iraklion and Chania, where you can also change money. These are usually open until 8.00 p.m. and also at weekends until 6.00 p.m.

Only 20,000 Drs. can be taken out of the country; there is no limit on the export of foreign currency.

> WE RECOMMEND: Take a quarter of your holiday money in cash and the rest in travellers' cheques, with a few Eurocheques as a reserve.

▶ **Diplomatic Representation:** *United Kingdom,* 1, Ploutarchou St. Athens, tel. 01/7236111 (Mon-Fri 9.00 a.m.-1.00 p.m.). *United States of America,* 91, Vassilissis Sofias, Athens, tel. 01/7212951 (Mon-Fri 9.00 a.m.-1.00 p.m.). *Canada,* 41, Ioannou Genadiou St. Tel. 01/7239511 (Mon-Fri 9.00 a.m.-1.00 p.m.). *Australia,* 37, D. Sotsou, Athens, Tel. 01/6447303 (Mon-Fri 9.00 a.m.-1.00 p.m.)

▶ **Hours of Business:** The siesta is a basic principle; hence the long opening hours in the evening when it is cooler, and shopping is more fun.

● **Museums, archaeological sites:** No general rule, and subject to constant changes. The notices at the entrances have usually had new notices stuck over them several times. Normally however, they are closed on Mondays or Tuesdays. Entrance fees range between £1-2. More detailed information can be found in the relevant chapters of this book.

● **Churches, Monasteries:** The siesta is taken very seriously. As a rule, these establishments are closed between 1 and 4 p.m. Make an early start when planning a visit. An important point to note here is that entry is forbidden to those wearing shorts and those whose shoulders are uncovered!

● **Banks:** Official opening hours are Mon-Thur 8 a.m.-2 p.m., Fri 8 a.m. -1.30 p.m. There may be slight local variations on

these times. The Agricultural Bank of Crete in Iraklion is also open in the afternoons and at weekends.

● **Shops:** Open in the mornings from 8 or 9 a.m. until around 1.30/2.30 p.m, afternoons from around 5/5.30 p.m.-8.30 p.m. Souvenir shops are often open all day until 9 or 10 p.m. A large proportion of business is mostly done in the evenings, particularly in the beach resorts.

● **Travel agencies:** These keep to the normal opening hours, but often remain open all day in summer.

● **Post offices:** see separate section.

● **Chemists/Drugstores:** These keep normal business hours, and there is also an emergency service. See under Medical Care, page 25.

▶ **Information:** You can ask the British office of the *National Tourist Organisation of Greece* (NTOG) - in Greek "Ellenikós Organismós Tourísmou" (EOT) to send you material free of charge, although this seldom contains any definite information. A *road map* of Crete is certainly useful, and there are also various brochures available. Try to let them know exactly what you want, otherwise you will only receive some very general brochures on Crete.

● **NTOG: London,** 195-7, Regent Street, London W.1. Tel. 01/7345997. **New York,** 645, Fifth Avenue, Olympic Tower. Tel. 212/4215777. Their main offices on Crete are in **Iraklion,** 1, Xanthoudidou St. Tel. 081/222487-8; **Chania,** 6, Akti Tombasi. Tel. 0821/26426; **Rethymnon,** El. Venizelou St. Tel. 0831/29148.

Apart from the information centres of the Tourist Organisation mentioned above, there are also the **Tourist police** (Tourístikí Astynomía) on Crete. They look after the interests of tourists, allocate rooms, and give information of every kind. If there is no local office of the tourist police, the regular police take over their responsibilities.

▶ **Maps**: No map of Crete is 100% correct. The best map at the moment is that produced by the Viennese cartographers *Freytag & Berndt* (1:200,000). It is revised regularly, and this is more than necessary in view of the spate of roadbuilding which is going on. If you wish to save money, the same map is a little cheaper on Crete from the Greek publishing house *Efstathiadis*.

Somewhat less accurate, but adequate for average requirements, is the map of Crete by *Nelles* (with contours, 1:200,000). Apart from those mentioned above, various other road maps are available on Crete; these are mostly reasonable in price (eg the Tourist Map of Kriti by D. & I. Mathioulakis), but are sometimes rather inadequate and incorrect.

You may be able to obtain the four-part cartographic work of the *Ethniki Statistiki Ipiresia tis Ellados* in specialist bookshops in Greece. There is a map for each administrative district (Iraklion, Rethymnon, Chania and Lassithi) on a scale of 1:200,000. The maps are, however, completely out of date, and the legend on them is written only in Greek.

▶ **Medical Care:** The cost of treatment in Greece is not, generally speaking, excessive. First Aid, hospitalisation and treatment in state hospitals are all free in emergencies. For treatment in private hospitals and surgeries, citizens of EC countries require Form E 111. This can be obtained from every office of the DHSS. With this, you can obtain a certificate from the Greek Health Service IKA, which entitles you to free medical treatment (getting the certificate can take a long time), but only from doctors who accept IKA patients, which is by no means mostly the case.

Travel Insurance taken out at home will cover both visits to doctors who do not accept IKA patients and chemists' bills, although you will have to pay cash on the spot and reclaim your expenses on production of receipts at home. Always ask for a proper receipt (*apódixi*) on which the diagnosis and treatment are clearly stated.

Many doctors have studied abroad and speak good English. There is a list of chemists who operate an emergency service at weekends on display at every chemist's shop. Many drugs can be obtained without a prescription.

▶ **Post office** *(tachidromíon)*: There are post offices in almost every village, although they are mostly only open until 2 p.m. Money can also be changed there.

● **Postcards and letters** to central and western Europe usually take about a week, but letters sometimes go more quickly. There is no point in marking them "Air Mail", as they generally all go by this method. Parcels may only be closed at the post office, after their contents have been inspected.

● **Hours of business**: generally Mon-Fri 7.30 a.m.-2 p.m. Often open until 8 p.m. in the cities.

• **Post office kiosks**: a relatively new institution in the larger cities (Chania, Rethymnon, Iraklion, Sitia). They are centrally located and are open for both the sale of stamps and the changing of money. Their long opening hours are an advantage; they are usually open until 8 p.m. on workdays and until 6 p.m. on Sundays.

• **Stamps**: These are available in most shops which sell postcards, as well as at post offices.

• **Poste Restante**: Every post office accepts mail which is to be called for. This can be collected on production of a passport and payment of a small charge. A letter will normally be held for up to 2 months. The sender should always write the name of the recipient (surname underlined!), the post office to which it is going and the information **Poste Restante** on the envelope.

A tip: if the post office clerk cannot find a letter under a surname, he should also be asked to look under the Christian name. Greek clerks understandably find it difficult to classify non-Greek names.

• **Telegraphing of funds**: This is the quickest way to obtain money when funds run out. Ring a reliable person at home and ask for the amount desired to be sent by telegraph in favour of a named recipient to the main post office of a particular city. This should ideally be one of the larger towns or cities. Normally (unfortunately not always!) the telegraphed funds arrive within 48 hours and the money is paid out in drachmas. There is a charge for the service, payable by the sender.

▶ **Telephone:** All towns and cities, and often the larger villages, have an OTE telephone office. Anywhere in the world can be reached with ease and reliability from the telephone cubicles there. However, in the high season, these offices are "besieged" by tourists from all over the world.

To make a phone call, it is necessary to go to the counter and be assigned a cubicle. When phoning, first dial the country code (United Kingdom **0044**, USA **001**), then the area code without the zero which precedes it and then the number of the person you are calling.

Important - dial slowly! If you hear an engaged signal, hang up and redial.

The lines are often extremely busy, especially in the evenings, in which case it is better to wait and try again later. In general, no great problem should arise.

The OTE telephone offices in Iraklion, Rethymnon and Chania are open from the early morning until midnight, and often in the other larger towns until 9 or 10 p.m. (For more details see under the individual places). They are often closed at weekends. In smaller villages without an OTE telephone office there is often an OTE telephone in a taverna, shop or other such place.

• COST OF CALLS: a meter on the wall shows the number of units you are using, and there is usually a table of prices on the wall of the booth from which you can keep a tally on the cost of your call.

When there is no OTE office at hand, or it is closed, it is also possible to telephone abroad from a **kiosk**. However, such calls are more expensive, and connections are not always very good. In the high season, these kiosks can be identified by the queue of people in front of them. Otherwise calls can be made from **hotels**, **tavernas** etc. However, the unit rate from the latter is almost double.

Miscellaneous

- All types of *photographic material, films* etc, should be purchased at home. Due to Greek import duties, they are at least 50% more expensive on Crete.

- In spite of rumours to the contrary, it is no longer possible to spend a night at a *monastery*. They are not, after all, hotels. Exceptions prove the rule . . .

- Because of the *time difference*, the whole of Greece is (in summer) one hour ahead of us in the U.K . . .

- *Toilets* of the traditional stand-up type are to a large extent still in use. When used correctly, they are really a more hygenic alternative to our sit-down type. Paper should not be flushed down the toilet; there is a bin in the corner . . .

- *Bathing shoes* will be of great use when bathing in rocky bays, and a *torch* is a must when visiting caves . . .

- The *spines of sea urchins* cause a lot of pain. Thinly-applied toothpaste will eventually get them out. Vinegar can help in the case of *wasp stings* . . .

- *Language Problems* will hardly arise in tourist areas. Every Cretan who has to deal with tourists speaks English. However, this is not always the case in isolated areas . . .

- *Petty thieving* is unfortunately on the increase. Above all, lone campers and those who sleep on the beaches in certain places are often the victims of robbery at night. For example, special care should be taken of valuables in Georgioupolis, Agia Galini and Paleochora. Our tip - bury your money and passport under your sleeping bag at night . . .

- As a rule, *students and schoolchildren* receive a 50% reduction on the entrance fees to museums and archaeological sites, on production of an international student card.

Travelling around Crete

Goats have priority; wide asphalt roads and adventurous gravel tracks; efficient network of buses

With your own vehicle

This brings the priceless advantage of mobility. So much more can be seen when you are not dependent upon bus itineraries.

Although it is great fun travelling around Crete by car, an exception has to be made where the large cities are concerned. Here, the columns of vehicles move forward at a tortuously slow pace all day. By contrast, there is hardly any traffic on country roads. You should, however, be prepared to meet a bus or a herd of goats around every corner.

A network of roads of northern European standards must not be expected. Large areas of the island are mountainous or hilly and for this reason it is difficult to incorporate them into the road system. In recent years however, considerable efforts have gone into closing the last gaps in the road network. Many roads originate from the pre-automobile era and donkey and cart tracks still link some small villages. But there are men at work everywhere on the roads and new lengths of asphalt are added to the network every year. Thus, the traveller often comes upon roads which are partly asphalted, but then degenerate unexpectedly into bumpy gravel tracks. Furthermore, the asphalt roads are not always in good condition. Potholes, bad curves with ridged road surfaces, undulating road surfaces and unexpectedly steep curves are common. For this reason, the golden rule is drive very carefully and take as few risks as possible.

Just as important - animals always have priority on the road. Goats, chickens, or dogs often lie in the road and will only acknowledge a foolhardy motorist with a bored grunt. An owner would be anything but bored, however, if he were obliged to clear the remains of his animal from the road.

▶ **Cretan drivers:** We had no bad experiences. Flashes of Mediterranean temperament at the wheel are not the rule here.

It is noticeable that priority roads are not sacrosanct in the cities. In spite of heavy traffic from left and right, vehicles turn carelessly into a main road, and the result is slowly-circulating traffic and a foot constantly on the brake pedal. In Cretan cities and towns there are of course mopeds and scooters, which overtake cars in an adventurous way by weaving in and out from left to right, and from behind and in front. Always check before swinging to the right; there is usually a scooter or moped just about to swish past.

▶ **Maps:** The inadequacy of the maps that are available is a small handicap on extensive tours around the island. There is no map which adequately describes the current state of the road network. At any time, the motorist can suddenly find himself on a narrow dusty track. The road may either be asphalted again after a few bends, or even after a distance of 6 or 7 miles. For this reason, we have tried to give detailed information about the state of the roads in our descriptions of routes and places. Warnings about the bad condition of roads should always be taken seriously. Who wants to find himself in the middle of scorching hot scrubland with a flat tyre?

▶ **Planning your time:** The length of time required to cover even short distances is a constant source of surprise. Cretan roads are full of curves, steep, and as stated above, not always made up. Therefore always allow more time for trips across country than you would at home; indeed, in the mountainous interior average speeds of 15-20 m.p.h are no rarity.

▶ **Tools/Breakdowns:** Always have enough petrol (even a full spare can), a spare tyre and tools with which to change a wheel. It is very important to carry out frequent checks that there is enough *distilled water* in the *battery*. This tends to evaporate very quickly in the Cretan "oven". The same goes of course for the water in the radiator and for oil.

▶ **Garages/Gas stations:** The network of garages on Crete has recently been greatly extended. In spite of this, there are still isolated areas and villages, in which petrol is not to be had. This applies especially to the small villages on the south coast.

As in the rest of Greece, it is always advisable to buy super-grade petrol on Crete. Diesel is nearly always available. As of very recently there are garages in Iraklion, Chania and Rethymnon which sell unleaded petrol.

▶ **Breakdown assistance:** This can be obtained from the Greek Automobile Club ELPA, but only in the area around Iraklion and Chania and on the New Road from 7 a.m.-10 p.m. Members of British automobile clubs can obtain breakdown assistance free of charge.

IRAKLION, 46-50 Papandreou St., tel. 081/289440. In emergency ring 081/104.
CHANIA, 1 Nik. Skoula St., tel. 0821/26059. In emergency ring 0821/104.

▶ **Motorbikes:** To explore Crete on your own motorbike is a wonderful experience. The curving mountain roads offer a new view around every corner, and there is little traffic on them. The New Road on the north coast can be very busy.

Nevertheless, drive very carefully! Potholes and stones in the road are no rarity, and the asphalt surface may have melted slightly in the heat (danger of skidding and falling off the bike). The chances of obtaining spare parts are slim, and authorised workshops are only to be found in the large cities, if at all. Take special motorbike tools with you: a Bowden spanner, nipples, fuses, contact spray, lamps, puncture repair kit and a small oil can.

ASPHALT, ASPHALT . . .

Since tourism has become a major economic factor, and especially since Papandreou became Prime Minister, the government has been spending a lot of money on road-building on Crete. Construction, improvements, improvisations, applications of cement or asphalt, widening and levelling of the road surfaces; these are going on everywhere. In my view, there are two sides to this activity. When the last coastal village has been connected to the asphalt network, when it becomes possible to speed through the White Mountains on a fast road, and when the most isolated beach coves attract columns of rented cars, then a lot of what makes Crete unique today will have been destroyed.

Road conditions

▶ **North coast:** The New Road along the coast from Chania via Rethymnon and Iraklion to Agios Nikolaos is the main artery of island communications. It is the best and most modern road on the island and is to a large extent constructed as a fast road.

Roughly parallel to it and mostly further inland is the curving Old Road, the older arterial road. The latter is often more interesting from the point of view of landscape, but time-consuming, and only worthwhile if you wish to visit places along it.

The eastward and westward continuations of the New Road have also been completed:

a) from Agios Nikolaos to Sitia and farther on to the palm beach at Vai.

b) from Chania to Kastelli and Phalassarna. There are plans to extend the New Road as far as Kastelli within the next 5-10 years.

▶ **South coast**: In contrast to the north coast, the south coast is not totally accessible by car. In the west the great ridge of the White Mountains (*Lefka Ori*), with mighty gorges running through it in a north-south direction, prevents the building of roads from west to east. There are, however, direct roads from the north coast to most of the coastal villages in the south-west (see north-south connections). Some of the places at the foot of the Lefka Ori can only be reached by boat.

Only from *Chora Sfakion* is the south coast completely accessible by car as far as the extreme south-east around *Ierapetra*. A curving panoramic road runs in an easterly direction over the foothills along the coast to *Plakias* and further on to *Agia Galini*. This road is still unmade over a distance of a few miles but this does not present any great problem. Road conditions on the *Messara Plain* are good. An asphalt road goes to *Ierapetra* in the extreme east of the island. Only a short stretch between *Ano Kastelliana* and *Demati* has not yet been made up, but this presents no problems for motorists.

The most important routes from north to south (listed from west to east)

There are now virtually no problems involved in travelling along these.

(1) **Platanos to Paleochora**: A panoramic road high above the west coast, with little traffic. This is an asphalt road until just south of Kambos, then it becomes a wide gravel track. There is asphalt again from Kefali onwards; then the road branches off beyond Elos through Strofles, and becomes a gravel track once again, this time with pot-holes. It proceeds via Archontiko to Voutas, whence it becomes an asphalt road again, with road works until Paleochora. The first part of this route can be shortened by travelling on the inland road from Kaloudiana via Topolia.

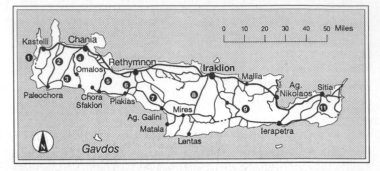

(2) **Tavronitis to Paleochora:** The main route from the north coast to Paleochora. The entire road is asphalted, narrow and winding in places, and consists partly of newly-constructed mountain stretches through the foothills of the Lefka Ori (White Mountains). Buses also travel this route.

(3) **Chania to Sougia:** This is the only road to the south coast village of Sougia. At first, it crosses the largest area of orange plantations on Crete, then the flanks of the Lefka Ori. In the latter there are beautiful lonely stretches of road, which have been completely made up.

(4) **Chania to Omalos to Agia Roumeli:** panoramic road up to the Omalos High Plateau at an altitude of 3,924 ft. From there a 10-mile hiking path leads through the famous Samaria Gorge to Agia Roumeli on the south coast, whence the journey continues by boat. All details on page 429.

(5) **Vrises to Chora Sfakion:** The road leads steeply into the mountains, through the beautiful Askifou Plateau and in breathtaking hairpin bends down to the coast. It is completely made up.

(6) **Rethymnon to Plakias:** One of the two narrow parts of Crete. Leads through several attractive regions and through the deep Kourtaliotiko or Kotsifou Gorge. Completely asphalted, but be prepared for potholes.

(7) **Rethymnon to Agia Galini:** At the beginning, the same route as that which goes to Plakias, but then via the green town of Spili and through a long, drawn-out valley. Recently made up, but the road is damaged in places.

(8) **Iraklion to Mires, Phaistos and Matala** (or **Agia Galini**): Main bus route towards the southern part of central Crete. Well-constructed stretch through the largest wine-producing area of the island; only steep in one place.

(9) **Iraklion to Ierapetra**: Long route through the wine-growing area of central Crete, then through Arkalochori and later along the slopes of Dikti. Not quite so well made up, but on the whole O.K.

(10) **Pachia Ammos to Ierapetra**: The shortest route from north to south - the distance from Pachia Ammos to Ierapetra is only 10 miles. Quite a level road, no problems.

(11) **Sitia to Ierapetra**: A beautiful, winding route over the mountains.

Buses

"Use the public transport bus - individually and inexpensive". *Everyone without a car of his own gladly follows the advice offered by this slogan of the Cretan Bus Company KTEL.*

Buses run to and fro across the island, and even isolated villages have a daily bus connection, provided of course that there is a road in existence. If there is no alternative, such boneshaker buses also travel along gravel or dirt tracks. Even 90° bends are no problem - they chug along over an abyss or go at a cracking tempo through narrow defiles. "Use the public transport bus. . . " Accidents are rare. The drivers know their roads and the vehicle fleet has to a large extent been recently modernised. However, from time to time the traveller still experiences a ride in one of these ancient jalopies, with loose wall panelling, springs jutting out of the upholstery and all available room around the driver's seat decorated with Holy Virgins, icons and crucifixes.

The Cretan bus network is divided into two areas and is orientated towards the political division of the island. *KTEL Iraklion/Lassithi* is responsible for central and eastern Crete and serves locations in the districts (Nomoi) Iraklion and Lassithi. *KTEL Chania/Rethymnon* serves all places in western Crete, that is, in the Nomoi of Rethymnon and Chania. Both have their own timetables, and points at which the two companies' services meet are Iraklion in the north and Agia Galini in the south.

The central points of the bus network are naturally the bus stations in the cities along the north coast and in the south east, namely *Kastelli, Chania, Rethymnon, Iraklion, Agios Nikolaos, Sitia* and *Ierapetra.*

▶ There are daily connections between these cities by long-distance bus:

Iraklion	20 x daily to Agios Nikolaos (via Mallia), 9 x daily to Sitia (via Agios Nikolaos), 9 x daily to Ierapetra (via Agios Nikolaos), 25 x daily to Rethymnon and on to Chania
Rethymnon	25 x daily to both Iraklion and Chania
Chania	25 x daily to Rethymnon and on to Iraklion, 13 x daily to Kastelli

▶ In addition there are also frequent connections to the villages on the south coast:

Iraklion	9 x daily to Agia Galini, 7 x daily to Matala, 2 x daily to Lentas, and also to Phaistos, Gortys, Mires, Agii Deka etc.
Rethymnon	7 x daily to Plakias, 6 x daily to Agia Galini
Chania	6 x daily to Paleochora, 4 x daily to Chora Sfakion, 2 x daily to Sougia
Ag. Nikolaos	9 x daily to Sitia, 10 x daily to Ierapetra.

▶ In addition there are also local connections to all the larger villages. Here is a small selection:

Iraklion	Anogia, Archanes, Fodele, Agia Pelagia, Limin Chersonisou, Mallia etc.
Ag. Nikolaos	Elounda, Kritsa, Neapolis
Rethymnon	Georgioupolis, Arkadi Monastery
Chania	Ag. Marina, Kolimbari, Meskla, Souda
Kastelli	Kambos, Kolimbari, Phalassarna, Platanos
Sitia	Paleokastro, Vai, Zakros
Ierapetra	Ano Vianos, Makrigialos, Myrtos

Try to obtain the two bus timetables as soon as possible:

a) For **Western Crete** (Iraklion to Rethymnon, Chania and on to Kastelli). This is obtainable from Bus Station C in Iraklion and at Rethymnon and Chania bus stations.

b) For **Central and Eastern Crete** (Iraklion to Ag. Nikolaos, Sitia, and Ierapetra). This is obtainable from Bus Station A in Iraklion and in Ag. Nikolaos, Sitia, and Ierapetra. Distances, length of journey and prices are always given in this timetable.

• TICKETS: These are available on the bus, and in the larger bus stations they can also be bought at the counter in advance. For longer journeys, they are usually issued with a seat reservation. This seat should always be occupied, otherwise problems may arise with other passengers, who for their part have found that the seat which they themselves have been allocated has already been occupied. Tickets should always be retained until the end of the journey, as there are frequent ticket checks!

• PRICES: Ag. Nikolaos £2, Iraklion - Sitia £4, Iraklion - Matala £2, Iraklion - Rethymnon £2, Rethymnon - Chania £2. Rule of thumb: 50 miles cost around £3.

• DEPARTURE TIMES: These are changed several times during the year. Neither the printed timetable nor the time-tables displayed at bus stops are one hundred per cent correct, and should only be used for rough orientation. Always be sure to ask and obtain additional information.

• FINDING THE RIGHT BUS: A delicate subject. How do I find the right bus? Basic rule - the destination shown on the bus is not always correct. Be sure to ask again. In the larger bus stations, buses are also announced over a loudspeaker, or someone may call out the destination of the next bus. Be sure to pay attention!

• CHANGING BUSES: Often a difficult exercise; the buses are rarely timed to each other. Be patient!

• LOCAL CONNECTIONS: When there is a bus connection to a place only 2 or 3 x per day, departure times are mostly planned to suit the local travelling public - that is to say, buses go from the village to the city in the morning, and in the opposite direction in the afternoon. Return buses from the smaller villages leave at the latest in the early evening for the larger cities. Generally, buses only run until 9. p.m.

• LUGGAGE: This is loaded into the large baggage compartments of the buses before the journey begins. Some elderly buses transport rucksacks in a wobbly pyramid on the roof. Do not take bulky luggage into a bus, except on city buses.

If day trips are planned, always determine whether a bus returns on the same day from your target destination!

Rented cars

These are a favourite on Crete. Countless firms in all the cities and larger tourist resorts offer car rentals and a lot of use is made of them.

The condition of the vehicles varies greatly. They are sometimes new, but have often been severely neglected. Loss of oil and water, worn-out clutches, badly-adjusted pedals and defective shock absorbers are common. At all costs, make a trial drive!

Greatly favoured and recommended in view of the road conditions are the various type of open Jeeps on offer. In these, it is possible to drive over stony dirt tracks away from the accessible asphalt roads. This is often necessary in Crete to get to interesting places. The smaller cars of the cheaper category are often very badly sprung.

There are two different possibilities:

1) Renting per day with a charge per kilometre

2) Renting for 3 or more days without a charge per kilometre

It is advisable, before entering into a rental agreement, to calculate what mileage is likely to be covered, and thus to see which tariff is the more reasonable. Rentals which include a charge per kilometre are always calculated by the rental company on the basis of at least 100 kilometres per day. As a rule of thumb, the cheapest prices (involving a charge per kilometre) are around £20-24 per day.

As prices and quality vary considerably, it is always advisable to check with several rental companies. Brochures with current applicable rental rates and conditions of contract are to be seen everywhere. It is nearly always possible to renegotiate rates, especially out of high season.

The conditions of rental should also be studied carefully. In the case of an accident, large sums of money may be demanded, especially by unscrupulous rental companies, of which there are unfortunately not a few among the mass of companies operating. The personal impression made by the renting agent should also be taken into consideration when making a decision.

Vehicles from the international car rental companies *Avis*, *InterRent*, *Hertz* and *Budget* are normally no better or worse than those of the Cretan rental companies, but they are usually a little more expensive (Budget is still the cheapest of these).

Important: 16% tax is always added to the prices (VAT, car tax, road tax)!!

• RENTAL CONDITIONS: The driver must be at least 21, 23 or 25 years of age, depending on the rental company! The driving licence must already have been valid for 1 year!

• INSURANCE: Most companies offer a third-party insurance which is only valid up to a certain sum. Any costs above this sum must be met by the driver from his own pocket.
Otherwise, the rental companies offer **fully comprehensive insurance** with a high personal liability for damage to the rented vehicle (this varies among companies and according to the category of car, but is mostly between £2,500-4,500). This personal liability can be waived for c. £4-5 per day (Collision damage waiver insurance).
Important: Damage to the tyres and the underside of the vehicle is never included in the insurance!

• OTHER INFORMATION: Most car rental companies do not like their vehicles to be driven on dirt tracks. If they are informed beforehand that the vehicle is to be driven along such tracks, they often levy a surcharge. If they are not told beforehand and there is a breakdown, the person who rented the vehicle must normally meet the cost.

• READERS' TIPS: "Only the rental company **Zeus** informed us that, for example, tyre damage and damage to the underside through rocks were not included in the insurance. This condition has to be signed and accepted in every rental contract . . .
"I would like to pass on my positive experiences with the car rental company **Fun**. We travelled over 1,000 km in a Suzuki (smallest category). It was our impression that prices are definitely negotiable."

On Two Wheels

"Rent a scooter, rent a bike." These signs are to be found everywhere on Crete. Motor bikes, scooters and mopeds can be rented in almost every larger town.

Also applicable here: before renting, make a test drive to check brakes, lights, gears, tyre profiles etc. Note: If there is any damage or breakdown while you are out and about, **you** will have to pay for it! Therefore, always make sure that you are renting a bike that is in the best condition.

It cannot be stressed strongly enough: always drive carefully!! The roads on Crete are especially treacherous for lighter traffic such as mopeds and scooters. Unexpected uneven surfaces, ridges and potholes are common. A speciality: channels across the road which have been cut by residents and not reclosed with cement. A momentary lapse in attention can ruin the whole holiday - we have seldom seen so many abrasions on the arms and legs of young people as on Crete.

Always ensure that there is enough petrol in the tank. On one occasion we had to push our bikes 4 miles to the nearest garage. Do not drive for hours on end in summer in shorts and a T-shirt. There is a danger of sunburn!

> If you have never had any experience with motor bike, you should not try to remedy this deficiency on Crete. Only rent a Vespa if you have already had some experience with one. Safest for beginners are the automatic mopeds.

• INSURANCE: Damage to two-wheelers is generally to be paid for in full, and only a third party insurance is included in the rental price. The rental contract must be carefully studied beforehand; insist that the third party insurance is noted on the contract, otherwise the rental company can talk its way out in cases of damage.

• PRICES: Mopeds cost £4.50-7, scooters £7-10, and motorbikes of 250 ccs. £15-17. If you are renting for several days, the daily rate is somewhat lower. 16% VAT should be added. Bargaining for a better price is usually difficult.

Taxis

A comfortable means of transport, very commonly available and cheap in comparison to the United Kingdom and the United States.

There are two kinds of taxi. Those which only move around the city or town (*Taxí*) and those which also go to areas farther away (*Agoréon*). The latter do not have a meter, but a list of fixed prices for certain journeys, which a passenger may examine. However, the meter is often not switched on in city taxis, but a fixed price demanded instead. The possibilities for bargaining are limited. It is recommended that the price be ascertained before starting the journey!

If the meter is used, always ensure that it is set to the correct tariff. The cheaper *tariff 1* is valid within the limits of the city in which the taxi is registered, while the more expensive *tariff 2* is only applicable outside the city boundaries!

The following prices are generally applicable, although they are not always adhered to:

• Basic charge c. £0.70, c. £0.14 per kilometre in the city (tariff 1), c. £0.17 per kilometre outside the city (tariff 2), surcharge of c. £0.17 at airports, railway stations, bus stations and harbours, c. £0.09 for every piece of luggage, and c. £0.20 per km. for journeys at night.

Some more tips: In Crete and the rest of Greece, taxis which are already occupied will often stop to take you on board, if you want to go in the same direction. In such cases, note the reading on the meter when you get in; the price will be calculated later from this figure. If two independent parties travel the same distance in a taxi, they must normally *both* pay the price shown on the meter at the end. This does not of course mean that when a *group* gets into a taxi *each member* has to pay the fare shown. Occasionally taxi drivers try to make inexperienced tourists believe that this is indeed the case.

Connections by sea

Above all, sea connections play an important role in the mountainous south west. The terrain between *Paleochora* and *Chora Sfakion* is extremely mountainous and prevents the building of any kind of road.

Chora Sfakion lies at the centre of sea traffic on the south coast

Instead, in the high season, passenger ships and converted fishing boats ply to and fro several times daily with interim stops at *Sougia*, *Agia Roumeli* and *Loutro*. The whole thing is a wonderful journey along the steep, rocky coast, which you should make at least once! *Agia Roumeli* is at the end of the Samaria Gorge. It is only possible to go on by boat from there, either to *Paleochora* or to *Chora Sfakion*.

There are also boats several times a week from Paleochora and Chora Sfakion to the lonely island of *Gavdos*, the southernmost island of Greece.

More detailed information on all boat connections under the relevant locations.

Hiking

Those who go on walking tours on Crete get to know the island from another angle. It is then the realisation dawns that the Cretans are not fishermen but mountain folk. By the same token, the island is not a beach paradise with "*dolce vita*", but an extremely mountainous island in an often very stormy sea.

It is possible to hike all over Crete; there is hardly a corner of the island which one would advise a hiker to avoid. Nature in its original, often grandiose form, no industry, few large towns. All these are advantages. However the terrain is often difficult and can place high demands on the hiker. Lone hikers should take especial care, particularly in the White Mountains *(Lefka Ori)* in the west of the island. This region is a dangerous one for the uninformed, and a number of hikers have already died of thirst there because they did not know about routes and wells. Whoever wishes to get to know the high mountains would be well advised to join one of the frequently organised hiking trips (For addresses see below).

A general rule is that **one should hike alone as little as possible.** At the very least, a contact person should know where a hiker intends to go. Crete is sparsely populated and there is lonely, wild and virgin country away from the roads. On many hiking routes there is a possibility that no other human being will be met throughout the whole day. What should be done, therefore, if an ankle is sprained, or a leg broken etc.?

A hike on Crete is not a stroll! Although as a rule climbing experience is not required, good "staying power" and enjoyment of physical effort are necessary. An extended test hike with a complete set of equipment should be carried out at home beforehand (a weekend is enough). The blisters on your feet will be painful, but they won't occur on Crete.

Hiking paths as we know them do not exist. Sporadic splashes of paint and loosely-constructed pyramids of stones are the only markers; rubbish and stones polished by the soles of boots are further pointers to a hiking route. The hiker learns, in the course of time, to distinguish these from watercourses, animal tracks and natural rock formations.

How frequent and how long the hiking trips are is dependent upon condition and staying power. The hiker should certainly get up at first light and **set off at sunrise**. It is not only a feeling of psychological security that is provided by the knowledge that, although the heat of midday is clearly felt, two thirds of the journey have been covered.

• SEASONS: Crete is wonderful in spring; in summer it is exhausting and brings out the sweat, and in winter is dangerous to impossible.

There is a lot of rain **until March**, which means mud and mire on the hiking paths. At higher altitudes, snow prevents progress.

The best months for hiking in low-lying and hilly country are **April**, **May**, and **June**; the myriads of flowers and fresh colours are unforgettable.

June and July are suitable for **mountain hikes**. There is seldom rain and sudden changes of weather are rare. A light, misty rain on the coast mostly indicates fog, thunder and cold in the mountains, easily visible from the sea. Rain means an increased danger of rock falls on all paths, since the friable cliffs are not stabilised through a network of roots. Thus a departure for the high mountainous regions should **only** be made when the weather is stable and the sun is shining; at altitudes of over 2,300 feet the heat is bearable, even in high summer.

September and the first half of **October** are also pleasant months for hiking; grapes and fruit are ripe, and the sun is not so oppressive.

— ★ —

• MAPS/ROUTE DESCRIPTIONS: There are no good hikers' maps of Crete. It is often necessary to go by a compass or by intuition and follow the directions of the local people, which are unfortunately often conflicting and imprecise in nature. You are also advised to be sceptical when the length of time necessary for a journey is mentioned.

The hikes mentioned in this book were all carried out in spring 1988. The plans were prepared from the exact sketches made by our researchers.

The very latest information: 5 new hiker's map will be available in West Germany from the middle of 1990 onwards. Each gives exhaustive information on a particular part of the island, including the roads, tracks and paths. You may perhaps be able to order these maps in the U.K.: Crete, Touristmap with Footpaths; harms-ic-Verlag, D-6741 Erlenbach b. Kandel, Waldstr. 18 / Fed. Rep. of Germany

— ★ —

• EQUIPMENT: The terrain of Crete is stony and full of thorns. Ankle-high **hiking boots** which have a firm sole with a profile are essential - those who have spent 8 hours hiking through the mountains in sandals will know what I mean! A pair of light jogging shoes is recommended as a reserve. A small folding canister for drinking water is advisable if a stay is intended on a beach, and perhaps climbing gloves for safety and long trousers for going through bushes.

Only use one of the newest types of **rucksack** without a carrying frame, which lies close to the body and does not move around like many "trampers' rucksacks". If a tent and sleeping bag are not to be carried, a small daytime rucksack will suffice.

Some beautiful hiking areas

*Hikes marked with an * are exhaustively described in this book.*

▶ **Central Crete:** The Ida mountain range is the highest on Crete. There are numerous possibilities here, and just as rewarding are hikes across the Lassithi Plateau.

* **Timios Stavros:** From the Nida plateau near Anogia in 4-5 hours to the highest peak on Crete (8,393 feet). The ascent can also be made from Kamares on the southern side of the mountain range (Kamares Cave), but it is longer and more difficult.

▶ **Eastern Crete:** There is beautiful hiking country in the Dikti range and in the Thripti mountains.

* **Valley of the Dead:** An easy route from Zakros to Kato Zakros.
Katharo Plateau: Longer hike up to an isolated plateau above the village of Kritsa.

▶ **West Crete:** Where hiking is concerned, this is the most attractive area of Crete. The White Mountains and the wild southern coast with their deep gorges are especially interesting.

* **Samaria Gorge:** This is the largest gorge in Europe, 10 miles long, highly exploited by tourism and accordingly over-frequented.
Gingilos: A path leads from the beginning of the Samaria Gorge up to this impressive six thousand footer.
* **Coastal hikes:** From Agia Roumeli (entrance to the Samaria Gorge) to Loutro or Anopolis (above Chora Sfakion); from Paleochora to Sougia; from Paleochora to the beautiful beach at Elafonisi.
Preveli Beach: From Lefkogia via Gianiou to Preveli Monastery and the palm beach which lies below it.
* **Gramvousa Peninsula:** The wonderful beach at Tigani is situated on the northwest side of this wild peninsula. Unfortunately, a road is being built to it.

> "KALLERGI HUT": This well-equipped hut is situated in the White Mountains high above the Omalos Plateau. There is a track for cross-country vehicles leading to it. The hut contains 40 beds and it is run in the summer months by the Austrian Alpine School at Innsbruck, which organises hikes from there through the White Mountains.

• ADDRESSES: Before embarking on a hike, a visit to the Greek mountain climbers' organisation **EOS** (Ellinikós Orivatikós Síndesmos) on Crete can be useful.
Iraklion, 74, Dikeossinis St. Tel. 081/287110
Chania, 90, Tzanakaki St. Next to Olympic Airways. (Open daily 8.00 p.m.-10.00 p.m.) Tel. 0821/24647
Rethymnon, Spandidakis Chemist Shop, 3, Gerakari St. Tel.0831/23666 (further details in Tourist Information). Many local travel agents and associations organise hikes, eg **Kedros Tours,** P.O. Box 125, 192, Machis Kritis St., Platanes/Rethymnon. Tel. 0831/24841. Ask for Mr. Leutsch.

Accommodation

Renovated houses in the old city; chipboard and swimming pool; hospitality given great importance.

Hotels/Guest houses

The building boom continues. Hotels are springing up in every corner of the island, holiday apartments are being constructed in rapid tempo, everyone has rooms to rent.

All this at the cost of quality; Cretan hotels are generally stereotyped in appearance, purely functional, lacking in the little details and offering little in the way of comfort. A table, a chair, and a bed - this is often all there is, even in the better establishments. Only the quality of the furniture rises with the price; instead of chipboard and cracked veneer there will be solid wood furniture, and sometimes carpeting. Demands for comfort should be moderated, at least where establishments in the lower categories are concerned.

However, things have changed somewhat in recent years. Most of the newly-built hotels, rooms for rent etc. display a clear trend towards modern living standards. Money has come to the island and many hotel owners have realised what the west European guest values most. In the historic old city quarters of Chania and Rethymnon, for example, more and more Venetian and Turkish houses are being renovated and converted into tasteful lodgings. Many hotel owners have previously worked abroad and know what their customers want. Quite a few have regular customers, which is an indication of sustained standards. Eventual deficiencies will be more than made up for by the hospitality and natural sincerity of the host.

While developments in tourism go ahead with greater speed in coastal areas, the *interior of the island* is to a large extent unspoilt. Here for the most part you will find simple inns, which certainly do not offer much in the way of comforts, but offer a true reflection of the real life of the island away from the "madding crowd".

The following often happened to us; when there was no room vacant in a house, we would be sent to a neighbour, because he might have a vacancy. In a place where everyone is more or less related to everyone else, the concept of competition does not play a major role.

In our descriptions of places to stay we have given extensive details of establishments which seem to us to be worthy of recommendation. The prices given are always those in the high season (July/August). In the low season, considerably reduced prices are often applicable. The abbreviation "DR" used in the recommendations for accommodation signifies "double room".

At this point, a request: Please write to me if you were especially satisfied with a stay in any one place! Your information will be carefully evaluated and mentioned in subsequent editions of this handbook.

Classification of accommodation

The hotels are divided into 6 categories: Luxury, A, B, C, D and E. In addition there are guest houses, private rooms and apartments or holiday flats. The tourist police keep a check on prices, which have to be displayed clearly in every room.

Luxury category: All of 8 hotels are accorded this description on Crete! 6 of them are situated in Agios Nikolaos and neighbouring Elounda, one is in Limin Chersonissou (near Mallia) and one between Agios Nikolaos and Pachia Ammos. These are most definitely super hotels with all the comforts: tennis courts, private beach, disco, air-conditioning etc. Prices in these centres of "quality tourism" range between £44-67 for a DR (half or full board is usually obligatory).

A category: Also for the more demanding guest, although somewhat simpler in furnishing and service than first class; sometimes however, they are completely compatible. Prices from £27-47 for a DR. (Half or full board are possible). Such establishments are to be found on the long sandy beaches of the north coast and in the cities and larger tourist locations there.

B category: Definitely better-quality establishments offering adequate comfort and service. Often well-established hotels which have been used by travel companies for a number of years, or newly-built hotels which are often pleasingly modern, with good plumbing and a cultured atmosphere. We were however obliged to wonder, in the case of a few of these B-class hotels, how they acquired their classification. DR for £24-34 (half board possible).

C category: Normal run-of-the-mill hotels, where there are considerable variations in quality, from very good to untidy and neglected. Prices for a DR from £12-17. Rooms usually have a private bath, but often there is only a separate shower cabin in the room. Half board is not always possible.

D category: Thoroughly simple "cheap hotels", furnishings sparse to absent. No private bath, but sometimes a more personal atmosphere than in the better categories. Here, too, the visitor can make both pleasant and unpleasant discoveries. Price for a DR £8-10.

E category: Cheap doss-downs, mainly beloved of rucksack tourists. A roof over the head, a shower on the hallway - much depends on the owner and how he keeps his house, what his attitude to cleanliness is etc. We seldom experienced a total disaster on Crete. Even this sort of accommodation is normally in a condition worthy of human beings. Above all in the larger cities, such accommodation is often found in "historic" houses, which have not been renovated for a long time. Price for a DR £5-10.

Guest houses (often called *Pensions* on Crete): These are also divided into A, B, and C categories. In guest houses of categories A and B the rooms have their own bath and are quite attractively appointed. Price around £12-15 for a DR. Often they are family businesses with a friendly atmosphere, which have established themselves in the cities and also in the smaller villages where there are no hotels. Guest houses of C category are on the same level as hotels of the D and E categories, but often as not they are a better choice.

Private rooms: In tourist locations it sometimes seems as though every inhabitant has rooms to rent. Signs with "Rent Rooms" are everywhere. These definitely provide a good source of secondary income in the coastal and bathing resorts. Many inhabitants build extensions or new storeys onto their houses. In spite of the large number of rooms on offer it can happen that, in the high season, in places such as Paleochora, Agia Galini or Plakias, you may have to spend a long time searching for such accommodation. Prices for a DR generally range from £5 upwards, but there are cheaper possibilities (eg inland or on the island of Gavdos).

Newly-built houses often have rooms with their own bath or even small apartments with a kitchen and a bathroom.

Apartments/Holiday flats

Mainly a reasonable proposition for families; living room and bedroom with kitchen and bathroom, mostly newly-built and offering totally adequate comfort. Can be reserved at home through travel agencies. Many owners offer their houses through advertisements in the travel section of British or American newspapers. A brochure can usually be requested. The details therein are not always one hundred per cent correct, but they are generally reliable.

When booking at home, the distance to the nearest village and shopping facilities etc. should always be ascertained. Sometimes the houses are rather off the beaten track. We met the father of a family who spent his holiday at a wonderful beach which was nearly 7 miles from the nearest shop. Prices from about £17 upwards, but these drop sharply out of season and it is possible to bargain freely. At this time, many houses are empty, and it is not necessary to book beforehand at home.

On Crete, you can book either through a travel agent or directly with the proprietor.

TIPS ... TIPS ... TIPS

- Prices drop by at least 20% out of season. Travellers to Crete at this time can make considerable savings on accommodation.

- Single rooms are rare, and those travelling alone must under certain circumstances be prepared to take a double room and accept only a minimal reduction on the price.

- There is often a supplementary charge of around 10% for a stay of only 1 to 2 days. Reductions for a longer stay. A surcharge of 30% can be levied if an extra bed is placed in a room.

- It is basically illegal for a proprietor to hold onto a personal identity card or passport for more than 24 hours. If you hold both a passport and an identity card, it is probably wise to take both on holiday with you, so that you can give one to the proprietor and keep the other for changing money, renting vehicles etc. U.K. citizens, of course, do not hold identity cards.

- It can happen that exorbitant prices are demanded in the high season. If difficulties arise, go with the proprietor to the nearest office of the tourist police (see also page 24).

- Be careful when there is only one room vacant in an otherwise full house in the high season. This is very often "the worst room". Always inspect a room before accepting it.

- If you are travelling around a lot and changing your accommodation frequently, try to obtain the brochure "Crete: A Guide to Accommodation". This contains the telephone numbers and short descriptions of the position and facilities of a large number of Cretan hotels and guest houses of all categories.

Youth Hostels

These are to be found in Iraklion, Rethymnon, Chania, Mallia, Agios Nikolaos, Sitia, Plakias and Mirthios.

Of course, there are the usual simple establishments on Crete too, with bunk beds in sometimes extremely musty sleeping quarters. Considerable differences exist, however, between the individual hostels. Indeed, some of them are not at all bad where atmosphere is concerned. Detailed information can be found in the individual chapter on places. Prices around £1.80-£2.20.

The following hostels are pleasant - *Rethymnon* (clean, centrally situated, German proprietor), *Chania* (not much going on because it is rather a distance from the centre), *Plakias* (near to the sea) and *Mirthios* (good view). In *Sitia* it is possible to pitch a tent on the land surrounding the building. The hostel in *Agios Nikolaos* is in the centre of town and a storey has recently been added. There is now much more space there than before. Least worthy of note at present are the hostels in Iraklion and Mallia.

GREEK YOUTH HOSTELS ASSOCIATION: 4, Dragatsaniou St., 105 59 Athens. Tel. 01/3234107.

Camping

At present there are 17 camping sites on Crete. We inspected all of them very carefully and give tips in the appropriate sections on the different places. New camping sites may be added in the next few years, but one should not expect too much.

The sites can be divided into "simple" and "better". On the south coast they are mainly of the modest, back-to-nature type with little in the way of comfort. On the north coast on the outskirts of the cities of Iraklion, Chania and Rethymnon there are larger, better-equipped sites. The advantage of the small sites is that you get to know people more quickly and the proprietors are mostly friendly. There is a personal atmosphere. Most sites are directly by the sea, a few are a couple of hundred yards away.

On the whole, camping sites are rather underrepresented on Crete. What used to be the nicest, situated at Mallia on the north coast, closed a few years ago and apartments have been built there.

A Summary:

▶ NORTH COAST *(from west to east)*

Camping Mithimna: Near Kastelli, lovely site, not very big, situated on a long shingle beach. Sanitary equipment adequate, small taverna and a pleasant, personal atmosphere. April to October, Tel. 0822/31444.

Camping Ag. Marina: Medium-sized site near Chania, well-equipped, long sandy beach and a lot of shade from attractive dwarf palm trees. April to October, tel. 0821/68555.

Camping Chania: Slightly nearer to Chania, small, simple site, adequate shade, personal atmosphere. 3 minutes from a cove for bathing. April to October, tel. 0821/31490.

Camping Elisabeth: Several miles east of Rethymnon, large, tolerably well-equipped, a lot of shade, long sandy beach, friendly atmosphere. April-October, tel. 0831/28694.

Camping Arcadi: Neighbour to Camping Elisabeth, not very large, moderately equipped, long sandy beach and a lot of shade. April to October, tel. 0831/28746.

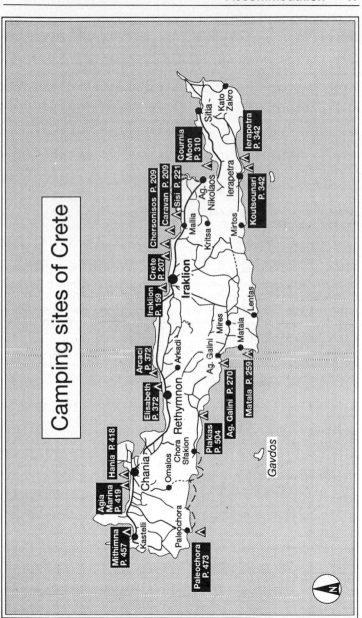

Camping sites of Crete

Sitia – Kato Zakro
Ierapetra P. 342
Gournia Moon P. 310
Koutsounari P. 342
Ag. Nikolaos
Ierapetra
Chersonisos P. 209
Caravan P. 209
Sisi P. 221
Mallia
Kritsa
Mirtos
Crete P. 207
Iraklion P. 159
Iraklion
Lentas
Arkadi
Mires
Arcaci P. 372
Ag. Galini
Matala
Matala P. 259
Ag. Galini P. 270
Elisabeth P. 372
Rethymnon
Plakias P. 504
Chora Sfakion
Omalos
Hania P. 418
Agia Marina P. 419
Chania
Palechora
Paleochora P. 473
Kastelli
Mithimna P. 457

Gavdos

N

Camping Iraklion: Comfortable, large site west of Iraklion. Little in the way of shade, however, sanitary equipment average, long sandy beach, salt-water swimming pool. April to October, tel. 081/250986.

Camping Crete: Medium-sized site east of Iraklion, unfavourable position next to a military area, and the shingle beach is not very attractive. May to September, tel. 0897/41400.

Camping Chersonisos: Opened in 1987, small site with a lot of grass. Bathing within walking distance.

Camping Caravan: Small site at the east end of the village of Limin Chersonisou. Shade under reed roofing, sandy bay nearby. April to October, tel. 0897/22025.

Camping Sisi : Small, simple site, about 1.25 miles west of Sisi. Bad approach road, but not very crowded. Only rocky cliffs on the coast here, but there is a swimming pool. April to October, tel. 0841/71247.

Camping Gournia Moon: About 9 miles east of Ayios Nikolaos. Small, peaceful situation, far away from any village. Little shade, pretty pebble cove between cliffs for bathing. May to October, tel. 0842/93243.

▶ SOUTH COAST *(from west to east)*

Camping Paleochora: Near Paleochora, a simple site with little shade, tolerably equipped, noisy disco. Pebble beach directly below site, 15 min. walk to a sandy beach. April to October, tel. 0823/41225.

Camping Plakias: Situated in Plakias, very simple, badly equipped, a lot of shade. A few minutes' walk away from a long sandy beach.

Camping Agia Galini: Medium-sized gravel area, adequate shade, a little back from a not very inviting pebble beach. Open all year round. tel. 0832/91386.

Camping Matala: Very simple, back-to-nature site, shade very unevenly distributed. However, dirt cheap and there is a sandy beach right in front of it. April-October, tel. 0892/42340.

Camping Koutsounari: East of Ierapetra, rather a poor site, and there could be more shade there, too. On the other hand, there is almost a mile of grey, sandy beach. Equipment is in order. May to September, tel. 0842/61213.

Camping Ierapetra: Almost a neighbour, similar to Koutsounari. May to September, tel. 0842/61351.

By the way, you are allowed to sleep on all camping sites *without a tent!*

Camping away from sites, sleeping rough

This is forbidden, as in the rest of Greece. The fact that it goes on everywhere despite the ban is another matter.

If the evening rush on the bushes on the beach is within limits, it will hardly disturb anyone. Only when the beds in the village are empty and the beaches full does discontent spread. Then complaints will be made about the "tramps" and the police will descend every few days.

Special care is taken in the high season to ensure that camping off site does not get out of hand in the coastal areas. Many beach and hotel guests could be disturbed by the sight of this picturesque group of individuals. Above all, the local people certainly begin to be disturbed when the general ceremony of ablutions begins in the nearest stream. Those sleeping rough should at least have the consideration not to undress down to the buff, thus injuring the morals of traditionally-raised villagers!

By now, the inhabitants of the hard-hit south coast have more or less grown accustomed to the herds of rucksack tourists, which descend on the small villages every summer, filling the tavernas in the evening, the disco at night, and the beach day and night. Whoever can do so takes a slice of the tourist cake for himself. Despite that, the elder generation of Cretans will not be able to accept the "new customs" quite completely; "Bay of Pigs" is the name given by the inhabitants of Souyia to the rocky cove at the end of the beach, which is almost entirely given over to a nudist colony.

There are particular places on Crete where extensive colonies of campers and those with sleeping bags come together every year. Among these are **Paleochora**, **Sougia**, **Damnoni** and **Preveli Beach** (both near Plakias) on the south coast, but also **Phalassarna** on the west coast, **Georgioupolis** on the north coast and **Sarakiniko Beach** on the island of Gavdos.

An exception is **Lentas**. The two taverna owners here are very much in favour of as many rucksack travellers as possible sleeping on the beach. The fact that the latter take all their meals there, from breakfast to dinner, means that the tavernas are not doing at all badly.

Those who sleep rough are very badly spoken of at the palm beach of **Vai**. Caravans, campers and rucksack travellers from all over the world have turned the beach here into what is more or less a rubbish dump in the space of a few years. Since then there have been strict controls and the police arrive at regular intervals, thus preventing any new developments; the "scene" has moved to a neighbouring beach.

Of course, this whole subject is often handled in a very delicate way by the communities. If camping off site and sleeping on the beach were rigorously forbidden, a loss of earnings would certainly soon be the result. After all, Crete attracts many young people because sleeping on the beach is so wonderful there.

Summary: The Cretans most certainly do not object to a single tent somewhere in the dunes. They are much too polite for that. In a place where man lives close to Nature, sleeping in the open air is certainly not disreputable. But the tone sets the mood, and a little more understanding and consideration on the part of rucksack tourists toWards the local people would not go amiss. Please do not leave rubbish behind you!

Always be prepared for petty theft when sleeping on the beach in well-known resorts!

Eating and Drinking

Local wines, chips and cordiality; delicacies from the grill; Kleftikó, the "bandit's meal"; 15 plates of Pikilía

Cretan food is simple and without ornament, appropriate to the conditions found on a rough, sun-scorched Mediterranean island.

Culinary high points and clever seasoning are rare. But there are steaming hot souvlaki from the charcoal grill, strong local wines and wobbly taverna tables, chips and a lot of sincerity.

The barren soil of Crete and the lack of stockraising only permit a limited variety, but this does not mean that the food is bad, it is just that the methods of preparation and variety of dishes available are only few. Individual ways of preparation are rare. A lot depends on the cook and the service; sometimes the food will be prepared with love and consideration, sometimes with negligence and no great effort put in. It is easy to notice when something tastes "different" in a taverna.

In recent years there has been an upsurge of restaurants of a thoroughly passable standard, especially in the large tourist centres. Their prices have remained realistic due to the hard competition around. It has become more noticeable that there is a trend towards serving particularly Cretan specialities when possible (see below for more details.)

Unfortunately, there is a dark side to tourism. The sheer volume of custom and frequently changing clientele have led many proprietors to perfect the art of "fast foods" in the larger resorts. Exorbitant prices are no rarity, either (when suspicious, check with the menu). In many hotels and established restaurants, international cuisine has made its appearance: roast chickens, Wiener Schnitzel and Cordon Bleu on a menu in four languages. Perhaps not quite what one expects from Crete?

On the other hand, after a hike through dried-up country, flimmering in the heat, after a lazy day on the beach, after a tiring tour of the Palace of Knossos or whatever else - a souvlaki, a country salad and *moussaká* will still taste good, even for the tenth time!

I had my greatest eating experience on Crete in an isolated village at the end of the season. I was the only customer in a taverna right on the beach. The sun went down, the trees rustled . . . the proprietress had a couple of pieces of steak in the fridge, otherwise nothing. So I had steak, and it had rarely tasted so good. Eating on Crete means imbibing the atmosphere, whether in a jolly retsina banquet on the beach or in the only taverna in a quiet mountain village. A simple meal can be found everywhere and perhaps the natural hospitality of the Cretan will do the rest.

Our Stifádo is polí kaló today (very good)!

Some typical local practices

The only things of which there is an overabundance on Crete are olive trees. Thus, all food is cooked in *olive oil*, and plenty of it! Even the old favourite "Greek salad" with tomatoes, slices of cucumber and *féta* (goats' cheese) is dripping with oil.

Perhaps it would be an idea to use olive oil for a while at home, in order to get acclimatised beforehand.

Many dishes in Cretan (and Greek) tavernas are prepared in the morning in huge pans and offered to customers during the day in a lukewarm state. The Greeks generally approve of this; northern Europeans do not always agree. If you wish to be sure of hot food, you should order souvlaki, grilled fish or casserole dishes that are freshly-prepared when an order is placed. Otherwise, it is quite possible to ask for the food to be heated up. In the tourist resorts, however, they have mostly become used to the demands of holidaymakers and everything is served hot.

Menus are generally printed in Greek and English; the only dishes available are those where a price is given. Usually, the price is in the second column.

Unfortunately, the menus are often old and the dishes are written in by hand - in Greek of course, and mostly quite illegible too. The best thing is to let them tell you what is available (in the resorts the waiters often speak English) or to go up to a counter where the day's specialities are displayed in casseroles or a special display cabinet. It is still quite normal to go into the kitchen and check the contents of the cooking pots in many tavernas. One should, however, always ask before doing this.

All dishes and accompaniments have to be ordered separately - there are hardly any set meals as we know them, and the individual puts his own meal together. As a rule, a full plate is brought of each item ordered. At the very most, Patates (chips) or noodles will be served as an automatic accompaniment to meat dishes.

If particular value is attached to the order in which dishes are served, it should be stated. Greek salad is always served as a starter.

When paying (*to logaryasmó parakaló* = the bill, please) a bill should be obtained for the whole table and you should settle up amongst yourselves later. Firstly, this makes life easier for waiters who are often under great stress, and secondly it accords with Cretan customs.

Prices are generally 20-30% lower than in the United Kingdom. A complete meal for 2 people might cost between £7-9.

The restaurants

There is hardly any difference today between *Estiatórion* and *Tavérna*. Previously, the Estiatórion was the "better" of the two with a larger choice of dishes; on the other hand in the taverna there was more atmosphere and often music. Today, both names indicate a restaurant or eating place. There is also the special *Psárotavérna,* or fish restaurant.

The *Kafeníon* is the favourite haunt of the Cretan male. It consists mostly of a few tables in a bare inside room with a few tables outside on the pavement. Cretan women only appear here behind the counter. The same goes for the *coffee bar.*

In the *Zácharoplastíon* (Confectioners'/cake shop) you can obtain cakes, sometimes ice cream and the tasty Lukumádes.

The *Ouzerí* offers the much-favoured mezedes in addition to ouzo and raki. These mezedes are little hors d'oeuvres and appetisers such as olives, mussels etc.

Meat

Meat is mostly imported from Athens. There are no cattle or pig-breeding establishments on the island, but more than enough sheep. Dishes served from the casserole are mostly very appetising. But a hearty meal of lamb should also be tried. It should not, however, be too fat.

• KEFTHEDES: "meat balls". These are usually rather more seasoned. Also called **biftéki.**

• KLEFTIKO: the "robbers' meal", consisting of potatoes and beef or lamb served in a clay pot or in aluminium foil. This is a Cretan speciality. The Kleftes (bandits) were partisans during the War of Independence against the Turks. They spent their life in hiding in the mountains and were fed secretly at night by their families. So that the food taken to them would not cool down too quickly, it was carried up to them in carefully sealed pots.

• KOKORETSI: offal wrapped round with the intestines and grilled on the spit.

• MOUSSAKA: A dish consisting of aubergines (eggplants), minced meat, sometimes potatoes, topped with a thick béchamel sauce. Prepared on a large baking tray and kept warm the whole day; mostly made with olive oil.

• PAIDAKIA: lamb cutlets. The lamb is grilled over charcoal and the best pieces are cut off. The more tender and lean, the better the lamb. It is a particular speciality in Vrises, near Chania. See page 394.

• PASTITSIO: A noodle dish with minced meat and tomatoes. Baked with cheese on top.

• SOUVLAKI: The national dish of Greece, known well enough to all travellers to Greece. These aromatic skewers of meat, either lamb or pork, are seasoned with origano and grilled over charcoal. They may be large or small, are mostly reasonable in price and can be obtained everywhere. A little lemon improves the flavour.

• STIFADO: A speciality which is all too rarely to be had. Tender, coarse textured beef with a delicious accompaniment of onions flavoured with cinnamon and mostly served in a clay pot.

• OTHER MEAT DISHES: **arnáki** (lamb), **arní** (mutton), **brizóla** (chops), **chirinó** (pork), **kimá** (minced meat), **kotópoulo** (chicken), **moschári** (veal), **sikóti** (liver), **vódi** (beef).

Fish and Seafood

These are much more expensive than meat. The fishing grounds around Crete have practically been fished dry, and the Cretan deep sea fishermen are often away for weeks, going as far as the Turkish or African coast. Much fish is imported, both from Piraeus, with its large fishing fleets constantly away in the Aegean, and even from Canada and Argentina.

Some fish are also caught around Crete by the method of fishing with dynamite, which is strictly illegal (see also page 79).The occasional accident is an occupational hazard here. The word for fish is *psári*. The price per kilo is normally given on the menu.

Swordfish is a delicacy on Crete

- GOPA: The simplest and cheapest of fish dishes. These tiny bogue, hardly as long as a finger, are sold in portions for around £1.30.

- KALAMARAKIA: squid. These are cut into pieces and deep-fried in oil.

- PESTROFA: trout. The only trout farm of this non-native fresh-water fish on Crete is at Zaros, on the southern slopes of Mount Ida (see page 265).

- PSAROSOUPA: fish soup. Only to be had in definite fish tavernas such as in the harbours of Rethymnon and Chania. Various fish are used, and even leftovers are made into a steaming stock with onions, potatoes and carrots.

- XIFIAS: swordfish. Quite delicious. These fine fish, which are several feet in length, are carefully cut into thick slices. The swordfish is a large fish, which can only be caught far out at sea.

- OTHER FISH AND SEAFOOD: **astakós** (lobster), **barbúnia** (red mullet), **chtapódi** (octopus), **fangrí** (sea bream), **gardiá** (crevette), **garídes** (prawns), **marídes** (sardines/sprats), **sfirída** (merou blanc), **tónnos** (tunny).

Other main dishes

- TOMATES YEMISTES: tomatoes filled with rice. These can be eaten everywhere. Less common are piperyés yemistés, stuffed peppers.

- MAKARONIA KIMA: spaghetti with a minced meat sauce.

- PIKILIA: A quantity of small dishes served all together on at least 10 to 15 plates. There are small meat balls, satziki, prawns, stuffed vine leaves, snails, olives, féta, and many other things besides.

Accompaniments

• **Arakádes** (peas), **angóuri** (cucumber), **fassólia** (beans), **gígandes** (large white "butter" beans), **karóta** (carrots), **melitzánes** (aubergines), **patátes** (potatoes or chips), **piláfi** (rice), **piperyés** (peppers), **spanáki** (spinach), **tomáta** (tomatoes).

• HORTA: A special Cretan wild vegetable, which grows everywhere like a weed. Resembling spinach, it is cooked with olive oil, flavoured with garlic, and sprinkled with lemon juice.

Salads

• CHORIATIKI SALATA: The favourite salad is, of course, the famous Greek country salad ("Greek salad"). It consists of tomatoes, cucumbers, green lettuce leaves and olives. The whole thing is crowned with a slice of aromatic, crumbly féta (goats' cheese). The choriátiki is mostly served as a starter, but can also be eaten as an accompaniment to a main meal. With a little bread, it can also provide an adequate midday meal.

• OTHER SALADS: **angourotomátasaláta** (tomato and cucumber salad), **láchano-saláta** (cabbage salad), **maroúlisaláta** (lettuce), **tomátosaláta** (tomato salad).

Starters

Perhaps first of all to an ouzerí, to drink an ouzo or a raki, the strong spirit made from the remains of the grape pressings.

Particularly here you will find the numerous mezédes (little appetisers): chunks of cheese, slices of tomato and cucumber, scampi, snails, olives, small pieces of melon, mussels and other delicious little things. Pistachios or almonds are mostly offered with raki.

• LIGHT APPETISERS: **arsinósaláta** (sea-urchin salad), **dolmadákia** (stuffed vine leaves) filled with rice and herbs, **taramosaláta** (fish-roe salad), **tonnosaláta** (tuna fish salad), **tsatsíki** (yoghurt with garlic and cucumber).

Desserts/Sweets

These are to be found in the *Zácharoplastíon*, a confectioner's/cake shop.

• BAKLAVA: sweet rolls of flaky pastry filled with nuts and honey, originating from Turkey.

• LUKUMADES: especially delicious! Light dough balls deep fried in hot oil and served with honey poured over them.

• BUGATSA: puff pastries filled with a yoghurt/cream cheese mixture. Highly recommended.

• RISOGALO: milky rice pudding, unfortunately seldom available.

• YAURTI: sheeps' yoghurt with honey (**méli**) is a speciality of the island. You should try it in Vrises near Chania.

• HALVA: a crunchy-sweet confection made from honey and sesame seed.

Fruit

A large part of the fruit harvested on Crete is immediately shipped to the Greek mainland and sent partly as exports to the countries of the EC. Cretan sultanas are especially prized. More details in the chapter on *Economy*.

● BANANAS (**banánes**): The sweet Cretan bananas, a hand's width in length, are a particular speciality of the island. They grow chiefly around Mallia and Ierapetra and are mostly ripe in the early part of the winter. Unfortunately, they disappear to a large extent on the Greek black market and reappear in the factories of northern Greece as baby food. They are prized on Crete and seemingly expensive.

● ORANGES (**portokáli**): There is a huge orange-growing area around Chania, and another around the small village of Fodele west of Iraklion. These citrus fruits are also ripe in the early winter, but in contrast to bananas they are cheap and easy to obtain throughout the island.

● CHERRIES (**kerásia**): Even if you don't believe it, the cherries which grow in the fertile Amari basin between Kedros and the Ida range are a favourite delicacy in the whole of Greece. The area of orchards lies around the village of Gerakari.

● GRAPES (**stafíli**): The noble **Rosakiá** grapes which produce a good wine grow in the vineyards behind Iraklion. There are huge drying frames to be seen everywhere, especially in the period from the end of August/beginning of September. The grapes are dried on these and thus become the famous sultanas. Their export is a main pillar of the island economy.

● OTHER TYPES OF FRUITS: **kolokíti** (pumpkin), **karpúsi** (water melon), **pepóni** (honeydew melon), **amígdala** (almonds), **mílo** (apple), **síka** (figs).

Miscellaneous

Bread (*psomí*): the main constituent of a meal. No meal is complete without bread, and it is always offered, even when the meal contains enough starch in the form of noodles or potatoes.

In many villages, families do their own baking, and the old-fashioned ovens blackened with soot can often be seen. The delicious dark bread (*choriatikó* = country bread) has now become a rarity and there is practically only white bread available, which is lacking in nutritional value - *áspro* or *léfko psomí*. It tastes good when fresh, but goes hard very quickly.

Some of the bread is baked for 24 hours longer; this produces *paximádi*, which can be kept almost indefinitely. A type of rock-hard toast is the result (before it can be eaten, it has to be soaked in water for a while, then it becomes soft again). It is also sold ready packaged in the shops.

Cheese (*tirí*): This is, of course, mainly produced from sheep's milk. Apart from the famous *féta* there is also a cream cheese called *mizíthra*, which is mostly produced in the cooler months of the year. Then there is *kefalotíri*, the hard, skittle-shaped "head cheese", which is mainly produced by the shepherds in the plateau of Katharo in eastern Crete (comparable to Parmesan).

Breakfast: As is the case in most Mediterranean countries, the Cretans do not have much for breakfast.
For tourists, however, "breakfast" is available in all cafés and tavernas, and consists of bread, butter, marmalade or something similar. If desired, an egg *(avgó)* or an omelette will be served, and it is often possible to order yoghurt *(gaúrti)*, milk *(gála)* or chocolate *(gála schokoláta)*. Fruit muesli and freshly-squeezed orange juice can often be had in the tourist resorts.

Drinks

Water *(neró):* traditionally the most important drink. As there is a constant shortage of water, everyone knows its value. It used to be the case that plenty of water was served both during a meal in a restaurant and then afterwards with coffee, but this practice is unfortunately becoming increasingly rare. Many Cretans view it as wasteful when a carafe full of water is placed on a table and the tourists drink only half of it at the most. If you are brought water, you should try to make use of it if you can! Even more so, when you have especially asked for it.

Coffee: If you want the typical Greek coffee, a strong, black mocca concoction in tiny cups, you should ask especially for *kafé ellinikó* or Greek coffee. The Cretans have become so used to foreigners that in cases of uncertainty they will always bring you a northern European-type Nescafé if you ask for coffee.
On no account order "Turkish coffee"!!

• KAFE ELLINIKO: **éna elafrí kafé** (weak), **métrio** (medium strong, with sugar), **varí glikó** (very sweet), **skéto** (without sugar), **varí glikó me polí kafé** (very sweet and strong).

• NESCAFE: **zestó** (hot), **frappé** (cold), **skéto** (black, without sugar), **me záchari** (with sugar), **me gála** (with milk).

Lemonade: Every place on Crete has its own lemonade factory . . . or at least nearly every place. For example, lemonade from Piskokephalo village, which is just under 2 miles away, is drunk almost exclusively in the Sitia area, while in and around Zakros there is lemonade from Zakros etc. It is mostly sold in very small bottles, cheap, very sweet and pleasant-tasting. At any rate, it is better than the well-known products of the US giants.
When *limonáda* is ordered, this means lemonade. The word for orangeade is *portokaláda*.

Beer: There are large quantities of beer on Crete, and a subsidiary of the Henninger Brewery even produces beer on Crete. The local people like this non-native brew and drink a lot of it.

Beer was introduced to Greece in the first half of the 19th century. At that time, Otto I, son of the king of Bavaria, was king of Greece. And of course he brought his beer and his brewer along.

It is mostly served ice-cold, wonderfully refreshing on hot days.

Wine: There is bottled wine and wine from the barrel. The latter is always preferable; it is cheaper because it is often a product of a local vineyard, and it is often better and simply the real thing. It is, however, seldom well-chilled, because it is stored in large barrels (ask for wine *ap to varéli* = from the barrel). There is good wine from the barrel, for example, in Chania and in Sitia *(Agrílos).*

One of the best bottled wines on Crete is *Minos.* It is not exactly cheap, but full in flavour and fruity. Other good names are *Gortys* and *Lato.* Cretan wines are generally strong, and you are urged to be careful at the beginning.

The famous resinated wine *Retsína* is an import from the mainland. It originally acquired its resin taste from the wooden barrels in which it was produced. These were made watertight using resin from the Lebanon cedar. Since then this wine, which tastes unusual when drunk for the first time, has become the emblem of Greek viticulture. Resin or an artificial flavouring is added to the metal barrels used today, in order to impart this typical flavour to the wine.

• **krassí** (wine), **mávro krassí** or **kokkíno** (red wine), **áspro krassí** (white wine).

Rakí: A clear spirit distilled from the remains of the grapes after pressing. This is produced in small distilleries or privately all over Crete in the autumn, and it tastes different in every village according to ingredients, method of preparation and quality of the grapes. The smaller and sweeter the grapes, the better the rakí. Characteristically, there is often a light after-taste, due to the fact that the distilling vats and storage vessels are often wiped out with sheep's fat. Rakí can only be obtained in bottles filled by farmers or taverna owners. There is no mass production of rakí by a factory. It is sometimes called *Tsikoudiá.*

Of course, *ouzo* can be obtained everywhere on Crete, as in the rest of Greece. This is the famous aniseed spirit. It changes colour to a milky white when diluted with water, but can also be drunk undiluted.

Sport

Strong-wind surfing in the south; tennis courses in the big hotels; diving for lost cities

The range of sports facilities on offer is relatively limited, and a lot is left to personal initiative.

Yachting

Only a few yachts have found their way to Crete up to now, although the distance from Athens is only around 150 nautical miles. There are well-constructed provisioning stations on the north coast, namely Iraklion, Rethymnon, Chania, Agios Nikolaos and Sitia.

The Aegean Sea is also a windy place in summer. Above all, the sometimes blustery *Meltemi* winds which blow from a north to north west direction can be unpleasant. As weather conditions in the eastern Mediterranean are often of a very local character, one can quickly be taken by surprise by a change in the weather.

• **Arrival by land :** There are no problems involved in bringing a private yacht by towing it behind a car on a trailer. Customs officers will note details of the car and the yacht in the passport at the point of entry. When leaving Greece, both must naturally be taken out of the country with you. Maximum sizes of yachts permitted are: length 15 m, width 2.5 m and height 3.5 m (c. 49.05, and c. 11.45 feet respectively).

• **Arrival by sea:** After reaching Greek territorial waters, you must make immediately for a **Port of Entry**. In the case of Crete, these are Chania or Iraklion; before these, there are Corfu (an island off the west coast of Greece), Patras (Peloponnese), and Zakynthos (an island off the west coast of the Peloponnese), amongst others.

On entering, the Greek flag and international signal alphabet flag Q must be flown. The harbour authorities will want to look at all passports and a list of crew members, and will then issue a **Transit Log** for a fee of £9, which is valid for a year. **The International Sports Boat Certificate** or a comparable document is obligatory. A Port of Entry is likewise the place from which the yacht may leave the country. Changes among crew members have to be reported! Berthing fees in harbours and marinas range between c. £10-13 per day.

• **Chartered boats:** A lot of care has to be taken here. Chartering permission is only granted to boats which sail under the Greek flag. The charter company or yacht owner must have a licence from the National Tourist Organisation or the Hellenic Ministry of Merchant Marine. The contract must be the **official Greek chartering contract** permitted by the Hellenic Ministry of Merchant Marine.

• INFORMATION: A list of harbours with provisioning stations and berths for yachts can be obtained from the **Greek National Tourist Office.** Further information for amateur sailors, eg advice on routes, is also available there.

Surfing

The magic word here is *Meltemi*. This strong, often blustery wind from a north to north-west direction frequently blows for days on end in the summer. Whereas it blows onto the flatter north coast as an onshore wind, it blows from the steep mountain slopes diagonally down to the south coast as an offshore wind. For this reason, beginners should choose the north coast as a surfing area. Advanced surfers with experience of strong winds can try their luck in the south.

● **South coast:** One of the best spots is undoubtedly the sandy cove of **Plakias**, the legendary wind tunnel of the south coast. The Meltemi can reach force 8 here, and the surfer should bring his own equipment for use in strong winds. Other good possibilities are to be found near **Ierapetra** and in the large bay at the exit to the Messara Plain (**Agia Galini, Matala**).

● **North coast**: At the most, the Meltemi reaches force 4 here. This can also produce high waves, but it is always an onshore wind. Generally, however, the sea is calm. There are many beaches suitable for surfing, surfboards can be hired almost everywhere, and a variety of surfing schools offer their services. The beach at **Rethymnon** between the two moles is especially suitable for beginners.

● RENTAL: Surfboards can be hired on many beaches for c. £3-5 per hour, and a week costs c. £57-67. There is no equipment available for heavy wind surfing.

● WINDSURFING SCHOOLS: **Crete Windsurfing Centre** in the Capsis Beach Hotel/Agia Pelagia; **Meltemi Surfing** in the Hotel Minoa Palace/Amnissos; **Vangelis Surfing School** in Limin Chersonisou, 16, Malikouti Street; **Sunwind** in the Hotel Istron Bay, east of Agios Nikolaos, among others.

Diving

Snorkelling is permitted almost everywhere, as is diving with bottles and diving suits, except in the immediate vicinity of an archaeological site. Such underwater sites are particularly common on Crete, since the west coastline of Crete has risen by a few metres in historical times, whereas the east coast has sunk.

The best possibilities exist along the jagged cliff coastline in the south, and also on the lonely west coast and in the east. For those who like exploring, the ancient sunken harbours such as *Olous* (near Elounda), *Limin Chersonisou, Itanos, Mochlos* etc. are of interest. It is only possible to dive with a snorkel and flippers at these places. There are severe penalties for the removal of archaeological material. Far too many amateur divers have found ancient "souvenirs" on the sea bed and "caused them to disappear".

● DIVING EQUIPMENT: This can be rented from some of the large beach hotels on Crete, and these also offer diving courses, eg in the **Hotel Peninsula**/Agia Pelagia (c. £17 for each diving session), in the **Hotel Kalypso**/Plakias (with vasili, c. £14 per diving session) and in the **Hotel Elounda Beach**/Elounda (Ski School, c. £20).
Apart from this, according to reports, equipment also available in Ierapetra, Limin Chersonisou and in a shop selling diving equipment in Iraklion, on the road to the airport.

• HARPOONS: These are permitted, but only without the use of diving suits and bottles and not for taking fish under 150 gr. in weight. Because of the further restrictions which are frequently imposed it is essential to obtain information from the tourist or port police.

▶ Fishing: allowed everywhere without any restrictions. A catch can hardly be expected from freshwater on Crete, and the sea around the island is no longer rich in fish. The only freshwater lake worthy of note on Crete is near Georgioupolis (north coast).

▶ Water skiing: the main centre is at Elounda, but also possible at the other larger cities on the north coast and at individual hotels.

▶ Tennis: Over 40 hotels in the Luxury, A and B categories have their own tennis courts. The larger hotel establishments mostly have several hard courts; thus the *Robinson Club Lyttos Beach* has 13 hard courts, the *Rythimna Beach Hotel* near Rethymnon has 6, and the *Creta Maris* in Limin Chersonisou has 4, to name only a few examples. Licensed tennis coaches, who offer courses for beginners and advanced players, are often employed during the high season.

The condition of the courts varies from place to place, however, and it depends on the hotel. Not all are in good condition, and most are completely open to the burning heat of the sun. High summer is therefore not a particularly good time for a tennis vacation on Crete.

▶ Riding: The only riding stable on Crete is to the east of Iraklion, on the beach at Amnissos. 40 horses are available here. There are day trips on horseback or with horse and cart to the rural hinterland, where the owner of the stables has a rakí distillery. Hotel guests from Limin Chersonisou and Mallia are picked up at their hotels. Price per day c. £17. Beginners are also welcome. Tel. 081/282005. Information available in Mallia on the road leading to the beach, opposite the Florella Hotel, and in Limin Chersonisou on the beach road leading to the Creta Maris Hotel, next door to the Hotel Castri. See also page 161.

▶ For Hiking see under the chapter *Travelling Around Crete,* page 39.

AT A GLANCE

SIZE: Crete is the largest of the Greek islands, and after Sicily, Sardinia, Cyprus and Corsica the fifth largest in the Mediterranean; it has an area of about 3,237 sq. miles, is 162 miles long, and 11-37 miles wide.

HIGHEST POINTS: The highest mountain peak is that of **Timios Stavros** in the Ida range, with a height of 8,031 feet. This is followed by **Pachnes** in the Lefka Ori (West Crete), which is all of 13 feet lower.

PLAINS: The largest plain is the **Messara Plain** in the southern part of central Crete, with an area of 54 sq. miles. There are other large plains around Chania and Rethymnon.

POPULATION: With just 600,000 inhabitants, Crete is relatively thinly-populated. A large area of the island is mountainous and sparsely inhabited. The largest cities are **Iraklion**/110,000 inhabitants, and **Chania**/52,000 inhabitants, then way behind these comes **Rethymnon**/19,000, **Ierapetra**/8,000, **Sitia**/7,000 and **Agios Nikolaos**/5,000. With the exception of Ierapetra, they are all situated on the north coast, which is easily accessible to air and sea traffic. Iraklion has resumed its function as the capital since 1972; previously Chania had been the capital for centuries.

TRAVEL CONNECTIONS: Crete has two large harbours: one at **Iraklion** and the other in the **Bay of Souda** (near Chania), apart from other harbours at Kastelli, Rethymnon, Agios Nikolaos and Sitia. There are three civil airports at **Iraklion**, **Sternes** (on the Akrotiri peninsula near Chania) and **Sitia.** International air traffic only lands at Iraklion.

ECONOMY: Just under 40% of the ground area is agriculturally useful. The small amount of industry there is on the island is centred around Iraklion.

GOVERNMENT: Crete is one of the 10 administrative districts of Greece, and is represented in the Athens Parliament by 13 members. The island is subdivided into 4 administrative areas (Nomoi): **Chania** (capital at Chania), **Rethymnon** (capital at Rethymnon), **Iraklion** (capital at Iraklion) and **Lassithi** (capital at Agios Nikolaos).

UNIVERSITY: The **University of Crete** consists of 5 faculties in Rethymnon (languages, philosophy, sociology, psychology, and education, with 3,000 students) and 4 in Iraklion (physics, mathematics, chemistry, and medicine, with 5,500 students). The Polytechnic is situated at Chania.

TOURISM: The following statistics are very revealing - In the administrative area of Iraklion there is to be found 53% of all sleeping accommodation for tourists on Crete (1,431,000 beds), in Lassithi 24% (648,000), in the Nomos Rethymnon 12% (324,000) and in the Nomos Chania all of 11% (297,000 beds). This gives a proud total of 2,700,000 beds, five times as many beds as there are inhabitants on the island!

A place to dream away the hours

Crete

A long drawn-out mountain range in the sea, its dark brown outline a long way off in the haze. There is far too little time to catch a glimpse of the striking profile of the island, before the plane begins its descent over the inky-blue sea off Iraklion.

Crete lies like a huge bar or bolt at the southern edge of the Aegean. The mountains are never far away, and four mighty mountain chains dominate the landscape. In a northerly direction, they progress gently into foothills and form great coastal plains, on which all the important cities are situated.

The picture is different in the south. Here, the six thousand footers end in abrupt, rugged precipices. It is a steep coastline with rocks, deposited sand and gravel beaches, and tiny villages between high cliffs, with the sun beating mercilessly down on them.

The beaches are well-distributed around the whole island. Long, light brown sandy beaches with less striking hinterland dominate mainly in the north. The big beach hotels have especially established themselves between *Iraklion* and *Agios Nikolaos*. But there are still beautiful spots to be found there.

In the south, the beaches are hidden in rocky coves, and the land-scape is more impressive, wilder and more primordial. Up to now, the area has rather been the domain of rucksack tourists, but now tour-ism on a big scale is on the march; *Agia Galini*, *Matala* and more re-cently *Plakias* are the front runners.

By contrast, the west is almost empty of people. A panoramic road runs high up along the coast, above the sea.

▶ **High plateaux:** These are a special feature of Crete. Whether it is Omalos, Lassithi or Nida, these round plateaux are to be found every-where in the mountains, well protected through their cliff walls. Soil which has been washed down from the cliffs collects in these places and provides the conditions for fertile cultivation. Fruit is chiefly grown on the famous Lassithi high plateau, and the windmills with their white sails pump up water from caverns in the porous lime-stone; these also constitute a great attraction for busloads of tourists.

▶ **Plains:** Only a tiny fraction of the island is flat, and this is mainly around the cities on the north coast. The largest plain is the beautiful *Messara Plain* on the south coast near Matala; it is a fine area with a cultivated, almost garden landscape with miles of olive, fruit and veg-etable plantations, and the mighty Ida range surging in the back-ground. Even the Minoans established one of their centres here.

In prehistoric times, the Messara Plain was probably still a sea bay, just like the flat "wasp waist" of Crete, between Pachia Ammos and Ierapetra. Sitia and its environs probably made up a separate island at that time.

▶ **Vegetation:** This is mostly sparse, and the mountains have been defor-ested; conquerors have helped themselves over the millenia. Only in the west is there a larger expanse of continuous forest. Instead, mil-lions of silvery-green olive trees characterise the face of the island. Harvesting of these small fruits does not bring in a lot of money, but it is an important branch of the economy. The vineyards with their terraces are surrounded by thorny scrub and herb bushes; everything is parched. *Bananas* are the chief crop in the southeast, around Ierapetra, and a sea of hothouses there ensures their rapid ripening. In some isolated places fine *date palms* flourish. The palm beach at Vai has been more than discovered from the tourist point of view.

▶ **Water:** A constant source of surprise are the strong springs which have gouged out deep furrows towards the sea in the valleys; these rise everywhere in the high mountains. Although the island is parched in high summer and most of the watercourses have dried up, glass-clear, ice-cold streams are to be found on many beaches. They are very refreshing and provide a welcome change to sea bathing.

Most attractive of these are *Georgioupólis* (between Rethymnon and Chania), *Preveli* (on the south coast near Plakia) and the *Samaria Gorge*.

The only fresh water lake on Crete is also situated near Georgioupolis.

▶ **Geology:** Crete is part of a large arc of mountains, which swings across from the western part of mainland Greece, through the Peloponnese and the southern Greek islands and deep into Turkey. The highest peak in this Tertiary mountain system is Timios Stavros in the Ida range on Crete, with a height of 8,031 feet. The Tertiary elevations and depressions of the earth's surface have had a very strong effect on Crete, due to its exposed position on the very edge of the Aegean basin, and have given rise to a complicated surface structure.

The four mighty mountain chains on the island consist mainly of schist and limestone, and they already existed in the Triassic period, 140 million years before the onset of the Tertiary period. The deeply-etched valleys, especially those in the south west (Samaria Gorge), are the result of strong erosion, which has been persistent due to the great height and steepness of the mountains. The surrounding hilly regions which are made up of limestone are much younger, and they have likewise been rendered quite barren because of forest clearance for cultivation.

Even today, eustatic movements continue. Changes in the land level have been taking place for millenia; the land in the western part of Crete is rising, whereas in the east, it is slowly sinking.

Sunken Cities

Even in historical times - that is, in the first few centuries AD - the land level in the west of Crete rose by around 26 feet, while the coastline sank below sea level in the east. The evidence for this is to be seen in the ancient harbour towns, which according to tradition were situated by the sea. Thus, for example, there is *Phalassarna* in the extreme west, the ruins of which are situated about 153 yards inland and above sea level; and then there are the walls of ancient *Olous* near Elounda in eastern Crete, which are visible several feet under the sea.

The raised coastline in the west can be clearly seen if a boat trip is made along the precipitous southern coastline from Paleochora to Chora Sfakion.

The main regions at a glance

Western Crete

This is the most mountainous and greenest part of the island, due to the constant south-westerly winds, which regularly bring rain with them in the cooler season of the year. The *Lefka Ori* (White Mountains) dominate the scene. Their bare, rocky peaks rise to almost 8,250 feet. Towards the south coast they are interrupted by huge ravines; the *Samaria Gorge* is one of the most impressive phenomena on the island. The spreading Cretan cypress trees once stood in thick forests in this region; conquerors helped themselves and acquired the wood they needed here. Today, there are only a few road passes through these lonely heights down to the small villages on the Libyan sea, and boats are the most important means of transport.

Central Crete

The hinterland of Iraklion is one large vineyard. The endless, gentle hillscape forms the largest continuous wine-producing area in Greece. Apart from *Knossos*, site of the world-famous Minoan palace, most worthy of mention is *Archanes*, at present the focal point where archaeology is concerned. Irrefutable evidence has been discovered there that the Minoans made at least one human sacrifice. This sun-scorched region is flanked in the west by the mighty *Ida Range*. *Timios Stavros* is the highest peak on the island with a height of 8,031 feet. Zeus, father of the gods, is reputed to have grown up in these mountains. A favourite starting point is *Anogia*, centre of the high mountain pastures for over one hundred thousand sheep. Mountain ramblers go further up to the *Nida Plateau* and the famous Cave of Zeus.

The *Dikti Range* in the eastern part of central Crete is easily reached from the north coast and from Agios Nikolaos. The impressive journey up to the top ends on the *Lassithi Plateau*, which is quite flat and almost circular in shape; this is where Zeus was born!

The south is characterised by the broad *Messara Plain*, one of the most fertile regions of the island. This served as an important base for the Minoans as well as for the Romans, who later ruled on Crete. The legendary caves at *Matala*, which were once used for habitation, are one of the many attractions of the region.

Eastern Crete

Eastern Crete is mostly barren, dry and rocky. It is dominated by the grey *Sitia Mountains*, which are only about 4,950 feet high but wild and not very accessible. A lively tourist resort has established itself in the shape of Agios Nikolaos, which still imparts an atmosphere in spite of the bustle. Other high points are the huge *Bay of Mirabello*, the legendary *Palm Beach* at *Vai*, and the Minoan palace at *Kato Zakros*. The endless grey pebble beaches near *Ierapetra* offer opportunities for bathing.

Climate/Time to travel

Truly an island of sun; you can be sure of a cloudless sky from the end of April to the middle of October!

After Cyprus, Crete is the island which receives the second largest amount of sun both in the whole of Greece and the Mediterranean, with 300 days of sunshine per year. It is even possible to venture into the water on the south coast in December.

Crete has a rainy and a fine-weather season. The transition periods are less definable; the spring is short but beautiful, and there is hardly an autumn in our sense of the word.

A Year on Crete . . .

From the *end of March* onwards the rains cease, and the whole island blooms in *April*, particularly the wonderful agave-aloe cacti. The temperature climbs to 17°C. *May* and *June* are the ideal months for travelling, because as a rule at that time it is not yet unbearably hot on the island. Everything is green, and there are pinky red oleander flowers in the gorges; the island has not yet dried up and become scorched.

It gets hotter from *July* onwards. Crete is transformed into a dusty, parched land of weak yellow and brown hues. You will come to appreciate the clusters of lush green vegetation all the more at this time - the fleshy, light green banana plants, the shady plane trees, the lofty date palms, and the grapes which are ripening everywhere. The best idea is to crawl into the shade in the burning heat of the midday sun; the sand on the beach gets hot so quickly that it is no longer possible to walk barefoot, and the sea is the only place to cool down. Taken as a whole, the high summer temperatures on Crete are quite bearable, because there is very little humidity. It could be described as having a relatively pleasant atmosphere, like that of an oven. The late afternoons and warm evenings are fabulous, once the heat has died down.

Then one begins to look forward to the next day, in the knowledge that there is no danger of rain or cold spells . . .

The heat only begins to die away from the *middle of October* onwards. The first indication of this is that the evenings and nights are cooler and damper. All activity now moves to the south coast, where the last few fine days can be enjoyed. Most of the tourists have gone, but some are only just arriving; the south coast of Crete offers the last chance to experience the summer in Europe, at a time when the leaves are turning brown at home. There are occasional clouds now; if it rains, it may teem down over a period of several days, then follows a stormy day and finally, as always, the sun shines again. The sea becomes choppier, boats have difficulty in leaving the harbours on the south coast, and there are only occasional trips to the small island of Gavdos. This is the southernmost island of Greece, 25 miles off the south coast of Crete.

From *November* onwards there is the rainy season. The tavernas, restaurants and hotels close. The last tourists leave the island, and only those spending the winter there move down to Ierapetra and the region around it, which now has the mildest climate on Crete. Meanwhile, in the chilly mountain villages, everything centres around the enormous heating stoves. Frost is extremely rare on the coast, but the rain is often accompanied by vigorous storms. It sometimes rains for days on end, but then the sun shines again.

The snow line lies at about 1,980 feet above sea level; in January it is possible to ski in the high mountains and bathe on the south coast.

APPROXIMATE AVERAGE TEMPERATURES (in Degrees C°)			
Month	**Air** (daytime)	**Sea**	**Days of rain**
January	15	16	13
February	16	16	10
March	17	16	8
April	20	18	4
May	23	20	3
June	27	22	1
July	29	24	0
August	29	25	0
September	27	24	2
October	24	23	5
November	20	19	8
December	17	16	12

The lowest daytime temperature ever recorded in Iraklion (in 1928) was **0.1 degrees centigrade!!**

The highest (in 1914) + **45.7 degrees centigrade!!**

The winds on Crete

The cool *north to north-westerly Meltemi* often blows for days on end in the summer. It brings pleasant, cool air, but is often strong to gusting in force. While it blows directly from the sea on the north coast, it whistles down the mountain faces in the south and develops forces of up to 8 Beaufort there. This can lead to little sandstorms on sandy beaches.

The south coast is mainly affected by the dreaded *Scirocco*, which is sometimes called Livas because it blows from Libya. This can also last for days. It brings with it sand and dust from the Sahara, which colour the atmosphere yellow and get into the finest crevices, as well as into clothes. Everything bad that happens on Crete takes place when the south wind is blowing; it is even supposed to have been blowing when Knossos was destroyed in a mysterious catastrophe. The Scirocco can increase to hurricane strength, but it can also produce an atmosphere thick enough to cut with a knife, extremely warm and immovable. Then, it lies like a thick blanket over everything, and it is hardly possible to breathe . . . a day later everything seems to have been blown away. These peculiar days can also be experienced on the north coast.

In the cooler half of the year, the damp west or south-westerly *Punentis* (Ponente) brings a proportionally large amount of precipitation to western Crete.

Vegetation

A typical Mediterranean picture. Where in previous times there were huge forests of cypresses and cedars, bare limestone rocks are to be seen today, dotted with an immense sea of silvery-green olive trees. Between these flourish thorn bushes, knee-high phrygana and countless fragrant herb bushes. A contrast is provided by aloe cactus several feet high, wild carob trees, lush vines and oleander.

In spite of the great drought in the summer months, there are today still over 1,500 different types of plants native to the island. Thus, Crete is amongst the Mediterranean islands which are richest in vegetation.

Nature particularly shows her best face towards the end of the rainy season (March, April). The huge meadow and limestone areas are a veritable sea of flowers at that time. Yellow-white daisies, brilliant red poppies and white narcissi constitute these huge fields of flowers which ripple gently in the wind. The vibrating hum of busy insects is everywhere. If the winter was a damp one, then everything grows twice as well. Crete in spring and Crete in summer - two very different aspects.

Trees on Crete

During antiquity, Crete was well-known for its huge forests of *cypresses* and *cedars*, which are reputed to have covered the whole island at the time. They now belong to the past. The Minoans feverishly cut down the huge trees in order to use durable but elastic pillars in the construction of their palaces (earthquakes!). However, the irresponsible plundering which took place in the middle ages and recent times has done serious damage to the once green island. Over a period of centuries, the *Venetians* and the *Turks* were vigorously engaged in chopping down the valuable forests, for the building of houses and ships, for the production of charcoal, and even in order to destroy the hiding places of the Cretan resistance.

Despite all this, Crete does still occasionally exhibit lush patches of green. Miles of cliffs wooded with chestnut trees, deep valleys with streams running through them and huge plane trees, and even wonderful palm groves along river courses characterise some regions. The largest areas of extensive forest are situated on the slopes of the *White Mountains* in the west, in the *Samaria Gorge*, which lies in the southern part of the west coast, and on the roads which run southwards from Kastelli. Apart from the chestnut trees already mentioned there are chiefly the broad dark green mountain cypresses. The unpretentious Aleppo pine has frequently been planted around Minoan sites and is favoured in forestation programmes (eg eastwards of Ierapetra).

Reforestation measures and the preservation of natural habitat are actually finding a wide area of application. Even foreign assistance has brought results. In the early eighties, saplings were flown in from the Federal Republic of Germany, along with a forestry expert, and these have flourished. They were planted near the little village of *Vlatos* on the road from Kastelli to the beach at Elafonisi. A drive along this road is the best of all experiences, where the vegetation of Crete is concerned. Thus the fact that there are always carelessly thrown cigarettes to endanger what has been so painstakingly achieved is all the more terrible. A few years ago, on the southern

The fine flowering stems of the aloe cactus are visible from afar

slopes of the Dikti range near Mirtos, a whole square kilometre of forest went up like a torch.

The dry eastern part of Crete today consists of large areas of scrub, phrygana and rocky desert without a tree or a bush.

Olive trees: Even when there are no more forests, these self-sufficient, often ancient trees with their knotty, weatherbeaten trunks are literally everywhere. Crete contains millions of them (according to estimates there are between 40 and 50 million), and the production of olive oil is a main branch of the modest island economy today. Everything is concerned with the harvest in winter. However, the profit margin is not very large, and citrus trees are a better commercial proposition.

THE HARVESTING AND PROCESSING OF OLIVES

Large nets or plastic sheets are spread out beneath the trees in the autumn; as soon as the olives are ripe, they fall off. What remains on the tree is knocked off with a stick or by shaking the tree. After the olives have been separated from the leaves and twigs they are collected into sacks and delivered to the *oil factory*. Nearly every larger town has such a factory; they are mostly financed by the village or by a farmers' cooperative (the factories are recognisable by the characteristic deposits of waste material from the pressings and by their smell, comparable to that of the soles of shoes or turf). There, the olives are pressed several times: firstly there are one or two cold pressings for high quality cooking oil, then a hot, hydraulic pressing which produces oil of lesser quality, eg for the production of soap. Rule of thumb - large olives yield little oil, small olives a lot. The solid material which is left over is used as animal feed or as heating material.

Carob tree: This striking tree with its evergreen, leathery leaves is chiefly seen in the area behind Rethymnon and in the eastern part of the island. At harvest time in early autumn, the sweet aroma of its long black pods fills the air. They are used for animal feed, in the manufacture of paper and for medicinal purposes, amongst other things, but they can also be eaten. Carob trees grow wild, but are also planted intentionally.

Cypresses: These are not to be compared with the thin pencil-like trees of Tuscany. Wild Cretan cypresses spread their branches wide, and are often huge trees which can reach a height of around 130 feet, especially in the mountains of western Crete. There are only remnants of the forests that once existed here. There are, for example, fine specimens in the Samaria Gorge around the chapel of Agios Nikolaos.

Chestnut trees: These are a real embellishment to the landscape when they occur in groups. The largest of these is around Elos in the far west of Crete. They bloom in early summer.

Aleppo pines: These are tall conifers, which grow chiefly on the slopes of the White Mountains and in the Samaria Gorge. They are related to the pines, which are more commonly met in the western Mediterranean.

Plane trees: also tall, broad-branched and leafy, giving a lot of shade. They need a lot of water and are mostly to be found on water courses, eg in Fodele (near Iraklion) and Vrises (between Chania and Rethymnon).

Eucalyptus: strong, well-developed trunks with thick foliage, with the bark hanging down from them in strips. Because they use up a lot of water, they are planted everywhere that a considerable amount of moisture has to be absorbed. The village of Georgioupolis on the north coast between Chania and Rethymnon is situated in a whole grove of eucalyptus trees. They are not native to Crete, but originated from New Caledonia (near Australia).

Tamarisks: These are generally thin trees with conifer-like, soft leaves, which are particularly prevalent on beach promenades and beaches, for example in Paleochora. They are the only trees that can grow very near the sea because they have special glands which are able to excrete salt.

And of course there is the **Date Palm**, not brought to Crete by the Saracens as legend would have it, but a native of Crete (*phoenix theophrastii*). Of particular beauty is the palm beach at Vai, and there is a forest of pines hidden below Preveli Monastery along the course of a river. The fruits are not edible.

Shrubs, flowers, herbs

Botanists could probably fill a whole treatise, for there are indeed about 1,400 different species of which a good 10% are peculiar to Crete - that is to say, they are only found on Crete. The extreme differences in altitude, the deep sheltered gorges and the isolated situation of Crete have made survival possible for a multitude of vastly differing plants from varying climatic zones.

Phrygana: The general name for an indefinable number of round-shaped bushes and shrubs which reach knee-height at the most; they cover large rocky areas of Crete. Phrygana is the equivalent of "garigue" in the western Mediterranean, but includes a number of plants peculiar only to Crete. It is the typical vegetation of Crete, visible everywhere and certainly felt, because it is extremely thorny and prickly. Phrygana covers the major part of the pasture area on Crete and also grows in extremely dry areas.

Macchia: an umbrella term for the various evergreen trees and bushes which cover the rocks as a tangle of thorns to a height of 6-13 feet in all places where nothing else will grow. *Prickly gorse, myrtle, convolvulus, juniper, mastica* and various other stunted types of tree, including oak-apple and arbutus; all these are present. This Macchia is almost impenetrable to anyone on foot.

Herbs: oregano, thyme, marjoram, sage and many others. These appear as fragrant, ankle-high bushes everywhere in the phrygana, on cliff faces and on plateaux. If you have a keen eye for these, you will easily be able to take your requirements in herbs for the year home with you. Cretan herbs are cheap, however, and freely available at all markets.

Diktamos: only native on Crete. A small labiate, with woolly, pale green leaves and violet flowers. Used to make a tea, but is also known for its healing properties and used as an aphrodisiac, hence its popular name "erondas". Diktamos is best in the high mountains, but is also produced in lesser quality on the plains. It is on sale everywhere.

Oleander: This blooms a brilliant pink from May onwards, at the beginning of the dry early part of the summer, and is mostly found at road edges and in dried up, stony river beds. It is of particular beauty, for example, in the *Valley of the Dead* near Kato Zakro. See page 327. It is, by the way, a very old cultivated plant, and is depicted in Minoan frescoes dating from the 2nd Millenium BC.

Aloe-Agave: This enormous, cactus-like plant actually originated from Mexico. The most striking characteristic is its metre-high flowering stem, which grows up like a tree out of a clump of thick, sword-like leaves. It also blooms in June.

Prickly pear: Careful! Very fine, but very unpleasant prickles cover the almost fist-sized fruits of these large cacti, which ripen in early autumn. According to their degree of ripeness, they are red to yellow in colour and have a pleasant taste. They often grow in large quantities on rocky slopes.

Horta: It is amazing how the Cretans conjure up edibles from nature! Thus for example, there is horta everywhere. This is a wild vegetable, somewhat resembling spinach. Cretan women collect it in large bundles, and it is even served in the tavernas.

Sea Onion: a thin stem bearing a whitish flower and reaching over 3 feet in height, with a bulb the size of a child's head, which projects a little out of the ground; these are the unmistakable characteristics of this plant. It can be seen especially in early autumn.

Asphodel: This plant, which is the symbol of the dead in the Elysian fields, often covers complete slopes. It can reach a height of up to about 2 feet, and has small white or pink flowers and long thin leaves.

Flowers: Orchids are now only seldom found in the valleys which lead off the Samaria Gorge. In spring, the brilliant red poppy fills the gleaming fields, and there are local variations of cyclamen, tulips, peonies and several hundred other varieties.

Cultivated Plants

Vines: After the olive trees already mentioned, the vine has the greatest importance for the Cretan economy. During centuries of domination by the abstinent Moslem Turks, viticulture almost came to a complete standstill. However, many villages once again possess large fields of vines, often with raised terraces at altitudes of up to 3,200 feet. The largest extensive area of viticulture is situated south of Iraklion, on both the left and right hand sides of the road to Matala. In September, the grapes are put out to dry everywhere on large frames, in order to produce *sultanas*. Their daily progress from green to dark brown can be followed. They are mainly intended for export to the countries of the EC.

Oranges, mandarins and lemons: These are mainly found in the plain around Chania. On the way to the Omalos Plain (entrance to the Samaria Gorge), the road goes for miles through the dark green groves. Harvesting takes place in winter, and the wonderful blossoms can be seen in March/April.

Bananas: These are a particular speciality of Crete! The small, very sweet bananas are found nowhere else in Greece. The first shoots were brought to Crete decades ago from the Near East. They are now grown in the whole of the eastern part of Crete, partly in the open and partly in hothouses. The greatest concentration is around Arvi, Keratokambos, Mirtos and Ierapetra (on the south coast), and also near Mallia and Pachia Ammos (north coast).

The banana plants are about 6 feet high with huge drooping leaves, recognisable by their soft green colour. Bananas are sensitive to variations in temperature, wind and dampness. For this reason, it is considerably more difficult to grow them in the open. The small, sheltered villages on the south coast around Ierapetra offer good opportunities. The "rapid ripening process" is of interest; the bananas are picked when they are green, placed in closed storerooms and treated with a chemical for 24 hours. After that, they spend 24 hours in the fresh air, and are yellow and ripe! Most of the bananas are sold "under the counter" on the Athenian market or to Macedonian factories which produce baby foods. For this reason, it is not at all easy to obtain them on Crete.

The climate of Crete is not suited to the production of the large bananas commonly found in countries of the EC. Large hothouses would have to be built to grow them, and these would be too expensive for most farmers.

HOTHOUSES

The area around Ierapetra, the extensive Messara plain, the bay around Phalassarna, west of Paleochora and around Mallia; everywhere there are these horrible greenish-yellow plastic "skins". Tomatoes, cucumbers and melons are raised in this breeding climate and are mostly intended for export to central Europe.

Almonds : These are grown especially in large areas in the broad plain from Neapolis down to Agios Nikolaos. They are in full bloom in February.

Corn, potatoes and pulses : These can only be grown in very modest proportion because of the bad soil and the lack of extensive areas for cultivation (see also the chapter on *Economy*).

Avocados, kiwis and pineapples : Yes, you have understood correctly. You are not reading a "Handbook to the South Seas" by David Staley. The Cretans have been experimenting with these tropical fruits for a long time and they have succeeded in cultivating them on the Messara Plain. The first harvests have already been made. Even coffee is the most recent crop to have been planted in the Messara.

The Animal World

This has been severely decimated due to the disappearance of the forests. There is practically no game.

An exception is the Cretan wild goat, *Ibex, Agrimi* or *Kri-Kri* as it is wrongly called (the latter was a small wild goat which was reared by a shepherd). There are now only a few hundred of these left; they live wild, mostly on the inaccessible rocky slopes around the Samaria Gorge. They are impressive animals with huge, wide-curling horns, but they are hardly ever seen, since they graze at night and hide during the day. Some can be seen in the city parks in Rethymnon and Chania, living out their days in mean enclosures. Do not confuse with the normal domestic goat, of which there are thousands on the island.

There are now, however, nature reserves on several of the uninhabited islands off the north coast: **Agii Theodori** near Chania, **Dia** off Iraklion, and **Agii Pandes** off Agios Nikolaos. As the wild goats can live in peace and reproduce there without disturbance, the preservation of the species seems to be assured.

At the most, you will only see small animals, such as *hares* or *rabbits* - apart from the countless goats, sheep, mules and donkeys, cats and dogs. The latter can however be troublesome, as they faithfully protect the land or house of their owners everywhere, and bark furiously at everyone who comes into their vicinity, even sometimes trying to launch an attack. Be careful!

The attractive emerald-green *lizards* are very common, and unfortunately so are the countless insects. The penetrating ratchet of millions of *cicadas* will follow you the whole summer long. They make this deafening noise by arching and contracting their bodies through the movement of platelets which are stiffened by ribs, in breathlessly rapid succession - 120-600 cracking noises per second! Only the males make this noise, a fact which led a philospher in antiquity to state that "*Blessed are the cicadas, for their females are silent . . .* " The cicadas are black and only a couple of inches long. They die in September; the quiet is almost uncanny in October.

There are hardly any *fish* left in the fresh waters of Crete, and the sea is also not very rich in fish (see also the chapter on Economy). There is, however, a trout hatchery in Zaros, on the southern edge of the Ida range. Otherwise, the setting out of *beehives* is particularly common on Crete. Care is advised.

There are no *poisonous snakes* on Crete; St. Titos banished them from the island! But there are scorpions! We never saw any. The sting of the type found on Crete is painful, but not fatal.

Economy

Crete is a poor island. There are no natural resources, and therefore there is hardly any industry worthy of mention. 60% of the inhabitants live on the products of their small fields or from the rearing of goats, sheep, pigs and poultry on a modest scale.

In view of this lack of alternatives, great importance is assumed by the services and trade sections of the economy. Above all, the steadily increasing tourist industry produces many jobs and possibilities for personal initiative, eg "Rent Rooms", tavernas, souvenir shops, travel agencies, tourist guides, boat trips, renting of surf boards, to name only a few. Those who are repelled by the incredibly rich assortment of services on offer would do well to remember that many Cretans have built their very existence upon it.

Cultivation of the fields, vegetables and fruit: Tilling and preparation of the soil is difficult. In the hilly and stony island terrain there is a lack of larger continuous areas of level ground which could be worked by machines. Apart from that, the limit of altitude under which vegetation will grow is very low; only thorny scrub, wild vines and olive trees will survive above 1,970 feet.

A further decisive factor is the system of sharing out inherited land, and dowries (see below, page 94). The constant subdivision of land amongst all sons, who have equal rights, and the provision of a dowry for the daughters of the family prevents any accumulation of land. Thus many farmers tend their own land, but by EC standards Crete is almost incapable of providing competition. The building up of agricultural cooperatives has been fraught with great difficulty, not the least because of the tendency to hold on to inherited land and a marked individualism (of the Greeks in general and the Cretans in particular).

Crete produces mostly for its own needs; on a larger scale, only sultanas, olive oil, tomatoes, cucumbers and citrus fruits can be exported. In particular, the large scale production in hothouses on the south coast makes the export of tomatoes and cucumbers possible the whole year round. In order to build these hothouses, most of the farmers have taken on large debts. For years, there has been an attempt, with the support of the Ministry of Agriculture, to broaden the range of fruit and vegetables on offer (see also the chapter on *Vegetation/cultivated plants*).

Grain can only be grown in the Messara Plain on Crete; most of it has to be imported from other EC countries at high prices. Thus EC membership has also had the effect of bringing strong price increases to Crete.

The occupation of charcoal burner has not yet died out

Animal Husbandry: This is mostly confined to the keeping of sheep and a couple of pigs and chickens in the farmer's own barn. There are hardly any beef cattle.

The Pastoral Economy is of great importance. The number of sheep and goats runs into the hundred thousands, and almost half of the island is pasture land. Also on Crete, the antagonism between shepherds with "nomadic tendencies" and ecological preservation of the land (reforestation, clearance for cultivation) is a problem. The voracious sheep graze so intensively on what little green there is that the soil, once laid bare, can hardly recover.

Fishing: This is undergoing a severe crisis at the moment, because the waters around Crete have been greatly overfished. All too often attempts are made to improve the yield by fishing with dynamite or nets of smaller mesh; the result is that innumerable young fish are netted before they have a chance to reproduce, and this causes a further reduction in the number of fish.

The Cretan fishing fleet often has to spend weeks and even months off the African and Turkish coast, in order to make a satisfactory catch. In spite of this, most fish has to be imported. It is quite possible that the delicious portion of fish served to you in a taverna originated from Canada or Argentina.

Charcoal burning: Charcoal burners can still subsist on Crete because tourists are so fond of their souvlaki and grilled fish. The taverna owners on the coast need a constant supply of good charcoal during the season. The Cretan charcoal burners cut down and saw up the wood from cypresses and other old trees, pile it up layer by layer into large heaps and burn it, by a long drawn-out procedure, into charcoal. The charcoal burners, bathed in sweat, are often seen at their hard work on the slopes of Ida in the hinterland behind Rethymnon, eg around Melidoni.

Handicrafts/art work: *see separate chapter*

Industry: This is only found in the area of greater Iraklion, with the main emphasis on local products such as olives, grapes and fruit being processed into soap, oil, spirits/wines and tinned fruits.

Otherwise, the *building materials industry* is of a definite importance. There are new buildings going up on a large scale everywhere on the island, most of which are connected with the tourist industry.

Tourism

This is taking on an increasing importance. More and more young people are leaving the poor mountain villages and hiring themselves out as waiters in the beach tavernas. The result is a high proportion of elderly people in the country districts, with traditions dying out and the loss of an identity which has grown up through history.

It is the dream of every Cretan to have his own shop or taverna; the turnover is massive in the tourist season, and it is not uncommon for considerable wealth to be achieved. Again and again one meets Cretans who have saved the capital for their business through years of sheer hard work in the Federal Republic of Germany. In spite of this, or perhaps because of this, most Cretans speak positively about the time they spent in Germany. However, nobody wants to return there. It is not uncommon for a taverna owner to place himself deeply in debt, in order to be able to achieve the right level of investment. He will then work to the limit of his ability in the summer months, in order to meet the needs of the hungry gluttons on the beach promenade.

Crete today: Since the tourist invasion began, the island has been in a state of upheaval. It is walking a tightrope between tradition and "progress", and moving more and more in the direction of the latter. Economic dependence on tourism, extensive migration from the land, emigration, EC membership and the confrontation with western European customs have all brought aggravating upheaval.

"Ambre Solaire" in the mountains of Crete

Since the flood of tourists began, everyone has wanted to get rich as quickly as possible. The Cretans are enlarging their houses; "Rooms to Let" signs are everywhere, and tavernas and souvenir shops spring up like mushrooms. There are more strangers than locals in the village kafenia, and hospitality becomes a blatant business necessity.

More and more farmers are choosing the easy tourist business in preference to the difficult working of the stony soil, and for many women the only source of income is in the sale of their woven goods. The consequence of this is that they no longer make everything themselves, but either "have things made" or even import them. This state of affairs naturally leads to an increasing economic dependence upon tourism in the holiday areas. Provisions have to be imported from other parts of the island, and prices rise. The danger of no longer being able to keep pace with the high level of prices can easily confront anyone who is not engaged in tourism.

Most conspicuous is the difference in living standards between the coastal area and the interior. Whereas life on the coast is affected by the continuous presence of tourists and thus by the flow of foreign exchange, poverty rules only a few miles inland. Villages in the interior are being increasingly depopulated through the migration of the younger generation to the coast and abroad. The few old people nourish themselves with difficulty from the barren fields, olive trees and sheep. As soon as tourism takes hold in a place, the inhabitants try with all their might to make it attractive to foreigners. Tourism means money and wealth, but the high price of this is social dissatisfaction and the breaking down of old-established traditions.

And just that is the other side of tourism; within the space of a few years the Cretans have been confronted with customs and modes of behaviour which are light years away. On an island like Crete, where family, marriage and morality have such deep roots, nude bathing, flirtations with local girls, non-observance of religious taboos and similar activities by "enlightened foreigners" are not exactly suitable means by which to make contact with the local inhabitants. The very fact of the matter is that, as a tourist, the individual is in an exceptional situation and *behaves differently away from home. He has a lot of time to spare, he wants to have a rest, but he also wants to amuse himself, and perhaps even, if it comes to that, go a little overboard. In short, he wishes to do everything that he would not dare to do at home.*

Of course, this clearly does not apply in the same degree to the high grade coastal strip, which has already been "infected" by tourism. There already, the Cretans have conformed considerably, they are familiar with western customs and have even taken them over themselves. Above all, the numerous former foreign workers are in the position here, thanks to their knowledge of foreign languages, to build up an existence in the tourist business. They have often spent 10 or even 20 years in Stuttgart, Duisburg or Mannheim, and have long since overcome the cultural differences between themselves and the "foreigners".

It is different in the countryside, and in the inaccessible mountain villages. These surely offer the most attractive possibilities to get to know the authentic Crete, but here one can wreak the most in the way of destruction.

Environment

In this age of dying seals and polluted algae in the North Sea I consider it inappropriate to criticise the wrecks of cars and rubbish tips along the roads of Crete. First of all we ought to put our own house in order.

Of course the landscape is no longer entirely as we would wish it to be. Little agriculture means little pesticide, however, and the waters around Crete are among the cleanest in the whole Mediterranean, according to the latest researches of *UNEP*, a UN organisation which monitors the quality of sea water.

Traditions

Lyra and Laouto; the war dance of the Curetes; celebrate the festivals as they come.

Migration from the land and tourism have to a considerable extent caused old customs and traditions to disappear. For example, the old folk costumes are only seen in a few villages.

Local costumes

The local costumes of yesterday varied from village to village and often exhibited Turkish or North African influence. Today, only the older men in the mountain country occasionally wear the *wráka,* the wide black breeches tucked into high boots (*stivánia)* or puttees, and the black fringed scarf, the *saríki,* wound round the head. The wráka has been in use on Crete since the 16th century. Originally, it is reputed to have been worn by African pirates.

The beautiful Cretan waistcoats with their complicated embroidery and the wide red cummerbund, which held the *bounialo,* a silver dagger, are hardly ever seen nowadays. The shepherds frequently use the *sakouli,* a colourful handwoven rucksack.

The richly decorated women's costumes, *sakkos* and *fusta,* have almost completely disappeared today, and the women in a village (particularly the elderly and widows) mostly wear black clothes and headscarves, which completely cover the head.

Young people everywhere wear western European clothing, jeans etc.

Cretan music

Cretan music is wild and unpredictable. Quite a different thing to the disciplined bouzouki music of the Greek mainland!

Endless melodies, one after the other in complicated 7/8 or 9/8 time, sometimes monotonous and archaic, sometimes almost ecstatic. The oriental influence cannot be missed. When on a bus journey across country, you will certainly get to hear some of the bus driver's cassettes.

The main role is taken by the *lyra*, the traditional three-stringed instrument made of mulberry wood. It resembles a violin, but is rested on the knee and plays the main melody; a theme is repeated with an infinite number of variations and embellishments. The *laouto* (a type of lute) and the *tambouras* (bouzouki) serve as accompanying instruments.

There is often singing, too, with the singer and the lyra leading the melody alternately. The verses mostly consist of *Mantinades*, which are 15-syllable couplets with a lot of humour and spirit. They are often created spontaneously. There are Mantinades for every occasion, and even children practice them; the pieces of music can be drawn out for as long as desired. This original form of making music is met at most Cretan festivals. Even young people are greatly interested in it, in spite of the existence of pop music, and there are even complete orchestras of lyras in the cities. The lyra is an exacting instrument to play, and with hard work and talent it can bring a masterful virtuosity to its player.

The flute is often seen in the countryside and in the mountains. The most common type is the *Askomantoura*, the squeaky double flute. At the entrance to the Minoan palace of Phaistos, for example, there are always keen flute-sellers, who greet every tourist bus with a penetrating fanfare.

The White Mountains of western Crete were the birthplace of the *Rizitika* ballads (riza = roots), at the time of the Turkish occupation. They expressed the passionate desire for freedom. Later, during the German occupation in the Second World War, they were sung again and brought back all the old fighting spirit and feelings.

Some well-known Cretan musicians, whose records are available everywhere, are the song writer *Jannis Markopoulos* and the lyra players *Nikos Xilouris* and *Jorgos Skoulas* from Anogia.

Cretan dances

The Cretans express their feelings and their mood in dance. Not only joy, but also sadness, anger and pain come to the surface.

Sirtos: This is a fast round-dance in 2/4 rhythm, found all over Greece. There are numerous versions of it on Crete alone. For example, the sirtos from Chania is called the *Chaniotikos*, that from Rethymnon the *Rethymniotikos* etc. In the sirtos, the dancers form an open circle, holding on to each other by the hand or on the shoulder. The first dancer in the row sets the steps, and can thus show his full capabilities. Traditionally, the circle was never closed, as it is sometimes seen today in dancing displays for tourists. The world-famous *Sirtaki* is not, however, a Cretan dance. It was created by Mikis Theodorakis for Anthony Quinn in the film "Zorba the Greek", and is a simple variation on the sirtos.

Pentozalis: Probably the most well-known Cretan dance is the Pentozalis (five-step) from eastern Crete. It may have originated during the Minoan period; perhaps it was even a war dance of the Curetes? As in the sirtos, several dancers form a line, hold on to each other by the shoulder and, without moving the upper part of the body, begin very slowly to follow through the complicated steps. The first in the row becomes the leader. The mood intensifies and the pace quickens, with the leader carrying out what are more or less acrobatic jumps, according to his ability. He slaps his heels, breaks away from the row of dancers and performs a short solo, subsequently being replaced by the next in the line. The wild, unbridled nature of this dance is its fascination.

Sousta: This is the only dance designed for a couple on the island, and probably originated in Rethymnon. It is sometimes seen at weddings.

Solo dancers are not unusual on Crete. Inspired by the music of the lyra, they get up spontaneously and provide an interlude. Older men often do this.

Cretan festivals

The Cretans like to celebrate and they do so lavishly. There will certainly be a chance to experience one of the numerous festivals celebrating a Saint's name-day or a political event.

In the larger villages, the atmosphere is often that of a folk festival. People are eating and drinking everywhere, and musicians play their lyra, laouto and tambouras for hours on end in the village square. Everyone especially likes to take part in the church festivals.

Easter: This is the most important festival both for the Cretans and for the rest of Greece; the Crucifixion and the subsequent Resurrection of Christ are relived with great fervour. Cretans return to their island from all parts of the world, and all ferries and planes are fully booked for days.

Preparations begin in the 49-day fasting period, which begins on the Monday before Lent. Fasting is, however, seldom strictly carried on, except perhaps in country areas and then normally by women. Services are held throughout Easter week. On Good Friday, Christ is put into his grave, and after the service of burial, a great procession winds its way through the village. The festivities reach their climax in the Service for the Resurrection on Saturday, shortly before midnight. With the call *Christós anésti* (Christ is risen), all the congregation light their candles - a wonderfully dramatic moment. A boisterous firework display follows. Then, families assemble to eat; firstly, there are the red-dyed eggs, symbolising the blood of Christ, and then a soup made out of the entrails of the lamb (*Magirítsa*). The end of the fasting period is celebrated on Easter Sunday, for which purpose countless lambs are slaughtered. There is dancing and singing everywhere. All in all a festival compared with which our Easter appears quite humble.

BOOK TIP: "Christ Recrucified" by Nikos Kazantzakis. This is not actually set on Crete, but the Easter customs described are typical for the whole of Greece.

Careful: Under the Greek Orthodox calendar, Easter falls on different dates to our Easter - in 1991 on the 7th April, 1992 on 26th April, and 1993 on 18th April!

Further important festivals:

6/7 January   Feast of the Epiphany, in memory of the Baptism of Christ. The waters are blessed everywhere. In coastal locations the priest throws a valuable crucifix into the water, and the young men dive for it. There is bitter competition. If by chance nobody finds it, the priest hauls it up by means of a string which he has very carefully tied to it. In the cities, this ceremony is performed by the bishop.

Carnival   Masquerades and processions take place, and celebrations are especially lavish in the cities. Everyone goes out on the first Monday before Lent. On that day, only fish, unleavened bread and Halvá, a sweet made from honey and sesame seed, are eaten.

25 March   Festival of the Annunciation, and at the same time a day of remembrance for the uprising of 1821 (Independence Day), celebrated with military parades.

1 May   Festival of Spring. Garlands of flowers are hung on the doors, and everybody goes out and eats in the open air. Lambs are often slaughtered.

Ascension Day   This is celebrated with services, folk festivals and fireworks.

20-27 May   Festivals of Remembrance for the Cretan resistance fighters of the Second World War in Chania. German paratroopers overran the island on 21 May, 1941.

24 June   Birthday of John the Baptist. Great Midsummer fires are lit, and the young men jump over them. A boisterous celebration with a lot of music and song.

17 July   Water melon festival in Limin Chersonisou.

2nd half of July Great wine festival in the city park at Rethymnon.

15 August   Feast of the Panagia (Assumption of the Virgin), one of the greatest festivals in the Orthodox Church. This is extensively celebrated in Crete and throughout Greece.

25 August   Festival of St. Titos. Large procession in Iraklion.

29 August   Beheading of John the Baptist. Two-day festival on the Rodopou Peninsula (to the west of Chania).

31 August   Important Lady Day festival on the Lassithi Plateau.

14 September   "Raising of the Cross". An ancient festival in the villages around the Ida range.

7 October   Festival of John the Hermit at the Gouverneto Monastery on the Akrotiri peninsula. Festive procession down to the cave of the hermit near the former monastery of Katholiko.

28 October   Ochi Day. A Greek national holiday in memory of the "No" (Ochi) given by the Greek government in answer to Mussolini's demand for capitulation in 1940.

7-9 November   National holiday on Crete, in memory of 8 November 1866, when Cretans besieged by the Turks in the Monastery of Arkadi blew themselves up, taking a large number of Turks with them. Mainly celebrated at the Monastery of Arkadi and in Rethymnon.

11 November   Festival of St. Minas, patron saint of Iraklion. Services and a procession.

6 December   St. Nicholas Day, patron saint of Agios Nikolaos.

Christmas   Not celebrated as extensively as Easter. Presents are only given at the beginning of the New Year. Christmas trees have now, however, been introduced to Crete.

New Year   Children go singing from house to house on New Year's Eve, and receive small presents. After celebrating with friends, everyone returns home by 11.00 p.m. at the latest and waits to see the New Year in with the family. The New Year's cake is cut. The one who finds the lucky coin hidden in the cake will have a lot of luck in the New Year.

Handicrafts

Traditional handicrafts are seldom carried on today; they take up too much time and bring too little reward. However, tourism has led to a certain revival.

Ceramics: The man-sized clay pithoi for storage are only made on the wheel in two villages, *Margarites* (Nomos Rethymnis) and in *Thrapsano* (Nomos Irakliou). They recall ancient Minoan prototypes. Most potters have changed over to the manufacture of pottery for everyday use, which only has a limited chance of holding out against competition from plastic (flower pots etc.). Thus there are more and more pottery souvenirs, ranging from tawdry to attractive, which are especially produced for the tourist market (vases, figurines, plates etc). Margarites is the place to look.

Weaving: Women weave on their own looms mainly in the mountain villages. They produce rugs and blankets of sheeps' wool, and crochet and embroider curtains and sheets edged with filigree lace. Thanks to tourism, this work has become lucrative. Young girls learn how to weave from their mothers. Wool is acquired through exchange for finished pieces of work. However, this business is so lucrative that one can no longer be sure everywhere of getting genuine Cretan work.

The beautiful *wallhangings* with the Byzantine patterns used to vary from village to village. Today there is in general a uniformity of style, with simple geometric patterns and brilliant colours. Inexpensive woollen rugs can best be acquired in *Anogia* or in neighbouring *Axos*, where without doubt most of the looms on Crete are situated.

Fine embroideries and crochet work are chiefly to be found in *Fodele*, not far from Iraklion, or in *Kritsa*, or indeed in the neighbouring village of *Kroustas,* near Agios Nikolaos.

Leather: Leatherworking is also of great importance today. Thanks to the extensive rearing of sheep there is no scarcity of raw materials and leather articles of all kinds (shoes, boots, bags, belts etc.) can be purchased quite reasonably, particularly in *Chania/Western Crete*. Cretan leather is often exported to EC countries and frequently turns up again on central European flea markets.

There are looms everywhere on the island

Icons: The icons which can be purchased everywhere are *not genuine antiques,* however old they may appear to be. Genuine icons, painted before 1830, are classed as antiquities and *may not be exported.*

In spite of that, however, the newly-produced copies of historic icons are attractive and often carefully painted; an attempt is made in part to reproduce the old colour compositions as faithfully as possible. There is a well-known icon painter living and working in Rethymnon, who can be visited (see chapter on Rethymnon).

EOMMEX

This abbreviation stands for the organisaton of small and middle-sized skilled craftsmen in Greece. There are offices everywhere, including on Crete. The purpose of this institution is to look after and promote craftsmanship. The finest pieces from a region are collected, exhibitions are arranged, awards are given to the producers and contacts established between buyers and producers. There are permanent exhibitions in Iraklion, Rethymnon and Chania (see the relevant chapters). You can be sure of finding quality craftwork here. There are no direct sales from the exhibitions, but the producer's address can be obtained, together with further advice.

TIP: If you intend to buy something, you should try as far as possible to visit the producer himself. You will get a better price there, and the largely poor inhabitants of the mountain villages could use the drachmas far more than the souvenir sellers on the coast.

The Church

The Cretan church is a real people's church and follows in the traditions of ancient Christianity. There is nothing distant or far-removed about it. Class barriers between priests and the Faithful are consciously kept to a minimum.

Numerous churches and monasteries on Crete are decorated with colourful frescoes

The Church, faith and life are all closely connected on Crete. Divine Service is an informal get-together without strict formalities, even at the most solemn moments of ritual. People like to go to church on Crete, as it is an important meeting-place and the centre of village life.

Structure and organisation: The Cretan Orthodox church is directly under the jurisdiction of the Patriarch of Istanbul. It has an Archbishop, whose seat is in Iraklion, and is subdivided into *dioceses,* each ruled over by a bishop. Such a bishop is the representative of Christ on earth, and the devout represent His followers. Together they form a unit, in which the bishop is leader, father, and brother of the Faithful. Representatives of the bishop, who cannot of course be everywhere at the same time, are his priests, the Papádes.

A *Papás* may marry, have children and live in the village. His theological training is mostly very modest and often consists of no more than a six-week intensive course (there are different categories of priest). He cannot be a bishop, for celibacy and monastic vows are necessary here. Educational or class barriers between him and the village inhabitants are carefully avoided; the priest speaks and thinks like everyone else in the village. What counts is his experience of life; he should set an example to the people, give them advice and help them to go along the right path in life. Thus it is not education, but godliness that is necessary. His remuneration is sparse (according to his level of education), and for this reason he has to tend his own field, his vines or a few sheep, like everyone else in the village. His services can always be acquired for payments in kind or in cash. Christenings, weddings and funerals afford such opportunities. On the other hand, the church does not levy any taxes.

"FREEDOM OR DEATH"

The present huge popularity of the Orthodox Church on the island can be understood in the light of its brave role in the forefront of the fight against the Turkish occupation over the centuries. Even during this period of the most severe repression, it emanated an unbroken will to survive and unflinchingly kept up the spirit of Crete and of Orthodox Christianity.

Above all, the monasteries on Crete were fortresses of resistance, sometimes secretly, sometimes openly fighting with weapons. The monks helped the resistance fighters in every way. They were able to meet in the monasteries and form new plans, and they always received something to eat there; the monastery was a place of hiding, a source of spiritual encouragement. But the monks did more; they founded secret schools in the monasteries and, putting their lives at risk, taught children in the Greek language. That the Greek and Cretan cultures were not wiped out in the 18th and 19th centuries and replaced by Turkish culture is largely thanks to the activities of these monks.

Among the most famous figures of the Cretan church even today is the highly revered Abbot Gabriel of Arkadi Monastery. In 1866, when the monastery was hopelessly surrounded by Turkish troops, he chose death with hundreds of Cretans rather than to hand over women and children to the Turks.

Church and resistance, this great tradition echoes right up to the present. Even in the Second World War, for example, the monastery at Preveli (on the south coast) worked closely together with the British, as did the monastery at Toplou (near Vai), where the abbot and several monks were shot by the German army.

One of the many miniature churches that are found on the side of every road

Orthodoxy today: The times described above have passed. The Orthodox Church of today still lives, however, in the past. Its doctrines have
not changed radically since the Seventh Ecumenical Synod in 787 AD.
Accordingly, it seeks to hinder social reforms whenever possible.
Because of its strong position in the State, it is often successful,
whether in the case of divorce law, family planning or marriage
contract. In the case of the latter, it has had to accept a defeat. Since
1983 civil marriage has enjoyed the same status as that of marriage
in church.
The efforts of the Socialist PASOK government over the last few
years were concerned with an attempt to separate the State from the
Church as far as possible, and to damp down the wide influences of
Orthodoxy. This went so far that in 1987 Papandreou actually
broached the subject of the dispossession of the Church, which owns
vast tracts of land in Greece. What the Orthodox Church actually does
with its wealth is uncertain; at any rate, nothing reaches the underpaid
Papádes. It is also interesting that the Greek Orthodox Church has no
social pretensions. Monks avoid any kind of charity work and follow a
mystical, ascetic ideal. There are virtually no deaconesses etc.

Many people, particularly young Cretans, want to escape from the strong influence of the Church today. On the one hand, the Church is seen as the upholder of tradition, but on the other hand it is criticised for its dogmatic rigidity, and for its constant attempts to increase its wealth and to interfere in all areas of private life.

But there is another side to Orthodoxy. *Bishop Irenaios* of Kissamos-Kastelli, who is nearly eighty years old, is one of the examples of how progressive and socially orientated an Orthodox bishop can be. Amongst other things, he is the main founder of the Cretan popular shipping company ANEK, which in the sixties put pressure on the mainland shipping companies, totally orientated as they were towards profit, and made room for shipping policies which were exclusively tailored to Cretan requirements. There is a small portrait of the Bishop on page 456. An interesting opportunity to get to know progressive members of the church presents itself at the *Orthodox Academy of Crete* near Kolimbari at the foot of the Rodopos peninsula. For more information see page 452.

> ICONOSTASIA: These miniature churches and simple monuments for prayer made of stone or metal are found scattered all over Crete, mostly on the roadside, in tortuous bends in the road etc. They contain a small icon or an oil lamp and indicate that, in that place, an accident or other event worthy of note has taken place.

Family and Society

As in all Mediterranean countries, the extended family is traditionally one of the most important institutions of society on Crete.

The isolated island position, a protective stance against the constant alienation caused by conquerors, and the mainly agricultural structure of the economy without any industry of note have all provided for a stronger maintenance of this tradition on Crete than on the Greek mainland.

To the family belong all relatives including nephews, nieces and third cousins. The most important function of the family group is that it, and not the State, takes over the task of social provision when a situation of economic emergency befalls an individual member. The nucleus of the family consists of at least three generations; the father has unlimited authority, even over his married sons. When he dies, this authority is transferred to the eldest son. Not infrequently the grown-up children continue to live with their parents even after marriage, usually with the bridegroom's father.

Marriage/dowry: An important task facing the head of the family is to take care of his sons' inheritance and his daughters' dowries. The marriage of a daughter is a very important affair, in which, especially in country areas, the parents often still choose the candidates. Position, possessions and the dowry *(príka)* can be expected to play the greatest part, not necessarily love. In traditional families it is even usual that the eldest son may not marry until his sisters have been provided for. On the death of his father, he has to provide for his sisters.

As always, it is of the greatest importance that the daughter enters into marriage as a virgin, or at least it must appear so to the outside world. A "sullied" daughter can only be given to a husband with difficulty and after allowances (usually of the financial kind) have been made. Of further importance is the size of the dowry. The more a family can provide for their daughter, the better her chance of marrying into a "better" position. Normally money, a piece of land and if possible, a house, will be provided.

Many mothers and grandmothers spend years crocheting their daughters' dowries

In earlier times, a father often had to place himself in serious debt, particularly when several daughters had to be provided for. The reason for this strict rule on dowries is that a bridegroom is to a certain extent paid off by a father, because he is freeing him from the burden of a daughter to provide for. Officially, the obligation of furnishing a dowry was abolished in 1983. This has been a great relief for families which are economically weak, and there are no longer grounds for a father to drink himself into a stupor when his wife brings a second daughter into the world.

Smaller family unit: Emigration to find work, movement from the countryside and the possibility of making easy money in the tourist resorts have led to the establishment of the smaller family unit and the apparent obsolescence of the enlarged family unit. Put more simply: when the children work abroad, they only come back for the great festivals, such as Easter. On the other hand, those who are engaged in tourism live mostly on the coast, whither their aged parents are not always willing and able to follow them, so that they only return to their villages in the winter months.

"Volta": The "Volta" will surely survive to the end of time on Crete. This is a stroll up and down a certain road every evening, and it has become a definite ritual, mainly in the larger villages and towns. Back and forth they stroll, mostly in family groups, whereby young daughters are especially guarded. Or a number of girls may stroll hand in hand, with young men sauntering after them and teasing them. Everyone joins in. People are especially dressed up at weekends, for the "Volta" is an opportunity to show oneself to the best advantage.

Hospitality: Here, tourism has destroyed the irreplaceable. Whereas before, it was almost a sacred duty to offer a stranger the protection of the family or the village, this ancient custom is only observed in pure form in very remote villages. Naturally the Cretans are mostly friendly and the stranger will surely be invited here and there, but this usually has nothing to do with real *philoxenía*. In spite if this, if you are invited anywhere, you should accept the invitation. It is also not exactly polite to refuse food and drink when it is offered.

However, when a young Cretan man invites a female tourist to his home, this is mostly in connection with quite another phenomenon . . .

Celebrations: The most important private celebrations are the christening and above all the wedding! Civil marriage has only been possible since 1983, thus a church wedding is still of paramount importance. The so-called "crowning" before the altar symbolises the union of the partners before God.

A wedding is an absolute high point. It is not uncommon that dozens of guests come to the huge marriage feast in the afternoon. In the smaller village, everyone turns up! There is a lot of eating and drinking to bursting point. Also, those who happen to pass by are enthusiastically persuaded to take a seat.

Blood feuds: These certainly do not exist any more today. The blood feud originated from the attempts of the family bands not to appear weak under any circumstances. Otherwise, a man could easily acquire the reputation for not being able to defend his own possessions. Every wound on the family's honour had therefore to be avenged immediately. A disastrous chain of events was the result, which could be added to indefinitely, for the other party thought in exactly the same way.

The last "vendetta" on a grand scale apparently took place between 1943 and 1952, and cost 20 lives. It persisted the longest in the wild area of *Sfakia*, the barren mountain region in the south west of Crete. The Sfakiotes are described as the most lawless people in Greece, and no conqueror of the island has ever been able to subdue them. They have always taken pleasure in opposing State intervention, and have always had their own unwritten laws.

Monuments to the brave freedom fighters against the Turks have been erected all over Crete

History

Crete lies at the crossroads of three worlds - Europe, Africa and Asia. Fertilised from Asia, and reaching out towards Europe, the island is seen as the germ cell of European culture.

The first highly developed civilisation on European soil emerges around 2000 years BC from the darkness of history. The *Minoans* build glittering palaces, create colourful frescoes, hammer out gold and produce finely-engraved jewellery. Nearly twice as many inhabitants as there are in modern times celebrate noisy festivals, full of the joys of life. For centuries they live without fortifications of any kind and without serious enemies, as the strongest power in the eastern Mediterranean, while people on the mainland are still walking around with stone axes and clubs.

Then the puzzling catastrophe takes place. The palaces burn, the Myceneans arrive from the Peloponnese, the Minoan civilisation disappears under a layer of dust and earth which is metres thick.

From then onwards, Crete suffers the fate of many islands; it is an independent culture with a proud sense of national consciousness, but occupied by enemies from outside, repressed, plundered. The Byzantines, Saracens and Venetians fall upon an island which, although helpless, is of immense strategic importance.

Then follow centuries characterised by the struggle between Turks and Greeks, centuries of horror and catastrophe.

Crete becomes a pawn of the Great Powers; illustrious admirals carry on their sea battles here, setting their plumed caps at glittering careers . . .

Crete belongs to Greece from 1913 onwards. Then, in 1941, the German army jumps out of the sky and once again the Cretans have to defend their island.

40 years later there is the last invasion. The tourists are coming! The Cretans are still defending themselves . . .

Mythology

The beginnings of written history. The inhabitants of the eastern Mediterranean related their fascinating chronicles about the creation of the world, the Titans, the gods and men only by word of mouth in the millenia before Christ.

Written histories of the birth of the gods, King Minos, and his island are only known from the 8th century BC, over 700 years after the Cretan-Minoan kingdom went to its doom. For this reason it is the ideas and thoughts of the ancient peoples of the mainland, who entered Greece in the course of the *Greek folk migrations* (Dorian invasion) from the north, which speak out from the myths that are well-known to us.

Actual remaining Minoan traditions have thereby been covered up and altered, and were probably also partly made up in a deliberate act. Above all, the mainland Greeks have certainly "polished up" their own, less significant role. The myths have therefore been given an alien Greek content, and it is almost impossible to isolate the Minoan elements which could perhaps give clues to what actually happened on the island. However, it is an undisputed fact in Greek mythology that the birth of Zeus on Crete marks the beginning of the world of the Greek gods, and with it Greece's own history.

1st Act

In the beginning, there is chaos. Gaia, or Mother Earth, escapes from it and, without male help, bears Ouranos (the Sky), Pontos (the Sea), and Ourea (the Mountains).

Ouranos is of the male sex. Gaia marries her son and they produce the Titans. Ouranos is now the absolute ruler of the world, but with the growing number of his children, he fears for his power. Gaia may become pregnant again, but she will not be allowed to bring any more offspring into the world.

Accordingly, Gaia forges a plot against Ouranos with *Kronos,* the youngest of the Titans. Kronos robs Ouranos of his masculinity while the latter is asleep. Thus Ouranos is no longer worthy to be a ruler, and Kronos is his successor.

He marries his sister *Rhea* and with her, produces many offspring. But Kronos is soon fearful of losing his power, principally because the children are seemingly ungodlike and exhibit human characteristics. He summarily gobbles up every newly-born child! However, as immortal gods, they live on in his stomach.

The horrified Rhea does not accept this, of course, and a new plot against the greedy ruler begins to form. Good-natured Gaia, expert on the subject of plots, renders her assistance. They feed Kronos a stone wrapped in swaddling clothes, representing a "new-born baby". Rhea hides in the Psychro Cave in the Dikti range on Crete (or was it the Idaian Cave in the Ida range?) and gives birth to *Zeus*. The baby is nourished with milk by the goat-nymph Amalthcia and honey by the bee Melissa, and thus brought up.

Zeus is a clever god. Secretly, he gives Kronos an emetic, which causes him to vomit and thus give birth to Zeus' brothers, among them Hades and Poseidon. Zeus and his allies then defeat Kronos, and Zeus, as the undisputed chief, takes his sister Hera as a wife and divides up the earth. Hades receives the Underworld, Poseidon becomes Lord of the Seas etc. The hierarchy of the Greek gods thus receives its permanent structure, with Olympus in northern Greece as its "seat of government".

In these stories of the gods, the fear of a son by a father always comes through; this is probably a memory from the grey mists of time, when it was not rare for the strongest son from a clan to take power through patricide. Incest was not forbidden at that time either. On the contrary, the son grabbed his father's better half along with his power!

After this Zeus, father of the gods, spends his time mainly in amorous adventures. An advantage here is his ability to change himself into any form desired. One day, he is sitting on the highest mountain on Crete when he sees, on a distant shore, the beautiful Phoenician princess *Europa* . . .

Europa is picking flowers. Suddenly there is a huge bull right in front of her, with snorting nostrils and a shaggy coat. He trots up and down in a good-natured way, Europa is trusting and bends over him to stroke him. Then suddenly the bull jumps up and begins to trot off, gathering speed and rushing towards the sea. Europa holds on tight, shaking with fear, and the bull plunges into the waves and swims over to Crete. It goes ashore at the sandy bay of Matala and allows Europa to slide from its neck. It shakes off the water, draws itself up - and suddenly Zeus stands in front of the confused Europa!

Not without Europa showing some displeasure at the audacious kidnapping, they retire happily to the nearby Messara Plain and take up position under a widely spreading plane tree, which Zeus quickly flies in from the Ida mountains. They spend their first night there and Europa conceives. She gives birth to three sons: *Sarpedon, Radamanthis* and *Minos*!! Thus Minos makes his first appearance; he is a demi-god, after whom Sir Arthur Evans, who discovered the Palace of Knossos, named the entire early culture of Crete.

The plane tree, under which this wedding night took place, is still to be seen on the archaeological site at Gortys; since that time, it has always had evergreen leaves. See page 241.

Zeus has soon had enough of Europa and moves in to other amorous adventures. Europa becomes the wife of the Cretan king Astarios, who adopts the three offspring of her liason with Zeus. End of the 1st Act.

2nd Act

As a youth, Minos goes up to the cave where Zeus' birth took place. He remains up there for 9 years in this mountain isolation.

In the cave, Zeus gives him instruction in kingship and finally gives him a number of law tablets; the parallels to Moses on Mount Sinai cannot be ignored here. Thus well-equipped, Minos comes down from the mountains, quickly drives out his two brothers and becomes the sole ruler of Crete! With the help of a mighty fleet, he builds up his sovereignty over the whole of the eastern Mediterranean; he need hardly fear any external enemies.

To discourage any other Cretan pretenders to the throne, he begs for a miracle from his uncle *Poseidon*, that a white bull should rise up out of the waves. To show his gratitude, he would then sacrifice the bull. However, the bull that comes ashore is so incredibly beautiful and strong, that Minos causes him to disappear among his own herd under cover of darkness, and sacrifices another, more delicate bull. Of course, Poseidon notices this and takes revenge in what is for him the usual way; he causes *Pasiphae,* the lustful wife of Minos, to become inflamed with love for the white bull.

Now that wonderful genius, inventor and all-rounder *Daedalos* comes into the picture. Originating apparently from Athens (probably an attempt by the Athenians to cull a piece of the glory in this exclusively Cretan story), he comes to Crete after an episode involving incest. The anxious Pasiphae turns to him for help, which he subsequently gives. He builds an ingenious wooden frame, over which he stretches the hide of a cow, and makes the queen get into it. He then pushes the contraption into the meadow; the stupid bull immediately mounts the "cow" and mates with Pasiphae! 9 months later, it happens - Pasiphae gives birth to a healthy child, a boy with a huge bull's head, a monster!

Minos rages, but spares the bull-like monster because of the moving pleas of his daughter Ariadne. Instead, he has it locked up inside a huge labyrinth, which is built by the great Daedalos. From now on, the half-man, half-bull is named the *Minotaur*.

The Minotaur

The fabled labyrinth of the Minotaur is a huge construction with angled false entrances, countless rooms and dark corners. Daedalos has achieved a masterwork; is this the Palace of Knossos? Probably not, but it fits into the whole story so well . . . .

Now the story switches to the Greek mainland. *Herakles*, the legendary son of Zeus and Alkmene, comes on to the scene. In a state of temporary mental derangement, he has just killed his children. In propitiation, the Oracle at Delphi directs him to carry out 10 heroic deeds. One of these is to capture the Cretan bull. This Herakles does, bringing it to the Peloponnese, where the bull rages through the countryside and devastates everything it comes upon. By chance, *Androgeos*, son of Minos, is staying at the court of King Aegeus of Athens. While hunting the bull, he is treacherously murdered, as it seems through jealousy over his newly-won victory in the pentathlon at the Panathenaic Games. When Minos hears the news, he immediately dispatches a fleet against Athens and conquers the city after a long struggle. He thereby becomes the absolute ruler of the eastern Mediterranean and the whole of Greece.

The Athenians have to subjugate themselves; in propitiation for the crime against his son, Minos demands human sacrifices. Every nine years, 7 youths and 7 maidens are to be sent to be devoured by the Minotaur!

On board ship on the third of these sad journeys is *Theseus*, the young son of King Aegeus. He wants to kill the Minotaur and end once and for all this terrible subjugation which has befallen Athens. He arranges with his father that if he is successful, he will hoist white sails on his return. If, however, he has been killed, his crew will hoist black sails ...

Although *Ariadne*, the daughter of Minos, is already betrothed to the god Dionysos, she immediately falls in love with the tall, audacious stripling with the long, flowing hair. On the advice of Daedalos, she gives him a ball of wool to take with him, fastening its end to the door of the labyrinth. Only by this method can Theseus ever find his way out of the labyrinth again.

She also gives him strange pills made of pitch and hair, which he is to throw into the jaws of the insatiable Minotaur. These are to make him unwell and distract him during the fight. Theseus actually goes into the labyrinth and pays out the thread slowly behind him. For a long time, nothing is seen or heard. Then, suddenly, he is standing at the entrance once again and triumphantly brandishing the scalp of the dead monster!

In the general confusion, Theseus flees to the harbour with Ariadne, where once again he follows the advice of Daedalos and destroys all the keels of the Minoan ships; then he sets course for home. In Naxos, the lovers are separated; perhaps Artemis shoots Ariadne with an arrow, or perhaps Dionysos takes his bride back for himself.

In his chagrin over the end of the adventure, Theseus forgets to hoist white sails. His father Aegeus is waiting with much longing and full of anxiety for his return. There - a tiny ship on the horizon; it must be him! Slowly the ship draws nearer and suddenly realisation dawns on Aegeus. The ship has black sails! Theseus is dead. Racked with sorrow over the apparent death of his son, the king throws himself from the high cliff into the sea. Since then, this sea has been known as the *Aegean* ...

And Daedalos? As soon as he discovers their treachery, Minos orders him and his son to be thrown into the labyrinth. But not for nothing is Daedalos a great inventor. In a labour which lasts for years, he collects wax and the feathers of birds nesting in the palace. One day, two very strange birds wing their way over the city in a seaward direction. *Daedalos* and *Ikaros* are on their way across the sea to Sicily!

At the beginning everything goes well, but suddenly the high-spirited Ikarus flies too near the sun, in spite of his father's warnings. The wax melts and Ikarus plunges deep into the Aegean Sea ...

DAEDALOS THE SECOND

Saturday, 23rd April 1988, 7.05 a.m. The pedal aircraft **Daedalos 88** takes off from a beach near Iraklion. After 3 hours and 54 minutes in the air, it safely reaches the beach of Perissa on the island of Santorini. Kanelos Kanellopoulos, the Greek cycling champion, has not made it as far as Sicily. Still, he has covered the 119 km to Santorini. Using only the muscle power of his legs, he maintained his US-built propeller-driven machine at a height of 5-7 metres above the Aegean sea. Never before was a human being able to fly so long and so far using only the power of his muscles - excepting Daedalos the First, of course.

3rd Act and Finale
King Kokalos is the ruler of Kamikos on Sicily. He takes in Daedalos as an artist at his court.

But Minos does not rest, and searches everywhere for Daedalos, using every kind of trick; he offers a large reward in gold for whoever can draw a thread through a shell. Kokalos also hears about the task and passes it on to Daedalos, who trickles honey through a shell and then ties a thread to an ant. The ant, following the path the honey has taken, then licks its way through the passages within the shell.

When King Minos hears that the problem has been solved by Kokalos, he knows exactly how and by whom. He marches on Kokalos with a great army and is killed in battle.

Another more fantastic myth tells us that Minos comes to see Kokalos and demands the extradition of Daedalos. While Kokalos retires to consider the demand, his daughters prepare a bath for Minos. They have however become fond of Daedalos, because he is always making them such beautiful jewellery, and they do not want to hand him over. So they pour boiling water into the bath and scald Minos to death.

What can we deduce from these myths?

Again and again, the historical base glints through these personifications in legend. The Athenians had to submit to their Minoan overlords (= human sacrifices to the Minotaur). This Cretan overlordship of the eastern Mediterranean is historical fact. The Mycenaean Greeks (= Theseus) were finally able to break out of this subjugation (= defeat of the Minotaur).The fact that the story of Minos ends on Sicily could point to Minoan refugees who fled to the western Mediterranean after the conquest by the Mycenaeans.

Furthermore, the later Greek poets seem to have taken pains to present Minos and·his kingdom in as bad a light as possible. Human sacrifices, a Minotaur blind with rage, the great artist Daedalos on the run . . . In other sources, King Minos is by contrast presented as wise and just, and after his death is accepted as a leading judge in Hades.

In spite of everything bad which has been said about it, the Greeks cannot avoid the admission that, at one time, Crete was a flourishing and influential empire, upon which even the Athenians were at one time dependent ...

A Minoan clay pithos, in which provisions were mostly kept

The History

On the basis of the chronologically arranged finds in the Archaeological Museum of Iraklion, the prehistoric and historical development can be followed very well.

Neolithic (New Stone Age) 6000-2600 BC

The beginnings are shrouded in darkness; the first settlers probably come to Crete between 6000 and 5000 BC, from Anatolia in Asia Minor, or even perhaps via Africa. There is dispute as to whether they came upon indigenous peoples on Crete at that time. At the beginning, they live a semi-nomadic life in caves, but are later able to build simple domiciles of burnt clay bricks. Simple clay and stone vessels have also been found, and even small figurines, idols, and representations of animals.

The earliest settlements are situated in central and eastern Crete, near Knossos, Mallia, Phaistos and Sitia. Under the Palace of Knossos, Evans found a layer containing the refuse from Neolithic habitation 6-8 metres thick.

THE "MINOANS"

From about 2000 BC onwards, a new era begins for Crete; great waves of immigrants sweep over the island, probably from the area of Asia Minor, where great cultures already existed at an early date. Thanks to their superior degree of civilisation, they are easily able to assimilate the indigenous inhabitants. The so-called "Minoans" are the product of the fusion of these two groups of people, and for the next 1200 years, they make Crete the centre of a highly-developed culture. They will establish a fully comprehensive rule over the eastern Mediterranean.

Prepalatial Period 2600-2000 BC
The new immigrants bring a mass of new techniques and knowledge with them.

They are able to work bronze and use it to produce weapons and tools. They also introduce the potter's wheel and with it various ceramic styles are developed, among which the best known is a type with a surface varying in colour, caused by uneven firing (mottled "Vasiliki" style). The art of cutting stone is also perfected, and the manufacture of individual sealstones is the greatest achievement of the early Minoans. It appears that everyone possessed his own seal, which was used to seal chests and doors, and also as an amulet.
Above all, the new lords of the island soon carry on a vigorous sea trade with Egypt, Asia Minor and Mesopotamia. A brisk cultural exchange is carried on with the more developed cultures on the Asiatic mainland, and a primitive type of pictographic script is developed. The inhabitants know how to tend the fields and to rear animals, and are already living in permanent houses. The dead are buried in large vaulted graves. The best preserved settlement of this period has been found between Ierapetra and Mirtos.

The Protopalatial Period 2000-1700 BC
The simple agricultural society develops into a society whose members are differentiated by class.

Great centres of power grow up on Crete, the mighty palaces at *Phaistos, Knossos, Mallia* and *Kato Zakros* are probably built by slaves. Both palaces and surrounding settlements are completely unprotected by fortifications. This is an important indication that the Minoans must already have extended their rule over the whole of the eastern Mediterranean!
In contrast to Knossos, which was dominant at a later date, the most important palace at this time must have been that of Phaistos, the

only palatial site to yield the wonderful, extremely thin "eggshell ceramics". These take their name from the most important archaeological site at which they were found, the *Kamares Cave*, in the southern Ida range.

The Minoans buried their dead in large clay vessels (pithoi) or in clay sarcophagi.

During excavations, archaeologists sometimes come across the pictographic script which had already appeared at an earlier date; but most frequently, clay tablets bearing the famous *Linear A Script* are discovered. Even to this day, the syllable-based script has not been deciphered.

All of the palaces are razed to the ground around 1700 BC as a result of a mysterious catastrophe. In all probability, this was caused by an earthquake.

> Even to this day, Crete lies in an area prone to earthquakes. Historians have been able to prove that earthquakes took place in the years 66, 365, 1246, 1304, 1508, 1665, and 1856. The last one took place in 1926 and among other things was responsible for raising parts of the coastline by around 20 cm. Elderly Cretans can remember it.
> The Minoans knew why they should build their palaces with wooden pillars and wood frameworks; only thus could the buildings collapse without crushing the inhabitants.

The Neopalatial Period 1700-1450 BC

The high point of Minoan culture. The palaces are rebuilt with a magnificence greater than ever before, with more floors, stairways and large courtyards.

Colourful frescoes decorate the passages and innermost rooms, and religious rites and festivals, particularly the curious bull cult, play a great role in the lives of the upper class. At a later date, Homer wrote of 90 cities which were reputed to have already existed at that time. Trade and handicrafts are flourishing, the fleet controls the Mediterranean and it is probable that Cretan traders went as far as Scandinavia. The standard of living is correspondingly high, and the impressive storage jars in the palaces are filled to the brim. Undisputed centre of the island is *Knossos,* but a typical workers' and artisans' settlement of the period can still be seen today, namely at *Gournia,* east of Agios Nikolaos.

Minos is ruler at Knossos. The former is probably not a personal name, but the title given to a ruler, similar to that of pharaoh in Egypt. There are reputed to have been 22 kings named Minos, and a throneroom with the oldest throne in Europe has been found at Knossos! Always conspicuous is the *role of women*. As statuettes and

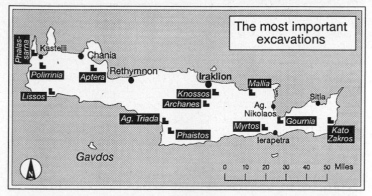

The most important excavations

in frescoes, they are depicted with bared breasts and exhibiting a great deal of self-confidence. They are wordly, elegant, and have valuable jewellery. When they are compared to the heavily veiled women of the strongly male-dominated Islamic society, the difference becomes apparent. Women were to all appearances the object of veneration and lead a free, self-determined existence, even perhaps sitting at the rudder of power.

Worthy of artistic mention, apart from the lifelike frescoes, are the wonderful pieces of gold jewellery and the pottery, excessively decorated with relief ornament. Linear A Script is overtaken by the Linear B Script, which has been deciphered! This work of art was carried out in 1953 by the young Englishman Michael Ventris, whose mother was Greek. He himself was not an archaeologist at all, but an architect. His method, too, was far less the result of a systematic study of antiquity, but rather the result of a logical process of genius. He employed a military technique of decipherment from the Second World War, and was successful! However, the texts from the clay tablets which have thus been deciphered are not very informative. They are expansive inventories and lists, and accounts from the domestic quarters of the palace. (They can be seen in the Archaeological Museum at Iraklion.) Interesting, however, is the fact that an early form of Mycenaean Greek has been identified in the Linear B Scripts, which leads to the conclusion that at that time, mainland Greeks must already have been in positions of authority on Crete. Perhaps they were already preparing for the later conquest and transfer of power.

Around 1450 BC, the palaces are destroyed in a terrible catastrophe. What happened at that time is still a puzzle today. The explosion of the volcano on the island of *Santorini,* the greatest volcanic eruption of all time known to us at present (75 miles north of Crete - today only the imposing rim of the crater remains), was for a long time believed to be the cause of this destruction.

The "Grand Staircase" at the Palace of Knossos

Within half an hour, a huge tidal wave is said to have washed over Crete and destroyed all the settlements near the coast. However, at excavations in the Cycladic-Minoan settlement at *Akrotiri* on Santorini, which was destroyed by the eruption, a discrepancy in time of around 50 years between its destruction and that on Crete has been established. The tidal wave would hardly have waited that long.

Today, strong earthquakes are preferred as the cause of the eclipse of the Minoan cities and palaces. The invasion of the Myceneans or other enemies is being increasingly discussed by researchers. Only the Palace of Knossos is rebuilt. Its final eclipse takes place in around 1400 BC, though whether it is due to an enemy invasion, a new earthquake or even a revolt of the Cretans is not clear. The exact year is not known, only the time of the year. During the blaze, there was a strong south wind blowing. It must have been a beautiful spring day, because it is only at this time that the strong south wind blows . . .

MINOAN PUZZLES

The mysterious eclipse of the Minoan culture between 1450 and 1400 BC is only one of many puzzles. The more the archaeologists unearth, the more the previous conclusions are undermined. One thing is certain. The soil of Crete is full of still undiscovered secrets. Much else is hypothesis and not definitely proven by science.

The Bull cult: The bull was to all appearances a sacred animal to the Minoans. Representations of bulls appear everywhere, on frescoes, on seal rings and in stone reliefs. The famous stylised bulls' horns probably decorated the walls of all the palaces, and the bull played a leading part in mythology.

Perhaps the Minoans venerated the sun or sky god through the bull; was thunder perhaps the angry bull-like ravings of the sky god, or did they sacrifice the bull to the angry deity, in order to propitiate him? Sacrifices are attested to many times over. Such a scene is shown in great detail on the sarcophagus of Agia Triada. Peculiar scenes of so-called *bull-leaping* have been found on frescoes and sealstones. The leaper waits for the animal which rushes towards him, seizes hold of him by the horns at the last moment and swings himself up in a high death-defying leap over its back. Young men and women are supposed to have carried out these acrobatic achievements. Experts today are in serious doubt as to whether the leap was at all possible. Perhaps such representations are to be seen as the *symbolic* overcoming of the brute strength of the bull by man? It is, however, certain that games dedicated to the bull cult took place at the Minoan palaces. The young acrobats were perhaps professional sportsmen, who presented their skills before the assembled citizens. At any rate, the games had a clear religious background, although the centre of attention - whether the bull or acrobat - is not known.

Double Axe: probably the sacred sign of the Minoans (similar to the Christian Cross). This was scratched into the walls and on columns dozens of times in all the palaces, particularly that at Knossos. The origins of this cult symbol are very ancient and go back to before 10000 BC. It probably came to Crete from Asia Minor. Its

significance has not yet been explained (in contrast to that of the Cross). Perhaps it was a sign representing strong divine assistance. On the other hand, it is believed that the double axe gave rise to the term labyrinth. The double axe was named after a pre-Greek word, *labrys*. Probably the later Greeks named the Palace of Knossos "Labyrinth" - the House of the Double Axe. The generally angular and puzzling nature of the architecture of all the Minoan palaces has given the modern meaning to the word labyrinth (labyrinth = a building with a confusing ground plan, in which it is not possible to find the exit). Even the myth of the Minotaur was placed in a Minoan labyrinth.

Lustral basins: These have been found in every Minoan palace on Crete. Wide steps lead down to a small square or rectangular room beneath floor level, which has been carefully lined with alabaster. These so-called "lustral basins" were mostly situated in the immediate vicinity of the ruler's apartments (at Knossos they are directly in the throne room), and must have played an important role in rites. Perhaps certain ceremonies of anointment took place, the purpose of which can no longer be discerned today.

Human offerings: Irrevocable proof of these was found just about 10 years ago on the hill called *Anemospilia* at the foot of Mount Juktas near Archanes. A human had been sacrificed in this temple sanctuary! The temple collapsed, probably during the earthquake of 1700 BC, at the very moment in which the ceremony of sacrifice took place, and preserved the dreadful scene for millenia. No other traces of human sacrifices have been found to the present day. Was this a single, desperate attempt by the priests to hold back the terrible earthquake and instil mercy in the hearts of the gods? The excavator, Professor Yannis Sakellarakis, is quite convinced that this is so. More on this under Archanes, page 197.

Postpalatial Period 1400-1100 BC
Some of the palaces are rebuilt on a smaller scale, but the power of the Minoans is broken.

The Mycenaean conquerors are now the undisputed rulers of the island, and Cretan domination of the Mediterranean is at its end. During the following period there seems to have been a kind of hybrid Mycenaean and Minoan culture, the centre of which was increasingly being transferred to the mainland. The great "Cyclopean" fortifications at *Mycenae, Tiryns* etc are built there. The Minoans establish several new settlements in eastern Crete, and arts and crafts continue, although they are visibly overshadowed and altered by coarser Mycenaean influences.

Dorian Epoch 1100-480 BC
Great folk migrations take place on the mainland in the 13th century BC.

The Dorians fall upon Central Greece, destroy the Mycenaean strongholds and force their way to Crete around 1100 BC. They form the new ruling class and establish a kind of class-orientated society following the example of the Spartans. Only they themselves have political rights and can hold office, while the indigenous population have to go into military service and farmers are turned into serfs.

One group of Cretans refuses to accept this system and flees into isolated mountain regions (these are the so-called *Eteocretans*, or real Cretans). The Dorians settle in the old centres of population, but also establish many new settlements. They build their well-fortified strongholds on steep hills near the coast, and there begins a warlike epoch, with bitter struggles for the overlordship of the island. The Dorians also bring the technique of ironworking with them - thus the new weapons are made of iron.

But the golden period of Crete is over. Athens and Sparta on the mainland are now the Great Powers which determine the course of Greek history. Crete becomes just a province. The island only seems to have maintained a certain importance in the field of legislation; the *Gortys Code* (found at Gortys near the modern Agii Deka) is the first written body of civil law in the ancient world and knowledge of it seems to have been widespread.

Classical and Hellenistic Period 480-67 BC

Crete has sunk into obscurity. The individual city-states are constantly fighting one another, and the power of Gortys surpasses that of Knossos.

In the last century BC the harbours of the island are primarily used as bases by pirates, who greatly disrupt sea trade; this is a reason why the ambitious Roman empire begins to take an interest in Crete.

The Romans on Crete 67 BC-395 AD

The Roman general Quintus Caecilius Metellus subjugates the island. For the first time for more than 1000 years, foreign conquerors set foot on Cretan soil!

Things are made all the more easier for the Romans by the disunity of the city states. The island becomes part of a Roman province, and the settlement at *Gortys* is built up into a powerful capital with theatres, baths and great temple complexes. The ruins can still be admired today. The whole of Crete is covered with a network of roads and even achieves an importance for distant Rome through the intensive production of grain in the fertile Messara Plain.

Christianity makes its appearance, too. The Apostle *Paul* is reputed to have landed on the south coast of Crete in 59 AD, on one of his missionary journeys. His companion Titos stayed behind in Gortys and became the first bishop on the island. Crete must almost have become Christian at a stroke; in spite of this Paul, in a letter which has been attributed to him, admonishes Titos thus:

"One of them said - indeed, it was their own prophet - that every Cretan is a perpetual liar, a bad lot and lazy to boot. For this reason, punish them severely!"

From the middle of the 2nd century onwards, the Christians were persecuted on Crete. The village of *Agii Deka* near Gortys is named after the 10 bishops who were executed there because they refused to sacrifice to the Roman gods. Their burial vault is situated right next to the ruins of Gortys and can be visited.

But even the period of the great Roman empire is drawing towards its close. In 395 AD it was divided into the *Western* and *Eastern Roman* empires. Crete passed to the Eastern empire, which had its seat of government in Byzantium (modern Istanbul).

First Byzantine Epoch 395-826 AD

The centuries of Byzantinism are characterised by the spread of Christianity. Churches were built everywhere, including on Crete. The most important of these is the Church of *Agios Titos* near Gortys, the ruins of which are close to the excavations of Roman Gortys.

Otherwise Crete assumes an insignificant position on the edge of world history, while the Arab world strives for power.

The Arab Conquest 826-961 AD

"La ilaha illa 'Ilah." (God is God!) This battle cry of the Saracen pirates soon becomes feared throughout the whole of the eastern Mediterranean.

In 824, Abu Hafs Omar, hitherto commander-in-chief in Moorish Spain, is obliged to flee from Spain with his Saracen-Arabian troops. Subsequently, they land on the south coast of Crete. Legend has it that Omar ordered the boats to be burned behind them, so that there would be no going back! Mercilessly, they destroy the churches and everything else in their way. Survivors have to submit to forced labour and renounce their Christian beliefs. Many island inhabitants flee into the White Mountains, the Ida and Dikta ranges, and carry on a partisans' war against the conquerors; it will not be the last time they do this. The Cretans' long history of suffering now begins.

For a long time, the Byzantines are not able to pull themselves together and offer serious opposition to the Arabs, who rule the island and a large area of the sea for 135 years. Abu Hafs Omar builds a large fortification on the site of what later becomes Iraklion. It is named *Rabd el Chandak*.

Only in 960 does the Byzantine general Nikephoros Phokas land a mighty fighting army west of Rabd el Chandak. The campaign which followed has been embroidered with numerous anecdotes in contemporary sources, although the element of truth in them is not always clear. Thus there is a story that the Cretans who come down from the mountains to join the Byzantines know of a Saracen relieving force of 40,000 which has just landed on the south coast. The Byzantines march to meet them by forced marches, prepare an ambush and wipe out the Saracens to a man. The story goes on to say that they arrange the heads in two circles around the walls of Rabd el Chandak, and use those that are left over as cannon balls.

The city falls on 7th March 961. Those who surrender without a struggle are allowed to live. Great blocks of the population are given into slavery.

Second Byzantine Epoch 961-1204

As the Cretan population has been severely decimated, war veterans and settlers from Asia Minor are brought to the island and domiciled there. Rabd el Chandak is rebuilt and refortified - the Byzantines now call it *Chandax*. Henceforth, 12 aristocratic families share power on Crete.

The division of the Church also takes place during this period into the Roman and the Orthodox Churches. The Cretans accept the Orthodox beliefs.

The Venetians 1204-1669

It is the time of the Crusades. During the Fourth Crusade (1202-1204), the united forces of western Europe attack Byzantium instead of Arabian Palestine.

They sack Constantinople and divide up the empire. For a ridiculously small sum, the *Republic of Venice* buys Crete, among other places. But years pass by before the Venetians take possession; in the meantime the arch enemies of the Venetians, the *Genoese*, establish themselves firmly on Crete. 15 castles spring up in the short period, and it takes Venice 5 years to be rid of them.

The four centuries under Venetian domination become the period of the cultural flowering of Crete, but the high price paid is the incapacitation and plundering of its inhabitants.

The Venetians reorganise the economy, and by means of exorbitant taxes they squeeze the last drop out of the farmers and shepherds, who are already impoverished. Whereas in the cities splendid buildings are erected and art and science flourish, one revolt follows another in the countryside, and there is a total of 10 revolutions in the first 150 years! It is notable here that Venetian settlers even side with the Cretans and enter into numerous "mixed marriages".

From the beginning of the 15th century onward a new danger looms on the horizon - the Turks! Constantinople (formerly Byzantium) falls in 1453 and the Turks move increasingly nearer to the Venetian area of power. Under conditions of relentless serfdom, the Cretans are forced to build up the Venetian fortresses of Gramvousa, Spinalonga and Souda. The necessary finance for this work is achieved through constant rises in taxation.

CRETAN RENAISSANCE

In 1453, many artists and scientists flee from Constantinople to Crete. The island becomes a reservoir for Byzantine culture, which receives new impulses from the Venetian Renaissance. The most important focal point is the **Church of Ekaterini** in Iraklion, an offshoot of the famous Mount Sinai School, which was at that time the most important high school in the Christian east. Theology, Philosophy, Law, Rhetoric and Fine Art are taught here.

Above all, Cretan literature can develop. In the epic poem **Erotókritos** by Vitzentzos Kornaros from Sitia, the Greek popular language is used in literature for the first time. This and other contemporary pieces are still held in high esteem in Greece.

Icon and fresco painting also reach a high point. **Michael Damaskinos** becomes the most important representative of the so-called "Cretan School", which enriched the strict Byzantine rules of form with Cretan stylistic elements and even used contemporary stylistic devices from the early Italian Renaissance. Several works by Damaskinos are on display today in the Ekaterini Church.

The famous **El Greco** (actual name Domenicos Theotokopoulos) was born on Crete in 1541. Today, he is recognised as the most important Greek artist. In spite of the fact that he painted most of his works in Toledo/Spain, it is possible to recognise Cretan peculiarities in his bizarre, long-limbed figures.

The Turks arrive in 1645; they are welcomed by the Cretans as a means by which to drive out the hated Venetians. Too late, however, they realise that they are fighting the Devil with the Devil. They ally themselves with the Venetians in order to begin the struggle against their larger, common enemy, but it is too late. Chania falls in 1645, Rethymnon a year later after a siege of only 23 days. Only three years later have the Turks covered the 62.5 miles to Iraklion, a fact which indicates the desperate resistance kept up by the Cretans and Venetians. The siege of Iraklion begins in 1648, the final battle for Crete has begun! Volunteers from everywhere flow into Iraklion, in order to save the last outpost of Christianity in the eastern Mediterranean from the grips of Islam. The Pope issues a call for defence, the French king sends troops, as do the German duchies.

The defence of Iraklion is led by the Venetian leader, Morosini, after whom the fountain in Iraklion is named. The Turks attack with unbelievable doggedness, and the slaughter goes on for 21 years. This war outdoes the First World War in its long years of trench warfare. The Turks lose 120,000 men, the Venetians 30,000. The end comes in 1669. There is hardly one stone left on top of another, but Morosini is able to secure the honourable withdrawal of the last defenders in the negotiations for surrender.

With the assistance of Cretan rebels, the Venetians are able to hold their fortifed bases at Gramvousa, Spinalonga and Souda until 1715. After that, the Cretans are on their own. Crete is now Turkish, and what goes on here under Turkish rule over the next two centuries defies all description.

The Turks on Crete 1669-1898

The population of Crete is severely decimated after the Turkish wars, and the basis of the economy has been seriously destroyed. Only half of the total number of olive trees has reputedly escaped devastation.

However, the Turkish colonists pay little attention to economy and trade, but try instead to bleed the population through exorbitant taxes and carry on an intensive exploitation. Where the Venetians left off, they achieve the final deforestation of the Cretan forests, and the cities and harbours fall into decay. The economy is to a large extent crippled, because the high taxation offers no economic incentive.

In addition, every Cretan has to become a Moslem. The Turks are most satisfied when whole villages convert to Islam at the same time. One of the methods by which they "convince" those who resist has survived: firstly, the village is surrounded, then a written declaration is demanded from the head of the village, to the effect that the entire village wishes to convert to Islam. If he refuses the demand, he is promptly strangled and the same demand is made of his deputy. If he refuses, he is also throttled, and a new deputy named, of whom the same demand is made . . . normally, someone is soon found to sign the declaration for the village. Most Cretans however keep their own religion under cover of Islam and work quietly against their new overlords.

Those who do not wish to play ball flee into the mountains; the rebels in the White Mountains and the Dikti and Ida ranges are known as the *Klephtes* (bandits), because in the face of Turkish encirclement, they can only acquire the provisions they need through robbery. Above all Sfakia, the province of the White Mountains, is a collecting point for the partisans and it is never conquered by the Turks. The Samaria Gorge is an ideal place to lie in wait for land troops from the south, and when the Turks want to move up to Omalos from Chania, they receive many a bloody nose on the steep rocky track.

Cretan Klephtis

Daskaloyannis, the famous leader of the Cretan partisans, gazes far into the White Mountains

In 1770, there is a great revolt against the Turks. Its leader is Yannis Vlachos, nicknamed *Daskaloyannis* (the teacher Yannis) from Anopolis (near Chora Sfakion). He places his whole, not inconsiderable, wealth at the disposal of the rebels and makes contact with the Russians, who are at war with the Turks. However, under the pretence of peace negotiations the Turks lure him to Iraklion, where he is publicly skinned alive in front of a huge mirror. The story of Daskaloyannis is well known everywhere in Crete today, particularly in Sfakia. A monument to him stands in Iraklion, in the square named after him.

From the beginning of the 19th century the unrest increases; the Cretans join the general Greek movement for independence. In 1821, a Greek revolt flares up against the Turks. After initial success on the part of the Greek freedom fighters it is quickly put down by Egyptian troops who have received a summons for help from the hard-pressed Turks. From 1827 onwards, the European Great Powers interfere in the Greco-Turkish conflict. The Turks are forced to withdraw from Greece and the proclamation of the independent Greek state can be made. Where Crete is concerned, the Great Powers are unable to decide on a united course of action. The island is promised to the Egyptians, and from 1840, the Turks are there again.

The struggle for Cretan freedom now enters its most bitter phase, in which the monasteries have a particularly large share. They offer shelter to the partisans and are centres of Greek and Cretan culture. The monks also fight with arms against the Turkish usurpers. In 1866, the monastery at Arkadi near Rethymnon becomes the symbol of the Cretan struggle for freedom, as several hundred Cretans under the leadership of Abbot Gabriel blow up not only themselves but also a large number of Turks, who are in the process of storming the monastery. The Greeks have written *Freedom or Death* on their flags and they really mean it. Some of the flags are preserved today in the Historical Museums at Iraklion and Chania.

Help then comes from a liberated Greece; the united Greek and Cretan troops are able to force the Turks back into their strongholds. In 1898, 17 British soldiers are killed by accident during an exchange of fire in Iraklion; they have been stationed there as observers.

At last the Great Powers interfere; they occupy the island and the Turks must leave Greece for good. Crete receives an autonomous status, under a protectorate of the 4 Great Powers - Italy, Russia, Great Britain and France. Prince George of Greece lands in the Souda Bay in 1898 and is established as High Commissioner. The reJoicing among the Cretans cannot be adequately described, but can be read about in "Zorba the Greek", by Nikos Kazantzakis.

The Autonomous Crete 1898-1913

The autonomous status can only be an interim solution. The Cretans do not wish to be under the command of the four Great Powers. They demand unity with Greece and unrest breaks out again.

Their spokesman is *Eleftherios Venizelos*, a Cretan by birth from Therissos near Chania, and at that time Minister of Justice under Prince George. He carries out a coup in 1905, together with numerous officers, and the self-important Prince is obliged to withdraw. A plaque marks the spot under a huge tree near Therissos where the rebels met together. The new High Commissioner is the former

Greek Prime Minister Zaimis.

The energetic Venizelos makes a career for himself on the mainland; in 1910, he is elected Prime Minister of Greece. He introduces compulsory schooling permits the forming of unions and initiates a general programme of basic reforms. But he has not forgotten Crete. From 1912 onwards, and without any constitutional basis, he summons Cretan members to Parliament. He carries on the war of the Balkan League (Greece, Serbia, Montenegro and Bulgaria) against Turkey which, because it is carrying on a simultaneous war with Italy in North Africa, is weakened and has to make concessions. Greece receives Macedonia, Epirus, the islands of the eastern Aegean and Crete in the London peace negotiations. **Crete is finally united with Greece on 30th May 1913!**

Countless streets and squares on Crete are named after Venizelos, and his picture hangs next to that of the current head of government in every official building. Up to the present, he is the most important politician that Crete has produced, for he achieved the union of Greece and Crete. His elaborate funeral monument stands high above Chania at the foot of the Akrotiri peninsula (see page 420).

1913-41

The First World War is only a peripheral experience for Crete, but in 1919, the Greek military and politicians see a great chance to extend the borders of Greece right into Asia Minor and above all, to take Istanbul.

They begin a *war against Turkey*, which they lose in 1922 with a blaze of trumpets. Greek troops have to flee from Asia Minor, and Smyrna (modern Izmir) is burned. Only a part of the Greek civilian population is able to save itself on the offshore islands, the remainder is butchered by the Turkish troops.

Through the *Peace Negotiations at Lausanne*, Venizelos is able to bring about a gigantic exchange of populations. All Greeks living in Turkey are to move to Greece, and all Turks living in Greece are to go to Turkey. 600,000 Turks thus leave the country (mostly against their will, as Pandelis Prevelakis from Rethymnon impressively describes in his *Chronicle of a City*), while 1.35 million Greeks arrive. They mostly settle in the large cities and found their own city quarters. Nearly 20,000 Greeks go to Crete, and at least half settle in Iraklion. The suburb of Nea Halikarnassos, which is passed through on the way from the airport to the city centre, is founded at this time.

In the years preceding the Second World War the seeds of tourism are sown, and the discoveries made by Sir Arthur Evans are the signal for archaeologists from all over the world to begin excavations everywhere on the island.

From the Second World War to the present day
The Greek mainland is occupied by German troops in 1941, and the British defenders withdraw to Crete.

On 21st May and the days following it, German parachutists and mountain troops land on Crete. This is a risky air-to-land operation, during which the attackers suffer heavy losses because the British and their allied troops are well-prepared for the invasion. Reichsmarschall Göring will never again be able to use his decimated élite unit by itself. The airstrip is only secured by the Germans after a week has passed, enabling reinforcements to land. The battle for Crete has been decided, and the British troops move to the south coast, where they are evacuated to Egypt in boats that have been quickly gathered together.

A total of 4,465 German soldiers, 1,527 Allies and an estimated 5,000 Greeks met their death in this week. The Commonwealth Military Cemetery at Souda and the German War Cemetery near Maleme are memorials to the fact. Even today, it is impossible not to be moved by the long, dismal-looking rows of graves there.

Crete remains in German (and Italian) hands until 1944, the west of Crete even until 1945. Again the Cretans reach for their weapons to fight the occupying forces. There is a bitter partisan war, which makes life difficult for the German army. Aided by British agents, the Cretan resistance fighters carry out guerilla actions time and time again, which are answered by the German authorities with the destruction of whole villages and the shooting of Cretan civilians on the principle of "10 Cretans for every dead German". Thus in June 1941 the village of *Kandanos* is levelled, and in September 1943 400 inhabitants of the village *of Ano Vianos* are shot, having been designated as partisans. On 15th August 1944 all the male inhabitants of the mountain villages of *Anogia* and *Gerakari* who can be found are shot. A high point in the partisan war is the successful kidnapping of the German General Kreipe in a joint Anglo-Cretan operation. The partisans bring him safely through 22 road blocks and finally to a British boat off the south coast (for more details see Archanes, page 196).

The last German troops leave Crete in 1945; behind them there remain the bombed cities, burnt-out, depopulated villages, destroyed roads. The economy of the island is at an end.

The merciless civil war that follows and which rocks the whole of Greece does not spare Crete. Many of the Communist partisans are executed by government troops, and those few that manage to escape the conflict only receive an amnesty in 1975. Two of the former resistance fighters hide themselves for 30 years in the mountains. Today, one of them takes tourists to the caves in which they lived during that period.

With the help of international and American organisations, in particular UNO and the Rockefeller Foundation, the economy, trade and communications are built up again, although not without ulterior motives, for in 1951 Greece enters NATO and Crete becomes the most important base for the United States 6th Fleet in the eastern Mediterranean.

Today, there are cruise missiles at the NATO base on the Akrotiri peninsula near Chania, and German troops are once more stationed on Crete, this time as allies. The NATO bases are anything but popular with most Cretans, and a relatively strong anti-American feeling is noticeable throughout Greece, especially since PASOK (the Panhellenic Socialist Movement) formed the governing party in 1981 with almost 50% of all votes.

The Cretans and Politics

The Cretan attitude to politics and politicians is still coloured by its history, which is to a large extent one of repression.

The Cretans reject anything to do with state patronage, exaggerated authority or strict conservatism. Traditionally, they choose the party which promises them the most freedom.

When a Panhellenic referendum was held on December 8th, 1974, to determine whether Greece should become a monarchy or a constitutional democracy, the following results were obtained:

Greece: For the monarchy   30.8%   against 69.2%

Crete: For the monarchy   09.0%   against 91.0%

The last two Greek general elections for Parliament also showed a similar tendency on Crete: when Karamanlis and his Conservative "Nea Demokratia" party were voted out during the "landmark" general election of October 1981, and the progressive, left-wing PASOK under Prime Minister *Andreas Papandreou* elected instead (having had a withdrawal from NATO and the closure of the American bases in Greece in their manifesto), the percentage of Cretan supporters of PASOK was 60%, in contrast to 48% for the rest of Greece.

The election of 1985 ended with a similar result, although Papandreou had not been able to fulfil his election promises, and despite the fact that *Constantine Mitsotakis,* the leader of the Nea Demokratia party, comes from Chania and is a very influential man on the island.

Now, as before, the US bases on the island constitute a great political problem (among others those at Timbaki/Messara Plain and Gouves/Iraklion), while the NATO bases are more easily tolerated. In the coming years, the American presence will provide the fuel for much political debate.

Central Crete

The heart of the island; the highest mountains, the largest plains, the greatest concentration of population and the most important archaeological sites. Focal point of the island in every way.

90% of all foreign tourists arrive at *Iraklion*, whether on charter flights or on the daily ferry-boats from Piraeus. Most of the large beach hotels are situated on the beaches *to the east of the city*. The flat coastal zone cannot quite be described as attractive, as the overtaxed infrastructure of tourism has made originality a rare quality here. However, its favourable position where road connections are concerned makes interesting excursions into the hinterland and the eastern part of Crete a possibility.

Wilder and more impressive is the north coast *to the west of Iraklion*. The mighty foothills of the Ida range plunge down into the sea here and bathing resorts have only established themselves in a few niches in the barren rocky landscape.

The inland area of the widest part of the island is largely hilly in nature and totally characterised by viticulture. One of the largest continuous areas of grape cultivation in Greece spreads across it. It is flanked in the west by the extensive *Ida range* which includes the highest peak in Crete, and in the east by the slopes of Mount Dikti and the *Lassithi High Plateau*, which is famous above all for its thousands of windmills.

The south is dominated by the *Messara Plain,* the largest and most fertile plain on the island. Several of the most-favoured beach resorts and the best beaches on Crete are situated here; above all, there is the legendary former Hippy-rendezvous *Matala*, and the fishing harbour of *Agia Galini*, which today, however, lives mainly from a steadily rising income from tourism. But the Minoans and their classical descendants had already discovered the Messara. The Minoan palaces at *Phaistos* and *Agia Triada*, as well as the Graeco-Roman *Gortys* are among the most interesting remains from the turbulent past of the island, and are overshadowed only by the world famous *Palace of Knossos*, which is situated a few miles from Iraklion and can certainly be counted among the world's greatest archaeological attractions.

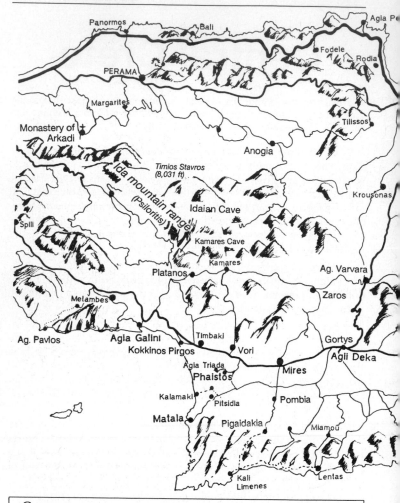

GEOGRAPHY: Central Crete extends from the **Ida range** in the west to the **Dikti Mountains** and the Lassithi High Plateau in the east. Hilly, vine-growing terrain stretches between the two mountain ranges, and the great Messara Plain lies in the south. The only city centre is **Iraklion**, capital of the island with over 100,000 inhabitants, and this is followed by the provincial centres of **Archanes**, **Mires**, **Anogia**, **Kastelli** and **Timbaki**.

ROADS: The motorway-like **New Road** runs along the north coast and forms the main axis of the Cretan road network. Most of the roads are of asphalt and in good condition. Exceptions are to be found in the gravel track from Anogia to the Nida Plateau, the dirt road south of Archanes (Vathipetro) and several approach roads to the south coast (Tsoutsouros).

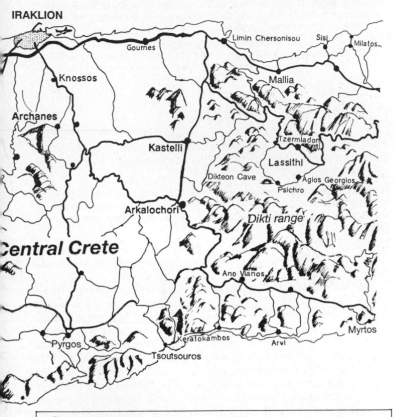

IRAKLION

Gournes

Limin Chersonisou   Sisi   Milatos

Knossos   Mallia

Archanes

Tzermiadon

Kastelli   Lassithi

Dikteon Cave   Agios Georgios
Psichro

Arkalochori   *Dikti range*

entral Crete

Ano Vianos

Myrtos

Pyrgos   Keratokambos   Arvi
Tsoutsouros

CONNECTIONS: The centre of the bus network is **Iraklion.** Connections in an **eastward direction** along the coast (Limin Chersonisou, Mallia), to **Rethymnon** and to **southern central Crete** (Messara Plain, Agia Galini, Matala) are particularly good. Buses leave less frequently for the inland villages. An exception however is **Archanes**, and buses also travel several times daily along the road to **Anogia.**

ACCOMMODATION: most of the overnight accommodation available on Crete is concentrated in Iraklion and on the coast to the east of the city (**Limin Chersonisou, Stalis, Mallia** etc). Bathing resorts on the south coast, particularly **Agia Galini** and **Matala**, are also well-endowed with hotels and guest houses. There are **camping sites** near Iraklion, Limin Chersonisou, Sisi, Matala and Agia Galini.

ARCHAEOLOGY: Central Crete has yielded the greatest concentration of archaeological sites. Just under 4 miles from Iraklion lies **Knossos**, the largest and most important Minoan palace on the island. **Phaistos**, the second largest palace, is situated in the Messara Plain, in the immediate neighbourhood of **Agia Triada**, another Minoan residence. There is another Minoan palace to be found at **Mallia**. Finally, the most recent excavations on Crete, which were concluded in the seventies, are to be found around **Archanes** (Temple of Anemospilia, Necropolis of Fourni etc).

BATHING: There are beautiful beaches in the north near Iraklion, Mallia and Limin Chersonisou, and in the south near Pitsidia, Kalamaki, Matala and Lentas.

Iraklion

"Little Athens" on Crete; economic pulse and a magnet for tourists; the Fountain of the Lions, the Venetian fort and the mighty city walls

Chaotic, indiscriminate development beside a deep blue sea. A grey spider's web, covering coast and hills. The first sight is not one for an aesthetic; uniform housing, reinforced concrete, dust, heat, and steaming asphalt.

This, the largest city on Crete, the economic and general gathering point for the whole island, is not distinguished by finely-tuned city planning. Anything goes, where building is concerned.

Today, over 100,000 Cretans live in the city and its suburbs. Not a large number, it might be thought, but that does mean one in five of the inhabitants of this sparsely populated island. Iraklion is a huge "head", out of proportion on the Cretan body, and also the fulcrum and hub of all the tourism on the island. Whole legions of tourists populate the city and its environs.There are cruise passengers, who are rushed off to Knossos and into the museum, people waiting for ferries and planes to depart or arrive, holidaymakers from the large hotels on the nearby beaches, and still others. Countless thousands make their way daily through this relatively small old city. They seldom pause for contemplation along these much-frequented sight-seeing trails.

Despite this, Iraklion has atmosphere; even though little has been preserved from its turbulent past. The focal point of the historic centre is the Platia Venizelou with the *Morosini Fountain*. One can have a quiet coffee here and absorb new impressions. It is only a few yards to the busy *pedestrian precinct*, to the *market passage* bursting with people, to the extensive, leafy *Eleftherias Square* and the world-famous *Archaeological Museum* with its unique collection of Minoan art. A chance to escape from it all and gain a general impression presents itself in the form of a stroll along the *fishing harbour*, with its sturdy Venetian fort and the long, quiet mole.

One constant factor amid the bustle of the streets is the fishing harbour and the Venetian fort

Of course, nobody omits *Knossos,* only a few miles outside the city; a visit to the breathtaking ruins of the world-famous Minoan palace is a must, with its elegant, roofed-over "King's Apartments", brilliant coloured frescoes, and flights of stairs thousands of years old. Sir Arthur Evans' daringly-constructed "archaeologists' Disneyland" has for decades been a sure guarantee of a steadily increasing flow of tourists.

In spite of the traffic noise and the hectic atmosphere of a large city, Iraklion does have something to offer those who happen to pass through. For the Cretans themselves, Iraklion particularly epitomizes the opportunity for economic advancement. Young people emigrate down from the barren mountain villages all over Crete, in order to seek their fortune in the city. Over half of all the industrial and commercial businesses on the island are concentrated here, and by the same token, the number of wholesale and retail businesses is increasing continuously. Of course there is always work to be found in the service sector - that means tourism! Last but not least, there are four faculties (medicine, mathematics, physics and chemistry) of the *University of Crete* situated in the city, with a total of 5,500 students. Iraklion is the only district on Crete where the size of the population is increasing.

LITTLE ATHENS ON CRETE

There are historical grounds for the sudden ascendancy of the city - In 1923 **Eleftherios Venizelos**, the Greek Prime Minister of the time, gained an agreement on an exchange of populations on a huge scale at the international conference in Lausanne. All Greeks in Asia Minor were allowed to leave the Turkish areas and return to Greece, where they were established in the big cities (1.35 million people altogether). In return, the 600,000 Turks living in Greece were transported back to their homeland. Thousands of new arrivals established themselves in Iraklion and suburbs sprang up overnight. Names such as Nea Alikarnassos recall the origins of the immigrants.

Blanket bombing devastated two-thirds of the old city during the Second World War and provided the conditions for a rapid reconstruction, which took everything into consideration except aesthetics and the preservation of historical buildings.

History

In Minoan times, there was only a minor harbour serving Knossos in the present city area of Iraklion. The real harbour for the settlement around the Palace of Minos was at *Amnissos*, a few miles to the east. There are only a few modest ruins there today (see page 161).

The small city of *Heraklea* was only founded during the Greek period. It was apparently named after the legendary Herakles, who captured the Bull of Minos alive on Crete and thus carried out the seventh of his Labours.

Both the Romans and the later Byzantine conquerors inhabited the harbour town. There is almost nothing left which can be dated to this period, and there are certainly no remains preserved.

Iraklion moves onto the stage of history in 842 AD, when Abu Hafs Omar and his Saracens conquer the settlement. They surround it with a strong wall, and a moat. *Rabd el Chandak*, the "stronghold with the ditch", is the name they give to the new fortifications. Right down into the 10th century, the city is feared as a pirates' lair.

Led by Nikephoros Phokas, the Byzantines conquer Rabd el Chandak in 961, and destroy it completely. However, the plan to abandon the city and build a well-fortified castle instead on a nearby mountain comes to nothing, because of the resistance of the inhabitants and the Byzantine colonists. There is nothing else for it but to rebuild and refortify the city. In imitation of the Saracen name, they call it simply *Chandax*.

During the 13th century, the Byzantine empire is worn down by the Fourth Crusade; the Venetians are able to buy up Crete from a weakened Byzantium for a ridiculous sum of money. Chandax becomes *Candia*, a new name for both the city and the whole island.

The Venetian occupation becomes a period of the flowering of culture in Iraklion. The economy and government are completely reorganised by the Venetians, and rich landowners are obliged by law to erect magnificent buildings in the city. Byzantine intellectuals and artists flee to Crete after the final fall of Constantinople in 1452. The *Mount Sinai School*, at that time the most important high school in the Christian east, establishes a teaching and research centre in the Ekaterini Church in Iraklion. However, the rigorous methods of colonial government practised by the Venetians provoke continual revolts among the local people.

From 1462 onwards, the walls of Candia are reinforced in a great show of strength; the *Turkish invasion* looms on the horizon. The fortifications at Candia are now amongst the strongest in the whole of the Mediterranean area. In spite of this, the siege begins after the fall of Chania and Rethymnon in May, 1648. It lasts for 21 years! Again and again, the Turks storm forward, force their way beneath the fortifications, and besiege the metre-thick walls with their prolonged bombardments.

Then, on 27th September, 1669, it happens. The Venetian governor *Francesco Morosini* is obliged to capitulate. He secures an unhindered withdrawal for the sparse remnants of his troops; there are only ruins left of the former proud walls and bastions. One of the longest city sieges in recent history is over; 30,000 Venetians and 120,000 Turks have paid for it with their lives.

Now Crete is Turkish; although Iraklion is named *Megalokastro* (great fortification) by the Cretans in the years that follow, it continues to lose importance, since the Turks make Chania into the centre of administration.

The city is given back its original name Iraklion in 1898 when the Turks withdraw and an *independent Crete* is declared, but only regains its earlier importance later in 1913 on the *unity of Crete with Greece*. The influx of Greek settlers from Turkey causes a dramatic rise in the population.

Iraklion is extensively destroyed by German and British bombs in the Second World War, but afterwards tourism, industry and trade soon allow it to become the most important city on the island. In 1971, Iraklion once again becomes the capital of Crete.

Information office of EOT (National Tourist Office of Greece): This is situated directly opposite the Archaeological Museum, on the corner of Eleftherias Square. Helpful, knowledgeable personnel. English is spoken, there is a lot of printed material, information about bus connections, opening times, accommodation, and medical care etc.
Open Mon-Fri 7.30 a.m.-8.00 p.m. (except outside the high season, when the hours of opening are shorter). Address: 1, Xanthoudidou St. Tel. 081/222487-8.

> **Tourist police:** These are situated in the Leoforos Dikeossinis, the wide traffic
> artery between the Morosini Fountain and Eleftherias Square (parallel to the
> pedestrian precinct, Dedalou St.). Generally not very helpful, but a source of
> good information on boat connections. Open daily 7.00.a.m.-10.00.p.m. Tel.
> 081/283190.

Connections

▶ **Flights**: The airport is about 3 miles east of the city centre. Not a very
big one, but in the high season charter flights sometimes land at 10-
minute intervals, with crowds and delays the result. A total renovation took place in spring '87; there is a new baggage carousel along
with various developments in the reception hall. These include an
official information counter, bureau de change, several car rental
companies, souvenir shops, and a waiting room with a snack bar in the
"Arrivals" area for Greek internal flights. There is a complimentary
telephone service to various travel agencies, hotels and car rental
companies etc. The firms that can thus be reached are listed with
their numbers on a board and calls are free (in the hall on the left,
when you come through from your plane). There is only one medical
room with a nurse, no doctor. In emergencies, a doctor comes from the
El. Venizelou Hospital. However, the airport personnel are very
helpful.

From the airport to Iraklion: if you have booked hotel accommodation,
you will be taken directly to your hotel by bus. Otherwise, you can go
into Iraklion by taxi or public bus.

• **Taxis**: Taxi drivers like to ask exorbitant prices, but you should not pay more than 400 drachmas (c. £2) for the journey to the centre. About £0.09 extra will be de-manded for luggage, and night journeys, those taking place between 1 and 5 a.m. cost around £0.21 per km. It is advisable to agree on the price beforehand, since there is a risk that the taxi driver will take a roundabout way if the meter is running. A useful destination: **Eleftherias Square** (Platia Eleftherías or Liberty Square), right in the centre.

> **Taxis** also go from Iraklion Airport to more distant destinations over the whole
> island, and prices for these journeys are given at the exit for international
> flights (see also the chapter on taxis below).

• **Buses**: the cheaper alternative.The **bus lines** do not unfortunately go directly from the reception hall (probably so as not to spoil business for the taxis), but from a bus stop situated opposite a barracks (Stratones), around 300 yards in the direction of Iraklion. A short walk along the road, buses (Nos.1 and 6) leave about every 20 minutes, and the cost of the trip to Eleftherias Square is just under £0.21.

In case you want to go to the camping site, the no. 6 bus goes from Stratones through Iraklion to the camping site on the other side of the city. Ask if in doubt, otherwise change at Eleftherias Square (bus stop for the camping site is in front of the cinema next to the Astoria Hotel).
Incidentally, one gets to know the worst side of Iraklion on the journey from the air-port to the centre - dusty suburbs, lifeless flat-roofed buildings, junk and rubbish.

• **From Iraklion to the airport**: Bus no. 1 ("Stratones") leaves about every 20 min. The best idea is to get on at Eleftherias Square; the bus stop is opposite the Astoria Hotel but in the middle of the square. Check with the conductor just to be sure, as not all no. 1 buses go to the airport.

1 hour before every departure there is a **transfer bus** for passengers of Olympic Airways only from the airline office in Eleftherias Square. It is rather more expensive than the ordinary bus.

▶ **Boats:** The large ferries from Piraeus dock about 0.6 miles east of the Venetian harbour and the centre of town. There is a large self-service restaurant and cafeteria here, as well as Bus Station A (see below).

To Piraeus: there is a connection twice daily at 6.30 p.m. with *Minoan Lines* (ships named *Ariadne* or *Knossos*), and at 7.00. p.m. with *ANEK* (ships named *Candia* or *Rethymnon*). Duration of journey 12 hours.

• **Prices:** berth in a cabin of A category c. £20, B category £16, pullman-type seat (tourist class) c. £12, deck class c. £10 per person, and cars of up to 4.25 m. in length £25, over 4.25 m. c. £34.

Other boat connections: daily by the Scandinavian hydrofoil "Nearchos" or a car ferry to *Santorini*, on some days continuing to *Ios, Paros* and *Naxos*.

On Mondays with Marlines to *Kuşadasi* (Turkey), and on Wednesday with Marlines to *Patras, Igoumenitsa, Ancona* (see page 14). Also every 8 days on the *Espresso Egitto* (Adriatica) to *Alexandria* (Egypt) and to *Piraeus* and *Venice*. From 1988 onwards there is a connection twice weekly with ANEK to Thessaloniki.

• **Information/tickets**: These are available in the numerous agencies on the **25th Avgustou Street** between the Venetian harbour and the Morosini Fountain. In particular, **Polytravel**, situated on the corner of Koronairou and 66 Avgustou St., sells tickets for all the shipping lines. The offices of **ANEK** are at 33 Avgoustou St. and **Minoan Lines** at no. 76.

▶ **Buses:** Iraklion is the fulcrum and hub of all bus traffic on the island. All of the larger towns on the island are reached several times daily by buses from the 3 bus stations (hereafter named A, B and C).

A good, free timetable is available for journeys in the administrative districts of *Iraklion* and *Lassithi* (eastern Crete) from bus station A. There is another available for journeys to the districts of *Rethymnon* and *Chania* from bus station C. In the timetables, the plans are to a large extent reliable and quite helpful in finding your way, but the actual departure times are nearly always at variance to those printed therein. There is an information counter, usually with English-speaking personnel, at every bus station.

• **Bus station A**: situated at the place where the ferries from Piraeus dock, about 400 yards east of the Venetian harbour. Buses go from here to the eastern part of the island. There is a small café here.

Iraklion

Key:

-  **A** Bus Station A/B/C
- **1** Morosini Fountain
- **2** Venetian Loggia
- **3** Nat. Arch. Museum
- **4** Bembo Fountain
- **5** Ag. Ekaterini (Museum)
- **6** Historical Museum
- **7** Venetian Arsenal

IRAKLION: Buses to **Mallia** every 30 min. from 6.30 a.m.-9.00. p.m., c. £1; to **Agios Nikolaos** around 20 x daily, c. £2; to **Ierapetra** 10 x daily, £3; to **Sitia** 8 x daily, £4; to **Lassithi** (Psychro) 2 x daily, £2; to **Sisi, Milatos** 2 x daily, £1; to **Archanes** 12 x daily, £1; to **Agia Pelagia** 4 x daily, c. £1; to **Mirtos, Ierapetra** 2 x daily, £3.

• **Bus station B:** c. 60 yards from the Chania Gate. Kafenia and tavernas in the immediate vicinity. Mostly buses to the southern part of central Crete.

IRAKLION: Buses to **Ag. Galini** around 9 x daily, c. £3; **Phaistos** 10 x daily, c. £2; **Matala** 7 x daily, £2; **Lentas** 2 x daily, £3; **Anogia** 6 x daily, £2; **Fodele** 2 x daily, £1.

• **Bus station C:** the most agreeable of the three, situated in a small square right next to the Historical Museum, c. 350 yards from the Venetian harbour and only a few steps from the quay road (opposite the Xenia Hotel). Frequent buses travel from here along the north coast to Rethymnon and Chania. Several kafenia help the long periods of waiting to pass more quickly.

The main artery serving the Cretan bus network is the well-constructed New Road from **Iraklion** via **Rethymnon** to **Chania**, along the north coast. Buses travel along it about 25 x daily between the hours of 5.30 a.m. and 8.00 p.m. Departures almost every half hour, and the trip takes just under 3 hours.
Be careful: Some of the buses use the Old Road, which goes further inland, and this journey takes almost 2 hours longer (ask at the bus station!). A ticket to Rethymnon costs around £3, one to Chania £4.

▶ **Inner city bus routes:** City buses are dark blue. *Bus no. 1* goes from Eleftherias Square to the beach at Amnissos, east of Iraklion.
Bus no. 2 goes from bus station A along Avgoustou St. (bus stop is in Plateia Kallergon, opposite the Venetian Loggia) and through the Jesus Gate (bus stop) to Knossos.
Bus no. 6 goes from the barracks at the airport (Stratones) right across the city (Eleftherias Square) to the town beach in the west (camping site and beach hotels).

▶ **Taxi:** There is a taxi rank in Eleftherias Square. Otherwise the drivers will stop when flagged down, provided they are "free" - this does not necessarily mean that they are unoccupied! Price per kilometre is c. £0.15 (*Tariff 1*), and c. £0.20 outside the city limits (*Tariff 2*). Surcharge for luggage is c. £0.15 and night rides between 1.00-5.00 a.m. cost c. £0.20 per km. The price should always be agreed on beforehand, in the case of long-distance trips.

Prices from Iraklion (as of 1988): to Mallia c. £8, to Ag. Nikolaos c. £14, to Rethymnon c. £7, to Ag. Galini c. £17, and to Chania c. £29.

▶ **Car and motorbike rentals:** There are dozens of agencies in the city centre, most of them in 25th Avgoustou St. and its side roads. Many of them give a discount of 20% out of high season. At the time of most recent research, **Hasstel**/54, Avgoustou offered the best terms. A friendly and reliable service is offered by **Ritz** in the Hotel Rea, 1, Kalimerakis St. The prices are no indication of the quality of the cars offered.

Useful addresses
AUTOMOBILE CLUB: The Greek Automobile Club ELPA is at 46-50, Papandreou St., south of the city wall, and is reached via the exit road for Knossos (signposted). Tel. 081/289440.

BOOKSHOPS: **International Bookshop** V. Kouvidis and V. Manouras is at 6, Dedalou St. (pedestrian precinct). There is a well-chosen selection of books, including travel guides, and among them is the German version of this book.

EOMMEX (Organisation of medium and small craft enterprises): there is an exhibition of specially-chosen fine handicraft products in Zografou St.

CHANGING MONEY: There are several banks on 25th Avgoustou St., which runs from the fishing port to the Morosini Fountain. (They are open Mon-Thur 8.00 a.m.-2.00 p.m. and Fri 8.00 a.m.-1.00 p.m.) The newly-erected **post kiosks** are most useful, and money, including travellers' cheques, can be changed there at a slightly less favourable rate every day from 8.00 a.m.-8.00 p.m. (Sun 8.00 a.m.-6.00 p.m.). There is one situated at bus station A, and another on the eastern side of El Greco Park. In addition, the **Agricultural Bank of Greece** at 44, Evans St. is open Mon-Fri from 5.30 p.m.-7.30 p.m. and Sat-Sun from 10.00 a.m.-2.00 p.m.

LEFT LUGGAGE FACILITIES: **Prince Travel**, 30, 25th Avgoustou St.; **Left Luggage** (Candia Motor), 48, 25th Avgoustou St. (opposite Bank of Greece, open from 7.00 a.m.-12.00 p.m!)

HOSPITALS: The **El. Venizelou** Hospital is a state hospital situated in the east of the city, on the exit road to Knossos. Very amenable to visitors, but the standard of hygiene there is not very satisfactory. Tel. 081/235921. A large **University Clinic** is being built a little outside Iraklion. This is to be finished in about 2 years' time and should be up to the latest technical standards.

FINE HANDICRAFTS: The **Grimm Gallery of Folk Art** is situated on the square which contains the Morosini Fountain. It is one of the best shops in the city, and owned by Eva and Helmut Grimm from W. Germany. A rich and carefully displayed collection of old, mostly brilliantly-coloured woven rugs, and also jewellery and musical instruments. The whole thing is a riot of colour and as pretentious as an oriental bazaar. Due to the beautiful presentation and the excellent range on offer it has already been mentioned in several guide books, and extracts from these are posted on the large notices in the windows. Expert advice is available in the shop.

POST OFFICE: at 10, Daskaloyannis Square, a few steps away from Eleftherias Square (can also be reached via Dikeossinis St.) Open Mon-Fri 7.30 a.m.-8.00 p.m for stamps, poste restante, and from 7.30 a.m.-2.30 p.m. for telegrams, money transfers.

DRY CLEANING: near the El Greco Park, next to the Hotel Hellas.

TRAVEL AGENCIES/BOAT AGENCIES: dozens of them on Avgoustou St. Most of them only represent certain travel companies or shipping lines, however. Tickets for nearly all destinations from Iraklion can be acquired at **Polytravel**, at 62, Avgoustou St./corner of Koronaiou; **ANEK Office**: situated at 33, Avgoustou St. (Departures from Iraklion and Chania to Piraeus). **Minoan Lines** (Minoikes Grammes) at 76, Avgoustou St. **Olympic Airways** are situated on the southern side of Eleftherias Square.

TELEPHONE: The OTE central office is on the El Greco Park. Open continuously, but there are long queues in the evenings.

LAUNDRY: **"Coin-Up"** at 25, Merambellou St., about 60 yards down the road from the Archaeological Museum. Several washing machines, self-service, take 20 drachma coins with you. Open daily 10.00 a.m.-7.00 p.m.

NEWSPAPERS/MAGAZINES: There are several shops which sell international newspapers and magazines near the Morosini Fountain.

Accommodation

The problem in Iraklion is to find a quiet room! Probably the best chance of this is to be found in the old quarter *between 25th Avgoustou and Chandakos St.*, where the narrow passageways have prevented any larger volume of through traffic up till now. Mostly simple accommodation is to be found in these streets. Hotels of the higher category are often new buildings somewhat away from the immediate centre, but they are not infrequently on noisy entry and exit roads.

Otherwise, noise can best be avoided at the beach hotels outside the city or on the camping sites.

HOTELS OF THE UPPER AND MIDDLE CATEGORIES

• **Xenia**: A class, certainly the best of the three Xenia hotels on Crete (Iraklion, Karteros, Chania). Modern and elegant, best possible situation directly on the sea front, but unfortunately it is right behind the busy shore road in the direction of Rethymnon; a room with a sea view is a must! All rooms have private bathroom, many have balconies. Lush green lawns around the hotel, and there is a pool. The Café terrace with its banana plants and comfortable bamboo armchairs is less enjoyable, because of the traffic swishing past it. Cost of a double room with bathroom and breakfast is around £22. Address: 5, Akti Sophocles Venizelou, five minutes' walk along the shore road from the fishing port in the direction of Rethymnon, opposite the Historical Museum and bus station C. Tel. 081/284000.

• **Dedalos**: C class, good location right in the middle of the main street for shopping (pedestrian precinct), 2 min. from the Morosini Fountain. Pleasant, cool lobby with windows the size of shop display windows looking out onto the pedestrian zone. Pleasantly furnished, various types of paintings in the hallways, and the rooms have (slightly worn) carpeting, private baths and balconies. Unfortunately it is very near Jam, a noisy music bar. Double room with breakfast costs c. £14. Address: 15, Dedalou St. Tel. 081/224391.

• **Metropole**: C class, tasteful and modern, near the market and with a view over the Cathedral of Ag. Minas. During the high season, however, it is often taken over by tour operators. DR c. £25. Tel. 081/244280.

• **Lato, Kris, Marin, Ilaira etc.**: There is a whole group of hotels of the C class behind the Venetian harbour (entering Epimenidou St. from Avgoustou St.). Their advantage is in their relatively quiet position, but the hotels themselves are stereotyped in appearance, although quite solid and with good sea views. DR c. £14-16.

• **Domenico**: C class, down from the El Greco Park in a northerly direction. The furnishings are unspectacular, and the place is in need of renovation. Worth it because of the central position, in spite of which it is wonderfully quiet. Some of the double rooms have balconies. DR costs around £18. Address: 14, Almirou Street. Tel. 081/288231.

• **Mirabellou**: C class, a sobering experience, with long silent hallways and few guests. Unbeatable advantage is the almost heavenly quiet for Iraklion, and there is hardly any traffic in the passages around the hotel. Room with a bath (shower cubicle) costs around £14, without a bath £12.00. Address: 20, Theotokopoulou St., a few yards down from the El Greco Park. Tel. 081/285052. Right next to it is the more expensive Hotel **Kastro** (B Class, tel. 081/285020).

• **Knossos**: C class. A simple, older city hotel next to the Venetian Loggia. A trace of elegance remains on the stairway and in the rooms; there are embellished doors, alabaster steps and beautiful tiled floors. All rooms have balconies and furniture which is no longer very new, and the back of the hotel is considerably quieter (view over the Church of Agios Titos, see under "places worthy of a visit"). The shower cabinets are rather stuffy. DR with bath costs c. £14, without bath c. £12. Address: 25, Avgoustou St., a few paces from the Morosini Fountain. Tel. 081/283247.

REASONABLY PRICED

There are various simple hotels, guest houses and private rooms for rent to be found in the old Turkish Quarter, which is bordered by Avgoustou and Chandakos streets. There are three of these alone in narrow Kantanoleon St. between the Morosini Fountain and the El Greco Park.

Mostly young people and those travelling with rucksacks use these cheap quarters. General observation: There are only communal showers on each floor, but to compensate there is an informal atmosphere. Single beds in dormitories are often available.

• **Hotel Hellas**: D class, with the house facade painted in brilliant blue and ochre. Rooms and passages kept clean as a whistle, which is astonishing for this price category. Small inside courtyard, where breakfast and drinks can be obtained. DR (without private bath) c. £9, spacious dormitory room with 6 beds at c. £4 per person, with 14 beds at c. £3 per person. There are three bathrooms in all. Yannis and Antonis impart a friendly atmosphere. Address: 11, Kantanoleon St, directly on the El Greco Park. Tel. 081/225121 and 243842.

• **Atlas Guest House**: picturesquely dilapidated, passages relieved by posters, plants and standard-lamps. High-ceilinged rooms with 2/3 beds and tiny balconies. A couple of ramshackle deckchairs on the "roof garden", where breakfast is also available. DR (without private bath) c. £9. Address: 6, Kantanoleon St., only a few paces from the "Hellas". Tel. 081/288989.

• **Georgiadis Guest House**: exactly opposite the Atlas. An elderly Madame rents out 17 rooms, most of which are clean and inviting. c. £9 for a double room (without private bath). Tel. 081/284808.

• **Hotel Rea**: D class; we liked it. Pleasant proprietress, light, clean rooms, DR c. £10. Situated at 1, Kalimerakis St., which branches in its lower part off Chandakos St., near bus station B (by the Xenia Hotel). Tel. 081/223638.

• **Vergina Private Rooms**: only two doors away from Rea, at 32, Chortatson St. Renovated house dating from the Turkish period, beautiful courtyard with banana plants and orange trees. Simple furnishings, passages and rooms carpeted, new beds. Shower on the pretty roof garden. Owners speak good English (son lives in Australia). DR c. £9, without private bath. Tel. 081/242739.

• **Hotel Lena**: E class. Newer building, relatively clean, rooms of varying quality. DR c. £9.50. Address: 10, Lachana St. About half way up Avgoustou St., turn into Byronos St., continue on for about 150 yards and then left. Tel. 081/242826.

• **Hotel Ideon Antron**: E class, very simple, but lovingly conceived. Pleasant inside courtyard with climbing gourds and a lot of plants. Rooms are small, with iron bedframes and old furniture. Whole place has lino flooring. DR. c. £7. Address: 1, Perdikari St., in the lane at the back of the Venetian Loggia. Tel. 081/283624.

• **Hatzidakis private Rooms**: converted house with c. 6 rooms, directly in the pedestrian precinct (opposite Dedalos Hotel). Pleasantly furnished, family atmosphere, c. £10 for a double room, and a three-bedded room is also available. Address: 22, Dedalou St. Tel. 081/242446.

• **IYHF Youth Hostel**: 24, Chandakos St., only a few paces from the Morosini Fountain. Stuffy accommodation with 6, 8, and 10 bedded rooms, c. £2 per person. Cramped breakfast room, staff not very friendly. Tel. 081/286281.

• **"Hotel" Hania**: E class, below the YH and around the corner. Not a hotel, however, but also a form of youth hostel. George, the owner, appears to be a surly, bearish individual at first sight, but he is good-natured. Prettily painted courtyard with the stunning fragrance of jasmin, and a relaxed atmosphere. There are dormitories with 10 beds in each. Take a sleeping bag with you. Showers poor. Doors close at 12.00 p.m. Cost about £3 per person. Address: 19, Kidonias St., a side road off Chandakos St. Tel. 081/284282.

• **Mary Private Rooms**: at 67, Chandakos St. Small house with a handful of twin and three-bedded rooms. Tel. 081/281135.

• **Iraklion Camping:** a large, level site on the long sandy beach west of Iraklion, c. 3 miles from the city centre. For description and directions see under Bathing/Surrounding Area page 159.

• READER'S TIP: "George at **Lions Rent Rooms** gave me a very friendly reception, speaking perfect English. The rooms are clean and quiet, in spite of the central position. There is a clean bathroom with constant hot water for every three rooms. One can have discussions with George in the reception hall, which is more a kind of living room. Sometimes he shows videos there. DR costs c. £10. Address: 9, Androgeo St, a side road diagonally across from the back of the Venetian Loggia. Tel. 081/241194."

Food

Iraklion is not only a place for passing through, but also a favourite excursion destination for the inhabitants of the large beach hotels in the surrounding area. Thus by Cretan standards, the city has much to offer gastronomically, not least because of the stiff competition.

There are dozens of tavernas, restaurants and souvlaki places in the centre, concentrated above all in *Dedalou St.,* the pedestrian zone between Morosini Fountain and Eleftherias Square. As far as Greek cuisine is concerned, the range of dishes on offer is rather uniform; we have listed particular culinary delights below.

Careful: The restaurants situated directly at the Morosini Fountain only partly live up to their ideal position, and you can't eat those pretty nightlights they use in the evening either!

IN THE AREA AROUND MOROSINI SQUARE

• **Cyprus:** At 1, Milatou St., behind the Venetian Loggia. Interesting dishes of Cypriot origin, eg Sikoti (liver) or Seftali, deliciously seasoned meat balls (similar to Yugoslavian Cevapcicci), served with parsley and onion. Competitively priced.

• **Maxim's**: Quiet situation on the lower edge of El Greco Park. Specialising in fish dishes, and also good vegetable dishes.

• **Rizes**: This is an old Turkish house with bay windows on wooden supports, probably the most attractive restaurant in the city. Patrons sit in a lovingly-decorated leafy courtyard with huge wooden beams, away from the hustle and bustle and only c. 60 yds. from the sea. Unfortunately, the quality of the food does not quite live up to the expectations of the surroundings. Address: 54, Chandakos St., five minutes from Morosini Fountain.

• The **"Dirty Alley"** is by no means worthy of its nickname today. The spick and span tavernas in the tiny alley between Market St. and Evans St. (officially called Archimandritou Fotiou Theodosaki St.) were originally cheap snack bars for provincial visitors to the market. They were already a hot tip years ago. Nowadays, they have been completely "discovered". There are delicious grills and fish dishes here, but the prices are not cheaper than elsewhere.

• **Ionia**: an old fashioned taverna, on Evans St., diagonally across from the entrance to "Dirty Alley" (on the upper floor of a guest house of the same name). Kalamari (squid) dishes are a speciality here, but beware of an exorbitant bill.

PEDESTRIAN ZONE DEDALOU STREET

• **Knossos**: If you like to dine in lofty halls with white table cloths and a cultivated atmosphere, this place at the beginning of the pedestrian zone is the right one for you. Address: Venizelos Square (Morosini Fountain), next to the Church of Agios Markos. Rather expensive.

• **Curry House**: The smell from this Mexican/Indian restaurant pervades to the next street corner. Manolis, who also owns the taverna Klimataria in the pedestrian precinct, is an old fox. He has been in the business for 25 years, and is attentive and affable. The magic word here is curry. He has been collecting recipes for years and is always developing new, more sophisticated mixtures. Curry is not one single spice, but has at least 13 different components. Above all the meat dishes here are excellent - eg Chili con carne (£2) and of course the flambés, carried out if you so desire, at the table. The sweet and sour dishes are also worth a try. The whole thing has its price, of course. The Curry House is centrally situated at 4, Perdikari St., a side street off the pedestrian zone (Dedalou St.), signposted at the junction.

• **Pizzeria Victoria**: situated in the pedestrian zone, and here too, one can sit comfortably. They offer 22 different pizzas at prices from £3-4, thick, succulent and satisfying. Try the Pizza Mexicana - peperoni, anchovies, olives. Address: 25, Dedalou St.

• **Giovanni**: for those who like a quiet, almost intimate atmosphere. A row of small tables, in a narrow passage parallel to the pedestrian precinct. Soft music, with the accompanying atmosphere and a good selection of dishes, including Tortellini and Stifado. Candlelight in the evenings, delightfully shady at midday. Address: 12, Adam Korai St.

ON THE VENETIAN HARBOUR

• **Ta Psaria**: There are several fish tavernas close to each other at the beginning of 25th Avgoustou St. Ta Psaria is directly on the street, and it is a place where you can have excellent and reasonably-priced fish.

• **Paralia, Muragio** and **Gorgona**: Those who wish to dine directly on the sea can do so in these three tavernas on the promenade west of the fishing harbour. Protective glass walls have been built around the tavernas because of the Meltemi winds, which are often very strong.

• **Ippokampos:** This is situated near Muragio; the chef speaks good English. Try the stuffed octopus or stifado (meat stew).

SOMEWHAT OUTSIDE THE CENTRE

• **Kyriakos**: a noble restaurant on the long Demokratias St., exit road in the direction of Knossos. Enjoys a very good reputation amongst local people, but is also very expensive.

KAFENIA

• **Mbougatsa Kirkos** and **Ta Leontaria**: two old-established kafenia, right next to each other on Morosini Square. They were already there when there was not a single restaurant or snack bar on the square. Their speciality is Bugatsa, puff pastry rolls with a yogurt/cream cheese filling; quite delicious!

• **Eleftherias Square**: Dozens of cafés fill the area, one next to the other, always full. Ice cream specialities here. Even **Crystal**, the favourite café of Iraklion's tavli and card players has acknowledged the rule of tourism with its English menu and large, striped awnings. It is somewhat hidden beneath a large sign advertising wine.

• **Ta Asteria**: Those who wish to try the famous Greek mezedes (appetisers, hors d' oeuvres) should drop into this kafenion on Daskaloyannis Square in the evening. A raki or an ouzo can be ordered and along with it a colourful assortment of mezedes - snails, scampi, olives, nuts, tomatoes . . . As of late, Ta Asteria also functions as a taverna, and there is a colourfully-lit eating area separated from the area with the small kafenion tables.

Nightlife

The best thing is to sit outside somewhere and observe the bustle. Ideally, sit near the Morosini Fountain - the square is filled to capacity in the evenings, but still has atmosphere. A lot of Greek students meet at the fountain every evening.

• **Four Lions**: elaborate roof establishment above the Morosini Fountain. The apparently impossible, where the historic fountain in the square is concerned, has been achieved here; at least one fountain is constantly playing. Always full.

• **Loggia**: three establishments in one, next to the Venetian Loggia. On the first floor there is the **Piano Bar**, with intimate lighting, colourful glass partitions, marble tables and a bar; naturally there is a piano there, too. On the second floor is the **Women's Café**, a modern kafenion, with daylight neon lighting, the feminists' answer to the male-dominated kafenia of Crete. Men are, however, allowed in when in female company. Nicest of all is the **Roof Garden** with bar, music, and a wonderful view out over Iraklion by night.

• **Jam**: prettily decorated students' café with large, colourfully-lit garden and a lot of loud music. Naturally, there are tourists here too. Unfortunately the prices are clearly too high, and for this reason it has lost a lot of custom. Daily 7.00.p.m.-2.00 a.m. 13, Pedestrian Precinct.

• **Flash Pub, All Juicy, To Avgo**: in a square which consists only of bars, at the new heart of student (night) life in Iraklion. Full to bursting point every evening, but hardly any tourists. Certainly in the case of To Avgo (the egg) the chick has hatched out; it has a comfortable interior with a lot of wood. A small beer costs c. £1. Can be reached from the pedestrian precinct through a small sidestreet near the Pizzeria Victoria.

• **Piper**: disco, a few paces away from Eleftherias Square (follow the illuminated signs).

• **Ariadne**: situated on the exit road to Knossos, this is one of the typical Cretan music and dancing establishments (so-called Kritika Kentra), which are to be found everywhere on the island. Music from the lyra and the laouto - live, of course, and electrically amplified. Very busy.

Sightseeing

Iraklion is a city with a rich historical past. Byzantines, Venetians, and Turks have built, destroyed and rebuilt here.

Not much has been preserved; the old city was devastated by intensive bombing in the last war. What little there is left often disappears between unimaginative and unattractive new buildings. One of the highlights is the Venetian city wall, which is almost completely preserved.

Most of what is worth seeing is situated a stone's throw from the Morosini Fountain. There are some renovated old Turkish houses in the quarter between 25th Avgoustou St. and Chandakos St.

The Morosini Fountain in Iraklion

Morosini Fountain: The water supply was always, and still is, the city's greatest problem. In 1628, Morosini, the ruler of the city, had an aqueduct of nearly 10 miles in length built from Mount Juktas to the city; at its end was the fountain. Today, it stands, old and covered over with moss, amidst the bustle of the traffic, with sad, almost toothless lions holding up the great basin, from which the water cascaded. Below them, there are reliefs depicting sea nymphs and gods, embracing each other or blowing trumpets, and Europa on the bull can also be identified here.

The fountain is one of the few well-preserved Venetian works in the whole city. The Venetians, however, did not derive much pleasure from it, since they had to surrender the city to the Turks 40 years after it was finished. There was hardly one stone left on top of another after the 20-year-long siege of Iraklion. The commander of the last Venetian troops was also a Morosini, the nephew of the former builder of the aqueduct.

Church of Agios Markos: Situated diagonally across from the fountain on the same square, and interesting from the point of view of Romanesque architecture. The church was built in 1239, but a little later it was twice almost completely destroyed by earthquakes. Thanks to the fact that the original plans had been preserved, it could be reconstructed in 1600. It has withstood time well since then, and was temporarily used by the Turks as a mosque. Agios Markos has a nave, the roof of which was previously of a much greater height, flanked on the left and right by side naves, and a wooden ceiling worthy of note. There is a collection of *copies of Byzantine frescoes* from various churches on the island (13th, 14th and 15th centuries). Apart from this, there are often visiting exhibitions there.

Venetian Loggia: This is a stylish and tasteful Renaissance palazzo with a fine entrance hall, semi-circular inner courtyard and arcades. A lengthy restoration of the building has almost been completed. The Loggia was built during the rule of *Morosini* (1626-9), and was used as a reception hall and representational building by the city authorities. Above all it served as a "Clubhouse" and ballroom for the Venetian aristocracy, and was the focal point of social life for the municipal upper class. The Turks could not put the unusual building to any use and let it decay.

Today, it is the *Town Hall* of Iraklion; those who wander through the passageways can observe Cretan burocracy at work. The doors are usually open.

Church of Agios Titos: This beautiful church is a little lower down from the Venetian Loggia. The dome and the oriental-looking intricate detail on the external facade were added in the 19th century by the Turks.

But Agios Titos is much older. When the Apostle Paul stopped off on Crete in 59 AD he left his companion Titos behind at Gortys, as the first bishop (see page 237). When however the Saracens landed in southern Crete in 824, the bishop's seat had to be moved to the north coast. Thus the first Church of Titos was built here at the turn of the millenium. It was destroyed time and again during its history, but always rebuilt; as stated above, the last rebuilding operations were carried out by the Turks.

The interior is elaborately decorated; brilliant, colourful glass windows, a huge chandelier and a richly ornamented altar screen with fine chiselled woodwork are notable points of interest.

The ancient icon of *Panagia Messapantitissa* (Virgin Mary), which is reputed to work miracles, is directly on the left hand side. The paintings on the side walls depict the most important scenes from the life of St. Titos; for example, his landing on Crete, or the moment when he received the famous letter from Paul.

To give the necessary note of vividness to the whole thing, there is even the skull of Bishop Titos on view! A small chamber contains the priceless relic, in the anteroom on the left. Only the roof of the skull can be seen, incorporated in a gold container. A small red lamp lights the whole scene. To one side there is a picture of the Bishop; numerous votive tablets there ask for arms, eyes, legs and hands to be healed.

The sacred skull was kept in Venice until 1966. Just to be sure, the Venetians took it with them when the Turks conquered the island.

Note: At the time of my latest researches, the anteroom was being rearranged. The skull has possibly been moved to a different location.

El Greco Park: a little oasis in an asphalt jungle, down the road from the Morosini Fountain. Shady and wonderfully cool, with a bust of El Greco, stone benches and busy gardeners.

The Market: This is the heart of present-day Iraklion. Whether local or tourist, everyone meets here. This bustling bazaar begins at the traffic lights a few paces up the road from Morosini Square, and runs along the whole of 1866 St. to Kornarou Square. First of all there are the loaded fruit and vegetable stalls, between them sponges, herbs and local seasonings of all kinds, and then meat and fish. The poor rabbits with their long ears hang there, completely shorn by the smiling butchers; only the rabbits' limbs and tails still bear their fur.

The market, a favourite venue of both Cretans and tourists

After the food stalls there is an ever-increasing amount of leather products, bags, souvenirs, bathing equipment and other articles for the needs of tourists. If a rest is necessary, there are several original kafenia.

The side roads in the southern area of the market are of interest. Craftsmen painstakingly carry on their trade here, and are grouped according to their guilds; shoemakers, metal workers and loudly gesticulating fish sellers sit in long, narrow shops which open onto the street.

Kornarou Square: The focus of this square is the former Turkish *Pump House*, an elegant building with a wide spreading tiled roof. It is used as a kafenion today, and one can sit there in comfort under the bushy stony oak and let the traffic rush past.

Right next to it is the Venetian *Bembo Fountain* with a headless alabaster statue.

Pedestrian zone *(Dedalou St)*: This begins at the Morosini Fountain and runs in a dead straight line to the large Eleftherias Square. It is the showplace of tourism in Iraklion, with its (expensive) souvenir shops, restaurants, boutiques, jewellery. A couple of tattered beggars crouch at the end of it every day, hoping in their own way to have a share in business.

The Venetian Bembo Fountain: People like to drop by for a coffee

Eleftherias Square: an extensive area with tall palms and eucalyptus trees. The cafés under the shady canopies are under constant threat from the traffic. The picture is relieved to a certain extent by an attractive wooden pavilion.

The world famous *Archaeological Museum*, a modest building from the outside, is situated on the north side of the square (more detailed information below). In the middle of the square there is a monument to the Unknown Soldier, and at the far (eastern) end, the high city wall with its bastions drops away steeply to the former ditch. Finally, on one of the bastions a short distance along Leoforos Demokratias, there is the larger than life-sized bronze memorial to Eleftherios Venizelos (see History, page 117).

Harbour

Going down 25th Avgoustou St. from the Morosini Fountain, one comes to the pretty fishing harbour of *Koules*, with the Venetian fort. The remains of the old city fortifications and lofty warehouses (so-called *Arsenale*, also Venetian) can be seen on the quay, and fishermen mend their nets at the water's edge. Unfortunately there is the steady drone of traffic passing by on its way to the big freight harbour.

On the other side of the harbour, opposite the fort, there is the shady **Harbour Café**. Almost all of those sitting on the long terrace are Greek.

Venetian fort: This lies at the beginning of a long mole, which protects the entrance to the harbour. The sturdy stronghold with its metre-thick walls, crenellated passages and two marble lions of St. Mark was built in the 15th century on the site of an earlier Arab fortification. It constitutes only a tiny part of the complete city fortifications of the time, whose size can thus be imagined. The fortifications of Candia were acknowledged as the strongest in the Mediterranean, until the Turks attacked them systematically with prolonged barrages for 21 years in the middle of the 16th century, and left not one single stone upon another.

One should not forego a visit; there are wide passages with rounded archways, wooden doors heavily clad in iron, and gloomy turrets with light shafts and tiny slits for shooting from, all of which impart a classic picture of a castle of the middle ages. A wide ramp leads up into the large courtyard, and it is possible to walk around this along the battlements. There are often music or theatre performances here in the evening. A narrow spiral stairway winds up to the highest point in the whole fort but ends in nothing, except room for 2 people at the most. It provides a fine view over the whole of Iraklion and its harbour. Try comparing the water on both sides of the mole; outside it is an inviting blue, but in the harbour basin it is a yellowish-green brew.

● OPENING TIMES: Mon-Sat 8.30 a.m.-12.30 p.m., 4.00 p.m.-6.00 p.m., Sun 9.00 a.m.-3.00 p.m. **Admission** just under £1, children/students half price. WC available.

Those who wish can now walk to the farthest tip of the quay wall, past the half-submerged steamer which has been rusting there for years. Even in the burning midday heat there is a cool breeze blowing here, and the huge breakwaters are wonderful places for sunbathing; even the occasional dip is possible (only for practised climbers, and bathing shoes are recommended!).

Off the coast lies the island of **Dia** in a haze. This is one of the few nature reserves which have been established to protect the threatened species of Cretan wild goat *(Agrimi)*:

Daily boat trips to the island of Dia are organised by **Skoutelis & Co**, at 20, Avgoustou. The cost, including lunch, is about £17.

Ekaterini Square

There are three churches on this generously-planned square not far to the west of the market passage. The square has almost a glistening white aspect in the sunlight, because of the white stone used in its building.

Cathedral of Agios Minas: The largest church on Crete, this dominates the square. It is a fine domed construction in Byzantine-Greek style with two clocktowers, many cornices and rich stonework. Focus for attention in the gloomy half-light of the nave is the huge golden chandelier under the dome, with the Pantokrator Jesus Christ gazing seriously down from above it on the congregation below. The walls are decorated with modern stylised frescoes which, as in all Cretan churches, are painted according to the strict orthodox rules of Byzantine iconography.

Agios Minas: This little church is situated a short distance down from the Cathedral, and contains a beautiful iconostasis, worked in gold.

Agia Ekaterini:

This simple single-naved and domed construction with a side chapel houses an important collection of well-worn icons from the 16th and 17th centuries. The most important works are six by the artist *Michael Damaskinos*, founder of the so-called Cretan School.

When Constantinople was conquered by the Turks in 1452, many scientists and artists fled from that centre of the eastern world to Iraklion. They instigated the so-called **Cretan Renaissance** on the Venetian-controlled island, which only came to a sudden halt in the 17th century because of the Turkish conquest. The Church of Agia Ekaterini was built in 1555 and became the Cretan headquarters of the Mount Sinai School, which developed into the most important high school in eastern Christendom. Subjects studied here were theology, philosophy, literature, rhetoric, law and painting. The most important exponent of icon painting was **Damaskinos**, as mentioned above. His pupil was probably the famous **El Greco** from Fodele (see page 184).

• VISITING TIMES: Mon-Sat. 9.30 a.m.-1.30 p.m., in addition on Tuesdays, Thursdays and Fridays 5.00 p.m.-7.00 p.m. Closed on Sundays. **Admission** c. £1.

Inside the Church: The paintings in the main nave are the most important items in the exhibition. As there are no works by El Greco preserved on Crete, the icons painted by Damaskinos are of central interest. In them, he has achieved a virtuoso combination of the techniques from the early Italian Renaissance with Byzantine and Cretan elements of style.

The historic frescoes, old liturgical books and colourfully embroidered priests' robes are also worthy of note.

LEFT WALL

1) The Adoration of the Magi (behind the cash desk). There are strong Italian influences in the spatial perspective and the presentation of human figures. The Byzantine austerity has given way to the warmth and versatility of western artistic trends.

4) The Last Supper. This is very well preserved, with strong Italian characteristics in its lively interpretation of forms and excellent presentation of perspective.

7) Mary in the Burning Thorn Bush. The last of the icons on the north wall. Byzantine and Cretan stylistic elements predominate here.

RIGHT WALL

• **Noli me tangere** (do not touch me). Next to the bishop's throne. The graceful and lively Mary Magdalene has a definitely modern appearance, in astounding contrast to the rigid Byzantine Jesus.

• **The Council of Nicaea.** In the middle of the wall. Mostly consisting of elements of Byzantine art, the rules for which have been laid down for centuries.

We also liked the fourth icon on the right side of the nave. This shows **the Second Coming**, and dates to the 17th century. It is not by Damaskinos, and contains a very detailed and graphic presentation of the Second Coming, which is also intelligible to the layman.

SIDE CHAPEL

Restored historic frescoes are kept here. There used to be around 800 churches and chapels on Crete which contained frescoes. In some cases walls and domed ceilings were very extensively decorated with paintings (best example of these is at Panagia Kera near Kritsa, see page 294).

The Venetian City Wall

The mighty city wall, just over 3 miles long and with seven large bastions situated on it, encircles the whole of the inner city. Its construction was begun in 1462, but it was only finally completed at the beginning of the 16th century. A strictly enforced labour programme made this work possible. Every Cretan between the ages of 14 and 60 had to work on the wall for one week in every year, and in addition provide two ashlar blocks or stone cannonballs.

Today, the walls and bastions are in part thickly overgrown with windblown pines and dried-up bushes. Narrow footpaths go through this wilderness in places. The most impressive gate is the *Chania Gate*. It has such an Arab appearance that the BBC once made a film about Jerusalem there.

Marengo Bastion: About 15 minutes from the centre, this is the southernmost part of the whole fortification. The nearer one gets, the more village-like the appearance of this quarter of Iraklion, with its narrow passages and stairways and low houses. In the late afternoon, the inhabitants sit everywhere on the steps.

High above the bastion is the grave of *Nikos Kazantzakis*, world famous through his book "Zorba the Greek", which was only one of his many works. He was not only a writer, but also a minister, and today he is still one of the most popular (and controversial) figures in more recent Cretan (and Greek) history. He died in Freiburg im Breisgau, W. Germany, in 1957.

An undecorated gravestone with a simple wooden cross, framed by a flowering hedge - this is all there is to indicate the grave of Kazantzakis. The view over the city is wonderful from here; the deep blue sea is visible between the television aerials and concrete. Inland, there rises the fabled Mt. Juktas. Its outline resembles that of a sleeping person; indeed, the father of the gods, Zeus, is supposed to be resting there. In all, certainly the right place for a man interested in the outside world, such as Kazantzakis was. He was a constant traveller during his life and lived abroad for a long time.

The inscription in Greek which is chiselled onto the gravestone gives food for thought: "I hope for nothing, I fear nothing, I am free." Pride emanates through this inscription, but also deep loneliness and sadness over the lack of understanding of his fellow men.

When Kazantzakis died, the whole of Iraklion turned out. He received a funeral of the first order, but in spite of this he had to be buried alone and forgotten high above the city; Katzantzakis was excommunicated because of his sharp criticisms of the Church. To the present day, the Greek Orthodox Church denies him a place in the cemetery.

Museums

There are only a few museums in Iraklion, but they are among the best on the island.

Historical Museum

A beautiful, aristocratic building from the last century, on the shore promenade west of the Venetian harbour and opposite the Xenia Hotel. The collection is a continuation of that to be found in the Archaeological Museum and comprises carefully collected exhibits from Cretan history, from the early Christian period to the present day.

• OPENING TIMES: Mon-Fri 9.00 a.m-1.00 p.m., 3.00 p.m.-5.30 p.m., Sat 9.00 a.m.-2.00 p.m. Closed on Sundays. **Admittance** c. £2.

Ground Floor: In the corridor there are yellowing photographs dating from times when there were no tourists on Crete.

There are various exhibits from monasteries and churches in the rooms on the right, including liturgical equipment of pewter and bronze, a bishop's chair, bookholders, icons, robes used for services, coins and seals from the Byzantine, Venetian and Turkish periods.

Straight ahead at the end of the corridor there is a reconstruction of a small chapel with lustrous, colourful frescoes.

The room to the left of the corridor is dedicated to the Cretan struggle for freedom against the Turks. There are portraits of the revolutionary leaders, old flags *(Freedom or Death!)*, a drinking glass belonging to the famous Abbot Gabriel of Arkadi, supposedly bearing splashes of his blood (see also the Monastery of Arkadi, page 378), and even Venetian weapons from the time when Iraklion was besieged by the Turks (1648-1669). The writing desk, uniform and a portrait of *Prince George of Greece* are also to be found here. He was the brother of the king of Greece and was established on the island by the Great Powers as High Commissioner for Crete, after the liberation from the Turks in 1898.

Basement: A notable collection of sculptures and chiselled inscriptions; mainly Venetian (middle ages and early recent period), but also some Byzantine and early Christian exhibits. Perhaps the nicest are the Turkish stones in the last room - grave posts with turbans on top, and finely worked Arabic lettering.

Upper floor: This contains a quantity of rarely published photographs of the Battle of Crete, fought between the British defenders and German paratroopers in the Second World War. There is also the study of the Prime Minister and scholar Tsouderos, with many valuable documents, including letters from Churchill and Roosevelt.

Above all, however, there is Kazantzakis' workroom, reconstructed exactly as it was! Simple, almost spartan, with its large bookshelves, writing desk, chair and bed. In the anteroom there are first editions of his works in numerous languages.

Up another stairway there are Cretan folk costumes, weavings, lustrous, colourful rugs, embroideries and various household articles on show.

Archaeological Museum

Cretan finds from the Stone Age to the Roman occupation. Focal point is the Minoans and their culture. An exceptional collection, which hardly anyone can afford to miss!

Although unprepossessing from the outside, the inside of the museum amazes the visitor with its huge volume of exhibits. Even after a lot of explanations and a dutiful round of the exhibits, the visitor is often left with only a confusing multitude of impressions.

My advice is as follows. When you arrive in Iraklion, go inside the museum, have a look round but not for too long, and not too intensively (headache and buzzing noises in the head!). Then go to Knossos and take a guided tour. As far as time allows, have a look at least at one further palace, ideally **Phaistos** or **Zakros**, and then come back to the Museum.

In my opinion, one has to visit this collection at least twice, in order to appreciate its exceptional nature to the full. Above all, the visitor has to have seen the locations of these discoveries, those ancient palaces of a civilisation which still puzzles us in many ways, in order to be able to relate to their everyday objects, jewellery and household equipment.

There are two further facts worthy of note:
The Minoan Culture is around 3,500 years old, thus considerably older than the culture of the ancient Greeks and Romans; at that period, the latter were probably still walking around with clubs and stone axes.
Furthermore, this quite enormous collection is no more than the proverbial tip of the iceberg. Most of the remnants of the culture have been irrevocably destroyed, plundered, burnt or still lie deep in the hard Cretan soil. The Archaeological Museum in Iraklion can only give an impression of the variety and wealth which must have been present on the island at that time.

Finding your way around: The collection is presented chronologically. In Galleries I-XIII on the ground floor there are ceramic finds, weapons, household equipment, jewellery etc. from the Neolithic (New Stone Age) to the Postpalatial Period and the so-called Geometric epoch (5000-650 BC). The places where the finds were made are indicated, and partly described on information boards. Here you will find such world famous pieces as the *Phaistos Disk*, the *Snake Goddess*, the *Bull Leaper*, the *Bull's Head* and much more.
On the first floor are the wonderful *coloured frescoes* from Knossos and various private Minoan villas. After a period of restoration lasting many years, this gallery was once more open to the public in 1984. It was renovated again, however, in 1987.

Tip: As the museum is nearly always very crowded, there is a good chance of being able to follow the explanations given by one of the many English-speaking guides, although these cannot be listed here because of the limitations of space. The museum is most empty at midday, although it is also at its hottest then.

We recommend the purchase of one of the coloured museum guide books for about £3. The contents of most of the showcases are identified and explained here, and apart from this, good photos help you to find your way around.

Arrangement of the exhibits: The showcases are arranged in a spiral formation in every room, facing inwards. Begin at the first case to the right of the door, then go along the wall and eventually into the middle of the room. See plan of museum, Gallery I. This system is, however, not always strictly adhered to.

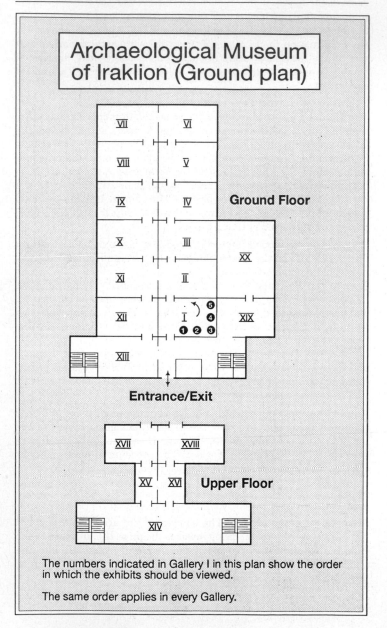

Archaeological Museum of Iraklion (Ground plan)

Ground Floor

Entrance/Exit

Upper Floor

The numbers indicated in Gallery I in this plan show the order in which the exhibits should be viewed.

The same order applies in every Gallery.

Idols, some with headdresses of poppy-heads which were apparently used as a drug in rituals

• OPENING TIMES: Tues-Sat 8.00 a.m.-7.00 p.m., Mon 12.30 p.m.-7.00 p.m., Sun 9.00 a.m.-7.00 p.m. **Admission** just under £2. Schoolchildren and students half price. A photography permit without the use of flash is free; one including the use of flash costs c. £2.00. Tripods prohibited.

Gallery I: Finds from the *Neolithic* (New Stone Age) from 5000 BC up to the *Prepalatial Period* (2600-1900 BC).

The earliest pottery, exclusively hand-formed (potter's wheel was not yet known). Numerous cult figures (so-called idols), stone vessels, jewellery, sealstones, weapons and tools. Originated mostly from graves and cult caves.

Showcase 1: hand-formed clay vases, crooked in shape and buckled. In **Showcase 2** there is a wonderful male idol made of marble.

Showcase 6: fine clay vessels with variegated surfaces due to uneven firing. Long-spouted "tea pots".

Showcase 7: fine stone vessels with veining of different colours from graves on the island of Mochlos. Worthy of note is the round stone box with a reclining dog on its lid.

Showcase 10: small clay models. A ship with a high prow, a votive bowl with a herd of animals and a shepherd on the inside (the most important piece here) and a four-wheeled wagon, the oldest model of a wagon in Europe.

Showcase 11: sealstones made of alabaster, ivory, steatite and other soft materials. Very varied forms and presentation; sometimes fully sculptured animal heads, whole animals etc. Of especial note is the large seal in the form of three dice on a stem.

Sealstones were worn as amulets, used to close containers and were taken by their owners to their graves.

Showcase 12: an original ritual vessel in the form of a bull, with little men climbing on its horns. The nonplussed expression of the bull should be noted.

Showcase 13: marble, alabaster and ivory idols of excellent workmanship. Mostly originating from the Messara Plain.

Showcase 14: daggers made from bronze, some even of silver!

Showcase 17: a focal point here is the wonderful jewellery made from thin gold sheet. The bands were laid across the eyes of the dead. There is also jewellery for the hair in the form of leaves and flowers.
The necklaces of semi-precious stones of various colours, such as rock crystal and amethyst, are especially attractive.

Gallery II: Finds from the *Protopalatial Period* (1900-1700 BC), mainly from the early palaces of Knossos and Mallia and the peak sanctuaries. At this time, the culture of Crete has already reached a high level; the island is thickly populated, the first palaces and cities have been established, trade and crafts are flourishing, prosperity is increasing. Thanks to the discovery of the potter's wheel more complicated pottery vessels can be produced than in the Prepalatial Period. The so-called *Kamares style* comes into being, in which the most diverse patterns and shapes are painted in white and red on the black background of the vessels and vases. This style of pottery is recognised to be the finest of those originating from prehistoric Greece.

Showcase 20: bell-shaped objects with projecting horns, probably representing masks used during rituals of the bull cult.

Showcase 21 B: a fine pendant in the shape of a drop; a snake, a scorpion and an insect are represented.

Showcase 23: Kamares ware. These extremely thin, richly decorated "egg-shell vessels" are exceptional. Their walls are only millimetres thick!

Showcase 24: numerous votive figures, on which details of the costume of the time are visible (men with loincloths, women with long bell-shaped skirts and headdresses).

Showcase 25: small faience plaques, which show the houses of the Minoans in miniature. Very detailed, and windows, walls and light shafts can be discerned.

Showcase 29: large Kamares vases; the pithos with the palms is a well-known piece.

Gallery III: Likewise finds of the *Protopalatial Period*, mainly from the older palace at Phaistos and especially from the Kamares Cave, not far away from Phaistos on the southern slope of Psiloritis in Central Crete. The main body of pottery with a black background on show in Gallery II was found here and subsequently named after the cave. The patterns have now become more defined; mussels, starfish and fish are now visible.
Main attraction in this room - the Phaistos Disk!

Showcase 34: particularly fine Kamares vases, eg the beaked jug with white double spirals and painted eyes, or the cups with the fine floral pattern.

Showcase 41: This is where the crowds gather. The **Phaistos Disk** is the most important find from this palace. It is a clay disc of 16 cm (6.29 ins.) diameter, with hieroglyphics arranged in a spiral pattern from the centre to the outside on it. It was found in 1908 and is dated to the period between 1700 and 1600 BC. A total of 45 signs were stamped into the clay while it was still wet; thus it is a first example of preclassical printing. Heads with helmets, figures, birds, flowers and other simple symbols are recognisable, but to this day the writing has not been deciphered! Experts do not even agree on the probable content of the text on the two sides of the disc. Perhaps it is a type of sacred hymn, since a number of repeated groups of signs, perhaps a type of refrain, are believed to have been recognised. Every sign indicates a syllable, and the words are separated from each other by a vertical line.

Showcase 43: here are the finest vases - up to 19.5 inches high, superbly preserved, eg the fruitstand with white, appliquéd flowers on the rim and foot, and the pithos with the fish and the nets. This definitely belonged to the favourite dinner service of the lord of Phaistos.

Gallery IV: The *Neopalatial Period* (1700-1450 BC). After the great catastrophe around 1700, when all the fine buildings on the island are destroyed, the palaces are rebuilt even better than before. This is the high point of Minoan civilisation and several of the masterpieces in the museum are gathered together here.

Showcase 47: the head of the royal sceptre. On one side there is the head of a panther, and on the other a double axe.

Showcase 49: a wonderful vase in "Floral style" (decoration of reeds), a bull's head rhyton and a "Marine style" rhyton.

Showcase 50: another focal point, this time the full-breasted **Snake Goddesses!** They come from the underground treasure chamber of the central shrine at Knossos and have almost become a symbol of the Minoan culture. Snakes were sacred animals to the Minoans. One of the goddesses (or priestesses) is holding a snake high above her head; in the case of the other, the snakes are winding themselves around her body. The unusual costume is worthy of note with its wide, long skirt, very narrow waist, the breasts totally exposed. The colourful shells probably decorated the base of both statuettes.

Showcase 51: the famous **Bull's Head** - made of steatite, only the right (darker side) is original; the rest has been reconstructed. Served as a type of cult vessel for blood sacrifices - there is an opening in the neck for filling, and one on the upper lip for pouring out. With such an offering, the bull deity could be appeased; the famous bull cult was a main component of Minoan religion. The eye is made of rock crystal and jasper and the nostrils are surrounded by mother-of-pearl. The golden horns are a reconstruction.

Showcase 52: a large royal sword with a crystal pommel from the Palace of Mallia. Also, the pommel of another sword, with the circus-like performance of an acrobat worked in gold: he is bending so far backwards that his head is touching his feet. There is also part of a rock crystal plaque, which shows a bull leaper (reconstructed).

Showcase 55: finds from the Temple Repositories (royal treasuries). Two wonderful faience plaques showing a cow and a wild goat, suckling their young. Also a large stone cross.

Showcase 56: model of a **bull leaper**, made of ivory. Unfortunately the surface is in bad condition.

Showcase 57: a large **Gaming board** made of ivory with inlaid work in rock crystal, silver, gold and glass paste. Ivory gaming pieces. Such games have also been found in Egypt. They resemble the game of tavli.

Showcase 58: superb ritual vases, with pointed bases. One of them in the form of a triton shell.

Gallery V: *Final phase of the Palace of Knossos* (1450-1400 BC). **Knossos alone of all the great palaces was inhabited once again after the puzzling catastrophe that struck around 1450, and this time it was inhabited by Mycenaean immigrants.**

Showcase 69: The two famous Minoan scripts are here shown in contrast to each other. On one side there are tablets with the early **Linear A script** - this replaced the hieroglyphic script and has not to date been deciphered. On the other side there is the later **Linear B script.** This was used on Crete during the period of Mycenaean domination and has been deciphered. These tablets are part of an inventory from the Palace of Knossos.

Showcase 70 a: a clay house model, with only one floor, a light well, and a terrace. Found in Archanes.

Gallery VI: Finds from graves of the *Neopalatial* and *Postpalatial* periods (1450-1300 BC).

The Mycenaean influence has now gained the upper hand. Particularly noticeable is the fact that weapons suddenly appear. This attests to the presence of the warlike Mycenaeans on Crete.

Showcase 75 a: a pile of bones, including jaw, ribs, and vertebrae. This poor horse was slaughtered and laid before the door of the burial chamber of a dead hero.

Showcase 78: another fine piece. A **leather helmet** with boars' tusks sewn onto it. Typically Mycenaean.

Showcase 84: contains mostly weapons - swords, knives, arrowheads. These are identical to finds of the same period from the Greek mainland.

Showcase 85: a fine **bronze helmet** with cheekpieces.

Showcases 87, 88: Gold jewellery, partly originating from Mycenaean graves.

Gallery VII: Once more, Minoan art from the *Neopalatial Period*; this time not from the great palaces, but from estates, villas and scattered isolated cult centres. There is no need for any of this to be hidden away in the presence of the art works from the palaces.

To the immediate right of the entrance there are three huge **double axes** from a lonely estate. The double axe was a sacred object to the Minoans.

Unique at this period are the **steatite vases** in Showcases **94**-**6**. They all originate from the villa at Agia Triada (near Phaistos).

Showcase 94: the beautiful, gleaming black **"Harvester Vase"** in the shape of an ostrich egg (lower half reconstructed). Depicts a procession of farmers with harvesting equipment - perhaps a procession giving thanks to the Goddess.

Showcase 95: the so-called "Chieftain cup".

Showcase 96: large, funnel-shaped rhyton with fine representations of boxing and bull leaping.

Showcase 99: monstrous 30 kg. (66.13 lbs) copper "talents", used as a form of currency. Obviously a little too heavy for a purse (it is thought that they were carried on the shoulder - hence the slightly curved sides).

Showcase 101: a lot of gold jewellery. Worthy of much admiration is the **pendant** with two bees (or wasps?) from a grave near Mallia. The insects are in the process of storing away a drop of honey in a comb.

Gallery VIII: Finds from the *Neopalatial Period* (1600-1450 BC), all from the Palace of Zakros in eastern Crete, which was only discovered in 1962.

Showcase 109: One of the finest remnants of the Minoan culture is this small **drinking rhyton** of rock crystal. This originated from the treasury at Zakros and had to be painstakingly reconstructed from a jigsaw puzzle of over 300 (!) single fragments. Its handle is made of pearls (the green shimmer is due to the oxidation of the wire) and there is a ring around the neck made of rock crystal pieces and gilded ivory rings.

Showcase 111: stone rhyton with a fine representation of a peak sanctuary. There are 4 wild goats with mighty curling horns above the entrance, and below this an altar with ritual horns.

Showcase 114: also a number of fine conical-shaped vases of precious materials such as marble and obsidian. Found in undamaged condition.

Showcase 118: stone cult vessels. Of exceptional elegance is the **Amphora** of variegated stone with a double rim and curving handles.

Gallery IX: Finds of the *Neopalatial Period* from eastern Crete.

Showcase 120: pottery vase in the "Marine Style", depicting an octopus whose tentacles curl around the flask.

Showcase 123: fine clay figures, the female figures resplendent with their elaborate hairstyles. These statuettes are among the most informative that the period has produced.

Showcase 128: numerous sealstones made of hard, semi-precious stones.

Gallery X: *Postpalatial Period* (1400-1100 BC)
The Minoan Culture in decline. Simpler materials are used, schematised representation becomes more frequent, and the coarser Mycenaean art conceals the former originality.

Showcase 133: large clay cult idols. Cylindrical skirts, hands raised up high and unusual headdresses with poppy-heads (probably used as a drug in certain rituals).

Gallery XI: *Sub-Minoan* and *Early Geometric Period* (1100-800 BC).
The Mycenaeans are defeated by Dorians pushing down from the north, and their strongholds are destroyed. The Dorians also arrive on Crete via the Cyclades. The indigenous descendants of the Minoans flee to the mountains. Art and crafts are at their lowest ebb.

Showcase 148: ungainly clay statue of a goddess with raised hands, perhaps a further development of the figures in the previous gallery (**Showcase 133**). There is also a peculiar votive model in the form of a team of oxen. Only their heads have been modelled, however, and the bodies are missing. Is this modern art?

"Bath" for a deceased person

Showcase 153: The secret of the overwhelming success of the Dorians in war; the first weapons made of iron! On the other side of the showcase there are so-called **fibulae**, which fastened the clothes of the Dorians together. The wide skirts and narrow waists of the Minoans are out.

Gallery XII: *Geometric* and *Orientalising Periods* (900-650 BC).

Minoan, Greek and Orientalising influences fuse together, and there is no real Cretan art any more. Mostly pottery, heavier and more severe in style than that of the Minoans, sometimes relieved through frivolous orientalising motifs.

Showcase 163: a favourite piece is this vase with a moving and innocent representation of a pair of lovers. They exchange deep glances, and "he" strokes "her" chin. As primitive as a child's sketch.

Showcase 170: gold jewellery from the Geometric Period. Not as fine as the Minoan pieces, but exhibiting a more advanced technique.

Gallery XIII: Minoan sarcophagi of the *Postpalatial Period* (1400-1100 BC).

Whereas the Minoans of the Palace Period interred their dead in wooden coffins (almost nothing has been preserved of these), it became fashionable in the Postpalatial Period to use **clay sarcophagi**. There are box-shaped sarcophagi with lids and oval tubs without lids. They are mostly beautifully painted, like the vases of the period. The small size of the sarcophagi is worthy of note; the dead were placed in a crouched position in the sarcophagi befor rigor mortis had set in.

Upper Floor

A highlight here are the remnants of the splendid **frescoes** which decorated the interior of the Palace of Knossos and various other palaces
and villas! They date almost exclusively from the *Neopalatial Period*
(1600-1400 BC).
There is almost nothing left of the frescoes which must certainly
have adorned the walls of the palaces at Mallia, Phaistos and Zakros.

Already at the beginning of the century, on the orders of the discoverer
of Knossos, Sir Arthur Evans, the frescoes were painstakingly pieced
together from fragments, in order to establish their composition and
subject matter. Evans commissioned a well-known Swiss artist, a
certain M. Gillieron, for this work. With unimaginable precision and
an almost detective-like approach, he worked at reconstructing the
original, large frescoes from the many and various fragments that
had survived. The modern observer can hardly imagine how metre-
high figures can be created from pieces the size of the palm of a hand,
but in scientific circles these frescoes are given more credibility than,
for example, the reconstruction of the Palace of Knossos! Thus it can
more or less be assumed that the reconstructions of the frescoes on
the upper floor of the museum are relatively accurate as far as their
original appearance is concerned. The dazzling colours are also considered authentic. However there is only a weak trace of this bril-
liance left on the original fragments; the reconstructed parts are far
more colourful.

Gallery XIV-XVI: These three galleries contain all the remaining
frescoes from Knossos and the area around it; some are even worked
in relief, and the subject-matter is mainly that of scenes from nature
and cult ceremonies. Men are always painted red, women have white
skin. Exuberant naturalism, pleasure in colours and a lot of fantasy
are the trade mark of the pictures. This is a huge contrast to the
strict stylised frescoes of the Egyptians, from whom the Minoans are
believed to have acquired the technique of fresco. They attest to an
enjoyment of life, and it was not without grounds that a French
scholar was reputed to have cried out "*Mais, ce sont des Parisiennes!*"
(But these are Parisian women!) when he saw the pictures of these
elegant women.

• On the left in the northern part of the long **Gallery XIV** are fragments from the **Corridor of the Procession** at Knossos. Originally, there are thought to have been 500
(!) figures here, moving in long rows towards a princess or goddess painted as the
central figure. They are holding vessels, and at the rear is the famous **Rhyton carrier**,
whose head is even preserved.

"The Prince with the Lilies" or *"Priest King"*

• Between the two doors to the next galleries is a representation of a **griffin** from the throne room at Knossos. He has the head of an eagle, the body of a lion, and a snake-like tail, and was badly damaged by the fire which destroyed the palace.

• To the right of the doors there are frescoes from Agia Triada. The finest is that of a **wild cat**, which is stalking a pheasant.

• On the opposite wall, amongst several other frescoes, there is the representation of the **"Three Ladies in Blue"**, together with the puzzling picture of the **Bull Leaper**, the pretty **Partridge Frieze**, and perhaps the most famous of all - the **Priest King** fresco from the end of the Corridor of the Procession at Knossos.

• In the middle of the Gallery there is the well-known **limestone sarcophagus** from Agia Triada, which dates to around 1400 B.C. and is the only stone sarcophagus ever to have been found on Crete. It is one of the most precious exhibits in the whole museum and its extensive painted decoration is in particularly good condition.

On both of the long sides of the sarcophagus, there are representations of cult ceremonies. On one side there is the **sacrifice of a bull**; this lies hobbled on an altar, below which are two more sacrificial animals. On the other side of the sarcophagus there are representations of priestesses. One has a yoke with baskets on her shoulders, the other is pouring the blood of the sacrificed bull into a container between double axes. On the right, three men are bringing calves and a boat to the dead man, who is standing in front of his grave.

• At the end of the gallery there is a very instructive **wooden model** of the reconstructed Palace of Knossos.

Gallery XV:

• Directly on the left (west wall) there are two **miniature frescoes** of crowd scenes. One depicts a ritual dance, the other a ceremony taking place in front of the three-pillared shrine at Knossos. Both originate from Knossos.

• **"La Parisienne"**, from the Piano Nobile at Knossos. One of the most famous frescoes from the palace. It depicts a priestess, as can be seen from the sacral knot in her hair. The excavators, however, recognised an attractive young woman, whom they could best imagine in Paris, the centre of elegance and fashion in their time.

Gallery XVI:

• On the west wall there are two reconstructed versions of the **Blue Saffron Gatherer**. Evans thought the figure to be that of a boy, but according to the more recent research of Professor Platon the figure is that of a monkey. On the same wall there is the **Dancer**, with her hair flying.

• On the east wall the **Blue Bird** and the **Monkeys** amidst lush vegetation are worthy of note.

Gallery XVII: This collection was formed by Dr. S. Giamalakis of Iraklion and bought by the Greek Government in 1962. It contains exhibits from all periods up to and including the Roman and Byzantine.

Of particular note: the wonderful amorphous clay idol of a seated woman from the Neolithic period (showcase 175, from Ierapetra) and the fantastic **collection of sealstones** (Showcases 187, 188).

Gallery XVIII: minor arts of the Archaic, Classical, Hellenistic and Graeco-Roman periods (700 BC-400 AD).

Gallery XIX: monumental art of the Archaic Period (700-600 BC).
An independent style develops in Cretan sculpture; this is the so-called "Daedalist Style". It is recognised as the precursor of Greek Archaic.

Gallery XX: Classical, Hellenistic and Graeco-Roman sculpture (500 BC-400 AD).

Only three works date to the Classical period (145, 363, 378); the rest originate from the period of the Roman occupation of Crete.

IRAKLION - BATHING/IMMEDIATE VICINITY

There are long sandy beaches on both sides of the city. Allowances have to be made here; the coast is overpopulated, the beaches rather dirty. This is the usual picture near centres of population.

Even the inhabitants of the large, sometimes carelessly situated hotels complain about it. However, for holidaymakers who have booked accommodation directly in Iraklion, these beaches near the city offer the only possibility for bathing.

To the west of Iraklion

We liked this extensive stretch of beach. There is a beautiful view out over the rugged mountains with the prominent *Stroumboulas* (2,616 feet) on the western end of the bay. Particularly pleasant towards evening, when the sun is going down. Unfortunately the picture is dominated by countless buildings under construction, the sand is covered with rubbish, and on top of that a huge oil refinery complete with transformer station and cement factory has established itself at the western end of the beach.

Ammoudara is the location of the camping site for Iraklion, just over 3 miles from the centre (see below). In addition, some of the largest beach hotels in Crete are situated just before the refinery. These are the *Akti Zeus, Agapi Beach, Apollonia* etc; package tourists are probably disappointed here. The busy through road is flanked by tavernas and souvenir shops and is the venue for a stroll in the evenings.

• HOW TO GET THERE/CONNECTIONS: A branch of the old main road to Rethymnon leads to the beach at Ammoudara. If you are driving your own car from the centre of Iraklion, go down Kalokairinou St. in a westerly direction, through the Chania Gate and go straight on down 62 Martiron St. At the crossroads, follow the signs which give directions for the beach hotels and camping site (keep bearing towards the right).

Bus no. 6 leaves Eleftherias Square every 20 mins. The bus stop is in front of the cinema next to the Astoria Hotel. The last bus to the camping site leaves at around 11.30 p.m. and stops directly in front of the camping site. Fare c. £0.33.

• CAMPING IRAKLION: Well-equipped site with decent sanitation, generously planned self-service restaurant (expensive), kitchen for private cooking, bar (television and video) and a supermarket. An attraction here is a swimming pool, but with sea water. There is just enough shade; small tamarisk trees and bushes separate the spacious individual tent sites, and in an few places clumps of reeds and trees have been left. An ideal place to get yourself acclimatised after your arrival, but readers of the first edition of this book complained about the impersonal atmosphere. Price: low season £2, high season £3 per person, large tent £2, small tent free. Car £1. Open from April to October, tel. 081/250986.

• OTHER INFORMATION: Directly in front of the entrance to the camping site there are the following - a **car rental company**, the small hotel/restaurant **Creta Sun** with a taverna which we recommend, and three bars/music bars next to each other. The latter are well-patronised every evening by the numerous camping and hotel guests.

The **Cottage Pub** is in the style of a Scottish/Irish music pub with a darts board and live music daily, provided by itinerant musicians who give their best on the little stage with the help of a microphone and an amplifier. Breakfast can also be obtained here in the morning.

To the east of Iraklion

After passing through horrid suburbs and in a wide arc around the airport and the large military area, the visitor comes via the Old Road to the actual city beaches - *Amnissos , and Tombrouk Beach.*

They almost continue into each other and are only separated by a small rocky promontory. Many tourists from the city and holidaymakers from the beach hotels are to be found here, especially at Tombrouk Beach (Tobruk Beach) where there are deckchairs, sun umbrellas and pedalloes.

The city cannot be seen from here, as the airport and a rocky ridge lie in front of it. However, the silhouettes of arriving jets and all the accompanying noises are "impressive". The region does not offer much in the way of landscape. It is a wide agricultural plain without any flair, crossed by two through roads; with a rocky desert of scrub and thistles behind it. Between the fields and the dusty wasteland there are carelessly scattered guest houses, hotels and tavernas; there is no village in the true sense of the word.

• CONNECTIONS: **Bus no. 1** goes from Eleftherias Square to the beach at Amnissos; the bus stop is opposite the Astoria Hotel, but on the other side of the road. Be careful, however, not every no. 1 bus really goes out there. Copy the local people, and ask where every bus is going.

There are several bus stops at the beach. In the evenings the crowds hurry to get back to the city.

Amnissos/Tombrouk Beach (from west to east)

Right at the western end, when the road from Iraklion emerges from the rocks in an S-shaped curve, there is a little point of interest on the route. This is the dazzling whitewashed chapel of *Agios Ioannis* and *Agios Nikonos*. It is tucked into the mountain under an overhanging rock roof and blends into the rock with its elegant curves. The whole thing is shaded by tall eucalyptus trees. Undressed rock forms the ceiling in the shadowy interior; a small church of unusual beauty.

The beach opposite the chapel is not much frequented, but it is also not tended. A small river flows into the sea here.

A little further on there is the *public bathing beach* of Iraklion with modest stretches of lawn, several shady reed roofs, paddle boats to rent, tennis and equipment for childrens' games. Open daily from 9.00 a.m.-7.00 p.m. Admission c. £1. The bus from Iraklion to Amnissos stops right in front of the entrance.

Ancient Amnissos: . . . *he was just able to escape from the storm in the dangerous bay of Amnissos and anchored there near the Grotto of Eileithyia* . . .

Homer already knew about the bay, as these lines from the *Odyssey* indicate. Amnissos was the harbour of Knossos in Minoan times, until in later years Iraklion took over and Amnissos fell into decay and silted up.

Remains of the ancient harbour city have been excavated, but there is not much to see. Best preserved are the fenced-off ruins of a *Minoan Villa,* on the eastern edge of the rocky promontory which separates the beaches. The wonderful Fresco of the Lilies was found here, and it is numbered amongst the most important examples of Minoan art (it can be seen on the 1st floor of the Archaeological Museum in Iraklion).

Tombrouk Beach: An adjoining beach to the east of the promontory, dominated by the Minoa Palace Hotel. There are several pleasant tavernas, eg *Plaz Amnissos* directly on the promontory (road leading to it) and the taverna *Kakondakis*, which is situated at the eastern end directly on the beach.

• ACCOMMODATION: there is nothing in the lower price class. But there are various immaculate hotels/guest houses, the best of which are situated directly on the Old Road, partly hemmed in between the Old and New Roads.

At Karteros/Amnissos Beach, for example, there are the friendly guest houses called **Villa Semeli** and **Villa Amalia**, situated next to each other on the road. Further along are the attractive apartments/rooms of **Ariadni**, with a lush green lawn and red hibiscus bushes (diagonally opposite the Hotel Ariadni). Accommodation of a rather more basic nature is offered by the guest houses **Xenios Dias** and **Blue Dolphin Inn**, both c. £14-15 for a DR.

Minoa Palace: A class; a rambling, complicated and massive construction at Tombrouk Beach. Luxury accommodation with all the possibilities - a pool, riding, disco, tennis, table tennis, billiards. Directly on the beach. Half-board c. £40 for a DR. Tel. 081/227802.

• OTHER INFORMATION: there is a **riding stable** on Karteros/Amnissos Beach, inland from the Old Road (shortly after the Blue Dolphin Guest House). Leonis, Agamemnon, Baby, Sirokos and whatever else their names may be are all standing patiently in their stables. There is a small area for riding. Lessons are available and excursions into the interior can be made. Customers are picked up in Mallia and Limin Chersonisou. Information is available in Mallia on the beach approach road, opposite the Hotel Florella, and in Limin Chersonisou on the road to the Creta Maris Hotel, next to the Hotel Castri. Tel. 081/282005.

GROTTO OF EILEITHYIA *(Spiléon Eileithyía)*

The condition of this place hardly suggests that it is one of the oldest sanctuaries in the Mediterranean region. Over a period of more than 3000 (!) years, from the early stone age onwards, it was used by devotees of the most diverse religions as a cult sanctuary. It was originally dedicated to the goddess of childbirth, and countless pregnant women came here, to plead for her help during childbirth.

This yawning cavern is about 33 feet long and its roof bulges deeply towards the floor. The entrance is almost completely overgrown by a fig tree and closed by an iron grille, although this is usually open.

To get there: When about level with the promontory between Amnissos and Tombrouk Beach, take the road which turns inland towards Episkopi from the Old Road (passes beneath the Old Road). This proceeds in wide curves for about 1.25 miles (beautiful view!) and the cave is directly after a sharp bend, on the left below the road (look for the illegible sign). There is a place to park about 200 yards down the road.

West wing of the Palace of Knossos, facade overlooking the Central Court (Reconstruction)

Knossos

The intriguing palace of the fabled Minoan kings, only a few miles from Iraklion and one of the most important architectural monuments of ancient history.

The huge area was laid bare in the early part of this century. More than 30 years of painstakingly detailed work revealed a desert of ruins with empty pillar sockets and the blackened foundations of buildings whose rooms had been destroyed; in all, a site of immeasurable importance for archaeology and our knowledge of antiquity. What lay here deep in the soil of Crete was a real sensation and exceeded the wildest expectations of all researchers. It was decisive proof of the existence of a highly developed civilisation, long before that of classical antiquity in Greece. What had up till then only come to light in a few intriguing finds was suddenly revealed to the eyes of the world in abundant measure - 2000 years of Cretan and European prehistory!

Listless tourists wandering aimlessly between sparse piles of rubble, disappointed expectations and a wasted afternoon; this is the fate of so many important archaeological sites but it has been spared the Palace of .Knossos. Even visitors without specialist knowledge can find pleasure, and perhaps a certain fascination too, in the remains of this huge complex of buildings. This is the result of the service that has been rendered by *Sir Arthur Evans*. With a lot of fantasy, enthusiasm and great powers of imagination, he made the palace what it is today - probably the most disputed reconstruction of a historic building that there is!

Where other archaeologists would have left everything exactly in its original condition, i.e. walls without roofs, bases without columns, Evans built floors, completed crumbling walls with concrete, erected new pillars on the bases, painted the rooms with bright colours. In short, he did everything he could to restore at least a part of the palace to the form which it *might* originally have had. On the other hand, walls which did not fit into his picture of the palace were rigorously removed, and not even marked on the plans. This latter fact is held deeply against him today.

While Evans took too little of a serious scientific approach, he had too much in the way of an intuitive and speculative approach. Thus, due to the presence of a simple clay bath he immediately recognised the function of a room; it was of course a bathroom. The absence of a drain did not disturb him in the least. He completely reconstructed an upper floor which had collapsed *(Piano nobile)*. Whether it really looked then as it does now is known only to the Minoan gods . . .

We must be fair and take into account the fact that archaeological knowledge was still in its infancy at the beginning of the century. Thus Evans thought he could protect the precious remains of the original rooms from the strong rays of the sun and from rain with a roof of reinforced concrete. However, this heavy concrete is rather a serious danger to the ancient foundation walls today because of its weight; supports will probably soon have to be installed or extensive rescue measures brought into operation.

Evans' daring and original reconstructions have at any rate played their part in making Knossos "attractive". The Cretans can only be happy about it; and most visitors take pleasure in it.

The Excavations

The existence of the mighty city of **Knossos** was known for a long time. Homer reported its existence as the capital city of Crete and seat of the fabled King Minos in his Odyssey.

But for centuries, nobody paid any attention to the ancient myths, until the German amateur archaeologist *Heinrich Schliemann* found Troy on the basis of his Homeric studies at the end of the 19th century, and proved the existence of a glittering culture long before the period of *Classical Greece*, through his sensational excavations at Mycenae and Tiryns.

Schliemann, too, was on the trail of the Palace of Knossos. According to tradition, Knossos was supposed to be situated on the hill of Kephala, near Iraklion. A quantity of finds had already been made there. The owner of the land, the Cretan business-man Minos Kalokairinos, had been carrying out test excavations there since 1878 and had thus discovered huge clay storage jars and stones with masons' marks. But the Turkish authorities of the time banned the excavations.

Schliemann came to Iraklion in 1886 and wanted to buy the whole area. But the price asked seemed too high to him, since he was at any rate sceptical about the place where the finds had been made. He returned in 1889 but could still not agree on a price with Kalokairinos. As he would have had to hand over all finds to the Greek authorities anyway, he left the island, thus making the biggest mistake of his scientific career!

Arthur Evans came to Knossos in 1894. He was the son of a wealthy lover of antiquities, quite independent financially and an enthusiastic amateur archaeologist. He was particularly interested in unusual sealstones with strange characters he had never been seen before, which he had discovered in the shop of a dealer in antiquities in Athens. When asked where the stones came from, the dealer had replied that they came from Crete. When he arrived there, Evans found the intriguing characters on a variety of chance finds from all over the island. Above all, he noticed that many women in country areas wore these ancient sealstones with holes in them around their necks. His interest was by now thoroughly awakened. When he saw what had been found on the Kephala Hill, he scented opportunity. He purchased part of the area and thus ensured himself of the right to veto any excavation by a third party. Six years later, the Turks left Crete and he was able to acquire the whole area.

The excavations began in March 1900. Even during the first month, it became clear to him that there must be a whole system of buildings under the surface of the hill. He wrote in his diary: *"Nothing Greek and nothing Roman found here; perhaps a single sherd among tens of thousands of fragments of much older pottery. Not even any fragments of vases from the Geometric period (7th century BC). A flourishing Knossos must have existed here at least in early Mycenaean times!"*

The first sensation takes place on 5th April. Two pieces of lime plaster from a fresco were brought to light. The first *"Minoan"* has been discovered. He has bronze-coloured shoulders, thick, black curly hair, and an unnaturally thin waist (the Rhyton bearer from the Corridor of the Procession, today visible in the Archaeological Museum in Iraklion). All are fascinated, especially the Cretan workmen; one of them keeps watch day and night from now on at what is thought to be a Byzantine sanctuary. While asleep on watch there he has night-mares, and hears lowing and neighing sounds. In short, the place is haunted.

The next surprise is on 13th April. What is considered at the begin-ning to be a "bathroom" reveals itself to be in fact a large ritual bathing room. A spacious rectangular room is discovered next to it, which has stone seats and artistic frescoes on three walls. Above all an artistically produced *throne* made of alabaster is situated against one of the long walls. It is 2000 years older than any other throne in Europe! There is no doubt that the throne room of Minos and his successors has been discovered, at the very centre of the Palace!

Further spectacular finds follow: the **Grand Staircase** in the East Wing, then the spacious **King's Megaron**, the tiled **Central Court** and more and more **frescoes.** In particular Evans and his colleagues are continuously finding representations of bulls - on frescoes, on sealstones, and as sculptures. The most important discovery is that of the **Fresco of the Bull Leaper**, which shows a young man leaping over a charging bull. The intriguing bull cult now becomes the focus of interest. Were these death-defying leapers perhaps the young Athenian men and women who were thrown to the Minotaur every year? (Compare the myth of Ariadne; see Introduction page 101.) Or were they daredevil acrobats, who carried out a circus-like performance in front of the assembled court? Was the bull myth connected with the constant earthquakes in the region? Did the Minoans try to appease the deity of the underworld, the Earth Mother, with their bull games? Questions, questions, the answers to which have still not been finally found . . .

Fresco of the "Bull Leaper" from the Palace of Knossos

Slowly Evans begins to realise what lay in store for him here - the complete excavation and reconstruction of one of the most important palaces of ancient history. In addition, there is the registration of finds, and the examination and dating of the complete Minoan culture, which had been unknown up to then. Evans spent over 30 years on this enormous task, and used a considerable part of his fortune. It seems doubtful that the archaeological societies or the British Government would have provided such enthusiasm or means.

The palace reveals itself as an architectural jewel; Evans and his people excavate over 1,200 rooms in the course of the years. The high point is the discovery of the fine Grand Staircase mentioned above, which leads down to the King's Apartments.

However, with the uncovering of walls which have lain hidden under masses of earth for millenia, the first problems arise, for a large quantity of wood had been used in the construction of the Palace of Minos. Heavy rafters had carried the weight of large masses of wall, rather like the half-timbering of modern times. Then there were the countless pillars, which were also made of wood: cypress trunks, with the roots pointing upwards and tapering towards the bottom. All of these wooden parts were burnt in the raging fires of 1450 BC. The sparse remains had long since rotted through dampness and exposure to air. In short, the whole construction is threatening to collapse and bury the countless treasures of the Minoans beneath it.

Evans and his architect try everything; first they use wooden posts and rafters, but these rot too quickly. Then they try the same thing with brick walls and carefully matched stone columns, but this is also too expensive (even for Evans). Finally, in the twenties, reinforced concrete is discovered. This is long-lasting and strong and can be applied to all joints and empty spaces. It seems to be the ideal material for restoration work. Thus the excavators replace all the former wooden parts with concrete, and paint it light brown, in order to imitate the appearance of wood. These concrete works can be seen today in many parts of the palace.

The most difficult task is the rescue of the large *Grand Staircase*; to avert the threatening catastrophe, the lower floors have to be supported by a solid concrete foundation, and in addition a whole wall has to be moved back into a vertical position from its tilted one.

But Evans desires something more: he wants a vivid reconstruction of the whole complex, which will be interesting to the eye. Not a pile of rubble, but something which people would otherwise have to picture in their imagination. So he begins to roof over the rooms, and has large frescoes made up in brilliant colours on the basis of the original fragments. He also has the shafts of the newly-placed concrete columns painted red, and their capitals and bases black, among many other measures. "*The Archaeologists' Disneyland*", as critics like to call it, begins to take shape . . . . . .

Ritual bulls' horns probably adorned the external walls of all Minoan Palaces

The Palace

Knossos is situated on a small hillock in the broad Kairatos Valley. It is directly on the left hand side of the road, when approaching from the direction of Iraklion.

The gate to the site, which is entered from the west side, is reached by passing dozens of buses, tavernas and souvenir shops. A thick band of Aleppo pines blocks the view of the palace which, with a total area of 22,000 sq.m., well over 1,000 rooms and up to four storeys, is by far the largest of the Minoan palaces on Crete. It stands in a completely undefended location, a symbol of what was apparently an absolute state of peace enjoyed by the Minoans. Their ships enjoyed complete domination over the eastern Mediterranean, and defensive walls were not necessary.

The ground plan of all the Cretan palaces is the same; the four wings of the building surround the rectangular *Central Court* on all sides. At Knossos the cult rooms and magazines (storerooms) are situated in the west wing, and in the east wing there are the Grand Staircase, the private apartments belonging to the ruling family, and the artisans' workshops.

It is an interesting fact that there are only a few windows, but instead there are those wonderful constructions known as *light wells,* which bring air and light to the farthest corners of the palace. These are the most original invention of the Minoans. The *drainage system* is also impressive; clay pipes and drainage channels of almost modern character are to be found everywhere in the palace. A clever system, which would almost do credit to a modern habitation.

In spite of the beautiful pine trees and cypresses around the perimeter of the site, the latter is itself, of course, completely devoid of both trees and shade. Thanks to Sir Arthur Evans, however, one can easily escape from the burning heat of the sun, by going down into the rooms that have been provided with a roof.

• HOW TO GET THERE/CONNECTIONS: If you are going by car, take the wide Leoforos Dimokratias from Eleftherias Square. This leads directly to Knossos (about 3.75 miles).

Bus no. 2 leaves for Knossos every 20 mins. from Iraklion. It starts from bus station A at the harbour, stops a little below the Morosini Fountain (opposite the Venetian Loggia) and at the Jesus Gate. Fare about £0.25. The buses are mostly overcrowded.

Taxis cost about £3.

• OPENING TIMES: Mon-Sat 8.00 a.m - 7.00 p.m. Sun 8.00 a.m.-6.00 p.m. **Admission** £2. Schoolchildren and Students half price.

Guided tours (1 hour) cost £3. You will be asked whether you want a guide at the entrance. Whether it is worth it or not depends on the guide, but those at Knossos are surely among the best on the island. Disadvantage: You will be rushed in quite a smart tempo through the whole site. But of course you can go round again in peace after the guided tour.

History

The hill on which the palace stands was already inhabited during the neolithic period; the remains of huts have been found beneath the Central Court. The first palace was built after 2000 BC, at the same time as the palaces at Phaistos and Mallia. Even at that time, there must have been a considerable settlement around the hill.

Knossos and the other palaces were probably destroyed by an earthquake around 1700 BC, but had already been rebuilt by 1600. They were then considerably larger in size and much finer than before. This was the period of the flowering of Minoan culture. Knossos was the absolute centre of the island, and with two harbours and considerably more than 100,000 inhabitants the city around the palace probably had more inhabitants than present-day Iraklion! The legendary "King Minos" and his successors are said to have ruled the whole of the island and the eastern Mediterranean from Knossos.

In 1450 BC a catastrophe which is still puzzling to us today struck Crete. According to older theories this was caused by a huge volcanic eruption of the nearby island of Santorini, which tore it to pieces and created a giant tidal wave that reached the north coast of Crete a little while after, causing terrible devastation. New research has called the relationship between the volcanic eruption and the destruction of the palaces seriously into question, mainly because a discrepancy of about 50 years between the two events is believed to have been established. Whatever the cause, the palace was burnt right down to its foundations. Traces of the conflagration can still be seen today on the west front. But in contrast to the other palaces, Knossos was rebuilt for a second time, probably by the Mycenaeans who conquered Crete at that time. The famous *Linear B tablets* also date from this period, and were found here. They contain what is probably the oldest form of Mycenaean Greek (the script was deciphered by an Englishman in the fifties - see *Crete/History*).

The final destruction of the palace by new marauders took place around 1400. The settlement at Knossos remained, however, as did its harbours; the Dorians inhabited the still powerful city from then on. It outlasted even the Roman and Byzantine occupations, until it was plundered and destroyed by the Saracens in the 9th century AD. It was once again mentioned in official records in 1271 and has been inhabited, with interruptions, up to the present.

THE LABYRINTH OF THE MINOTAUR

Knossos is reputed to have been the scene of this gruesome myth (compare History, page 101). Even today the palace is confusing because of its size and diversity; but what must the mainland Greeks have thought about it, when they stumbled through it after the intriguing conflagration that took place in 1450 BC? Walls and light wells that had caved in, long puzzling passageways, floors full of rubble, dark stairways . . .

"Labyrinth" was the name they probably gave to the palace because of the countless double axes (labrys) which had been engraved on the walls and posts there. The word probably became synonymous with chaos and maze, because no normal human being could find his way around the place . . .

Tour of the Palace

West Wing

First of all, there is the large, flagged **West Court** *(1)*. It probably often served as the venue for ritual ceremonies, since it is crossed by slightly *raised walks,* and vessels which were used at the ceremonies have been found in the three large *walled pits (2)*. The ruins of early Minoan houses from the Prepalatial Period are visible in the second of these. There are also the remains of an *altar (3)* in the court, which Evans surmised was used to sacrifice animals. There is a *bronze bust* of Sir Arthur Evans under the tree to the right of the path.

Only the foundation walls of the famous **West Facade** of the palace are still extant, and the upper part and pillar bases are reconstructions. There are still clear signs of the terrible conflagration of 1450 BC on the sharply-edged alabaster panels, with which the blocks are covered.

The interior of the palace is reached via the *west entrance and porch (4)*. A round column, of which the *base* is still preserved, supported the door jamb. There are two small rooms on the right in which gatekeepers were probably stationed.

The long passageway has been named the **Corridor of the Procession Fresco** *(5)* because of its wall paintings (remains of the frescoes are on the upper floor of the Archaeological Museum in Iraklion; there were originally more than 500 figures). Notice the *floor*. It has been reconstructed according to its probable original appearance using white alabaster flagstones, grey schist and red mortar (there are several original pieces on the far side facing towards the palace).

By turning to the left before the end of the corridor the visitor arrives at the **South Propylaea** *(6),* the monumental south entrance to the palace with walls several feet thick. It consists of two halls with two columns in each and was partly reconstructed by Evans. Point of interest here: the reconstructed *fresco copy* which depicts people carrying ritual vessels. This is probably the end of the Procession fresco, which extended to this point. The concrete vertical and horizontal beams in the walls are intended to imitate wooden beams, which gave the walls elasticity in the form of half-timbering.

On the southern crest of the wall there are enormous **cult horns**, which probably decorated one of the palace windows. These cult horns were an important symbol of the Minoan bull cult, and were often used to decorate the upper edge of the palace facade. Incidentally, the "mythical" Mount Juktas with its startling outline of Zeus can be seen in the background.

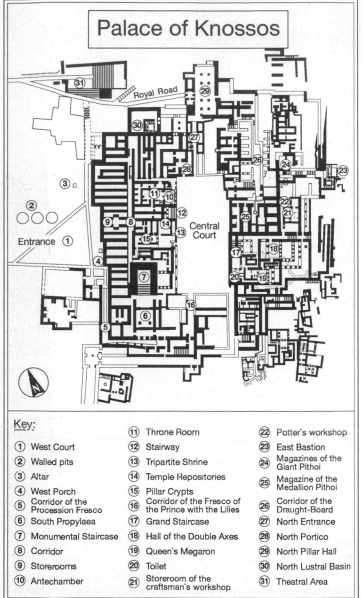

Palace of Knossos

Royal Road

Central Court

Entrance

Key:

1. West Court
2. Walled pits
3. Altar
4. West Porch
5. Corridor of the Procession Fresco
6. South Propylaea
7. Monumental Staircase
8. Corridor
9. Storerooms
10. Antechamber
11. Throne Room
12. Stairway
13. Tripartite Shrine
14. Temple Repositories
15. Pillar Crypts
16. Corridor of the Fresco of the Prince with the Lilies
17. Grand Staircase
18. Hall of the Double Axes
19. Queen's Megaron
20. Toilet
21. Storeroom of the craftsman's workshop
22. Potter's workshop
23. East Bastion
24. Magazines of the Giant Pithoi
25. Magazine of the Medallion Pithoi
26. Corridor of the Draught-Board
27. North Entrance
28. North Portico
29. North Pillar Hall
30. North Lustral Basin
31. Theatral Area

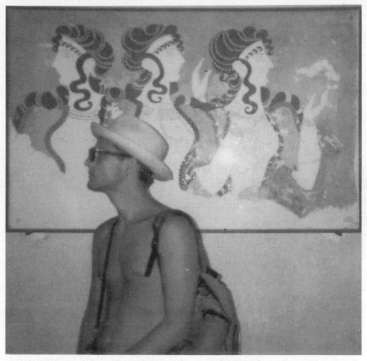

"Three Ladies in Blue" and one perspiring tourist

The upper floor is reached via a wide stairway *(7)*. This is the so-called **Piano Nobile**, which had completely collapsed and was rebuilt by Evans (the reconstruction is hotly disputed). A few yards on, the visitor enters a room with three pillar bases and three column bases, the so-called *Tricolumnar Hall*. To the right of this is Evans' *central treasury*. Below, on the ground floor and to the west there is the long *Corridor of the Magazines (8)* flanked by 18 *storerooms (9)*, in which huge clay pithoi containing wine, oil and grain were situated. Some are preserved in their original condition and location. Narrow walled *boxes* were sunk into the floor here; they probably functioned as "safes" for the most precious articles in the palace. None of the contents have been found, however. They were thoroughly plundered after the great catastrophe.

A little further to the north on the Piano Nobile there is a small roofed *room* on the right, directly above the throne room (the latter is described below). Copies of various *frescoes* can be seen here, so that the visitor receives a small impression of the rich decoration of the original rooms. In the right half of the room there is a *light well* surrounded by columns; looking down it, the ritual basin in the throne can be seen.

The **Central Court** can be reached via a staircase from the raised terrace of the Piano Nobile. The former official rooms of the palace were situated above one another over several storeys, directly on the left next to the stairway. Only the ground floor with the famous throne room is preserved. Visitors today may only enter the *Antechamber (10)* of the throne room. The well-preserved alabaster floor has been worn smooth by the feet of countless visitors. In the middle there is a large *basin made of porphyry*. A great attraction is of course provided by the wooden replica of the oldest throne in Europe. The characteristic wave-like edge of the seat back is striking, and the seat is especially well-formed, suiting the shape of the human body perfectly. Everyone sits down there and is allowed to feel like King Minos for a moment.

The *Throne Room (11)* can be seen through the doorway - there stands the real "*Throne of Minos*" in its original location, surrounded by alabaster benches! On the right and left, and on the side walls, there are representations of mythical beasts, so-called *griffins* with the head of an eagle, the body of a lion and snake-like tail. These symbolise the comprehensive power of Minos in the heavens, on earth and beneath the earth. The king's priests probably sat on the benches. On the other side of the room and separated from it by reconstructed columns, there is a wonderfully preserved *lustral basin* with a light well over it (above it is the room with the frescoes). These lustral basins or basins for ritual cleansing have been found in all the Minoan palaces, but their exact purpose has not been explained.

Evans found this room in a chaotic state. Cult vessels had been strewn everywhere, and a large oil ewer had been thrown in the corner. Did the priests in desperation make a last-minute attempt here, perhaps even during the catastrophe, to appease the earth deity? It must all have been over within a few hours, with the palace a pile of rubble and the throne room conserved for millenia . . .

The oldest throne in Europe has naturally always fired the imagination of men. It is thus not surprising, that the President of the International Court of Justice in the Hague sits on a replica of the throne of Minos.

On the other (right hand) side of the *stairway (12)* from the Piano Nobile into the Central Court are the remains of the facade of the so-called *Tripartite Shrine (13)*. This is entered through an anteroom with benches and directly beyond are the (inaccessible) so-called *Pillar Crypts (15)*. A massive, four-cornered pillar stands in the middle of each of these two rooms; small, sacred double axes have been engraved on both pillars. Shallow troughs have been hewn into the bases of the pillars for the blood of sacrificed animals. By turning to the right in the anteroom, the visitor can see the *Temple Repositories (14)*, the last of the walled rooms in that area. Here, in a rectangular pit, several objects including the "Snake Goddess" were discovered (in Gallery IV in the Archaeological Museum).

By crossing the Central Court you can now make a short visit to the **South Wing**. You will find the famous fresco of the *Prince with the Lilies* or *Priest King fresco (16)* here, in the corridor leading into the court. This is only a copy, of course. It derives its name from the elaborate flower and peacock feather crown.

The extensive **Central Court** served as a source of ventilation and light for the adjoining quarters. There are traces left of the original paving here. In all probability, apart from other rituals and festivals, the notorious *bull-leaping* also took place here (see Introduction, History page 109). Some fine frescoes have been preserved, which show the thronging of the grandstands (in Gallery XIV in the Archaeological Museum at Iraklion).

East Wing

This is situated on the other side of the Central Court. It originally stood five storeys high; two of these storeys towered over the Central Court, the other three were built on the edge of the hill, which falls steeply to a river bed at this point. Down below were the apartments of the ruling family (the centre of power), and there were also workshops and magazines (storerooms).

The *Grand Staircase (17)* is perhaps the most wonderful structure in the palace. The steps are wide and overhang each other, and a spacious light well runs from above to below and provides light for every floor. The landings of the individual floors are separated from the light wells by a low balustrade, once again with reconstructed, brilliant red columns. Strangely, the steps are made of gypsum, a soft, smooth material, which is worn down extremely quickly. This fact led the German archaeologist Hans Georg Wunderlich to his own theory about the function of the Palace of Knossos (see below, "Knossos as a City of the Dead?"). The walls at the side of the stairway were probably decorated with frescoes.

Further down is the so-called *Ramp of the Royal Bodyguards* with frescoes depicting figure-of-eight shields. (The recessing in the middle serves to reduce the weight of the shield; Homer writes about them 800 years later!) It is likely that the sentries guarding the entrance to the royal apartments were accommodated here.

At the foot of the stairway there is a corridor leading to the *Hall of the Double Axes (18)*. This name is derived from the tiny double axes that have been scratched into the west wall of the light well (look carefully, they are difficult to find). Perhaps this was a kind of audience chamber; on the wall, there is a limestone formation preserved behind glass on which the imprint of what was either a wooden throne (or altar) has been recognised.

Right next to this is the *King's Megaron*. The architectural arrangement here is ingenious and characteristic of Minoan building construction. There are wide doorways in three walls of the room. When the wooden doors were opened, they disappeared completely into depressions at the sides, so that the room gave the impression of being surrounded only by columns and must have been a wonderfully airy place. The lower floor is in general pleasantly cool and shady. In summer it is undoubtedly the most pleasant part of the palace. These so-called *multi-doored rooms* are also found in the other palaces at Zakros, Mallia, Agia Triada and Phaistos.

The "Queen's Megaron"; airy and full of the joys of life

A small dark passage leads from the Hall of the Double Axes into the so-called *Queen's Megaron (19)*. This is undoubtedly the room with the most atmosphere because of the wonderful dolphin frescoes alone - dark blue on a light blue ground, with fish and spiny sea urchins. A stone bench runs round the Megaron, and there are a number of windows and light wells on two sides. It is a pleasant, inviting room today with its frescoes, ornaments and brilliant colours! Evans found it feminine, and this is why it is called the "Queen's Megaron".

There is a tiny room next to it; according to Evans this is the Queen's bathroom! Strangely, however, the "bath tub" here has no drain; perhaps it really was only a sarcophagus for a dead person, as Wunderlich has suggested? This clay tub was found a little away from the place where it stands today.

A narrow passage leads to the so-called *Queen's Toilet (20)*. Here is the biggest surprise of all - a *toilet* with a flushing system, commonly known as a "stand-up" toilet! There was a construction in the wall to house a wooden seat (traces have been found), a hole down below which connected with a drain, and a space next to the seat for a vessel with which to pour water down the toilet. The drainage pipes ran to the neighbouring river. Beyond the toilet there was an *archive room*, where clay tablets were stored.

The former workshops were situated to the north of the King's apartments. In the *storeroom of the craftsman's workshop (21)* were found pieces of Peloponnesian basalt, a material used for the production of sealstones. Potter's wheels lay next door *(22)*. The remains of the wonderful drainage system originating from the first palace can be seen in a nearby court. Directly ahead are the *magazines of the giant pithoi*, in which there are huge clay pithoi with many handles *(24)*. To the right, a stairway leads down to the *east bastion (23)*, allowing access to the river bank directly below. The door is blocked today.

You will find one of the most remarkable examples of the art of Minoan drainage on this stairway. A narrow channel runs down the right side of the stairs. The Minoan engineers have constructed it with such ingenious bends (parabolic curves) and catchment basins for earth carried down by the water, that the water flows only half as quickly as it would do if it were to flow in a straight line. On the other hand the water arrives at the bottom in such a clean state that it can be used for laundering. Perhaps the palace laundry was situated here.

Going back up the stairway, you arrive at the so-called *Corridor of the Draught Board (26)*. The famous gaming board that can be admired in Gallery IV of the Archaeological Museum was found here. Once again the clay drainage pipes, reminiscent of a modern system, can be seen in the corridor and particularly in the room over its southern end. There is also a neighbouring *magazine*, in which there are large pithoi with medallion decoration, still in their original position *(25)*. Above this, but no longer preserved, there was a large room decorated with frescoes; this might have been the ruler's actual throne room, in contrast to the rather more ritual throne room in the west wing, and a place in which political decisions were made.

North Wing

A narrow, shelving *corridor* leads from the central court to the **North Entrance** of the palace *(27)*. There are two high *bastions* on either side of this entrance, of which Evans reconstructed the one to the west *(28)*. On the wall behind the columns there is a reconstruction of a *fresco relief*, which may show the capture of a wild bull. At the lower north end of the corridor there is a large *Hall (29)* with 8 pillar bases and 2 column bases. The road from the harbour of Knossos ended here and this room may have been used for the sorting and stacking of incoming goods. Evans called it the *Customs House*.

To the west of the bastion containing the representation of the bull there is a further large *lustral basin (30)*. This is roofed over today. It is lined with alabaster and was previously decorated with frescoes. Perhaps a place for newly arrived visitors to the palace to cleanse themselves.

The so-called "*Royal Road*" runs a few yards to the north of the lustral basin. In Minoan times this road went in a westerly direction as far as Amnissos, the harbour of Knossos; possibly there were frequent festive processions along it. In the middle of the road there was a double row of rectangular slabs, thus enabling wagons to travel comfortably along it. Another, more ancient way has been found underneath the road: this is thought to be the oldest roadway in Europe.

A few yards on, you come to the so-called "*theatral area*" *(31)* on the north side of the road. Here, there are two rows of steps built at right angles to each other around a paved court. The audience must have stood on these steps. The royal box might have been situated at the point where the steps meet; the base of it is still preserved. This was probably used as a place where receptions, audiences or gatherings were held during religious ceremonies, or it may sometimes have been used as a court of law.

A paved way leads from it to the west and soon meets the Royal Road. After just under 100 yards there are the foundation walls of some *Minoan Houses*; several fine frescoes have been found here (there are copies in the room over the throne room). The road ends today with a closed gateway on the main road to Iraklion. You can reach the West Court, where our tour began, by going to the left up a few steps under the trees.

Surrounding area

Numerous other buildings have been excavated around the palace. They can only be visited with special permission.

● **The Little Palace**: This is just before the tavernas on the right side of the road when approaching from the direction of Iraklion. The "Royal Road" leads from here to the Palace of Knossos.

● **The Royal Villa**: Probably a luxuriously appointed private villa. Situated slightly to the north east of the large excavated area.

● **The Guest House**: a little to the south of the palace (on the left below the motor road). Evans called it the "Caravanserai".

● Further to the south there are the so-called **House of the High Priest** and the neighbouring **Temple Tomb**, which was probably a royal burial place.

What was the Palace of Knossos? There are always new suggestions, speculations, and theories:

KNOSSOS AS A CITY OF THE DEAD?

A new sensational theory was put forward by the German archaeologist Hans Georg Wunderlich in his book "*The Secret of Crete*" in 1971:

Completely unfortified walls, without battlements or watch towers; can this be the residence of a mighty king?
Angular, narrow entrances to the palace, living quarters located in a cellar position; can these be the staterooms of the ruler of all Crete?
Nearly all the stairs made of gypsum, an extremely soft material. Were they really intended for use?
Bathtubs without drainage, huge clay vessels in what are supposed to have been living rooms, and not a kitchen in the entire complex?

In short - Wunderlich considers the Palace at Knossos to be an over-dimensional *grave complex*! The light wells served to ventilate rooms filled with the smell of putrefaction, the complicated drainage system was used during the embalming of the dead, the statues of the snake goddesses represented keening women, who bared their breasts as a sign of mourning.

Although Wunderlich might have been able to cause a sensation with this amazing theory, as the "Däniken" of Minoan archaeology, it is more or less discounted today. For one thing, a *kitchen* has been found at the palace of Kato Zakro which was built to the same pattern as that at Knossos. For another, the large *Cemetery of Fourni* has been excavated near Archanes. The typical vaulted graves found there present quite a different picture to the complex at Knossos.

NOT A PALACE BUT A SHRINE?

The prominent French archaeologist **Paul Faure**, who himself has spent many years conducting excavations in Crete, has ventured an opinion that the Minoan palaces are in reality large shrines, in which the huge priesthood, not the "priest king", resided as a religio-economic community.

Faure's main argument is that extremely spacious building complexes have been found in the immediate vicinity of all 4 of the great Cretan palaces, and these have mostly been given names

such as "the Little Palace" or "the Royal Villa". But would Minos
have built a second palace c. 300 yards from his main residence
(as at Knossos?) It is more likely that the smaller building is the
palace and the larger one is the "temple"; the gods always lived
better than men in antiquity. Minos would have come over from
the little palace for great religious ceremonies several times in
the year, but worldly political power was not wielded there.
Faure gives Solomon as an example; he too built a temple - the
Temple of Jerusalem - near his own royal palace.

IRAKLION/SURROUNDING AREA

From Iraklion westwards

While stereotyped hotels dominate the picture in the area to the east of Iraklion, the west is wild and mountainous in the direction of Rethymnon. The foothills of the central Ida range characterise the coastal area.

The New Road traverses mountain and valley here in wide curves and there are only few centres of tourism, for example the hotel village *Agia Pelagia* and much further to the west the former fishing village *Bali*. The village of *Fodele*, said to be the birthplace of the painter El Greco, is much-frequented, whereas the terraced village of *Rogdia* is hardly visited; from it, there is a breathtaking view over Iraklion and up to the flowering oasis that is the *Nunnery of Savathiana* above it. This is undoubtedly one of the most beautiful monastic complexes on Crete!

Rogdia: A fine excursion from the western end of the beach at Iraklion. A winding road 3.75 miles long begins at the refinery and goes to this isolated village, high up on the cliff. From here there is a stunning view out over the sea and the bay of Iraklion, almost as if from an over-dimensional amphitheatre.

Leave your vehicle at the entrance to the village (the buses from Iraklion stop there too) and stroll along the main road. After a few yards on the right hand side below the road there are the remains of a fine Venetian *palazzo*. There are several kafenia which offer a panoramic view situated on this road, and further on there is an ancient baking oven.

NOTE: the road from Rogdia to **Achlada** is not asphalted, but it is wide and relatively well-constructed. The five mile stretch presents no problem. At Achlada the road goes in steep curves down to the New Road.

NUNNERY OF SAVATHIANA

Those who have made it as far as Rogdia should also manage the 2.5 miles to the nunnery. At the entrance to the village a path, which is only cemented at the beginning, winds off to the left up to the mountains above Rogdia. Always take note of signposts at crossroads and memorise the way you have come. The way back to Rogdia is not signposted.

The whitewashed nunnery complex lies hidden in a cleft in the rocks between tall cypresses. The first thing which the visitor notices is the unbelievable abundance of water. There is the sound of water splashing everywhere and there are lush clumps of flowers on the sides of the path. A Via Dolorosa with the Stations of the Cross leads behind the buildings to the fruit terraces of the nunnery. The elderly *Papas* of Savathiana, who has been in charge of the nunnery for 32 years, has transformed the complex into a flowering showpiece with the help of around two dozen nuns living there. When we arrived there, he showed us around the little twin churches and the nunnery. Among other things to see there are various icons and the skull of a priest killed by the Turks. To round off the little tour we were served with a spoonful of home-made quince jam and a glass of raki or water.

VISITING TIMES: 8.00 a.m.-1.00 p.m., 4.00 p.m.-7.00 p.m. The recent use of building materials at Savathiana shows that the nunnery has the will to carry on. The tourists' drachmas are essential for this purpose. Please leave some money behind you.

From Iraklion to Agia Pelagia

After the wide coastal plain to the west of Iraklion the well-constructed new road winds up to a rocky peak and the cliffs on the right fall steeply away to the sea. Again and again there are wonderful views back over the bay of Iraklion, and fine mountain vistas!

Not far after the road enters the mountains, there is a small *shingle and sand beach*, directly beneath the bridge over the road, picturesquely framed by cliffs. Behind this an area containing several hotels and apartment complexes extends deep into the green hinterland, and high above on the slope there is the village of Rogdia (see above). A stay in this valley is not really recommended; the busy main road is right on top of you.

Palekastro: There are the ruins of a Venetian stronghold on the rocky hill on the right hand side of the beach. Not much is preserved, but in spite of this it is an important structure. This is where the governor *Morosini* negotiated with the Turks for an honourable surrender of the fortress of Iraklion in 1669 (at that time called Candia).

Agia Pelagia

Seen from the New Road, Agia Pelagia lies far below in a barren dried-up rocky landscape. A fine view.

What from a distance appears to be a quiet, unworldly fishing village reveals itself on closer inspection to be a tourist resort of the first order. Here, in the middle of a rocky, jagged coastline a tiny nest has been nurtured into an almost stylish holiday resort. There are apartment complexes and hotels, crowded together and built in indiscriminate fashion; only occasionally between them are the former humble habitations of the local people visible. While some agricultural activity is carried on in the hinterland with olives, oranges and vegetables, one taverna next to the other vies for the favours of the holidaymaker. Those looking for a little comfort and a lot of hubbub have surely come to the right place in Agia Pelagia.

(Almost) everything that money can buy is on offer. **Water-skiing** (£5 per trip), **Paragliding** (£14), **boat trips** - "an unforgettable trip on which you will see wild geese and pigeons in their natural habitats" (£6), and **water taxis** are always available to go to the surrounding coves. For £3 you can watch the fishermen bringing in their nets. Of interest to **divers**: You can borrow diving equipment from the Austrian diving instructor Peter Engert in the Hotel Peninsula (£17.00 per dive).

• CONNECTIONS: Buses go 5 times daily to and from **Iraklion**, and the bus stops are at the Hotels Capsis Beach or Peninsula. In 1988 the first bus left at 9.45 a.m. for the city and the last bus from the city left Iraklion as early as 5.00 p.m. Hotel guests in Agia Pelagia are advised to get together and share taxis if they wish to go into Iraklion in the evening.

Accommodation

As everything is very close together here, the position of most of the houses is not exactly ideal, and in part they block each other's view.

• **Capsis Beach Hotel**: A class, the best and most comfortable address in the place. It occupies a complete long peninsula with its more than 1,000•beds. A wide, branching complex of two-storeyed houses in the middle of an extensively laid-out and lovingly tended park landscape. There are wild vines growing here, along with bush roses, rubber and eucalyptus trees and flowers of all kinds; a really fantastic sight in this barren area. A long private beach, tennis, 2 pools, watersports and motorbikes for rent. Costs around £34 for a DR. Tel. 081/233395.

• **Perla Apartments**: B class, very nice and quietly situated, a little above the village on the entrance road to the Capsis Beach Hotel. Surprisingly modern and tastefully furnished, large 2- and 4-room apartments (bedroom, living room, kitchen, bath). Light-coloured wooden doors, tiled floors, rough, whitewashed walls and cleverly simple beds on whitewashed stone foundations. Balconies. A two-roomed apartment costs c. £17. Tel. 081/289408.

• **Hotel Panorama**: B class, also recommended. A long distance from the sea, however, situated above the village on one of the turnings off the New Road. There are several terrace-shaped blocks with bungalow-like architecture, arranged in tiers. Fine swimming pool, very quiet and a super view down over the landscape of branching cliffs and the village. Somewhat more expensive than Perla Apartments. Tel. 081/285632.

• **Akti**: private rooms in the middle of the village on the first floor of a house standing relatively alone, opposite the supermarket. Rooms have beds made of light-coloured wood, a small kitchen niche, shower and toilet, and a balcony. Owner's son has a cafeteria in the village. About 100 yards to the beach. Price about £14 for a DR. There is no accommodation of a considerably cheaper kind to be had in the village.

• READER'S TIP: "Two years ago the Hotel **Peninsula** was built in Agia Pelagia (A class, tel. 081/289404). It is of medium quality and has a narrow shingle beach, which is reached by 250 steps."

Author's Note: The Hotel Peninsula has 250 well-furnished rooms in several tiers of buildings, a freshwater pool, a dining room and two tennis courts.

Going further along the New Road in the direction of Rethymnon, there is a little-frequented beach near a petrol station. This beach is not very clean. A number of fishermen and farmers spend the summer here in simple wood and reed huts, and grow a few vegetables. There is one taverna directly on the beach, and another near the petrol station. At present a new hotel complex is being built here.

The turnoff to Fodele (1.9 miles) is here; the road is made up, but there are several potholes.

Fodele

This simple whitewashed village is situated on a strongly-flowing little river in the middle of lush green orange groves.

In spite of increasing numbers of visitors the village has retained something of its original character. Off the main street, you are quickly in a maze of angular passages with old houses, balconies overgrown with flowers and shoulder high walls, which often conceal pretty gardens behind them. The signs of prosperity are recognisable; the occasional modern, recently-built house stands between the old cottages.

Going along the main road, past a long row of souvenir shops, you will reach the large square at the end of the village where you can sit comfortably beside the little river under thick, shady plane trees. And here it is, not far from his bust, engraved on copper in the Spanish language:

"The Faculty of History at the University of Valladolid, spirit of the heart of Castile, donates this stone to Fodele. It was hewn in Toledo to commemorate the immortal fame of Domenicos Theotocopoulos. July 1934".

DOMENICOS THEOTOCOPOULOS

Better known in the history of art under his pseudonym *"El Greco"* (this is what he called himself). He was reputedly born in Fodele in 1545, but researchers are not completely sure. Even if it is true, he went to Iraklion at an early date, in order to receive an education at the Mount Sinai School there. The great Damaskinos is said to have been his teacher (see Iraklion page 143). At the age of 25 he left Crete for good and went to Venice, probably armed with very good testimonials, because Titian, certainly the best known painter of his time, took him into his workshop. In 1577 he moved to Toledo, where he soon achieved great recognition and remained until his death in 1614. Although the Spanish royal house rejected him, he received many commissions for paintings from churches, monasteries and wealthy private patrons from all over Spain.

El Greco is recognised today as the most important exponent of Spanish Baroque. His pictures are alive with visions and he brought a spiritual dimension into his works which fell on fruitful ground in a deeply religious Spain. He often went too far, and faked reality; ophthalmic surgeons have suggested that his predilection for elongated figures comes from a disease of the eyes, astigmatism. His most famous work is the *Funeral of the Count of Orgaz* in Toledo, which is nearly 16.5 feet high.

Above all, the name El Greco means money to the inhabitants of Fodele, and who can blame them? Whole busloads of tourists arrive there every day during the season. The women of Fodele earn themselves a considerable pocket money from the sale of lace, weavings, tablecloths and runners. Even the children are brought into the business at an early stage. Crochet and embroidery are everyday activities, and they also have to hold their own when selling their wares. Their products really are fine, and in addition they are cheaper here than in Iraklion.

Fodele has also become a favourite destination for excursions with Cretan and Greek families. Near the large square at the end of the village and on the other side of the river there is a park where a fountain plays, with picnic tables and a children's playground - the latter has been a rarity up till now on Crete. Unfortunately there is a lot of building and investment evident at the end of the village; it will not be long before the first hotel opens its doors there.

El Greco in Fodele: It is difficult to track down El Greco in Fodele. Apart from the inscription and the bust, there is practically nothing else to remind the world of him. There is a book containing reproductions of his pictures in the village church.

And of course there is the *house where he was born* about half a mile outside. An attractive path leads from the main road over the river (signposted) and through the orange grove to a small cruciform-vaulted Byzantine church, a real jewel made of flat schist slabs. The walk is worth it for this alone. Inside the church there are frescoes from the 14th century (unfortunately, the church is usually locked). Continuing on to the left under a couple of tall oak trees, it is only a short way to the house, where a small memorial was recently set up.

• CONNECTIONS: **Buses** go to and from Iraklion twice a day, one leaving in the morning and one at midday.

• ACCOMMODATION: available in the kafenion **El Greco** at the beginning of the village. A "café" of the old, original type with a lot of bric-a-brac and photos of the family from christening to wedding. The rooms are on the 1st floor, and are very simple, with old furniture, including the beds. The room on the front has a fine balcony, looking out onto the road. There is a shower on the landing. In all it is a simple farmhouse, in which high expectations cannot be placed. A DR costs around £7, and a room with several beds c. £10. There are also simple rooms for rent in the neighbouring house.

There are other possibilities at the end of the village, where there is constant building activity, for example the new **Hotel Domingo**.

• FOOD: There is the **Taverna El Greco** on the shady village square under the plane trees; the speciality here is "grilled pork chops". The two charming daughters of the house are Maria and Katrina, who with much enthusiasm and business panache attempt to persuade holidaymakers to buy their carefully embroidered and crocheted table cloths and lacework. They speak good English and one easily gets into conversation with them.

A new taverna **Piraiko** with a young polyglot proprietress and an international crew to serve customers is a few yards further on.

From Iraklion to Anogia

A mountain trip into the outskirts of the mighty Psiloritis massif. Anogia is the largest mountain village in Crete and noted for its sheeps' wool rugs. Apart from that, it is the best point of departure for climbing the highest peak on Crete.

Travelling from Iraklion, pass through the Chania Gate onto the New Road and do not miss the turning to Anogia. Shortly after *Gazi*, and near a cement works, there are two former Venetian rest houses with striking Turkish domes, situated on the mountain slope. These served as hostels for all travellers who were not able to reach the city gates of Iraklion before sunset. The gates were closed overnight.

Tylissos

A village in the middle of vineyards. It is worth stopping here not only because it is the site of the excavations of three large Minoan villas directly in the village, but also because it is a typical Cretan agricultural village. There are chickens cackling everywhere, donkeys braying, dogs barking. The best time is probably that of the grape harvest - the whole village joins in then.

The round village square with its kafenia is rather away to one side, and tourists seldom seem to find it.

Minoan villas: These are signposted from the bus stop at the kafenion, and are about 3 minutes' walking distance away. A beautiful location under huge pines, with farms all around. There is a view far into the vineyards.

An amazingly large complex dating from the Late Minoan Period (from about 1600 BC onwards). Very well preserved, but partly covered over by later buildings. The walls stand to a height of about 6.5 feet, and the stairways to the now non-existent upper floors can be seen. There is also a cistern for storing water. Three huge bronze tubs were found here; they are now in the Archaeological Museum at Iraklion.

• OPENING TIMES: daily 9.00 a.m.-3.30 p.m. Sun 10.00 a.m.-3.00 p.m. **Admission** c. £1.

• CONNECTIONS: see Anogia, about half an hour difference in times.

• ACCOMMODATION: The restaurant **Akropolis** at the beginning of the village in the direction of Anogia rents out simple rooms.

Beyond Tylissos the road goes up through silvery-green olive groves into the mountains. A super journey through a rugged rock gorge with almost vertical walls. At the beginning of the gorge on the left there is a *memorial* to the Cretan partisans who defended the gorge during the Second World War and were shot by members of the German army on 21st August 1944. At the exit from the gorge on the left of the road there is another noble Minoan villa, known as *Slavokampos* (signposted). A seal impression with a bull leaper motif was among finds made here (Archaeological Museum of Iraklion). The house was discovered during roadworks.

Soon **Gonies** comes into sight; it is an extended mountain village, with the houses terraced to mould to the slope and clinging there beneath the hilltop. Even here, vines have been planted everywhere on the slopes and in sheltered hollows. There is a striking cruciform-vaulted church with two clocktowers.

The road winds on up to Anogia through a wonderful mountain landscape with wide vistas. At the entrance to the village the left branch of the road leads up to the *Nida High Plateau*, whence *Psiloritis* can be climbed by the shortest route (for details see below).

Anogia

Crystal clear mountain air, the sun even more brilliant; the largest mountain village on Crete lies spread out within a garland of barren mountain ridges.

The wonderful peace and solitude is deceptive. Anogia has been "discovered" by tourists and is a preferred destination for tour operators who offer "Cretan nights" up here in an original setting. At the entrance to the village from the direction of Iraklion they have even built a kind of stadium for displays of folk dancing. This was not a chance development; Anogia had always had an excellent reputation on Crete where music was concerned. Several of the best families of musicians originate from here (Xilouris, Skoulas). Thus an evening in Anogia may certainly be interesting.

Unfortunately the recent history of Anogia tempers such unrestricted enjoyment. On 15th August 1944 German soldiers shot all the male inhabitants of the village that they could lay their hands on. The village was burned right down to its foundations.

Why? Because of the kidnapping of a commander-in-chief of the German forces on Crete by partisans, who passed through Anogia on their escape route and some of whom came from the village. With the help of British officers, they had kidnapped General Karl Kreipe of the Tank Corps from his staff car at a crossroads not far from Archanes. Using clever camouflage measures (they passed through 22 German checkpoints!) and by a march straight across the Ida range they were able to bring him to the south coast, whence he was taken on by ship to Egypt. Even today the presence of many women without male relatives is noticeable in the village. (More about the spectacular kidnapping under Archanes page 196.)

Resistance to every type of occupation is a tradition in Anogia. Even during the Turkish period partisans from there were known to be the most dangerous and dedicated on the whole island. This memory has been nurtured up to the present; there is no café which does not proudly display the map of Greece, or often photographs or pictures of the famous Greek resistance fighters, and in one café there is even a picture of Fidel Castro. Traditionally the people of Anogia are left-wing voters. The mayor is a communist and the communist news-paper of Greece is read in the kafenia. However in the meantime, the Conservative Nea Demokratia party are trying to gain ground with the slogan "*For a new Anogia*", and not without success.

No politics, however, prevent the inhabitants from making the village attractive for the tourists. A long avenue of trees forms the main road in the upper part of the village. The white houses are enhanced by blue or green flights of steps, and the angular stairways fall steeply away to the lower village where, at the exit to the village in the direction of Axos the real centre of Anogia is located. There is no house there on the square without the brilliant and colourful sheeps' wool rugs hanging on its facade in their dozens. No other village on the island contains as many weaving looms as there are here. There are two main reasons for this. Firstly, Anogia is the centre of sheep and goat rearing on Crete. The shepherds find huge grazing areas, which cannot be used for any other purpose, here in the rough mountain landscape. Secondly the disproportionately large number of women has certainly played a part in the weaving boom. Although the sales technique of the women can sometimes be obtrusive, good, reason-ably-priced pieces can be obtained everywhere.

• CONNECTIONS: Buses go from Irakion to Anogia about 6 x daily from bus station B, but only twice on Sun-days. Fare one way is around £2.
The bus stops several times in Anogia; the best idea is to get out at the Town Hall Square (large open square with Town Hall, post office and a memorial) and walk down into the lower village. There is also a bus stop at the square in the lower village.

• ACCOMMODATION: only a few chances of simple accommodation, all of which are in the upper village.
Hotel Psiloritis: E class, on the right hand side of the main road when coming from the direction of Iraklion (hotel sign is almost hidden, and there is a grocery store underneath the hotel). The friendly proprietor rents out 9 rooms, which are pleasantly

cool due to their stone-paved floors. Bath with a bathtub and toilet on the landing. DR costs £6-7. Tel. 0834/31231.

Arkadi: private rooms opposite the shady square with the kafenia, situated on the main road a little above the Town Hall Square. A mother and her daughter have three rooms for rent here and sell their rugs and woven goods on the ground floor. Very simple, but right in the middle of village life. DR cost around £6, and there is one room with several beds available. The private rooms at **Ideon Antron** on the Town Hall Square are newer.

• FOOD/KAFENIA: In the upper village there is a taverna at the exit to the village in the direction of Iraklion. There are several nice kafenia on the main road - in the prettiest of these you sit about 200 yards above the Town Hall Square on a small **Church Square** which has plenty of atmosphere (bus stop). There is a lot of greenery, shade provided by several plane trees and the side facades of the small white church are covered with flowers. The older men of Anogia meet here, mostly wearing the traditional black cloth (sariki) wrapped round their head, to read the newspapers or play tavli. When you order coffee you also get a glass of water with it, without having to ask for one; this is very seldom the case on the coast.

The kafenion belonging to **Nikos Manousos** is situated on the Town Hall Square (diagonally across from the village church). He is a patriot, a fact attested to by numerous pictures of militant Cretans from the last century (struggle for freedom from the Turks). Everything costs 40 drachmas here, whether it is a coffee, an ouzo or a raki.

In the lower village, everything centres around the square with the plane trees. There are a number of pleasant tavernas with charcoal grills here, and there is the tiny kafenion **Xilouris**, named after the famous lyra player Nikos Xilouris, who was born here.

Come and look, very cheap!

• SHOPPING : There is a large quantity of woven rugs, covers and bags, as well as lace cloths and embroideries, to be had in the lower village. They mostly cost £4-14. The **Sarikis**, the traditional black headscarves, are well-made (c. £4). A unique spot is the shop owned by **Alkibiades M. Skoulas**, in which the sculptures made from cypress wood and nearly two feet high are worthy of note.

• OTHER INFORMATION : The **Bank**, **Post Office** and **OTE Telephone Office** are on the Town Hall Square.

Sightseeing

The bare **Town Hall Square** on the main road in the upper part of the village is completely paved with alabaster. On the side wall of the Town Hall there is a *memorial plaque*, also of alabaster. The order given by the German army commander to burn down the village and execute all the men is engraved here in the Greek language in the form of an open book. There is also the *Memorial of the Unknown Soldier* in the square; he is represented as a sturdy Cretan with a sabre and a musket.

On the lower edge of the square there is the little *Church of Agios Ioannis,* with its double nave; the interior is beautifully decorated with a gilded wooden iconostasis and many pictures of the Saints. Directly to the right of the entrance, there is yet more palpable evidence of Cretan religiosity: the Second Coming. At the back of the nave there are old frescoes, almost completely blackened by soot from the candles. The colours have faded strongly and are hardly recognisable. Themes are from the life of Jesus - the Crucifixion, burial etc. Unfortunately this little church is usually locked.

The way down to the **lower village** passes through narrow stairways and passages, in which tubs of basil and flowers stand before the doorways. The *Main Church* of Anogia, which is situated a few paces from the central square with its tall plane trees, is lavishly painted with frescoes.

From Anogia westwards you can drive via Axos to Mourtzana on a good asphalt road, which meets the Old Road to Rethymnon there. Then on via the large provincial town of Perama to join the New Road, on the coast to the east of Rethymnon. Detailed information on this route and on the whole region (*Axos,* the potters' village of *Margarites,* the *Cave of Melidoni, Arkadi Monastery* etc) under Rethymnon/Surrounding area.

The Nida High Plateau on Psiloritis; pure solitude

Climbing Psiloritis

To climb the peak of Psiloritis is surely the dream of every hiker on Crete. It can be achieved in 8 hours, including the time taken for the descent, from the Nida plateau. Not however, for those who fear solitude.

The Psiloritis massif (or Ida range) is the roof of Crete. Its highest peak is *Timios Stavros* with a height of 8,013 feet. The Nida High Plateau is a relatively small enclosed plateau, about 12.5 miles from Anogia. It is situated right in the middle of Psiloritis.

A round trip there from Iraklion by car takes 4 hours, therefore the whole thing could be done from Iraklion in one day if an early start is made. A disadvantage is that you will thus only be able to spend a maximum of one hour on the peak, to avoid the onset of darkness during your descent.

But there are enough possibilities for extending your time on the peak, if for example you spend the night in Anogia or in the guest house on the Nida Plateau, and begin your ascent in the early morning. The most attractive alternative is undoubtedly to spend the night (armed with sleeping bag and provisions) on the peak itself. Your stay on the peak will be the climax of the whole hike not only from the point of view of height!

▶ **Getting there:** The distance from Anogia to the Nida Plateau is about 12.5 miles. A difficult road with asphalt only at the beginning, the turning for the Nida Plateau branches off the road from Iraklion shortly before the eastern entrance to Anogia (signposted). Cars can only pass slowly along it, and there is no bus service. Reckon with just under one hour for the trip through the wild stony landscape, where you will meet nobody except the occasional shepherd with his flocks. From a height of 2,289 feet (Anogia) the track climbs up to a pass at a height of 4,905 feet (about 10 miles from Anogia), whence there is a sudden overwhelming view of the plateau. Then on to the Nida High Plateau (4,479 feet). The road winds tortuously around half of the plateau and ends by the *Ideon Antron Hut*, on the edge of the plateau. It is staffed in summer, a meal can be obtained and with any luck there will be one of the 4 beds free. The guest house was comprehensively renovated in summer 1987.

Shortly after the guest house the track turns off and goes up the cliff. After a few yards there is a little plateau with the *Chapel of the Analipsis*. Cars can be parked here and the four and a half hour ascent of Timios Stavros can begin. If there is time a visit can be made to the Ideon Cave, situated at the end of the track (about half an hour on foot); it can be reached by car but the track is narrow and there are sharp stones.

▶ **Ideon Antron or Idaian Cave:** A huge dark hole in an almost vertical rock wall. There are moss-covered limestone formations in the hollows of the roof, and numerous birds nest in the darkness. At present there is no access to the cave because of excavations, but if you are lucky the workmen may let you go in. The cave floor falls away steeply but is made accessible by terracing, and a wooden stairway leads downwards. At a height of about 26.5 feet a hole is visible in the back wall of the cave. This leads to a further cavern. A truck railway is used by the excavators to transport debris out of the cave, so that it can then be examined.

Even Zeus was Young Once

The Idaian Cave has the claim to fame of having been the place where the young Zeus spent his childhood. It is here that his mother Rea is reputed to have hidden him from his terrible father Kronos, after his birth in the famous Cave of Psychro on the Lassithi High Plateau. Kronos wanted to eat all of his children to keep himself safe from usurpers. Whenever the baby Zeus cried, the Curetes, or priests of Rea, beat their bronze shields together, to drown the give-away noise. More details on the myth in the chapter on Crete/History.

As a result of this overwhelming importance, the Idaian Cave was an important cult sanctuary already in Minoan times. Even in Roman times pilgrimages were made to the place where Zeus is thought to have spent his childhood.

Archaeological expeditions there had already begun to sift through the cave at the end of the last century, but it was only in 1955 that new excavations, directed by Paul Faure, brought definite results. Faure discovered the side chamber of the main cavern as mentioned above and found countless Minoan offerings there. In particular there was the great bronze shield of the Archaic Period (650-500 BC) which is generally referred to as the **Shield of the Curetes**. This can be seen today on the first floor of the Archaeological Museum in Iraklion.

New excavations have been carried on for several years, and for this reason the cave is not officially open.

An Assault on the Peak

• **Duration**: ascent about 4.5 hrs, descent just under 3.5 hrs.

• **Track markers**: The way up to Timios Stavros is marked out by red dots and occasional pyramids of stones. They can only be distinguished with difficulty in some places.

• **Condition of the route**: not a terribly difficult hike, but partly consisting of terrain without a path through sharp stones and low thistle vegetation. Good shoes, perseverance and sureness of foot are necessary.

• **Take with you**: provisions and water for 8 hours. If you wish to stay up there overnight, a good sleeping bag and warm clothing are essential. Even in the high summer the temperatures sink down close to freezing point at night.

• **Weather/Season**: from early summer to early autumn. Only when the sky is cloudless. In the early part of the year there is often snow on the slopes.

> **Please do not go up there alone! If you sprain an ankle or suffer another injury it could be days before anyone appears.**

▶ **Description of the route:** The path to the summit begins 220 yards after the chapel at the first steep turn in the gravel track. You climb up the slope on the left (in a south-westerly direction) through debris, thistles and ankle-high thorn bushes. After just under half an hour you reach a ravine, which leads upwards to the right in a north-westerly direction. Follow this for about another hour until it reaches a "saddle", behind which there is the *Kolita Alpine Pasture*, a flat depression. You will come upon the path which leads up from the south side of Psiloritis at this point (see below), and should perhaps take a break here.

Not a sound is to be heard except for the humming of insects, twittering of birds and occasional tinkling of a sheep's bell. Suddenly a shot rings out among the cliffs and only dies away after many echoes . . .

From the Kolita alpine pasture there is another ravine leading upwards in a north westerly direction. After 1.5 hours' trek there is a crater-like depression, which you skirt round on the right. Then upwards to the right onto the ridge of Psiloritis, where you will come

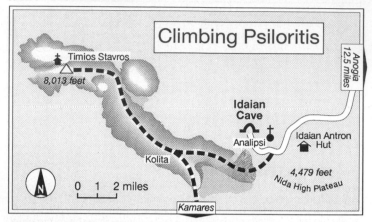

Climbing Psiloritis

Timios Stavros
8,013 feet

Anogia 12.5 miles

Idaian Cave

Analipsi

Idaian Antron Hut

Kolita

4,479 feet
Nida High Plateau

N
0   1   2 miles

Kamares

upon a shepherd's hut built out of piled up rubble. It is daubed with the graffiti of climbers from all over the world. The north coast of Crete can now be seen for the first time. You then climb up a path along the ridge in a westerly direction to the peak (from the crater to the peak just under 1.5 hours).

Here on the highest point in Crete there is a chapel made of layers of undressed stones with a small side building, which is occasionally used by hunters and mountain climbers overnight. The gloomy interior is unfortunately rather neglected, and pictures of saints and remnants of candles lie scattered there. A few steps beyond there is a well with brackish water, which originated from melted snow. There is a bucket which can be used to draw up this unappetising-looking water.

The view and the atmosphere up there just cannot be described. If visibility is good, the sea on both sides of the island can be seen. The peaks of the neighbouring mountains are often shrouded in cloud, and there is not a sound to be heard. The way down again takes about 3 - 3.5 hours.

ASCENT FROM THE SOUTH: The peak can also be reached in a difficult 7-hour climb from the mountain village of **Kamares**, on the southern slope of the Ida range. The way up from there converges with that from the Nida High Plateau on the Kolita alpine pasture. On the way, a visit can be made to the famous **Kamares Cave**, situated at 5,027 feet on the southern side of Mount Mavri (about 3 hours from Kamares). Unusual, paper-thin pottery vessels of the Minoan period were found here and named after the cave (**Kamares vases**). They can be admired in **Gallery II** of the Archaeological Museum in Iraklion.

On the roof of Crete

IRAKLION/HINTERLAND

The hilly hinterland of Iraklion is one complete vineyard. Green vines cover the slopes everywhere. In between there are small, silvery olive groves, gigantic cacti, and slim, tall cypresses.

The gentle landscape of vines between two mountain ranges (the mighty Psiloritis in the west and the steep-sloped Dikti massif with the famous Lassithi Plateau in the east) is worthy of one or two extensive excursions. It offers everything from the latest archaeological discoveries at *Archanes* (recognised as a sensation by experts) to the potters' village of *Thrapsano* and the new *Kazantzakis Museum* in Mirtia.

Almost every village is fully orientated towards grape production. In particular, everyone is busy with the grape harvest at the end of August/beginning of September. Whole families work in the vineyards, their heads wrapped in thick cloths to ward off the burning sun. Little three-wheeled vehicles, filled to the brim with the sweet grapes, trundle between the slopes and the villages. Grapes are hung up to dry everywhere or simply spread out on large sheets. The sultanas produced here are almost exclusively for export.

From Iraklion to Archanes

Take the exit road to Knossos from Iraklion for Archanes (20 miles from Iraklion). The good asphalt road makes the journey a pleasure.

A little to the south of Knossos there is a two-storeyed aqueduct directly on the road. This dates from the period of the Egyptian/Turkish occupation (19th century). At the large fork in the road, where the road turns off to Archanes, is the place where a troop of British commandos and Cretan partisans kidnapped the German General Karl Kreipe in 1944 (see also Anogia). Via Kato Archanes there is a way along the flank of Mount Juktas through an extended valley.

A DARING OPERATION

26th April 1944, about 9.00 p.m. **General Karl Kreipe**, commanding officer of the German 22nd Tank Regiment, is on his way home in his spanking new Opel staff car from his headquarters in *Archanes* to the *Villa Ariadne* at Knossos, where the German officers have been given quarters. It is already getting dark, and apart from Kreipe there is only a chauffeur in the car. At the crossroads where the road from Archanes turns into the main road to Iraklion, men in German uniforms appear and the car is flagged down with lights. The driver is used to frequent checks and he stops. Then everything happens very quickly; both the occupants of the car are pulled out and disarmed. Two Englishmen jump into the front seats, and three Cretan *Andartes* (partisans) squeeze themselves into the back with the General. The British passenger in the front puts on the General's conspicuous uniform cap and the journey proceeds to Iraklion. The ambush has only lasted about two minutes. In the course of the journey to Iraklion they pass through 22 German checkpoints! The General's car is well-known everywhere and can pass freely. The car goes right through Iraklion and turns left at Eleftherias Square. There is one final roadblock at the Chania Gate, and this too is passed. The journey continues along the coast road in the direction of Rethymnon. When they are about level with the village of Sises, the kidnappers leave the car, which is driven to one of the nearby coves in order to feign an evacuation by submarine. A letter is left behind in the car, in which a group of British commandos claim that the kidnapping is all their work and was carried out without the help of Cretans. The purpose of this is to prevent any reprisals against the civilian population (unsuccessful, as the later course of events showed). Then the trek begins across country to the mountain village of *Anogia*. They

---

meet up with other Andartes near this village and start on the
long march across the Ida range to the south coast. In close co-
operation between British agents and Cretan partisans, the
General and his kidnappers are whisked safely through German
lines. The German Wehrmacht combs the Ida range with considerable expenditure of time and energy, and places a cordon of
one thousand men in the mountain landscape. But the Cretans
know the terrain and are always one step ahead. The odyssey
takes over two weeks, until finally the British and their captive
can be evacuated to Egypt by submarine from *Rodakino Beach*,
one of the few unguarded beaches on the south coast. The operation is a complete success and signifies a stinging rebuff for the
occupying forces. The Cretan resistance, reinforced by British
commando troops, receives a new boost through this "coup de
main". (A replay of the kidnapping, in which the General's successor is the new target, fails at a later date, supposedly because
of treachery on the part of Cretan communists.)

In the early autumn of the same year German troops razed the
mountain villages of Anogia and Gerakari to the ground because, amongst other things, Kreipe's kidnappers met up with
their helpers here.

RECOMMENDED READING: **Ill Met by Moonlight**. W. Stanley Moss, one of
the two British leaders of the operation, later wrote a book about the kidnapping of General Kreipe. It was published by Efstathiadis in 1985 in English,
and can be bought everywhere on Crete (c. £3). A gripping story, certainly
prejudiced at times, but a worthwhile source of first-hand information.

Archanes

A little provincial town at the foot of steep Juktas on which, according to
ancient Cretan legend, Zeus is buried. With the large wine producers' cooperative at the beginning of the village, it is the focal point of wine production in the region today.

Shortly after entering the village the visitor comes upon a broad
square with the pretty *Church of the Panagia,* which has three naves
(usually closed), and the free-standing *clocktower.* The actual centre
of the village is situated at the southern exit. From the large square
with the monument to Cretan resistance fighters, there is a fine view
over the lengthy, extended flank of Juktas. There is also a small
taverna, and several kafenia, and on the winding main road going into
the village small fruit and vegetable stores and other shops. On the
left hand side (in beside house no. 227) there is a hidden whitewashed chapel.

The main attractions at Archanes are the various *Minoan* and
Mycenaean Sites in and around the town. They have turned Archanes

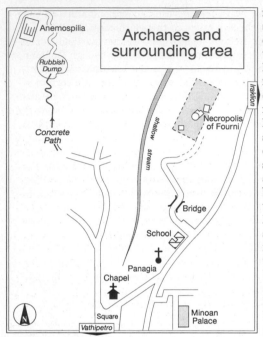

Archanes and surrounding area

Anemospilia

Rubbish Dump

Concrete Path

shallow stream

Necropolis of Fourni

Iraklion

Bridge

School

Panagia Chapel

Square

Minoan Palace

Vathipetro

into the **site of the most important excavations in Crete** at the present time. It has been recognised recently that a second important Minoan centre (similar to that at Knossos or Phaistos) including a palace, a surrounding city and a cemetery has been found around the mythological Mount Juktas. The settlement was also inhabited later by the Mycenaeans. Unfortunately the sites are completely closed to visitors because of current excavation work.

The ascent of Juktas is pleasing and in itself particularly worthwhile; there is a grand view from the top in every direction.

• CONNECTIONS: c. 12 buses daily from and to Iraklion. The ride starts from the Venetian Loggia in Iraklion, and the last bus leaves for the city from Archanes at about 8.00. p.m. The bus station in Archanes is in the square at the southern end of the village, as mentioned above.

• ACCOMMODATION: **Hotel Dias**, B class. Superb position shortly after the southern exit to the village. A building of noble appearance in a spacious park with dwarf palms and pine trees, rather resembling a sanatorium. It has, however, been closed for a long time due to lack of custom and is in need of renovation.

• FOOD: I **Folia** (the leaf), a small taverna and grill beneath tall trees on the square where the buses stop. Directly opposite the Church of the Panagia there is the taverna **Rodakinies** with a large courtyard beneath the tendrils of vines.

The Excavations at Archanes

The finds from Archanes are closely bound up with the names of *Yannis* **and** *Efi Sakellarakis.* **This Greek couple, both of whom are archaeologists, have been digging here since 1964 and have made spectacular discoveries.**

They discovered the foundation walls of another Minoan palace directly under the houses of the town (Sir Arthur Evans had already suggested the presence of a summer residence for Knossos here). The climax of their research came however in 1979, as the couple were excavating the little temple of *Anemospilia* about 1.5 miles outside Archanes. There they found the first and until now the only proof that the Minoans carried out human sacrifices! The place has retained its hold on the Sakellarakis, in spite of the fact that Yannis Sakellarakis was made director of the National Archaeological Museum after his discoveries. Today he lives in Archanes in the immediate proximity of the newly-discovered palace, and has committed himself to the excavations in and around the town. Excavations only take place in July and August when the farmers are not in their fields. At those times, students and archaeologists come together from all over Greece to work under the direction of the Sakellarakis. Their house is the *Dig House* of Archanes. It functions as a "command headquarters" and a collection point for all the finds. Information from farmers who have come upon ancient foundations, painted pottery etc. when ploughing proves itself again and again to play an important role in excavations.

The Minoan Palace: This had already been located by Sir Arthur Evans but it was only excavated in the sixties by the Sakellarakis. They only exposed a part of the complex because of its unfavourable position in the middle of the town, and this is enclosed behind railings today. Apart from the foundation walls there is a passage with a channel to collect water, and a paved room with benches has been discovered (resembling the throne room at Knossos).

Finding your way there: Arriving from the north, the road forks into two one-way streets shortly after the church square. Go a little further on and take the first alley on the left. Then take the second turning on the right (opposite vines that have been fenced in) and go on c. 60 yards to the railings, behind which the excavations can be seen.

Necropolis of Fourni: This is the largest cemetery that has been discovered up till now on Crete and contains numerous graves of the Prepalatial Period up to the Mycenaean Period (2500-1250 BC). This was also excavated in 1965 by the Sakellarakis and should be viewed as having a close connection with the neighbouring settlement and palace. It is hardly possible to explain the presence of such a huge cemetery without the existence of a city with living inhabitants nearby.

The first and most significant find was that of **Tholos Grave A** (vaulted grave). The upper part of the vault had been used by unsuspecting farmers as a hut. Sakellarakis recognised it to be a tholos grave, and discovered the cemetery of Fourni. In a side room he found the first unplundered sarcophagus of a Mycenaean noble, which contained among other things a necklace, gold rings, and the remains of clothing and bronze dishes.

The excavations continue today. The site is fenced off, and trees and scrub bushes prevent any view into the site. If you are lucky you will find the keeper of the site, who may eventually open it up for you (ask in the kafenion on the main square with the church). If not, the little walk is worth it just for the view; the hillock is covered with sage and other bushes, and in the valley below a vigorous stream gurgles along even in August. The view over Archanes is definitely worth the walk.

Finding your way there: Fourni is situated on a hill at the entrance to the village of Archanes and on the right hand side, when approaching from Iraklion. Turn off the road shortly before the church square at the pastel-coloured school building, then walk or drive down the road to the bridge (leave your car). After the bridge, proceed c. 440 yards straight on to where the path is closed, then take the stony track to the right up to the top of the hill.

Anemospilia: The little temple of the *"Wind-caves"* is situated a good 1.5 miles outside Archanes, in a breezy "saddle position" on the north slope of Juktas. The wind blows continuously over the mountain ridge. Along with the fantastic panoramic view of the vineyards as far as Iraklion and the sea, there is a touch of the mysticism to be felt which perhaps predestined this place to be the site for a temple. It is incidentally the only Minoan temple to have been discovered until now. Unfortunately, it too is fenced off.

Here, in this almost unpretentious building, the excavators found irrefutable evidence that the Minoans offered a human sacrifice at least once.

> . . . around 1700 BC all the Minoan palaces on Crete are destroyed by a puzzling catastrophe, probably an earthquake. Signs of what is coming can be felt days beforehand. In a feverish hurry, the priests try to appease the angered earth deity with valuable offerings, as in the temple at Anemospilia. In the middle of one of these ceremonies, it happens; the severe earthquake causes the temple to collapse. It is not rebuilt over the following centuries and the walls preserve for millenia what echoed round the world as a sensation in 1979 - a young man of about 18 years of age was sacrificed to the gods in the temple at Anemospilia! Was this a final desperate attempt to hold back the inevitable force of nature? Or was it even normal practice in this civilisation of the Minoan priest kings, which until now has always been considered peaceful and certainly not of a barbaric nature? Research is being carried on today, but until now no other proof of human sacrifices has been found.

(after I. Sakellarakis)

The Human Sacrifice

What kind of image was crystallizing in the minds of the husband and wife team, as together with their helpers they removed layer after layer in the temple? On the altar block in the westernmost of the three adjacent rooms, they found the skeleton of a *young man* whose limbs had been bound. In it, there was a *bronze razor blade* almost 16 inches long, with which the *priest* who had been killed by the debris from the falling temple and who lay beside the altar had, to all appearances, just severed the jugular vein. A *priestess* (?) was found a short distance away in the south west corner of the room, and a further *corpse* lay in front of the room containing the sacrifice. The corpse had a *basin* with the blood of the sacrifice by it, which was probably being taken to the statue of the deity in the middle room of the temple when the walls caved in . . . .

How to get there: After passing through the square with the Church of the Panagia, take the one-way street at the fork in the road and go on down to another square. Go sharp right there, out of the village and take the cement track which leads up sharply to the left from the next large crossroads. At the beginning this passes through vineyards, then the cement track comes to an end and a bumpy path passes through the municipal rubbish dump. Shortly after this the cement road continues and at one point goes very steeply up the slope (1st gear!) to a windy "saddle" on the north slope of Juktas. During the ascent and on the right hand side several grottos can be seen, which give the rock the appearance of a skull with their deep hollows. These are the **Anemospilia** (wind-caves) which owe their name to the wind that constantly blows into them. Shortly after this the road makes a sharp curve and falls away in a westerly direction. The temple is situated on the inside of the curve, a little above the road.

Juktas

The Archanes area is dominated by the rocky profile of the sleeping Zeus, 2,651 ft. high. The climb is especially worth it because of the wonderful view.

A bad stony track branches off the road to Vathipetro about 1.25 miles to the south of Archanes (the road forks down by the signpost, and the right fork leads up to the peak, a distance of about 3 miles). There is no problem involved in driving along this track, in spite of the sharp gravel, and taxis will also go along there if required.

The motor road ends on the middle peak, exactly on the *tip of the nose* of the sleeping Zeus. There is a cross on this peak which can be illu- minated at night, and in addition the brilliant whitewashed Chapel of *Afendi Christou Metamorfosi*, which has four naves. Every year on the evening of the 5th August, there begins a church festival which lasts for several days. Many Cretans come to it, either driving up or climb- ing up in a long procession.

A characteristically rich vegetation flourishes all around the church; the fragrance of herbs hangs in the air, there are several varieties of flowers, mountain tea, wild tangled oak apples and juniper trees. The western side of Juktas falls away from the church as an almost verti- cal wall, and the hilly vineyards resemble closely cut green lawns from up here. The mighty outline of *Psiloritis* pushes up out of the haze in the west, and in the south the Asterousia Mountains which surround the Messara Plain are visible. The northern peak of Juktas has been taken over by a receiving and transmitting station.

Vathipetro

Two and a half miles to the south of Archanes. Probably used as an agri- cultural estate by the Minoans, who even then grew grapes in this fertile area.

Vathipetro can be reached on an unmade road which leads away from Archanes to the south. Only at Choudetsi do the wheels of your vehi- cle meet asphalt once again.

The estate is situated in the middle of vineyards on a hill plateau di- rectly adjacent to the dusty road (a small access path leads to the en- trance, where there is limited parking space). It was abandoned as early as 50 years after building first started there around 1550 BC (perhaps because of earthquakes) and remained in an unfinished state. Unfortunately this site is also closed, but in order to gain an impression one can walk along the fence a little way. The owners at the time enjoyed a wonderful view out over the adjoining plain to the south west.

Choudetsi is situated in the deep cleft of a valley with a vigorous stream, lush vegetation and a thick cover of trees of all kind. A small detour is worth it here to the Nunnery of *Spiliotissa*, which is well-hidden on the floor of the valley. Follow the sign to the left at the north exit of the village and keep straight on this road. Below, there is an oasis with the splashing of water, old plane trees, willows, cypresses and eucalyptus. The nunnery huddles close to the rocks, and is inhabited by only a few nuns and a handful of orphans. Let them show you around the nunnery church which is pushed deep into the rocky cliff; with the help of a candle the remains of very old wall paintings can be seen in a corner.

From Iraklion in the direction of Kastelli

A round trip taking in the new Kazantzakis Museum at Mirtia and the potters' village of Thrapsano on the slopes of the Dikti massif.

From Iraklion take the exit road to Knossos. A few miles after the Palace an asphalt road (signposted) branches left to Mirtia and the new Kazantzakis Museum (almost 7.5 miles from Knossos).

Mirtia *(Varvari)*: a friendly wine-producing village in the middle of fertile slopes full of vines. Pretty village with whitewashed walls, in some places with lush green and tubs of flowers wherever you look. The centre is the village square with several kafenia and the Kazantzakis Museum, which was established in the house of Kazantzakis' father in 1984.

Kazantzakis Museum: a comprehensive documentation of the life and achievements of the Cretan poet and author, spread over two floors. Apart from photos, letters and manuscripts there are costumes from his plays on exhibition, and photos of the shooting of the film "Celui qui doit mourir" (*The Man Who Must Die*) in Kritsa/Eastern Crete, which was made by Jules Dassin and based on the novel *The Greek Passion* by Kazantzakis. One room contains all the editions of his works in dozens of languages (the cover illustrations alone make a detour here worthwhile) and there is a slide show (in Greek) about the most important stages of his life.

OPENING TIMES: closed on Thursdays, otherwise from 9.00 a.m.-1.00 p.m. and in addition on Mon, Wed, Sat and Sun also from 4.00 p.m.-8.00 p.m. **Admission** c. £2, children/students half price.

Do they know him?

To the south of Mirtia the traveller soon joins the beautiful road from Agia Paraskevi to Kastelli; there is thick vegetation with cactuses several feet high, cypresses and huge boulders. There is an opportunity to turn off to the right, via Voni, and go to the potters' village of Thrapsano.

Thrapsano: Set at a complicated angle away from the main road. All the roofs have clay vessels for chimneys. Next to Margarites near Rethymnon Thrapsano is the second village in Crete in which professional potters carry on their work. However, pottery is no longer a profitable business because the competition from cheap plastic and metal products is too great. There are accordingly few potters left.

The places where the pottery is fired are situated somewhat outside the village on both sides, directly on the road. Storage vessels of up to two feet in height are the main products, made on wheels turned by hand from several layers of clay (*so-called clay pithoi*). Firing takes place in giant kilns, which are used simultaneously and heated from a pit in the middle. The potters were pleased at our interest. However it was difficult to find something to buy because of the size of the vessels.

Too heavy for souvenirs; clay vessels the size of a child in the potters' village of Thrapsano

Kastelli: A sober provincial town on a plain between vineyards. Bus stop at the crossroads in the town centre, where there are also two kafenia. There is another at the exit to the town in the direction of Agia Paraskevi. On the road to Xidas there is the newly-built establishment *Veronika* with rooms to rent and an adjoining cafeteria.

Xidas: A quiet farming village half way up the slope of the Lassithi mountains. Fine view over Kastelli and the surrounding plain including the military airstrip (photography is prohibited from up here). Shady kafenia at the entrance to the village, an old chapel and what used to be a fountain at the highest point. On the ridge above there are the bases of windmills, for which the region is noted (see Lassithi Plateau).

A brand new asphalt road leads between rusty-red schist cliffs, wild pear, fig and olive trees to **Aski** in the upper ranges of the Dikti Mountains. The trip is especially worthwhile because of the wonderful stillness. It may be possible to continue on along a bad track to **Gonies**, which lies on the asphalt road leading up to the famous Lassithi High Plateau (ask in Aski about the state of the road).

From Iraklion eastwards

Unlovely, over-inhabited coastal landscape without any highlights. One hotel after the other, right up until Mallia, firmly in the clutches of package tourism.

Happily there are no cement boxes 20 storeys high à la Spanish Mediterranean coast. Despite this, it is a boring area without charm; there are villages that have hardly grown at all, and the beaches are sometimes bad, with a lot of shingle and rubbish.

The beaches of Karteros, Amnissos and Tombrouk are directly to the east of Iraklion; for the chapter on *Iraklion Bathing/Surrounding area* see pages 160-162).

To the east of Tombrouk Beach and about a further 1.5 miles on there is a coastline of rough black cliffs, where no building has taken place. Then comes the beach of *Vathianos Kampos*, which is around 650 yards long. Deck chairs and beach umbrellas can be rented here. Shortly after this there is the village of **Vathianos Kampos**, directly on the road, which has almost merged into the adjacent village of **Hani Kokkini** to the east. There is only an inadequate deposit of shingle which serves as a beach in the immediate area of the village, but there are various hotels, for example the inviting-looking bungalow hotel Knossos Beach, which is situated directly on the sea (with a swimming pool), and the newly-built Iris Apartments.

• CONNECTIONS: Buses leave from bus station A on the harbour at Iraklion. Buses to Mallia every half an hour from 6.30 a.m.-9.00 p.m. See also under Mallia, page 212.

Gournes: A colourless place to pass through, with nothing attractive about it, and certainly a beach to forget about - narrow patches of sand and horrible piles of shingle. Not worth a mention. Despite this fact there is keen building activity everywhere, and there are a lot of rooms and apartments.

The only good piece of beach has been commandeered by a military base belonging to the US Air Force. A barracks with a sandy beach and a sea view is certainly something new for the servicemen. They are often seen sitting in the few cafés on the road at Gournies. The two parabolic antennae on the prominent table-top mountain, visible from a considerable distance, also belong to the Base.

East of the Base in particular, in the direction of **Kato Gouves**, there begins one big area of indiscriminate development; there are hotels, unfinished constructions and rooms to rent, in spite of a beach of middling quality. The big complexes, such as *Creta Sun* (A class, over 300 rooms, 4 tennis courts), *Marina* (A class, wind surfing school, tennis) and *Afroditi* (B class) are all down on the beach.

• CAMPING CRETA: directly to the east next to the high barbed wire of the military area. Completely without any shade, only a handful of reed roofs and a few sparse tamarisks to keep off the sun. Sanitation O.K. Market, bar and self-service restaurant. The beach in front of it is quite mucky, and is part gravel, part sand. There is not much going on here even in the high season, and it often closes its doors between the beginning and middle of September because of the lack of custom.

Can be reached from the through road from Kato Gouves (bus stop). Tell the bus conductor quite clearly that you want to get out here. Follow the signs, and at about 1.5 miles along the beach go across the premises of the Marina Hotel, then about 550 yards down the cement path along the beach. Open from 01.05.-30.09. Tel. 0897/41400.

A little to the west of Limin Chersonisou the road branches off to the Lassithi High Plateau, which is signposted (see page 225). Just before the turning there is the spanking new Camping Chersonisos; see below under Limin Chersonisou.

Then over a rocky spur, and suddenly there is a view miles wide over the whole bay of Mallia! This is one of the happiest experiences to be had on this coastal strip. On the left hand side of the road some caves which have been gouged deeply into the sandstone of the spur can be seen. There is also the way down to a long sandy beach below the hill (see Limin Chersonisou).

Bay of Mallia

Almost a bay out of a picture book. Deep blue water, spacious coastal plain, with the gentle foothills of the Dikti range behind it.

Tourism has firmly established itself. At the water's edge there is the near "skyscraper skyline" of Limin Chersonisou, then Stalis and Mallia, which are hotel settlements firmly in the hands of package tourists. The hubbub dies down at the western end; the fishing villages of Sisi and Milatos are not yet capable of dealing with the assault but are included in the building development.

The region is worthwhile as a starting point because of its developed tourist infrastructure and because of the possibilities it offers for excursions into the Lassithi Plateau.

Limin Chersonisou

Used to be a quiet fishing village. Since then, the meagre sandy beach has been relentlessly closed off with cement blocks of three to four storeys. Hotels, tavernas and cafés project out over the water with their wide, extending terraces.

For many years Limin Chersonisou has been the mecca of organised tourism and enjoyed an unbroken growth. The main road with its side streets resembles a noisy fair ground; there are neon signs, colourful tavernas, bars and discos. There is nothing discernible of the old village centre because of the countless hotels of every type. Away from the main thoroughfare the village dissolves into nothing; there is no business to be carried on there.

A positive point is the attractive landscape in the surrounding area - see under Excursions/Walks.

● CONNECTIONS: Buses operate a shuttle between Iraklion and Mallia every half hour. However the buses to Iraklion are often so over-full when they leave Mallia that they do not even stop in Limin Chersonisou. For this reason there is often a long waiting period. We recommend forming a group and taking a taxi, which costs about £5.

— ★ —

● CAR/MOTORBIKE RENTAL: any amount of companies renting these on the main through road.

● SHOPPING: The third house on the left in Sanoudakis Street (coming from the beach promenade) offers beautiful handmade **icons,** deceptively like the real thing, with gold leaf and glowing colours. There are also attractive but rather tawdry landscapes.

Nick's Cretan House: on the beach promenade, an average souvenir shop, but with an original line in advertisements: "Animals can be friends for life, why not people". Nikos Chourdakis has made it his mission to bring up dogs, cats and mice together. They would never hurt each other; the mice are however only documented on a video tape, but the dog gets his bottle and the kitten also sometimes gets a lick at it.

● POST OFFICE: at the beginning of Eleftheria Street, which branches off the main thoroughfare at the western end of the village in the direction of the interior and goes to Piscopiano and Chersonisos. Signposted.

● TELEPHONE: OTE telephone centre on the main through road (no. 65), in the direction of the eastern exit. Open Mon-Fri 7.30 a.m.- 9.00 p.m., closed on Sat/Sun. Long queues are the norm here.

Accommodation

A humble selection - only 60 hotels! Even so, it is almost impossible to find a bed free in the season.

● **Creta Maris**: luxury class, a huge complex with 1,000 beds on the beach west of the town, and the most traditional and sumptuous house in the place. Its construction made Limin Chersonisou "acceptable to society" and started off an incredible building boom. Half of it is a comfortable beach hotel, the other half a tasteful bungalow complex with white houses, passages covered with vines, little stairways and wooden balconies. Built after the style of a Greek island village, with much expense and a wealth of fantasy; there are winding passages, village squares and fountains, but there are also lush green lawns and an air-conditioning system. In all, a smoothly-running holiday "factory" with all the refinements - cinema, bowling, tennis, pool, disco etc. There is a private beach in front of the premises. Cost including half board c. £40 for a DR. Tel 0897/22115.

• **Vrito**: B class guest house, centrally situated on the beach promenade. Stylishly furnished and not too big, only 11 rooms. Around £17 for a DR. Tel. 0897/22401.

• **Avra**: C class, beautiful position on the fishing harbour, around £14-15 for a DR. Tel. 0897/22203. An immediate neighbour is **Zorbas**, in the same category and at the same price. Tel. 0897/22075.

REASONABLE

• **Selena**: a guest house in the old part of the village, only a few yards away from a narrow beach. Well-kept rooms with old lamps and dark wooden furniture, costs c. £11 for a DR without private bath. Address: 13, Em. Maragaki St.,

which leads off the main through road in the centre of town.
• In parallel Giampoudaki St., there are several D class hotels, eg **Cristal**, c. £11 for a DR without a private bath, tel. 0897/22546, and **Argo** opposite it, c. £12 for a DR. Tel. 0897/22558.

— ★ —

• CARAVAN CAMPING: situated at the eastern end of the village below the road to Mallia, directly at the sea's edge. A smaller site with shady reed roofing and few trees. There are also some interesting sites amongst thick reeds, and there are some huts with lush greenery for rent. Sanitation is alright and there is of-

ten hot water in the showers. The restaurant is passable. There are low rock ledges in front of the site, and a sandy beach without shade a few yards to the west. Price per person in the high season £2, small tent £1, large tent £2, car £1. Open from 01.04.-30-09. Tel. 0897/22025.

— ★ —

• CAMPING CHERSONISOS: Approaching from Iraklion, this is situated shortly before the turn off to Kastelli. Opened for the first time in 1987, it is a small site with

enclosed green lawn areas, taverna, bar and minimarket. Shade is only offered by reed roofs. Brisk building activity in the vicinity. Price per person £2, tent £2, car £1.

Food

Any number of open-air restaurants on the main road and in the side streets, often with live music. Unfortunately the waiters in the tavernas on the beach promenade are very persistent ("come on, come on, very cheap").

• **Maxim**: a great favourite, live music daily. From the main through road, go down the alley opposite Disco 99 Degrees.

• **Castello**: a beautiful garden under fig trees, with a music-loving proprietor. Also in an alley between the main road and the beach promenade.

• **Il Camino** : on the beach promenade. Pizzas out of a wood-fired oven.

• **Lorenzo's Grill**: in a small side street off the beach promenade. Lorenzo speaks at least five languages and offers spare ribs and steaks.

• **Votsalo**: impressive roof garden restaurant, prettily illuminated with candlelight, subdued atmosphere. The correct address for a refined meal. International menu with a Greek tinge. Address: Sanoudakis St., which branches off the beach promenade.

• **Pharos**: excellent position on the rocky cape by the fishing harbour, super views. It has retained something of its original character, and has good mezedes (appetisers). Readers of the first edition of this book met with unfriendliness when they only ordered drinks. The proprietor wants customers who eat.

• **New China**: Chinese restaurant in G. Petraki St. This is a side road off the main thoroughfare in an inland direction.

• BARS/NIGHT LIFE: The best place to sit is on the beach promenade. The café-bar **New York** lures you with its neon lights, the **Bolero Pub** has its seating directly down at the water's edge (cocktails and large ice cream cups), and the **Black Rose** is in the style of an English Pub.

• **Time**: a favourite souvlaki place on the main road, opposite Disco 99 Degrees.

• **Pithari**: an excellent tavern and grill in Koutouloufari, a few miles above Limin Chersonisou. Also much frequented by the local people. The other taverna **Rustico** in the village offers the better view. A worthwhile alternative to the bustle down below.

— ★ —

The bouzouki centre **Sirocco** is situated at the beginning of Sanoudakis St., 55 yards from the beach promenade (next to the Votsalo restaurant). There are several discotheques, eg **99 Degrees,** on the main through road.

Sightseeing

The *beach road* with its many souvenir shops, restaurants and cafés is an attractive place to stroll. There is a considerable bustle there, particularly in the evenings. You come quite unexpectedly to an ancient Roman *mosaic fountain* in the form of a flattened pyramid, on which there are several scenes depicting fishermen.

Limin Chersonisou was founded in ancient times by immigrant mainland Greeks. It achieved importance in the Roman and Byzantine periods as a harbour city. Water was brought down from the Lassithi Mountains to the city by an **aqueduct**, the remains of which are preserved on the road up to the Lassithi Plateau.

The beach promenade leads to the little *fishing harbour* at the left end of the bay. It is totally protected by a rocky limestone cape. Down below there is the *Chapel of Agios Nikolaos*, and on the plateau above it there are the remains of a triple-naved *basilica* of the 5th century, with fine mosaic floors and overturned column bases. This is unfortunately fenced in.

▶ **Bathing:** The actual town beach is hardly worth a mention; there are two mean strips of sand, narrow and crowded.

The fine white sandy beach to the west of the fishing harbour is better. It is c. 450 yards long, but directly behind the large complexes of the Creta Maris and other hotels, thus it is always rather crowded. There is a surfing school and paddle boats are available. You will find more peace on the rock slabs at the nearer end of the harbour cape; there is never very much going on there.

You will find the best beach, however, if you are not afraid of a short walk: leave the town in a north-westerly direction and go along the road past the Creta Maris Hotel. Follow the dust road along the coast, go past the strange-looking bathing coves of very fine sand that have been gouged deeply out by the sea. Then there is a rocky cape with a small white church and the stump of a disused windmill, at the extreme end of the bay of Mallia. If you look back there is a wonderful panorama of the "white city" of Limin Chersonisou.

Now comes the point of the whole excursion; a seldom-frequented *sandy beach*, which extends to the west for miles. Shade is provided by a number of tamarisks. Unfortunately several large living complexes have been built there in recent years.

• **How to get there**: can also be reached by car from the road to Iraklion. Wide field paths lead down there from the ridge west of Limin Chersonisou, distance about 1.5 miles.

Limin Chersonisou/Hinterland

The mountains rise up directly behind Limin Chersonisou. Tourism is already spilling over, but in spite of this the little villages on the slopes are still considerably "more authentic" than the city of hotels by the sea.

About half a mile behind Limin Chersonisou lies *Piscopiano*. A pleasant kafenion and a beautiful view from here, and there are also appartments for rent. Just a little to the east, in *Koutouloufari*, there are two tavernas which are highly rated by local people (see under Limin Chersonisou/Food).

A little to the west there is the actual village of *Chersonisos*, a favourite destination for hotel guests from Limin Chersonisou. Excellent food can also be had in the tavernas on the oval village square there.

Stalis

Between Limin Chersonisou and Mallia, Stalis is a colourless place without authenticity or charm. It consisted originally of a handful of houses. In the meantime, hotels and new apartment complexes have extended into the flat coastal plain and climbed up the slopes. Stalis has almost amalgamated with neighbouring Mallia.

Moderately suitable for a pure bathing holiday, with a good beach of fine sand.

• CONNECTIONS: buses every half hour in both directions. See also Limin Chersonisou and Mallia.

Accommodation

There are about 20 hotels, which are mostly occupied by package tourists in the season.

• **Blue Sea**: B class, attractive bungalow complex, only separated from the beach by the cemented "beach promenade". Several apartments are contained in each of the long units, everything on ground level, with areas of lawn in front of the small terraces. Pool and restaurant. Address: take the access road from the main through road down to the beach, and turn left at the bottom. Tel. 0897/31371.

• **Stalis**: D class, a simple house with a gallery of sun reflectors on the roof. Roomy accommodation with balcony; new beds and light blue tiled bathrooms. Price with breakfast c.£14 for a DR. Address: turn right shortly before the end of the access road down on the beach, c. 175 yards. About 2 mins. from the beach. Tel. 0897/31246.

• **Marina**: guest house shortly before the Hotel Stalis. Simple rooms without breakfast for £12.

• The large beach hotels are somewhat outside the village in the direction of Mallia - eg **Anthoussa Beach** (A class. Tel. 0897/31381) and **Palm Beach** (B class. Tel. 0897/31666).

• FOOD: There are certainly a dozen tavernas on the beach, some of them with attractive gardens and palms. Pleasantly shady and cool, and high above the beach you can sit in the **Panorama** taverna, with a beautiful view.

▶ **Bathing:** The sandy beach is relatively narrow, but long. Low cliffs adjoin the beach in the direction of Mallia, and there are further little sandy beaches in coves, for example near the Hotel Smaragdine Beach. Crowds!

Mallia

A highlight, at least as far as provisions for tourism, loss of original character and numbers of holidaymakers are concerned.

This previously insignificant village along the road has grown into one of the most favourite Cretan holiday centres because of its beautiful beach and its proximity to Iraklion. An access road about 1.5 miles in length leads down to the beach from the main thoroughfare with its closely packed souvenir shops, restaurants and hotels. A true record has been set here; there is practically no house which is not involved in tourism! In long rows on both sides of the road there are tavernas, restaurants, bars, hotels, souvenir shops, discos, car rental companies . . . In the evening there is a fairground atmosphere, and each bar drowns the other out with the newest hits from abroad, coloured strobe lights, lavishly laid tables and fashionably chic clientele from the United Kingdom, France, West Germany, and Austria. The only Greeks to be seen here are the waiters or the proprietors of the tavernas.

The day is spent mainly on the beach, normally in the same closely-packed fashion as in the evening. Those who like this sort of thing will certainly have a lovely holiday here, as contact with others is guaranteed.

Mallia is a good starting point for excursions, if only to the Minoan palace a couple of miles outside, or up to the famous Lassithi High Plateau.

The actual village is situated beyond the long main through road - luckily for the inhabitants, who have a place of refuge here from the pleasure-seeking masses. Hotels and restaurants are (still) in the minority in these winding alleyways.

• CONNECTIONS: The stretch of road from **Iraklion** - **Limin Chersonisou** - **Mallia** has the best bus service in Crete! The buses leave Iraklion every half hour daily - Mallia (6.30 a.m.-9.00 p.m.) and Mallia - Iraklion (7.00 a.m.-10.00 p.m.). The cost is around £2 and the journey takes about 1 hour. The reason for this is, of course, the numerous tourists who stay in the beach hotels along the route.

The buses are used to get from hotel to bathing beach and vice versa, and they are especially overcrowded in the evenings!
There is also a connection twice daily to **Sisi** and **Milatos** and once in the morning up to the **Lassithi Plateau** (returning in the afternoon). See also under the respective places.

— ★ —

• CAR/MOTORBIKE RENTALS: Most of these are to be found on the access road to the sea.

• CHANGING MONEY: There is the Bank of Crete opposite the Hotel Zeus, and another bank at the beginning of the narrow alley which leads in the direction of the beach and is situated about 55 yards to the east of the beginning of the access road. They are often overfull in the season and long queues must be expected.

• MEDICAL SERVICES: very good, and there are several doctors in the village, for example in the **Hotel Elkomi** on the right hand side at about the middle of the access road leading to the sea. Or there is the **Koinotes Malion**, a small clinic on the main road near the western end of the village, next to the church.

• MINOTAUR TOURIST SHOP: a good selection of English language books, international newspapers and magazines. At 106, Main Road.

• PHOTOS: There are a number of shops offering a 1 hour service on the main road. "Get your colour photos in one hour".

• POST OFFICE: behind the church at the western end of the village.

• SOUVENIRS: There is quite a "department store" called Mallia Maria Market on the left hand side of the access road to the beach. Cannot be missed and is completely unbelievable.

• TELEPHONE: OTE office at the western end of the village. Open Mon-Fri 7.30 a.m.- 3.00 p.m., closed on Sat/Sun.

Accommodation

Here again there are numerous hotels, which are up to 95% taken over by package tourists in the season.

• **Pension Grammatikakis**: B class, one of the oldest houses on the square at the end of the long access road, and directly at the beginning of the beach. Excellent central position, but quiet in spite of this because the road ends here and there is hardly any vehicle traffic. All rooms have balconies and bathrooms, and there is a large restaurant overlooking the beach. Bus stop in front of the door. Only half board is available in the season, cost around £25 for a DR. Tel. 0897/31366.

• **Ermioni**: B class, quiet situation away from the bustle. Time has been spent on the furnishings and there is a friendly dining room, Cretan wall hangings, a lot of plants, tasteful furniture and curtains. Costs around £20 for a DR. Address: Go down a little alley from the main road in the eastern area of the town (follow signs for the hotels Sireus Beach and Phaedra Beach), then turn left into a narrow unpaved passageway about 110 yards on. Tel. 0897/31093.

AROUND THE CROSSROADS

The hotels and guest houses directly on the main road and around the crossroads of main road and access road to the beach cater rather for travellers who are just passing through.

• **Hotel Zeus**: D class. Although on the main road it can be recommended, if you are able to secure a room on the attractive inner courtyard. Inviting dining room on a terrace in the courtyard. Costs around £14 with a bathroom. Address: 77, Main Road, a few paces from the beginning of the access road in a westerly direction. Tel. 0897/31464.

• **Hotel Rousakis**: D class, simple and loud but with fine balconies over the bustle over the main street. The quieter rooms face towards an alleyway towards the back. Costs around £13 for DR with bath, or £11 without bath. Address: 74, Main Road, directly opposite the Hotel Zeus. Tel. 0897/31251.

• **Sarpidon**: situated 60 or so yards from the crossroads down the access road. A long tube-like building with a terrace. Mostly frequented by rucksack travellers, costs about £10 for a DR. There are further possibilities around the crossroads at the Guest Houses **Mary**, **Sokrates** and **Sophocles.**

OLD PART OF THE VILLAGE

Inland from the main through road you will find what is certainly the cheapest and also the simplest accommodation.

• **Aspasia**: friendly guest house. When all the rooms are occupied, there is a possibility of sleeping on the roof (wooden bedsteads). Beautiful view out over the roofs to the sea. Around £9 for a DR.

— ★ —

• YOUTH HOSTEL: This moved premises recently. It is now situated at the western end of the village. Take the turning by the church and go right after the Post Office, then about another 100 yards

Situated in the eastern part of the town. There are several comparable establishments nearby, eg **Athinas** and **Menios**, which are cheap in price.

further on. Quite desolate-looking corrugated iron sheds, but there is room in the courtyard for a handful of tents. Costs around £3. Open from 01.04-30.10.Tel. 0897/31338.

• READER'S TIP: "We stayed in the newly-built **Pension Kastri** and had very comfortable rooms. A room with three beds costs c. £15. The Pension is situated in the second road crossing that which leads from the bus stop in an easterly direction."

Food

All restaurants offer everything in at least three languages.

• **Milos**: an attractive garden restaurant situated within the first third of the way down the access road, on the left hand side. The refined restaurant **Elisabeth** almost opposite the Milos is also recommended.

• **Olympic House**: also on the access road. Has mainly young people as its customers, and offers both Greek and international dishes (Wiener Schnitzel, cutlets, and pizzas too). Opposite the Olympic there is an (up till now) nameless **Café**, which offers German-type breakfasts, muesli and fruit cakes.

• **Metoxi**: situated on the lower part of the access road. Original Greek food is still served here.

• As of recently, the old part of the village south of the main thoroughfare has been more than adequately provided with eating places. Since the locals have discovered that foreigners often prefer eating in romantically winding alleys to the bustle of the access road to the beach, new eating places are being established on every corner. Above all the tavernas are clustered around the two church squares. Many of them offer local wines from the barrel. Try **San Georgio** directly by the little church, which offers a good selection and many special dishes.

— ★ —

• KAFENIA: There is the kafenion run by **Nik. Mrelivanis** directly on the main crossroads where the access road to the sea branches off the main road. This is the meeting place of the elderly men of Mallia and mostly younger tourists who have had enough of the synthetic fairground atmosphere of the main road. A nice place to sit and enjoy company; a lot of British people go there and there is a more than adequate flow of alcohol there every evening. Another good café is the **Cabana** at 50, Main Road, to the east of the church at the western end of the village.

• NIGHT LIFE: There are at least 4 discotheques - Highway, Flash, Krypton and George's Place, and apart from these there are countless **music bars.** There is good live bouzouki music in **Scooby Doo.**

• READER'S TIP: "Our tip for a restaurant in Mallia is the **Eva.** This taverna is situated about 0.75 miles outside in a north-easterly direction, between hothouses where bananas are grown. Good food (Kalamari!), nicely furnished, a broad terrace, slightly higher prices. It is signposted from the access road to the sea on the right hand side."

Author's Note: Careful here. There is another Restaurant Eva, to the west of the road leading to the beach.

The Palace of Mallia

On a flat site near the sea, between olive groves and thorny phrygana bushes. Unfortunately, there is practically no shade.

Not as attractive from the point of view of position as the other palaces, and also smaller than Knossos and Phaistos. But worth a visit because there is less bustle, and there is a place to bathe only a few yards further on.

The palace dates from the period around 1650 BC; there are only a few traces of the older palace which stood on the same spot. The building follows a similar plan to that of the palaces at Knossos, Phaistos and Zakros, whereby four wings of the building are grouped around an extended central court which has a south-north orientation. In general, however, it is of a simpler aspect than the lavish complexes of Knossos and Phaistos. For example, the extravagant alabaster facings are absent, and only limestone and sandstone from the area have been used as building materials, apart from dried mud bricks. The number of rooms is also smaller and there is no theatre complex.

Thus it was a kind of "provincial palace", but still the centre of a large settlement, extending from the modern road to the sea. It has only been partially explored, and the excavations of the *École Archéologique Francaise d'Athènes* are still going on (the most recent excavations are situated under corrugated iron roofs in the area).

In 1450 BC the palace and the settlement fell prey to the same puzzling catastrophe as the other cities on the island.

• OPENING TIMES: Tues-Fri 9.30 a.m.-3.00 p.m. Sat/Sun 9.00 a.m.-2.30 p.m. Closed on Mondays. **Admission** c. £1. The palace is situated 1.75 miles from Mallia. A signposted way leads towards the sea from the road in the direction of Iraklion. There is a bus stop on the road.

A tour around the site

After entering the site the visitor first arrives in the **West Court** which extends to the front. Remains of the paving can be seen and a slightly *raised path (1)* runs parallel to the facade. A branch off the way goes to the south-west corner where there are the foundation walls of 8 *circular structures (2)*, which were probably grain stores.

The walls of the very angular *facade* are only shoulder-high, and the *entrance (3)* to the interior is roughly in the middle. Through the entrance, a *corridor (4)* passes numerous storerooms and goes left to a boundary wall and then right towards the so-called *"Robing Room" (5)*. This is where the ruler prepared for his official appearances - a sceptre decorated with a panther's head, a large sword with a pommel of rock crystal and a gilded razor were found in this room. In a raised position next to it is the *Loggia (6)* containing the bases of columns and the foundations of an altar and a throne. This hall was open to the central court, and a few steps lead down to it. Here, from a slightly raised platform, the "king" took part in ceremonies and rituals which were also followed by those assembled in the courtyard.

Directly next to it there was a wide *stairway (7)* leading to an upper floor (no longer extant today). Next to this again there is the large *hall (8)* leading into a pillar crypt, with the remains of a bench; perhaps a type of audience hall. Behind that is the *Pillar Crypt (9)* itself with two striking square pillars, into which small double axes and other cult signs have been chiselled (can be seen today).

Right down in the south-west corner of the central court there is another wide *monumental stairway (10)* which may have constituted some kind of theatre. Right next to it is the famous *Kernos (11)*, a circular sacrificial stone of just under 3 feet in diameter and with 34 small depressions all around the outer rim. The use of this stone is unknown, but it is suggested that seed grains and early fruits were

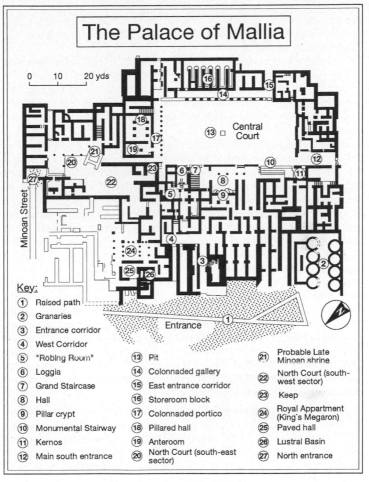

The Palace of Mallia

0   10   20 yds

Central Court

Minoan Street

Entrance

Key:

① Raised path
② Granaries
③ Entrance corridor
④ West Corridor
⑤ "Robing Room"
⑥ Loggia
⑦ Grand Staircase
⑧ Hall
⑨ Pillar crypt
⑩ Monumental Stairway
⑪ Kernos
⑫ Main south entrance
⑬ Pit
⑭ Colonnaded gallery
⑮ East entrance corridor
⑯ Storeroom block
⑰ Colonnaded portico
⑱ Pillared hall
⑲ Anteroom
⑳ North Court (south-east sector)
㉑ Probable Late Minoan shrine
㉒ North Court (south-west sector)
㉓ Keep
㉔ Royal Appartment (King's Megaron)
㉕ Paved hall
㉖ Lustral Basin
㉗ North entrance

placed in the depressions as an offering of thanks to the deity. This type of thanksgiving for the harvest and fertility was widely practised on Crete, and several of these offering stones have been found in Minoan excavations.

The paved corridor in the **South Wing** is the *main entrance (12)* to the palace. In this part of the complex there were workshops and a small shrine, where ritual vessels have been found.

The **Central Court** is smaller than those at Knossos and Phaistos. It was probably completely paved, and in the middle opposite the crypt is a *pit,* which may have been an altar for burnt offerings *(13)*; 4 supports for a grid have been identified there. No such construction has been found in any other central court.

Pillars and columns divided up a long *gallery (14)* on the **eastern side** of the court; perhaps this served as a kind of spectators' room during events in the central court, for example the famous bull-leaping. Behind this there is a *storeroom block (16).* This was used for the storage of oil and is roofed over and closed today. To the right is the *eastern entrance (15)* to the palace.

There is also another *colonnaded portico (17)* in the **north wing.** Behind it and separated from it by a wall, there is an *anteroom (19)* with a pillar and a striking *pillared hall (18)* containing 6 pillars. The king's official banqueting rooms were probably situated directly above it; there is a stairway leading upwards on the right.

A narrow passage leads to the *south-east sector of the north court (20)* with columns on two sides. The *shrine (21)* which has been built diagonally into it probably dates from the period after the destruction of the palace. From *south-west sector of the north court (22),* three steps lead into the the *Keep (23).*

A short distance away to the west there is the *King's Megaron (24).* This room, which was originally paved and had many doors and light wells, must have been impressive. Next to it there is a small paved *hall (25)* and, as in every Minoan palace, a mysterious *lustral basin (26).* Around the north court there are storerooms and workshops. A paved way leads to the harbour through the *north entrance (27).* There are two large multi-handled clay pithoi here, too. If you go further on, you can see some of the new excavations under the large corrugated metal roof, but there is no access to them.

▶ **Mallia/Bathing:** A long sandy beach with fine, soft sand interrupted repeatedly by rocky cliffs extends in both directions from the end of the access road at Mallia. There are several bathing attendants, and water-skis, pedalloes, canoes and surf boards are available. Opposite the beach there is a small, rocky *island* with a white chapel on it. It is easy to swim the 100 yards or so across to the island.

To the east there are alternate areas of sand and gouged-out sandstone formations. There is a small church between thick tamarisks on a promontory; the occasional lone tent is pitched here.

Still further to the east, where the camping site used to be, there is a cleaner, finer sandy beach of about 0.75 miles in length. Behind it there are low dunes, large areas of reeds and an almost undisturbed plateau with the rusty skeletons of windmills, rust-red fields and hothouses used for growing bananas. Up till now this has remained a peaceful area, but hotel buildings are going up everywhere.

The eastern end of the beach forms a large sandy bay, which is in the immediate vicinity of the Palace of Mallia and can easily be reached from there. There is a very unique and original taverna here called *Monachos*. There is no electricity, and in the evenings the light sputters out of petroleum and gas lamps which are certainly out of the ark. A basin of water is used to cool the drinks, the water being brought up out of the ground by means of a motor pump. Georgia prepares simple dishes such as Greek salad, omelettes, and sometimes fish. Those with a car or a motor caravan could spend a couple of days on the beach here: according to information there would be *no problem*! However, a notice announces that tents are forbidden here.

How to get there: Follow the signposted way to the **Palace of Mallia** from the main road a few miles to the east of Mallia. Turn left shortly before reaching the palace, and then proceed for a few hundred yards along the bumpy dust track. There is also a bus stop on the road.

Bananas in particular are grown around Mallia

The *coast in the direction of Sisi* is thoroughly rocky and can only with difficulty be negotiated on foot. Small bays alternate with rough-cornered stone blocks, between which mosses and patches of herb bushes grow. Shimmering green scrub extends inland. Low stone walls separate old grazing pastures.

There is a small beach of sand and large shingle not far from the sandy bay mentioned above, but it is rather dirty and for this reason seldom frequented.

Sisi

Situated at the exit from a wide, hilly plateau with several ravines and a sea of olive trees. There is hardly any village to speak of. A handful of old houses is grouped around the pretty fishing harbour, which is well-protected in a rocky fjord. But the future has come to Sisi. Stereotyped white apartment buildings are being dropped in among the rocks in the area.

The only potential that this place still possesses is its peacefulness. Mostly Greeks find their way there, apart from a few British stragglers. There are a lot of rocks, a fine bathing cove, a camping site, no disco; instead there is accommodation to be found off the approach road, and it is very quiet out of season. Several car/motorbike rental companies offer their services.

• CONNECTIONS: There is a bus twice daily from Iraklion to Paralia Milatos via Sisi and back.

Accommodation

Apartments and private rooms predominate here. There are a number of new establishments on the approach road, eg *Eleanna* apartments and rooms for rent at *Sofia* and *Iris*.

• **Petsalakis**: a taverna on the road a little up from the harbour. Modern spacious rooms with good bathrooms and beds on stone foundations. You can still snatch a view of the harbour from the balcony. About £11 for a DR. The friendly propietor has built a new house exactly opposite, in which he also has rooms for rent. The **Hotel Sisi** a few houses down was closed at the time of our visit.

• **Triena**: private rooms directly on the harbour, with a fine view over the cliff coastline and the sea. Clean, tiled floor, good bathrooms with small bathtubs. The rooms have small balconies, where you can sit comfortably in the evenings. Costs about £10 for a DR.

• **Elena**: E class hotel, diagonally opposite. Simple, but modern, nice rooms with roughly-plastered walls and original bedside tables made of stone. Price with private bathroom around £10 for a DR.

• **Porto Sisi Apartments**: on the way to the beach (signposted) and directly on the low cliff coast. Attractive complex with cube-shaped white houses, balconies, shady stairways and a small swimming pool. The apartments consist of a spacious living room, a small but modern kitchen niche, shower/toilet and a bedroom. Rough plastered walls, sparse but immaculate furniture, with beds and seating arrangements on stone bases (pleasantly cool). A 2-roomed apartment costs c. £25. Tel. 0841/71385. There are more apartments in the neighbourhood.

• CAMPING SISI: a small, simple site directly on the cliff coast. No beach, but a convenient swimming pool. Little shade at present through thin tamarisks, and the sanitation could be better. Restaurant and bar available. In the low season particularly there are few visitors and the site is very peaceful. Costs around £1 per person, and the same for a tent. Bad approach over a bumpy, stony road, about 1 mile to the west of the harbour (signposted from the New Road). There is also an approach road from the harbour. Open from April-September. Tel. 0841/71247.

• FOOD: There are several tavernas and cafés down on the harbour. Try **Zorbas**, (next door to Triena Rooms) or **Porto** at the end of the harbour.

• SHOPPING: Have a look in the souvenir shop diagonally across from the Hotel Sisi. It has a sagging wooden ceiling, old sofas, wall hangings and a lot of embroideries.

▶ **Bathing:** about 500 yards east of the village there is an attractive gravel/sandy cove between eroded cliffs. Somewhat polluted by seaweed and plastic rubbish, no shade, and only a couple of sparse tamarisks at the very back.

Bay of Milatos

Take the turning off the Old Road after Sisi, and about 200 yards on take the road on the right to Milatos (3.75 miles, signposted). The road goes in snake-like curves over the backbone of a mountain; here, there are gaping holes in the rust red earth, large boulders and olive groves. There is a tiny village on the way, semi-derelict and almost abandoned.

Milatos: The old village is situated about half a mile in from the sea and up on the slope. Winding alleys and low white houses brood silently in the fierce sun and the church square, devoid of people, brings to mind pictures of dusty Mexican villages. Tourists rarely lose their way up here. The men sit in long rows in front of the village kafenion in a side street off the main road and look the exotic strangers up and down in a friendly way.

There are rooms to rent across from the kafenion for about £7.

Paralia Milatos (Milatos Beach)

This once intimate harbour village with a handful of fishing boats and two tavernas has noisily woken up to reality. There is building, building everywhere, and in 1988, amongst other things, a large cement mole was under construction. This did not do much good to the peace and sense of security that Paralia Milatos once emitted.

On the right hand side of the village there is a 200 yard long shingle beach, which is not particularly inviting.

Accommodation

This consists almost entirely of apartments with kitchens for self-catering, well-suited to families. Up to now there is hardly a visitor in the low season, hence lower prices.

• **Diamerismata**: on the left hand side of the entrance road, shortly before the harbour. A house of original design with several semi-circular bays and balconies. Absolutely new, tip-top clean rooms, invitingly furnished with furniture of light wood. Living room, bedroom, kitchen (with a large fridge) and bathroom - cost in the low season only £12-14.

• **Thalia Village**: a distance to the west of the harbour, only a few yards from the sea. Attractive complex with little houses arranged in a square, small gardens with flower-beds and high hedges. Ideal for families; there is a kitchen, a bathroom and a choice of 1 or 2 bedrooms. Costs around £14 (low season). Tel. 232301. The neighbouring **Villa Village** is similar, but has a restaurant and double rooms.

• **Akrogiali**: private rooms on the harbour, and there are more rooms/apartments in the fish restaurant **Psaris** a short way to the west of the harbour.

Cave of Milatos: high in the mountains above the village of Milatos. Reached by a bad dust track, of about 2 miles in length, clumsily cemented in places. Signposted from Milatos. Possible with a robust vehicle, but best by motor bike or moped. There is a wonderful view over the whole bay from up here. It is a short walk to the entrance of the cave along a consolidated secured path through wild rocky landscape.

The entrance is in the greyish-red, vertical rock face; you grope your way inside on the uneven floor between stalagmite columns. In part the cave is only of shoulder height and pitch black, so take a torch! At the lower end of the chamber, which is about 150 feet deep, there is an exit. There is a white *altar wall* built into the cave, and there are human bones in the stone shrine here - a memorial to the bloody massacre which took place here over 150 years ago.

In February 1823, 2,700 Cretan women and children under the protection of only 150 men hid themselves in the cave from the murderous Egyptian and Turkish hordes. Their presence was discovered and the cave was besieged. The narrow entrance could easily be defended and the siege lasted for weeks. Relief attempts by Cretan partisans failed several times, and the inhabitants of the cave starved. They were finally forced to surrender. The men of fighting age were killed immediately, the women and children were given to the officers as slaves, and the remaining people were either trampled by horses or thrown into the ravine.

Unfortunately, the white sails of the windmills are only rarely seen

Lassithi high plateau

Windmills, apple trees and barren chasms; the birthplace of Zeus; the village museum at Agios Georgios

A circular enclosed plain in the Dikti massif, 2,616 feet above sea level. Steep rocky crests project up into the sky all around it, and there are only two winding road passes that penetrate these towering rock barriers.

Farming activities have been carried on in this mountainous isolation for thousands of years. Many more than 10,000 windmills with their characteristic white sails used to pump vital water from hidden caverns in the underground limestone. At least that many photos owe their finishing touches to these picturesque sails.

However these white "wind wheels" have become a rarity; fewer and fewer farmers can afford to make the irrigation of their fields dependent upon the wind. Above all, because the water table underground has sunk considerably, diesel-powered motorised pumps have reduced these picturesque relics of days gone by to the status of film extras. About a dozen are said to be in use on occasion for the benefit of tourists, a very pale reflection of the delights often promised in the brochures. But the Lassithi Plateau is worth a visit even without the windmills, in order to get an impression of one of the most character-istic, and at the same time, most fertile types of landscape on the is-land. In spite of a constant stream of tourists, it has remained typical Cretan farming land, shielded from the hustle and bustle down on the coast. There are countless fields and fruit plantations crammed closely together; shimmering green in early summer, they are brown and dried up in autumn, when the harvest has taken place. Then the apples and pears are ripe - one can wander in peace in every direction over the dusty field paths.

Only the daily air-conditioned buses signal the importance of the Lassithi Plateau for tourism. They usually have only one target desti-nation - the legendary birthplace of Zeus, the cave at Psychro.

Dates/figures/facts: c. 5-6.25 miles long, c. 3.25 miles wide, comprising 21 villages in all. These are all situated on the lower mountain slopes, in order to sacrifice as little of the precious farming land as possible. The road also goes in wide curves around it, and only dead straight field paths cross this completely level plateau. The main crops pro-duced here are apples, pears, potatoes, wheat and various vegetables. The vital water is provided by the melting of the snows in the early part of the year. Such a great volume of water is washed down from the surrounding six-thousand footers that the whole plateau is flood-ed to a depth of 3-6 feet, and a huge lake is created. Only the fruit trees and the windmill structures can still be seen sticking out above the surface. When the water drains away, it collects in the limestone under the ground in huge caverns, which are connected to the surface by clefts in the rock. The water is then brought back to the surface by means of motorised pumps and used for irrigation.

In spite of adequate water, soil fertility and lush vegetation, the farmers of the Lassithi Plateau are poor. The intensive subdivision of land is a particular hindrance to prosperity. The simple village houses are constructed from rough unhewn stones, there are hardly any new buildings, and few cars. A donkey or mule, a few chickens, one or two fields - these are the possessions on which most families have to base their upkeep. The tourists bring money, but hardly anyone remains there for longer than a day trip.

The surrounding mountain chains are also of light-coloured marble and limestone, and the highest mountain is *Dikti*, also called Kako Kephali (literally: "bad head") which lies directly to the south and has a height of 7,023 feet. It is 23 feet higher than the neighbouring *Afendis Christos*.

History: More than 5,000 years ago in the Neolithic Period, the Lassithi Plateau was already inhabited because of its unusual fertility. The remains of settlements and cult centres of the Minoan period have also been found, including the legendary *Cave of Zeus*. It is probable that the plateau also enjoyed continuous habitation in later centuries and was an ideal place of withdrawal when conquering armies gained the upper hand . . .

When the *Venetians* occupy the island in the 13th century, the Cretan rebels withdraw into this natural fortress with its huge walls. In 1263, the Venetians storm this nest of resistance, drive out all the inhabitants and turn it into a prohibited area. The Lassithi High Plateau becomes a lonely mountain wilderness, remaining so for nearly 200 years, with only the occasional straying of a shepherd and his flocks into the area.

In 1463 the Venetians' corn reserves run out; then they remember the once fruitful plateau in the Dikti massif. Experts on farming are hurriedly given the task of bringing the flooded land up to standard. Within a few years there is a criss-cross system of canals on the plateau, and fields that have been reclaimed for agriculture are given to Cretans on compulsory lease. In future they have to hand over one third of their harvest to the Venetians. The Venetian irrigation system is still in existence today.

The Lassithi Plateau again became a place of refuge for Cretan resistance fighters in the 19th century, this time from the Turks. The constant state of siege there becomes a fact of everyday life, and the houses are converted into small fortresses (one of them is preserved; see under Agios Georgios). Attacks are successfully repulsed for a number of years, until 1867. Then the much-feared army commander Omar Pasha advances with an army of almost 40,000 Turks. Everyone they come upon is put to the sword and the villages are razed to the ground.

• GETTING THERE: There are two roads up to the Lassithi Plateau. One branches off the road from Iraklion to Mallia slightly to the west of **Limin Chersonisou** and goes up into the mountains. It reaches Tzermiadon, main village of the plateau, via the Ambelou Pass (3,433 feet).

The other road leads up from the east and can be joined at several places from the direction of **Agios Nikolaos** and from **Neapolis** (between Mallia and Agios Nikolaos).

• CONNECTIONS: Buses go along the first of the roads mentioned above from Iraklion and Mallia, and from Agios Nikolaos on the road from the east. The end of the bus route in both cases is the little village of Psychro with the famous Dikteon Andron cave (birthplace of Zeus).

Iraklion - Psychro twice daily, bus returns at around 2.00 p.m. and 5.00 p.m. (Duration 2 hours, fare £2).

Mallia - Psychro once daily, bus returns at 2.00 p.m.(1.5 hrs. Fare £2).

Ag. Nikolaos - Psychro twice daily, Sat/Sun only once. (2 hrs. Fare £2).

From Limin Chersonisou up to the Lassithi High Plateau

The landscape is so breathtaking and there is so much of interest on the wag that a short stop is worthwhile.

There is a good asphalt road (signposted) to the west of Limin Chersonisou. Shortly after the turn off to the little provincial town of Kastelli (see page 205), there are the remains of a large Roman *aqueduct* next to the road on the right hand side. At one time, this transported masses of water from the Lassithi mountains to the harbour town of Limin Chersonisou. The road runs along a ravine, amidst a landscape of deep green olives and cypresses. Shortly before the village of **Potamies** there is the small weathered church of *Afendis Christos*, on the left amid vine-covered hills. Above this is the old monastery of *Panagia Gouverniotissa*, built of roughly-hewn stones. It is abandoned today, but in the Byzantine church (which unfortunately is usually locked) there are fine 14th century frescoes. It is signposted on the road.

There are also frescoes of the same period in the little church of *Agios Antonios* in the next village, **Avdou**. The village of **Gonies** is situated at the foot of the steep rock walls that border the plateau. The road winds adventurously up to the pass in snake-like curves, there is a wonderful view over the green plateau far below and the surrounding mountain chains seem to crowd in on one another! Be careful of potholes, this is a tortuous stretch of road.

A road branches off to the left towards **Krasi**, a small diversion of about 1.5 miles which is especially worthwhile at midday. A meal can be taken in comfort on the shady village square, and the huge, swollen plane tree in the middle is supposed to be the largest in Crete! In the rock face above the square there is a large but simple *Venetian fountain,* surrounded by a long white wall with a rounded archway.

Try the Raki at Krasi. The sweet, seedless grapes of the village are particularly suited to its production.

Shortly before Kera there is the attractive monastery of *Panagia Kera* on a cypress-clad slope to the right below the road. The great festival of the Panagia is celebrated on September 8th, and thousands of Cretans come up here, blocking the road for miles with their cars. The few tavernas at Kera do a great deal of business then.

The inner court of the monastery has a lot of atmosphere, and there are many plants there. Particularly worth seeing are the wall paintings which were discovered a few years ago in the simple monastery church. They had been painted over in fear of the Turks.

Behind Kera there is a wonderful view back towards the sea, and in front the deep indentation formed by the pass can be seen in the distance. The striking rocky peak above Kera is called *Karfi* ("Nail") because of its characteristic shape.

The Pass of Ambelou: 3,433 feet high. The bus stops for 5 minutes, and rightly so. The view in both directions is fantastic! Deep down below is the plain, whence you have just come; the sea is far in the distance, and in front of you is the almost unrealistic-looking Lassithi Plateau. The windmills are all facing you; here, the strong Meltemi wind blows from the north in the summer.

In previous years the sharp winds that sweep across the pass into the plateau were also put to use here, on the right and left hand sides of the cutting that forms the pass; the substantial remains of former *corn mills* can be seen. Their giant wind wheels measure almost 33 feet in diameter and are set in a fixed, unchangeable orientation, due to the fact that the wind is almost always blowing from the north.

• FOOD: The **Selli** taverna is situated directly at the pass and is of course fully geared to tourists. Lamb is sometimes still roasted in the old-fashioned stone oven outside the taverna. The elderly proprietor stands on the roadside proudly wearing the Sariki around his head and offers herbs and Diktamos from the Dikti Massif for sale. Diktamos is one of the most favourite of Cretan herbs and is mainly drunk in the form of tea. See also the chapter on Vegetation.

From the pass down to the plateau: This is as flat as a board and is 100% given over to farming activity. Dead straight paths lead everywhere through the fields and fruit orchards, and only the iron towers of the windmills project above the tops of the trees.

The road goes in an almost complete circle through the villages at the edge of the plateau. The last stretch of road between Psychro and the monastery of *Vidianis* has now been completed, so that it is possible to go right round the Lassithi High Plateau.

Tzermiadon

The "capital" of the Lassithi Plateau. An attractive village whose centre is full of luxuriant green wild vines growing on streets and flower-decked balconies, which all forms a tasteful contrast to the low white houses with their doors and windows of turquoise or blue.

The main road runs through the whole village in a number of curves. There are several tavernas, a noticeable number of kafenia and a whole nest of souvenir shops, which cover the fronts of complete houses with their rugs and woven goods.

• CONNECTIONS: All buses to and from Psychro stop here (about half an hour earlier than the estimated time of arrival in Psychro, and half an hour after leaving Psychro on the return journey). The bus stop is in the direction of the northern end of the village, near several kafenia.

• ADDRESSES: The Post Office, bank and OTE telephone office (Mon-Fri 7.30 a.m.-3.10 p.m.) are situated in the immediate vicinity of the main crossroads in the middle of the village.

• ACCOMMODATION: **Kri-Kri**, E class. An old house in a central position on the main road opposite the church, in the middle of village life. Rooms are very mediocre, and the mattresses, woollen blankets and sheets have obviously seen better days. During our recent researches the water supply in the room was out of order and the only shower on the landing was dirty. Cost around £5 for a DR. Tel. 0844/22170.
Kourites Hotel, B class, well-run, clean and has a large restaurant. Situated at the exit from the village in the direction of Psychro. DR without a bath costs c. £7. Tel. 0844/22194. Also recommended is the new **Hotel Lassithi** opposite, for the same price.

• FOOD: **Kronio**, about 300 yards to the east of the bus stop. Run by a Cretan and a young French woman, a combination which enhances its quality. You must try the "Lassithi Salad".

Agios Georgios

A simple, peaceful farming village. The only sight worth seeing and the pride of the inhabitants is the really attractive and original *Folk Museum*, situated only a few paces from the main road on Eleftherias Square (signposted). Open daily 10.00 a.m.- 4.00 p.m., admission fee around £1.

The museum is accommodated in one of the few remaining village houses of the 19th century; because of the constant threat posed by the Turks there are no windows. Light and air only enter via an opening in the ceiling, which is pitch black from the smoke of the oven that used to be there.

The interior provides an excellent insight into Cretan village life during the last century. The main room is in front; it is a living room/bedroom and kitchen all in one, with a stone oven for baking and a raised bed on a stone foundation (this is often copied in hotels today). At the back there is a storeroom and a stall, and there are numerous authentic utensils used in crafts and agriculture: an anvil, shoemakers' tools, distilling apparatus, bellows, and a weaving loom. There is also a bag of goats' leather on the wall; the *Tsambouna*, a musical instrument similar to the bagpipes, is made from this. Right at the back there are the provisions - large clay pithoi filled to the brim with beans, maize and other pulses.

The next room is dedicated to traditional **home furnishings**; there is intricately carved and decorated furniture with colourful embroideries both of which were a normal part of the furnishing of a well-to-do city house or a rich farmhouse.

There is a small **picture gallery** on the first floor; a mine of information is the series of photographs about the life of **Kazantzakis.** There are pictures from different periods of his life from his schooldays until the splendid funeral attended by the whole of Iraklion. It includes pictures of Kazantzakis at the Great Wall of China, in Cannes, Paris and Pisa - taken together with Albert Schweitzer, Melina Mercouri and many famous personalities.

• CONNECTIONS: Buses to and from Psychro stop on the main road (Platia Eleftherias). There are also several kafenia here.

• ACCOMMODATION/FOOD: **Hotel/Restaurant Rea**, E class, lovingly furnished restaurant with huge ivy creepers, stuffed mountain animals and embroidered rugs on the walls. Simple room costs c. £6. Tel. 0844/31209.
Similar and directly opposite there is the **Hotel/Rest. Dias**, E class. Tel. 0844/31207.

Psychro

A simple village, seemingly untouched in spite of tourism, with its steeply climbing alleys and crumbling stone dwellings in the upper part of the village. Business is only carried out on the shady main road with its huge plane trees. There, you will find the tavernas and the kafenia, and also the village church, right next to the clear village spring.
In the evening, after the air-conditioned tourist buses have returned to Iraklion, only a handful of strangers is left in the village and peace prevails.

• CONNECTIONS: Psychro is the final destination of the buses from Iraklion, Mallia and Ag. Nikolaos. For further information see under Lassithi High Plateau, how to get there.

• ACCOMMODATION: **Hotel Zeus,** D class, probably the best address in the village. A detached house a little outside on the road between the village and the bus park at the Psychro Cave. Terrace on the 1st floor, rooms partly with balcony; simple, but the beds are O.K. Spacious bathroom on the landing. About £10 for a DR with breakfast and a hot shower, or £9 without. There is a taverna. Tel. 0844/31284.
A little cheaper, but also simpler, is the **Dikteon Andron**, an E class hotel with only 8 beds. Tel. 0844/31290. It is in a rather hidden position in the upper part of the village, up by the little church.

— ★ —

• FOOD: the tavernas **Platanos** and **Stavros** are centrally situated near the plane trees on the main road from Psychro and are a favourite meeting place.
At the place where the buses park at the foot of the Dikteon Andron Cave there is a good **Xenia Restaurant** (its speciality is Stifado - stewed beef with onions!) and also the kafenion belonging to **G. Androchlakis**, where you can treat yourself to a second breakfast. There is a fabulous view over the whole Lassithi Plateau from up here.
The taverna **Milos** in the nearby little village of Plati is a very attractive place, and offers wine from the barrel.

Dikteon Andron (Cave of Psychro)

The most famous cave on the island, this is the second of the magnets which draw visitors to the Lassithi Plateau, after the windmills. This is where the mighty Zeus, father of the gods, was born!

Well, probably. Nobody is absolutely sure, since a second cave in the Ida range also makes the same claim (see page 192). Thus the problem has been solved according to Solomon and quite in the spirit of the Cretan flair for business; Zeus was born here in the Diktaian Cave, and grew up in the Idaian Cave in the Ida range.

The cave at Psychro is definitely the more impressive of the two. If you look down into this deep cavern (or better still if you look up out of the black depths!) it seems eminently possible that the mighty Zeus first saw the light of day down here amidst peals of thunder, fire, dense smoke and stench.

THE MYTH

Kronos, the ruler of the world, is warned by his predecessor Ouranos that his son will one day dethrone him and take power for himself. Kronos is disturbed and does not know what to do, so he gobbles up all his children: **Hades**, **Poseidon**, **Hera**, **Hestia** and **Demeter**. When his pregnant wife discovers the tragedy she is horrified and hides herself in a cave on Crete. Secretly, she gives birth to a son, **Zeus**. She hands Kronos a lump of stone wrapped in swaddling clothes to swallow. He is satisfied, and Zeus is secretly brought up in the Ideon Andron and the Ida mountains . . .

Much later, Zeus has taken control of the world for himself, as was prophesied. He receives his son **Minos** at the cave which was his former birthplace, gives him lessons in kingship for 9 years and makes him the ruler of Crete. Minos even brings up tablets, on which the laws are written for his new Cretan kingdom, from the depths of the cave - just like Moses and the Israelites.

This is the story extracted from the primeval myth. The ancient Cretans knew about the story, of course; this is attested to by the quantity of dedicatory gifts and offerings that has been found here. The cave must once have been one of the most important sanctuaries of the Minoans.

3000-4000 years later:

For centuries the existence of the cave is only known to the shepherds of the area. In bad weather they sometimes spend the night here and drive their herds into the protection of the rocks.

In 1866 one of the shepherds discovers glittering objects in the crevasses in the stalagmites; these later prove to be Minoan objects intended as offerings. In the same year, the cave is examined by the well-known Italian archaeologist *Halbherr*. He can report nothing, since the upper part is almost completely blocked by debris. *Hatzidakis,* Director of the Archaeological Society of Crete, has the same experience in 1894. Again and again farmers bring in bronze figurines, small double axes and other Minoan finds. But the Turkish authorities on the island at the time rigorously ban any systematic excavation.

At last the island is liberated in 1898, and in 1900 the time has come: *D.G. Hogarth,* Director of the British School of Archaeology at Athens, arrives on the scene. The explosive charges set by his demolition workers make, in his own words, "short work" of the rubble; now the real process of excavation can begin. For this purpose, Hogarth engages both men and women (a minor sensation in those times of opposition to women)! He has in fact discovered that men work much better when there are women around . . .

The small upper cavern has already been partly plundered by farmers from the area, but the excavators still find small bronze artefacts, knives and bracelets, and also pottery. The deep cleft on the left seems to be of more interest and much more promising.

This is where the workers, wading knee-deep in mud, have more luck: by chance, one of them fixes his candle into one of the stalactites hanging from the roof, and sees the blade of a bronze sword wedged in there. Immediate examination reveals it to be Mycenaean (post-Minoan). Now the men and women no longer scrabble around in the mud, but look upwards. They discover a breathtaking mass of undoubtedly Minoan offerings in the clefts in the formations hanging down from the roof. There are miniature double axes, knives, pieces of jewellery and figurines. The innermost sanctuary of Zeus has been discovered!

Way to the cave: The public bus service runs through Psychro and stops at a parking place situated further up the road below the cave. A stone path that is smooth and somewhat difficult to walk on leads up through a thinning forest of oaks to the entrance to the cave. This is a walk of about 20 minutes and not 1 hour, as some of the donkey drivers will assure you! You can also allow yourself to be carried up there in a leisurely way on the back of a **donkey** - the return trip costs c. £4, or about £3 for the ascent only.

Admission to the cave costs under £1 and the obligatory candle £0.25 (this is not necessary when a group is just about to go down into the cave - which is mostly the case). A guide, who with few words will show you one or two things, will demand about £5 per group. Finally, a trip by donkey from the bus park down to the village will cost you around £1. A tip: take a torch with you!

Visit to the cave: You can perhaps get a weak glimpse into the secretive cult of the Minoan palace period when you go down inside the earth . . .

The chasm falls away almost vertically to a depth of about 230 feet, into pitch black darkness. The whole thing is lit by dozens of smoking candles, which are pressed into your hands at the entrance. Like a procession of pilgrims, the groups of tourists grope their way down through the dampness over makeshift stone steps, hewn out of the rock - a chain of flimmering points of light, the murmuring of voices, the smell of incense. The burning heat of the sun dies away, and you are surrounded by an intense cool dampness. Bizarre stalactites grow down from the wet, moss covered rocks, like icicles. There are also columns of stalagmites, several feet thick, growing upwards from the floor, but they can only be reached in dry high summer, and are otherwise nearly always under water. If you have engaged the services of a guide, he will definitely show you the various ludicrously-named rock formations, such as the *young Zeus in nappies,* his *cradle, Zeus' coat* . . .

From Iraklion southwards

Go out of the centre of town through the Chania Gate and along 62 Martiron St. Turn off in a southwards direction after the bridge over the river *Yiophyros.* The legendary *Juktas* (2,651 feet) soon comes into view in front of you on the left hand side. From a particular angle, its profile resembles that of a human head to such an amazing degree that, as legend would have it, this is the sleeping Zeus (can be seen very well from the grave of Kazantzakis on the Martinengo Bastion).

You will now cross the largest single area of wine production on the island. This is a gentle, almost middle-European hill landscape - for miles there is one slope after another covered with green vines, and between them small silvery forests of olive trees and slim, lofty cypresses. Details and worthwhile destinations in the chapter on *Iraklion/Hinterland.*

At length, the landscape loses its "charm", and the mountains become more barren, jagged and rocky. The *Ida Range* appears on the right and its rugged rock mass starts to get nearer. The dazzling white *Chapel of Pantaleon,* on a mountain table top on the right hand side of the road shortly before Agia Varvara, is visible in the distance. Two ancient temples were found next to it at the beginning of this century.

The long village of *Agia Varvara* lies at the geographical centre of the island. To the south of it, the road climbs up to the highest point; the Ida range towers majestically and from up there, a splendid view can be had out over the great *Messara Plain,* into which the road now descends in slow, winding curves.

• CONNECTIONS: About 7 buses per day leave Iraklion from the bus station at the Chania Gate for Phaistos, Matala, Lentas and Agia Galini on the south coast. Duration of journey c. 2 hours, fare just under £2.

Messara Plain

The historic granary of Crete; avocados, kiwis and coffee; the archaeologists' El Dorado; miles of sand

A huge garden and agricultural landscape, 25 miles long and up to 7.5 miles wide. Hothouses, olive trees, cornfields and small white villages make the picture here.

This seemingly huge plain is driven like a wedge between the mountain slopes. It narrows at length to the east, until the slopes of the Dikti Mountains rise up as a barrier. The *Asterousia Mountains* form a natural windbreak towards the Sea of Libya in the south.

There are thus optimal conditions for agricultural exploitation. Tomatoes and cucumbers are by no means the only crops grown in the hothouses. Apart from bananas, pineapples and kiwis are also grown, and even *coffee* was planted for the first time in 1988. The first crops are expected in six years' time.

Even in antiquity the Messara was the granary of Crete. The Romans built up *Gortys* into a magnificent island capital here. Its ruins, which have been excavated near Agii Deka, give some impression of its former wealth and grandeur. The great Minoan palace of *Phaistos* is situated on one of the few hillocks in the plain. The view of the surrounding area is stunning.

Messara Plain/East

Hardly developed from the point of view of tourism, in contrast to the west. The beaches can only be reached via difficult dirt tracks through the high Asterousia Mountains.

A well-constructed through road connects the farming villages situated between vineyards and olive plantations. As there is usually little traffic, there is great enjoyment to be had when driving through this fertile landscape. Until recently, however, this enjoyment ended in *Mesochori*, and the road onwards to Ierapetra via Martha was a terrible dirt track, along which even taxi drivers refused to go. These times are past, and there is only a small piece of road between *Ano Kasteliana* and *Demati* which has not been made up. It does not, however, pose any problem. Thus there is no difficulty involved in going by car from the Messara Plain through the foothills of the Dikti Mountains into the south east corner of the island, or vice versa.

Buses do not yet travel along this stretch of road; it is necessary to return to Iraklion in order to go from the Messara Plain to Ierapetra.

The only place suitable for bathing that is worth a mention is *Tsoutsouros*, at the eastern end of the plain. An excursion there is still a little adventure. A bumpy and extremely rocky dirt and gravel road climbs up from Kato Kastelliana onto the jagged ridge of the coastal mountain range, and drops away in steep hairpin bends to the sea. The 7 miles can only be covered at walking pace, but on the way there are wonderful views out over the backs of the mountains, which are only covered with ankle high phrygana bushes. The size of the village of Tsoutsouros attests to the fact that such approach roads were an everyday occurrence on Crete a few years ago.

Tsoutsouros

Not exactly beautiful. Unwhitewashed, half-finished houses of hollow bricks are crammed into a broad bay, and the cliffs rise up steeply behind. Hothouses and dusty banana plants indicate the agricultural purpose behind the settlement, which seems mostly to serve as a summer habitation for farmers from the Messara Plain.

A sand and shingle beach of about 1 mile in length attracts the occasional foreign holidaymaker, but in spite of this your time here can be almost exclusively spent in the company of Cretans. The growing numbers of tavernas, bars and pizzerias on the beach promenade indicate that investment in tourism is already being made, since land is still cheap. The road will be completed at some stage.

• ACCOMMODATION: **Hotel Giorgios**, D class, on the beach promenade. Of a thoroughly pleasing standard. Tel. 0891/22190. A few paces in front of it are the new **Priasos** apartments. Otherwise there are number of private rooms to be had, eg at the **Michaelis** Pizzeria in the middle of the beach promenade for c. £9.

• FOOD: Many tavernas have been built directly at the water's edge on the beach promenade. There are several cafeterias (e.g. Gianna, o Takis) and 2 pizzerias, where there is a wonderful opportunity to sit beside the sea.

For Keratokambos, Arvi and other coastal villages in the direction of Ierapetra, see under Eastern Crete page 347. The track from Tsoutsouros to Keratokambos is catastrophic, but not impassable.

Messara Plain/Central area and West

This is where the tourists conglomerate. Various archaeological excavations here show that this part of the plain was already thickly populated in antiquity. Several wonderful sandy beaches open into the plain from the west.

Matala, with its famous cave dwellings and *Agia Galini,* a beautiful former fishing village slightly outside the plain, are at the centre of the flow of holidaymakers. Where Agia Galini in particular is concerned, it is possible to book a package holiday there at your local travel bureau. It is not very far to Rethymnon and the west of Crete from there. The small bathing resorts such as *Lentas* and *Kalamaki* are also attracting more and more guests, mostly young people.

A drive along the slopes of the Ida Range, which borders the plain to the north, should not be missed if at all possible, even if its sole purpose is to taste the only trout on Crete at *Zaros.*

Agii Deka

A simple agricultural settlement on the main road. The centre of the village, full of twists and turns, is situated below the road. Its name *(Agii Deka = Ten Saints)* derives from the early Christian martyrs, who were beheaded here because of their faith. A visit can be made to what are presumed to be their graves (see below). At the beginning of this century Agii Deka was still the seat of a bishop, and the beautiful old church in the middle of the village is a witness to its previous importance.

The greatest point of attraction is the huge site of ancient *Gortys,* about 1 mile to the west of the village, where the oldest written body of civil law in Europe was found! The road to Mires goes right through the site.

Thanks to this attraction the inhabitants of Agii Deka are noticeably geared up for tourism; there are several tavernas on the long main road and also rooms for rent. However, most visitors only come for a short excursion into the realm of archaeology and soon disappear in the direction of the beach.

• CONNECTIONS: buses to Iraklion, Gortys, Mires, Matala, Ag. Galini and Lentas (the last bus leaves at around 2.30 p.m.). Bus stop in the middle of the village near the kafenion.

• ACCOMMODATION/FOOD: There is the taverna **Dimitris** at the eastern end of the village. Delicious souvlaki here, and friendly proprietors. Rooms available in a newly-added upper floor, beds OK, clean. About £9 for a DR. There is another taverna with rooms in the centre, called the **Elpida**.

• OTHER INFORMATION: **OTE Telephone office** on the main road in the centre of the village, and the **Post Office** is a couple of houses further to the east.

Sightseeing

Pompeios, Euarestos, Saturninos, Theoloulos, Euporos, Gelasios, Zotikos, Basileidis, Eunikianos, Agathopous: these 10 martyrs are buried a little to the side of the main through road at the western exit from the village. The low, whitewashed vault with the simple tombs (6 can be seen, 4 are situated inside the foundation walls) lies under a small, attractive **church** with a shady verandah. This was erected in 1927 when the bones of the saints were discovered here.

The way there is signposted *(Tombs Ag. Deka)* from the main through road. If you carry out the tour of the excavations of Roman Gortys described below, you will come to the church of the Martyrs at the end of it.

A LEGEND

Until sixty years ago there was a circular village pond on the site of the present church. This was used for watering the animals, and a child of a family from Rethymnon often used to play there. One day, a woman clad in black appeared before him under a fig tree and told him the story of the 10 martyrs who had been beheaded by the Romans at this spot. The child did not believe the story and suddenly had a fit of shivering and a high fever. When it had passed, he went to the pond again. Once more the female figure appeared and once more she told him about the martyrs. When the child had a renewed attack of fever on the following day, his parents went to the bishop who had his seat there at the time, and told him about the strange occurrence. In summer, when the pond had almost dried up, the bishop had the ground dug over. The workmen soon found the bones of 10 human beings and a *marble slab,* on which impressions had been left by knees (the slab, they say, on which the martyrs knelt for their execution). Thus the pond was drained, dried out, and graves were prepared to house the mortal remains. In December of the same year the construction of a memorial chapel began at the holy place. That was 1927. However the drying out of the pond was only partly successful, and even today the little church stands under water every winter.

Mr. **Vouvakis** lives next to the church with his German wife. He owns a workshop and sells ceramic vases (Antik-shop). He might tell you the legend of the founding of the church. He knows it better than anyone else because he has lived in his present house since he was a child.

The Village Church of Agii Deka: This rough stone building, with a definite beauty of its own and situated in the middle of the village, has just been restored. The foundation walls of an older, much larger church building have been discovered during excavations around the church. It probably collapsed during an earthquake and was only partially rebuilt. Several old columns have been preserved, eg in front of the main entrance portal.

Faded frescoes can be seen inside the church in some of the columned archways, and the iconostasis (altar wall) of dark cypress wood is a fine example. The famous *marble slab* of the martyrs is preserved today under glass, because in days gone by the villagers grated away the surface of the stone, mixed the splinters with liquid and drank it as a healing medicine.

Gortys

Evergreen plane trees; legal texts in ancient Greek; the Roman capital; about Titos and Paul

An impressive expanse of ruins in the middle of the sparse olive groves to the west of Agii Deka.

The ancient theatre of Gortys

Not only traces of the Minoans have been left behind on Crete. Gortys only became famous at a much later date, in the Greek period, for its progressive legal system. When the Romans occupied Crete centuries later, Gortys really embarked upon its career. The Latin conquerors made this place in the fertile Messara Plain their capital, and used the remains of the tablets on which the Greeks had inscribed their laws as a decoration for their theatre.

Only a small part of the former Greek/Roman city complex has been excavated till now; the rest probably lies hidden under Agii Deka and the olive trees.

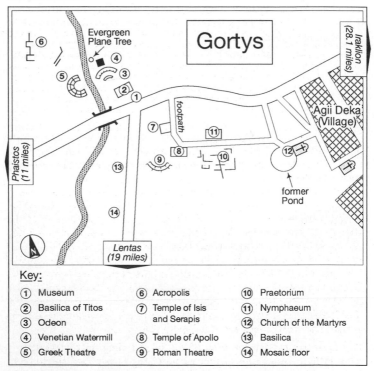

Key:

① Museum
② Basilica of Titos
③ Odeon
④ Venetian Watermill
⑤ Greek Theatre
⑥ Acropolis
⑦ Temple of Isis and Serapis
⑧ Temple of Apollo
⑨ Roman Theatre
⑩ Praetorium
⑪ Nymphaeum
⑫ Church of the Martyrs
⑬ Basilica
⑭ Mosaic floor

• SITUATION/CONNECTIONS: Ancient Gortys lies about 1 mile to the west of Agii Deka, and the road to Mires goes practically right through the site. Buses to and from Iraklion, Matala, Ag. Galini and Lentas stop directly at the Church of St. Titos (tell the conductor which bus stop you require). There is a large car park, directly opposite the turn-off to Lentas (the bus to Lentas stops there).

• OPENING TIMES: Mon-Sat 8.45 a.m.-6.00 p.m. Sun 9.30 a.m.-2.30 p.m. **Admission** c. £1, schoolchildren/students half price.

To the north of the road

Museum *(1)*: built in 1988. It is situated right next door to the entrance to the Basilica of Titos (about 50 yards north-west of the ticket kiosk). Its contents consist largely of marble statues dating from the Graeco-Roman period.

Basilica of Agios Titos *(2)*: This is only a few steps away from the road, directly after the kiosk where tickets are sold. It originates from the 6th century AD, ie from the Byzantine period, and is built on the site where the Church of Saint Titos stood.

According to tradition, **Titos** was established as the **first bishop** of the island by the Apostle Paul in 57 AD (Paul had landed at Kali Limenes not far to the south of the Messara Plain). Titos began his mission to the island from the Messara Plain and had the first cathedral church on Crete built here. Nothing remains of this today.

The famous **Letter of Paul**, in which he describes the Cretans as "liars, wild animals and lazy dogs" who must be brought to obedience by any means possible, is addressed to Titos. It is impossible to say whether Titos succeeded in doing this; at any rate almost the whole of Crete is supposed to have been won over to Christianity within a few years. This may have been all the easier for them, because their old belief in Gaia, the Earth Mother, and her son Zeus has noticeable parallels with a belief in Mary and her Son . . .

The eastern apse and the two small side apses are the only parts of the cruciform vaulted church of the 6th century still standing. The church was plundered and thoroughly destroyed by the Saracen hordes in 824 AD.

The great blocks used in the roof and placed together in such a way that no join is visible are very impressive. The way in which the stones support each other without the help of mortar can easily be seen where the roof breaks off and the stones reduce in size as they get lower. The archways of the doors also consist of wedge-shaped corresponding ashlar stones. There is a small altar with a picture of the Virgin in the left apse, and above it hovers the Holy Spirit in the form of a dove with a censer in its beak. Only the foundations of the actual nave are preserved, and the bases of columns and capitals (Corinthian and Ionic) are strewn around. A couple of beautiful, tall cypresses and sturdy olive trees complete the picture.

The most impressive building of the later Roman city of Gortys is reached by crossing the former *Agora* of the Greek city settlement. This is the **Odeon** *(3)*, a theatre which dates from the 1st century AD. The marble floor in the *Orchestra* (stage area) is wonderfully preserved, as are the semicircular tiers of marble seats. Statues stood in the niches of the building structures surrounding the stage in the Roman period. Part of the brick entrance has been reconstructed, but it is unfortunately fenced off, so that visitors are only able to peer through the opening. Inside this most famous part of the whole site are the stone blocks on which the legal code has been inscribed.

This was drawn up between 500 and 450 BC and had originally been placed in the Agora in a location so easily visible that every citizen could read it. The Romans built the 42 stone slabs into the round wall of the theatre, although it is not certain whether they were able to read the writing on them. It is probable that they were only intended for decoration.

AS AN OX PLOUGHS . . .

The ancient Greek legal code from Gortys consists of 12 columns, is 33 feet long and over 6 feet high, and is made up of about 17,000 letters. It is written in an old Doric dialect and follows the direction in which an ox ploughs; that is to say the writing runs from left to right, then from right to left and from left to right again. As a consequence of this the lines beginning on the right hand side are in mirror-writing. This can be clearly seen in the case of the letter E.

The subjects dealt with, apart from the everyday problems of agricultural life, include legal pronouncements on problems which seem surprisingly modern ones and can be found in our modern body of civil law: libel, adultery, rape, divorce, inheritance.

The Legal Code of Gortys: every other line is in mirror-writing

The legal relationship between slaves and free people is also described here, particularly where the problem of "mixed marriages" is concerned.

Much has been learned about social conditions in Greek antiquity from this code; it was probably binding for most of the cities on Crete and the mainland.

There are the ruins of a *Venetian Watermill (4)* behind the Odeon. Its
chimney is particularly well preserved.

A paved way leads to the "botanical wonder" of Gortys - an apparently
evergreen *plane tree* grows here, fenced off on the bank of a river
which is mostly dried up. It is even supposed to retain its leaves in
winter when all the other trees in the area are bare. The beautiful
king's daughter Europa is supposed to have conceived Minos with
Zeus under this plane tree (see also Mythology, page 99). Even today,
it is probably still the nicest place on the whole site; at any rate this
is certainly so during the burning heat of high summer, when it is
pleasant to sit here in the shade while the leaves rustle overhead . . .

Various other ruins which have been excavated lie in scattered positions on the other side of the river bed - the *Acropolis (6)* is situated
on the top of a hill, and on the slope in the direction of the road there
are the remains of a Greek *theatre (5)* etc.

To the south of the road

There are further excavated areas of the Roman city here, well hidden between the olive trees. Only narrow paths lead through the
parched fields. A visit is definitely worthwhile, as solitude is practically always guaranteed and you can explore and discover these
picturesque and scattered ruins in peace.

About 200 yards from the crossroads by the Church of Agios Titos in
the direction of Agii Deka there is a small signposted path. After following it for about 80 yards there is a sanctuary of the Egyptian de-
ities *Isis and Serapis (7)* on the right hand side. The lustral basin (used
for ritual cleansing) is the best preserved part of the sanctuary, on
the southern side. The forecourt and entrance are on the west side,
otherwise there are overturned columns, a few remains of sculptures,
and a frieze around a door with inscriptions in Greek. The partly-pre-
served sculpture probably depicts the goddess Isis.

100 yards further on is the fenced-off *Temple of Apollo (8),* the largest
temple in the city. There is an altar in front of the entrance in the
east, an entrance hall (outer temple), and in the main temple the
three wings were separated by rows of columns. Adjoining this to the
north is the treasure chamber of the sanctuary. The remains of a
semicircular *theatre (9)* have been excavated in the immediate neighbourhood.

On the long side of the temple, in an eastwards direction, the visitor
comes to what is actually the centre of the whole excavation - the
Praetorium (10), or palace of the Roman ruler of the city. A couple of
impressive high walls are still standing, and the open square was
adorned with large portrait statues, whose bases can easily be seen.

The path now leads along the long northern side of the complex in the direction of Agii Deka. To the left of it is the *Nymphaeum (11)*, a large fountain structure with water troughs. It was later roofed over with a dome by the Byzantines. The impressive remains of the Praetorium can still be seen on the right. The huge columns in the eastern part of it are most noticeable, with their diameter of over three feet.

At the entrance to the village of Agii Deka there is the most attractive *Chapel (12)* where the 10 martyrs are buried (on the right; see under Agii Deka).

There are further finds directly along the road to Lentas; namely the foundation walls of an ancient *basilica (13)* with the remains of a mosaic floor, c. 300 yards to the south of the crossroads and on the right. 200 yards further on are the fenced-off foundations of a *trefoil-shaped chapel*, with mosaic floors consisting of finely-worked geometric patterns *(14)*.

Mires

A lively little town with a lot of shops and workshops, at the centre of the Messara Plain and the junction where all the buses meet. A visit on a Saturday morning is particularly worthwhile; there is a large market which attracts people from all over the Messara Plain.

• CONNECTIONS: Buses to Matala, Agia Galini, Lentas, Iraklion etc. The bus station is directly on the main road, but on the market day, Saturday, the buses are diverted through the parallel road down from it, and passengers have to join and leave buses there too.

• TELEPHONE: The **OTE Telephone Office** is in the lower (southerly) road parallel to the main road. Open Tues-Fri 7.30 a.m.-3.00 p.m. Closed on Sat, Sun and Mon.

• POST OFFICE: 44, Koraka St. Mon-Fri 7.30 a.m.-2.30 p.m.

• ACCOMMODATION: Several guest houses are signposted. They are all situated up from the main road, about 5-10 minutes' walk from the bus stop.
Festos: the best address, an attractive guest house in a quiet residential area. Clean rooms with new furniture, and the bathrooms are O.K. (bathtubs). Some rooms have balconies. Friendly proprietress. Cost around £9 for a DR. Address: Metropoleos St., signposted from the bus station. Partly along the same way is the **Gortys** Guest House at 11, Arkadiou St. Tel. 0892/22528.
Olympic: D class, the only hotel in the village. Directly on the main road and can be noisy. Cost around £9.00 for a DR. Address: 135, Main Road. About 200 yards to the east of the bus station. Tel. 0892/42777.

• FOOD: There are several kafenia and tavernas on the main road. Delicious **loukoumades** (little doughnuts fried in oil and served with honey) are to be had in the kafenion owned by Mr. **Karitakis**, a few paces from the bus stop.

Sightseeing

Oriste, oriste (come on, come on)! This can be heard everywhere, as everybody tries to win customers at the Saturday morning market. For spoilt northern Europeans such as us the range of goods on offer is certainly not overwhelming; mainly old clothes, shoes, materials, even woven goods and embroideries. However, a short stop here is worth it just for the atmosphere. Of most interest are probably the fruit and vegetable stalls, where country people sit perspiring behind their apples, grapes, cabbages, peppers, beans and potatoes and drown out each other by shouting their latest prices.

Some of the market people park their donkeys at the western entrance to the village; not everyone can afford a car. There is a craft shop there too, selling ceramics, glass, and fine copies of icons (opposite the church).

The market in Mires is a weekly meeting-point for the inhabitants of the Messara Plain.

From Mires/Agii Deka to Lentas

Mires and Agii Deka are places where it is necessary to change buses for Lentas. This is one of the favourite bathing resorts of the south coast, particularly for rucksack tourists.

A fine journey along a road whose snake-like curves do not seem to want to end, passing through the *Asterousia Mountains* which border the Messara Plain to the south. Again and again there are grand views between the rust-brown thorn bushes and bare rocky slopes; If possible sit on the left hand side on the outward journey. *Miamou* is an attractive mountain village with houses built of natural stone, some painted white and some unwhitewashed, and narrow alleys. When the crest is reached, the striking peak of *Kofinas* appears to the east, while sandy beaches and bays which can be reached from Lentas via hiking paths can be seen along the sea edge down below. The road descends in steep curves to Lentas, an oasis in a rocky desert.

Lentas

A handful of houses at the foot of a steep rocky promontory, a few bumpy dust tracks, and a grey shingle and sand beach about 200 yards in length. The whole thing is crammed in between steep coastal mountains.

Lentas certainly does not have much to offer to hotel holidaymakers who are used to comfort. By contrast there are masses of rucksack tourists, especially on the half mile of finest sandy beach to the west of the village. By kind permission of the three taverna proprietors you are allowed to pitch your tent on the beach. Thus a supply of regular customers is assured.

Worthy of mention in the actual village itself are the gardens, some of which are really superb, and the shady greenery with vine creepers, oranges and many other trees. Lentas was already renowned for its healing waters in antiquity, and even today there is a lemonade factory there.

On the eastern edge of the bay there is the Chapel of *Agios Ioannis* which contains frescoes dating from the 14th/15th centuries.

• CONNECTIONS: buses to and from Iraklion via Agii Deka 2 x daily, and from and to Mires once daily.

• ACCOMMODATION: Almost every house in Lentas has rooms for rent. Probably the nicest place to stay is in the **Themistocles** taverna at the western end of the bay, directly below the large promontory. In a slightly raised position, and thus affording a wonderful view over the bay to the mountains on the opposite side. Try the moussaka here! The rooms are very simple, concrete floors, iron bedsteads, with a shower/toilet behind the house. Price around £6 for a DR, or a simple single room for £5. More rooms are to be found at the **Apostolakis** kafenion on the main village beach and in the neighbouring **Why Not Pub**, and also at the back of the village, where there is less bustle than directly on the beach.

• OTHER INFORMATION: There is a small "supermarket" in the upper part of the village, and a disco in the **Paradise** Pub/taverna in the evenings. There are **paddle boats** and **canoes** for hire on the main village beach.

▶ **Bathing:** A narrow path winds its way over the lower slopes of the rocky promontory to the next bay in a westerly direction. After a walk of about 15 minutes, most people will have reached their target destination: a wonderful grey sandy beach, a good half mile long and up till now the domain of individual campers.

The tavernas *Oasis* and *Odyssea* take care of the creature comforts here; the Oasis is reputed to offer the largest selection of dishes. There are also showers there. The Odyssea taverna rents out very simple rooms for c. £5, as does another taverna, which is newly-built. Quite a number of rucksack tourists spend weeks and months here; there are several cliques and at the beginning it is not at all easy for a newcomer to rub shoulders with the "old hands". In the evenings people meet with guitars in the tavernas or around a fire on the beach. Even a spacious *disco* with very "modern" equipment has opened its doors recently.

▶ **Excursions/Moving on:** The road westwards via *Peramata* to *Kali Limenes* is terrible but passable, according to information from some drivers of rented vehicles.

From Mires to Kali Limenes

To the south of Mires, the road soon winds up in steep 180 curves to *Pombia*. The view looking backwards over the Messara Plain is stunning! The asphalt finishes in *Pigadakia*, and even the buses only go as far as there (twice daily from Mires). There is a broad gravel track from Pigadakia down to Kali Limenes (7.5 miles). The presence of machinery for road construction indicates that this will soon be asphalted.

Kali Limenes

Arrival at "Fair Havens" is heralded by a brown sand and shingle beach of about 0.5 miles in length. Whether St. Paul would land here today is questionable. There are derelict huts made of wood and corrugated cardboard, and drinks can be bought in one of them.

Even in the high season there is not much going on; the four large oil tanks on a small island off the coast here are probably to blame for this. They belong to the Motor-Oil Company, and are used to store the crude oil which the tankers bring over from nearby Africa (mostly from Libya). The oil is then transhipped into Greek tankers, which go up to Piraeus. There is a stranded tanker on the reef off the beach.

After passing a magnificent building with a luxurious garden, which rumour has it belongs to an oil magnate, you proceed in an easterly direction to a tiny harbour, which is directly opposite the island with the oil tanks. Several huts where the oil workers live and two simple tavernas are all that is to be found here. It is an extremely odd, original place, far from the tourist track, and only very occasionally do the rented cars find their way down here.

• ACCOMMODATION: There is a tolerable **hotel** with a taverna near the crossroads where the road from Mires and the road to Lentas (also passable) come together. It is mostly used by travellers concerned with the oil business. Price c. £10 for a DR.

• BATHING: Apart from the long beach, there is a tiny sandy bay to the right of the harbour after a climb over a couple of rock ledges.

• MOVING ON: The track to Lentas is passable, as is the track via the Monastery of Odigitrias to Sivas, where the road is once more made up.

From Mires to Matala

At a point roughly midway between Mires and Timbaki, the two largest villages in the Messara Plain, the road to Matala branches off in a southerly direction from the main axis of communication that crosses the Plain. Two important Minoan sites, *Phaistos* and neighbouring *Agia Triada*, are situated on the nearby hill which can be reached via several winding curves of the road. On top of the hill you will be greeted by the quivering sound of the flutes of souvenir sellers.

Before this, however, it is worthwhile making a visit to the Monastery of Kaliviani.

MONASTERY OF KALIVIANI

This is a little town of its own. The extensive complex lies on the road from Mires to Timbaki, a little to the east of the turn-off to Phaistos and Matala. Kaliviani is one of the few remaining monasteries on Crete that is still completely intact. It functions today as an orphan's home, boarding school for girls, home for the elderly and sanatorium, and also contains a large **school of handicrafts** with numerous weaving looms and sewing machines. Some particularly fine pieces of work (woven and embroidered) are on show in a separate room and can be bought. The rich variety of plants is noticeable all over the complex; there are white oleanders, bougainvilleas, dwarf palms and so on. The remains of old frescoes can be seen in the chapel behind the richly decorated main church, and at the entrance to the monastery there is even a deer pen. You can have a rest in the kafenion in front of the entrance.

Phaistos: not a "Disneyland", but a scientifically conducted excavation

Phaistos

The second largest Minoan palace after the Palace of Knossos. Wonderful position on a hill in the Messara Plain. No less fantastic is the panoramic view over the broad plain and the steeply rising slopes of the Ida Range.

The Palace of Phaistos was built around 1900 BC but destroyed by an earthquake as early as 1700. After sporadic attempts at rebuilding failed during the 17th century, a new building was started around 1600 (Neopalatial period), which was intended to be even more lavish than the old palace. However, as in the case of the other Minoan palaces, it was destroyed during the puzzling catastrophe that struck around 1450 BC, before building could be completed.

From 1900 onwards, the *Italian School of Archaeology* carried out the excavation of the palace under the direction of Professor Federico Halbherr.

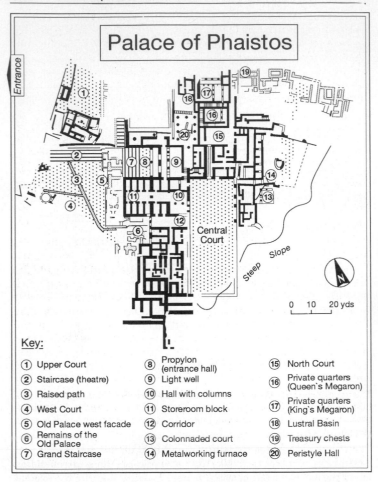

Palace of Phaistos

Key:

1. Upper Court
2. Staircase (theatre)
3. Raised path
4. West Court
5. Old Palace west facade
6. Remains of the Old Palace
7. Grand Staircase
8. Propylon (entrance hall)
9. Light well
10. Hall with columns
11. Storeroom block
12. Corridor
13. Colonnaded court
14. Metalworking furnace
15. North Court
16. Private quarters (Queen's Megaron)
17. Private quarters (King's Megaron)
18. Lustral Basin
19. Treasury chests
20. Peristyle Hall

In view of the fact that it was easier to uncover and conserve the sites here than at Knossos, the excavators were content to undertake what was, by contrast, a minimum of restoration. The present-day tourist pavilion on a hillock a little above the palace served as a headquarters for the archaeologists. During the First World War it was used as a field hospital and in the Second World War it was a command centre for the German army.

The palace is built on the usual plan of the Minoan palaces: a large west court, from which the palace is entered, and a paved central court-yard inside, with buildings grouped around it. The most important rooms are in the north wing. As hardly any articles of value and no frescoes have been found in the building of the Neopalatial period, it has recently been suggested that the Minoan rulers used the nearby Palace of *Agia Triada* as a residence instead (see there also).

The excavations in the area of the Palace of Phaistos have not yet been completed. The extensive Minoan settlement reaches down as far as the little hamlet of *Agios Ioannis* at the southern foot of the hill.

• CONNECTIONS: Phaistos is the junction from where all the **buses** go to Agia Galini, Matala and Iraklion. You must change buses here when going from Agia Galini to Matala and vice versa. Connections are very frequent. A few taxi drivers are always on the look out for customers and also give the occasional piece of false information.

• OPENING TIMES: daily 8.00 a.m.-7.00 p.m. **Admission** c. £2, students and schoolchildren £1. The **Pavilion** above the pay kiosk functions as a cafeteria, and more recently as a self-service restaurant, and offers guides to Phaistos and souvenirs. The little hotel has been closed.

A tour of the site: Access is via a stairway from the *upper court (1)*, which was once perhaps the market place, down to the large *west court (4)* which is situated on two different levels. The lower part of the west court is crossed by a paved *raised path (3)* and belongs to the older palace complex of 1900 BC. During the rebuilding operations the palace facade was relocated further to the east and the court was reconstructed and enlarged three feet above its former level. The *west facade of the old palace (5)* constitute the western border of the area thus newly-created. In the northern part of the court there are 8 wide steps, which finish at a vertical wall *(2)*. This structure may have served as a *theatre*: spectators would have been able to follow a ritual procession in the west court in comfort from here. There are numerous rooms belonging to the old palace preserved in the *southeast corner* of the west court *(6)*. A branch off the way leads into the interior of the palace here; in 1988 this whole sector of the palace was closed because of excavation.

There is a wide flight of stairs with flat steps in the present west facade *(7)*. This is the *main entrance* to the later palace; it is supported above the steps by a massive column, the base of which is still preserved. The rooms behind may have constituted the official throneroom area of the palace; this might be indicated by the fine entrance way (8). The last of the three adjacent halls, which was separated from the previous one by three columns, could have been a large *light well (9)*.

We now proceed down via a little stairway to the corridor of the *Storerooms (11)*. There is a massive pillar in the middle of the passage, and chambers run off to the left and right where large clay pithoi stood and indeed can still be seen in some places. The last room on the right is roofed over; the rooms probably all looked like this. At the eastern end of the corridor there is a magnificent *hall* with a paved floor and alabaster panelling around the base of the walls. This was probably a cult room (10). Directly to the south and adjoining it there is a wide *corridor*, which connects the west court to the central court *(12)*.

The **central court** was paved with limestone slabs. There were long halls on the long sides, from which the games or cult ceremonies in the court could be watched. Our attention is attracted by a strange rostrum with two steps in the north west corner. One original interpretation holds this to be a construction used during bull-leaping. The bull stands on the lower step, and the brave acrobat on the upper, ready to grasp the bull by the horns at the right moment and leap up onto his back.

There is hardly anything left of the **east wing**; most of it has fallen down the steep slope. It is thought that the little *peristyle hall* was the appartment of the king's heir. Next to it is a court with a colonnade on two sides *(13)*. There is also a light well and basin for ritual cleansing. A wonderful view along the whole of the Messara Plain can be had from the steep slope with its shady Aleppo pines. Henry Miller thought it the Garden of Eden from up here. Further into the east wing there is a large court with a *smelting oven or furnace* for metal in the middle *(14)*.

The royal apartments are situated in the **north wing**. The importance of this wing is recognised from the facade facing onto the central court; it is lavishly decorated with half columns and watchposts.

Going along the corridor we come first of all to the large *inner court* of the north wing *(15)*, through which there is access via a further corridor to the so-called "Private Apartments" At first, on the left, there is the *"Queen's Megaron"* (16); a magnificent hall with alabaster panelling, bench and paved floor, a hall of columns and a light well in the middle. Behind them are the neighbouring *King's apartments (17)*. The centre of these is the large hall with many doors, which is paved with alabaster slabs. All around it are several smaller halls and again a light well. To the west and adjoining the hall there is a basin for ritual cleansing, probably *"the King's bath"* *(18)*.

The official rooms of the palace were situated above the ruler's private apartments. These included another hall with many doors and a square *Peristyle Hall (20)*, the latter bordered on all four sides by a colonnade.

To the north east of this section are the *treasury chest* of the palace *(19)*. The famous Phaistos Disc was found in the fourth of these (counting from the stairs). It can be seen today in the Archaeological Museum in Iraklion.

A 3,500 year old water conduit

Agia Triada

This Minoan palace lies well-hidden between bushy Aleppo pines only 2 miles away from Phaistos on the western slope of the same hill. It is often still described as a *Villa* **in the older literature.**

Agia Triada was only built around 1550 BC, a considerable time after the first palace of Phaistos. Because of intensive trade contacts with North Africa it soon attracted a number of craftsmen and business people, who settled down in the neighbourhood. The houses and shops comprise the only known example of a *Minoan commercial town*.

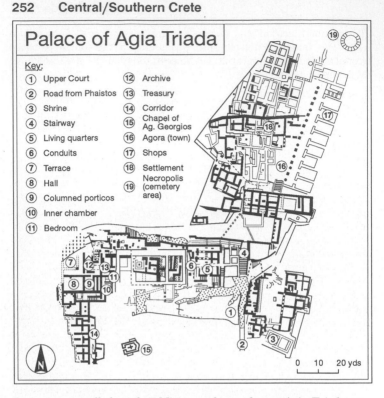

Palace of Agia Triada

Key:
1. Upper Court
2. Road from Phaistos
3. Shrine
4. Stairway
5. Living quarters
6. Conduits
7. Terrace
8. Hall
9. Columned porticos
10. Inner chamber
11. Bedroom
12. Archive
13. Treasury
14. Corridor
15. Chapel of Ag. Georgios
16. Agora (town)
17. Shops
18. Settlement
19. Necropolis (cemetery area)

0   10   20 yds

In contrast to all the other Minoan palaces, that at Agia Triada consists of two wings, which are built at right angles to each other (in an L-shape). The settlement and commercial area adjoin it to the north.

Suggestions that Agia Triada was a country estate or a summer villa for the ruler of Phaistos have today been largely discounted. As more valuable treasures, more comprehensive archive material and finer frescoes have been found here than at Phaistos, Agia Triada may have been the actual residence in the Neopalatial period, while the Palace of Phaistos remained unfinished and functioned more as a religious and cult centre. In particular, very fine vases of steatite (chlorite) have been found in the rooms at Agia Triada. These can be seen in the Archaeological Museum at Iraklion, in Gallery VII.

Getting there from Phaistos: The narrow motor road to Agia Triada turns off to the right directly after the little church, 50 yards along the road to Matala from the car park at Phaistos. Rather a lengthy way on foot, but it is a lovely walk around the southern flank of the hill. During the second part of the way there, and from the small car park above the site, there is a wonderful view across the plain around Timbaki, the majestically soaring Ida Mountains, and the sea.

• OPENING TIMES: Mon-Sat 9.00 a.m.-3.00 p.m. Sun 10.00 a.m.-2.30 p.m. **Admission**: just under £1, schoolchildren/students half price.

Tour of the site: Visitors descend by a few steps from the custodian's kiosk into the large paved *upper court (1)*, which is entered by a similarly paved *road* that ran from Phaistos *(2)*. There are the foundations of a Late Minoan *shrine (3)* to the east of the beginning of this road. In the north-east corner of the court a well-preserved *stairway (4)* leads to the *agora* and the residential quarter in the north wing of the complex. Adjacent to the stairway and to the west of it there are *living quarters* of which several rooms have many doors *(5)*. These living quarters are roofed over today. The *Minoan conduits (6)*, which brought rainwater from the south court down to the wells below it, are in a fine state of preservation here. The best way to go round this section is via the lower (north) side, descending by the stairs *(4)* and turning left where a paved way leads right along the front in a westerly direction. The private apartments are at the western end, and are bordered by a large *terrace (7)* in the direction of the slope. The complex, which was built facing the north-west, was open here to the frequent winds from that direction; winds which had a much-desired cooling effect. Passing through a large *hall (8)* and two adjacent *columned porticos (9)* leading to a light well, the visitor comes to an *inner chamber*, roofed over today, in which the wall panelling and the bench running around the walls are superbly preserved *(10)*. The little room immediately adjacent to this in the north has been identified as a *bedroom*, because a wooden couch is supposed to have stood on the platform there *(11)*. In the so-called *workroom and archive*, the room situated to the north-west *(12)*, numerous sealstones and tablets bearing Linear A script have been found. In the next room to the east, the narrow *treasury (13)*, there were 19 solid bronze bars, which can now be seen in the Archaeological Museum in Iraklion (Gallery VII, showcase 99). To the south of the section of private apartments there are *living* and *storage rooms* and a long *corridor (14)*. The famous *Chieftain Cup* was found in this sector (Gallery VII, case 95). On a small hillock here there is the *Chapel of Agios Georgios (15)* which contains a number of beautiful old frescoes. It is locked, but the custodian may provide the key.

The north wing of Agia Triada contains houses and the market area, the so-called *agora (16)*, dating from the Late or Subminoan periods. This is recognised as the oldest known agora in Greece! The long row of alternating pillars and columns, which supported a stoa-like hall, is of particular note here. Beneath it (but today beside it) were eight identical rooms next to each other, which were certainly *shops (17)*. Further down from these there are the remains of the *settlement (18)*. Outside the site (the gate is closed) there is the *necropolis (19)*. The famous sarcophagus from Agia Triada, which is on the upper floor of the Archaeological Museum in Iraklion, was found here.

From Phaistos to Matala

Passing the small village of Agios Ioannis with the tiny Chapel of Agios Pavlos, the asphalt road drops down through the undulating foothills of the coastal mountains towards Matala.

Kalamaki

A tiny hamlet on the beach, with the houses directly built on the soft white sand dunes, some of them half blown away. The west wind blows sand into every nook and cranny, and the nearest asphalt is a long way away.

Until a few years ago the village was far off the usual tourist tracks. However, intensive building has recently taken place, and new, two-storeyed buildings contrast with dusty alleyways and low huts of hollow brick. There are bars, tavernas and discos, contacts are easily made and the beach is as beautiful as it ever was. The atrocious, bumpy approach road guarantees that the great wave of tourism will not reach Kalamaki so quickly.

• GETTING THERE: When approaching from Phaistos, take the dirt track to **Kamilari** shortly before reaching Pitsidia (signposted). This wide, jolting path leads on to Kalamaki.

• ACCOMMODATION: **Philharmonie**, the leader in the market, is a spanking new house at the entrance to the village. Also recommended is the **Ilios** Guest House, just before the main square.

There are simple, cheap rooms to be had in several houses, eg on the main square next to the shop (iron bedframes). At **Kostas** the rooms cost even less than £3.

— ★ —

• FOOD/CLUBS: The best (and most crowded) is the large taverna by the name of **Vangelis/Philharmonie**, a few yards from the square, above the beach. You can also sit directly on the beach at **Scorpios** next door. There are several other possibilities at the southern end of the village, for example the handful of tables in the comfortable **Kostas Bar**, in a narrow passage between houses. The **Zig-Zag** dancing bar is a little further on.

▶ Bathing/Walking: There are wonderful opportunities all along the beach; small tamarisks have been planted everywhere to stop the huge sand-drifts. Dunes, eroding soil formations and ash-grey rocks give the landscape an unrealistic appearance.

Kalamaki Beach is separated from its northern neighbour, the beach at Kokkinos Pirgos (also miles long - see below, page 263), by a long sandstone cliff of not very great height. Adjoining it in a southerly direction is Komo Beach (see Pitsidia).

Pitsidia

Situated in a level hollow in the hill to the left of the road. A refreshing contrast to the bustle of Matala.

A farming village which still retains its original character in many ways, with narrow alleys, shady gardens and small courtyards, in which chickens run freely. The disproportionally large television aerials are almost obligatory!

Tourism has, of course, spilled over from Matala in this direction - "rent rooms" signs are springing up out of the earth, and Pitsidia is no longer a well-kept secret. In spite of this, it is still to be recommended, if you do not wish to join in the bustle of Matala all the time but still want to be nearby.

The beach at Pitsidia, called *Komo Beach*, is about half an hour's walk from the village. You will find people of your own kind, relaxation, and peace and quiet in this corner of the island, while the bodies roast side by side in the sun in the small sandy bay at Matala, only a few miles away.

• CONNECTIONS: **Buses** to and from Matala stop on the main through road, below Pitsidia. The village centre is a few paces on, and the way to the beach is on the other side (see below).

Accommodation

There is a whole mass of private rooms on offer and a short stroll through the village will help to make your choice. They are all very simple, but here you will be able to partake of the village atmosphere.

• **Georgia Emm. Kiradakis**: a low, whitewashed house on the way from the bus stop to the centre. With terrace and flowers.

• **Petros**: situated on the large village square, and probably the best address. Two houses connected to each other by steps and with small shady terraces in front of the rooms. Cost around £9 for a DR.

• **Manolis**: opposite Petros, new rooms in a house to which a storey has been added.

• **Nikos Fasulakis**: friendly, up an alley on the main square.

• **Panorama**: outside the village, at the entrance to it in the direction of Matala and 150 yards off the road. Friendly Manolis Daskalakis and his wife run this relatively new house and the taverna. Advantage: quiet position and a beautiful view down over the gulf. Manolis is very musical and often gets out his mandoline. Price c. £9 for a DR with bathroom.

• Those who are not particularly keen on village life can also find rooms at the tavernas down on the main through road, eg in the **Miranta** Guest House (taverna at the bus stop) or at the new **Agapi** private rooms.

• FOOD: The best food is to be found at **Nikos** on the main through road, and there is also wine from the barrel here. There are two coffee bars (one of them already has video!) on the main square.

▶ **Komo Beach:** From where the bus stops, there is a dusty field track which leads through gentle hills down to the beach. An easy drive by car, and takes about half an hour on foot. The tracks ends a couple of hundred yards above the beach; the descent is on foot over a wide area of sand dunes, overgrown with thorn bushs.

Below, there are several miles of the finest sandy beach, and tamarisk trees afford good shade there. To the right there is a superb panorama of the Ida massif behind Agia Galini! In the low season, at least, you can establish yourself here; all is at peace, and there is great solitude.

Matala

Sandstone cliffs and cave dwellings; the finest sunsets; Europa and the Bull

A singular position at the exit to a long valley, which opens to the west between two huge sandstone bluffs.

Above the long and softly-drawn out curve of a beach cove, the little white houses of Old Matala are pressed into the gap between two cliffs which descend to the sea diagonally in layers. The famous *cave dwellings* of the Neolithic period make the northern wall seem almost like a gigantic termites' nest.

Over the last two decades, Matala has had an almost breathtaking career where tourism is concerned. It was the Hippies who discovered the "living caves" of Matala in the sixties. They lived here during the summer months for many years, far from civilisation and near to Nature, marvelled at by the handful of local people, but tolerated. Then came the rucksack tourists; Matala's reputation as a place "where the scene was" on Crete went right round Europe; people slept in the caves or right on the beach. The first clever taverna proprietors scented business. The next point on the agenda was clear; the authorities wasted no more time observing the brisk goings on in the caves, but declared these millenia-old holes in the rocks an ancient monument - sleeping in the caves was forbidden!

Of course the beauty of the bay did not remain a secret. For several years now, Matala has been on the programme of absolutely every travel company. Every day, busloads of tourists from the large beach hotels on the north coast roll up by the dozen. They crowd the beach and the dozen or so tavernas which border it until the early afternoon. But the legend of Matala attracts more and more overnight guests. New hotels and guest houses are constantly being opened in the narrow valley, and the simple camping site directly on the beach is always overcrowded. Every night the numerous disco-bars bombard the whole bay with their "Kleine Nachtmusik". The level of prices is noticeably higher here than in other places where tourism is less developed.

Matala offers something for everyone with its grandiose, rocky landscape; but it is not for those who seek solitude. This is only experienced by the 15 "real" inhabitants of Matala in winter. The flood of tourists has brought the simple fishermen and farmers of the bay an income which they could not have dreamed of earlier, but the high price of this is the total "marketing" of their village. This means standing in the kitchen, serving, washing up and serving again for Evangelia, Maria and all the others, whatever their names may be. Yet only a minority of tavernas belong to local people today, and the owners are people from Iraklion and as far away as Athens.

In spite of the bustle, Matala is, as it always was, an experience, and those who have the chance to spend a few days here should certainly do so, ideally in the low season. At that time, when the sun sinks far out to sea in the evenings and you can have the previously crowded beach all to yourself, the bay is perhaps at its most beautiful.

Like the holes in Swiss cheese - the cave dwellings at Matala

History

This begins in ancient times, wrapped up in mythology. The lusty *Zeus* kidnaps the king's daughter *Europa* from Asia Minor and goes ashore with her at the bay of Matala. They soon move on, however, to Gortys in the Messara Plain; there, King Minos, ancestor of the Minoans, is conceived under a plane tree which remains evergreen to this day.

The caves are dug into the soft sandstone during the *New Stone Age*. These neolithic inhabitants create a perfect style of living with stone beds, fires and passages through to other caves.

The bay of Matala is probably the harbour of Phaistos in *Minoan times. Menelaos* is stranded here on his return from the Trojan wars; the united cities of Greece had begun the decade-long struggle against Troy because of the abduction of his beautiful wife Helen.

The *Romans* use Matala as a harbour for their capital Gortys in the Messara Plain. The first *Christians* bury their dead in the caves in the rock face (rock-hewn sarcophagi have been found).

The greatly feared Saracen *Abu Hafs Omar* lands with his troops in the bay in 824 AD. He orders his ships burned behind him and his troops, thus indicating that there is no going back, and conquers the island.

- CONNECTIONS: buses from Iraklion - Matala 7 x daily (via Mires, Phaistos). Change at Phaistos for Agia Galini, around 6 x daily.

- CAR/MOTORBIKE/MOPED RENTALS: several companies on the large main square, where the buses stop.

- CHANGING MONEY: There is a **Post Office kiosk** at the beginning of the "road with a bazaar", and money can also be changed at the travel agency **Matala Travel**, on the corner of the "road with a bazaar" and the main square. Reasonable exchange rate.

- POST OFFICE: There is only a post office kiosk, open Mon-Sat 8.00 a.m.-7.00 p.m. Sun 9.00 a.m.-5.00 p.m.

- TRAVEL AGENCY: **Matala Travel**. Money changed here, tickets for ANEK boats, organised excursions, cars for hire. **Festos Travel** offers a similar range of services.

- TELEPHONE: There is no OTE telephone in the village. International calls can be made from the **Kiosk** in the "road with the bazaar". They are not cheap.

- LAUNDRY: situated on the approach road, opposite the entrance to the camping site.

- NEWSPAPERS/MAGAZINES/BOOKS: There is an international selection in the shop next to the Hotel Zafiria, a little back from the road.

Accommodation

Hotels and guest houses are constantly springing up, and there is also the camping site. You should not be sensitive to noise, however, as disco-bars and an all-night moped rally echo round the valley.

ON THE APPROACH ROAD

Hotels and guest houses extend into the hinterland over a distance of several hundred yards.

• **Matala Bay**: C class, one of the best establishments in the place, immaculate, large car park and much greenery, even small palm trees. Quite a solidly built entrance lobby with a goldfish pond. Passages have linoleum flooring, rather austere, but the rooms are attractive, with rough, whitewashed plastered walls, nice curtains, dressing table and mirror. There is a pool behind the hotel. Price c. £14 for a DR with a bathroom. Address: on the approach road to Matala, a few hundred yards from the beach. One of the first buildings on the right hand side when you reach the village. Tel. 0892/42300.

• **Bamboo Sand**: C class, furnished in an original way, with walls made of synthetic material and ancient Greek columns which give an impression of ancient glory. The dining terrace is completely roofed over with reeds, to keep out the heat. The rooms vary, with the best at the back of the hotel where the beach is immediately behind a green curtain of reeds. DR with shower c. £10-12. Address: on the approach road (noisy!), but right at the beginning of the actual centre of Matala. 100 yards to the beach. Tel. 0892/42370.

• **Zafiria**: D class, next to the Bamboo Sand, light and airy and friendly. Central position (noisy!), and only a few yards from the beach. It has its own restaurant, bar, terrace and large balconies. DR with private bathroom c. £12, three-bedded room £14.00. Tel. 0892/42366.

• **Romantica**: E class, attractively decorated, with a large square in front of it where you can sit under trailing vines. Above it is a roomy terrace, with a lot of plants. Rooms have shower/toilet. Cost around £9 for a DR. On the right hand side of the approach road, near the Matala Bay Hotel. Tel. 0892/42357.
Of a comparable standard is the **Chez Xenophon** next door, D class.
Tel. 0892/42358.

• There are more rooms to be had, eg in the **Acropol** Guest House, and at **Rena** (situated opposite the Matala Bay Hotel and established 1987).

ON THE ROAD OPPOSITE THE ZAFIRIA HOTEL

About eight to ten new guest houses have been built in the street which branches off the main road opposite the Hotel Zafiria (footpath to Red Beach). They are all quite clean and reasonable in price. The further away, the quieter.

• **Nikos**: the third house on the right. Nikos Kephalakis speaks good English. There is a comfortable inner courtyard and bar. A three-bedded room costs £12, DR with bath £10, without bath £8. Tel. 0892/42375.

• CAMPING MATALA: barren, unimproved site on the sand dunes at the back of the beach. Thick tamarisks provide good shade but are very unevenly distributed over the site; shady spots are quickly occupied. Primitive sanitation, no restaurant. But it costs only £1 per person, tent and car, and slightly less for motor bikes. Open 01.04.-31.10. Tel. 0892/42340.

• READER'S TIP: "We stayed in the **Silvia** Guest House in the street opposite the Hotel Zafiria. This is the last house on the left hand side, away from the the bustle. DR with bath costs just under £8. It was the best room we had on our whole trip to Crete."

Food

Restaurants are naturally 100 % geared to tourists. All the tavernas
are crowded into an area below the little "bazaar passage" on the
beach. Access down there is via a few steps.

● **Pizza Bar**: Only pizzas and spaghetti are served here. Those who are looking for them have come to just the right place here. Run by an elderly couple.

● **Plaka**: a large taverna on the southern tip of the bay, specialising in delicious fish dishes. A little more expensive, but in spite of this there is hardly ever a vacant seat. Come early.

● There is a simple **souvlaki place** in the little "bazaar passage" with the fruit and souvenir shops.

Bars/Clubs

There is a surprising amount of entertainment and diversions for
such a small place as Matala. It is completely westernised, however;
in the evenings, loud pop music thunders from all the bars and
kafenia and chic young Cretans arrive with the clatter of mopeds for
their disco-dancing.

● **Two Brothers of Matala**: on the small square, right at the beginning of Matala. Muesli, orange juice and yoghurt in the mornings here, and in the evening people meet here for a beer before the buses leave for the disco. Unfortunately over-priced and the service is often unfriendly.

● **Café-Bar Valentina**: opposite the "Two Brothers". You can sit comfortably in a room with warm lighting and décor in light coloured wood on the first floor here.

● **Café-Bar Matala**: in the "bazaar passage". Run by a dear old grandmother, who moves around with astounding agility when serving her customers. Rather a pleasant place for breakfast, but has a limited menu.

● **The Rock Bar**: situated a little before the Plaka Restaurant at the south end of the bay, with a relaxed atmosphere and a lot of music. There are other pubs in this corner, some of them imaginatively furnished, eg **Pub George**, the **Marinero Pub** or the **Odyssey Bar**, right out in front on the rocks, and worthy of mention because of their superb position at the southern tip of the bay, where the rocks push out into the sea.

● **Cactus Bar**: on the main square. At an advanced hour this is a sight with its empty beer bottles, and there is deafeningly loud music too.

● DISCOTHEQUES: **Zorbas** is situated at the end of the valley, quite a distance back along the road. Large disco, with plenty of room to move or to sit around. Moderate prices. From 9.30 p.m. onwards a bus leaves every 15 minutes from the main square for the disco.

The **Malibu** disco is more convenient - it is directly on the beach.

Sightseeing

Matala consists of only a handful of houses grouped around two
squares. They are connected by the colourful little *bazaar passage*,
where people can stroll amongst the juicy fruit and tawdry souvenirs.
As mentioned above, the tavernas are all on the beach, which can be
reached via a few steps from the shopping street.

Due to the fact that the bay of Matala opens exactly in a westerly direction, the highlight of every day is the *sunset* with its wonderful long-lasting red hues, which takes place directly out to sea.

Cave dwellings: The actual sightseeing attraction of Matala. To this day, it is not possible to give an exact assessment of their age, but they are probably over 8,000 years old!

The huge sandstone bluff resembles a Swiss cheese with its many holes; indeed the soft rock must have offered the people of the Stone Age an almost irresistible invitation to gouge out caves. They are situated only a little way up from the beach and you can spend a while climbing over them. Some of them comprise almost comfortable 2/3 room apartments, of course without a bath, but there are elegant rounded archways, little niches in the rock for provisions and comfortable stone couches with headrests. The many *cave paintings* seem to be of a later date, probably painted by inhabitants there during this century. It must have been very pleasant to sit up here and watch the beach; we even found a kind of draughts game scratched into the rock there. The countless thousands of visitors today only scratch their names into the walls.

Unfortunately the caves were often used for another unmistakable purpose, and a certain smell pervades the air.

Bathing

You can bathe very well in the softly rounded sandy bay of Matala, but it is very crowded during the season. There are paddle boats, canoes and surf boards for hire.

On the right hand side at the end of the rocks there is a diving platform several feet high, whence you can dive into the sea. The very daring swim out to the farthest tip, where the ridge disappears under the sea, and climb up the layers of rock formations to a height of at least 100 feet. This "sport" can only really be recommended for those who have absolutely no fear of heights and are sure of foot.

Komo Beach: This is a long beach near Pitsidia, not much visited. Go along the road by bus or on foot and turn off towards the beach at Pitsidia (about one hour's walk from Matala). For details see under Pitsidia.

Kokkino or Red Beach: This beautiful beach is situated in the next bay to the south of Matala. It can be reached across the rocks behind the houses of Old Matala (turn in by the Hotel Zafiria). Solitude soon takes over; there are only little goat tracks into this rocky wilderness. By climbing up a path stamped out between rocks that have been hollowed out and washed away by erosion, a place can be reached from where there is a fine view over to Matala, its beach, and the cliff with the cave dwellings. This rocky plateau is covered with sage and ore-gano, and far below on the other side you can see the narrow Kokkino Beach (Red Beach) with its light brown to reddish shimmering sand. The view over the rocky coast to the south is grandiose; jagged chalk plateaus seem to slide everywhere into the sea.

From Phaistos to Agia Galini

A sea of hothouses extends around Timbaki. Tens of thousands of melons and tomatoes ripen under the dirty yellow plastic sheets. The intensive agricultural exploitation of this part of the Messara Plain makes it less attractive for tourists, who mostly drive straight through it.

Timbaki

A transit town of the larger, dustier variety, with a lot of workshops and shops. The sun beats mercilessly down on the broad main street. Timbaki is a typical business and agricultural centre, and the second most important town in the Messara Plain after Mires.

The attractive main square to the south of the main through road is recommended for a short rest. You can sit drinking coffee or playing tavli in one of several kafenia here, under sturdy eucalyptus trees.

There is a large *road market* in Timbaki every Friday, rather similar to that in Mires on Saturdays.

• CONNECTIONS: Buses from Ag. Galini to Iraklion, Ag. Galini to Phaistos and Ag. Galini to Matala stop on the main through road.

• CHANGING MONEY: There are several banks on the main road.

• POST OFFICE: situated on El. Venizelou Street, on the opposite side of the square and up the alleyway on the other side of the main road.

• TELEPHONE: The OTE office is in the road which runs parallel to the north of the main through road, on a level with the bank "Agrotiki Trapeza tis Hellados" (ATE). Open Mon-Fri 7.30 a.m.-9.00 p.m.

• ACCOMMODATION: only when really necessary, and then probably best at the Hotel **San Giorgio**, C class. Agreeable lounge on ground floor, rooms with balconies. Costs around £10 for a DR. Situated on Ag. Georgios Street, to the south of and a little back from the Main Street. Tel. 0892/51613.

It is only 1.25 miles from Timbaki to the beach at

Kokkinos Pyrgos

This little village is a mixture of tattered plastic hothouses, half-fin-ished cement frameworks and faceless new buildings, with hotels and tavernas scattered amongst them. The advantage: miles of grey beach. You will have the beach all to yourself in the low season.

• CONNECTIONS: Some of the buses from Ag. Galini to Iraklion and Phaistos/Matala make the short detour to Kokkinos Pirgos.

Accommodation

In spite of the modest demand there is a surprisingly large number of rooms to rent, and new hotels are constantly being built.

• **Brothers Hotel**: C class. A relatively new building with a garden and a restaurant, and a fine view of the sea. Run by two brothers, rooms have lino floors and tolerable beds, with tiled bathrooms. Price around £10.00 for a DR with breakfast. Near the harbour mole, a little back from the road. Tel. 0892/51462.

• **El Greco**: E class, and surprisingly attractive for hotels of this category and price. Recently renovated, rooms have good wooden furniture, private bath/toilet. Costs c. £10. Address: on the road to Timbaki, near to the end of the village,

but still in the immediate vicinity of the beach. Tel. 0892/51182.

• **Galini**: A class apartments. We recommend this attractive, carefully planned house, with a quiet situation and somewhat back from the road. Mr E. Kamnakis spent 16 years in Germany, hence the many regular German guests here. The eight rooms are all equipped with a kitchen niche, bath and balcony. Breakfast on request. DR costs £10, a three-bedded room costs £13. Tel. 0892/51127.

— ★ —

• READER'S TIP: "We came upon a hotel at Kokkinos Pyrgos which we liked very much. It is called **Mary Helen** and is a little outside the village. The hotel is only one year old, and has a lift, good (new) furniture and swimming pool, which was half-finished in 1987. A short path leads from the hotel to a gravel and shingle beach at the exit from a ravine."

Author's note: The Hotel Mary Helen is situated to the north of Kokkinos Pyrgos in a quiet, isolated position almost direct-

ly on the water's edge. This modern hotel is run by a friendly family from Timbaki. There are 60 rooms, all furnished with furniture of light-coloured wood, some with a superb view of the sea. The hotel's own taverna also offers a fine view. The approach road, bumpy and about 500 yards long, is signposted from the main through road north of the village. DR with bath and breakfast just under £14. Tel. 0892/51268.

— ★ —

• FOOD: Because of the proximity of the tourist centre Ag. Galini, there are several tavernas in Kokkinos Pyrgos, which specialise in fish dishes, eg **Ta Delfinia**. During the season there are even boisterous "Cretan Nights" with lyra and laouto to

which, particularly at weekends, holidaymakers are transported from Ag. Galini.

A very pleasant place to sit is under the knotted tamarisks in the **Taverna** on the little harbour mole.

▶ **Bathing:** The grey sand and shingle beach extends for several miles along the whole bay to *Kalamaki* in the south. At the beginning it is narrow and dirty in places, then becomes noticeably wider. Tamarisks afford good shade in the first part in particular, and the little harbour mole with its fishing boats has a lot of atmosphere. There is a US military airstrip in the hinterland.

The beach becomes very narrow in a northerly direction and is dominated by the low rocky bluffs behind it. You can have a fine walk from here to *Agia Galini*, keeping close to the sea all the way; it will take you about one and a quarter hours. For further information see under Ag. Galini.

Messara Plain/Hinterland

Probably the finest way to explore the mountainous hinterland of the Messara Plain is by going along the road through Platanos, Kamares and Zaros, along the foothills of the Ida Massif.

There are simple mountain villages and a handful of monasteries here, far away from the bustle on the coast; the loneliness of the mountains soon descends when you leave the villages behind you. A highlight here is certainly the trout farm at Zaros. Mountain hikers can use the neighbouring hotel as their headquarters. The ascent of Psiloritis from Kamares does, however, require quite a bit of staying power and good training.

• ACCOMMODATION: There is very simple private accommodation in **Kamares**, **Vorizia** and **Zaros**. In the latter village there is also the **Hotel Idi**, probably the best hotel in the Cretan interior (see under Zaros).

Kamares: A simple mountain village, and starting point for the 7-hour ascent to the peak of Psiloritis. This trip requires mountain experience and should never be attempted alone. A total of two days should be allowed for it.

The climb up to the famous *Kamares Cave* is easier. It is situated at a height of 4,986 feet, a good 3 hours above the village of Kamares on the southern flank of *Mavri* (6,477 feet). In Minoan times, the cave served as a cult centre for the people of the Messara Plain. Research has gone on there since 1894, and unusual, very thin pottery vessels of the Minoan period have been found in front of the cave entrance. These vessels are characterised by a black background with very varied patterns painted on them in white and red. They contained seeds and wild fruits that had been placed there as offerings, and were probably made in the palace workshops at Phaistos and Agia Triada. This pottery form has been named the *Kamares style*, after the place where they were found (Gallery II of the Archaeological Museum in Iraklion).

Vorizia: 2.25 miles to the east of Kamares. The village was almost completely destroyed by German troops in the last world war. At the western end of the village a road branches off to the former *Monastery of Valsomonero* 2.25 miles to the south east of the village on the other side of a small ravine. The small monastery church with its triple nave is the only part remaining, and can easily be seen from the road to Zaros. A path, also clearly visible, goes over to it through the little ravine from below the Monastery of Vrondisi. The interior of the monastery church with its triple naves is competely covered by frescoes which, next to those at Panagia Kera in Kritsa, are amongst the finest in the Byzantine-Cretan style. Even the famous El Greco is supposed to have gained inspiration here. Unfortunately the monastery is always closed, so that the way over there is hardly worth it.

The Monastery of Vrondisi: This lies above the road 2.25 miles to the east of Vorizia. A steep roadway around 800 yards long leads up to it. In front of the monastery, which is laid out simply in the form of a square, there are two massive plane trees, and on the left water bubbles out of the mouths of three bearded heads from a *Venetian fountain.* Adam and Eve, unfortunately headless, can be recognised above them. The *monastery church* in the courtyard has two naves of differing heights. One of the two Papades (priests) at the monastery will be pleased to open up the church for you. The lowest of the two naves can be illuminated and is decorated with wonderful frescoes in deep dark red, turquoise and white shades, which to all appearances have recently been restored. There are scenes from the life of Jesus, and the Last Supper is depicted in the apse (donations are used to extend the electricity supply here).

There is a splendid view from the courtyard over the broad cypress-clad and mountainous landscape of southern Crete.

Nunnery of Agios Nikolaos: At about 500 yards from the western entrance to the village of Zaros, a roadway leads up c. 1.25 miles to the small, immaculate nunnery. There are three nuns here, supported by four men who do the heavy work. Visitors are given a hearty reception, and have to try the homemade raki, as well as the cheese and milk from the nunnery's 80 goats and 10 sheep. The nuns still make their own candles, and this is a complicated process carried out by hand; you may be shown their workshop. The low church has two naves and a lot of icons, and there are the remains of old frescoes in the back part. Everything is lovingly looked after.

Zaros

The village lies at the foot of a mighty gorge. Those who only keep to the main road will hardly be able to get an idea of the quite unbelievable abundance of water in the region. There are countless springs above Zaros and they transform the landscape into an oasis of chuckling water.

GOING TO CRETE FOR A TROUT DINNER

The overabundance of fresh spring water gave a local farmer the idea of building up a *trout hatchery* in Zaros 6 years ago. He had read about a similar venture in northern Greece in a Greek agricultural newspaper. The state financed the importation of Canadian trout eggs for him, and two years later Petros Gianaki had a passable number of these pleasant-tasting freshwater fish in his ponds. However, the Cretans were sceptical. Why drive deep inland to eat fish, when there are good sea fish to be had everywhere along the coast? The breakthrough came in the form of an article written by a Scottish professor, who talked enthusiastically at home about the trout from Zaros. When as a result flocks of British tourists began to arrive, the local people themselves became curious. Today, Zaros is a well-known secret and a much visited attraction, where people can sample these delicious *pestrofa* (trout), which are not native to the island.

Above the village there are two tavernas with large, well-filled fish ponds, in which the nimble trout cavort in their thousands in constantly-flowing, oxygen-rich water. Right next door is a hotel which is by far the best in the region. The bumpy approach path is c. 400 yards long and signposted from the through road from Zaros.

• CONNECTIONS: There is a daily bus from Mires and there are also other buses from Iraklion.

• ACCOMMODATION: **Idi Hotel**, C class, in a wonderful position in the middle of a lush green park with lawns and a swimming pool. Quite immaculate inside and tastefully furnished, with a large restaurant, terrace, and rooms which are carpeted and have modern furnishings. DR with breakfast costs just under £17.00. It is a good idea to telephone and make a reservation as groups of travellers or hikers sometimes stop here. Tel. 0894/31302.
There are several opportunities to find very simple private accommodation down in the village.

— ★ —

• FOOD: Right next to the hotel there is a large **fish taverna**, with 6 trout ponds and an old mill powered by the water which rushes down from all over the mountain; it functions almost as a museum. A large carafe of spring water is served automatically with every meal. There is another **taverna** offering a similar menu, five minutes' walk above the last one. Up to the present, there have always been fewer tourists here.

• HIKING: The lush surroundings are a pure invitation to hikers. There are several interesting routes hanging on the wall in the hotel, and you can also get further information there. The path into the **Rouvas ravine** above the tavernas is well built-up.

A fishing harbour and tourist centre

Agia Galini

From fishing harbour to fairground; the atmosphere has been preserved; the beach of rather middling quality

The turmoil in the village is overwhelming, especially when you have just had what seems a never-ending journey through Cretan mountain villages and rocky landscapes with not a soul to be seen.

It is almost impossible to take in the number and variety of hotels, restaurants, bars, discotheques etc that have collected here. Even at the entrance to the village, let alone in the centre, one hotel sign after another beckons to you.

And Agia Galini is really a beautiful place, with whitewashed houses crammed into a deep river valley. Down below, everything has long since been built up and in particular, hotels are advancing up the slopes and along the approach road. The harbour square with its house facades piled up on top of one another, is surely one of the most attractive in Crete.

This former fishing village has gone through stages of development similar to those at Matala, but to a greater extreme. Whereas 10-15 years ago it was still a "secret" among the young generation, a meeting place for rucksack tourists and drop-outs, Agia Galini today has been 90% taken over by package tourism. The few passages in the centre are filled to overflowing every evening, the taverna passage is swarming with people and every hotel bed is taken. The fact that the Lord of Commerce and King Mammon reign here has unfortunately wreaked a lot of destruction. Business acumen and exaggerated desire for profits often cover up the traditional cordiality of the people. But in spite of this Agia Galini has atmosphere, perhaps because everything is so near to and on top of everything else here. Hubbub and close proximity can often impart a feeling of security.

It is thanks to the inhabitants that the place does not degenerate into a sterile hotel settlement without charm. The black-clothed matrons sit in front of their houses, seemingly unimpressed by the light summer attire of the mostly young tourists. Something of the original colour of this attractive Mediterranean village can be particularly felt in the area at the back of the village.

Those who come here for bathing should be warned; the so-called "beach" consists exclusively of heavy stones, on which it is hardly possible to lie down in comfort, let alone go into the sea without bathing shoes. Those who are not afraid of a little expedition, however, can find good, isolated places. Agia Galini is also a good point of departure for trips into the rich hinterland. For example, what about a tasty fish meal in the mountain village of Zaros, which has the only trout hatchery in Crete?

• INFORMATION: available at the travel agency **Candia Tours** (see addresses below).

The local police station takes over the function of the **tourist police**, only a few paces from Candia Tours.

CONNECTIONS

• **Bus**: The bus station is at the back of the village. Departure times are listed there, but as they are constantly changing, there is not much point in this. Thus we give only a little general information: you should ask for all other times and routes.

To and from Iraklion about 8 x daily/£2.50, to and from Rethymnon c. 6 x daily/£2, Phaistos c 8 x daily, Matala 6 x, Plakias 4 x (1 x direct, otherwise change in Bale - see page 269), Chora Sfakion 1 x.

Above all, you should check in advance on the the departure times of the last two connections mentioned above. The route to Chora Sfakion is among the most scenic in Crete, but it is seldom travelled because of the difficult terrain.

• **Boats**: There are daily boat excursions from the harbour to the bathing beaches in the area, and to Matala. Information and bookings at the travel agency Candia Tours (see also under Travel Agent).

• **Taxi**: There are three taxis in the village. Tel. 0832/91245.

• **Car/Motorbike/Moped rentals**:
Galini/Rent a Car and Moto Tours are on the square diagonally opposite the Post Office. Soulia cars are in the west road to the harbour, Biggis Bikes are opposite the bus stop, and Horiatis at the upper end of the taverna passage.

• CHANGING MONEY: There is a small branch of the National Bank below the Post Office and round the corner. Money can also be changed at the Post Office.

• POST OFFICE: in the road leading from the bus stop to the harbour (square which has a fountain that does not function).

• TRAVEL AGENT: There is no competitor to **Candia Tours,** the best source of information in the village. Have a look through the lovingly-compiled English-language file there - you will find good tips on hiking and walks, vehicle rentals, excursions etc.

Various excursions to different destinations can be booked here, eg to the Samaria Gorge, Matala, Agios Nikolaos, Plakias, Rethymnon etc. All the excursions cost between £9-10. Tel. 0832/91278.

• SOUVENIRS: Original carvings in olive wood can be bought from a shop in the western road to the harbour. The shop is also the workshop here. Whimsical figures and faces, but also some functional pieces such as bowls etc.

• TELEPHONE: There is a small **OTE office** in the passage parallel and to the west of the approach road, at the back of the village (signposted). Open Mon-Fri 7.30 a.m.-3.00 p.m. There is another telephone at the kiosk and one in a shop at the end of the "food passage".

• LAUNDRY: diagonally opposite the Post Office in a passage. Once washed, the laundry is dried and ironed.

• NEWSPAPERS/MAGAZINES/BOOKS: well-arranged shop with an international selection in the middle of the taverna passage.

Accommodation

With over 30 hotels and countless private rooms, it is difficult to make a choice. However, when almost everything has been taken in the high season you will often have to take what is still available.

The best establishments are situated up on the approach road to the village, with the more basic accommodation in the old centre of the village. Hotels of the B class and upwards are completely absent.

AROUND THE HARBOUR SQUARE

A fine view and the best place to drink in the atmosphere. Can be noisy.

• **Akteon**: E class. If you look back from the harbour it is above and on the right hand side. Prettily overgrown terrace and friendly people. Rooms only tolerably modern, but with shower/toilet. Extremely fine view from the two terraces. Costs around £9 for a DR. Tel. 0832/91208.

• **Acropol**: C class, next door to the Akteon. Similarly fine position with same view, thickly overgrown terrace, shower/toilet on the landing. Cost as at the Akteon. Tel. 0832/91234.

• **Selena**: C class. Every room has its own shower cabin, but some of them do not have sea views. Cost around £10 for a DR with balcony, or even slightly less. Also has terrace. Tel. 0832/91273.

• **Ariston**: opposite Selena. Simple rooms with older furniture, primitive showers (shower pipe attached to the wash basin) and no sea view. Fine view from roof garden. c. £9 for a DR.

• **Pantheon**: E class, directly on the "food passage", noisy and very simple, and only the uppermost rooms have a sea view. Costs c. £8 for a DR. Tel. 0832/91293.

• **Soulia**: C class, directly down on the harbour. All rooms have a sea view but not all have their own shower/toilet. Tiled and very clean, beds not the newest. Costs around £10 for a DR. Tel. 0832/91307.

IN THE MIDDLE OF THE VILLAGE

There are hotels on the steep slope and around the bus station, and also countless simple private rooms for rent, eg Moderno and Kivolos.

● **Manos**: E class, attractively appointed with blue window shutters, doors and overgrown balcony. Simple interior, older furniture. Prices of rooms rise from ground floor upwards, c. £7-10. Shower on the corridor. Address: only a few paces from the bus station. Tel. 0832/91394.

● **Dedalos** and **Candia**: C class, both on the steep slope at the upper end of the "food passage". Dedalos has nice balconies with vine creepers growing over them. DR with bath £10, without £8 Tel. 0832/91214 and 91359.

AT THE BACK OF THE VILLAGE

The further back you go, the quieter it is, but there is no panoramic view any more.

● **Kriti**: where the exit road makes a large curve. New house run by the family of Mr Kostas Jasafakis. A lot of light coloured wood inside, 9 rooms with balcony and bathroom (small bathtubs), and attractive paved floor. Around £10 for a DR. Tel. 0832/91324.

● **Michalis**: E class, the last house in the village, with spacious rooms, most of which have a balcony and private shower/toilet. Very quiet, apart from the clucking of hens. Costs c. £9. Tel. 0832/91231.

IN THE UPPER PART OF THE VILLAGE

A fine view far out over the water, but purely a hotel area, thus there is not much else going on. In addition there are a lot of steps to be climbed when going to and from the centre.

● **Adonis**: C class, one of the best addresses. Attractive building somewhat off the approach road; most rooms have balconies, good bathrooms, but the view out to sea is partly blocked by new buildings. There are rooms with a sea view in a small side annex. Costs c. £15-17 for a DR. Tel. 0832/91333.

● **Galini Mare**: C class, situated directly on the approach road on the left hand side. Spacious complex building with superb sea view. The rooms have tiled floors and are clean. Tiled shower/toilet, simple furniture. Cost c. £12, and there are also apartments with cooking facilities. Tel. 0832/91358.

● **Rent Rooms Michael:** a whitewashed building with a small inside courtyard directly on the approach road on the left hand side. Very clean, but the rooms are quite simple, with lino flooring and beds with simple iron frames. Fine view out over sea from the balcony running round the house. Shower/toilet in the courtyard. Cost c. £8 for a DR.

● There are other possibilities up here, for example **Areti** (D) at the beginning of the village, where the wind whistles in, or the solidly built **Astoria** (C) opposite Galini Mare, or **Athina** (C) with its fine sea views, situated in the bend of the road where it descends into the village.

● CAMPING AGIA GALINI: a large gravel site beneath plane trees and olives. Mostly shade, with passable sanitation, good taverna and shop at hand. Situated in a little forest hidden behind the beach. There is a bumpy cement track leading to it from the road to Timbaki, a few yards east of the junction with the road from Rethymnon (watch out for a small signpost). Can be reached from the beach by crossing the

• **Sleeping on the beach** is still quite usual at Agia Galini. Dozens of rucksack tourists find their way down there every day, in spite of the occasional police raid and a lot of petty thieving. A couple of tamarisks afford sparse shade, otherwise it is quite a "hard" experience because of the shingle.

Please write to us if you have any tips for overnight accommodation: we will be pleased to print them in the next edition.

Food

A large variety on offer; there are certainly no problems of the culinary kind in Agia Galini. Dishes of the more elaborate kind are also offered, eg *Stifado*, served in a casserole, often with rice and vegetable pilaf. The local speciality *Sachanaki* is particularly delicious with its rich sauce (see below/Tav. Phoibos). As the inhabitants of Agia Galini also make their living from fishing as well as tourism, there is a good selection of fresh fish to be had.

IN THE "FOOD PASSAGE"

In one of the three passages to the harbour there is one taverna next to the other; this is the "food passage" of Agia Galini. It is often so crowded in the evenings that people on their own are brusquely compelled to sit at tables with others travelling alone (this happened in *Livii* at the lower end of the passage).

• **Ariston**: Try the succulent Stifado here - tender beef with stewed onions in a casserole. Arrive early, otherwise there will not be any room for you.
• **Christos**: various pizzas, which are also available at **Babis**.
• **Greenwich Village**: roof garden and a view out over the roofs, at the upper end of the taverna passage. International dishes.

AROUND THE HARBOUR

Those who know the harbour from earlier days will probably receive a little shock here. Where previously there were a few tavernas grouped around the large open square, everything has now been taken over by sprawling tavernas with huge canopies.

• **Phoibos**: Previously called Galini and a favourite taverna on the square. Today the most westerly of the restaurants. A small, raised side garden carries on the earlier tradition. You must definitely try the Sachanaki here. This is a kind of casserole dish with a highly piquant sauce made of sausage, paprika, mushrooms, aubergines and other ingredients. There are several variations of it costing from £3-5, and it is one of the best things to be had in Agia Galini.
• **O Faros**: around the corner from Phoibos, parallel to the "food passage". Less bustle, and mainly fish dishes available.

ON THE BEACH

• **Kostas**: has a garden in front of it with a shady roof. Known for its good fish. Try fish shish-kebab.

• **Kyriakos**: large, Greek/Austrian run snack bar/taverna to the east of the bridge, near the camping site. A lot of room and worthwhile, if you want to have a snack while bathing.

OUTSIDE

• **The Garden Taverna** (Perivoli): on the road to Melambes, c. 1 mile from Ag. Galini. A small taverna with terraces under vine creepers. Wonderful view over the coast as far as Matala.

Kafenia/bars

• Kafenion **Synantisis**: A praiseworthy exception among the thumping pop music of the bars in Ag. Galini. Here, you can indulge in the illusion that you are sitting in an old Greek café; simple, wobbly chairs, bright neon lights and occasionally (good!) Greek and Cretan music from the loudspeakers. Even in the high season, this is the meeting place of the men of Agia Galini, where they drink raki and chew pistachios. The village elder looks in every evening, dressed in his traditional garb. A good place for watching the world go by, because it is in the best position at the upper end of the middle passage with steps which leads to the harbour.

• **Sweet Corner Pub**: diagonally across the way from "Synantisis" and the "alternative" to it. You can sip milkshakes here and, according to the sign, enjoy "fresh strawberries with special ice cream". The popping of champagne corks can sometimes be heard here, too.

• **Zorbas**: With its two floors this is the largest bar in the village, down on the harbour. Seating is in upholstered bamboo chairs under large canvas marquees. Absolutely crowded in the evenings, when the heat begins to die down. Wonderful view out over the sea. The prices of cocktails, juices and coffee etc. are naturally rather exaggerated.

• **Soulia**: a video bar on the harbour, on the ground floor of the hotel of the same name (most westerly building). Friendly service and the newest pop videos.

• **Stelios**: an agreeable breakfast café with a good selection: muesli, omelettes, home-baked cakes, fruit salad etc. Under a shady canopy on the square diagonally across from the post office (next to the fountain).

— ★ —

• DISCOTHEQUES: The **Juke Box** disco is at the lower end of the "food passage". There are two open-air discos directly on the beach, a little outside the village. A torch is recommended, as the bumpy path around the rock bluff is not lit. We preferred the **Soroco** disco to the **Diagonisos**, because of its easier-going, informal atmosphere and spaciousness. A small beer costs c. £1.

▶ **Bathing:** Follow the hilly path to the left of the harbour square around the rocks, a walk which lasts c. 5 mins. After a small, attractive shingle cove you reach a narrow piece of sandy beach. Then the actual beach begins, made up of shingle of all sizes from that of a fist to a head, some of it sharp-edged but most of it well-rolled and smoothed by the water. Everywhere there are small, semi-circular pitches marked out by stones; every couple has its special territory. There is hardly any shade, and bathing shoes are recommended. There is a shower at the taverna Kostas.

The little rivulet *Platis* with its cool water flows down from the hinterland to form an estuary right on the beach. There is even water in the rivulet in high summer, and it can be crossed by means of a newly-built wooden bridge. Behind it, the beach really begins. You can walk for miles here along the water's edge, either down on the narrow shingle beach or on the dirt track slightly above it. A very lonely experience, and there are only a few solitary swimmers here. We also saw a tent.

Agia Galini/Surrounding area and hinterland

It is possible to walk along the beach to the east of Agia Galini towards *Kokkinos Pyrgos*. The route goes along the water's edge all the way, but there is no shade anywhere. The narrow shingle beach extends for miles, then there are rust-red broken rock formations and low coastal cliffs. Duration about 1.5 hours, return by bus.

Bathing coves to the west of Agia Galini

The two bathing coves of *Agios Georgios* and *Agios Pavlos* are situated to the west of Ag. Galini in the middle of a lonely rocky landscape. Getting there entails a little bit of an adventure with a car, but it can be done. Otherwise there are boat excursions there every day from Agia Galini. It is also possible to get there on foot.

Agios Georgios: Take the road to Melambes. At a distance of about 2.5 miles, a rusty sign points down to *Niko's Café Bar*. Here you come on to a very bad, bumpy track about 2.25 miles in length, which leads down to a modest sand and shingle beach. The owner of the snack bar on the beach hires out umbrellas and sells refreshments. This is greatly resented by the taverna proprietors up the hill, because he is taking away what little business there is to be had, and is said to have no permit. The two tavernas are the main focus of interest in this bay.

• **Niko's Taverna**: the taverna nearest the beach. Simple meals and a lot of peace and quiet are to be had on the little terrace with its fine view. Niko's rooms for rent are spanking new, likewise their furnishings. Cost £10.

• **Georgios' Taverna**: A unique experience. Because the distance to his taverna from the beach is the greatest, he has done everything possible to attract custom. His premises are bursting with hand-painted signs bearing poems and philosophical precepts, eg "The absolute connection of universe is 1 x 1 = 1". Georgios announces his homemade philosophy in Greek, English and German. It all seems to have an effect, because the terrace is always well-occupied, and there is Cretan and classical music, a small library and a panoramic view. Money given for tips is used for a new world (ie Georgios buys new music cassettes), and if you eat at his taverna, Georgios promises to bring you back to Agia Galini.

Marketing Cretan style

Agios Pavlos: Take the road to Melambes. This is a wonderful mountain drive with fine views out over the Kedros range and the road to Rethymnon deep below in the valley. Soon after passing through Melambes, take the turn-off to Saktouria. The road now goes downhill again. Turn right where the road forks before *Ano Saktouria*. This road goes around the village. The asphalt comes to an end after *Kato Saktouria*. A bulldozed gravel track gives your vehicle a considerable shaking-up and drops continuously down to the beach of Agios Pavlos.

Agios Pavlos is a really beautiful cove for bathing with fine gritty sand and high dune-like drifts piled up behind it. The beach is bordered at the sides by eroded cliffs, and the little chapel of Agios Pavlos clings to the slope above. Access to the water is over rock slabs which are covered in seaweed and extremely slippery; be careful. The Paximadi islands are visible far out to sea. There are usually several dozen people in the cove, as there are daily boat excursions there from Agia Galini.

• ACCOMMODATION/FOOD: There is a **taverna** with extremely simple rooms (there are fly screens on the window instead of glass panes), and a hotel/taverna **Ag. Pavlos** (to the east above the bay), which is only open right in the middle of the high season. There is another simple hotel **Livikon** with green shutters, situated on the approach road and quite a distance up from the bay.

PURE SOLITUDE

Those who find that there is too much going on in the bay at Agios Pavlos can climb over the dunes in a westerly direction or drive a little way back along the approach road and then turn off to the left shortly afterwards into the track with the deep sand drifts. (Having left their car behind!)

A few yards on there is a promontory covered with fragrant oregano, beneath which there is a totally deserted beach of sand and shingle, extending westwards for at least 500 yards. Huge grey sand drifts close it off at the back. Far away opposite the *Monastery of Preveli* appears as a tiny white speck with the striking river gorge of Megalopotamos below it, along with one of the most beautiful beaches on Crete (for the Beach at Preveli see page 511).

Amari Basin

An unknown piece of Crete, hemmed in between the high mountain ridges of Kedros and Psiloritis.

This broad, hilly plain is a lush green garden landscape with a sea of olive trees, small vineyards and fruit plantations. In fact the former *Monastery of Asomaton* in the middle of it functions as an agricultural college today.

A good asphalt road runs once around the plain via Fourfouras, Moni Asomatos, Apostoli and Meronas. A generous amount of time should be allotted to travel the winding road along the mountain slopes, down to the plain and far up the slopes again.

45 YEARS AGO

During the German occupation, the Amari Basin was frequently used as a transit area by partisans and British agents, who found a lot of support here among the population. Those who kidnapped General Kreipe also passed through the region and hid for a while near the village of *Gerakari*. The village was razed to the ground a few months later by German troops. In the villages on the slopes of the *Kedros* in particular, there are other visible monuments to the "retribution measures" meted out by the German army.

A Round Trip

The best point of departure is Agia Galini. First go in the direction of Platanos, but turn off a few miles before it in the direction of Apodoulou and Fourfouras. The road to Fourfouras runs along half way up the slopes of Psiloritis.

Apodoulou: There is a Minoan vaulted grave (tholos) directly above the road on the right hand side at the northern end of the village. A rusty sign on the slope points to it. The door grille is usually open and it is possible to climb down into the low, dark burial chamber. Around the next bend in the road a small signpost announces the little church of *Agios Georgios* which is hidden in the greenery below the road, about a 10-minute walk away. There are well-preserved frescoes dating from the 13th century inside, but it is mostly closed.

Fourfouras: A larger village at the foot of the highest peak of Psiloritis, which can be climbed from here. There is a refreshing fountain at the northern end of the village. You should now turn off to the left where the road forks, towards Vizari in the plain.

Vizari: There are Roman excavations under the olive trees below the village and in a westerly direction. They are signposted from the main through road.

You now drive along a dead straight avenue with robust eucalyptus trees, amidst a fertile landscape of olive groves and vineyards. Scant traffic here makes the journey a real pleasure. There is a thick cover of trees, including ancient twisted olives.

Monastery of Asomaton: This dates from the 17th century and has been a flourishing agricultural college and the cultural centre point of the Amari Basin since 1935. Orange groves, various types of trees, and even palms grow on the premises. Old Byzantine icons can be seen inside, and one monk still lives here.

A short diversion can be made via Opsigias up to Amari. There is a superb panoramic view out over the plain on the way. The road is winding and, around **Opsigias** in particular, there is a sea of trees, with huge oaks at the end of the village. The road ends at **Amari** in a circular Platia with a kafenion. The inhabitants are quite amazed when a foreigner strays up here.

Apostoli: The Amari Basin ends here, and it is possible to continue on to Rethymnon. The village takes its name from the Ten Martyrs, who were captured here by the Roman occupying forces and subsequently executed in Agii Deka on the Messara Plain (see page 236). There are several hospitable-looking kafenia offering shade along the road.

Meronas: There are a lot of trees here, and a kafenion under tall plane trees. You are now coming into the fruit-producing area of the plain. Nuts, apples, oranges, peaches and even large quantities of cherries are growing on each side of the road.
On the side of the road between Meronas and the next village, **Elenes**, there is the church of *St. Ioannis Theologos*, dating from the 11th/12th centuries. This picturesque little ruin is a real jewel, containing the remains of old wall paintings in the main church.

Gerakari: This is the centre of the cherry-growing area. The village consists entirely of new houses, because the village was razed to its foundations by the Germans in August 1944 as retribution for the kidnapping of Kreipe (see above). All the men in the village were shot for the same reason.

Ano Meros/Chordaki: In contrast to the farming villages to the north and east, the villages on the curving mountain road are simple, almost poor shepherd's settlements, in which there are often only a few inhabitants, most of whom are elderly. Large memorials to those killed by the German occupying forces are often to be found here.

From Agia Galini to Rethymnon

A pleasant journey, particularly until Spili, which leads up a broad, extended valley. On the right there is the rugged Kedros range, bleak and barren, and only occasionally can a small white village be seen, clinging to the slopes.
The asphalt road surface has partly subsided and broken away, but some stretches are being widened and renewed.

The water in Spili is ice-cold and refreshing

Spili

The "Garden City" at the foot of a sheer rock wall, situated in a wonderful forested area.

An attractive place to have a rest is at the Venetian *Lion fountain* in the middle of the village. There are 19 lion's heads, and 6 further openings out of which water gushes with incredible force from springs above the city. It is wonderfully cool and refreshing and the local people say that it can be drunk without qualms. There are agreeable tavernas and kafenia on the winding village road. The side alleys in Spili are particularly attractive. For example, if you go further up the street to the left of the fountain, you will soon find yourself in steep winding passages with little balconies, climbing vines and rich floral decoration.

Spili, incidentally, is the seat of a bishop. The ochre-coloured building above the road at the exit from the village in the direction of Rethymnon houses a priest's seminary. The priests can often be seen in the streets.

• ACCOMMODATION: **Hotel Green** (C class), at the exit from the village in the direction of Rethymnon. Covered with flowers; a wonderful sight. There is a wide view out into the green surroundings from the rooms. DR c. £10-12.

Tel. 0832/22225.
In addition, there are numerous private rooms for rent, eg **Pandocheion Private Rooms**, 50 yards from the fountain in the direction of Agia Galini, opposite the church.

• OTHER INFORMATION: There is a moped/motorbike rental company called **Rent Moto Spili**, and a car and tyre repair workshop at the exit from the village in the direction of Rethymnon.

Bale: A place to change buses, a little to the south of the turn off towards Plakias (via Koxare). Consists of a single, small taverna. Those wishing to go to Plakias must wait here for a connection. Plakias can only be reached through the narrow *Kourtaliotiko Gorge* (Ta Kourtala = rattles, the name deriving here from the noise made by the strong winds) or through the *Kotsifou Gorge,* further to the west.
For details about Plakias and the western part of the south coast see the chapter on *Western Crete.*

The rest of the journey to Rethymnon is of lesser interest; the route becomes pleasant again when the descent begins from the high hills down towards the city, when there is a fine view of the peninsula with its red roofs, and the large fort with the mosque and harbour.

Rethymnon and the surrounding area are described in detail below. See page 354.

Eastern Crete

The Dikti Massif with the Lassithi High Plateau forms a sudden barrier, drawn between the centre and the narrow, mostly barren eastern part of the island.

In particular, the south eastern area around Ierapetra is among the regions of Crete which have the least rain. But there are landscape highlights here too, for example the fantastic *Bay of Mirabello* south of Agios Nikolaos, together with the *Thripti Mountains*, which adjoin it

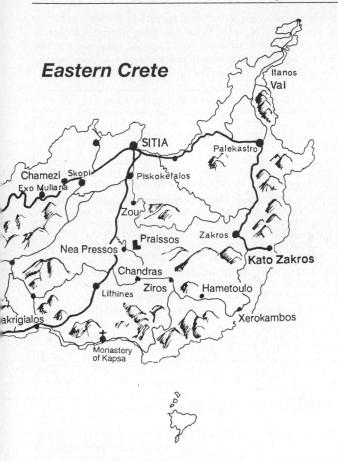

Eastern Crete

in the east. Because of its picturesque position, *Agios Nikolaos* developed into a booming tourist centre a long time ago. *Sitia*, the city of the Venetians, has remained peaceful by contrast and is a worthwhile headquarters from which to make excursions into the lonely, barren extreme east of the island. The legendary *palm beach at Vai* and the Bay of *Kato Zakros*, site of another Minoan palace, are the most prominent landmarks here. This fact has not been ignored, but there are still beautiful stretches, particularly inland, where a holidaymaker is hardly ever seen.

And finally there is the south coast, characterised by long grey shingle beaches and plastic hothouses. The small Cretan bananas ripen in a particularly short time here. *Ierapetra* is one of the hottest places on the island and is a favourite place in which to spend the winter.

As the road over to the Messara Plain has been almost completely asphalted, it is also possible to make very pleasant excursions in the south eastern part of Crete. Foreign tourists are very seldom seen in the little coastal villages to the west of Ierapetra.

GEOGRAPHY: The narrow eastern part of Crete begins to the east of the high Dikti Massif. The narrowest point of the island is between Pachia Ammos and Ierapetra, and is only just over 10.5 miles wide. While the south coast near Ierapetra consists of miles of sandy beaches, the north coastline is steep and characterised by deep bays. The Thripti Mountains dominate the interior.

ROADS: The main connections are good, but aside from them there are only dust or gravel tracks, eg to the **Monastery of Kapsa** and to **Keratokambos** in the extreme south east. A wide asphalt road goes to the **palm beach at Vai**.

CONNECTIONS: **Agios Nikolaos, Sitia** and **Ierapetra** are the centre points of the bus network. Connections are especially good from the first of these, and apart from long distance destinations, there are frequent connections to some interesting villages in the vicinity (Kritsa, Elounda). The palm beach at Vai can be reached without any problems by bus from Sitia, and there is also a connection to remote Kato Zakros with its Minoan palace.

ACCOMMODATION: There are dozens of hotels in **Agios Nikolaos** and countless possibilities in **Sitia** and **Ierapetra**. In all, there are only three **camping sites**; one near Gournia, and two near Ierapetra.

ARCHAEOLOGY: Minoan palace at **Kato Zakros**, a Minoan town at **Gournia**, the Dorian city of **Lato** and several smaller Minoan excavations.

BATHING: There are long grey sand/shingle beaches near Ierapetra, and the palm beach at Vai is famous. There is also a beach near Sitia.

From Mallia to Agios Nikolaos

The New Road goes through rust-brown fields and little forests of olive trees until it reaches the turn-off to Milatos. After that, it follows the alignment of a steeply-walled gorge, which separates the slopes of the Lassithi Mountains (Dikti) from the peninsula around Cape Ag. Ioannis in the north.

The Church of *Agios Georgios of Selinari*, which is directly on the road, beckons invitingly to those wishing to take a rest. An attractive complex with a slim, white bell tower, several chapels, a spring and benches under wide, spreading pines. There is a fine view along the gorge, and nearly always a refreshing wind blowing. There is a kafeteria/pizzeria on the road below the church, with steps leading up to a taverna. A home for the elderly is situated next to it.

The road goes on through one of the two road tunnels on Crete (about 300 yards long) to Neapolis, which has a cathedral.

Neapolis is situated on raised ground at the beginning of a long valley, which falls away level to Agios Nikolaos. The centre is the large square next to the cathedral church, and the buses stop there, too. There is a shady park with tall pines next to the church.

• ACCOMMODATION: **Hotel Neapolis**, D class, around £7 for a DR. Tel. 0841/33268.

The road now continues along the beautiful, gently undulating valley towards Ag. Nikolaos; a green sea of olive and almond trees. On the crests of the hills on the left hand side of the road there are old corn mills, of a type similar to those in the Ambelou Pass (see Lassithi High Plateau). There are tiny hamlets scattered here.

• CONNECTIONS: There are buses from Iraklion (bus station A) via Mallia to Ag. Nikolaos and vice versa about 25 x daily.

Agios Nikolaos

Tourism in its purest form; modest beaches; a worthwhile area

Pay a visit to the Historical Museum in Iraklion sometime. The yellowing photos there capture the old Crete. There was a time when Agios Nikolaos was a sleepy nest with only two kafenia on the harbour!

You can hardly believe it any more today; Agios Nikolaos is absolutely *the* tourist centre of eastern Crete. To be blamed for this in the first instance is the fantastic situation of the city on a hilly peninsula, jutting far out into the sea. The panoramic view out over the tremendous steep coastline of the Bay of Mirabello is also wonderful.

It cannot be denied that the centre also has a certain charm, too; there are several shady avenues, and the fjord-like harbour, slicing deeply into the coastline, and dark green landlocked lake behind it add a picturesque accent. An historical connection is absent, however. Agios Nikolaos has grown from a village into a city within a few decades. The picture is filled to a large extent by colourless, indiscriminately built hotel complexes of several storeys. The older houses dating from the turn of the century are hardly a sight worth seeing; they are two-storeyed, square, sturdy and built without taste. Agios Nikolaos is growing; the "skyline" extends far into the bay, and half-finished skeletons of buildings are pushing their way far up the slopes in the outer suburbs.

For those who like to sample the city life with its non-stop bustle and tourism in its purest form, and can afford the correspondingly high prices at the same time, this is the right place. The surrounding area also has something to offer.

The city on the green lake

The Information bureau of EOT is situated on the bridge between the Voulismeni Lake and the harbour. Information, room reservations and brochures. Open Mon-Sat 7.30 a.m.-9.00 p.m., Sun 8.00 a.m.- 3.30 p.m. Tel. 0841/22357.

The Tourist Police are located at the municipal police station quite a long way up at 17, Konstantinou Paleologou St (exit road to Iraklion). Tel. 0841/22321.

Connections

● **Bus**: The bus station is directly on the sea, just under 500 yards from the lake, and can be reached from the harbour via Venizelou Square. Connections to Iraklion about 25 x daily (from 6.30 a.m.-9.30 p.m.), to Sitia 9 x daily, Ierapetra 10 x, Elounda 16 x (from 7.15 a.m.-9.00 p.m.), Kritsa 17 x (from 6.00 a.m.-7.30 p.m.), Kroustas 6 x, Psychro (Lassithi Plateau) 2 x.

● **Boat connections**: There are interesting connections to the Cyclades and the islands of the Dodecanese, but they are irregular and change from year to year. To **Rhodes** via Sitia c.2 x weekly in the high season, duration of journey 15 hours and cost about £11. To **Santorini** 1 x weekly (Friday at around 11.00 p.m. in 1987), duration of journey 6 hours and cost around £6. There are also trips to **Anafi** etc. Information on all the boat connections can be obtained from travel agencies.

● **Car/motorbike/moped rentals**: The largest selection is to be found at **Adonis** on the harbour promenade (about 200 yards in a northerly direction from the harbour, near the Coral Hotel). Unfortunately, readers of the last edition of this book had bad experiences here. **Avis** car Rentals are right next door.

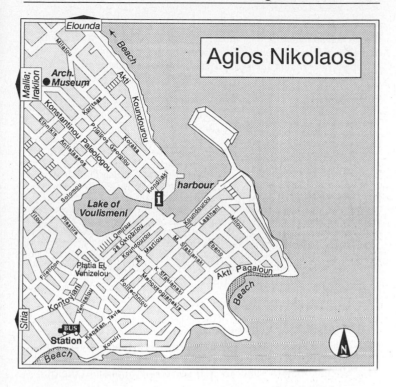

• **Excursions**: Boats make trips several times daily to the former leper colony on the island of **Spinalonga** (see Elounda for more details). The journey there and back lasts around 4 hours, including a guided tour of the island. Cost c. £5. The island of Kolokythia on the way there is also usually visited (nesting place for birds).

— ★ —

• CHANGING MONEY: There is a bank at 42, 28th Oktobriou St (a couple of paces from the harbour).

• POST OFFICE: at 9, 28th Oktobrou St. Open Mon-Fri 7.30 a.m.-2.30 p.m. Poste restante until 8.30 p.m.

• TRAVEL AGENCIES: There are several at 29, Koundouri St. (shady alley going down from Venizelou Square to the harbour), eg **Massaros Travel** or **Nostos Tours** diagonally opposite. Various excursions can be booked here, including a one or two-day trip to Santorini.

• TELEPHONE: There is an OTE office at 10, Kons. Sfakianaki St (a little below Venizelou Square). Open daily 6.00 a.m.-12.00 p.m.).

Accommodation

There are about 60 hotels, most of them belonging to class B and C, and only few in the lower price class. On the other hand, there are a lot of private rooms for rent. Everything is well booked out in the high season; the information bureau can book rooms for you.

● **Coral**: B class, one of the huge "boxes" on the promenade. Over 300 beds, with most (but not all!) rooms facing the sea front. Inviting wooden balconies, rooms are wallpapered and functionally furnished with wooden and plastic furniture. The sea water pool high up on the roof is a good idea; there is a super view! DR (with half board) in the high season costs around £30. Address: 21 Akti Koundourou (harbour promenade). Tel. 0841/28363. About 5 mins. from the harbour basin.

● **Panorama**: C class, on the right side of the harbour and cannot be missed. Solidly furnished, all rooms with balcony and a superb view, cost c. £22 for DR with breakfast. Tel. 0841/28890.

● **Du Lac**: C class, in the best position with a view out over the dark green lake, but on the front there is a busy road. Functional elegance here, with an agreeable lounge area in the reception hall from which the lake can be clearly seen. All rooms with bathroom, balcony and breakfast. DR facing the lake costs c. £22. Address: 17, 28th Oktobriou St. Tel. 0841/22711.

● **Alkistis**: C class, on the harbour promenade, 2 mins. from the harbour basin. Furnished in typically sober Greek hotel-style, and in need of a thorough renovation, but worth it because of its central position and the superb view of the harbour and the open sea. Costs c. £17 for a room on the front. Address: 3, Akti Koundourou. Tel. 0841/22454.

REASONABLY PRICED ACCOMMODATION

There are cheaper guest houses and private rooms particularly in Kapetan Tavla St. and its continuation, Modatsou St. (up the hill from the bus station). They are also scattered throughout the city.

● **Pension Atlantis**: for footsore bus travellers, directly at the bus station (follow sign). Rambling house on the hill, and access from the ground floor to the first floor is by means of a ladder (if you fail to land straight on the first floor when entering from the rear). Rooms of varying quality, and a couple of box rooms with a bare light well instead of a window are among them. Beds are OK. Shower/toilet on the passage, could be cleaner. DR from £7-9. Tel. 0841/28964.

● **Triptolemos**: "The Green House", a "character" like Kapetan Tavla himself. The house really is green; it is painted brilliant green, and access is via a little flight of steps to a raised inner courtyard

full of plants. A simple room costs c. £7. The friendly landlady offered to let us sleep in the courtyard for £2 per person. Address: 17, Emm. Modatsou St. Tel. 0841/22025.

● **Pension Argiro**: a few paces further up the hill at 13, Kastel. Mirambellou St., parallel to Modatsou (next to the large building which houses the Prefecture of the Nomarchia Lassithiou). Tel. 0841/28707.

Behind it and one crossroads higher up, at 7, Solonos St., there is the **Hotel Dedalos** with a beautiful sea view from some of its rooms. Going down the hill in the direction of the harbour below there is the **Hotel Ikaros**, with a view out over the gulf.

• **Egeon**: E class, in a very central position on the harbour front. The cheapest hotel in the place, mainly known and loved by rucksack tourists, and often full. There are five high-ceilinged rooms in this old building on the harbour, rather stuffy and crumbling, but not bad for the money. Shower/toilet in the little terrace courtyard. DR costs c. £7-9. Tel. 0841/22773.

• **Perla**: guest house on the promenade, with a fine view out over the water. With bathroom and small balconies, costs in the low season including breakfast c. £10, and £4 more in the high season. Friendly people. Address: 19, Akti Koundourou, about 300 yards from the harbour after the Hermes Hotel. Tel. 0841/23379.

— ★ —

• YOUTH HOSTEL: two blocks from the landlocked lake in the direction of the sea. The large blue sign is visible above the houses from a considerable distance. Was renovated two years ago and a storey was added, and now offers a lot of space. Guests are awakened in the morning by the bells of the neighbouring church, which seem threateningly near. Cost c. £2. Address: 5, Strategou Koraka St. Tel. 0841/22823.

— ★ —

• CAMPING: The nearest camping site is Camping Gournia Moon, about 8.75 miles in the direction of Sitia, shortly before Pachia Ammos. Buses to Sitia and Ierapetra will stop if the conductor is told in advance. The last bus goes at 8.00 p.m. The site is described under Cretan Riviera.

Food

Completely geared to tourists, with little originality. Of a passable standard, however, because of the strength of competition. Most of the tavernas are on the harbour and the little town beach to the south west of it. There are kafenia in a row on the inland lake.

ON THE HARBOUR AND VOULISMENI LAKE

The best food is not necessarily on offer in this central situation. A lot of bustle and a clientele which changes every day, few established customers.

• **Cretan Restaurant**: lavishly equipped and furnished, and the tables can hardly be seen for stuffed animals, wall-hangings, plants etc. As suggested by the presentation, quality and prices are far above average. International dishes: smoked trout, flambées, chefs specialities and much more. On the right hand side of the harbour basin.

• **Haris**: at the very front of the harbour basin, on the right hand side, where the big ships anchor. Worth a visit, because you can sit at small tables in a uniquely attractive setting directly at the water's edge. Prices within bounds.

• **Limni**: directly on the lake. Judiciously advertises the fact that the members of the TV crew who made the British TV series "Who pays the Ferryman" took 90% of their meals here. Beef dishes are quite good, e.g. "stewed beef in a clay pot" for c. £3. Readers of the first edition of this book were not satisfied with the food here.

• **Bella Pizza**: situated on the bridge between the lake and the sea. There is a "special pizza" with paprika, tomatoes, mushrooms and ham for c. £3. Middling quality, but filling.

On the Harbour Promenade in a Northwards Direction

The number of tavernas and restaurants here is also increasing in leaps and bounds. Very pleasant walk along the harbour.

- **Zephyros**: good food, exorbitant prices, a lot of bustle.
- **Ikaros**: shortly after the Hotel Cora. Always well patronised, and there is Greek dancing between the tables on Mondays and Thursdays. Great activity.

On the Town Beach

The somewhat quieter alternative to the noisy harbour basin. The candle-lit tavernas are built around the beach, with the gurgling of water and moonlight thrown in. Can be reached from the harbour by going along Sfakianaki St. in a south easterly direction.

- **Trata**: shortly before the town beach on the right hand side of the road. Well organised, friendly service, and moderate prices. Very good Kleftiko (lamb with potatoes baked in aluminium foil).
- **Delta**: the second taverna on the beach, situated on the left hand side.

Convivial atmosphere, specialities such as Stifado and Kleftiko.
- **Itanos**: near Venizelos Square, a good place to eat with relatively reasonable prices.

— ★ —

- Snacks: The centrally situated confectioner's shops on the harbour offer a large variety of cakes and an opportunity to sit right at the centre of action. Fast food places are to be found in the 25th Martiou St. which leads inland from the harbour: eg **Ciaou Ciaou** with its pizzas, spaghetti and sandwiches of many kinds, and **Meeting Point**. There is a large selection of ice cream available, eg in the **Casa del Gelato**, at 8, 25th Martiou St., in the **Apple Pub** on the harbour promenade in a northwards direction, and in **Penguin Gelato** in Sfakianaki St. which leads from the harbour to the town beach.

- Kafenia: Around double the normal price is paid for everything under the shady canopies of the cafés on the inland lake. A beautiful position, almost exclusively filled with tourists. A little more Greek are the kafenia and tavernas on Venizelou Square.

- Night Life: The area around the harbour and the lake is almost bursting at the seams with people at the time of the volta, or evening walk. Everyone parades by, everyone wants to see and be seen. The strollers go along the long harbour promenade in a northwards direction, then make an abrupt turn and come back to the city.

After dark, the lights of the tavernas and bars on the inland lake twinkle in colourful array, and you can choose your disco from those in the 25th Martiou St. Dart players meet in the **Bolero Pub** on the harbour promenade. The whole thing is particularly amusing when there is a power cut, and the whole of Agios Nikolaos is plunged into total darkness for a few seconds. This happens every evening . . .

Discos are springing up everywhere like mushrooms, especially in 25th Martiou St. and on the harbour promenade. In the centre of town, try **Bananas** or **Lipstick**, which according to information from insiders, is a superbly equipped disco with the best disc jockey on the island. It gets crowded from midnight onwards. The **Yachting Club** is open into the early hours of the morning.

Sightseeing

Voulismeni Lake: A mysterious pool with murky green water, only a few yards from the harbour. It is connected to the harbour basin by a canal about 23 yards long, which was constructed in 1870 by the Turks. Today, it is flanked by a long row of cafés, there are fishing boats tied up there, and paddle boats for hire. The local anglers haul fish one after the other out of the canal.

The most amazing rumours surround the pool, which is unique of its kind on Crete; for example the marine explorer Jacques Cousteau is supposed to have dived there and not been able to find the bottom, and German soldiers are supposed to have sunk quantities of tanks and guns there, but divers have never found any traces of them. Even the lorry which ran into the lake a few years ago has disappeared. In short, the Cretans firmly and doggedly believe that the lake is bottomless. Others in the know will tell you that the depth is exactly 64 metres (209 feet), and was measured years ago.

Whatever the truth of the matter is, the lake is always providing fuel for puzzles and surprises. Now and again, dead deep sea fish are found in it, which reinforces the theory that an underground passage connects it to the sea, perhaps even with the island of Santorini.

A thickly wooded rock wall of moderate height rises up at the back of the lake; in Venetian times there was a castle on top of it. At the foot of the wall there are stone benches, where you can sit undisturbed in the shade and watch the fishermen mending their nets. There are also several turkey pens, store rooms built into the rock and a small church.

It is an attractive walk up to the top of the rock wall, whence there is a grand view out over the roofs of Agios Nikolaos to the massive, soaring coastal mountains on the other side of the Bay of Mirabello.

Archaeological Museum

In spite of the fact that relatively few people know of its existence, a visit to this museum should not be missed. Since 1970, it has housed the extraordinarily rich finds from east Crete, which at an earlier date were all held in the Archaeological Museum of Iraklion.

In many ways, we liked this at least as much as the huge collection in the capital of the island. It is a smaller collection, easy to comprehend and there is less hubbub in the museum. The numerous finds and their relationship to each other can be studied in peace and quiet. They range from the Neolithic period (New Stone Age) through the Minoan period to the Graeco-Roman period. The development and progress of pre-classical and classical art on Crete can be followed perfectly in this limited space. The museum is situated in the upper part of Konstantinou Paleologou St., a few hundred yards up the hill from the lake (see map).

• OPENING TIMES: Mon-Sat 8.45 a.m.-3.00 p.m. Sun/holidays 9.30 a.m-2.30 p.m. Closed on Tuesdays. Admission c. £1.

A visit to the museum: The exhibits are arranged in chronological order. There is a striking Neolithic "idol" right at the beginning. With a bit of fantasy, a certain phallic similarity can be recognised, but it could also represent a human figure with body and head. Its function is puzzling, but it is probably meant to represent a deity.

Room 1: Early Minoan pottery, including vases in the so-called mottled style with chestnut red surface, irregularly marked through the application of objects to the surface immediately after firing. There are also bronze objects, eg the earliest fishing hooks on Crete (**Showcase 4**).

Room 2: The numerous idols in human and animal forms are particularly attractive here; amongst these are little doll-like figures, of which there is often only the head left (**Showcases 14, 15**). In **Showcase 9** there is wonderful jewellery made of paper-thin gold leaf (c. 2300 BC), which was found in graves on the small island of Mochlos (see under the place of the same name below). The vessels made from stone with veining of different colours are also very fine, and are a highlight of early Cretan art. There are huge clay pithoi, too, and well-preserved bronze weapons, partly with inlaid ivory handles.

Room 3: This room mostly contains large clay sarcophagi. The Minoans buried their dead in them. One of them contains a very carefully arranged skeleton.

Room 4: beautiful vases, richly decorated with ornaments and curved lines. Eastern influences are noticeable. The frequently stylised lotus flower has been turned into a bee on a vase in showcase 33. This room also contains the well-known burial of a child in a clay pithos. During its transport to the museum from the place where it was found (a very difficult operation), only the thin plate which covered the opening was moved from its position. Otherwise it is exhibited here exactly as it was discovered.

Room 5: In the large showcase in the middle there is a whole collection of clay animals: pigs, tortoises, lions etc. Young visitors will be especially charmed by these exhibits. Once again, striking heads and figures can be seen in **showcases 39** and **45**.

In the final rooms of the museum there are finds from the Greek and Roman periods. The prize exhibit right at the end is a skull adorned with a garland of thin gold, which has remained in position for 2,000 years without slipping. A silver coin was found in the mouth, provided for the dead person as an obulus for Charon, the ferryman of the Styx.

Agios Nikolaos: A Byzantine church north of the town. One of the oldest churches on Crete, but it has been restored and hardly attracts attention from the outside. There are faded wall paintings in lime-based colours in the interior, which date from the 9th-11th centuries. Go along the harbour promenade Akti Koundourou in a northerly direction, past Ammoudi Beach and the Minos Beach Hotel, to the little yacht harbour. The little church is situated opposite on the spit of land, up the steps by the Spilia Bar. It is normally closed but the key can be collected from the Hotel Minos Palace above it, on deposit of a passport.

Bathing/Town

There are only very modest opportunities in the immediate vicinity of the village. There are 3 small beaches in all, and they are completely overcrowded. A better plan is to take a bus or rent a vehicle and drive out of the town in a southerly direction.

● **Town Beach:** There is a small shingle bay 5 minutes to the south east of the harbour, which can be reached via Sfakianaki St. It is almost completely without shade, and there are only a few thin tamarisks. It is densely built up with tavernas.

● **Ammoudi:** A beach in the north, about 10 minutes along the harbour promenade from the harbour. A barren piece of sandy beach, with shade provided by several tall eucalyptus and tamarisk trees. There are paddle boats and surf boards for hire here. The beach seems rather dingy.

● **Southern beach:** To the south of the bus station there is a very narrow piece of sandy beach in front of a wall, then a shingle beach about 200 yards in length, and behind it there is a stretch of lawn with trees - this is the bathing beach of Agios Nikolaos (admission £0.50). Water skiing, surf boards, canoes or paddle boats are available. Very clean, and the best beach at Agios Nikolaos.

Bathing/surrounding area

In the direction of Elounda: Shortly after the great box-like Mirabello Hotel there is a long, little-frequented shingle beach in a bay with olive trees, below the road. No facilities.

In a southerly direction: Just over half a mile after the main crossroads at the exit from the town there is a fine, small, sandy beach with low clumps of beach grass behind it. Directly on the road, with surfboards for hire and a mobile snack bar. Crowded.

Almost a mile further on there is a sandy beach about 100 yards long in a cove on the road. Shade is provided by several trees, there are a number of well-frequented tavernas, a hotel, and villas/apartments to rent. Very full.

The beaches in the wide Bay of Pyrgos, about 5 miles to the south of Agios Nikolaos, are much better. See below under the heading **Road from Agios Nikolaos - Sitia**.

Kritsa is famous for its crochet work.

AGIOS NIKOLAOS/
SURROUNDING AREA

Kritsa

The pastel-coloured and snow white houses are grouped closely together in terraces on the slope. Above them is a row of olive trees, then the bare rock . . . Kritsa is the archetypal Cretan village, and without doubt one of the prettiest!

Jules Dassin thought so too, when in 1956 he made the film "The Man Who Must To Die" (see page 203), based on the famous novel "The "Christ Recrucified" written by Kazantzakis (see page 86). Although the action really took place in a Greek village in Asia Minor under Turkish occupation, the scenery fits exactly: the whitewashed houses, the little craft shops, the harsh landscape.

But there is another reason why nearly every holidaymaker in Agios Nikolaos comes up here. Just outside the village there is Panagia Kera, the church containing the best-preserved Byzantine wall paintings on Crete.

It is thus hardly surprising that the houses on the long, winding village street are completely geared to tourism. Souvenir shops, woven goods and kafenia are crammed together, and there is even "Fast Food". The village is a hive of activity during the day, and hundreds of holidaymakers, armed with cameras, saunter up and down or sit in the agreeable little village square. It is noticeably quieter in the evening, the cloak of anonymity disappears and the inhabitants examine the strangers more carefully. Hardly anyone stays overnight.

In spite of all the hustle and bustle, Kritsa maintains a genuine village atmosphere only a few yards from the main raod. There are narrow stairway passages, whitewashed walls, tubs of flowers, and brown, green and blue window shutters. Elderly matrons often sit in front of their doors, crocheting or spinning wool.

• HOW TO GET THERE: about 5.5 miles from Agios Nikolaos. The road climbs up gradually through extensive terraces of olive trees, and there is a wide view of the Bay of Mirabello. Suddenly, Kritsa appears half-way up on the rock wall in front of you. The shape of the village noticeably resembles a scorpion. The arm of the village which curves off to the left is the tail with the sting, and the two parts of the village which lie above each other on the right are the pincers. Park somewhere at the beginning of the village and walk the last few yards. The main road through the village is not closed to traffic, but only those who find it really necessary drive right into the middle.

— ★ —

• CONNECTIONS: Ag. Nikolaos - Kritsa about 17 x daily, last bus at 7.30 p.m. Kritsa - Ag. Nikolaos about 16 x daily, last bus at 8.15 p.m. It is essential to check on the times of the buses back to Ag. Nikolaos at the bus stop at Kritsa, as they are changed frequently. The **bus stop** is in the lower part of the village: Go past the church and up into the centre. Fare one-way c. £0.50.

— ★ —

• ACCOMMODATION: There are no hotels, but private rooms are available. **Kritsopoula**, a new building down from the square containing the bus stop, offers reasonable rooms for c. £7. There are further private rooms on the road from the bus stop into the centre, and on the small village square right in middle. Prices about the same.

— ★ —

• FOOD: The taverna **Siganos**, on the square where the bus stops, is not bad. There is a taverna near the Panagia Kera, just before Kritsa, in rural surroundings.
Some of the kafenia and small taverns on the narrow main road through Kritsa have attractive little balconies with a wide view over the terraces of olives below the village. The cafés on the atmospheric little village square are always full. Here, you can dream away the day under sun umbrellas. The most attractive is perhaps the kafenion **Saridakis** just before it, this consists of only a few tables under a shady plane tree.

• SHOPPING: Crocheted and woven goods of high quality - sheets, coverlets, table-cloths etc. They are enhanced by fine filigree lace patterns and flowered ornaments.

The Panagia Kera - simple from the outside, but a beautiful interior

Panagia Kera

Simple in appearance from the outside, the church is full of architectural refinements. Its dream-like setting under tall, slender cypress trees has certainly provided the cover picture material for a dozen travel guides.

The Panagia Kera is over 600 years old. The oldest part is the middle nave, while the two side naves were added at a later date. A high round dome sits above the three high-vaulted naves. The strong supporting walls on both sides almost taper off into the ground; this gives a feeling of unity with the earth itself, even a sense of thrusting power, but at the same time suggests elegance.

The highlight is, however, the interior. The Panagia Kera is exhaustively decorated with colourful Byzantine frescoes. It is a pictorial Bible of the 13th and 14th centuries, as were so many Byzantine chapels on Crete in earlier times. The whole development of Cretan art can be followed here in a confined space, as though one were looking through a quick-motion camera. It is exemplary, indeed, for the whole of European painting, which went through a similar process during the transition period from the Middle Ages to the Renaissance; the breakthrough from stiff, established rules of form and painting according to unreal pre-established patterns, to genuine representation of people with mimicry, liveliness and feeling.

• LOCATION: Shortly before the entrance to the village of Kritsa, there is a driveway up to the church on the right hand side of the road.
• VISITING TIMES: Mon-Thur 8.45 a.m.-5.00 p.m. Fri/Sat 8.45 a.m.-3.00 p.m. Sun 9.00 a.m.-2.00 p.m. **Admission** c. £1.

The Middle Nave

The oldest frescoes are here. Dark colours, stiff physiognomy, immobile faces without feeling in them, stereotyped forms.

Apse: The paintings here have been largely destroyed; there are only remnants of the large portraits of the *hierarchs* with their vestments, situated in the lower part. An indication that the search for new stylistic devices has already begun is to be found in the comparative lightness of the colours used, and the intensity of the expressions on the faces.

The *Ascension of Christ*, depicted on the ceiling of the apse, is more in the traditional iconographic style. The trees are of particular note here, as the form of their representation was not preordained by Orthodox rules. In front of them are the large figures of the kings *David* and *Solomon*.

Dome: Partly destroyed, but divided into 4 scenes by the ribs of the dome: the *Presentation of Christ in the Temple*, the *Entry into Jerusalem*, the *Resurrection of Lazarus*, and the especially attractive representation of the *Baptism of Christ*. All are in traditional style; restrained, without individuality, dark colours.

Vaulting: The paintings are best preserved here. There are several scenes covering large areas on both sides, both next to and beneath one another.

The most impressive of these is the large scene of the *Birth of Jesus*. Mary, depicted with sharply defined features, lies exhausted in front of the cave. On her right is Jesus, wrapped in swaddling clothes and watched with curiosity by ox and ass. The bath scene in the lower part is wonderful; Jesus is being scrubbed in a square bath tub while a seemingly thoughtful Joseph sits beside Him. The Three Wise Kings and the Shepherds are approaching from that side. The reports on the Nativity by the Evangelists Matthew and Luke are given pictorial representation here together with those originating from the so-called *Apocrypha*, which does not belong to the Bible, but deals partly with the same subjects, albeit in elaborated and changed form. Matthew and Luke, for example, know nothing about the birth taking place in a cave.

Frighteningly macabre is the representation of the *Slaying of the First-Born* by Herod, on the same side; there are horribly realistic pictures of little boys speared through by the soldiers' lances. Below, on the right, Rachel mourns with the heads of her three murdered children

The Birth of Christ in the middle nave at Panagia Kera

in her lap, and above on the right, Elisabeth hides John the Baptist in a cleft in the rock.

On the same side there is the descent of Christ into *Hell* and a scene which depicts *Paradise*: the Patriarchs Abraham, Isaac and Jacob hold the Souls of the Dead in their laps.

The *Last Supper* is depicted on the other side of the vaulting. The inability of the painter to cope with perspective can be seen in the case of the table. This almost looks like a child's painting. Judas is especially highlighted; he is intentionally ugly in appearance, and is putting his hand into the dish.

Other representations: *Mary in the Temple,* accompanied by her parents Joachim and Anna (these are also scenes from the Apocrypha, which deals exhaustively with their lives). There is a lot going on at *Herod's Feast;* the wine is flowing, the executioner is beheading John the Baptist at bottom right, and in the upper right hand corner Salome is dressed in red, dancing, and holding the head. Beneath this is the monumental figure of *St. George,* the slayer of the dragon, and by way of a surprise on the northwest pillar there is *St. Francis of Assisi*! His presence here is due to the influence of the Venetians, who were the rulers of Crete in the 13th century.

Above and beside the main entrance there are the remains of the *Crucifixion*, which have largely been destroyed. There is also the *Punishment of Sinners*, who are roasting in the everlasting fires of Hell, bound hand and foot.

The South Nave (right side nave)
The frescoes seem fresher, more lively, more animated. Some of the faces are wonderful, full of expression and true to life, full of passion and dramatic. Perhaps not as valuable as the Orthodox paintings in the middle nave from an artistic point of view, but considerable progress has been made in human representation.

On both sides of the vaulted roof there are rows of scenes from the *Life of Mary*; the subjects are mostly taken from the Apocrypha. Typical: the same problem existed then as today. Mary is having a baby. She is hunched in a chair, while Joseph is in the opposite corner with a worried expression on his face. He is not looking forward to the baby at all! But soon the Angel of the Lord appears and tells Joseph that the whole thing is not as bad as it seems.

In contrast to this is the *Annunciation to Joachim,* who has been sitting and fasting for 40 days in the wilderness because of his inability to father a child. An angel appears and informs him that his wife is pregnant. You can see here the unhappy face of Joachim, who does not yet know of the luck about to befall him.

The Three Hebrew Priests who bless the baby Mary seem almost strange. The morose little figures of the old men with their beards and shoulder-length hair remind us of the Druids in the Asterix comics. Other paintings in this nave are the *Embrace*, the *Way to Bethlehem*, the *Sampling of the Water, Prayers in the Garden etc.*

The North Nave
Painted by a different artist to that of the south nave, with good colour composition but less attention to mimicry. Darker colours. Very damaged in places.

Nearly half of the wall in the area in front of the altar is taken up by a representation of the Apostles, with a crowd of angels standing behind them. Beside this picture is one of *Paradise*. Peter hurries to open the door with his key, while behind it Mary and the Patriarchs are throned in magnificence, holding the souls of the pious in their laps.

On the front wall, opposite the apse, there is a representation of the *Weighing of Souls,* and below it on the right the torments in Hell are shown again; this time the sinners are hanging upside down on chains.

Quite out of context, next to the torments of Hell in the corner, is a painting of the individual who financed the building of the church, shown with his wife and child. Of less value from the point of view of art, but of great significance because it is one of the few representations of ordinary people of this time. The three figures are shown in the apparel of persons of high rank.

Kritsa/Surrounding Area

Lato

An ancient settlement, built around the 12th century BC, long after the Minoan period, by Dorian conquerors. Superb position on a mountain "saddle" above Kritsa. The long grey walls of the settlement run like terraces down the steep slope beside a deep crater-like hollow.

The difference cannot be ignored: the Minoan palaces, carelessly situated on the plains, without defences of any kind, and here, high up in an isolated mountainous position, a settlement with walls several feet in thickness, virtually impregnable. Fear and the need for security determined the site of this settlement.

There is a wonderful peacefulness about the grass-covered ruins of this mountain stronghold. A couple of birds can be heard singing, and bees are humming; otherwise there is no sound to be heard. The visitor's eyes scan the wild mountain environment; looking along the valley to the north west, a number of small, box-like structures can be seen at the end on the slope. These are the corn mills on the road to Agios Nikolaos (see page 283).

THE WAY TO LATO: Go along the road to Kritsa and shortly after the sign bearing the name of the village, turn right along the field path by the cemetery. The path winds upwards between almond and olive trees, into the increasing solitude of the mountains. There is a wonderful view out over Kritsa and the olive terraces. The site can be reached by car, and the journey on foot takes about 1 hour. There is hardly any shade there.

A tour of the site: Visitors approaching from Kritsa arrive in the upper part of the settlement, at the market place. There is a large *well* in the middle of this so-called *agora*, and a small *sanctuary* further on; the *exedra* is in the shade of a stony oak.

There are wide *terraces of steps* between the foundations of two watchtowers on the other side of the square. These steps are considered to be the forerunner of the ancient theatre, since all the activity in the Agora could be watched from them. If you go up the steps, you will come to the rooms occupied by the *Archontes*, or city authorities.

The way down to the actual settlement is on the left. Walls of roughly-fitted stone blocks several feet thick surround small rooms used for both residential and commercial purposes. A well, several handmills, vats, and mortars have been found in the lower rooms.

The Bay of Elounda

There is something of a dream bay about it. Even when going down the long, curving road from Agios Nikolaos towards the bay, its unique situation can be recognised.

The peninsula of *Spinalonga* (long thorn) lies like a long branch of land off Elounda, and is only connected to the mainland by a very narrow causeway. The sea forms a large, natural lagoon, protected from the wind by the steep mountain slopes which rise directly behind the coast.

The ancient harbour city of *Olous* sank into the sea here between one and two thousand years ago; guides proudly point out several underwater ruins to visitors, which *could have* belonged to the city.

Another highlight is a boat trip to the little island of Spinalonga at the northern end of the peninsula of the same name. It enjoys an extremely strategic position in the only approach channel to the bay, so it is not surprising that the Venetians established one of their strong coastal forts here. The later function of this rocky island was a much eerier one, and more attractive to tourists; it served as a *leper colony* from 1903 to 1957! All those affected by this illness had to leave their homes and families, and spend the rest of their lives until a bitter death in this sea-bound quarantine station. More about them below.

Elounda also has several things to offer; managers in the tourist business recognised its potential at an early stage, and a large part of the bay has been taken over by some of the best hotels on Crete. And this is the other side of the coin. Elounda is totally given over to mass tourism and is crowded with people on package holidays. Dozens of buses arrive there daily and in particular there are boat trips from nearby Agios Nikolaos. The village itself is accordingly not very prepossessing, extends impersonally along the road and is full of hotels and tavernas geared to tourists. There are no good opportunities for bathing.

In spite of all this, the landscape in general is extremely attractive and certainly worth a visit.

• CONNECTIONS: buses to and from Ag. Nikolaos about 16 x daily; bus stops on the fishing harbour and the main road.

Boat excursions several times daily from Ag. Nikolaos. Information and bookings in the travel agencies in Ag. Nikolaos.

Boats leave for the leper colony about every half hour.
The car and motorbike rental company **Albatross** is under British management. Bicycles can be rented from **Motor Fun**, right next door to Albatross.

Accommodation

• The three hotels **Elounda Beach** (Tel. 0841/41412), **Elounda Mare** (Tel. 41512) and **Astir Palace** (Tel. 41580), are all of the luxury category and form an enclave of "top class tourism" on Crete. The Elounda Mare has pretty bungalows, built in Cretan style. With almost 600 beds, the enormous Elounda Beach is almost a city by itself; it has its own beach, water-skiing, diving courses, paragliding, and every kind of facility.

• **Aristea**: C class, well-run establishment, modern and functional. Just over 5 yards from the sea, with the best views possible. Also has a good restaurant. Cost c. £17 for a DR with private bath

and breakfast. Address: c. 20 yards in front of the large main square, where the excursion boats anchor. Tel. 0841/41301.

• **Kalypso**: C class, balconies with a lot of greenery, good taverna, fine view of the fishing harbour. Same price class as the "Aristea", at the lower end of the large square next to the church. Ask for a room on the front. Tel. 0841/41367.

• **Olous**: E class, a larger building with attractive balconies on the main road, in the direction of the southern end of the village. Very pleasant and friendly atmosphere, cost c. £9 for a DR. Tel. 0841/41357.

— ★ —

• PRIVATE ROOMS: available in a house opposite the main door of the church on the harbour square. Simple, rooms with tiled floors, in general clean and OK. Cost c. £8. The room available for c. £6 on the ground floor is not recommended.

There are more rooms at the taverna **Olous** on the main road (next to the Hotel Olous) and in the neighbouring house. The Restaurant **Venus** on the harbour square rents rooms with a fine sea view.

— ★ —

• FOOD: most of the tavernas and cafés are situated on the large main square and the fishing harbour. There is even one taverna on a little artificial peninsula in the fishing harbour.
Vasilis, reached by going from the main

square along the sea in the direction of the causeway, is quite a normal, average type of waterside tavern. It was probably chosen by the BBC for the TV serial "Who Pays The Ferryman" for this very reason.

• OTHER INFORMATION: The **Post Office** and the **Bank** are on the harbour square. Diving equipment can be hired from the Elounda Ski School (Tel. 0841/41017) for the considerable sum of £20.

Sightseeing

There is not much to see in the village itself. There is a modern marble memorial with two huge bronze doves in the wide harbour square. The large village church is only a few paces away and is at its most beautiful shortly before sunset, when the sun shines through the colourful glass windows, throwing out reflections everywhere in the form of points of coloured light.

If there is time, you should take a walk over the narrow *causeway* to the stony peninsula of Spinalonga. A unique atmosphere prevails on the lagoon, and you can feel a little of the peace and privacy of this secluded little spot. Aside from the path there are several salt lakes, which were used as salt pans at an earlier date. A small *bridge* crosses the narrow canal; the latter is the only connection by water on the south side of the bay, and only navigable by small boats. The causeway was cut through here by the French in 1897, and since then Spinalonga has been an island!

If you go along the shore past the remains of windmills on the right hand side, you will find a *taverna* a few yards on, which is in a really ideal position. It is away from the bustle, quiet, and well and truly designed for relaxation. It is a comfortable place to have coffee in the afternoon. Simple dishes such as spaghetti and souvlaki are available, and it is called the "Canal Bar".

50 yards behind the café there is the attractive mosaic floor of an early Christian basilica. Here, a couple of lively dolphins and other smaller fish are depicted within an ornamental frame of garlands and flowers, the whole composition carried out in only three colours - black, white and red.

A little way on, at the small white church, the seaweed and algae-covered foundations of several houses are clearly visible only a few feet below the surface of the water. There are more foundations further out, but they can only be seen from a boat. These are probably the remains of *Olous*, the legendary sunken harbour city, but experts are not quite sure.

Olous is already mentioned in Homer; the city was one of the most important harbours in eastern Crete and even the Dorians still used it. The last mention of Olous was made by the Greek author Pausanias in the 2nd century BC; the city must have sunk after that time. This was probably due to land movements; while parts of the coast of eastern Crete sank below the surface of the sea, the western part of the island rose up by several feet.

But not only the ruins in the water make this little diversion worthwhile. You can go on walking along the rocky cliffs for quite a distance and climb down into the water without being disturbed, then stretch out on the rocks and enjoy the wonderful view out over the steep, inaccessible slopes of the Mirabello mountains on the mainland. If you look carefully, you will be able to recognise the road to Sitia in the far east of Crete. This appears as a thin line chiselled into the rocky slope. You can also cast a glance over the complex of luxury hotels opposite.

Bathing

The best beaches have unfortunately been commandeered by the luxury hotels. The only public beach in Elounda is the narrow strip of sand on the mainland side of the causeway. It is crowded, of course, and dirty. The beach does not shelve at all, and there are surf boards for hire.

A better plan is to walk over the causeway and go on for about 0.75 miles to the other side of the peninsula. This can also be reached by car, and there is a small car park at the end of the bumpy track. Then there is about a ten-minute walk down a stony path between crude stone walls and through an extensive grove of carob trees, after which there is a sandy beach over 70 yards in length. This consists of the finest white sand, and is called *Kolokythia*! Unfortunately its whereabouts are all too well-known and there is plastic refuse lying around there. Offshore opposite is the rocky little island of *Kolokythia*.

There are more small beaches and opportunities for bathing on the road to Plaka at the northern end of the lagoon (see below).

Elounda/Surrounding area

Mafrikiano: A tiny village on the crest of a hill behind Elounda. While the holidaymakers tread on each other's toes down below, time has stood still up here. It is necessary to climb up a couple of steep passages in order to get up there. But it is worth it; the village is attractive, with paved ways which are inacessible to traffic, whitewashed houses and low walls of ashlar stone. The raki is good, and the view of the bay is wonderful.

Pano Elounda: This is situated high above Elounda (which is really called Kato Elounda), but the only thing it has in common with the bustling harbour village is its name. Sauntering along the winding alleys, the visitor almost feels like an intruder. The main road clearly passes the village by, for it is a little world of its own, intimate, labyrinthine and protected.

Leaving Elounda in a northerly direction, the road runs along the bay to Plaka. There are several small beaches, and the occasional lone camper can be seen.

Plaka

Plaka is situated exactly opposite the little island of Spinalonga. When the leper colony was still in use, Plaka was its ferry port. This is where the sick arrived, sometimes with their whole families, and where the terrible farewells took place. All provisioning for the leper colony and all contact with the outside world took place through Plaka. When the leper station was closed, Plaka sank into obscurity. There is a strange atmosphere here today. New apartments and villas have grown up amongst weathered ruins and empty cave like windows seem to stare across from Spinalonga. In the low season in particular, this place seems to be in the middle of nowhere.

Both of the fine, clean shingle beaches each side of the village are worth a visit. Plaka is mainly known for its fish tavernas. If you want to eat fish, this is the place to come. Unfortunately exorbitant prices are often asked here for fish.

• CONNECTIONS: buses 2 x daily at the most from Elounda.
Fishing boats go across to Spinalonga, and are a little cheaper than boats from Elounda.

• ACCOMMODATION: private rooms (c. £9 for a DR) in the tavernas **Castellos** and **Maria** etc. There are also **Kalidon** Apartments.

Spinalonga, the Lepers' Island

"Visit the island of pain and living death"; cheap-jack advertising by the travel agents in Ag. Nikolaos, but the visit is worthwhile.

A steep fortified hill out to sea and surrounded by bastions on all sides; impregnable. Inside the walls are the crumbling houses and alleyways of the leper colony. Some of them spent nearly their whole lives here. Very few visitors seem to be affected by the fact today; well-disposed tourist guides hurry their groups once around the site at a brisk marching pace, while fanatical souvenir hunters systematically plunder the charnel houses and graves. The fishermen of Elounda are also carrying on a ferry business here.

From a strategic point of view, the position of the island is unique, and it totally dominates the entrance into the bay of Elounda. The Venetians liked to construct their coastal forts on such outposts, and there are others, for example in Souda Bay near Chania and on the long peninsula of Gramvoussa in western Crete. Crete fell to the Turks in 1669, but the latter were not able to conquer the Venetian island forts. The Venetians only handed over Spinalonga in 1714.

Turkish fishermen settled on the island in the 19th century. In 1903 they left there in droves, because the Greek Government had decided to make Spinalonga a collecting point for all lepers on Crete! The lepers were to settle into the former Venetian and Turkish houses and stay on the barren, waterless rock until the end of their days. The police rounded up the sick all over Crete; up to that time, many had been living far away from civilisation in caves and broken down, rotting huts.

At length, about 400 Cretan lepers were gathered together on Spinalonga. In addition there were several dozen lepers from the rest of Greece, who had been confined under subhuman conditions in an Athens hospital and had eventually gone on a hunger strike before they were finally brought to Spinalonga. They came mostly from orderly,

View across the bay of Elounda to the leper colony of Spinalonga

middle class families, had finished their professional training, some as lawyers or teachers, and were, in spite of their illness, full of a desire to lead active lives.

Under their direction, the lepers began to turn the island into their home. They renovated the Venetian and Turkish houses, built small homes on the old foundations, laid out gardens and even kept sheep, goats and chickens. They also brought the crumbling Venetian wells back into use; they collected rainwater from the roofs in butts and stored it in the water reservoirs of the former fort, which were almost as large as tunnels.

Over the years, a real little village grew up, with four tavernas, two churches, small shops and many houses. The lepers often practised their former professions, and there were cultural activities such as performances of puppets and film presentations, and even dances. Marriages took place among the younger lepers, and they sometimes produced healthy children who were taken to an Athens orphanange because of the danger of infection.

The lepers received a monthly pension from the State, and all provisioning took place via the small village of Plaka on mainland Crete (see above).

A large disinfection chamber was built, and every visitor to the island had to go through it. Thus relatives could visit their sick at any time. Some healthy couples even had their children baptised in the little church on the island.

Medical care and conditions of hygiene improved steadily. In 1937, a hospital and laboratory were built, and doctors who came over from mainland Crete operated on a shift basis which changed regularly.

However, all these successes and improvements could not hide the fact that nearly all the inhabitants of the little island were incurably sick.

Many of them had to have whole limbs amputated at frequent inter-vals, and not a few died after these operations. Those who had saved enough money (or received enough from relatives) were able to give the island's carpenter an order for a wooden coffin, and thus could be buried in a single grave marked by a simple wooden cross. Others were buried in a cement tower set deep into the ground at the end of the cemetery. This mass grave can still be seen today.

In 1957, the last living lepers from Spinalonga were brought to an Athens hospital.

THE LEPERS

Leprosy was widespread and feared in the Middle Ages, and the "unclean" of the Bible were lepers. They were expelled from society and forced to live far away from every human settlement (Jesus once visited them before the gates of Jerusalem). Indeed, this was the usual practice on Crete until 1903!

Leprosy is transmitted by bacteria, and the period of incubation lasts 3-5 years. At first the nerves are affected; they swell and burst, causing typical lep-rosy wounds. This phase can last decades. When the nerves have been totally destroyed, it is the turn of the bones. The destruction of both can cause the death of whole limbs.

The illness is transmitted via blood, that is from open wound to open wound. There is no vaccine today that is 100% effective, and leprosy is widespread in large areas of the Third World. Not commonly known is the fact that a large number of lepers can still be found in Europe. The sad record holder is the area of Andalusia in southern Spain, where over 1,600 cases have been definitely diagnosed by the medical authorities, but the actual figure for the number of lepers in Andalusia is put at over 2,500.

There is no risk involved in a visit to Spinalonga.

• CONNECTIONS: Fishing and excursion boats go there frequently from **Elounda**. Duration of trip around 15 minutes, cost c. £3 return, with one hour spent on the is-land. You may even make the trip with Yannis and Kostas, two nice fisherman who are actually father and son with an incredible likeness to one another in their striking facial profile.

The crossing from **Plaka** is slightly cheaper, and there are also several boat tours organised daily from Ag. Nikolaos (see under **Ag. Nikolaos**).

A tour of the colony: The whole island was built up as a fortress by the Venetians. There are several rings of walls around it, and the massive bastions are equipped with 35 strong cannons.

The boats land today at the *south bastion*, which is the finest and larg-est. High up in the wall, the Venetian marble lion roars across at the Spinalonga peninsula.

The best plan is to go up the stairs and left through the *tunnel*, c. 66 feet long, which leads into the interior of the fortifications. The long *street of shops and houses* of the leper colony begins here. Immediately on the right, half way up the steps, there is a building that has been completely *reconstructed* and *restored (2)*. This is what the houses looked like when there were people living in them.

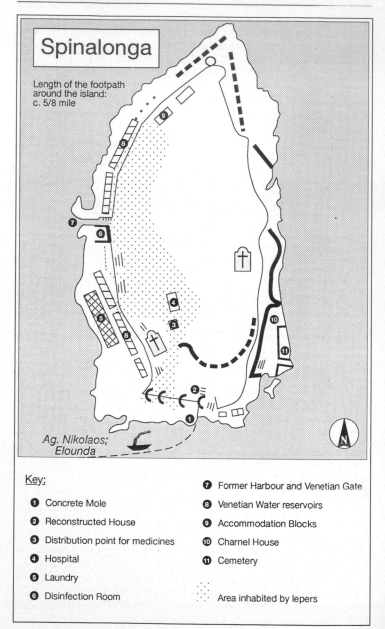

Spinalonga

Length of the footpath
around the island:
c. 5/8 mile

Ag. Nikolaos;
Elounda

Key:

1 Concrete Mole

2 Reconstructed House

3 Distribution point for medicines

4 Hospital

5 Laundry

6 Disinfection Room

7 Former Harbour and Venetian Gate

8 Venetian Water reservoirs

9 Accommodation Blocks

10 Charnel House

11 Cemetery

Area inhabited by lepers

The narrow, dead straight passage now leads to the westerly long side of the island. There are the well-preserved ruins of houses on both sides of the road, with their crumbling walls, rotting wooden balconies, empty window openings. Many houses are wooden framed, and there is debris and waste inside them, along with the remains of whitewash, old house numbers, and paper cartons moving about in the breeze. Grass grows on the walls everywhere.

Passing two houses, from which stones have been removed, you come to one of the small *island chapels*. Above it is the *hospital (4)*, which was built at a later date. On the other side of the path there is one of a total of 15 Venetian *wells (8)*. Be careful when you look in, the opening is not secured! Behind it there are cement basins, which belonged to the *laundry (5)*.

After the chapel there are houses which once had gardens. In the meantime they have become full of flourishing cactus figs, tamarisks and pines, and flowers of all kinds are growing wild here. These gardens were lovingly laid out and tended by the lepers.

At the end of the row of houses on the left there is a large building with a deep-sunk floor; this is the *disinfection room (6)*. Every visitor and indeed every object leaving the island had to pass through here. Go down the steps and out through the magnificent *Venetian Gate*. You are now at the former *landing stage* of Spinalonga *(7)*. The Gate, with its columns, Latin inscriptions and the Venetian lion is very well preserved.

Further on is the northern facade of the island. The cliffs on the shore fall away almost vertically here, and most impressive of all are the walls and the semi-cicular *bastion*, with the huge openings for the cannon that were used to cover the entire width of the narrow channel.

You return to the landing stage along the side of the island which faces towards the open sea. Shortly before you come to the bastion, you can see the little *burial chapel*. On the left is the *cemetery (11)* of the lepers; there are 4 rows of long graves, covered with cement slabs. Curious tourists are always lifting these lids, but there is nothing more inside. The bones of the dead have all been collected in the *charnel house (10)* alongside the cemetery. There, when your eyes grow accustomed to the darkness, you can see dusty skulls and bones lying right at the bottom.

The charnel house was filled to the brim a few decades ago. Unscrupulous souvenir hunters and "students of archaeology" have been secretly carrying the bones piece by piece home with them. Today the ferrymen and guides watch what the visitors take away with them.

The "Cretan Riviera"

A panoramic stretch of road south of Agios Nikolaos. The winding road snakes up high over the rocky coves of the broad Bay of Mirabello (*Kolpos Mirabellou*).

The contrast between the glittering turquoise sea, white rocks and silvery-green olive trees is a delight to the eye. Jagged cliff falls alternate with deeply-cut fjords and lonely sandy beaches.

The degree of settlement here seems within reason, given the immediate proximity of Agios Nikolaos. There are occasional holiday homes, villas "to rent", and bungalow-hotels. The actual mountain road up among the massive rocky walls of the Sitia mountains begins to the east of the wide bay of *Pachia Ammos*.

Unfortunately, the great bay of Mirabello serves as a natural catchment area for all the rubbish from Agios Nikolaos when the winds are unfavourable. A lot of plastic bags and other articles of rubbish are to be seen floating in the sea.

For beaches directly to the south of Agios Nikolaos see under Agios Nikolaos/Bathing.

Bay of Kalo Chorio

A wide, deep green agricultural plain, with the coastal mountains rising directly behind it. Very fertile, with fruit and olive plantations, and several wonderful beaches. There are developments in hand where tourism is concerned; tavernas, apartments and hotels indicate that there is already considerable business to be made here. Many holidaymakers from Agios Nikolaos and the surrounding area come here to swim.

The two villages of *Pyrgos* and *Kalo Chorio* are situated a few miles inland.

• ACCOMMODATION: **Golden Bay**, C class, immaculate and modern, with a cool, shady entrance lobby, and a lot of plants. All this for the pleasing price of £14 (up to the present) for a DR with balcony and private bathroom. On the left hand side of the main road (northwards), near the large bathing cove. Tel. 0842/61202.

Otherwise there are a lot of villas with apartments to rent, eg **Villa Maria**, **Villa Lidia** or the **Villa Andrea**. There are signposts everywhere on the road.

• FOOD: There are several well-frequented fish tavernas on the road, eg **Kavos** and **Vrokastro**.

▶ **Bathing:** There are several beaches at the exit to the fertile flood plain; one is situated at the point where the road from Agios Nikolaos comes down from the cliffs. At least 500 yards long, with fine sand, but difficult to reach. There are dusty field tracks through olive plantations, where you can easily lose your way.

A better idea is to go on to the neighbouring beach at *Kalo Chorio*. The entrance to it is under the tall eucalyptus trees on the road, and there is an even better approach a little further on. About 500 yards long, this is a beach which gives the impression of being wild and un-touched, and a lot of shade is provided by large tamarisks. A mobile café sells refreshments, hamburgers, souvlaki etc. Camping should be discreetly possible. There is an old German army bunker built into the sand here, as on so many of the beaches of Crete, where an Allied landing was feared.

Last but not least, at the eastern end of the plain and not far from the road there is a large rocky *bay* with a wonderful sandy beach. The scenery is unusual; the beach does not shelve at all and you can wade out in the shallows for about 50 yards. Superb light turquoise water here.

▶ **Hinterland:** *Pyrgos* is a tiny mountain nest, practically untouched by tourism. Steep alleys with rough concrete floors, poor-looking stone-built houses, a modest kafenion. The best thing to do is to leave your vehicle at the entrance to the village, after the bridge, and walk into it. There is a fine view out over the bay from the upper part of the village.

The neighbouring village of *Kalo Chorio* is larger and boasts more activity. There is a primary school here, with a large church next door to it, and there are signs of a greater prosperity. Tourists from the hotels and apartments down on the main through road are seen here more frequently.

• HOW TO GET THERE: Turn-offs (asphalt roads) from the main road lead up to both of these villages. The one leading to Pyrgos is slightly to the west of that which goes to Kalo.Chorio.

• FOOD: The taverna **Panorama** is situated at the eastern entrance to Kalo Chorio. There is a wonderful view from the vine-covered balcony out over the green plain, which falls away gently to the sea. Agile proprietress, good food, and billiards. The tiny kafenion **To Koutouki** below the main road also offers an attractive place to sit.

The scenery becomes rocky and desolate to the east of the bay of Kalo Chorio. A little further on in the direction of Sitia, in a deep bay below the road, there is the Hotel *Istron Bay* (luxury class, tel. 0842/61303). Clinging to the grey rock wall, this white terraced construction resembles a space station on the moon. There is a fine, long, sandy beach directly in front of it, and a bus stop.

A few bends further on to the east there is a deeply-cut fjord, around which the road runs in an accordingly deep curve. At the front of the fjord there is a small and rather lonely shingle beach with a couple of shady trees. Approach is via a bumpy field track at the eastern end of the bay.

• CAMPING GOURNIA MOON: c. 2.25 miles west of Pachia Ammos, the nearest village; peaceful and far away from the bustle, this is the only site in the region. An attractive, small terraced complex below the road on a bizarre rocky bay. Agios Nikolaos can be seen directly opposite. Sanitary facilities cramped, but relatively new. Not much shade at present, but the little trees there are growing! There is a taverna, but only a modest shop selling the barest essentials (a disadvantage, if you do not have transport!). Only a few yards to a small shingle beach, perfect for snorkelling. However, a lot of plastic refuse floats over here from the tourist centre of Agios Nikolaos. Cost per person £2, vehicle £1, same for tent. Open from 01.05.-31.09. Tel. 0842/93243.

Connections: Buses from Agios Nikolaos to Sitia and Ierapetra (and vice versa) will stop, if you ask the conductor beforehand. Last bus to Agios Nikolaos c. 8.45 p.m. and last bus from Ag. Nikolaos at 8.00 p.m. Note: You are rather "cut off" on the site in the evenings.

Gournia

The only Minoan town to have been excavated on Crete up till now. Thus it has an extraordinary significance, because it enables research into the living standards of people over 3,500 years ago.

From the amount of bronze tools, knives, needles, fishing hooks, pottery and such like that has been found here, Gournia must have been a large centre for handwork. The maze of paved alleys and little houses greatly calls to mind a mountain village in present-day Crete.

Gournia is just under 1.25 miles to the west of Pachia Ammos, on a hill directly on the road, only 100 yards from the sea.

• CONNECTIONS: Buses from Ag. Nikolaos to Sitia and Ierapetra stop directly at the entrance.

• OPENING TIMES: daily from 8.45 a.m.-3.00 p.m. **Admission** free. Smoking is strictly forbidden!

A tour of the site: Today, the whole settlement consists only of walls of up to no more than shoulder height. The rooms in the small houses were tiny, but nearly all had a second floor, reached by an external stairway. Remains of the stairways can still be seen, along with parts of the original drainage system.

The plateau on top of the hillock with its broad *agora* is reached via a small, stepped alleyway. There is a superb view out over the sea as far as Agios Nikolaos from up there. A flight of steps leads to the former palace, the rooms of which are grouped around an inner court. Only foundation walls and the bases of columns there can be seen today. To the left of the steps there is a large round slab of stone, a so-called *Kernos*, which was probably an altar for animal sacrifices.

A little to the north of the palace there was a small *sanctuary*, in which numerous votive offerings have been found.

TIP:. Make friends with **Marcos** from Pachia Ammos. He has been custodian of the site for 25 years and is an inexhaustible source of information; he knows, as it were, every stone in the place. If he takes to you and feels in a good mood, he will certainly give you a private guided tour. He may even show you the newest excavations, for example the recently-examined burial chambers.

Pachia Ammos

The landscape is grandiose. This little bathing resort lies in a wide bay at the foot of the mighty rock wall of the Thripti mountains. The steep cleft of the *Monastiraki Gorge* can be seen in the background, with the jagged silhouettes of the mountain crests to the left and right of it. The little island of *Psira* lies out to sea.

Unfortunately the beach has gone totally to ruin; it is neglected and full of refuse. There is more plastic than sand.

We questioned a couple of the inhabitants. They said that, unfortunately, Pachia Ammos was rather like the sewer of Ag. Nikolaos, and that all the rubbish from the big hotels, together with that of passing ships, accumulated in this huge natural bay. In order to keep the beach clean, it had to be cleaned several times a week. This was done in June, July and August and there were a lot of visitors there at that time; but then, in September, it was no longer worth the effort.

There are several hotels, private rooms and a grocery store in Pachia Ammos. The huge "hotel ruin" in the background rather seems to indicate the capitulation of managers in the tourist business because of prevailing local conditions. In the low season, you will surely be among the very few guests here; and the predominant atmosphere is almost that of a ghost town.

• CONNECTIONS: buses from Ag. Nikolaos to Sitia or Ierapetra or vice versa stop here.

• ACCOMMODATION: **Golden Beach**, C class hotel directly on the beach. The name seems rather sarcastic in view of the quantities of rubbish here. DR with bathroom costs around £10 in June, July, and August, and £8 in September. Despite everything, it is a very agreeable place to eat. There is a fine sea view, and the beach is hidden from the terrace by trees. Tel. 0842/93278. The **Xenios Zeus** seemed to us to be in better condition (D class), situated on the main through road. Tel. 0842/93289. There are immaculate **private rooms** in a modern villa at the western exit to the village.

• OTHER INFORMATION: There is a small **grocery store** with an overdimensional "Supermarket" sign (big, cheap!) in the middle of the village, and a **garage** near the ruins of the hotel to the east of the village, shortly after the turn-off to Ierapetra.

▶ **Bathing:** A long beach of fine sand with large shingle stones, a few shady trees directly on the beach. But, as stated above, in the low season you get the feeling that you are on a rubbish dump . . .

The "Wasp Waist" of Crete

(Pachia Ammos to Ierapetra)

The narrowest part of Crete lies between Pachia Ammos and Ierapetra; it is only just over 10.5 miles wide.

The road branches off to the south coast at a point to the east of Pachia Ammos. Dominant on the left hand side is the towering, sinister cleft of the Monastiraki Gorge.

The journey to Ierapetra (see separate chapter) continues through lowland, and along past several mountain slopes, passing through **Episkopi** with the little domed church of St. Georgios and St. Charalambos (12th/13th century, situated to the east below the main through road), and **Kato Chorio** (Turkish fountain in the village square).

From Pachia Ammos to Sitia

The road to Sitia runs through a flat plain of olive trees as far as Kavousi.

Kavousi: A pretty village at the foot of a high rock face. There are a lot of oleanders on the main through road. The upper part of the village is labyrinthine, with several well-hidden little churches. The taverna *The Canyon* at the eastern end of the village is a favourite stopping place for tourist coaches.

Tholos: An asphalt road about 2.25 miles in length leads from Kavousi down to the sea through olive groves. All that can be found there is a semi-circular sand and shingle beach, which is not very clean, a couple of trees and a taverna (mostly closed). However, the water seems as clear as glass here. The barren island of *Psira* lies offshore; the amateur archaeologist Robert Seager discovered the modest remains of a Minoan harbour settlement there in 1906-8.

To the east of Kavousi, the road becomes steep. It winds up the bare, rust-brown mountain slopes, and there are grand views in every direction. At the top there is a place to rest and a vantage point called **Platanos**: a tall, shady plane tree, two tavernas, a spring and the little church of *Agios Nektarios*. There is a wonderful view out over the whole of the Bay of Mirabello as far as Agios Nikolaos, and in particular over the island of Psira down below.

The journey continues by means of a winding mountain road along the "Cretan Riviera". Occasional villages cling to the mountain ridges. East of *Tourloti*, there are constant fine views out over the tiny fishing and bathing resort of Mochlos and the offshore island.

Sfaka: A pretty little village on the main road. Built in a steep position on the slope with wide, white steps. If there is time, take a walk up to the very conspicuous church at the highest point and enjoy the view from there. On that side of the main road there is a kafenion, and the buses stop here, too.

A dusty track five miles long leads down to Mochlos from Sfaka. Tight hairpin bends, potholes, some smaller sections of the track have been cemented. No bus connection, only taxis (c. £3), or go on foot.

Mochlos

There is only a handful of houses on the little landspit between broken coastline and eroded rocky coves. Peace rules here, outside the tourist season.

Particularly among rucksack tourists, Mochlos is one of the few "secrets" of the north coast. There is not a lot to do here, but that is exactly the beauty of Mochlos; people meet in the two tavernas on the tiny harbour bay, play tavli, write their postcards, and there is usually a guitar lying around. Or they sun themselves on the weathered rock slabs and the little shingle beach, doze, or enjoy the view out over the bizarre, torn coastline.

"Big" tourism is not far away, however, and the Club-Hotel Aldiana has established itself only just over a mile outside. A small surfing and sailing school is already there, too.

• ACCOMMODATION: **Sofia**, D class. Quite habitable rooms, but not as good as they were a few years ago. Directly on the sea, has a taverna. The proprietor's daughter speaks good English. Cost with breakfast c. £14. 10% surcharge for a stay of less than 3 days. Tel. 0843/94240.

Mochlos, E class, a pleasant place to stay. A little back from the sea, therefore quiet. Inviting rooms with original beds on stone plinths, wash basin, and balcony. Shower/toilet on the passage, newly installed. Agreeable courtyard at the back covered with fine vines, a nice place to sit, or have breakfast etc. Also has a taverna. Cost c. £10 with breakfast. Tel. 0843/94205.

There are private rooms for rent in the taverna **Kavouria** (Nikos) for c. £7.

— ★ —

• FOOD: most of the rucksack tourists meet at **Nikos**. He is very friendly, when he is not overworked. There is a larger selection of dishes at the taverna **Sofia**, which belongs to the hotel of the same name. Also a well-stocked **supermarket.** There is a nice **kafenion** with a spreading carob tree on the way from the Club Hotel to Mochlos.

Bathing: A small shingle beach lies a few hundred yards to the west of the village, in a rocky cove. Otherwise the area is very rocky, with crumbling cliffs and rock slabs. There is a tiny shingle beach directly below Nikos' taverna.

The little island of *Mochlos* lies only about 150 yards opposite the harbour bay. It was probably connected to the mainland in Minoan times, thus forming a peninsula. All that remains of what must have been a very important harbour settlement at that time is a number of rock-cut graves, which are empty and overgrown today. There is a small white chapel on the island. It is easy to swim over there, but bathing shoes are necessary, as the rocks have sharp edges and there are also sea urchins.

From Sfaka to Sitia

The road passes through a beautiful mountain and hill landscape, with the occasional white village clinging to the slopes. A view of the "white city" of Sitia in the middle of a broad bay unfolds just before Chamezi.

Chamezi: The village is completely white, with a lot of steps and a wide view towards the mountains. It boasts a simple *Museum of Folk Art* (key obtainable from the kafenion below it, admission c. £0.50). A small room with a heavy wood beamed roof contains a richly decorated bedstead, and a weaving loom with accessories. There are also several old costumes and some pottery vessels on exhibition.

Sitia

The "White City"; Venetian influence; has remained peaceful

The white and pastel-coloured houses cluster in terraces like the tiers of an amphitheatre in the gentle curve of the harbour bay.

Narrow passages with steps interrupt the long parallel roads at right angles in the centre of the town. They run up the slope to the striking *Venetian castle*, behind which the desert of rocks and thistles soon begins. Tourism is concentrated on the harbour promenade; there are long rows of restaurants with hotels between them, and souvenir shops. The place is bustling in the evenings, but an air of introspection still prevails during the daytime. Directly adjoining the line of tavernas is the sandy beach, which is about 1 mile long.

Sitia is not a real Cretan city, but its groundplan of roads set at exact right angles originated from the Venetians, who wanted to establish their fourth largest coastal fort here (the administrative district of Lassithi probably took its name from La Sitia, the Venetian name for the city). But the ambitious project failed because of earthquakes and pirate attacks, and the fortifications gradually decayed. The Turks completely rebuilt Sitia in the 19th century. In the last war, Sitia was not occupied by the Germans, but instead by Italian soldiers.

Sitia is an introspective place, at least in the low season

In all, a pleasant little city, in which strolling is a pleasure. It is even peaceful out of season. It is also an ideal base from which to make excursions into the far eastern corners of Crete; the famous palm beach at Vai is on its doorstep.

Last but not least: a good, strong wine is produced on the hills around the city (see under Food).

Information: There is an information kiosk on the central square or Platia Iroon Politechniou (side of the square towards the sea). Some brochures available, but not much else.

CONNECTIONS

● **Flights**: There has been a small airport on the hill above the city of Sitia for a number of years. There are no international flight connections, but Olympic Airways operates a service about 2 x daily to and from Rhodes. Tickets can be bought at Olympic Airways, 56. Venizelou St.

● **Boats**: At present, there is a boat connection twice weekly to **Rhodes** via **Karpathos**. The journey to Rhodes takes about 15 hours, and from there, there are good connections to the other islands of the Dodecanese. There may be other connections and a check should be made on these in Sitia itself.

• **Bus**: recently the bus station has been moved to Itanou St., a few yards from the shore promenade. There are connections to Iraklion via Agios Nikolaos 9 x daily, to Vai via Palekastro 6 x daily, to Kato Zakros 2 x daily, and to Ierapetra 6 x daily.

• **Taxi**: There is a taxi rank on the Platia Iroon Politechniou (central square with the war memorial).

— ★ —

• CHANGING MONEY: Several banks are to be found in El. Venizelou St., and on the Platia Iroon Politechniou. There is also a Post Office kiosk behind the city park.

• FRUIT/VEGETABLES: There are a number of stalls on the corner of Kazantzakis/Fountalidou St.

• POST OFFICE: situated on the Platia Ethniki Antistasis. Open for business Mon-Fri 7.30 a.m.-3.00 p.m. There is a post office kiosk behind the city park, open Mon-Sat 8.00 a.m.-7.00 p.m. and Sun. 9.00 a.m.-5.30 p.m. Money can also be changed here.

• **Car/motorbike hire**: There are several companies at the lower end of Itanou St. and on the shore promenade in an eastwards direction, eg Hermes, Sitia, Vai (cars) and Petras, Kazamias, Moto Sitia (motorbikes and mopeds). There is a garage in the immediate neighbourhood.

• TRAVEL AGENT: **Tzortzakis Travel** on the fishing harbour, a short way along the shore promenade El. Venizelou in a northerly direction. Boat excursions, ferries to the mainland, and flights. Tel. 0843/22631 and 28900.

• TELEPHONE: **OTE Office** at 22, Kapetan Sifi St. (opposite Hotel Crystal), Mon-Sat 7.30 a.m.-10.00 p.m.

• NEWSPAPERS/MAGAZINES: An international selection is available at the **kiosk** next to the large kafenion Tsirikales, on the square with the war memorial.

Accommodation

There is no lack of accommodation in the middle to reasonable price categories. On the other hand there is a complete dearth of hotels of the A and B class. The Sitian Beach Hotel (A class) directly on the beach has been taken over by a French club.

• **Itanos**: C class, the largest hotel in the place with 130 beds. Situated directly on the shore promenade, next to the square and the small city park. There are leather sofa suites on the ground floor, and a television; the dining room is on a slightly raised floor in the background. Rambling passages, rooms with linoleum-covered floors and dark wood furniture. Telephone, radio/cassette player, and balcony. Solid middle class hotel. Cost c. £16. Tel. 0843/22900.

• **Elena**: C class. Unusually tasteful furnishings. Elaborately paved floor and heavy upholstered furniture in the lobby, and the rooms have air conditioning which functions. Cost. c. £14 for a room with breakfast and bath. The Elena is only a few yards from the shore promenade, at 4, Itanou St. (Noisy street, and the double glazing does not help very much). Tel. 0843/22681.

• **Denis**: hotel-like guest house in a central position on the shore promenade. Magnificent view of the sea from the upper floors. Clean rooms with washbasins and passable beds. Toilet/shower on the passage. Plain, but spacious. Cost c. £10-12. Tel. 0843/28356.

• A very new addition is the C class Hotel **Elysee** (on the promenade in an eastwards direction), and there is also the **El Greco** (C class) at 15, Gabriel Arkadiou St. (diagonally across from the Folk Museum).

REASONABLY PRICED

• **Archontiko**: D class, with an informal, personal atmosphere and a lot of established custom. The owner, Mr Kamali, lives with a charming lady from Berlin, Brigitte, who is responsible for the extreme cleanliness and particular flair apparent in this guest house which used to be the old Town Hall (dates from 1910). Hotel guests meet under the orange tree on the terrace in the evenings, and the ouzo is free! Situated in a quiet side street, which leads up to the castle. The rooms are simple, but very clean; washbasin, toilet/shower on the passage. Cost c. £9.00 for a DR. Address: 16, Joan. Kondilakis. Tel. 0843/28172.

• **Apollonia**: A young Greek/German couple, Terry and Daggi Aerakis, have recently become proprietors of this guest house at 22 Daskaloyannis St/corner of Misonos St. It is recommended by many satisfied guests, and a DR costs c. £9. Shower/toilet are up on the roof garden, where it is very nice to sit in the sun.

Farewell feasts for guests who are leaving also take place there. If the house is full, it is possible to sleep up there on mattresses. Breakfast is accompanied by music.

• **Viktoria**: on the right hand side at the exit from the town in the direction of Ierapetra. Attractive little guest house with two gardens, simple rooms and friendly owners. Use of kitchen possible. DR for £9. Tel. 0843/28080.

• **Windstille**: residential premises in a quiet side alley, doors with decorated glass panels, simple, use of kitchen. Balconies with greenery. About £9 for a DR. Address: 26, 4. Septembriou St. Near the bus station.

• **Akrogiali**: E class, on the shore promenade next to the taverna To Paragadi. A little cramped, with a view of the sea from some rooms. Terrace at the back. Cost with private bathroom c. £10, without bath £9. Tel. 0843/22357.

— ★ —

• PRIVATE ROOMS: Countless citizens of Sitia rent out private rooms. These are scattered over the whole city, especially in the old passages up to the castle. They are, of course, quite simple, but reasonable. Large clean rooms with new beds can be found, for example, at a certain house at **37, Fountalidou St** (direction of the castle). Cost c. £9.00. The

small rooms for c. £6 are less recommended. The "lady of the house" will let you sleep on the roof for c. £3.

Those who want quick access to the beach will find various other possibilities on the road which runs along the beach, just over half a mile out of the city (eg **Michel, Demetra, Petras**).

— ★ —

• YOUTH HOSTEL: situated on the edge of the city, on the road leading into it from Agios Nikolaos (go back along Itanou St. for a few yards from the bus station, turn right by the traffic signs and go about 440 yards up a low hill). A simple establishment with musty-smelling rooms, but a quiet position. You can sit comfortably on the terrace in the evenings, and there is sometimes hot water in the showers.

The "warden" Lakis Dimakis is very seldom around, but there is usually a seasoned traveller there who will show you where everything is. Please do not check out before 9.00 a.m., as people want to sleep in. You can also pitch a tent in the burning sun in the stony "garden" behind the house. Cost c. £2. Address: 4, Therissou St. Tel. 0843/22693.

• READER'S TIP: "By chance we landed in very clean and pleasant accommodation in Sitia. **Finikias** is near the Archaeological Museum at the exit from the city in the direction of Ierapetra, and can be reached via a field path. There are three double rooms (cost c. £8), a very good bathroom, a communal kitchen and an agreeable courtyard with a large round table. Tents may also be pitched on the premises if the house is full. The owner, Manolis, likes to invite his guests for coffee. Tel. 0843/23741."

Food

There is one taverna next to the other on the shore promenade; fresh fish and lobsters with their claws and feelers still waving are put on show in large refrigerated displays. Unfortunately, touts from these establishments can be quite persistent.

A speciality of Sitia is the local *Agrilos* wine, which is of a particularly intense red colour.

• **Zorbas**: the market leader, a large restaurant on the shore promenade, right next door to the square containing the war memorial. It is a top address, directly on the water's edge, but usually so full that there is a long wait for food.

• **To Paragadi**: recognisable from its long green sun canopies. Quicker service, good food and a large selection of dishes. Georgios, the proprietor, likes to laugh and it is important for him that his customers are satisfied. The speciality is fish soup. Situated on the shore promenade in an eastwards direction.

• **Yuras**: at 4. Dimokritou St., behind the little city park. Smaller than the big places on the sea front. Local people also eat here, and it is still relatively cheap. Less fish, but more meat dishes.

Try the local Agrilos wine here; white, rosé and red are all the same low price.

• **Da Capafresco**: a friendly pizzeria, newly renovated in gleaming immaculate white. Run by Salvatore from Sicily for many years; simple pizzas, and a good local wine from the barrel. Address: Itanou St., right down on the water.

• **O Baklavas**: "Come on! If the food's no good, you won't pay!" This and other tempting statements are plastered in German over the front of a little **kafenion/taverna** of the old sort. There are primitive wall paintings inside, and a bouzouki hangs on the wall. Only offers a few dishes, hearty simple cooking. Rucksack tourists like to come here. Address: 27, Bitzentzo Kornaro.

• SNACKS: There are simple souvlaki and fast food places in El. Venizelou St., which runs a little behind the sea front and then meets it.

KAFENIA

• **Mitzakakis**: situated on the seafront near the Hotel Itanos. A speciality here are loukoumades (small doughnuts deep-fried in oil, with honey). Two huge oil paintings of Sitia and the palm beach at Vai hang in the café.

• **Tsirilakes**: on the square with the war memorial, and originates from the "good old days". You can sit here without placing an order; and with every order you automatically get a glass of water. A nice place to read a newspaper.

• **Melissa**: a little way along the sea front from Zorba's Restaurant in a northerly direction. A quiet place to sit, and there are various pastries to be had, apart from Risogalo (cold rice pudding).

• NIGHT LIFE: **Cavi Club**, also called Kalamia (which means bamboo/reeds). Large, very pleasant beach bar with good music. Very crowded, a colourful assortment of Greeks and tourists. On the shore promenade in an easterly direction. Opposite is the large open-air disco **Black Hole** (entrance fee). Smaller and with a more personal atmosphere is **Zorbas** disco, at 121, Bitzentzo Kornarou St. parallel to the harbour promenade.

Sightseeing

Many attractive little alleyways can be discovered by going up the steps behind the shore promenade, and there are also occasional town houses dating from the last century.

A marble monument representing a dying, pain-wracked hero stands under palm trees in the central Platia Iroon Politechniou. Here, too, there is the little *city park* with a couple of palms, orange trees, and hibiscus interspersed with the busts of important Cretan personalities. Unfortunately, there is nowhere to sit here.

On your way up to the castle you can look in at the *Folk Museum* (10, Gabr. Arkadiou St., well-signposted). This features traditional household and work equipment; worthy of note are the plough, which has been fashioned from rough wood, and the old weaving loom, on which the colourful wall hangings are woven from sheep's wool. There are also many other examples of crochet and woven work.

OPENING TIMES: Mon-Sat 10.00 a.m.-2.00 p.m., 5.00 p.m.-8.00 p.m. Admission c. £0.50.

Venetian castle: This still has a military appearance today, with its firing slits and massive walls. There is almost nothing else left apart from the well-preserved walls and the tower-like main building, as the castle was totally destroyed three times by the Turks. Restoration has been going on here for several years; new wooden doors are being put in, and battlements and watchtowers are being restored. The ascent will draw the perspiration out of you, but it is worthwhile for the fine view over the bay of Sitia from the top.

Archaeological Museum: This is situated on the exit road to Ierapetra. A modern atrium-building with a lot of light and space. It serves as the depository for the countless finds that have been made at over 80 places in eastern Crete. The exhibits, which date from the Neolithic to the Hellenistic/Roman period are exhibited chronologically and well-presented. Even the finds from the most recent excavations in 1987 have been included. Exhibits from the palace at Kato Zakros take up a considerable amount of room. The final exhibit consists of several moss-covered Roman amphorae in a water-filled aquarium, meant to represent their original location at the bottom of the sea. Owing to the fact that there are not many visitors to the museum, there is adequate room and the exhibits can be studied in peace.

OPENING TIMES: workdays 8.45 a.m.-3.00 p.m. Sat 9.30 a.m.-2.30 p.m. Closed on Sunday. Admission £1.

▶ **Bathing:** A sandy beach, not very wide and about 1 mile in length, runs the whole length of the bay of Sitia. Directly behind it is the very busy stretch of road to Vai. The beach does not shelve at all. The main attraction in earlier years, a freighter that had run aground and whose rusting hulk could be seen sticking out of the water, has unfortunately now disappeared.

From Sitia to the extreme east of Crete

Barren mountain ridges without trees or bushes extend eastwards from Sitia. Only ankle-high brown phrygana covers the mountain slopes.

This is one of the areas of Crete with the lowest amounts of precipitation. The broken rims of bays and bizarre cliffs coloured rust-red to dusty yellow give it the appearance of a barren moon-landscape. The few villages can be counted on one hand, and there is no sign of life for miles on end. Thus the beach at Vai seems like an oasis in the desert, and other places worth a visit are the Monastery of *Toplou,* the beach at *Palaikastro* and of course the beautiful bathing cove at *Kato Zakros,* site of another Minoan palace.

At the eastern end of the bay of Sitia, the well-built asphalt road winds upwards in snake-like curves. Passing weathered cliffs and coves, there is a constant fine view of the sea and the bay of Sitia. A wide asphalt road leads to the Monastery of Toplou and further on to Vai (signposted).

Monastery of Toplou

This stands like a Mexican hacienda in the middle of the lonely wilderness of rocks. The nearer you come to it, the more Toplou seems like a fortress of the Middle Ages. An outpost of civilisation, with walls several feet thick, military and forbidding in appearance.

Left on their own, the monks were constantly on the watch for pirates and the Turks. The cannons were ready (*Toplou* in Turkish means something like "cannons"!), and with a permanent watch posted at the top of the high bell tower, the monastery was equipped for resistance against conquerors of any kind throughout its whole history. It was attacked many times during the Turkish occupation, and also destroyed. Even during the Second World War, Cretan partisans used to meet with the British here.

According to reports, the Monastery of Toplou owns rich lands, including for example the beach at Vai; thus its financial position seems to be a firm one, in contrast to that of many other monasteries on the island. The whole complex was even lavishly restored a few years ago. The two monks who still live there talk to visitors, take the role of tourist guide and sell postcards. A souvenir shop and a small taverna have established themselves in front of the main door.

A tour of the monastery: Passing beneath the bell tower, visitors enter the intimate little *inner courtyard*, which is surely one of the most beautiful of its kind in Crete. Closely paved with round shingle stones, surrounded by a shady arcade, flights of steps and the protective wall of the monastery, this is a world all of its own.

The *text of a treaty* dating from the 2nd century BC hangs under glass next to the door to the little *monastery church*. In places, the letters have almost worn completely smooth, as the slab was used as an altar table for many years before its value was recognised. There are several old frescoes preserved in the dome of the chapel, and in particular there is one of the most magnificent icons of Crete: *Megas i Kyrie* (You are almighty, Lord), painted by Ioannis Kornaros around 1770.

Finally, visitors can go up the steps from the monastery courtyard. There are several walkways around the top of the walls, from which there is a view out over the barren landscape, a few farm buildings, and the fields belonging to the monastery.

Vai is an area of nature conservation today

Vai, the Palm Beach

A sea of tall green date palms pushes its way between the rocks far into the hinterland. In front of it, there is a wonderful beach of fine sandy gravel. Vai is a wonder of nature, with lush vegetation in a stony wilderness, the rustling of palms and that South Sea feeling. Legends abound, and everyone wants to see it . . .

The more recent history of Vai is identical with that of so many beautiful places. It was almost unknown 20 years ago, and travellers to

the easternmost part of Crete only occasionally strayed there, giving amazed reports of a great palm beach on their return. Then came the "hippies", followed by rucksack tourists; some stayed for weeks, some for months, others even longer. The wonderful palm beach turned into a rubbish dump. Its bad reputation even got into guide books, and travellers were warned against staying in the dirty, polluted palm forest. Then a few years ago, the authorities reacted; the whole palm oasis was designated as a nature conservation area, a fence was put round it, and entry was prohibited!
There is an area of beach with a few palm trees outside the fenced-in area, and this is the only part which is accessible today.

In spite of all this, an excursion to Vai is part of the standard programme of almost every visitor to Crete. All day long, dozens of air-conditioned buses deposit whole droves of trippers there, and then there are those who have rented cars or motor bikes, and those who come here by regular bus. If you dislike crowds of people, you should perhaps come here out of season, for then it is still an idyllic setting. Behind you are the shady palms, in front of you there are bizarre-shaped rocky islands. And even when the palms are perhaps not quite such a lush green, but rather somewhat dusty, with wild oleander, thorn bushes and tufted grass growing between them, Vai still remains one of the most beautiful places on the coast of Crete.

What legend tells us about Vai:
. . . it was in the Year of our Lord 824, when the bloodthirsty Saracen rabble under its godless leader Abu Hafs Omar arrived once more on the island of Crete. This time he issued an order that all the ships should be burned; there was no going back and the hordes of Allah stormed through the plains and the cities of the north. Those who did not convert to the true Mohammedan religion were hanged, hacked to death, or even worse. One of mighty Abu Hafs Omar's divisions landed in the rocky bay of Vai, too. Tired and hungry, the Arab pirates ate the dates that they had brought with them, carelessly throwning the stones away behind them . . .

Quite apart from the tendentious and summary judgement on the Saracens, whose conduct, as described here, is far less apparent to experts, this theory about the origin of the trees is doubted by modern scientists. They contend that the date palms at Vai are indigenous trees, at home on Crete long before the Arabs arrived, of the type *Phoenix theophrastii*. They are also found in other places on the island, eg on the beach at Preveli (see page 511). The fruit is inedible.

• HOW TO GET THERE/CONNECTIONS: With your own car, it can be reached by a good asphalt road from Sitia via Palaikastro (17 miles). Or take the road to the left about 3 miles before Palaikastro, which leads there via the Monastery of Toplou (also asphalted and a little shorter). A recommended day excursion: **Sitia - Monastery of Toplou - Vai - Itanos - Palaikastro - Sitia**.

Public buses run several times daily from Sitia via Palaikastro to the beach at Vai, and vice versa.

• FACILITIES: There is a large new car park at the beach, public toilets, a large snack bar and a restaurant (half-way up on the rocks). There is also a surfing school/board hire at the northern end of the beach. The beach is open from 7.00 a.m.-9.00 p.m.

• ACCOMMODATION: not available, either on the beach or near it. The nearest private rooms for rent and hotels are to be found in Palaikastro (5 miles away).

As always, however, rucksack tourists are drawn magically to Vai, but sleeping on the palm beach there is expressly forbidden! Despite this, there are always a few undeterred individuals who try it. Police presence and operations there vary. If there are only a few likely sleepers around, there may be no checks made at all. But on no account make a fire!

A much better possibility to spend the night and one which has been tolerated by the police up to the present: to the right of the main beach, and after a climb of about ten minutes (past the restaurant), you come to a wonderful **beach of dunes**, which is only about 100 yards long. This extends far up the slope, but there is hardly any shade, only low bush cover. There is another narrow beach, surrounded by rocks, to the left of the main beach. This can also be reached over a rocky path and is about a 10-minute walk away. It is sad that some people seem to view beaches as rubbish tips!!

Thus a sign at the entrance to the beach states:

"The beautiful forest of Vai is a unique habitat, created through the indigenous species of palm known as *Phoenix theophrastii*. This is the northernmost occurrence of the species and therefore it is a place of international interest. For this reason, its conservation and the creation of excellent environmental conditions here are essential; thus, its development may continue undisturbed, while at the same time the entire habitat may be the subject of thorough research."

Itanos

Vai in miniature. While the tourists tread on each others' toes at the famous palm beach, a wonderful peace prevails here, at least out of season. One or two rented cars certainly stop here for a flying visit, but only very few stay here, mainly because of the problem of amenities. Palaikastro, the next village, is just over 5 miles away.

Of the three beaches, the southernmost is by far the finest, with its white sand, several slim palm trees, and bushes. Camping is possible. Please do not expect solitude in the high season, for Itanos has been discovered.

The historical origins of the place are only suggested by a couple of column bases and the remains of walls. Itanos was probably inhabited as early as Minoan times and remained an important harbour city until early Christian times. In 148 BC Itanos allied itself with Hierapytna (modern Ierapetra), and the treaty is incorporated into the external facade of the little church at the Monastery of Toplou. Sometime later, parts of Itanos sank into the sea (as at Olous, see chapter on Elounda). However, the last inhabitants left the city only in Venetian times.

● HOW TO GET THERE: Itanos is about 1.25 miles north of Vai. When coming from the direction of Palaikastro, do not turn off to Vai but continue straight on. Turn right at the next fork in the road. No bus connections.

From Itanos northwards

This is almost the end of the world. A good road runs over to the north-easternmost tip of Crete, but the sign at the crossroads near Itanos indicates a Greek military base here. Only a few drivers of rented vehicles have enough curiosity to stray further along the road. But it is worth it; there is a fascinating play of colour between the rust-brown and white rocks, with their covering of green bushes, and the deep blue of the sea. Absolute solitude. Far out across the glittering water you can glimpse the outline of Karpathos. A sign saying "Restricted Military Area" once again warns you when you get to the narrow spit of land of *Ormos Tenda*, in the midst of a desert of glistening stones.

Palaikastro

The quiet main town of the region, situated on a hill in the middle of extensive olive plantations. The white alleyways are scorched by the sun during the day, and in the evenings the tourists meet in the colourfully-lit tavernas on the square by the church.

Palaikastro is a typical farming village, where the inhabitants live almost exclusively from their olive trees. The village has a factory for producing the oil, and in the months of December, January and February everyone is busy with the olive harvest.

Thus there is nothing particularly interesting about the place, but in spite of this Palaikastro is "on the way up" where tourism is concerned. Its proximity to Vai and the fine sandy beaches about 1.25 miles outside the village, plus the fact that a Minoan settlement has been excavated there, are all to blame for this.

It is not a bad place to relax for a few days, away from the bustle.

● CONNECTIONS: see under Sitia. **Buses** stop on the main square, from which point there are roads to Vai/Itanos, Sitia, and Zakros.

● TELEPHONE: There is an OTE office up the passageway opposite the main door of the church. Mon-Fri 9.00 a.m.-12.00 p.m. and 5.00 p.m.-8.00 p.m.

● MOPED HIRE: at Hotel Hellas and elsewhere.

Accommodation

● **Marina Village**: C class, wonderful quiet position in the middle of olive trees slightly outside the village on the way to the beach. Especially ideal in the low season for quiet, relaxing holidays. DR with shower/WC costs c. £14, including breakfast. The approach road is unfortunately very bad, a bumpy, stony track, well-signposted from Palaikastro. About 10 mins. to the beach on foot, and 20 mins. to the village. Tel. 0843/61284.

• **Hellas**: central position on the main square. Very neat interior, recently renovated. Extravagant marble floor in the little entrance lobby and in the passageways. Rooms rather modest by comparison, with private bathroom, balcony, new wooden beds. "Art works" made of wrought iron on the walls. DR c. £10. Has a large taverna, which can be noisy in the evenings. Tel. 0843/61240.

• **Itanos**: E class, exactly opposite the Hellas. Very simple, but spacious, airy landings, shower/WC on the passage, all rooms with balcony, view over the square. Costs £8 for a DR, Tel. 0843/61205. Also has a much-frequented taverna.

• **Haus Margot:** guest house at the exit from the village in the direction of Sitia. The German proprietress, Mrs. Margot Paladakis, and her Cretan husband are very friendly and helpful. They not only promise a family atmosphere in their advertisements, but they actually offer one. The style and furnishings are very appealing and the price is moderate by comparison, c. £9-10 for a DR. Breakfast and German coffee are available after a swim. The Margot Guest House is frequently booked out, so reservations beforehand are essential. Tel. 0843/61277.

• PRIVATE ROOMS: The best of these are offered by **Ioannis Perakis**, a little below the village on the road to the beach. Rural atmosphere, with goats grazing nearby, and the occasional farmer passes by on his clattering three-wheeler. DR costs £8. There are more private rooms for rent in Angathia, a little below the house of Mr. Perakis (see below).

• FOOD/CLUBS: There are two tavernas on the village square and a pizzeria. The discotheque **Space** is situated on the road to Sitia (diagonally across from the Margot Guest House), and there are also several bars, eg the **Enigma Pub**, which is the last house in the direction of Vai.

Angathia: A tiny village on the side of the road to the beach, on a mountain slope just over half a mile from Palaikastro. The pretty cruciform-domed church with the light blue roof is visible for miles around. Far away from the hectic world, or thus it seems; the women sit in front of their low, whitewashed houses doing crochet work or knitting, and look up in curiosity when a tourist strays by. Almost no cars find their way up here, and the cement road ends at the entrance to the village. There are only unmade stepped paths in the village itself. You can try a raki in the tiny kafenion belonging to I. K. Kocharakis. There may only be two or three wobbly chairs here, but there is a peace that does you good, and a wonderful view out over the silver-green olive trees and the sea. There is already a taverna in the village.

• ACCOMMODATION: **Papadakis** private rooms are our tip here. Nikola Papadakis and her husband only built the house in 1984. Extremely tasteful and immaculate, with a fine view, modern rooms with tiled bathrooms, and a well-stocked garden. Good middle European standard. DR costs c. £9. Breakfast is offered. The house is signposted from Palaikastro ("beautiful view").

▶ **Bathing:** The 1.25 mile trek from the village to the beach through dry, dusty olive groves will draw the perspiration out of you. But it is worth the effort; there is a striking table mountain beside the sea, and to the left of it a *sandy beach* about 1.5 miles long, which curves slightly in a northerly direction. Still a very peaceful place, with shade provided by a lot of trees. Also recommended for motor caravans, camping etc. There is a wonderful semi-circular *sand and shingle cove* to the right of the table mountain. There is rather more activity here; tourist buses come here several times daily, and their occupants stumble through the Minoan excavations at Roussolakos.

Roussolakos: The excavations lie directly behind the beautiful bathing cove and were carried out at the turn of the century. Today, the site is partly overgrown again, and quite neglected. This was a Minoan city settlement rather like that at Gournia (see page 310). However, only the very modest remains of crude, dark grey foundation walls have been preserved. It is still possible to make out the right-angled pattern of main and side streets, on which the houses were situated.

• FOOD: A visit to one of the fish tavernas on the bathing cove is very worthwhile. The best position is enjoyed by the taverna **Chiona**, whose elderly owners are very pleasant people.

From Palaikastro to Kato Zakros

There are just under 19 miles of curving road through a desolate mountain region between Palaikastro and Kato Zakros. A handful of little nests of houses is the only sign of human habitation in this parched landscape. There has been a marked rural exodus here, and the coast is almost inaccessible.

Fascinating: about half way along this stretch of road, the soil is an intensive lilac colour. The landscape is characterised by contrasting colours over a number of miles. Minerals such as oxide of copper etc. are probably responsible for this colouration.

Zakros

A place to stop on the way down. Zakros is attractively situated on the slope and has lush green gardens. The picture is also relieved by a lot of slim cypresses.

The secret of this fertile oasis in the middle of barren limestone mountains is easily explained. The strongest spring on Crete gushes forth directly above Zakros. 800 cubic metres of water bubble out of the mountain every hour, if the inhabitants are to be believed. The water has for a long time been channelled through the alleys of the village by means of small conduits.

Because of this, of course, Zakros also has its lemonade factory (the grey building on the main square, next to the taverna of "Maestro") and bananas have also been grown in the open air here for about 50 years.

• CONNECTIONS: only two buses daily to and from Sitia (via Palaikastro). Fare around £2. Apart from that, there is a school bus between Palaikastro and Zakros in the morning and afternoon, on which you can also travel.

• TELEPHONE: there is a telephone with a meter in the cigarette shop.

• ACCOMMODATION: **Zakros**, C class, the only hotel in the place. This has a monopoly, because there are no private rooms! The cost of a room with balcony and private bathroom/WC is about £10. Situated right on the village square, where the buses stop. Tel. 0843/28479.

Alternatives: either spend the night in **Kato Zakros** (more choice) or at "Maestro's", far down on the road to Xerokampos (Ambelos). There you can have a simple DR for c. £6, but the approach road is not made up and full of potholes. Ask at his taverna.

— ★ —

• FOOD: The few tavernas are nearly all on the main square. The nicest place to sit is at **Erotokritos**, where there is a shady canopy and breakfast can be ordered. At **Maestro**, the chatty, friendly owner with his excellent knowledge of languages (English, German, French, Italian) will attract your attention. He will gladly give you information about any-

thing in the region, and also knows a little about archaeology. Unfortunately, he is not always there, as he has to tend to his banana plantation. A speciality of his taverna is goat's meat with garlic and wine. There is also a **Pizzeria** with a terrace affording fine views of the countryside at the exit from the village in the direction of Kato Zakros.

From Zakros to Kato Zakros

The road from Zakros to Kato Zakros has recently been made up. Public buses from Sitia go down to the beach. The road winds sharply through a wild, seemingly primeval landscape with some superb views out over the coast and the deep blue sea.

Walking from Zakros to Kato Zakros

Those who wish to do so can take a very worthwhile hike from Zakros to Kato Zakros through the famous *Valley of the Dead*. From Zakros, the hike takes around one and a half hours.

Description of the route: From the village square, take the road along by the Hotel Zakros, then follow the road which is signposted to Kato Zakros. The turn-off to Keratokambos (see below) soon appears on your right and straight after it there are the ruins of a *Minoan Villa* (signposted), directly on the road to Kato Zakros. It is just under 5 miles to Kato Zakros from here.

Valley of the Dead: So-called because the Minoans interred their dead in the numerous caves along the ravine. Only one intact, undisturbed grave has been found, however, which contained the remains of 5 women dating from the period 2300-2100 BC. All the other graves had been robbed.

In order to find the entrance to the ravine, you must first of all follow the normal motor road to Kato Zakros. The ravine with its steep slopes can be seen on the left, about 100 yards after a pale yellow house directly on the road. The descent begins here. Shortly before the pale violet-coloured vehicle track which leads up to the left, the path descends steeply beneath telegraph poles. A barely discernible goat track leads through a gate (with "please close after you" in Greek written on it) to the bottom of the ravine.

After reaching the bottom, the way continues through huge oleander bushes and moss-covered boulders and along a dried-up river bed, although you feel the way here rather than see it, and you will probably stray off the track for a few yards from time to time. It is wonderful to see what is growing here in this untouched environment; asphodel, wolf's bane, and the slopes brimming with oregano, amongst many other plants. There is the absolute quiet, too. The huge, shimmering, rust-red to grey cliffs are above you, with windswept little trees and bushes clinging desperately to them. Thus the river cutting winds down, gouging its way deep into the limestone massif. Perhaps you will climb up to one or another of the huge holes in the weathered rocks, but there is not much to be seen there. Then, the valley opens up, and suddenly you are in the midst of fleshy banana plants, and orange and lemon trees - you are in Kato Zakros! A fertile hollow, almost subtropical. The ramble should take about 1 hour from the beginning of the descent.

Kato Zakros

A dream of a bay; "table mountains" weathered to terraces fall sharply into the deep blue sea. Between them is a wonderful sand/shingle beach, about 550 yards long.

The sun beats mercilessly down during the day, and shade is only to be found under the knotty tamarisks on the beach. Here too, are the six tavernas of the "village" in a row, like pearls on a chain. They are always quite crowded in the summer. Directly behind the beach in an area of pale violet-coloured soil is the huge complex of the Minoan palace, while in the background, deep green banana plantations indicate the most important source of business for the region.

Kato Zakros is a typical destination for a day trip. During the day, various tourist buses make the tortuous trip down the winding road. Only very few visitors stay here overnight. The accommodation available is very limited. Some rucksack tourists sleep on the beach, but this is only tolerated when the rooms are all occupied. The beach tavernas are very busy in the evenings. There is smoke from the charcoal grills, from which souvlaki and grilled fish are served, and there is also music, wine and the sound of the sea. Yes, this is the way one imagines Greece . . .

• ACCOMMODATION: Apart from the few rooms that are available in the tavernas, there are two main houses which have **private rooms** for rent. You will find them if you go on for a few yards after the last taverna.

The first house seems almost like a youth hostel, and mostly young people stay here. Well-kept double rooms with wooden beds, a large sun terrace with a little table, open air shower, and a small grocer's shop - cost of a DR £9-11.

Poseidon Private Rooms: A sweet elderly couple have several rooms to rent in the next house, although these are not very clean. The rooms have washbasins and beds with simple iron frames, and there is a shower on the passage. Probably quieter than the other house, with a superb view from the terrace. Cost around £8 for a DR. Cigarettes can be bought here, and it is also possible to eat here in the high season.

— ★ —

• FOOD: The six tavernas are strung out like a necklace, an amenity and meeting place all in one. They offer simple, hearty dishes, as already mentioned - the souvlaki and grilled fish are the best. Good food is to be had, for example, at

Nikos. An attractive place to sit in daytime is at the kafenion owned by **G. Daskalakis**, where you can see the skull of an Agrimi (wild goat) with its curling horns.

Bathing: A wonderful stretch of sea in the midst of superb rocky scenery, and several caves can be seen in the sides of the cliffs.

The Palace of Zakros

The palace was found all of 100 yards behind the beach in an area of pale violet-coloured earth. A beautiful position between tall cypresses and other trees and bushes, with the bare limestone cliffs rising behind it.

Several surprises lie in store for the visitor at the smallest of the four Minoan palaces on Crete - eg its immensely rich water supply, which more than adequately feeds three wells. In addition, it is the site of one of the earliest metal-smelting ovens in world history. Here too, the excavations have not yet been completed.

The palace dates from the period between 1600 and 1550 BC, was in close contact with that at Knossos, controlled the entire sea area around Crete, and carried on a regular trade with Asia Minor and Egypt. Zakros, too, was destroyed during the great catastrophe of 1450. In contrast to the other palaces, there was no rebuilding on the rubble. The existence of the palace was forgotten, it was never (!) plundered, and it retained its precious treasures until excavation took place in this century. Some of the most important finds of the Minoan culture have been made here.

In 1901, the Director of the British School of Archaeology, *D. G. Hogarth*, tried his luck here. He dug in the wrong place, and only found a few remains of houses belonging to the extensive Minoan settlement on the slope behind the actual palace. By a great stroke of luck, an owner of land in the area decided to build a hothouse for growing tomatoes in 1961, and came upon jewellery from the palace in the process. Since then, the excavations have been led by the Greek archaeologist, *Professor Nikolaos Platon*. Amongst other things, a search is being made at present for the harbour of Zakros, which is thought to lie deep under the surface of the sea.

• OPENING TIMES: Mon-Sat 9.30 a.m.-3.45 p.m. Sun 9.00 a.m.-2.30 p.m. **Admission** c. £1.

A tour of the site

The entrance to the complex is at the little custodian's kiosk, which is mostly unoccupied. You then come upon a paved way, which led from the palace down to the harbour. Right at the beginning, on the left hand side and under a protective roof, there is the most peculiar structure in the whole palace; this is a pit-like depression, with 3 channels of about 6.5 feet in length leading into it. This was probably a foundry for the smelting of metal. The path leads via steps down into the paved *inner court (1),* and then the central court is reached through a narrow passage. The small rectangular construction in the court in front of the main entrance is the remains of an *altar (2).*

The central court was bordered on both of its long sides by two main wings, which probably had three storeys. On the other two sides, there were side wings with workshops and rooms used for commercial purposes.

East Wing: When approaching from the entrance to the complex, the East wing is situated on the left hand side of the central court. It housed the so-called *royal living quarters (3/4),* but has unfortunately been severely destroyed by centuries of agricultural exploitation in the area. With a little imagination, you can still make out the two rooms with their many doors and neighbouring light wells. Of interest is the circular water tank *(5)* in the rectangular *cistern hall* next door; the latter was probably the audience hall. Perhaps the circular tank was used as a private swimming pool (!) or as an aquarium for rare fish. The water still flows so strongly today that the palace is sometimes under water in the winter. Directly to the south of it there is another enclosed *well (6),* and in addition there is a round *well (8)* in the south east corner of the central court, with a stairway leading down to it.

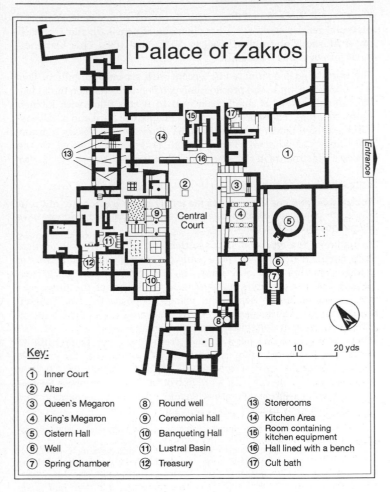

Palace of Zakros

Central Court

Entrance

0   10   20 yds

Key:

1. Inner Court
2. Altar
3. Queen's Megaron
4. King's Megaron
5. Cistern Hall
6. Well
7. Spring Chamber
8. Round well
9. Ceremonial hall
10. Banqueting Hall
11. Lustral Basin
12. Treasury
13. Storerooms
14. Kitchen Area
15. Room containing kitchen equipment
16. Hall lined with a bench
17. Cult bath

The **South Wing** mainly housed workshops and magazines. Rock crystal was worked here, among other materials.

West Wing: Directly adjacent to the central court is the great *ceremonial hall (9)* with its many doors, columns and a paved inside court. Strange partitions made in mortar are recognisable in the floor. Next to it, and formerly connected to it by three doors, is the smaller so-called *banqueting hall (10)*. The inner rooms in the west wing were reserved for cult ceremonies, and a *lustral basin* can clearly be seen here *(11)*. Next to this again is the *treasury (12)*. Numerous ritual objects of great worth were found here, the finest of which is a wonderful rhyton of rock crystal with a handle made of pearls (in the Archaeological Museum at Iraklion, Gallery VIII, case 109). This had shattered into over 300 fragments.

The **North Wing** is dominated by a room with six internal pillars. This is the first and, up to the present, only *kitchen* to have been found in a Minoan palace *(14)*! A small room next to it was filled with kitchen equipment *(15)*. There are also several Magazines here and a hall containing a fixed bench construction *(16)*. There was probably a dining hall above the kitchen. The *cult bath (17)* was connected to the Queen's apartments in the east wing by a corridor.

Xerokambos (Ambelos)

Rocks, wind and sea characterise the lonely south-east corner of Crete. There are only a few small houses here, widely scattered amongst olive plantations and plastic hothouses.

Xerokambos is a typical summer settlement for farmers who particularly maintain hot houses there. Only occasionally do bold drivers of rented cars find their way down the 6.5 miles of dirt track from Zakros to this superb yet untidy beach, with sand of the finest sort and low dunes (to the west of the "village", opposite the two little offshore islands). There is an impressive panoramic view of the high, almost completely uninhabited mountains on all sides.

Since there is a second approach from the road from Sitia to Ierapetra, the whole thing can be done as a round trip, for example **Sitia** - *Chandras - Ziros - Xerokambos - Zakros - Palaikastro - Sitia*. A *trouble-free*, reliable car with a full petrol tank is prerequisite for this trip, which goes through areas devoid of human occupation and hardly touched by tourism (more information below).

• APPROACH FROM ZAKROS: about 7 miles of stony, bumpy dirt track. The road to Xerokambos runs off to the right about 100 yards after the factory at the exit from Zakros in the direction of Kato Zakros. There is a rusty, almost illegible sign at the crossroads (shortly before the Minoan Villa on the way to Kato Zakros). At the beginning, the road passes through rich olive plantations, then through the bare limestone slopes of the coastal mountains and past a deeply-cut ravine. On the final stretch down into the plain there are numerous hot houses everywhere, with dirty plastic sides; bananas, tomatoes and cucumbers etc are grown in them.

The second approach road, which can be reached from the road from Sitia to Ierapetra (the turn-off has been asphalted as far as Chandras and Ziros, then it becomes a dusty track), presents no great problems and goes through varied terrain. Those approaching from Zakros, and wishing to make the journey up from Xerokambos via Hametoulo to Ziros, should be prepared for a steep winding road. It is better to make the round trip in the opposite direction.

• ACCOMMODATION/FOOD: There are about three houses in Xerokambos which have simple rooms for rent, and there are two kafenia.

From Sitia in the direction of Ierapetra

A curving mountain road from the north to the south coast of eastern Crete. On the right hand side of the road, about 2.25 miles from Sitia, there are the remains of a Minoan mansion (signposted). Immediately after it and on the left is a turn-off to the Minoan villa at Zou (see next paragraph). There is a lemonade factory in nearby Piskokefalo. The road climbs in curves. Passing little hamlets and the larger village of *Lithines*, the road reaches the Sea of Libya at *Makrigialos*. A detour on the way up to the Chandras Plateau and perhaps even further on to Xerokambos is worthwhile.

• VILLA OF ZOU: Approaching from the direction of Sitia, there is a turn-off to Zou just before Piskokefalo. At the beginning it is a gravel track, then it widens and, after about 2.5 miles, becomes an asphalt road. Shortly after this, the foundations of the Minoan villa, with about eight rooms, can be seen directly to the right above the road (not clearly signposted). The village of Zou is a little further down the road.

Up to the Chandras Plateau and further on to Xerokambos

A little to the north of *Ag. Georgios*, the narrow asphalt road branches to the left via Nea Pressos towards Ziros. A winding journey through the hills, with the possibility of a visit to the ruins of ancient Praissos at *Nea Pressos*.

Praissos: The city originates from the 12th century B C, that is, from the post-Minoan period, and was founded by the so-called *Eteocretans* (true Cretans), who at that time fled into the isolated mountain regions from the Dorian conquerors (see also History). There is not much left of the city, but the detour is worthwhile for the wonderful peace and quiet to be found amongst the overgrown remains of the walls. It is reached by turning to the left down a field path at the beginning of the village of Nea Pressos, and continuing along it for about 1.25 miles to a hill on which there is the so-called *first acropolis*. Keep going left at the many forks in the path on the way there. The track is bad, but passable to cars. A sign stating "First Akropolis" marks the former hill site where there was once an acropolis, the highest of three such in Praissos. The slope is thickly covered with sage and oregano bushes today, and the view ranges far over the quiet hillscape to Sitia, which was once the city's harbour.

Chandras High Plateau: This quiet, sun-drenched plateau with its lush green vines and the few houses that are Chandras makes a relaxing contrast to the bustling tourism of the coast.

A well-preserved Turkish fountain at Chandras

Just over half a mile to the east of Chandras and at the foot of a rocky hill, there are the ruins of an abandoned village, dating from the Middle Ages (there is a roadway off to the left from the main road by the playground in Chandras). A Venetian *habitation tower*, of a type often seen in the Aegean region, can be seen here. The interior contains lofty barrel-vaulting, and there are two cypress trees and an axe chiselled over the entrance. Slightly further up, there is a cool *chapel* with a double nave, containing some badly-preserved wall paintings over a grave. On the south side of the village there is a wonderful Turkish *fountain,* still in use and providing water for a garden down below, which contains a huge nut tree.

It is possible to go back from Chandras via Armeni and Etia to the main Sitia-Ierapetra road.

Ziros: A pretty village on the slope above the plateau. Here, a colourful picture is provided by pastel coloured and whitewashed houses, together with vines. There are traditional-type windmills, like those of the Lassithi High Plateau, in the area, and on top of the mountain there is a radar station belonging to the Greek army.

Xerokambos is now a distance of about 11.25 miles. A good asphalt roads winds up from the plateau and ends in a restricted area. On the right, there is a good gravel track (used by the military) to *Hametoulo*, an almost deserted village amongst barren rocks. From this point the track deteriorates progressively, but is passable to cars. It curves steeply down to the beach at Xerokambos and can only be taken at a snail's pace. On the way, there are superb views of the wild, rocky coast and the turquoise blue sea!

The South-east

The largest concentration of hothouses is to be found on the coast to the east of Ierapetra. The narrow coastal plains are plastered with yellowish-brown plastic for miles.

The little villages here also seem less attractive, the shingle beaches are often dirty, and here and there holiday homes and bungalows occupy the landscape. The rocky foothills of the Thripti mountains, which rise directly behind the coastal strip, are relieved in part by light green pine forestation. There are, however, a few beautiful bathing coves on the main through road.

In the extreme east, there is only a desert-like wilderness of stones, dried-up earth and dust tracks. In the midst of this is the brilliant white *Monastery of Kapsa*.

The miles of fine, grey, sand and shingle beaches near Ierapetra are worth a visit . . .

Ierapetra

Pole of heat in the south; Africa is not far away; a beach in the middle of the city

The only city on the south coast is situated on level ground in a broad coastal plain. Modern, less attractive buildings almost exclusively dominate the scene here. There is little sightseeing, and hardly anything of historical importance here.

But perhaps it is just this lack of attraction which allows Ierapetra to keep some of its original atmosphere.

It is only a few steps from the centre to the busy shore promenade, the nicest part of the city. The long grey sandy beach begins here, practically in the centre of town, and extends about 1.25 miles to the east. In spite of numerous tavernas and the bustle of tourism, the

Fishermen mending their nets in Ieraptera

fishermen have their permanent meeting-place here; there are thick bundles of dark red and yellow nets everywhere, and small cats rub around your legs. The elderly men of the city sit at wobbly tables, drinking their raki, munching olives and playing tavli, while right alongside them the holidaymakers from the large beach hotel crack open their lobsters and spread out their towels among the fishing boats. Out of season particularly, the scene often seems almost idyllic. The western end of the beach is bordered by the small but solidly-built *Venetian castle* and the fishing harbour, secured by breakwaters of several tons in weight. The former old Turkish quarter is also situated here; there are small paved alleys, too narrow for cars, and children are at play everywhere. Somewhere, someone is proclaiming the excellence of his tomatoes, and women are sitting in groups and chattering. You can often look right into the little houses, and some have tiny inner courtyards, protected from the sun by the creepers of vines. Building, improvement and improvisation are being carried on everywhere and noticeably new, immaculate houses are appearing in the alleys.

• **Information**: There is a small information office on the main Emmanuel Kothri Square (in the building which used to house the Archaeological Museum). Mon-Fri 9.00 a.m.-3.00 p.m. Sat 9.00 a.m.-4.00 p.m. Sun 9.00 a.m.-2.00 p.m.

• CONNECTIONS: As of late, the **bus station** is situated to the east of the centre, in Lasthenous St. If you follow the signs in the direction of the centre, you will come to El. Venizelou Square.
Connections from Ierapetra-Iraklion (via Ag. Nikolaos) about 10 x daily, Ierapetra-Iraklion (via Ano Vianos) 2 x daily, Ierapetra-Sitia (via Pachia Ammos) 3 x daily, Ierapetra-Sitia via Lithines 7 x daily, Makrigialos 7 x, Myrtos 6 x, Kalamafka (via Anatoli and Males) 2 x.
There is a taxi rank on the central square, Platia Eleftherias.

— ★ —

• CHANGING MONEY: There is a bank on Platia El. Venizelou, and two more are to be found on Platia Eleftherias.

• MARKET HALL: a rich selection of fruit and vegetables in the passageway between Kostola Adriano and Stilianou Houta St, about 100 yards from Platia Emm. Kothri.

• MOPED/MOTORBIKE RENTALS: **South Crete Tours** and **Rena** both on Stilianou Houta St., only a few yards from the Post Office; **Motus**, next door to the "California" in Kyrba St. There are more on the road in the direction of Sitia, and there is a branch of Rena at the Petra Mare Hotel.

• POST OFFICE: situated on Platia Emm. Kothri (signposted from the bus stop). Mon-Fri 7.30 a.m.-4.00 p.m.

• TRAVEL AGENCIES: **Ierapetra Express**, at 24 Platia Eleftherias, tel. 0842/22411.

You can book a whole-day tour from here to the island of Chrisi for c. £5. See below under "Excursions". There is also an **ANEK** office on Platia Eleftherias, tel. 0842/23179. **Olympic Airways** can be found on Platia Venizelou, tel. 0842/22444.

• TELEPHONE: There is an OTE office about 100 yards from Platia El. Venizelou (where the buses stop), on Nikiforou Foka St., the road to the Post Office (signposted), directly next to the little sports ground. Open Mon-Fri 7.30 a.m.-10.00 p.m.

• LAUNDRY: in a square on the exit road to Sitia.

• MAGAZINES/NEWSPAPERS: An international selection is available at 3, Dominiko Theotokopoulou, only a few paces from Platia Eleftherias.

Accommodation

A large range is available, and Ierapetra is waking up to tourism. Various hotels have opened in recent years.

• **Petra Mare**: A class, the most southerly beach hotel in Europe, as it describes itself. A large "box" with every facility, directly on the beach at the eastern edge of the city of Ierapetra (the road to Sitia passes it). Most rooms are carpeted and have a sea view, and the hotel is furnished in rustic Cretan style (eg beds on stone foundations). Large swimming pool on the terrace, private beach, disco, water sports, restaurant, cocktail bar and many other amenities. Frequented by German package holidaymakers. Cost in the high season c. £44 for a DR, in the low season c. £40. Tel. 0842/22412.

• **Camiros**: C class, attractive new hotel. Solidly furnished, marble flooring everywhere (even in the rooms), good beds, beautiful pewter lamps with tinted glass. Excellent bathrooms, with small bathtubs, and a large balcony on the first floor with a view over the roofs to the sea. Cost with breakfast c. £15-17 for a double room. Address: 17, Michali Kotri St., at the centre of the city, in a street parallel to the shore promenade. Tel. 0842/28704.

• **Ersi**: C class, a smaller establishment with inviting rooms and balconies on the street. Good beds, bathrooms tiled in blue. Considerate service, lift, recommended. Cost with breakfast c. £15-18 for a DR. Address: 23, Platia Eleftherias, very central position. Tel. 0842/23208.

• **Creta**: C class, on Platia Eleftherias. Rather older, partly renovated, rooms of varying quality. Inspect them beforehand. Also with breakfast, bath and balcony. Cost c. £14 for a DR. Tel. 0842/22316.

REASONABLY PRICED

There are numerous possibilities in the lower price category. The smaller guest houses and private rooms are mainly to be found in the maze-like quarter behind the shore promenade, especially in quiet Ioannidou St. which runs parallel to the beach promenade. Apartments with kitchens are also available.

• **Cretan Villa**: D class, near the bus station. Two-hundred-year-old house, lovingly restored, with wooden ceilings, rough white plastering and Cretan furniture. The courtyard with its mass of greenery is a gem. DR for just under £10, and there are also three studios (room, kitchen niche, shower) in a separate house for £14. Vasilis' Cretan Villa is at 16, Oplarchegou Lakerda St., which branches off Platia El. Venizelou by the Rex Restaurant. Tel. 0842/22439.

• **Gorgona**: We have had only good reports of this guest house. Very attractive and clean, DR with a bath costs c. £10. Owned by a Greek couple, who actually live in Switzerland. They cannot always be found, so you are often confronted by a locked door here. The nicest part of the guest house is the roof. Situated in Ioannidou St., parallel to the shore promenade. Tel. 0842/23935.

• **Hera**: Agreeable private rooms offered by Theo Achlatis and his family. With shower, some with a kitchen, c. £8-9. In the same alley as **Gorgona**, a few houses further on, at no. 44. Tel. 0842/23394. **Angela** rooms are diagonally opposite.

• **Coral**: D class. A small city hotel opposite the Hera. Cost c. £10 for a DR. Belongs to a Greek named Niko who can mostly be found in one of the cafés on the shore promenade. If you are looking for a room, you have come to the right man; he knows everyone (and everyone knows him), and also rents apartments with kitchens (£12) and private rooms (£7-9), some of them directly on the sea.

• **Kastro**: relatively simple rooms, not particularly large, some with simple iron bedframes. Directly on the shore promenade, however, almost at the castle. Ask for a room with a sea view. Some rooms have their own shower/WC. Cost around £8-9 for a DR.

• **Café-Bar Diagoras**: also on the shore promenade, the first house when you turn off from Platia Emm. Kothri (Town Hall, Information) towards the sea. Simple, clean rooms with new furniture of light pine. Here also, ask for a room with a sea view. Cost c. £10 for a DR.

• CAMPING: There are two sites about 5.5 miles east of Ierapetra, between the main through road and the beach. Absolutely flat and rather boring sites, but miles of grey sandy beach. Buses to Makrigialos and Sitia (via Lithines) stop here. For a description see Ierapetra/Surrounding area.

Food

There is one taverna next to the other on the shore promenade, and between them an ever-increasing number of bars and cafés. In the evenings, flashing lights and a fairground atmosphere, and unfortunately there is considerable pestering from persistent restaurant touts. The tavernas charge outlandish prices and I recommend, for this reason, a careful comparison of the bill with the menu.

SHORE PROMENADE

• **Acropolis**: offers you, amongst other things, a menu in Finnish, conveyor-belt like service, good food (try the Kokkinisto) and Middle European prices.

• **Manthos Palace**: simple, original type of fish taverna, the only one on the shore promenade that has resisted the trend towards middle European "standards" until now. Who knows how long this will last? For this reason it is the only taverna still frequented by Greeks. Offers mussels and snails, apart from fish.

• **California**: home-made fresh cheesecake, pancakes, omelettes, salads, filter coffee and ice cream. There is also an entrance on Kyrba St.

• **Pizzeria 1**: Here, the pizzas are made by Ralf from Düsseldorf. There are Italian ice cream specialities, too. Also on the shore promenade, a few paces from California in the direction of the Venetian castle.

• READER'S TIP: "Many dishes that are not included in the repertoire of most of the tavernas can be found in the taverna **Napoleon**, on the shore promenade towards the castle. One such dish is tiropitta. Closed on Sundays, for religious reasons."

Apart from those on the hectic shore promenade, there are unfortunately not many other places to eat. There is a cluster of tavernas around Platia El. Venizelos, eg *O Michalis*, where there are always a couple of sizzling spits being turned over a charcoal grill.

• **Miramare**: large, immaculate restaurant with regular customers from the neighbouring Petra Mare Hotel. Very good Greek dishes, and an excellent local wine. There is an exhibition of Greek dancing almost every evening on the dance floor, which is later given over to a disco. Everyone can join in, and there is a good atmosphere. No outlandish prices up to the present time.

• **Taverna Karin**: run by Karin and Hans from Cologne; situated to the east, next to the Petra Mare, and directly on the beach. Agreeable bar, serving schnitzels, fillet steaks, and chips, and in the mornings a lavish breakfast, continental-style: sausage, cheese, yoghurt, fruit juice, and high prices.

• KAFENIA: The traditional kafenia under the mulberry trees on **Platia Emm. Kothri** (near the Post Office) are much loved by the local men. A particularly lovely little spot is the small kafenion on the square next to the **mosque** (see under sightseeing).

• BARS: a seemingly uniform selection here. Particularly at the weekends, the large bars on the shore promenade are frequented more by Greeks than by holidaymakers; hence the prices are more within limits. There are good drinks (also international ones) in the **Le Figaro Bar**, but the **Aquarius Bar** has better outside seating. **Chez Victor** is run by a German couple.
There is live Greek music almost every evening in the pleasant **Bora-Sita Club** (except Mondays), on Kyrba St.

• DISCOTHEQUES: **Zanadu Club**, on the shore promenade, and **Santé** on the road behind it, amongst others.

Sightseeing

Ierapetra is not all that big, and the alleys behind the shore promenade are quickly explored. There is the obligatory war memorial on the central *Platia Eleftherias*, its message blatantly obvious this time: a soldier with hand grenades shields his fallen comrade with his own body. The whole thing is flanked by two rusty cannons. The richly decorated *market hall* is only a few yards away in Kostola Adrianou St.

(road to Myrtos). As always, there is a small kafenion right in the middle of it.

The *Venetian castle*, which is in need of restoration, is not accessible to visitors. Right next door to it there is a strange, completely free-standing *bell tower* with an iron spiral stairway, rounded arches and a viewing platform. A little inland from the castle is an old ruined *mosque*, the restoration of which, contrary to information from other sources, had not yet been completed. The slim *minaret* is definitely attractive and so, in particular, is the elegant Turkish *fountain house* in front of the mosque. Right next to it is a kafenion under spreading tamarisks, where Cretans are mostly among themselves, playing cards, eating mezes and drinking raki. The quiet old city quarter is a few paces from here.

NAPOLEON is said to have stopped off in Ierapetra on the way to his Egyptian campaign. Sometimes people there point out the house in which he is supposed to have spent the night.

Archaeological Museum: The small but fine museum of Ierapetra has recently moved to Kostola Adrianou St. (the road to Myrtos, a few yards from the Post Office). At the time of my last researches it had not yet been opened.

The former museum building next to the Town Hall housed several superb sarcophagi and pottery finds from various Minoan periods up to Classical times. These are decorated with almost modern drawings of chariot races, cows being suckled by calves etc. By far the most beautiful piece is an impressive *statue of Demeter* dating from the beginning of the 2nd century/end of the 1st century BC. Snakes are entwined around the head of the goddess, and she holds ears of corn in her hand. The fingers of the right hand are an addition, hence the little supports. The play of shadow in her face and the different colours in her robes and skin should be noted. The statue was found by a farmer while ploughing.

▶ **Bathing:** The long, grey, shingle and sand beach begins in the middle of the city and extends from the castle for several miles in an easterly direction. Perhaps it is not quite what you hoped for in your wildest dreams, but is well-suited to families with children, as it is completely level and there is a lot of space. There is, however, hardly any shade, only a few sparse tamarisks. A windsurfing school has established itself near the castle.

The beach also continues to the right of the castle and the harbour, but this part of it is less frequented. Rocky slabs, promontories and cliffs prevent access to the water in some places.

There are more good sandy beaches to the east of Ierapetra, eg near the camping sites.

The jewel of Ierapetra: an elegant fountain house with a minaret and a ruined mosque

▶ **Excursions:** There are daily boat trips to the offshore *Chrisi-Island* (Donkey Island), with its beautiful cedar forest and soft sand dunes. There are several tavernas open in the summer, and nude bathing is normal. Departure at 10.00 a.m. every day from the pier where the excursion boats moor in Ierapetra (on the shore promenade). Bookings can be made at the Ierapetra Express travel agency (see under addresses).

From Ierapetra eastwards

A flat stretch of land along the sea. Inland there are the slopes of the Sitia mountains, and at the beginning there is grey beach as far as the eye can see. Various beach hotels and villas are scattered over the bare landscape, and trees are only to be seen again from Ferma onwards, where there are also some beautiful bathing coves. Here too is the little fishing village of *Makrigialos,* the nicest village on this strip of coast.

About 5.5 miles east of Ierapetra, just before Koutsounari, there are two camping sites near to each other, and there are villas and apartments for rent in the area.

• CAMPING KOUTSOUNARI: rather depressing gravel site about 5.5 miles to the east of Ierapetra. There is a little shade afforded by a large reed roof and low olive trees, and the site is fenced in. One advantage is the huge beach, which is almost empty in the low season. Sanitation OK. There is a taverna with a terrace and loud piped music in the middle of the site, but this is only open in the high season. Open 01.05.-30.09. Tel. 0842/61213.

• CAMPING IERAPETRA: 500 yards to the east. Similar to Koutsounari Camping, with reed roofs and low tamarisks. Sanitary facilities are useable (stand-up toilets, however), and restaurant also open only in the high season. Open 01.05.-30.09. Tel. 0842/61351.

• OTHER INFORMATION: There is a nice taverna, called **Anamnesis**, opposite Camping Ierapetra. Breakfast is reasonably priced here, and in the evening, it is a favourite meeting place for campers. Michaelis, the owner, also rents double rooms for c. £9.

Koutsounari: A small village inland on the mountain slope, consisting almost entirely of holiday homes, with no recognisable village centre.

• ACCOMMODATION: **Traditional Cottage Koutsounari** is a settlement in the style of old Cretan villages. Unpainted houses with living rooms and bedrooms, bath and kitchen. Very attractive, with several floor levels in the cottages, stone floors and substantial pinewood ceilings. In addition, there are coloured bedspreads and wall hangings in Cretan style. Bathroom and kitchen are very spacious. For 2-4 people, cost c. £22-25. There is also a **taverna** in the same style. Tel. 0842/61291.

Ferma: This is a village along the road comprising widely scattered houses, in front of the grey slopes of the Sitia mountains. There are some little sandy coves to the west of the village, otherwise cliffs with a small rock and shingle beach. Several tavernas on the road, plus a car rental company.

• ACCOMMODATION: **Ferma Beach**, A class, a luxurious, large complex between the road and the low cliffs on the coast, with several hundred yards of sandy beach directly below it. The rooms are mainly in one or two storey houses amidst an immaculate garden with palms and tamarisks. There are many extras such as a swimming pool, tennis court, disco, air-conditioning. Cost of a DR with full board £37. Tel. 0842/61341. Many local and long distance excursions are offered here, including one to Chrisi Island opposite.

Coriva Island, B class, greatly recommended. Also directly on the road, at the beginning of the beach which is nicer here than by the Ferma Beach Hotel. Surrounded by greenery. Cost c. £24 for a DR. Tel. 0842/61263.

There are **apartments** for rent in a lonely rock, pine and olive landscape between Ferma and the bay of Agia Fotia to the east of it (Ferma Solaris and Ferma Hill).

Agia Fotia: a deeply gouged-out bathing cove. A rock mass juts out high over the road, almost like Hinkelstein in the Obelix stories. There is also the large, newly-built *Hotel Eva Mare*. Bumpy track leads down to the sea from the road below the hotel. At the bottom there are vines, olives and bananas, and a taverna on the beach. It is to be expected that tourism will increase here in the coming years.

The most beautiful stretch lies in an *easterly direction*; it is mountainous, with pine and olive trees, and there has hardly been any building activity here.

There is a good place to swim several miles further on, in a tempting rocky cove with a wide sandy beach, with adequate shade provided by tamarisks. Private rooms can be found at a really attractive house with a lot of greenery at the western end of the bay. There is also the large taverna *Fri-Hamn* with a shady terrace and paddle boats for hire. Another bay further on boasts a small shingle beach with tamarisks and the taverna *Panemidi*.

Koutsouras has a shingle beach. Rocky slabs and low cliffs extend as far as Cape Makrigialos.

Makrigialos: A small, quiet fishing village beneath a steep headland. A sandy beach extends about 770 yards to the east, with the village of **Analipsi** on the road at the end of it. The little white houses of Makrigialos, the tiny fishing harbour, the narrow promenade and a few tavernas under tamarisks still seem wonderfully introspective. The beach here is quite level.

• ACCOMMODATION: there are various private rooms in Makrigialos, and in Analipsi there is the newly-built Hotel **Irini** and the **Vivi** Guest House, both on the road.

Shortly after the huge box-like Sun Wing Hotel, which seems out of place here, the road leaves the south coast and goes up over the mountains to Sitia. For tips here see page 333.

A detour to the Monastery of Kapsa

A little way before Pilalimata, a catastrophically bumpy track branches off to the east and follows the coast. This is a worthwhile trip for all those who wish to punish their vehicles. Not recommended for mopeds. Impressive landscape here, with a cliff coastline torn to shreds, bare, stony mountain slopes with neither tree nor bush but characterised by dried-up earth and sharp edged-boulders.

Kalo Nero is the only village on the way, consisting of a couple of lost-looking houses between hot-houses above low cliffs, surrounded by a desert-like stony wilderness.

• FOOD: The little taverna **Oasis** really does seem like an oasis in the desolate surroundings. The facade is painted with butterflies, flowers and plants, red hibiscus and bouganvillea cover the large terrace, and behind the house there are shady olive and fig trees, which keep off the burning sun. A really agreeable covered porch with a fine view of rocks and sea. There are simple fish dishes to be had, as well as souvlaki etc.

To the east of Kalo Nero, the stony dust track makes its tortuous way along rust-red rocky slopes with deep clefts and yawning caverns. On the right, only 20 yards below, the sea beats against weathered rocks. Suddenly the monastery appears after a bend in the track; brilliant white, it clings to a rocky bluff above a ravine. With its little green gardens, flourishing prickly pears, olive trees and cypresses it seems to belong to another world.

There is a small shingle beach, together with a shady tamarisk copse, below the monastery; this is a nice place for a picnic.

Monastery of Kapsa

A complicated construction on several levels, and partly pushed into the rock. A flight of steps leads into a shady courtyard with a spring; the refectory is situated here, and below this are modest areas set aside for cultivation. Up a few steps again there is another court with a bench running around it in the shade of several slim cypresses. The *cave church* with its two naves has a beautiful shingle floor, and there are two old black icons hanging on the carved wooden iconostasis, which is divided into two.

Kapsa was probably founded in the 15th century; at any rate, there is an icon there dating from that century which might be presumed to have been in the possession of the monastery since its foundation. It was probably razed to the ground in 1640, on one of the numerous Turkish onslaughts on Crete. It was only completely renovated or rebuilt between 1861 and 1863, thanks to the efforts of one man, Ioannis Yerontakis, who is nicknamed *Yerontoyannis*.

Today the Monastery of Kapsa is under the jurisdiction of the Monastery of Toplou, and is ruled by a representative from Toplou. A few nuns live and work with him.

A DEATH-LIKE SLEEP

Until Easter Week in 1843, Yerontoyannis was a simple man, more than partial to wordly pleasures. On the night of 4th-5th April he fell into a death-like sleep, which lasted 43 hours. When he regained consciousness, he brought about healing miracles, and cured the critically sick child of the Turkish city commandant of Iraklion, thus rapidly becoming famous on the whole island. At that time he conceived of the plan to rebuild the Monastery of Kapsa, where he was born. People flocked to him, donated money, and helped him with their labour. Yerontoyannis became a monk and established his cell in a rather remote cave. Later, he renovated yet another monastery in the region (Agia Sophia near Chandras).

When the Monastery of Kapsa came under the jurisdiction of the Monastery of Toplou after 1901, Yerontoyannis received an order to serve there from then onwards. For this reason, he fled to friends of his who were sponge fishermen on the island of Symi. His name is still famous and revered in the whole of south-east Crete today.

• VISITING TIMES: daily 8.00 a.m.-12.30 p.m., and 3.30.p.m.-7.00 p.m. Decorous clothing is required of visitors (legs and shoulders should be covered), but slipover smocks can be borrowed.
More information on Yerontoyannis and the Monastery of Kapsa can be acquired from a little **brochure**, which can be bought at the monastery church (c. £2).

From Ierapetra westwards

At the beginning, hothouses and villages stretching along the sides of the main roads determine the character of the flat plain. The slopes of the Dikti mountains are only encountered for the first time at Myrtos.

Myrtos

An attractive little village at the exit from a long, fertile valley, set between barren sandstone rocks without a tree or a bush.

There is no shade on the long shingle and sand beach here either, but all the more greenery in the few narrow alleys between the low, whitewashed houses.

Over recent years, Myrtos has developed into a favourite meeting place for rucksack tourists. In the high season, the village is bursting at the seams, the rooms are booked out, and not a few people sleep on the beach. Even "ordinary tourists" are more frequently seen here; a large and very comfortable hotel is situated on the main through road.

• CONNECTIONS: There are about 6 **buses** daily to and from Ierapetra. The bus stop is at the taverna near the new church (the main road from Ierapetra to Iraklion goes past the edge of the village). The distance to the centre is about 200 yards.

• TELEPHONE: International calls can be made from both kiosks in the village.

Accommodation

There are two hotels. However, all the other inhabitants of the village are also geared up to tourism, and many rent rooms - even when there is no sign hanging outside. Things have gone so far that there are even signs to be seen which announce "*We do* **not** *rent rooms!*"

• **Esperides**: C class, the best address. Large establishment on the main through road to Ano Vianos. Rooms and passages have carpeted floors, good bathrooms, and there is a large swimming pool; all is immaculate. Good service, and fresh linen almost daily. Cost around £14-15 for a DR. Tel. 0842/51207.

• **Mirtos**: C class. Although in the same category, there is no comparison with the Esperides. In the middle of the village, gloomy passages and rather uninviting; older furniture. Generally OK, however. Rooms with shower/WC, and balcony. Only 50 yards from the beach, some rooms with sea views. Cost c. £11-12 for a DR. Tel. 0842/51226.

Private Rooms, Guest Houses

• **Yorgo**: a new, white house at the western exit from the village, shortly before the Beach Café. DR for £7 or with kitchen niche, shower/toilet for a maximum price of £10.

• **Katerina**: a little after Jorgo's, on the right hand side. The sun beats mercilessly into the house during the day, but it is only 50 yards from the beach. In spite of frequent calls, we were unfortunately not able to talk to anyone here.

• **Villa Mare**: one of the tallest houses in the village, with a super view from the top floor. Well-run.

• **Sleeping on the beach** is a possibility, but the inhabitants are not particularly fond of this and the police often arrive in the morning. Better to avoid this by going to the next bay to the west.

Food/clubs

It is really nice to sit in the tavernas, which are built on a cement platform directly above the beach.

• **Beach Café**: the last house at the western end of the village, where the widest part of the beach begins. **The** meeting place for young people, run by two young Germans. Good food here, eg Cordon Bleu steaks or schnitzel, but also vegetarian meals such as baked aubergines or soya dishes. To accompany the food there are 34 different cocktails available.

• **Alibi Bar**: below the Beach Café. Michalis offers good music and a refined atmosphere. Gays and heteros.

• **Straight Pub**: at the eastern end of the promenade, specialising in loud music.

• **Mountain Pub**: above the village, and a disco has been planned here for a long time (by the son of Yorgo).

Sightseeing: In the village itself there is nothing. Incidentally, the cement shore promenade was constructed in order to protect the village from landslip.

A *Minoan settlement* has been excavated on the crest of a hill right next to the road, about 15 minutes to the east of Myrtos. It was probably inhabited during the period from 2000 BC to the great catastrophe around 1450 BC. A fantastic site, with beautiful view out over the sea and a strategically advantageous position high above the wide, dried-up river bed. In particular a long stairway can be seen, which leads right up to the top, and also foundation walls, the bases of columns and a court paved with alabaster.

In order to find the site, go a little way down the road from Myrtos to Ierapetra. Take the track to the left after the bridge over the riverbed and then turn right immediately up a narrow path between oregano bushes. A rather tiresome climb, but you are greeted at the top by a relaxing stillness and a wonderful view.

▶ **Bathing:** There are about 1.5 miles of sand and shingle beach directly in the village, but there is hardly any shade, only two or three bare tamarisks. Mostly very crowded in July/August, but there is plenty of space here.

A driveway full of potholes runs along the sea in a westerly direction. You pass numerous shingle/sand beaches and bizarre rock formations and arrive, after a distance of about 3.5 miles, at the tiny hamlet called *Tertsa*, which only consists of a handful of houses and plastic hothouses. In addition there is a bad, stony beach, an original café and a mostly original clientele to match. The track goes on to Arvi, but is said to get increasingly worse and to be only passable on foot in places.

From Myrtos westwards

The road winds steeply up in mighty curves into the Dikti Mountains. Wonderful view of the valley of Myrtos and the surrounding mountain ridges. Terrible forest fires raged here in 1984, but almost all traces of these have now vanished.

The further you go, the more the landscape resembles that of the Alps, with a lot of fresh-looking greenery between the jagged rock walls, most of it pine trees, and the occasional little church or small village.

A curving asphalt road runs from *Amiras* through wonderful mountain scenery down to Arvi, about seven miles away.

Arvi

A village concealed amongst hothouses, banana plantations and reeds. Mighty rock walls jut up immediately behind it, interrupted by a great ravine through which a little river has forced its way to flow into the sea at Arvi. The inhabitants of Arvi live mainly from their fertile plantations, but the new asphalt road has also brought tourism here. There are already souvenir shops on the main road parallel to the long sand and shingle beach, and on the beach itself there are several tavernas.

A good tip for a couple of quiet days in the low season, but the beach is not very nice.

• CONNECTIONS: Buses from Ierapetra to Iraklion go along the road via Amiras and Ano Vianos c. 2 x daily, in both directions. Get out in Amiras and walk the rest of the way. The **school bus** goes down to Arvi at around midday.

• ACCOMMODATION: **Ariadni**, C class, at the beginning of the village. Seems a little neglected, but in general OK. Spacious rooms with balcony and good bathrooms (bathtubs), and lift. Cost of a DR about £12. Reduction for more than 2 days' stay. Tel. 0895/31200.
Gorgona: in the middle of the village, with a taverna. Definitely an attractive place to stay. Nicely presented, with plants on the open passage leading upwards. Rooms not particularly big, but wonderful terrace with a view of the sea. Cost of DR with private bath c. £10, without bath c. £8. There are also several private rooms in the village.

▶ **Sightseeing:** The *Monastery of Arvi* is perched half way up the mountain slope on the right hand side next to the very narrow ravine. It is extremely small and seems also to be half in ruins. Can be reached from the main square of Arvi by going along the service road running inland for about a quarter of a mile. Then turn left and go along a narrow footpath through fleshy banana plants, along a river bed which is dried up in summer.

▶ **Excursions:** 7.5 miles of bumpy, dusty track lead to *Keratokambos,* the next village to the west. Large amounts of sharp stones here and deeply uneven patches of road and large stones, especially in the bends in the road. Can be negotiated with a four-wheel drive vehicle.

Ano Vianos

Remarkable position on a steep slope amidst lush green. Thanks to the great abundance of water in the region, viticulture can be carried on everywhere, and there are also cypresses, olive trees and many other plants. The torrent which runs through the village is dried-up in the burning heat of summer, but in spite of that the vegetation flourishes in the narrow paved alleys away from the main road: flowering oleander, and small gardens with flowers, fig trees and lemon trees . . .

Ano Vianos is an attractive little place, and most of the tourist buses to and from Iraklion stop here for coffee. A quarter of an hour later they are on their way again, and peace returns once more. There is no allusion here to the fact that the Germans shot over 400 of the inhabitants as suspected partisans in September 1943.

• ACCOMMODATION: There are private rooms available at the kafenion opposite the church on the main square. DR costs c. £7.

• FOOD: several **kafenia** and **tavernas** both on the winding main road and above it.

A little to the east of **Kato Vianos**, a turning leads down to Keratokambos (5 miles). This road has recently been completely made up. Be sure that you have a full petrol tank, as there is no garage in Keratokambos (although there are two in Ano Vianos). At the fork in the road at **Chondros**, turn left and go as far as the church, then turn right and go on. The road now follows the ravine of Ano Vianos, and continues steeply down over bare rocky slopes, making wide curves. The view is terrific!

Keratokambos

A peaceful little fishing village with miles of sand and shingle beach. Seems far away from the centres of civilisation, and we counted just about half a dozen visitors here in the middle of September. But time has not stood still here, either, and as soon as the road becomes completely asphalted things will change.

At any rate the beach is wonderful, and beautiful washed pebbles and shells can be found there. You can take long walks, and there is no problem in pitching a tent amongst the trees behind the beach in the low season.

The nicest time to sit in one of the few tavernas on the shady shore promenade is when the wind is rustling the tamarisks and the pounding of the waves can be heard . . .

• ACCOMMODATION: Approaching from Kato Vianos, right at the entrance to the village on the left hand side, there is a house which offers **private rooms** for rent. Probably the best address at present; good rooms with an oven/sink/refrigerator, and spacious bathroom. The house is attractive too, with its hibiscus, bouganvillea and wild vines. DR costs c. £9.
At the western end of the village, directly on the beach, there is the guest house **Kastri**, belonging to Emm. Somarakis. Simple, but nice, and rooms have built-in sinks and an electric oven, and narrow balconies. Shower in the open air, and another one on the beach. At present costs only £6 for a DR.
The kafenion **Nikitas** at the eastern end of the village offers very simple rooms for c. £4. Near the pretty little church.

• FOOD: The favourite taverna here is the **Morgenstern Coffee Bar**, otherwise there is a grocer's shop.

Bathing: The beach rises up into high sand dunes at the eastern end. It takes about 20 minutes to walk there. There is another bathing cove at the western end of the beach.

Excursions: There are about 7.5 miles of catastrophic dust track to Arvi. Hilly terrain, sharp gravel, and in particular, deep potholes in the bends. Possible with a vehicle that can take punishment!

Further towards the Messara Plain

The road via Martha to the Messara Plain has now been almost completely made up! There is only a longer stretch of dusty track between *Demati* and *Ano Kastelliana*, although this does not present any problems for drivers. The next coastal village to the west is *Tsoutsouros*, which can only be reached via an adventurous mountain track from Kato Kastelliana. The long Messara Plain begins there. Information thereon in the chapter entitled *Central Crete/Messara Plain*.

• CONNECTIONS: Up to the present, there is no **direct bus connection** between Ierapetra and the Messara Plain. The buses always return to Iraklion first. Then you can change onto one of the frequent buses to Phaistos, Matala, Agia Galini and Lentas in the southern part of central Crete. One might expect that a bus connection will be started, as soon as the asphalt road has been completed.

Western Crete

The wildest, most mountainous part of the island, and the greenest. The former extensive forests have, however, been severely decimated.

The *Lefka Ori*, the "White Mountains", form the rocky backbone of Crete. Partisans retreated to their inaccessible hideouts here during the wars against the Turks, and also during the last World War. It has been possible to maintain tradition and customs in their most unaltered form in the region of *Sfakia*, on the steep south coast. The *Samaria Gorge,* which is said to be the longest gorge in Europe, is one of the many highlights of the landscape there. A walk through the gorge is practically a must, if one wants to experience a little of the Crete that is not served up at the beach bars.

Incidentally, western Crete has a wealth of excellent sandy beaches. To name a few examples: those on the *Plain of Rethymnon*, which is miles long, or the Bay of Plakias, and there are the hidden beaches on the west coast, which are among the most beautiful in Crete (a name to note is *Elafonisi*). And if that were not enough, there are the two cities of *Rethymnon* and *Chania,* which offer the most in the way of sightseeing, thanks to the historic nature of their buildings with their old alleyways, Venetian harbours and Turkish minarets. If you wish to have the history of the island pass colourfully before your eyes, a visit to these cities is almost a must.

However, the west is also synonymous for "highlights" of another kind. Thus the plains of Kastelli and Chania were the places where, during the last war, German parachutists and alpine troops jumped out of the sky. For thousands of young men, this was their first and last action, while the civilian population of the mountain villages had to suffer the later "retribution" meted out by the German Wehrmacht. Today, there is once again a military presence on the *Akrotiri Peninsula*; this time it is NATO.

Until now the west has been rather neglected where excavations are concerned; no Minoan palaces have yet been found. On the other hand there are various monasteries, which make a detour into the lonely world of the mountains worthwhile. Above all there is the *Monastery of Arkadi*, which has become a symbol of the spirit of Cretan resistance.

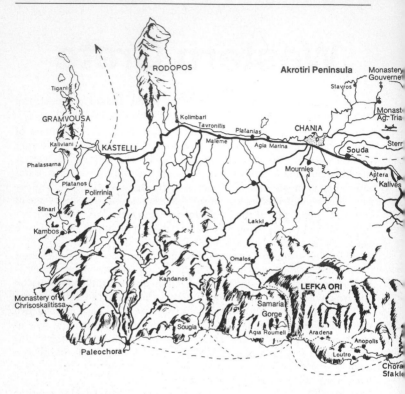

GEOGRAPHY: Western Crete begins at about Rethymnon, which is roughly on a line through the second narrowest part of Crete. It is the most mountainous part of Crete, with the **Lefka Ori** forming the dominant landmark in the southwest. Their peaks rise to over 7,800 feet. Further "heights" are reached by the slopes of the Ida and Kedros mountain ranges to the south west of Rethymnon.

ROADS: The New Road from Iraklion via Rethymnon to Chania is built like a motorway. There are several good north-south connections (to Plakias, Chora Sfakion, Sougia and Paleochora). In the heartland of the White Mountains there is a road only up to the Omalos High Plateau, where the famous Samaria Gorge begins, but this is only passable on foot. There are still a number of gravel roads in the extreme west.

CONNECTIONS: The centres of the bus networks are at **Chania** and **Rethymnon**, with frequent connections between the two cities and to Iraklion. There are also connections several times daily between the resorts of the south coast and the cities on the north coast. **Boat connections** play a large part along the steep southern coast of the Lefka Ori. Because of the difficult terrain, the villages there are not connected by a coastal road.

Western Crete

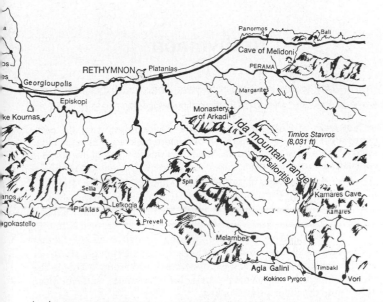

ACCOMMODATION: There are countless possibilities in **Chania**, **Rethymnon**, **Plakias**, **Paleochora**, and **Georgioupolis**, and further accommodation is available in Sougia, Kalives, Chora Sfakion, Loutro, Kastelli etc. **Camping sites** are to be found at Rethymnon, Georgioupolis, Chania, Kastelli, Paleochora and Plakias.

ARCHAEOLOGY: No Minoan palace has been found in the west up to the present, but there are archaeological sites (Minoan to Hellenistic) at Chania, Phalassarna, Polirrinia and Aptera.

BATHING: There are miles of sandy beach **between Rethymnon and Georgioupolis**, and further beautiful beaches at Kalives, Chania, Phalassarna, Paleochora, Sougia and Plakias. Special mention must be made of the superb beach on the island of **Elafonisi** in the extreme south west, which is without doubt one of the most beautiful places for bathing on the island. There is also a wonderful palm beach near the Monastery of **Preveli**.

From Iraklion to Rethymnon

An impressive mountain and valley trip along the New Road through the wild rocky landscape of the Ida foothills. The few villages in the bays on the steep coastline can be counted on one hand. *Agia Pelagia,* the most important bathing resort, is situated in the catchment area of Iraklion; for details, see under Iraklion. For *Bali* and *Panormo* see chapter "From Rethymnon eastwards". Shortly after Panormo there is the extensive *Plain of Rethymnon* (see also below).

Rethymnon

Wooden bay windows and minarets; the beach begins in the centre of the city; the fortifications overlooking the city

The first sight of Rethymnon can be a disappointing one. Its outer suburbs are a horrid conglomeration of austere concrete buildings, indiscriminately thrown together. In particular, the eastern area of the city is in a constant state of expansion.

But, as is often the case, this first impression is deceptive; Rethymnon is fighting with Chania for the title "most beautiful city on Crete". The Turks have left their mark for posterity in the old city, with its narrow alleys, and low, 2-3 storeyed houses. Several slim *minarets* are still standing, and the bulging domed roofs of former mosques can also be seen here and there. Above all, though, there are beautiful, latticed *wooden bay windows* scattered around. This is the typical architecture of the earlier oriental inhabitants, and can often still be found in modern-day Turkey.

On the other hand, the houses themselves, with their fine doorways and arches, are of Venetian origin. The old houses with their faded pastel colours, wrought-iron balconies and large window shutters, which are to be seen especially on the shore promenade and in the almost intimate, circular *Venetian harbour*, seem thoroughly Italian.

The whole thing is crowned by the walls of the mighty *fortezza*. It sits in splendour on a hill above the red roofs, and covers the whole tip of the peninsula on which the historic centre of Rethymnon is situated.

You can bathe and shop very well in Rethymnon. Many shops selling jewellery, souvenirs and leatherware provide colour in the narrow passages, while the wide beach with its soft sand begins in the middle of the city and extends for miles to the east. No wonder that the Old

City of Rethymnon mostly lives for the tourists in the season. There is one restaurant next to the other on the long shore promenade; all are well-filled, busy and west European-orientated.

But the calming atmosphere of a sleepy little Cretan city greets you a few streets behind the "tourist mile" on the sea. Take a stroll during siesta time . . .

As a tourist, you will hardly notice that there are five Arts faculties of the *University of Crete* in Rethymnon. About 3,000 students from the whole of Greece are enrolled here for philology, philosophy, education and related sciences.

Kostas Giampoudakis, the explosives expert of Arkadi Monastery.

Information: available from a pavilion on the beach promenade, El. Venizelou. Mon-Fri 9.00 a.m.-5.30 p.m. Sat/Sun 9.00 a.m.-2.00 p.m. Dimitris gives expert information and helps you find rooms in an emergency. A variety of printed information is available here, eg about the Samaria Gorge, boat departures etc. There is also a left luggage facility. Tel. 0831/29148.

CONNECTIONS

• **Boat**: The actual harbour of Rethymnon is well silted-up, and thus larger ships have only been able to berth there with difficulty. It is said, however, that from the end of 1988, a converted Japanese ferry called **Arkadi** will make a regular run from Rethymnon to Piraeus. The large landing and departure quay is a little to the north of the Venetian harbour. The ship (built in 1984) was bought by a cooperative joint stock company formed by people from Rethymnon. It moored at the mole in Rethymnon for the first time at the beginning of March 1987, at which time it was open to the public. The necessary conversion work should be finished by the end of 1988. Information, tickets etc are available at the main agents Kedros Reisen (Kedros Tours). For their address see below under Travel Agencies.

There is also the **Nearchos**, a Scandinavian hydrofoil, which undertakes day cruises 2 x weekly to Santorini (leaving at 8.00 a.m; trip takes about 3 hours). The same boat also goes 2 x weekly from Iraklion to Santorini. It was originally intended that the Nearchos should make the crossing to Piraeus, but it became apparent that the hydrofoil is not suitable for such long trips.

• **Bus**: The **bus station** for longer journeys overland is situated on a large, dusty square at **Moatsou St.**, which runs parallel to Kountourioti St., the great main thoroughfare of Rethymnon, on its southern side. Right next door to it is the striking Hotel Olympic with its overgrown facade. Dimokratias St. leads down to Kountourioti St. There are 2 bus stops, with 2 large waiting rooms/kafenia, situated opposite one another.

Buses leave from the southerly bus stop for the **south coast**, to Plakias (7 x daily), Agia Galini (6 x daily), Chora Sfakion (1 x, via Plakias) etc. It is sometimes necessary to change at Bale. Country people laden with their purchases sit here after their visit to the city, and wait for the bus to take them back to their home villages. On the north side of the street is the bus station for areas of the **north coast**. There are connections roughly every hour to Iraklion and Chania along the New Road (a few buses go along the Old Road, which is a longer journey). The last bus is around 9.00 p.m. There are also frequent buses to the beach hotels and camping sites to the east of the city (some of the buses to Iraklion also stop there). There are further connections to the Monastery of Arkadi (c. 4 x daily).

Another smaller bus station is situated at **Platia Iroon**, only a few yards from the water at the eastern end of the Old City. Buses go from here to most of the villages in the province of Rethymnon, for example Perama, Axos, Anogia, Amari.

• **Car/motorbike rentals**: These can be found in various places throughout the city.

• **Bicycle rentals**: A few paces from the Arimondi Fountain, at 14, Paleologou St., and at a house opposite it. Cost per day £3, three days for £6. Worthwhile in Rethymnon because of the extensive plain to the east of the city. Even Greeks can sometimes be seen on these metal donkeys.

• **Taxis**: There is a taxi rank on Platia 4 Martiron.

• **Excursions**: Daily in the high season, otherwise 2 x per week, a boat takes bathers from Rethymnon to the Bay of Manolis, in the direction of Bali. It is possible to eat there, and there is a cave and also a lagoon. Information available from the Socrates taverna at the Arimondi Fountain or directly on the harbour.

— ★ —

• ANEK: at Platia 4 Martiron. Boat reservations.

• CHANGING MONEY: The Bank of Greece and the Bank of Crete are on the square containing the monument to Eleftherios Venizelos, on Kountourioti St. a little down from the bus station.

• MARKET: only on Thursdays, on Platia 4 Martiron.

• OLYMPIC AIRWAYS: above Platia 4 Martiron, at 6, Dimitrakaki St. (in the Hotel Joan). Tel. 0831/22257 or 24333. There is a special bus to Chania for every flight.

• POST OFFICE: The new main Post Office is in Moatsou St., up from the city park, where there is also the bus station. Mon-Fri 8.00 a.m-1.30 p.m., 5.00 p.m.-7.30 p.m. There is a Post Office kiosk (also for changing money) on the beach road next to the Restaurant Delfini.

• TRAVEL AGENCIES: **Kedros Reisen**, at 2, Messolongiou St. Tel. 0831/21179. Run by Mr Harald Leutsch, who has lived on Crete for more than 6 years. He can arrange accommodation of every kind, hires out cars, motor bikes and mopeds, and organises excursions and hikes.

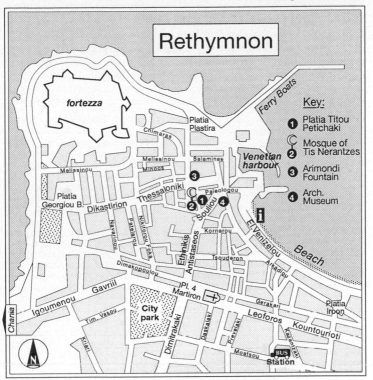

Key:
1 Platia Titou Petichaki
2 Mosque of Tis Nerantzes
3 Arimondi Fountain
4 Arch. Museum

• TELEPHONE: OTE office at 28, Kountourioti St., a little to the east of the city park. Open daily 7.00 a.m.-12.00 p.m.
• LAUNDRY: next to the youth hostel in Topasi St. Mon-Sat 9.00 a.m.-2.00 p.m., 5.00 p.m.-9.00 p.m.
• NEWSPAPERS/MAGAZINES: At 13, Kountourioti St., opposite OTE.

Accommodation

Numerous possibilities; there are 13,000 beds available in hotels and guest houses alone. The better-class hotels are centred around the bus station, and the large beach hotels are in the *newly-built quarter* on the beach to the east. Some of the best hotels on Crete (class A) are to be found outside Rethymnon on the *beach* to the east of the city (see page 372).

Simple accommodation is mostly to be found in the Old City, especially on *Arkadiou St.*, the long main road which runs behind and parallel to the sea front. Here you are at the centre of action (at full volume, too). In some cases, there are rooms on the front with a wonderful view of the shore promenade and the city beach. Such accommodation is, however, often booked out during the season.

Another focus of rooms for rent is to be found on the *left hand side of the Venetian harbour,* a little way along the road at the water's edge and situated directly on the sea almost below the castle. Advantage here: much quieter and perhaps an even more beautiful view.

HOTELS OF THE UPPER CATEGORIES

• **Olympic**: B class, perhaps the most comfortable hotel in the upper price range. Its facade is largely covered with wild vine creepers, it has an immaculate lounge and bar on the ground floor, and air conditioning. Used by tour operators, and there are mostly only a few vacant rooms. Cost c. £22 for a DR with shower/toilet and breakfast, and there are often considerable reductions available in the low season. Address: Moatsou St., directly at the bus station. Tel. 0831/24761.

• **Jo-an**: B class, a modern building on a moderately busy road. Quite immaculate, almost sterile. Carpet floors everywhere and interiors in dark wood, all rooms with balcony (not much of a view, however). Beautiful tiled bathrooms with green ceramic washbasins, sound-absorbing walls and doors. 50 rooms, but only a very narrow lift. Friendly service. Cost just under £24 for a DR with bathroom and breakfast. Address: 6, Dimitrakaki St., a little way above Platia 4 Martiron.

Tel. 0831/24241. The office of Olympic Airways is situated on the ground floor.

• **Brascos**: B class, only a few blocks from Jo-an. The comfort and furnishings here are not quite as good as at the latter, but the hotel is larger and more lively, with a friendly atmosphere and a lot of package holidaymakers. Cost c. £22 for a DR. Address: Daskalaki St., Tel. 0831/23721.

• **Ideon**: B class, beautiful position on a small square directly on the sea, a short way to the west of the Ventian harbour. Same price category. Address: 9, Nikolaou Plastira, tel. 0831/28667.

• **Park**, **Astali** and **Valari**: all C class, three hotels of the middle class on loud Kountourioti St., and for this reason less recommended. Price c. £15 for a DR (Valari has quiet rooms at the back, and the Park is situated, as its name suggests, opposite the city park).

ARKADIOU STREET AND SIDE ALLEYS

There are mostly guest houses and private rooms here.

• **Zania** (guest house): our tip. Simple, but a really nice place to stay. An old Turkish house; rooms with very high wooden ceilings, wooden floors and in part immaculate new furniture in the rooms. Shower on the landing only. Proprietress speaks French and is obviously very concerned with cleanliness. Only a few rooms, unfortunately. DR costs c. £9. Address: Pavlou Vastou St, a small side alley off Arkadiou St. Tel. 0831/28169.

• **Leon** (guest house): more expensive than the Zania. An old Venetian Palazzo with wrought-iron balconies and a lot of wood inside, also with wooden floors and ceilings. Decorated with numerous

examples of Cretan handwork - eg a carved wooden chest and brilliant red wall hangings. Small breakfast room and bar on the ground floor. Rooms with or without private shower/toilet. Clean. Cost c. £12-14. Address: in Arkadiou St., at the entrance to Vafe St. Can easily be recognised from the conspicuous sign depicting a lion. Tel. 0831/26197.

• **Rethymnon House** (guest house): stylish house of Old City type in a quiet side street off Arkadiou St. Quite immaculate interior with new wooden floors and a bar on the ground floor. About £14 for a DR. Address: 1, V Kornarou. Tel. 0831/23923.

• **Achillion**: E class, an originally furnished oddity, with wobbly lino floors and torn carpets. Some rooms are on the front overlooking the beach promenade, others have no windows, just skylights. Mostly patronised by rucksack tourists, moderately clean. Cost in the high season c. £9 for a DR, otherwise c. £8. Address: 153, Arkadiou St. Tel. 0831/22581.

• **Minoa**: D class, simple, rambling and cool. Whitewashed passages, rooms in part painted with linden green gloss paint. Simple furniture, and simple shower/toilet. Friendly proprietor, but there are unfortunately only a few rooms at the front overlooking the interesting and lively street. Cost c. £10 for a DR, or £12 for a three-bedded room. As the hotel is very large, there are usually vacancies, even in the summer. Address: 62, Arkadiou St. Tel. 0831/22508.

• **Rent Rooms**: house without a name, opposite the Hotel Minoa. Rather a maze-like place, with rooms of varying quality. The room with the balcony and view of the shore promenade is wellrecommended. Cost according to room £8-9.

Souliou Street

There are several well-kept guest houses in this narrow alley in the Old City, at Petichaki Square.

• **Olga's House**: rather angular in appearance, but pretty. The steps lead up into an agreeably appointed roof garden with a lot of plants and places to sit. Friendly proprietor and atmosphere. 7 rooms with shower/toilet for c. £9. Address: 57, Souliou St. Tel. 29851 (office) and 23493 (home).

• **The Lane**: a new guest house with steep stairs and a lot of wood, with Venetian remains in the stairwell. Rooms with shower and modern-styled metal beds. Often booked out by tour operators. Address: 7, Souliou.

On the Venetian Harbour

Advantages here are the quiet position and the fine sea views.

• **Seeblick**: rather a crooked house with narrow passages and stairways, rooms either with or without private shower/toilet. Generally OK, but rooms of varying quality (prices range from £9-10). The German proprietress, her husband Pandelis and son Manolis have a lot of established customers, thus it is often booked out. Address: 17, Nikolaou Plastira, a little way along the water's edge to the west of the Venetian harbour. Tel. 0831/22478.

• **Lefteris Papadakis Sons**: two houses after the Seeblick Guest House; recommended. Clean and solidly furnished, run by the young couple Manolis and Gabriela (a Swiss girl). Readers of the first edition of this book were very satisfied there. £10 for a DR with bathroom, £8 without. 26, Nikolaou Plastira, tel. 0831/23803.

• **Mikonos**: directly on the Venetian harbour, at 303, Arkadiou St. Spartan, and some of the furniture has tears in it. Only to be used in an emergency. About £8 for a room on the front.

• YOUTH HOSTEL: friendly house in the middle of the Old City - a good place for making contacts, and a lot of travellers stop here. Comfortable place with a lot of wood, and a total of 83 beds in dormitories with 8-18 beds. It is also possible to sleep on the terrace. There is a small garden and the toilets and showers are clean. The owner, Barbara, came originally from Germany and has lived on Crete for 33 years. The cost for one night is £2, and breakfast and drinks are available. There is no closing time in the evening. Address: 45, Topasi, tel. 0831/22848.

• READER'S TIP: "The **Pension Anna** is situated directly below the Fortezza, at the beginning of the footpath which leads to the entrance. It is a small Turkish house with a wooden bay window; newly-renovated, clean and tastefully furnished. The proprietors are very friendly. About £10-11 for a DR. Tel. 0831/25586."

There are two camping sites a few miles to the east of the city, directly on the beach. See below.

Food

There are two focal points: the area around the *Arimondi Fountain* and neighbouring Platia Petichaki, and the good dozen fish tavernas around the *Venetian harbour*. The latter is certainly a beautiful spot, but it is often packed to the limit of its capacity in the evening.

Otherwise, there are some worthwhile addresses scattered among the alleys of the *Old City*.

AROUND THE VENETIAN HARBOUR

More or less the same is on offer everywhere: bass, swordfish, kalamares, red snapper, fish shish-kebab, lobster and fish soup (Psarósoupa). The menus are normally printed in several languages, so there is no problem here.

• **Seven Brothers**: definitely the taverna with the least air of affectation among those around the harbour. Dimitrios Markulatses, the moustachioed proprietor, is in charge of the smoking charcoal grill here and has run the taverna with his son for 12 years, having worked before that in West Germany. His specialities are fish from the charcoal grill, and fish soup for c. £2. The wines available here include a red wine from his own vineyard. Dimitrios also has apartments for rent outside the city, on the beach.

• **Vassilis**: one of the market leaders on the harbour; an exceptionally fine interior with old photos, paintings, wall hangings etc. Take a peek inside!

• **Chelona**: at the eastern corner of the Venetian harbour. For the romantically inclined. Soft, caressing music, shimmering lights, and a gurgling fountain. The barbounia (red mullet) are mouthwatering!

FISH FROM CANADA

Those who believe that the fish offered on the Venetian harbour originate from fishing grounds around Rethymnon are mistaken! The sea bed is now completely made up of sand, and there are hardly any rocks any more, thus no breeding ground for fish. The large trawlers have to go off around the whole of Crete for days and weeks on end, or even as far as the Cypriot, African or Turkish coasts. The fishing areas off the Turkish coast have proved to be particularly productive; during the month of fasting, or Ramadan, little fish is eaten or caught. But the Aegean as a whole has already been fished dry, and so a lot of seafood has to be imported via Athens from abroad. In particular, deep-frozen products from Argentina and Canada land on the plates in the Venetian harbour at Rethymnon.

Pikilia is a speciality of Rethymnon

THE BEACH PROMENADE

This adjoins the fishing harbour to the east. In the season, it is one big mass of café-bars with flashing lights, snack-bars, ice-cream bars, tavernas, pizzerias, Fast Food places and sauntering tourists.

Several establishments here are much favoured by Greek students, since they can eat at a slight reduction using the meal coupons issued monthly by the university (there is no union building in Rethymnon).

• **Samaria:** low prices, good selection, also vegetable dishes. Particularly full of students at lunch time. The same applies to the Tassos. You are invited into the kitchen to place your order.

• **Labyrinth:** a large taverna/café, where you can enjoy your "Frappé" (iced coffee) directly on the sand. There are also pizzas, spaghetti, canneloni and hamburgers here.

• **Delfini:** a little to the east of Labyrinth. There is a disco on the lower floor; meals are also available on the upper floor, and there is bouzouki music. See also under Nightlife.

ARIMONDI FOUNTAIN/PETICHAKI SQUARE

The two adjacent central squares in the Old City still offer a homely atmosphere, in spite of their being well-known venues. In particular, the little square by the remains of the Arimondi Fountain offers a place for introspection with its candlelight, decorative gourds and creeping vines.

• **Sokrates**: on the fountain square, small, intimate and definitely cosy. Specialities change every day; eg the casserole of beef is delicious. Also special pizzas.

• **Vangela**: on the same square. The motherly, high-spirited proprietress Vangela takes her guests into the kitchen and tells them about the dishes in excellent French or English. The partisans' dish of Kleftiko (in aluminium foil) is very good here, but Stifado and Yuvetsi are also available.

• **O Platanos** and **Neratze**: two typical souvlaki places of the old kind, at the southern end of Petichaki Square (at the back of the large mosque). Christos in the latter taverna is in charge of the "Special" Gyros, with its sausages, hamburger, tzatziki, tomato and chips. The polite service you receive here is very pleasant.

Old City

• **Stelios**: on a small square at the end of Thessalonikis St. Quieter than in the very centre; fish in particular served here.

• **Gounakis**: original taverna with live music and reasonably-priced food. At 8, Panou Koronaiou St. (see also under Nightlife).

• **Kostas Pallepakis**: diagonally opposite Gounakis (no. 25). A very friendly family, and prices are reasonable.

• **Avli**: offers a romantically lit garden with the stunning perfumes of flowers, and prices in the upper bracket. Cookery with an international bias, immaculate. 22, Xanthoudidou St.

• **Alana**: newly-opened and generously appointed. Thus a larger garden, and a little more expensive. In Salaminos St., from the harbour in the direction of the Fortezza.

• **Ta Tria Delphia**: a unique establishment. It is really amazing that all of 11 tables and two lemon trees fit into the tiny courtyard! A simple taverna on Arkadiou St., only a few yards away from the Venetian harbour.

Scattered around the City

• **Iliovassilemata** (sunset): on the shore road, to the west below the mighty walls of the castle, directly on the water. The speciality here is Pikilia, a quantity of little plates containing kalamares, tzatziki, meat balls, olives, tomatoes, but also sea urchins, mussels and snails. The table buckles under the strain! Especially lovely when the sun sinks over the mountains of Cape Drepanon.

• **Ambrosia**: the only vegetarian restaurant in the city. Large and with plenty of light; excellent food, eg soya moussaka. Prices a little higher here. Can be found in Daskalaki St., near the City Park.

• **Astoria**: a good souvlaki place downstairs in the Hotel Leo on Arkadi St. Young Greeks mostly meet here, and the portions are generous.

• **Kafenia**: There is a row of cafés and restaurants about 500 yards long, one beside the other, on the beach promenade! Most of them are smart places, offering milk-shakes, fresh juices, ice cream, pop music . . . Those who find the crowds too much here can sit in attractive surroundings in the kafenia on the central Platia Titou Petichaki. **Athanasios Zamphotis** is mostly the favourite here because of his charm, and in the evening there is Greek music.

Nightlife

Rethymnon probably has the most to offer of all the cities on the north coast of Crete. On the one hand, what is on offer is determined by the vigorous demand from the young student population, and on the other, it is easier to get a total picture of what is going on here than it is in Iraklion or Chania; thus particular "scenes" have developed here.

GREEK-CRETAN MUSIC VENUES

• **Nikos Gounakis**: a favourite address for those who wish to hear Cretan music. You can eat at a reasonable cost here in the comfortably gloomy arcades of an old Venetian Palazzo. Nikos plays the lyra up on the stage almost daily during the season, accompanied by his sons

Iannis and Stefanos. Address: 8, Panou Koronaiou St.

• **Odysseas**: around the corner from the Venetian harbour, at the beginning of the beach promenade. Live Greek music every evening, from 9.30 p.m. Address: 82, El. Venizelou.

DISCO-BARS

• **Loggia Pub**: a large music bar, with loud pop-videos (quality from miserable to top). The variety of cocktails is a speciality, and a small beer cost £0.50. Address: 16, Nearchou St., just round the corner at the Venetian harbour.

• **Rooli's**: on the beach promenade, reputed to offer the cheapest beer in the city. Self-service.

• **Fortezza**: on the Venetian harbour; sometimes a pianist and guitarist play well-known Greek songs.

• **Lesci**: bar with dancing in Petichaki St., on the harbour.

• **To Melo** (Apple Pub): bar with neon lights, pop music and popular songs, and also a disco. At 287, Arkadiou St.

COFFEE BARS

• **To Diporto**: at 7, Vafe St., a side alley off Arkadiou St. Cosy, quiet bar, where Greeks mostly meet.

DISCOTHEQUES

• **Libra**: An insiders' meeting place for the young student population, on the main road (78, Kountourioti). Student bands sometimes play here.

• **Sound Motion**: modern furnishings. Minimum price of c. £3. On the beach in the eastern segment of the city.

• **Delfini**: Disco and bouzouki music, on the beach promenade.

Shopping

Next to Chania, Rethymnon offers the best chance to obtain reasonably-priced leather goods, ranging from bags of all kinds to belts and shoes. These are particularly cheap in September, at the end of the season, when reductions of up to 30% are possible. The range of jewellery on offer is just as large. A stroll amongst the many shops is worthwhile, even if you are only "just looking".

• EOMMEX: In the **Pavilion** on the beach, which also houses the Information Office, the Greek Organisation for Small and Medium-sized Craftwork Producers exhibits selected fine examples of

Cretan handwork, including woven rugs, leather goods and crochet work. Open daily from 10.00 a.m.-2.00 p.m. and 7.00 p.m.-11.00 p.m.

• WORKSHOP FOR ICON PAINTING: **Andreas Theodorakis** sits all day, every day at his easel, in his agreeably-furnished studio, and you can watch him work for a little while there. He paints his icons strictly according to the traditions of Cretan icon painting; that is, he uses only natural colours, varnishes and bases. Apart from his own works, which are mostly of a biblical nature, Andreas Theodorakis also sells lithographs by famous Greek painters. Address: 15, Souliou St.

• HERBS/SPICES: The little shop owned by Panayiotis Kontoyannis in the maze of alleys in the Old City is mainly conspicuous due to its many handwritten signs, which offer herbs of all kinds that have mostly been freshly gathered in the mountains of Crete. Those who wish to take home Diktamos from the Samaria Gorge, or sage, lavender or oregano, have come to the right place here. Address: 58, Souliou St. (not far from the Museum).

— ★ —

• MUSICAL INSTRUMENTS: **Emmanuel Stagakis**, one of the few remaining manufacturers of musical instruments on Crete, produces the traditional lyras and laoutos in Dimakopoulou St., a small side alley off Platia 4 Martiron. The shop is open to the street and visitors can watch him for a while. His basic material is wood from nut or mulberry trees.

— ★ —

• LEATHER: **Manolis Botonakis**, according to himself the "greatest partisan of leather on Crete", has a Colt stuck into his belt, a picturesque-looking Sariki around his head and smart boots on his feet. Some of his eloquent favourite slogans are "Stop Strauss (no longer necessary!), Stop Ghaddafi, Stop Neutron bombs . . ." He reportedly fought against the occupying forces during the war, and today he sells leather goods (no better and no worse than those in other shops). A "Socialist" of the real Cretan variety, he would never describe his own business acumen as capitalist. There is a picture of Olaf Palme greeting Erich Honecker in the entrance to his shop (Manolis says that the murdered Swedish Prime Minister was his guest three times!) Otherwise people are occasionally invited to an ouzo here. Address: 52, Arkadiou St.

— ★ —

• JEWELLERY/SOUVENIRS: There is an especially large range on offer, though naturally some of it is tawdry, or factory-produced jewellery of lesser value, in the little alleys behind the Venetian harbour. One good shop, for example, is located diagonally opposite the Venetian Loggia at the corner of Arkadiou/Nearchou St., and another is Gamma, in Petichaki St. on the harbour. There are several "serious" jewellery shops in Souliou St.
There is the shop of an **onyx cutter**, who produces beautiful, inexpensive vases, containers, ash trays etc, situated at 3, Katechaki St., at the way up to the Fortezza. The stone comes from Iraklion, and you can also watch Mr Theodorakis at work here.

— ★ —

• BOOKS: **Agora**, with its good selection of books, is situated in Joulianou Petichaki St. on the Venetian harbour. A mine of information for everyone interested in the history of the city is the book **"Rethymnon - A Guide to the City"**, by A. Malagari and Ch. Stratidakis, costing c. £3.

— ★ —

• CONFECTIONERY: Loukoumades can be bought, along with a large selection of cakes, biscuits and sweets, from the large Zacharoplastion **Kavakakis** (confectioner's shop), on Platia 4 Martiron.

Sightseeing

The Old City is a place on its own. You can stroll in peace through the maze of narrow alleys between Venetian doorways, artistic latticed wooden bay windows and wrought-iron balconies.

The condition of the buildings varies, however. In some places there is busy renovation and rebuilding going on, but there are dozens of

Turkish wooden bay windows characterise the alleys of Rethymnon

Palazzi, decorated with filigree work, which are wasting away their time as sad ruins. It is generally to be hoped that the city authorities and private owners will pay more attention to the upkeep of their valuable buildings. However, there is a growing tendency to use old, renovated buildings as guest houses or shops.

Platia 4 Martiron: This central square is the gateway to the winding alleys of the Old City. It is situated on the long Kountourioti St., which separates the Old City with its narrow alleys from the New City with its vehicle noise. A striking point of attention in the square is the monument to *Kostas Giampoudakis*, the famous explosives expert of the Monastery of Arkadi. In proud stance, with an audacious expression and armed to the teeth, he looks out into the mountains, where the monastery is situated. His ramrod figure, silhouetted against the slim Turkish minaret of the Valide Sultana Mosque in the background, seems particularly symbolic (more on the Monastery of Arkadi in the chapter entitled Rethymnon/Hinterland). The similarly-named church of the *Tessaron Martiron* on the square is worth a visit because of its colourful frescoes. It is named after four Cretans, who were hanged in the square because of their faith.

City Park: Situated on the upper side of the Platia 4 Martiron, and an oasis amidst the frenzy of the traffic. Tall Aleppo pines, eucalyptus, flowering oleander, orange trees, palms and hibiscus provide shade here. The shrieking of the cicadas is deafening, for they can really let off steam here! There is a central, round area of asphalt, on which theatre performances are sometimes given; colourful stage scenery is then erected here. Otherwise, there are a few modest animal enclosures with turkeys, marabus, peacocks, geese and ducks in them. There are even a couple of wild goats in shady stone-built pens.There is a great *Wine Festival* in the park in the second half of July.

Porta Guora: This is the former city gate on the north west corner of the Platia 4 Martiron, and the entrance to the winding alleys of the Old City. The narrow market passage called Ethnikis Antistasseos leads in a dead straight line down to the long *Platia Titou Petichaki* with its palm trees and tavernas; some interesting little shops can be found here, especially in *Souliou St.* (see chapter on Shopping).

Mosque of Tis Nerantzes (also called the Odeon): Situated at the southern end of Platia Petichaki, this is a large rose-pink coloured mosque with three bulging domes and a tall minaret. The second platform in the minaret can be reached by a narrow spiral stairway; from here, there is a superb view out over the city with its red tiled roofs. Psiloritis, the highest mountain massif in Crete, is also clearly visible. The interior of the mosque functions today as a public meeting place and concert hall. A music school is housed here, and sometimes the little ones can be watched as they practice on the lyra.

VISITING TIMES: daily from 11.00 a.m.-7.00 p.m. **Admission** free.

Arimondi Fountain: This stands on the introspective-looking little side square off Platia Petichaki. It was built in 1629 by the Venetian governor of Rethymnon, Arimondi, probably because he was jealous of the beautiful Morosini Fountain in Iraklion. Unfortunately it has not been completely preserved. The water gushes out of the mouths of three bulging-eyed lions, polished and shiny with age, and the Latin inscription has been partly broken away. The Turks built a dome over it, parts of which can still be seen.

The Venetian Loggia on the long *Arkadiou St.*, the shopping street of Rethymnon, is reached from Platia Petichaki by means of busy *Paleologou St.* Arkadiou St. runs like a long ribbon through the whole of the Old City, parallel to the shore promenade.

Today, the Venetian Loggia houses the Archaeological Museum of Rethymnon (see below). It is only a few paces from here to the almost circular *Venetian harbour*, from which you can take a beautiful stroll along the water's edge round the castle hill in a westerly direction (see below under heading "Walks").

From the Arimondi Fountain westwards: After going a few yards down narrow *Thessalonikis St.*, you leave the commercial area and reach the quiet residential area. This road and its side alleys are amongst the most beautiful in the whole city. There are large Turkish wooden bay windows everywhere, and between them many remnants of Venetian finery, eg doorways and stone window surrounds.

At the end of Thessalonikis St. you come upon a little square with a chapel, and on the right hand side the mighty Venetian Fortezza can be reached. A small side alley off Melissinou St. leads up to the great gateway of the fortifications. There is also the simple *Catholic Church* of Rethymnon, dedicated to St. Francis of Assisi, on Melissinou St. (statue at the altar, Mass every Sunday at 10.00 a.m.).

The Fortezza

This was built between 1573 and 1580 by the Venetians, on a peninsula bordered on three sides by the sea and by steep rocks.

Its main purpose, with its thick walls and bull-like bastions, was to protect against the new danger presented by cannons in the 16th century. It was so planned that, in times of danger, the entire population could find an emergency refuge here. But as early as 1645, when it was first put to the test, the fort was taken by the Turks after a siege of only 23 days, and completely destroyed; this was due to severe deficiencies in the construction and a number of unsuccessful operations.

The remains were destroyed by the bombardments in the Second World War.

Very little of the fort is preserved apart from the walls with their great bastions and the main gateway. Despite this, a visit is worthwhile, because of the peaceful atmosphere and the beautiful view of the city and the sea. From the architectural point of view the *cisterns* are especially interesting; they were used to collect the rainwater that was brought down from the flat roofs by means of long conduits.

OPENING TIMES: Sat-Mon 9.30 a.m. to 6.00 p.m., Tues-Fri 8.00 a.m.to 8.00 p.m. **Admission** £0.50.

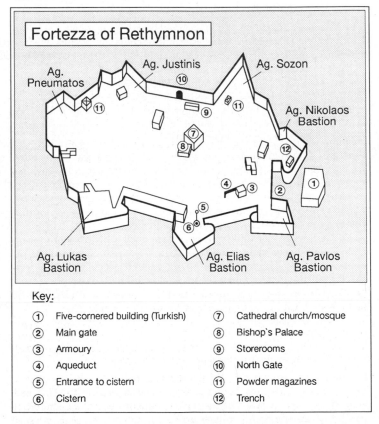

Fortezza of Rethymnon

Key:

①	Five-cornered building (Turkish)	⑦	Cathedral church/mosque
②	Main gate	⑧	Bishop's Palace
③	Armoury	⑨	Storerooms
④	Aqueduct	⑩	North Gate
⑤	Entrance to cistern	⑪	Powder magazines
⑥	Cistern	⑫	Trench

A tour of the site: In front of the Main Gate on the eastern side of the Fortezza there is a *five-cornered building complex (1)*. This was built to protect the Main Gate after the Turkish conquest, and was the jail of Rethymnon until the seventies. A museum is to be established here.

The unusually thick wall is penetrated by a passage with a barrel vault, which runs slightly uphill, behind the *Main Gate (2)*. The ticket office is in a side dome.

A relaxing stillness reigns within the massive walls; there is only the chirping of cicadas, and lizards race over the stones. Immediately and on your right, as you come out into the open, there is the former *armoury (3)* of the fort with four arched arcades. The rainwater that is collected on the flat roof is brought via an aqueduct *(4)* over the modern main path in to one of the numerous cisterns.

Straight ahead, you come to the *Ag. Elias Bastion* with several wide, spreading Aleppo pines, and there is a superb view of the whole city from here. The position of Rethymnon on a peninsula jutting out into the sea can be clearly seen. There are places to sit on this bastion, and refreshments can be purchased.

A visit to the deep *cisterns* in this bastion is very impressive. Passing through a door-opening *(5),* you reach a walled room, from which a vaulted passage, almost 18 yards long and with low steps, leads with a slight gradient down to the cistern (you should get used to the darkness first before going down carefully!). The round chamber at the end of the passage has a diameter of 13.2 feet and contains a deep well, in which there is still some water today *(6)*. Light comes in through the roof from an opening in the courtyard above.

At the centrally-situated highest point of the Fortezza there is the massive building of the former *Cathedral Church (7)*; the Turks added a dome to it later and used it as a mosque. The inside is almost empty, and to the right of the entrance there are some steps leading to the minaret, which has been destroyed and does not exist today. Opposite is the *mihrab*, a prayer niche which was once richly decorated; traces of the strongly faded colours can still be seen there. In former times the *Bishop's Palace (8)* stood next to the church, but there are only scant remains of it to be seen.

If you now go to the north side of the Fortezza, you will come to various lofty *storerooms (9)*. A passage leads down to the *North Gate (10)*, which opens onto the steep seaward side of the fortified hill. Originally, relief troops from the Venetian fleet were supposed to be able to enter the fort here, but the ships were unable to anchor because of heavy seas. Instead, those defending the fort fled down to the sea from here in the final phase of the Turkish siege. The Venetian *powder magazines* were also situated on the north side of the Fortezza; there, they were at a safe distance from the south side, which was in danger from cannon fire *(11)*. The view out over the sea is particularly fine from the north side.

If you proceed now to the *Ag. Nikolaos Bastion* on the eastern side of the fortification, you can finish your tour of the Fortezza but at the same time glance into a gloomy chapter in the history of this century.

The buildings which have been preserved on this side of the bastion are less spectacular. However, there is an unwalled *trench (12)* parallel to the wall; at the end of this you will see a door. This is where the German firing squads carried out their dirty work during the Second World War, when they executed Cretan resistance fighters.

Archaeological Museum: Finds from the Neolithic to the Roman period are on exhibition in the former Venetian Loggia, at the corner of Arkadiou/Paleologou St. It is only a small collection in a single room, but well worth a visit. The cases are arranged according to the period, in a clockwise direction; start by going round to the left.

Worthy of note is the case in the middle of the room, which contains numerous *coins* from the Greek, Roman and Byzantine epochs, all in first class condition.

The *gold jewellery* and the *sealstones* of various materials and dates in the case next to it are also fine examples, ranging in date from the Minoan, Greek, and Hellenistic to the Roman period.

Next to the case on the other side there are *red-figure vases* of the 4th century BC. Notice the risqué scene on the vase on the upper shelf, where a brave maid is escaping from the overtures made to her by the lecherous Pan, only to walk straight into the clutches of another gnome.

Finally, on the extreme right there is a case containing small *bronze sculptures* from various periods. These range from the Minoan pieces, which still exhibit a certain woodenness, to the routine mass-produced wares of the Romans.

OPENING TIMES: on working days 9.00 a.m.-3.00 p.m. Sundays 10.00 a.m.-3.00 p.m. Closed on Tuesdays. **Admission** c. £0.50.

▶ **Walks:** Continue straight on along the shore road beside the sea in a western direction from the Venetian harbour, around the castle. Above you on the thistle-covered castle hill there are the massive walls of the Fortezza, with its narrow shooting slits and little round towers. Below the road, there are black, hollowed-out cliffs. The local people like to prise away the countless sea urchins from the rocks here with their knives, so be careful, if you want to go for a swim. The nice tavern on the western side of the castle is an inviting place for a rest (see under Food).

▶ **Bathing:** The long shadeless sandy beach begins in the middle of the city, directly to the east of the Venetian harbour; varying in width, it extends for a good 9.5 miles along the whole coastal plain towards the east (see below for details on places to swim outside Rethymnon). Originally, there was a plan to build a large harbour here in the city area, between the two moles, but this turned out to be impracticable. The harbour kept silting up and had to be abandoned. It is very shallow and level underwater, and is thus a good place for children. Surf-boards and paddle boats can be hired from the Café Labyrinth. However, as the water is only replaced very slowly here, its quality is, as you might expect, not good.

There are a couple of smaller shingle/sand beaches on the road to Chania, but the sea is not very clean there.

THE HARBOUR OF RETHYMNON

Because of the several hundred yards of lightly shelving sea bed, a lot of sand and also dead sea animals and plants are washed into the harbour by the currents. Even the local author Pandelis Prevelakis wrote in his little history of the city about the ships which constantly used to run aground in the harbour; these could not be refloated and eventually had to be abandoned by their crews. After a long period of inactivity, the harbour basin at Rethymnon was dredged in March 1988. Huge cranes lifted black mud from the sea by the cubic metre and loaded it onto lorries, which tipped it back into the sea at another place. For several days, the water took on a black colour.

From Rethymnon eastwards

There is an extensive area of agricultural flatland to the east of the city. Not very exciting to look at; the ground is absolutely level, with fields of vegetables and corn, hothouses, reeds, and wasteland.

A point in its favour is the long sand and shingle beach - a good 9 miles of it - which (with interruptions) borders the plain on the seaward side. No wonder, therefore, that some of the best hotels on the island are to be found here; these include the modern *El Greco,* the *Rythimna*, the *Golden Beach* and the conspicuous box-like structure of the *Marelina*, standing all on their own. Tavernas and souvenir shops on the road indicate a high degree of tourism here. The villages are more or less places to pass through, and the fact that this is a catchment area for Rethymnon is quite apparent.

The two camping sites *Elisabeth* and *Arcadia* are directly on the beach, a few miles to the east of Rethymnon.

• CAMPING ELISABETH: a very nice, spacious site about 2.5 miles from Rethymnon, with numerous shady tamarisks and reeds, even patches of lawn, too. Sanitation good, but at the present there is only a very small restaurant. Has a more personal atmosphere than Camping Arcadia and belongs to Elisabeth, an American who is married to a Greek. Friendly staff, and a nice lady named Bopi is usually on duty at reception. There are motor bikes, mopeds, bicycles and sun umbrellas for hire. Cost per person is £2, tent £2, car £1, and overnight stay with a sleeping bag £2. Open from April to October. Tel. 0831/28694.

— ★ —

• CAMPING ARCADIA: a few hundred yards to the east of Camping Elisabeth. Simpler site, not all that much room; there are both advantages and disadvantages here. Extremely nice sites to pitch your tent, eg under reed roofs, which are partitioned off from each other by dense bushes. On the other hand, the sanitation is not of a high standard. The self-service restaurant is well-appointed. The surroundings are less spectacular, rural and flat. The beach, by contrast, is all the more beautiful, but there is no shade there at all. Prices as at Camping Elisabeth. Tel. 0831/28825.

— ★ —

• **How to get there/Connections**: Both sites are on the Old Road, a little to the west of Platanias; take especial notice of the signposts, which are not very clear. There is a bus connection into the city with the long-distance bus from Rethymnon to Iraklion, and with the frequent blue city buses (about 20 x daily, c. 6.30 a.m.-9.00 p.m.).
A taxi to or from Rethymnon costs around £2.

TIP: you can walk along the beach to Rethymnon!

Platanias: A place for passing through, with a noisy main road, but the tavernas are very popular here.

Monastery of Arseniou: This is at Stavromenos, just over half a mile inland (signposted). The monastery dates from the 17th century, but seems modern because of the comprehensive renovation that has been carried out. The church is worth a visit for its carefully restored iconostasis and wonderful frescoes, which were only painted in 1986/7. There is a terrace behind the church with a view out over the valley and stream below.

Further to the east the beach becomes excessively narrow, and is constantly interrupted by cliffs. There are only a few tracks providing access from the New Road to the shore, and the area is purely given over to agriculture.

At the point where the New Road goes a little away from the shore, there is a beach completely without shade, with a few trees behind it. It is easily reached from the road, and there is an opportunity for parking there.

Geropotamos Beach: A favourite destination for those who have rented mopeds. The Geropotamos flows down from the Ida mountains and forms an estuary at the eastern end of the plain. The New Road crosses over it by means of a bridge; beneath this, the river forms a dark green pool on the beach, and in front of that there is a a fine, semi-circular shingle beach, surrounded by cliffs. There are no facilities here. Leave your vehicle on the road and climb down to it. Particularly nice at sunset.

The low coastal mountains begin to the east, and continue until Iraklion. Fine view over the plain of Rethymnon. Low coastal cliffs extend to the little bathing resort and fishing village of Panormo, and are given over to modest attempts at cultivation, eg pumpkins. There are hardly any trees, and no approach roads to the sea.

Panormo

A refreshing peacefulness has been maintained here. A stroll through the few old alleys with their whitewashed houses is a very agreeable experience, and the blue, brown and turquoise-painted doors and window shutters provide splashes of colour.

However, it is becoming geared up to tourism. The crumbling stone ruins are being increasingly hemmed in by new buildings, and apartments and private rooms are often occupied by regular guests. But there is no bustle here, even in the high season. One reason for this might lie in the poor opportunities for those wishing to bathe. The large hotels on the plain of Rethymnon, of course, have their beaches right before their doors. Thus, the introspective character of this village quickly takes hold of you.

The most attractive spot is the tiny fishing harbour below it, with its view out over the low, shimmering, black to rust-red rocks of the area.

The frequent west wind blows strongest at the promontory to the east of the harbour, and the stormy seas thunder against the weathered cliffs and the wall of the quay. A place to sit for an hour or two, and dream . . .

• CONNECTIONS: The **buses** from Iraklion to Rethymnon and vice versa stop up on the main road. The village is only a few yards away on foot.

Accommodation

For the most part there are apartments with kitchens and shower/toilet to rent. Thus it is difficult to find anything under £15.

• **Panormos Beach**: C class, relatively new building in a quiet position, a short walking distance to the west of the harbour, on the coastal cliffs. All the rooms except one have their own small balconies, mostly with a fine sea view. The neighbouring bathing cove is only a few yards away. Cost c. £15 for a DR with bathroom and breakfast (large breakfast room). Tel. 0834/61321.

• **Captain's House**: very fine position directly above the small harbour, but only

apartments for 4 for £15, and some apartments for 5/6 people. Often booked out. Has its own taverna.

• **Kastelli Rooms**: likewise a new building with a sun terrace, rooms partly with balconies. Situated in the upper part of the village below a through road, and a little noisy because of this fact. Only a few yards' walk from the centre (signposted). Apartments for two also cost £15. Tel. 0834/51226. Details available at Tourist Information, see below.

— ★ —

• FOOD: An attractive place to sit is in the tavernas on the harbour, eg in **Kastelli** or in the **Captain's House**. The taverna **Agkyra** (anchor) is situated down below to the east, almost directly on the water. But undisputedly the best situation belongs to the little taverna of **Kostas** on a tiny sand/shingle beach to the west of the village (a few paces on from the Hotel Panormo Beach). Mainly fresh fish is

served at the handful of tables under the windswept tamarisks (the fishermen stop by every morning). The taverna **Panorama**, with its shady mulberry trees and view of the sea, lies in the upper part of the village (and also has rooms for rent). The modest **kafenion** at the lower end of the slightly crooked "main street" (a few yards down from the Post Office) seems to have the monopoly of peace and quiet.

• OTHER INFORMATION: **Kasteli Tours**. This all-round establishment calls itself "Tourist Information". It hires out cars, motorbikes and mopeds, and has apartments for rent (see above). Excursions are organised if there is enough demand.

▶ Bathing: There are low coastal cliffs, interspersed with small patches of beach. There is a modest brown strip of sand, right by the harbour. The tiny sandy cove which contains Kostas' taverna to the west of the village and a little to the west of the Panormo Beach Hotel is much nicer. 2 minutes' walk further on, there is a shingle cove with cacti growing on the bluff above it. There is a very nice walk along the lonely coastal cliffs in a westerly direction. This corner is a real windbreak, a fact which makes the heat bearable in summer, but also causes all types of things to be washed up here.

Bali

A small fishing village and popular bathing resort, tucked in between rocky coves. The last remnants of its original character have unfortunately been thoroughly destroyed in the last few years. Only the harbour has a cosy atmosphere about it, and you can sit here in the shady tavernas and watch the fishermen mending their nets.

Although a stay in Bali can no longer be wholeheartedly recommended, it is a fact that there is hardly a bed free there in summer. One of the reasons for this must be the impressive landscape in which Bali is situated. In an inland direction, thorn and phrygana-covered slopes rise up to a massive mountain corrie; in the immediate vicinity you can find solitude in a number of small, rocky coves. The opportunities for bathing are not stunning, however, and apart from the coves there is only a fine but overcrowded beach to the north of the village. Unfortunately, the long pebble beach at the beginning of the village is very dirty.

• CONNECTIONS: The buses from Iraklion to Rethymnon and vice versa (c. 23 x daily) stop at a large bend in the New Road, a few yards from the Shell garage. Bali is about a further mile on foot along the asphalt road. A lovely walk between rust-red soil formations and thistle bushes.

Accommodation

A lot of possibilities here, and new buildings are being added every year. A small neighbourhood of hotels has grown up on the hill shortly before the beginning of the village (*Bali Beach, Marian, Zoa*). But the nicest place to stay is actually in the middle of the village.

• **Bali Beach Hotel**: C class, a large bathing hotel. Cube-like apartments, smothered in bougainvillea, stretch out down the terraced slope between the first bathing cove and the actual village. Below is its own little shingle beach, in a pretty rocky cove with some shade in places. Cost of a DR c. £25 with private bath and breakfast, and a considerable supplement for half-board. Tel. 0834/22610.

• **Pension Charlot**: This is our tip! Immaculate furnishings, marble floors, doors and beds of light-coloured wood, modern baths, plants in the passages, large roof garden. Situated directly on the little harbour. Vassili, the owner, looks like Charlie Chaplin in the "Great Dictator". His son Georgios speaks English. Cost c. £11 for a DR with a bath-room. There is a shady taverna on the ground floor (see under Food).

• **Pension Panorama**: not called this for no reason. Situated high up on the left hand side, above the harbour square, and has a shady terrace. Advantage: you can see everything, but at the same time you are a little away from the centre. The cordial proprietress, Maria, offers simple rooms for c. £11 with a bath (the room with the balcony is the best). To get there, take the path which leads up to the left by the souvenir shops.

• **Elena Rooms**: run by Evangelia Papa - yianaki. Situated directly behind the Panorama on the slope. Modern, with tiled toilet/shower, but unfortunately other buildings rather block the view from here. Same price as the Panorama. Tel. 0834/22525.

• **Rent Rooms Sophia**: on the crest of a hill just before the village and directly on the approach road. Modern and clean, rooms with Shower/WC, spacious roof garden, breakfast terrace.

• **Sunrise:** Private rooms situated on a wonderful sandy bay north of the village (see under Bathing). Nobly furnished, superb view. Cost about £12 for a DR.

• **Taverna Dimitri**: As of recently, fine, spacious rooms with shower/WC are also available in this taverna, situated above the large shingle beach before you get to the village (c. 300 yards from the bus stop). Its position is rather a disadvantage, however, if you want to spend the evening in the village (see also under Food).

Other guest houses and hotels which give a favourable impression are situated above the sandy beach in the first bay before the village (and before the Bali Beach Hotel). Some of them have tavernas, and rooms with a bath cost around £10-12.

• CAMPING IN THE OPEN: Dimitri, the proprietor of the taverna above the shingle beach has no objections to people pitching their tents on the beach. This is unfortunately a rather neglected beach; the beach has not been looked after up to the present, and there is hardly any shade, only a couple of fig trees. At present, you can have a shower and get water free from Dimitri; he expects you to eat in his taverna now and again.

Food

The places to eat are clustered around the little harbour. As the fishermen of Bali still carry on their business, there is mainly delicious fish to be had here.

• **Charlot**: a taverna under massive trees which offer complete shade. Georgios recommends the fish soup (psarósoupa).

• **Panorama**: a wonderful view of the harbour, and a spot for contemplation even during the daytime.

• **Dimitri**: If you go down the asphalt road which leads off the New Road you come quite unexpectedly upon this taverna, long before you reach the village. It has a wonderfully shady terrace, flower beds and superb view over the little vine plantations to the sea. A few yards below it there is the shingle beach, as mentioned above. Dimitri's specialities are his fish dishes, but there is also a type of pizza, baked with a lot of cheese. Dimitri likes to join you at your table in the evenings, but conversation takes place in Greek.

• **Karavostasi**: situated on a pretty bathing cove north of the village. There is a friendly atmosphere here, and the food is good.

▶ **Bathing:** Unfortunately, the *shingle beach* of about 500 yards' length, before you come to the village, is not very inviting; it consists only of stones and is dirty in places. Deposits of tar and people camping there do not exactly contribute to its cleanliness. A handful of tamarisks offer a little shade, and the eastern edge is formed by rust-brown rocky slopes and shimmering green thorn bushes.

The little *sand/shingle* beach surrounded by rocky cliff walls, a short distance further on in the direction of Bali, is rather better. However, it is mostly crowded, and the water is not absolutely clean. Paddle boats, deckchairs, canoes.

The best beach is situated after a few bends in the road, to the north of the village. It is purely a *sandy beach* in a bay surrounded by rocks (follow the footpath along the water's edge or take the motor road round the back, signposted Evita apartments). The green, shimmering water is as clear as glass here, and there is a small rocky island only a few yards offshore which is a wonderful place for sunbathing and climbing around (also for nudists). There are deckchairs, sun umbrellas and paddle boats for hire.

Behind the bay, the rocks fall into the water in diagonal layered formation on the seaward side. Possibilities for walking here.

● OTHER INFORMATION: There are motor boats, rowing boats, paddle boats, canoes, surfboards, and water skis for hire around the harbour, as well as cars and motor bikes and mopeds. If you want nightlife, there is quite a large bar on the harbour. The only disco here is said to have closed temporarily.

Monastery of Agios Ioannou *(Moni Baliou)*: Situated on a terrace on the slope, exactly above Bali. There is a steep approach road c. 400 yards long, leading from the New Road. The monastery is an extremely attractive and rambling complex with a wide view over the valley and the sea. The classical facade of this little church with its two naves is flanked by two cypresses, and behind it partridges are kept in cages. The rest of the monastery buildings are partly in ruins. The inner courtyard behind the first house facade, with lovingly arranged tubs of flowers and lush arrays of plants, is most attractive. There is only one monk still living there.

VISITING TIMES: daily 9.00-12.00 a.m., and 4.00 a.m.-7.00 p.m.

From Bali towards Iraklion: At the beginning, the New Road to the east of Bali runs close to the sea. Passing jagged rocky bluffs, cliffs and rocky offshore islands, the road soon turns off into the interior, and to the left of it there is the little village of *Sise*, with its white patchwork of houses spread out on the crest of a hill.

Rocky wilderness now alternates with thickly-wooded green hills, and in between there are rust-red soil formations. The pungent aroma of herbs, resin and oleander comes in through the car window. Deep below, *Agia Pelagia* appears only a short distance from Iraklion; it is the only village for miles on this stretch of the coast.

For a more detailed report on this region see under Iraklion/Surrounding Area, page 181.

Rethymnon/Hinterland

This is characterised to a large extent by the mighty Ida Massif, which dominates the region between Rethymnon and Iraklion. There are several interesting destinations in its foothills, suitable for day excursions. Most notable of these is the famous *Monastery of Arkadi*, the

symbol of Cretan resistance against centuries of Turkish occupation.
There are two main routes on the south coast *(Plakias/Agia Galini)*.
The road via Armeni and Spili is the quickest way, and is used by the
buses. Attractive from the point of view of landscape, but more pro-
tracted, is the stretch of road via Apostoli and Fourfouras through
the beautiful *Amari Basin*, which played an important role as a route
used by British agents and Cretan partisans during the last war. Details under Agia Galini/Hinterland, see page 275.

The Monastery of Arkadi

This has almost become a kind of sanctuary or place of pilgrimage. For
Cretans, it is the most important building on the island, and is a constant
reminder of the terrible period of Turkish domination and the heroism of
their forefathers.

Although its appearance is unpretentious from the outside, this monastery was the scene of one of the most gruesome tragedies in the
struggle for Greek/Cretan independence. Hundreds of men, women
and children committed mass suicide here on 9th November, 1866, so
as not to fall into the hands of the Turkish troops who were storming
the place. Although the news of this terrible event shook many people
around the world, it was more than 30 years later that the island was at
last freed from the Turkish yoke, with the help of the Great Powers.
Today, Arkadi Monastery is the symbol of the unqualified desire for
freedom that is a Cretan characteristic. A visit is worthwhile not because of any spectacular sights to see, but because of this conscious
fact alone.

• CONNECTIONS: about 4 buses daily from Rethymnon and back, fare c. £1 one-way.

How to get there from Rethymnon: Arkadi Monastery is situated c. 14.5
miles from Rethymnon, and 1,648 feet above the sea. The road,
which is signposted, branches off a little to the east of Rethymnon (a
few miles after Camping Arcadia) into the interior. It winds up into
the mountains through olive groves and small villages.

• FOOD TIP: the taverna **Panorama**, shortly after leaving the village of **Loutra**.
Friendly people, few tourists and wonderfully peaceful, with a fine view out over the
mountain ridges, which are densely covered with olive trees, as far as the sea. Try
the red or white wine from their own vineyard; the best is 20 years old, and a litre
costs £3. Their home-produced raki is almost better!

The journey continues through the olive groves to *Kiriana*, a small,
picturesque mountain village, with its houses pushing their way up
the slope. Then follows a wonderful drive through the wooded, rocky
landscape; the road winds higher and higher upwards, with wide

views over deep gorges and sheer rock faces. The last part of the road follows a winding ravine. It has recently been given a new layer of asphalt and a crash barrier along its side, for the sake of safety.

The Monastery

A rectangular building of roughly-hewn stone, with the facades left unplastered. Not unlike a fortification.

A superbly beautiful position on a little plateau amongst lonely mountain ridges, ravines and cliffs. The surrounding area is barren in places, but there are occasional forest oases in the valley bottoms, with pines, cypresses and oaks. The predominant element here is the quiet, which is only occasionally interrupted by one of the air-conditioned tourist coaches winding its tortuous way up the curving road.

The few monks of the monastery carry on a little farming activity in the immediate vicinity; there are fields and little vineyards, and pigs are also kept.

In front of the monastery there is a taverna and a souvenir shop.

It is the year 1866. The whole of Crete has risen up against the Turks. The centre of resistance is the Monastery of Arkadi. On 1st May, 1,500 rebels gather here to choose their leaders for the different provinces. Abbot Gabriel, who is host to the meeting and the Abbot of Arkadi, is elected for Rethymnon and surrounding area. The monastery itself is declared the headquarters of the revolutionary committee of the province of Rethymnon.

These activities do not escape the Turkish Pasha of Rethymnon, who demands that Abbot Gabriel dissolve the revolutionary committee and withdraw from its leadership. Otherwise, his troops will destroy the monastery. Abbot Gabriel refuses, in spite of many warning voices which fear the destruction of the monastery by the Turkish authorities. Even the Greek officer Panos Koroneos, who arrives from the mainland with 150 men in order to give the Cretans support, can recognise the position at a glance: it is hopeless. Arkadi Monastery cannot be defended and, because he can see its certain destruction before his eyes, he once again urges Abbot Gabriel to give in, and withdraws with his troops.

In the meantime, numerous inhabitants of Rethymnon and the area around the monastery have fled within the monastery walls in fear of the Turkish soldiers. On 7th November they number 964 people; only 325 are men, the rest women and children.

On 8th November, 5,000 Turkish troops march up to the gates of the monastery! Those inside know what will happen to them if they surrender and fall alive into Turkish hands. But they also know that the struggle is futile. Despite this, they carry on a desperate defence. Again and again the Turks attack, bombarding the old walls with heavy cannon and trying to scale them. Inside the monastery, women and children fight alongside the men, loading the guns and tending the wounded. In the evening it begins to rain and still the battle has not been decided. The area around the monastery is covered with Turkish bodies, but the defenders have also suffered heavy losses.

During the night, there is a chance to send two messengers to Koroneos; but he does not come. Instead, one of the two monks sent as messengers returns of his own free will, with certain death before him. The defenders hold their last service together, for they know that there is no escape for them. It is at this moment that they conceive the idea of blowing up the powder magazine at the monastery and facing death together. Abbot Gabriel and most of those present, including the women and children, give their consent. Kostas Giamboudakis will do it.

The final decisive battle begins on the morning of 9th November. Although they are heavily outnumbered, the Cretans put up a dogged defence; but it is only a matter of time until the Turks gain the upper hand. Abbot Gabriel gives his last order: "Everyone into the powder magazine, the time has come!" The Turks take advantage of the lull to push their way through the West Gate. In the meantime, the couple of hundred Cretans who have survived gather together around the barrels of gunpowder. Kostas Giampoudakis loads his pistol with one of the last bullets. He can hear the Turks bellowing on the other side of the door to the Arsenal. Suddenly they burst in, and at the very same moment Giampoudakis shoots among the barrels. The Arsenal is blown sky-high in a monstrous sheet of flame, taking the desperate band of defenders to their death along with dozens of Turks.

But the slaughter has not yet finished. 36 young Cretans have taken shelter in the Refectorium, but without ammunition. The Turks break down the door and butcher them. In all, 750 Cretans have been killed by the evening of that day, among them Abbot Gabriel and Kostas Giampoudakis, the "explosives expert of Arkadi". Only 114 Cretans have been left alive and taken prisoner by the Turks. The latter have suffered twice as many losses; the bodies of 1,500 Turks are scattered in and around the monastery.

And so the solitude of the mountains takes over again.

The defenders of Arkadi have made their mark; up till now there has been little reaction to the constant flood of terrible reports from Greece, but this time, world opinion takes notice. People are made aware of the sufferings of the Cretans under the violent rule of the Turks; money is collected for the Cretan struggle for freedom, and a wave of indignation sweeps Europe. But the European Powers have their own problems. The Austro-Prussian war is taking place, and 4 years later the Prussians march into France. It is only many years later, after repeated revolts on Crete, that Russia, Italy, France and Great Britain intervene and the Turks have to withdraw from Crete. To this day, their deeds have not been forgotten by the people of Crete.

Every year, on 8th November, the Cretans celebrate their **National Day**. A great procession winds up to the monastery, and festive services are held both there and in Rethymnon.

A Tour of the Monastery

In the *round building* under the trees on the left, quite a way in front of the main entrance of the monastery, there are the skulls of some of those who fell at Arkadi. The holes and cuts made by bullets and sword slashes can still be seen. A macabre sight; they are placed in an orderly row in a semi-circular showcase . . .

Passing through the *doorway*, which was completely destroyed in 1866 but has been rebuilt, you come to the interior of the fort-like building. Directly ahead is the attractive *monastery church*, whose architect must have been in a playful mood. With its rich mixture of Renaissance and Baroque elements it almost resembles a church in the Spanish colonial style found in South America. It boasts two naves, and a beautiful *iconostasis* (altar screen), which was added after 1866, when the old one was completely destroyed.

On the left hand side, in front of the facade, there is a tall, thickly-wooded *cypress*. It is said that one Cretan hid himself in the branches during the storming of the monastery by the Turks, and thus survived.

There are monks' cells in the long left-hand wall of the monastery, and the entrance to the *Refectory*, or dining room, is situated in the middle of this wing. It is entered via a forecourt, and there are long, rough tables and benches inside, on which traces of blows and cuts can clearly be seen. They are reputed to have been caused during that act of butchery in which the Turks killed the 37 Cretan rebels here. Right next to it there is the gloomy *kitchen*, which almost seems to resemble a castle kitchen of the Middle Ages with its old-fashioned equipment. A door leads out into the open, where there are a couple of pig pens and some agricultural implements.

In the far corner of the wing there is the famous *powder magazine*, the vaulted roof was completely destroyed by the great explosion, and today this long room still yawns open to the sky. A small memorial plaque in Greek proclaims: *The flames which were ignited in this crypt, and which illuminated the whole of the glorious island of Crete with their light, were the fire of God, in which the Cretans died for their freedom.*

There are some monks' cells at the back of the monastery; these are still inhabited today.

The little *museum* is on the first floor of the right wing. There are many exhibits here which either survived the storming by the Turks, or are a reminder of it. For example, the embroidered vestments and sacred vessels were hidden by the monks in the crypts of the monastery, shortly before the attack. There is also the freedom banner of the rebels, torn to shreds by bullets, which was hoisted over the West Gate and remained there during the struggle; and then there is the door of the Refectory, punctured by sword slashes. There are also photos and portraits of the rebels, and many other items. In the last room there is a model, in relief, showing the *"Holocaust of Arkadi"* and the marching lines of the Turkish forces.

VISITING TIMES: from sunrise to sunset. **Admission** to the museum c. £1 (opened on request, and especially when a group of tourists arrives).

RECOMMENDED READING: **Freedom or Death** by Nikos Kazantzakis. A moving description of one of the many uprisings of the Cretans against the Turks.

From Rethymnon to Anogia/Ida Mountains

A trip much varied in character, through a richly-wooded region. The occupation of charcoal burner has not yet died out here.

Favourite destinations are the potters' village of *Margarites* and the *Melidoni Cave* at Perama. Further on, the road goes through *Axos* (worth a visit if you wish to buy a sheeps' wool rug!) to *Anogia*, the highest mountain village in Crete, from where Psiloritis can be climbed. For a thorough description of Anogia see under Iraklion/Surrounding Area.

If driving your own vehicle, take the New Road in an eastwards direction from Rethymnon. Turn off inland on the Old Road in the direction of Perama at the *Monastery of Arseniou* (signposted; for a description see Rethymnon/Coastal Plain). Between *Viranepiskopi* and *Hani Alexandrou*, the narrow road winds through a huge area which consists almost exclusively of carob trees. Then, around Hani Alexandrou, there are a lot of oranges, vines and olives. Just under 2 miles before the village, on the right, there begins a stretch of bumpy road to Margarites (about 3.25 miles). It is unmade in places.

Margarites

The potters' village is situated high above the shore plain amidst extensive olive groves.

Angular alleyways with bright blue walls, little whitewashed houses, flights of steps decorated with flowers; these are all an invitation for a careless stroll through this village. But many places have been abandoned and are empty. Years ago, there were numerous potters at work here, following the old traditions. They mostly produced the huge *clay pithoi* which were once used by the Minoans; these are fired in the enormous kilns of rough, piled-up stone blocks. Formed from grey clay, the pithoi can be seen quite a distance outside the village on the side of the road, while the black smoke from the kilns rises up into the sky.

Today, however, Margarites is going through an upheaval. The few potters that have remained there mainly produce simple everyday ceramics, such as flower pots, crockery etc, apart from pithoi. They have also begun to cater for the wishes of tourists. In particular, the occasional arrival of young, foreign potters has brought new ideas; delicate vases, plates and vessels are increasingly being produced, and make good souvenirs and gifts.

However, the bus connections are bad and tourists do not stray into Margarites all that often. Apart from the presence of several kafenia, there are no other amenities.

• CONNECTIONS: The bus journey there reveals itself to be a trip half way round the globe. There is only one bus at midday, every day, from the Platia Iroon in Rethymnon to **Perama**, the main town in the region. There, you have to change buses, and take the one that brings the schoolchildren back to their villages from their school in Perama. The bus winds its way upwards through tiny village nests and green olive groves by means of a mass of detours and short-cuts. The view out over the sea is beautiful. At last, at around 2.00 p.m., you arrive in Margarites. Be careful, the same bus returns immediately to Rethymnon, and there are no further connections! The only possibility is to return to Perama by taxi, and then take the 5.00 p.m. bus to Rethymnon.

• SHOPPING: Before the actual beginning of the village there is the conspicuous house of an Austrian potter, directly on the road. In the village itself, there are several newly-opened shops which sell attractive pottery.

Perama

A larger village, almost a small town. There are a lot of workshops, shops and kafenia on the long main road, but there is not much shade.

Perama is the point of departure for a trip to the nearby *Melidoni Cave*; this too has earned its place in Cretan history, because of a massacre which took place there during the period of Turkish occupation.

From Perama to the Cave of Melidoni: The way is signposted. At the eastern end of the village, the road to the coastal village of Panormos crosses over the narrow Geropotamos Bridge. Immediately afterwards, on the right, there is the turn-off to Melidoni (2.5 miles to the village, 4.75 miles to the cave).

Melidoni: The picture this village presents is dominated by the decaying ruins of houses, overgrown courtyards, areas of rubble and empty door frames. Melidoni has been half-abandoned, and the barren landscape brings little agricultural yield. Charcoal burning is the only occupation which is common here. It is a very agreeable pastime to sit in the kafenion on the village square and watch the men playing cards, which they do every day.

A signposted road leads up through massive, old olive and carob trees in winding curves to the cave on the mountain slope. The black heaps of the charcoal burners are a frequent sight everywhere here. The road ends at a chapel. The crater-like cave entrance is reached by going up a few steps.

Melidoni Cave: Around 300 Cretans hid inside this cave in 1824. When the Turks discovered their whereabouts, they threw in burning clothes and bushes and set fire to branches before the entrance, so that those inside suffocated in agony. An altar stands as a memorial to this event in the first chamber of the cave.

The Cave of Melidoni is a damp and slippery stalagmite cave, where torches and good shoes are essential. Beneath the first cavern, to which there is comfortable access, there are two further caverns, for which potholing equipment is necessary.

NOTE: Unfortunately, there was no access to the cave in recent years , apparently because of archaeological excavations in progress there. But the square under the trees by the chapel just offers itself as a picnic place. There is a wonderful calm here, and the view extends far over the plain of Perama.

From Perama to Anogia

Two roads run into the mountains, and the more southerly of these goes up to a higher altitude and is a lonelier road. The mountain villages around *Livadia* and *Zodiana* in particular still seem to be untouched by tourism. Both on the roads and in the kafenia there seem to be more Cretans than usual wearing the sariki and heavy boots. Quarrying and stone-working constitute an important part of the economy here. There is a stalagmite cave worthy of note near the village of Zodiana.

Axos

Attractive village on the mountain slope. A pale reflection of Anogia where the production of sheeps' wool rugs and blankets is concerned, but prices are a whole lot more reasonable here, and the village is not yet as given over to tourism as its famous neighbour.

The shops are grouped around a cosy little village square with a huge plane tree and a Venetian fountain decorated with lions.

Those wishing to make some purchases should perhaps visit *Mr and Mrs Patelaros*, a little below the square. They are both exceptionally friendly, and not stubbornly intent upon making a sale. They offer carpets with very interesting Byzantine designs. Mrs Patelaros has already won 6 diplomas from EOMMEX (the Greek/Cretan handicrafts organisation) for her weaving. Mr Patelaros, for example, explains one of his pieces in the following way: "*The name of this rug is the Way of Love', because the design is very complicated, like love. Once you are in it, you cannot find your way out any more*" . . .

Mr and Mrs Patelaros are happy to see all visitors

• ACCOMMODATION/FOOD: Rent Rooms **Etearchos** at the upper exit from the village, near the Church of Agia Irini. The only taverna is **Ta Fanarakia**, on the main through road above the village square.

• SIGHTSEEING: In the Dorian period, Axos was a powerful city with a large **acropolis**. Sparse remains have been excavated on the hill above the village. Otherwise there are some beautiful Byzantine churches. The little cruciform-vaulted Church of **Agia Irini** at the upper exit from the village dates from the 14th century, and is attractively built from quarried stone with noteworthy arcading around the dome. **Agios Ioannis** is situated at the cemetery above the village, and contains several frescoes from the 14th/15th centuries (ask for the key at the kafenion).

For Anogia and the Nida High Plateau, see under Iraklion/Surrounding Area page 187.

From Rethymnon to Chania

The New Road runs continuously along beside the sea, while the Old Road branches off inland shortly after Rethymnon. There are more bends along the latter and it is narrower and not as well constructed. It is only a worthwhile proposition for residents of the region and for detours into the mountains.

• CONNECTIONS: There are frequent connections along the New Road between Rethymnon and Chania (every half hour, c. 26 x daily). The Old Road is only used by a few buses, and the journey then takes considerably longer (c. 2 x daily).

To the west of Rethymnon the road is at first dominated by the striking rock and cliff coastline, with no village to be seen far and wide. A beautiful journey, not too high up above the sea, with the occasional little bathing beach between the cliffs. The best place to bathe is in a little patch of forest below the road, with a small beach and a taverna. An access track leads down to it.

Shortly before the turning to Episkopi the road descends to the plain, and there is uninterrupted sand and pebble beach from here to Georgioupolis! The road runs directly alongside the beach here; and the tavernas along it offer access to the beach and parking facilities.

About 2 1/2 miles to the east of Georgioupolis there is a whole cluster of relatively new hotels on the New Road (*Silver Beach, Happy Days Beach, Akti Manos* etc). There is enough room for everybody on the long sandy beach in front of them.

• ACCOMMODATION: **Akti Manos** (Manos Beach). A small, hospitable hotel which we heard about from readers' letters. Half board here costs £15 per person, and in addition to rooms there are also bungalows between the beach and the hotel, although these do not have kitchens (the prices for the bungalows and the rooms are the same). Manos and his brother Ioannis are concerned round the clock with the comfort of their guests. The evening meal is a little celebration, even if there is only one set meal. For breakfast you can choose between home-made yoghurt and fresh eggs from their parents' mountain farm. There is an almost tropical wilderness of banana plants etc. between the house and the beach. The little houses are situated on the edge of this "garden". Tel. 0825/61221.

Georgioupolis

This little, seemingly rural village is almost hidden under very tall eucalyptus trees.

To the left of it there are the rugged rocky slopes of Cape Drepanon, while on the right there is an absolutely endless sandy beach. The superb panorama of the White Mountains forms a splendid background. But what really makes Georgioupolis so attractive is the river, clear as glass and ice cold, which flows into the sea in several tributaries. A fleet of colourful fishing boats rocks gently on the water in the widest of these; the scene is almost idyllic.

That its charm has not remained hidden is evident. In the few alleys around the large, rectangular village square the number of houses with "Rooms to Rent" far exceeds the number of those which have not yet turned to the tourist business. Whereas a few years ago it was only the rucksack tourists who had discovered the village, it is now the ever-increasing number of package holidaymakers who populate the coffee bars on the square. As several hotels work together with

There is the estuary of a strong river at Georgioupolis

British tour operators, there are mostly British tourists here, apart from the Germans. In winter, by contrast, peace returns to the place again, and everything closes down except for the two old kafenia on the main square.

• CONNECTIONS: Buses from Rethymnon to Chania and vice versa stop on the New Road. The few buses which travel the Old Road stop on the village square. There is a bus every day at 6.00 a.m. to Lake Kournas (see below).

• CHANGING MONEY: There is no bank in the village. A **mobile bank** (Trapeza tis Hellados) comes to the village square on Tuesday, Thursday and Friday around midday. Otherwise the Pizzeria on the approach road will change money, and also cheques.

• SHOPPING: a traditional **kiosk** on the village square. Whether you want chewing gum, biscuits or Cola, you can get everything here for a small price. The fishermen of Georgioupolis often spread out their catch next to it, and fruit is also sold there.

• OTHER INFORMATION: Rent a car/bikes at the entrance to the village.

Accommodation

Although there is hardly a house in the village which does not rent out rooms, and although numerous new buildings are completed there every year, Georgioupolis is still completely booked out in August! To find a room there is a matter of pure luck.

• **Gorgona**: C class, directly on the beach, a few hundred yards to the east of the village. A larger establishment with its own restaurant, and you can sit in the open air directly at the water's edge. Most rooms have a balcony and their own shower. Price c. £12-14 for a DR. How to get there: Turn off to the right from the large village square. Tel. 0825/61352.

• **Nicolas**: C class, pleasant building with a facade of natural stone, small terrace and comfortable lounge with bar. Ground floor completely furnished in light-coloured wood. Rooms all with their own shower/WC and (very) small balcony. Cost c. £12-14. Situated at the beginning of the village of Georgioupolis, on the road which goes to Lake Kournas. Also caters for package holidaymakers, hence the large variety of tours and excursions on offer. Tel. 0852/22482.

• **Zorbas**: C class hotel, modern, and built only a short time ago. Rooms with private shower/WC, shady position under tall eucalyptus trees down below the square on the right (turn into the road by the Hotel Penelope). An extension was being built in 1988 (if it has not yet been completed you should reckon with building noise). DR costs around £12-14. Tel. 0852/61381.

On the Village Square

• **Penelope**: E class, the oldest house in the village. It was completely renovated and modified in 1986. Simple furnishings, but every room has a shower and WC. You are right at the centre of life on the village square here, and tall eucalyptus trees provide shade. DR without breakfast costs c. £9. Tel. 0825/61307.

• PRIVATE ROOMS: **Anna**, a larger house, newly-built, on the west side of the river. Probably the best address at the moment, although it only has shared showers on the passages. **Irina**, with a quiet position on the eastern edge of the village, is a large whitewashed house with an arched arcade and wide balconies. Unfortunately, the cleanliness left a

• **Amfimala**: E class, diagonally opposite the Penelope. Cheapest hotel in the village and furnished accordingly. DR c. £7. Tel. 0825/61362.

• **Almyros**: E class. Turn into the alley by the Hotel Amfimala. Slightly away from the bustle. Tel. 0825/22363.

— ★ —

lot to be desired in 1988, and there are only shared showers again (cold water only, if indeed they work at all). DR for around £9. Take the first road on the right from the village square (by the Hotel Penelope) and turn to the right at the Hotel Zorbas. Another possibility is **Eleftheria** behind the Bar To Steki (see under kafenia/bars).

— ★ —

• IN THE OPEN AIR: The little sandy beach on the left hand side of the village is a favourite place to spend the night among rucksack tourists. Although there is no shade, there are regular new arrivals in the evenings. An ideal place for a wash in the morning is, of course, the refreshing little river which flows into the sea here. However, the exposed position of the beaches makes it easy for the police

to carry out checks. I suspect that things will soon change here.

Long-staying guests prefer the other side of the village. Here too, you can find one spot or another behind the beach, but you will have to walk quite a way.

Motor caravans are occasionally seen on the open stretch of land by the sea, down from the village square.

• READER'S TIP: "**Paradise** is a brand new pension with an excellent taverna. Turn left at the Café Anatoli, and continue on for about 50 yards."

Food

• **To Arkadi**: exposed position on a landspit right by the sea. In front of you are the jagged cliffs and you can hear the gurgling of the water. Fine view. The proprietors and their son Yannis are very attentive and readers of the first edition were very satisfied with the food here. Sometimes specialities could be had which were not available elsewhere.

• **Yorgo's Taverna**: the meeting place in Georgioupolis, right on the New Road, before the actual village itself, and directly at the bus stop. In the evening, everyone sits here comfortably under the reed roof in front of the house, and western pop music emanates from a cassette recorder. The menu changes every day, according to what Yorgo has been able to buy - eg fish soup, moussaka, stuffed aubergines, sometimes fruit salad, and the country salad with eggs and olives is particularly delicious. Yorgo also offers wine from the barrel, eg a full-bodied retsina and a heavy red house wine.

• **Almiros**: on the village square, opposite the Hotel Penelope. Even in the burning heat, you can always find a place to sit in the shade here, amidst the greenery.

• **Aposperila**: on the village square, diagonally opposite the Almiros. Good fish, but there is also Stifado.

— ★ —

• KAFENIA/BARS: There are numerous coffee and cocktail bars around the village square, eg **Anatoli** with a much-favoured roof garden. **To Steki**, on the north west corner of the square, is run by Hans and Susanne from Berlin. There is a full menu with muesli, cakes, cornflakes and also Pikilia (various types of sausages and cheese, shrimps, zatziki etc). A nice place for breakfast. **Iliovasilemata** (Sunset Bar) on the eastern side of the village square is a pleasant place for breakfast or for cocktails in the evening.

▶ **Bathing:** *To the west of the* river there is a beautiful bathing cove, which is almost exactly semi-circular, with beautiful sand dunes. Immediately behind these there rise the sparsely covered rocky slopes of Cape Drepanon. At the end of it a rivulet flows into the sea, and careful inspection will reveal the little tributaries that flow into it; the water is slightly salty and ice cold. They can be reached by crossing the bridge which spans the river and its fishing boats.

Immediately *below the village* on the right hand side next to the river there is a barren area of grass and sand. A narrow, artificially-constructed causeway leads to a chapel on a rocky cliff.

A sandy beach several miles long extends in the direction of Rethymnon. The further you walk along it, the more lonely it becomes, but there is frequent vigorous building activity. Little rivers also flow into the sea here, and it is necessary to wade through them, in order to move on. There are places to park along the New Road which runs along directly behind the beach.

> **Warning**: Although the sea seems so harmless, it is dangerous to swim far out from the beach at Georgioupolis. Treacherous currents constantly claim human lives!

▶ **Walking:** It takes just under an hour to walk from Georgioupolis up to **Exopolis**, at the entrance to Cape Drepanon (take the road over the bridge; shortcuts along certain paths are possible here). It is very nice to sit under the mulberry trees at the Panorama Taverna, run by Georgia, and there is a superb view!

Cape Drepanon (from the East)

A great rock bluff with sides which fall away vertically into the sea in places. Little villages are scattered here, and they are often half in ruins as a result of the vigorous emigration of young people from the area. There are only elderly men in the kafenia; peace and quiet prevail. The agricultural basis for the area consists of modest vineyards, plus some fruit and olive trees, interspersed everywhere by tall cypresses. The central region around Vamos is very green.

The peninsula is a worthwhile place to visit, either on four or on two wheels. The road, which is entirely of asphalt, runs from Georgioupolis via Exopolis, Kefalas and Drepanos through the lonely eastern half of the promontory. There is a striking "table mountain" at Drepanon. The long sandy beach at *Kalives* is reached via Kokkino Chorio and Plaka (for details on the villages of Kokkino Chorio, Plaka and Almirida see under Kalives, page 397).

The journey via Vamos through the central hilly area of the peninsula is also very nice. There are wide panoramic views over a sea of dark green cypresses and olive trees. **Vamos**, the main village, is picturesquely situated on the slope amongst a lot of greenery, and there are kafenia on the wide crossroads in the middle of the village. A modern hospital has recently been built there.

Lake Kournas

You almost feel as if you have been transported to the Alps: deep blue water at the foot of a steep mountain slope, surrounded by scrub and thorn bushes, with trees dotted here and there.

Lake Kournas is the only freshwater lake on Crete. It is not large, but its waters are as clear as glass and it is a place where a contemplative stillness can be felt. Increasing numbers of holidaymakers, mostly those who have transport, are finding their way there, but all is still as it should be on the extensive areas of grass and bushes around the lake. There, you can roast in peace in the sun, but at the same time you can watch fat green grasshoppers and cicadas with their transparent wings. A couple of ducks paddle on the quiet waters of the lake; a beautiful little piece of this earth.

The lake is only a few miles behind Georgioupolis. It is only accessible on the long north eastern side, where the road passes by and there is also a taverna, the only house on the shores of the lake. The hills around it are thickly wooded, and although there is a path which runs along the shore for quite a way, the undergrowth on the far side is practically impenetrable and the ground is marshy. In addition to this, there are said to be giant crabs around . . .

The whole scene seems so un-Cretan that, if it were not for the burning heat, you could almost imagine yourself to be on the beach of an Austrian lake resort.

• CONNECTIONS/HOW TO GET THERE: A bus travels once daily at about 6.00 a.m. from Kournas, a little above the lake, via Georgioupolis to Chania. It returns in the afternoon.

The lake can be reached from Georgioupolis in a few minutes with your own vehicle. A road full of potholes goes past the Hotel Nicolas directly to the lake (signposted). But it is much nicer to cover the 3.75 miles along the slightly hilly road on foot - a swim is then all the more refreshing.

— ★ —

• ACCOMMODATION: Available at **Frangiadakis**. A friendly, elderly couple rent out a few rooms in the house behind the taverna. Simple but with your own shower, and the beds are OK. DR costs c.£8. The house is situated on the right hand side of the approach road which goes down to the lake. Tel. 0825/96385. There are more rooms with a view of the lake available at the **Panorama** Taverna (see below under Food).

— ★ —

• FOOD: **Limni**, a little way up from the lake, on the through road to Kournas. There is a wonderful view from the balcony, the cicadas chirp away, and the air sparkles. Try the Greek salad here. The homemade goat's cheese is in a class of its own, crumbly and very full-flavoured. **Panorama** is a taverna on the shore of the lake, and from the large terrace you can get a wonderful view of the lake through the arches of the reed roof. The wiry proprietor rushes nimbly around, and the presence of lambs' skins in the kitchen signals the fact that lamb chops are on the menu in the evening. Another taverna was under construction in 1988.

• OTHER INFORMATION: **Kayaks** and **paddle boats** can be hired for £2 each.

▶ **Bathing:** Ideal for freshwater fans. The lake is beautifully clear, without odour and wonderfully warm. Those who feel their way into the water through the rocks on the shore, which sometimes have sharp edges, can enjoy one of the nicest experiences that Crete has to offer in the way of bathing. It is particularly beautiful in the evening, when the sun magics forth a play of shade and glittering light on the water. There are extensive stretches of lawn on the shore, and behind them peppermint bushes with blue flowers. A lot of rucksack tourists, particularly riders of motor bikes, spend the night at the lake, but the tents are very well scattered - there is little activity here, even in August.

From Georgioupolis to Chania

The New Road goes round the solid mass of Cape Drepanon and only reaches the sea again at the almost fjord-like cutting that is the Bay of Souda. It crosses a superb area of forest, one of the few on Crete. There are massive pines and deciduous trees on both sides of the road, and the panorama of the White Mountains is always in the background.

The unclouded joy of a swim in fresh water: Lake Kournas

Vrises

A little off the New Road. Here, the road branches off to Chora
Sfakion on the south coast. The massive old plane trees on the village
stream (which is usually dried-up) offer an ideal, shady place to rest.
It is thus no wonder that some tavernas have established themselves
on both sides of the bridge, in order to profit from the tourist buses
which frequently stop here. Local specialities are the mild sheeps' yoghurt with honey, and lamb.

Thanks to the superiority of the yoghurt and lamb there, Vrises has
edged its way up to becoming a favourite place for an excursion
among tourists from the beaches around Chania and Rethymnon.
Every seat is taken beneath the colourfully lit trees in the evenings,
and the lambs are turned on spits over the smoking charcoal grills . . .

• CONNECTIONS: frequent buses to
Chania and **Rethymnon**, bus stop a little
to the west of the river across the stream
bed. It is also the place to change buses
when coming from Chania and Rethymnon to **Chora Sfakion**. One of the most
beautiful mountain roads over to the
south coast begins here, and it is also
the shortest way between north and
south in western Crete (Vrises - Chora
Sfakion 25 miles). It passes through the
Askifou Plateau and then descends to
Chora Sfakion in breathtaking hairpin
bends (see below for more information).

• ACCOMMODATION: **Paradisos Rooms** at the exit from the village in the direction
of Georgioupolis.

• FOOD: As already stated, grilled lamb
is the speciality here, but you should keep
an eye on the quality. However, c. £3 per
portion for lean meat is surely not too expensive. In addition there are casserole
dishes of every kind, eg courgettes baked
with cheese or egg, and good beer on
tap. The market leader is the first
Estiatorion to the west of the bridge,
with tables by the river bed.
Those who do not wish to eat a full meal
should at least try the sheeps' yoghurt
(not the prepacked variety) served with
(thyme) honey. The honey can also be
purchased.

From Vrises to Chora Sfakion

**The journey into the Sfakia is only 25 miles from Vrises, but offers a won-
derful experience where landscape is concerned.**

After the greenery of Vrises you soon wind up the narrow, curving
road into the bare mountain slopes of the Lefka Ori. Beforehand, however, it may be worthwhile to make a short detour to the *Church of the
Panagia* at *Alikambos* (on the left hand side below the road before you
enter the village, and surrounded by a cemetery). Inside the church
there are beautiful frescoes by Ioannis Pagomenos (14th century).

After passing the *Gorge of Katre*, which was many times the scene of
the annihilation of Turkish troops by Cretan resistance fighters, the
road soon runs through a pass into the fertile *Askifou Plateau*. The
houses lie between lush vines, and the ruins of a Turkish castle can

be seen on a striking double hilltop on the left hand side of the road. Some of the peaks of the Lefka Ori are visible on the right.

The road continues through another pass into the *Imbros Gorge*, a steep-sided ravine with beautiful cypresses, which finally opens high above the coast towards the Sea of Libya. The journey proceeds around unbelievable hairpin bends down the denuded slopes to the precipitous south coast near Chora Sfakion. There is one panoramic view on top of the other, and you can look along the coast almost as far as Plakias.

Details on Chora Sfakion and the surrounding area on page 486.

Kalives

A long farming village on Souda Bay, nestling between vineyards and olive groves. Miles of sandy beach in front of it, which are almost deserted in August.

While the crowds flock to the little villages on the south coast, you can still usually find peace and quiet here. The beach tavernas are only unbearably crowded at the weekends because of day trippers from Chania. However, the spectacle ends every Sunday evening, as quickly as it began, and once more you have the beach to yourself.

Kalives is actually only made up of the long main road and the many whitewashed side alleys, which extend up the slope behind it by means of a few steps. The women of Kalives sit before their doors here in the evenings, while the men gather under the thick plane trees on the cosy village square and examine every new arrival with curiosity.

In spite of the proximity to Chania only the beginnings of a tourist infrastructure are visible in Kalives. There are only a few rooms for rent and the village seems thoroughly Greek without the obligatory souvenir shops. Village life seems to be intact too, and the village square is bursting with life in the evenings.

Further points in its favour are the good opportunities for excursions into lonely Cape Drepanon, to the ancient city of Aptera, or to Chania and the neighbouring Akrotiri peninsula.

● CONNECTIONS: Buses from Chania - Rethymnon and vice versa stop on the New Road, and from there the centre is a distance of just under 1.25 miles on foot.

● POST OFFICE: diagonally opposite the village square.

● TELEPHONE: **OTE Office** at 162, Main Street, near the western end of the village. Mon-Fri 7.30 a.m.-3.10 p.m.

● OTHER INFORMATION: **Kalives Travel**, on the main street near the village square, changes money and sells boat tickets.

Accommodation

● **Haus Karoline**: the best accommodation in the village. Situated in the eastern part of the village on the slope, and clearly signposted with blue signs. Mrs Gisela Xirakis from Germany and her Greek husband built this new house only a few years ago. They offer double rooms for £10 and apartments (bedroom, living room, small kitchen) for £18 with modern plumbing, attractive furniture and a wonderful sea view. Gisela keeps everything scrupulously clean, and breakfast is available. A hearty welcome is guaranteed. Open from Easter to September/October. Tel. 0825/31703.

● **Corali**: E class, the only hotel in the village, and unfortunately under conract to a tour operator for package holidays. The resourceful hotel owners have recently added some simple wood-panelled private rooms, c. £7-9. The Corali is situated at the western end of the village directly on the beach. You can sit on a concreted terrace area under the trees here, and enjoy the view over the sea and the Akrotiri peninsula opposite. Cost c. £12 for a DR. Tel. 0825/31356.

— ★ —

● PRIVATE ROOMS: **Rent Studios**, a new building at the western end of the village. Tel. 0825/31537. There are also simple rooms in the **Stelios** Taverna, near the eastern end of the village, where the service road comes up from the New Road (200 yards to the east of the village square).

Food

● **Alexis Zorbas**: on the village square facing the church; clean, reasonably priced and good food. You will be surprised with a new speciality every day and receive excellent service.

● **Stelios**: situated in the eastern part of the village, where the service road to the village runs up from the New Road to the main street of Kalives. The taverna is right on a little river which flows into the sea here. Passing through a type of conservatory, you enter the reed-covered "garden" on the river via a bridge; bouzouki groups often play here at the weekends. When this happens, there is a supplementary price to be paid.

● **Iraion**: a pizzeria on the main road, 50 yards from the village square in a westwards direction.

● KAFENIA: There are two on the village square. Steph. Frangioudakis, the owner of one of them, is an extremely nice person. You can play billiards in the other.

● NIGHTLIFE: **Kalives Club** Disco; a pleasant beach disco, to which tourists seldom stray. Much patronised by young local people from 11.00 p.m. onwards. Situated in the western part of the village, down on the beach. Drinks from about c. £1.50.

Sightseeing: The actual attractions are in the surrounding area; see below. The nicest place in the village itself is the village square. There is the mouth of a small stream here and the scene is somewhat reminiscent of a little Venice. Next to it there is the ornamental *village church*, visible from afar with its typical Byzantine dome and bell tower. The inside is exhaustively decorated with modern frescoes. In particular there are scenes from the Passion of Christ, and He looks down with austere eyes on the Faithful gathered below.

Bathing: The *long, sandy beach* extends along the whole bay. There is an impressive view on both sides; on the right, the flattened out table mountain of Cape Drepanon, and to the left, the mighty complex of Izzedin, the former Turkish fort, with the ruins of the ancient city of Aptera above it. An ice-cold, strongly-flowing stream runs into the sea in the western part of the beach, just before the taverna.

There is rather more going on on the beach in the *eastern part of the village,* which is rounded off at the foot of a rock wall by the fishing harbour. Going along a path, you can still clamber over the rocks in an easterly direction and discover another lonely beach in the next cove (a dusty track leads down to it from the road on Cape Drepanon).

Cape Drepanon (from the West)

The coast road from Kalives passes through vineyards along the white cliff coast. There are little beaches scattered along here, with field paths leading down to them. The impressive lone peak of the table mountain lies in splendour before you.

Almirida: An insignificant village on a branching shingle and sandy bay, framed by white limestone cliffs. Up to now, it was known at the most to the inhabitants of Chania as a place to swim, but it is increasingly turning to tourism. However, the beach is only narrow and consists mostly of shingle, but you can sit comfortably by the sea in the few tavernas there and enjoy the view out over the Akrotiri Peninsula.

• ACCOMMODATION/FOOD: There are various private rooms available. Good food can be had at **Fagopoti**, especially from the charcoal grill, and there are also unusual dishes such as snails and horta (a wild vegetable).

The road climbs up the mountain from Almirida to Plaka, which is at a considerable height above sea level.

Plaka: A village which consists almost entirely of newly-built houses, and an old village nucleus is hardly discernible. In the mid sixties, a terrible whirlwind swept through the village in a wide path of destruction.

The road continues through a barren and lonely rocky landscape to a radar installation belonging to NATO: access is prohibited beyond this point. The journey as far as the sign is worthwhile because of the wonderful peace and solitude and the view out over the whole of Souda Bay. On the way back, the White Mountains rise up in their full height and majesty in front of you.

A concrete track leads up to

Kokkino Chorio: This tiny village is situated high up, right at the foot of the steep table mountain. It is a quiet mountain village of old houses, their frail roofs weighted down with heavy stones so that the wind will not blow them away. You can stroll in peace up the steep alleys between whitewashed walls and flower-decked inner courtyards to the vantage point on the terrace by the little church, whence there is a grandiose view of the White Mountains and Souda Bay. The journey continues via Drepanos and does not present any problems (see page 391).

From Kalives westwards

A fantastic drive along the Bay of Souda. On one side there is the turquoise blue sea, and on the other the rugged rock walls of the rust-red coastal mountains.

Kalami: This tiny nest is situated at the western end of the Bay of Kalives; its few houses climb up the slope between the New and the Old Road. There is a wonderful view out over Souda Bay from the 4 tables that make up the little kafenion at the beginning of the village; a dear old lady brings your drinks, and you can also watch the ferries coming in and going out. There is a particular atmosphere when the sun goes down over the flat Akrotiri peninsula. Here, at the narrowest part of the Souda Bay proper, the three "White Islands" protect the entrance; they are so called because of their steep white cliffs.

It is no wonder that the Turks established their mighty *Fort Izzedin* at this point of extreme strategic importance. It dominates the place and the whole Bay of Kalives, and stands directly beside the New Road, with its encircling wall and watch towers. Today it houses a barracks bristling with weapons, but during the Junta period of the sixties and seventies it served as one of the many jails for political prisoners.

There is still a large block of stone bearing a Turkish inscription from the year 1884 in front of the entrance to the fort. It is possible to walk along a little path around the walls to the modern guard rooms. Photography is forbidden.

Bathing: There are several isolated beaches below the road. They are reached by bumpy field paths.

Aptera

The widely scattered ruins of an ancient city high up on a mountain crest, opposite Kalami.

Aptera was founded by Mycenaean conquerors, added to by their Dorian successors and used as a settlement up into the Byzantine period. In contrast to the unfortified settlements of the Minoans, which were mostly placed without care or caution by the sea, the Mycenaeans and Dorians were more afraid of hostile marauders. Most of all, they liked to build their cities in protected mountain positions. *Lato* near Agios Nikolaos is another example of such a place (see under that name).

Even if the ruins are not exactly very imposing, the way up there is worthwhile; the view is staggering! The Bay of Souda is spread out in front of you like a huge blue carpet, the silver grey band of the New Road passes through the mottled hills with their olive groves, fields and vineyards, and the mighty chain of the White Mountains rises in the south. Directly in front of you are the broken white cliffs of the Akrotiri peninsula, like the chalk cliffs of Dover. Behind that you can make out the airport, and right over in the west lie Chania and Souda, with its tall cement factory. The whole thing seems all the more impressive because you are nearly always quite alone up here.

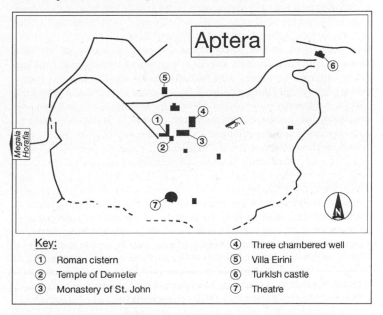

Key:
(1) Roman cistern
(2) Temple of Demeter
(3) Monastery of St. John
(4) Three chambered well
(5) Villa Eirini
(6) Turkish castle
(7) Theatre

History: The Mycenaean conquerors founded a settlement at the economically and strategically important entrance to Souda Bay. In the subsequent Dorian period this grew to be one of the most important trading cities on Crete. Aptera also remained an important city in the Classical and Roman periods and later, until it was plundered and finally reduced to ashes by the Saracens in 824 AD. The fort on the edge of the plateau, which is visible for miles around, was built by the Turks in 1816.

• HOW TO GET THERE: A winding road leads up from the New Road a few miles to the west of Fort Izzedin. A road branches off to the left (signposted) after the little village of **Megala Horafia**. The site is c. 1.25 miles further on.

A Tour of the Site: The ruins of Aptera date from various periods and are scattered over a gentle hollow in the plateau.

Perhaps it might be an idea, first of all, to take the right fork in the path on the plateau. This will bring you to the *Monastery of St. John of*

Patmos (3). Before you get to it, on the left, you can recognise a large Roman *cistern (1)* from its typical brick walls, and on the right there are the foundation walls of a Hellenistic *Temple of Demeter (2)*. The monastery itself dates from the Christian Byzantine period. Only a chapel, the high exterior walls and some house ruins are left of the monastery itself. The monumental three-chambered *well (4)* below the monastery is a very impressive sight and dates from the Roman period. The three well-preserved, lofty chambers seem almost eerily dark and deep, and no sound is to be heard there.

Now walk back to the place where the path forks, or go straight across to the Turkish *castle (6)*. This impressive rectangular building has a superbly preserved row of battlements around it, and round corner towers. All that remains of the internal structures is a section of their walls with some attractive window arches. A cement roof and a stairway has been built in one house, so that it is possible to climb up to the battlements. A longer section of the ancient city wall is preserved on the eastern slope of the plateau.

VILLA EIRINI (Peace)

This conspicuous Villa *(5)* belonging to the artist *Maria Orfanoudaki*, who counts many important Greek artists and politicians amongst her friends, is situated on the road to the castle. The house has an almost fortified appearance, and is fenced in by heavy wire netting. There are stone plaques with inscriptions such as "Peace", "Eirini" etc. to be seen everywhere. This monument to peace is surely in the right position above the military installations of Souda Bay. Mrs Orfanoudaki is very hospitable and is active world-wide in the cause of peace.

Souda

The harbour of Chania, a place for the transhipping of industrial cargoes and tourists all in one, with a towering cement factory right next to the quay.

In general there is not much to see here; it is a typical harbour town, with only through traffic and no atmosphere. There is also a large navy barracks here.

By contrast, there is a beautiful panoramic view of the mountains rising behind it. A short respite is possible in the kafenia under the shady trees on the harbour square.

Of significance here is the once proud monument to **Prince George** in the middle of the square; it is now crumbling away. The Prince first set foot on Cretan soil here on 21st December 1898, and proclaimed the autonomy of the island amid incredible festivities and jubilation. The years of subjugation under the Turks had thus come to an end for all time (see also our chapter/History, in the Introduction). The rejoicing did not last for long, however, for the Cretans did not want to be under the knout of the Great Powers and Prince George soon fell into disfavour with his autocratic style of leadership. His statue has been accordingly neglected and allowed to fall into ruin today.

CONNECTIONS

● **Boat**: There is a car ferry to Piraeus at 7.00 p.m. every day. The regular evening ferry from Piraeus arrives at about 7.00 a.m. in the morning, and the occasional morning ferries arrive at about 7.00 p.m. There are transfers by bus to Chania to and from all the ferries. Prices: luxury class cabin £21, A class £18, B class £15, tourist class (pullman seats) £11, C class (deck) £9, private cars up to 4.25 metres in length £25, over 4.25 metres £34.

● **Bus**: There are buses from the harbour square to Chania and vice versa about every 20 minutes (departure and arrival times are listed in front of the big market hall in Chania). Fare c. £0.50 one-way.
Only some of the through buses from Chania to Rethymnon go via Souda; check beforehand.

— ★ —

● ACCOMMODATION: **Knossos**, D class, a little way below the kafenia under the shady trees on the western front of the harbour square. Simple, but all rooms have a balcony, and it is seldom full. Cost around £9 for a DR. Tel. 0821/89282.

Nikos, D class, over the Nikos taverna on the upper side of the harbour square. Clean, relatively new rooms with good wooden beds. There are, however, only two rooms with balconies on the front. Same price.

● FOOD: **O Michalis**, a few yards from the harbour square on the road to Chania. Best place in the village.

● OTHER INFORMATION: **OTE Office** and **Post Office** on the same road, diagonally opposite.

Souda Bay Cemetery

The British War Cemetery is opposite the harbour at Souda. It is in a wonderfully peaceful situation at the head of the bay; a gently sloping site with lush lawns and flowers directly by the sea, and surrounded by massive eucalyptus trees.

One of the most beautiful military cemeteries that I have ever seen - even if such aesthetic criteria are out of place here. The remains of over 1,500 servicemen who fell in a terrible war are buried here under long rows of standing gravestones: 862 British, 197 Australians, 496 New Zealanders, 9 South Africans, 5 Canadians, 1 Indian, 1 Pole, 1 Yugoslavian . . . hundreds of them could not be identified. The whole site radiates peace and dignity. You should certainly let the heavy atmosphere take its effect; perhaps the madness of war will then be all the more evident.

In the middle there is a tall marble cross with a wrought iron sword set into it. This symbolises "perpetual resistance to enemies of peace".

If you stroll along the rows and read the inscriptions chiselled into the stones of the fallen, some of whom were hardly 20 years of age, you will hardly be able to resist deeper emotions:

"I shall always remember you smiling, your loving wife Joan" (Aged 22)

"Life's work well done, Life's crown well won" (Aged 18)

"Sadly missed. Memories linger of youth's happy days" (Aged 29)

"Softly the winds over his dear young head . . ." (Aged 34)

"A soldier of the 1939-45 war, known unto God"

The story of the German assault on Crete can be read in the **Cemetery Register of the Commonwealth War Graves Commission** in the entrance hall.

• HOW TO GET THERE: At a distance of about 3.25 miles from Chania, a road branches off from the New Road to the Cemetery and further on to the Akrotiri Peninsula. The cemetery is about 1.5 miles down this road.

Chania

A lot of atmosphere on the Venetian harbour; "leather alley" with a huge assortment of goods on offer; market hall built on the model of that at Marseilles

The second largest city in Crete. Apart from the quiet outer districts with their symmetrically planned roads, this is a city full of life and bustle.

Those who arrive here for the first time think that they should make an immediate exit. Long lines of cars hoot their way through roads which are much too narrow, and buses advance tortuously inch by inch around the corners; the city is practically being suffocated by the traffic.

But only a few yards from the petrol-impregnated through roads, you can plunge into the alleys of the Old City around the *Venetian harbour*. This is full of life of its own kind; shops and stalls are crammed together, pastel-coloured house facades and tourists jostle around the harbour mole, and right behind them there are zigzagging flights of steps with gateways climbing upwards. Pleasant guest houses or small hotels have often established themselves in the centuries-old Venetian palazzi. Everywhere you go in the harbour, you are following in the wake of history. In places, the houses are piled up on top of each other and built on ancient walls, and some parts of the Venetian city wall have also been incorporated in them, as have Turkish minarets and the remains of the old harbour fortifications and the

Sunset in the Venetian harbour at Chania

arsenals. It is clear that tourism in the purest form is paramount here. There is one taverna next to the other around the atmospheric harbour basin, and unfortunately there are always junk food shops between them. Half the population of Chania strolls here in the evenings. In spite of this, however, it is still possible to find hidden corners, if you deviate only a few steps from the usual tourist paths.

Another point worthy of mention: there is no city on Crete which boasts as much greenery and vegetation as Chania. Even when approaching from Souda you drive for miles through a shady avenue of plane trees. The quiet *city park* is situated in the middle of the modern business and office quarter, and by passing through the immaculate former diplomatic quarter, *Chalepa* (a remnant from the time when Chania was still the capital city of Crete), you quickly arrive up at the spacious complex which contains the tomb of Eleftherios Venizelos. From there, under the wide, spreading pines, the whole city seems spread out in front of you.

Those who have had their fill of city life can quickly drive out to one of the many beaches to the west of the city. In addition, Chania is the best point of departure for the trip through the grandiose *Samaria Gorge* and for excursions to the monasteries on the lonely *Akrotiri* Peninsula.

In short, Chania is definitely worth a few days' stay, and not only for the countless leather articles on sale there. They are cheaper here than anywhere else on the island.

Key:

ℹ️ former Mosque of the Janissaries

❶ Minoan excavations

❷ Arch. Museum

❸ Nautical Museum

❹ "Leather alley"

❺ Market hall

Information: situated up till now in the striking former mosque right on the Venetian harbour, at 6 Akti Tombazi. Friendly service, English spoken, and good information of every kind, including the booking of rooms. Open July/August Mon-Sat 9.00 a.m.-2.00 p.m., 4.00 p.m.-9.00 p.m. Sun 9.00 a.m.-2.00 p.m. *Notice:* the information bureau is apparently going to move to 40, Kriari St., in the centre of the city.

Tourist Police are at 23, Karaiskaki St.

CONNECTIONS

• **Flights**: c. 5 x daily with Olympic Airways from the airport on the Akrotiri Peninsula to Athens, West Terminal. Same frequency in the opposite direction. Price c. £25, night flight (11.00 p.m.) £20. Often fully booked at weekends - make sure of your tickets early.

One hour before flight departures, transfer buses leave the office of Olympic Airways at 88, Tzanakaki St., opposite the City Park, to go to **Sternes Airport**, which was fully modernised recently. There is no connection by public bus.

• **Boats**: The harbour of Chania is **Souda** in the large bay of the same name to the east of Chania. An **ANEK** ferry boat leaves for Piraeus every day at 7.00 p.m., and in addition there is a ship 3 x weekly at 6.30 p.m. operated by **Minoikes Grammes** (Minoan Lines). Tickets can be obtained at the city offices of both companies (see under addresses). For prices see under Souda.

Municipal buses run continuously between Chania/Market Hall and Souda/Harbour.

• **Bus**: The large **bus station** is in the newer part of the city centre on a large square between Kidonias and Smirnis St., near to 1866 Square (see city plan). There are frequent bus connections to Rethymnon, Iraklion, Kastelli, Kolimbari, Chora Sfakion, Omalos (Samaria Gorge), Paleochora, Souyia etc. There is a left luggage office (7.00 a.m.- 6.00 p.m., c. £0.50 per piece), loud speaker announcements are in English, and there is a large kafenion, which also serves as a waiting room. There are usually bustling crowds here. A free bus timetable can be obtained.

— ★ —

• ANEK: Tickets for the boats to Piraeus are obtainable at the office on Platia 3. Venizelou, opposite the Market Hall (next to the National Bank).

• CHANGING MONEY: There is one bank next to the bus station, two opposite the Market Hall, and another on Platia 1866.

• MINOIKES GRAMMES (Minoan Lines): boat tickets at the agency at 8, Chalidon St. right down on the left.

• OLYMPIC AIRWAYS: at 88, Tzanakaki St. opposite the City Park. The transfer buses to the airport also leave from here. Daily 7.30 a.m.-8.30 p.m. in the season. Tel. 0821/27701-3.

• POST OFFICE: in the road of shops and businesses which runs slightly uphill

Corner of 1866 Square/Kidonias Street: Buses leave here for the western suburbs and beaches, eg Galatas and Kalamaki (Chania Camping).

Market Hall: There is another important bus stop for municipal buses here. They run to the outer suburbs, to Souda, the Youth Hostel, up to the Tomb of Venizelos, and to the Akrotiri Peninsula etc.

• **Taxi**: There are taxi ranks on Platia 1866, Platia El. Venizelou, and at the bus station.

• **Car/motorbike rentals**: These are to be found especially around Platia El. Venizelou and on the Venetian harbour. Good bikes are to be had at **Zeus**, next to the former Café Costas.

• **Round Trips by Carriage**: These line up on the Platia Venizelou at the harbour. Not very special; you can see just as much on foot. Cost c. £5-7 per trip.

• **Excursions**: You can undertake reasonably-priced day excursions to the Samaria Gorge from the big hotels and the two camping sites at Chania, on buses operated by the KTEL bus company.

from the Market Hall to the City Park, at 3, Tzanakaki St Mon-Fri 7.30 a.m.- 8.30 p.m. Post Office kiosk on the square in front of the cathedral, in Chalidon St. (Mon-Sat 8.00 a.m.-8.00 p.m., Sun 9.00 a.m.-6.00 p.m.).

• TRAVEL AGENCIES: There are several in Tzanakaki St. (City Park) and more, for example, in Kanevaro St. to the east of the Venetian harbour. **Bassias Travel** in the "leather passage" offers cheap flights (Skridlof St.).

• TELEPHONE: OTE Office at 5, Tzanakaki St. (left hand side, next to the Post Office). Open daily 6.00 a.m.-12.00 p.m.

• NEWSPAPERS/MAGAZINES: There is an international selection at the kiosk on the corner of Chalidon/Platia 1866.

Accommodation

Countless possibilities, from A class hotels to private rooms right by the bus station. Most accommodation is in the area around the Venetian harbour; some of it is in lovingly restored Venetian/Turkish houses in a fine position and with a fantastic view. It is not always easy to find something in the high season, however.

● **Samaria**: B class, tasteful city hotel directly next to the bus station, comfortable to luxurious. The tinted window panes keep out the heat, and it is air-conditioned. Solid-looking coffee lounge with wood panelling and a lot of brass, and a fine roof garden. All rooms have balconies. Cost c. £29 with shower/toilet and breakfast. Address: Kodonias St. Tel. 0821/51551.

● **Doma**: B class hotel in Chalepa, the former diplomatic quarter of Chania. This neo-classical villa is directly on the low coastal cliff with a wide sea view. Solid, antique-type folklore interiors, with upholstered suites, a lot of wood, and Cretan art handicrafts. Probably the best address for those who want to stay in a place with style, away from the bustle. Cost c. £24 for a DR with shower/WC and breakfast. Address: 124, El. Venizelou St., several miles to the east of the centre (keep going along El. Venizelou St. from the Market Hall, until you reach the sea). Tel. 0821/21772.

● **Porto Veneziano**: B class, modern hotel in a wonderful position on the old fishing harbour right next to the Venetian harbour. Very soberly furnished, not much of a personal atmosphere, and seldom full. Air-conditioned. Cost of a DR with shower/toilet and breakfast c. £27. Address: Akti Enoseos, tel. 0821/29311.

● **Xenia**: B class, on a former bastion of the city wall to the west of the Venetian harbour, almost directly on the water. The hotel was comprehensively renovated two years ago - passages and rooms with carpeted floors, solid furniture in dark wood and very attractive tiled bathrooms have greatly improved the quality of the accommodation there. In addition there is a marvellous view of the sea and a large public swimming pool directly next to it. DR costs c. £27 with breakfast. Address: Theotokopoulos St., tel. 0821/24562.

● **Contessa**: An A class guest house, and our hot tip in Chania. Superbly restored house, 200 years old, with a large wooden bay and rich interior; beautiful wooden floors and ceilings, lace curtains and valuable old furniture. One room even has a gaily painted ceiling. In contrast to the historical nature of the house, the showers and toilets are absolutely new. Manolis Androulidakis, the owner, is a nice elderly gentlemen who is incredibly proud of his house, and rightly so, in our opinion. The expressions of gratitude in his guest book certainly attest to this. Perhaps he will invite you to a little guided tour round the house; the view from the upper rooms out over the harbour basin is unparalleled. However a DR with shower/toilet and breakfast cost c. £27. Address: 15, Theophanous St., which is a passage almost at the middle of the Venetian harbour (turn up by the Akti Restaurant). Tel. 0821/23966.

● **Porto del Colombo**: A B class guest house, a very short distance away from Contessa. Immaculate historic building with fine wooden floors, a little gloomy, but carefully restored. There is a view of the harbour from some of the rooms. Costs c. £19 with breakfast, £16 without. Tel. 0821/50975.

● There are more A class guest houses in the immediate vicinity; these are also restored Venetian palazzi, eg **Amphora**, with tall four-poster beds and a view of the harbour basin, and **Captain Vassilis**.

Reasonably-Priced Accommodation

• **Piraeus**: E class, and the furniture is no longer of the newest, but the very pleasant owner and the friendly atmosphere make up for this fact. Price for a DR just under £10 (without private bath). Address: Zambeliou St., behind the harbour promenade. Tel. 0821/54154.

• **Manos**: in the same alley; fantastic views of the Venetian harbour from the lofty rooms on the front. Simple but well furnished, with roughly cemented walls in Reception and on the passages, and wooden floors in the rooms. According to readers' letters, the cleanliness occasionally leaves something to be desired. Some of the rooms are quite small, and at night there is a lot of noise from the promenade. DR costs £14 with a private bath, or £11 without. Tel. 0821/52152.

• **Lucia**: in the middle of the waterfront on the harbour. Solid, without any extras, but clean and spacious. Thus, there are usually vacancies there, even in the high season. About £15 with bathroom and a small balcony. Tel. 0821/21821.

• **Thereza**: guest house at the north west end of the harbour promenade (Angelou St., by the Nautical Museum). Former Turkish house with the upper part of the facade made of wood. Friendly proprietor, and everything inside the house, including the carpets, is in white and light blue. 8 high ceilinged rooms with appealing furniture, and some of them with private bathroom and balcony.

Super view of the harbour from the roof garden, and there is a refrigerator which is at the disposal of guests. Around £11 with bathroom. Tel. 0821/40118. Next door are the guest houses **Meltemi** and **Stella**, the latter an angular house and a fine old establishment, but without private bathrooms.

• **Pension Erato**: Our tip. Old Venetian palazzo with 5 lofty rooms, in which the beds are located up in wooden galleries. Everything is spotless, and furnished with beautiful old furniture. About £14 for a DR. Address: 17, Lithinon St., a quiet side alley on the right hand side of the harbour.

• **Kastelli**: well-kept guest house with clean rooms, at 39, Kanevarou St. east of the harbour. The rooms only look onto the road, however.

• **Fidias**: E class, a favourite destination among rucksack tourists. A larger inn with 20 rooms, all with balconies. Informal atmosphere, about £8 for a DR, and there are some rooms with several beds. Address: 8, Kalin Sarpaki St., behind the cathedral and not far from the Venetian harbour. Tel. 0821/52454.

— ★ —

• **Private rooms**: **Amarilis**, a Venetian house with a Turkish wooden upper storey, on Skoufon St. **Port**, at 73, Sifaka Street (second road which runs parallel to the fishing and yacht harbour). Quiet and clean, with a pleasant proprietress. Costs about £12 for a DR with breakfast. **Monastiri**, at 18, Ag. Markou St., above the fishing harbour and built on the rubble of an old Venetian palazzo. It has

a beautiful terrace with a picturesque gateway. There is a superb view of the harbour from here, too, but the rooms are, by contrast, rather simple. For all of those whose legs will no longer carry them, there are private rooms directly at the **bus station** (c. £8 for a DR, £4 in a shared room with several beds). Clearly signposted and cannot be missed.

• **Youth hostel**: friendly establishment with a shady terrace and a wide view of the White Mountains. Situated on a hill in an outer suburb of Chania. Can be reached by taking the bus to Agios Joannis from the Market Hall, and getting off at Dexameni Square. Address: 33, Drakonianou St. Tel. 0821/53565.

There are two **camping sites** a few miles to the west of the city. For a description see under Bathing/Surrounding Area.

• **Readers' tip**: "We had a pleasant stay at **Amfitriti**, a little way above the Venetian harbour; there was a superb view of the harbour and the Old City, the proprietors were friendly and the price reasonable. Address: 33, Lithinon St. Tel. 0821/56470."

Fresh octopus for supper this evening

Food

The masses crowd into the tavernas on the *Venetian harbour*. There are several dozen tavernas in a row, and they are all full! There is a lot of atmosphere here in the evenings, the harbour is attractively illuminated and there is much to see. Personally, I prefer to sit in one of the fish tavernas in the neighbouring *fishing and yacht harbour*, which is still a meeting place for fishermen and those who live in the vicinity. Above all, there is very little activity here in the early evening, and the atmosphere is calm and relaxed. People from Chania come out here to eat in the late evening.

Some of the places that are really worthy of recommendation to gourmets are a little outside the centre, and in addition there are some restaurants under foreign proprietorship. This is a consequence of the fact that there is a clientele with a good supply of ready money among those stationed at the Namfi Base on the Akrotiri Peninsula.

On the Fishing and Yacht Harbour

● **To Karnagio**: This is a hot tip amongst insiders at the moment. Situated on the promenade between the Venetian and the fishing harbour in an external corner of the old city wall, at 8, Platia Katechaki. Its rather hidden position has not saved it from discovery, however, and every chair is taken within minutes in the summer months. It is essential to arrive early or make a reservation.

● **Elisabeth**, **Apostolis** and others: the fishing boats are often tied up directly in front of the tables in the little tavernas near the Hotel Porto Veneziano. There are simple fish dishes to be had here, as well as wine from the barrel. One reader recommends the **Faka** taverna, where the food is good and prices reasonable.

On the Venetian Harbour

● **Akti**: one of the best tavernas on the Venetian harbour. A house which juts out about half way along the promenade. The Stifado is highly flavoured with cinnamon. Very reasonable Chania wine, half a litre for just under £1.

Behind the Harbour Promenade

● **Les Vagabonds**: French food in one of the narrow alleys behind the harbour. No tables in the open air, but an invitingly furnished restaurant. At 48, Portou St.

● **Oleander**: also rather hidden behind the harbour promenade, and somewhat more expensive. Bought up in 1987 by a British team. In the dim, agreeable interior, with its candlelight and old film posters (Bogie and Marilyn) you can enjoy delicious meat dishes, eg fillet steak for £4. Vegetables are extra. Potatoes are served in aluminium foil, and

worthy of special mention is the lavish Oleander salad. Apart from tourists, officers from the NATO base at Akrotiri find their way here. Open evenings only 7.00 p.m.-12.00 p.m., and closed on Mondays. Address: 7, Skoufon St. (branches off Zambeliou St, the alley which runs parallel to the harbour front).

● **Semiramis**: opposite Oleander, also with candlelight and serving good Greek food. It is possible to sit outside here.

Chalidon St. and its Side Alleys

● **To Diporto**: a tiny, reasonably-priced taverna run by M. Kostakis in the middle of Skridlof St., the "leather passage" of Chania. Apart from simple fish dishes, tasty lambs' testicles are also served. Half a litre of wine costs £0.50 (!)

● **Tasty**: a favourite place for a quick snack, at 80, Chalidon St. (runs from Platia 1866 down to the harbour). Souvlaki, hamburgers and Löwenbräu beer are obtainable here. Some seating is available, and the food can also be taken away.

In the New Part of the City

● **Vouli**: reasonably priced and uncompromisingly authentic. The "Parliament", as it is called, is one of the great traditional eating places in Chania. In this restaurant with a high vaulted roof you are often completely among Greeks. The selection of simple dishes on offer is in the numerous pans on the stoves, and in the glass display case. Following the old tradition, the dishes are prepared in the morning and kept warm the whole day. Worth a mention is the good wine here, which is drawn off from the array of gigantic barrels in the background. Address: 27, Hatzimichali Gianari St. (in the centre, not far from Platia 1866).

A Little Outside the Centre

● **Retro**: surely one of the nicest restaurants in Chania; situated in Chalepa, the former diplomatic quarter of the city. Young people have brought an old villa on the quiet Platia Elena Venizelou up to scratch, and have furnished it in a surprisingly attractive way and with loving nostalgia. Carpeted throughout in light blue, with playful "Jugendstil" pictures, plants and elegant swinging chandeliers completing the picture. The nicest part, however, is the garden in front, where you can sit by candlelight and with soft music in the gentle evening breeze, under two towering palms and a lot of thickly-foliaged orange trees. It is obvious that style is of great importance here, from the festive white tablecloths and good tableware. You begin with a rich collection of appetisers, which are brought on a tray for you to choose from. Then there are a few main dishes, and a speciality of the house is beef in a mild white sauce for c. £4. Meals are served in the evenings from c. 9.00 p.m. onwards, and are somewhat more expensive than usual. Chalepa is to the east of the centre, on the road which goes to the Akrotiri Peninsula.

● **Jetée**: This excellent restaurant is run by two Irishmen, John and Vince, and is situated on the EOT beach, about 2.5 miles from the centre in the direction of Kastelli. In 1986 it was raised to the first class category by the tourist police. It offers middle European dishes with a French tinge; no olive oil, everything is cooked in butter. The dishes are served in aluminium foil (eg fried Schnitzel with potatoes) but there are also generous salads, and the special Jetée salad is particularly delicious. Open daily from 7.00 p.m.-11.30 p.m. Address: 209, Krisi Akti.

Kafenia/Cafes

A favourite area for these is the harbour promenade, especially on Platia El. Venizelou. *Fresh orange juice* is available everywhere.

● **Costas**: a reasonably-priced café on Platia El. Venizelou at the beginning of the harbour promenade, next to the place where there are motor bikes for hire. Traditional meeting-point for rucksack tourists, with an informal, relaxed atmosphere. In addition to music and the usual drinks, "breakfast", omelettes and perhaps even contacts can be had here.

● **Pharos**: the café behind the mosque, with a large terrace and a beautiful sea view.

● **Ideon Antron**: the café in the alleyway, named after the cave which was the birthplace of Zeus. Almost as if you were in a cave, you sit here in the long, narrow, almost tunnel-like garden behind the entrance gate, under a wide spreading plane tree, and can enjoy a cocktail for the price of £2 upwards. Address: right at the end of Chalidon St., only a few steps away from the Venetian harbour.

● **Kafenion in the City Park**: a traditional coffee house in the park, where extensive rows of chairs and table invite you to sit in the open air; there is a bit of a "Vienna coffee house" atmosphere. Above all, this is a favourite meeting place for the inhabitants of Chania in the evening, and in the conservatory the elderly men are constantly engaged in games of tavli or cards. If you ask, they will gladly show you how to play and perhaps you can even join in. You can borrow the games. A speciality here is "Hanum Borek", a kind of puff pastry with nuts, honey and whipped cream - sweet and crunchy, costs c. £1. Open daily 6.00 a.m.-11.00 p.m.

Nightlife

Chania certainly has the largest number of discos and music bars on Crete, and there are just under a dozen of these in and around the harbour. With their noise and bustle they are particularly clustered around the central harbour square, El. Venizelou, and at the north west end of the harbour.

It is much nicer in the evenings just to sit at one of the promenade cafés, which are quite bursting at the seams at this time. Everyone is dressed up, and tourists and Chaniots alike saunter up and down - the *volta* on the Venetian harbour is definitely one of the most striking and turbulent scenes of activity on the whole island.

Music Bars

● **Fagotto**: comfortable bar with electric piano and an atmosphere. Old Singer sewing machines have been converted into tables here, using sheets of marble. There is often live music, and you can read what is in store for you on the programme at the door. For example, there could be classical music of the Renaissance and Baroque periods from 7.00 p.m.-9.00 p.m., and from 9.00 p.m. onwards blues and jazz with Duke Ellington, Miles Davis, Keith Jarrett, Al Jarreau, Eric Clapton, B.B. King . . . no beer is available until 2.00 a.m., only cocktails. Address: 16, Angelou, a small alleyway at the end of the harbour promenade (near the Nautical Museum).

● **Disneyland**: not a music place, but an absolutely incredible amusements hall on Platia El.Venizelou. Much loved by the youth of Chania.

● **Café Port**: a first floor establishment on the same Platia, high above the crowds.

● **Tesseres Epoches**: a large, newly-opened bar on the fishing harbour. A lot of activity here in the evening, but nice and quiet during the day and adequate shade until late afternoon.

● There is a large **bouzouki place** built into the ruins of the former harbour fort, on the long mole which closes off the fishing harbour from the sea.

Discothequfs

● **Canale Club**: about 50 yards to the right of the mosque on the harbour, a favourite meeting point. People mostly gather in front of the entrance, and when it is cooler, you can go inside to dance or sit around. A popular with young tourists.

● **Ariadni**: further on from the Canale Club. The interior is entirely in green and black, with reflecting walls and columns.

● **Star-Majestic**: in Kondilaki St., behind the harbour front. Not very many tourists there up till now.

There are more noisy disco bars at the north west end of the Venetian harbour.

Shopping

Chania is famous above all for its *leatherwork*; thanks to the emphasis on rearing sheep in the White Mountains, there are enough raw materials at hand.

● Leather: **Skridlof St.** is the "leather alley" of Chania. There are dozens of shops here, one on top of the other, and there is a huge selection of boots (from c. £17), large bags (from c. £20), sandals, pouches etc. Prices are especially good out of season, when the shops are clearing their stock. Shoes can also be made to measure here. Skridlof St. branches off to the right from Chalidon St., on the way down to the harbour.

• MARKET: The large cross-shaped **Market Hall** of Chania was designed on the plan of the famous one at Marseille. It is in the middle of the noisy New City, on Platia S. Venizelou (see under sightseeing).

— ★ —

• EOMMEX: **(Hellenic Organisaton of Small and Medium Size Industries and Handicrafts)**: this organisation holds an exhibition of Cretan handicrafts; well worth a visit, in the former mosque on the harbour. The Tourist Information Office is there too. There are much better things to be found here than in the countless souvenir shops. The original and ingenious ceramics are particularly worthy of note.

If you are interested in a particular article, you can ask for the address of the producer and, through EOMMEX, even purchase some pieces. Otherwise, the exhibition serves merely to present handicrafts to the public, not to sell them. Open mid-July to mid-August from 7.30 a.m.-2.30 p.m., otherwise from 8.00 a.m.-1.00 p.m. Note: The Eommex will move from the mosque to another place.

— ★ —

• HANDICRAFTS: "Chess, like music and love, has the power to make people happy". This quotation seems to be appropriate for the nice owner of the original shop called **Mat** at 51, Potie St. He sells chess and tavli games of all types, and a very diverse selection of figures in bronze, clay and wood, some of them based on mythology. Apparently he makes some of them himself and is the Chess Master of Chania.

There are other interesting workshops and shops scattered in the alleys behind the harbour promenade; for example in long Theotokopoulou St., where there is a **potter's workshop**, and in neighbouring Zambeliou St. at no. 61, where there is a **weaver's workshop**, in which mostly wall hangings are produced on the loom.

Sightseeing

Chania is rich in history. Above all, the old quarter around the Venetian harbour invites you to wander up and down, without any particular purpose in mind.

New City

This surrounds the historic centre around the harbour, and houses most of the public buildings such as the post office, banks, telephone office, air and shipping agencies, travel agencies etc. The City Park is the only place to escape the noise and bustle here.

Platia S. Venizelou: The central traffic junction of the city. Here is the cross-shaped *Market Hall*, which is without parallel elsewhere in Greece. Built in 1913 on the plan of the market hall in Marseilles, it has a lot to offer both from an architectural point of view and from what is on sale there. You should not miss taking a stroll through it; the atmosphere is business-like, sometimes it is noisy, but not hectic. Worthy of a special mention are the stalls of the fish and meat merchants and the tiny tavernas, where you can eat very simple dishes at a reasonable price. The market is open Mon-Sat 8.00 a.m.-1.30 p.m., 5.00 p.m.-8.00 p.m. It is closed on Monday, Wednesday and Saturday afternoon.

Opposite the main entrance on Platia S. Venizelou, wide *Tzanakaki St.* with its travel agencies, boutiques and other shops and offices leads to the City Park.

City Park: A shady oasis in the midst of the traffic noise. A lot of benches, a large kafenion (see under kafenia) and even a little zoo. There are all kinds of birds in the cages here, eg turkeys, budgerigars, swans and peacocks. There are also monkeys and even a few Cretan wild goats (*Agrimi*) with their magnificent curling horns; they gaze sadly out through the wire netting.

If you go up Tzanakaki St. from the City Park to the next crossroads and turn left into Sfakianaki St., you will soon come to the *Historical Museum* of the city (for its exact position see the plan of the city; it is described in the chapter entitled Museums).

Platia 1866: To the west of Platia S. Venizelou, next to the bus station. The lush green is noticeable here; there are the busts of some valiant Cretans, and the bubbling Venetian fountain with eight outlets for water is a refreshing sight here.

The Old City

This was enclosed within the former city wall, which is still preserved in the west and east. In place of it in the south there is wide *Hatzimichali Gianari St.*, which forms the boundary with the New City.

In the "leather alley"

Chalidon Street: This runs from Platia 1866 down to the harbour; a lot of souvenir shops, jewellery shops and bustle. A few yards on to the left, behind the Tasty Fast Food Bar, the little alleyway Em. Baladinou turns off towards the large *Schiavo Bastion*, and there is a path leading up to it. From on top, there is a wonderful view over the old shingle roofs around the harbour, the hilly Kastelli Quarter and the White Mountains to the south. *Skridlof St.,* already mentioned under Shopping, branches off to the right from Chalidon St. This is a narrow alley where you can buy anything that can be made from leather. Further down the road, on the square with the great *Cathedral*, there is the facade of the Venetian Church of San Francesco, inconspicuous from the outside. This houses the *Archaeological Museum* of Chania (on the west side of the road; for details see under Museums). The domed roof of a former Turkish *bath-house* can be recognised diagonally across the road from it.

Around the Venetian Harbour: Behind the western harbour front with its tavernas you will find picturesque little alleys with crooked house facades, hidden thoroughfares, angular flights of stairs and wrought-iron balconies. There are lush plants in pots in front of the entrances, and children playing everywhere; cars cannot pass through here. The whole quarter almost seems village-like. The restored palazzi are often real jewels, but much has lain in ruins here for a long time. You will discover scattered historical treasures, for example at 45, Zambeliou St., where only the once proud facade of an aristocratic house remains. Over the portal, there is this noble inscription: *Nulli parvus est census, qui magnus animus* (Nobody with a great spirit will be thought of little account).

The striking former *Mosque of the Janissaries* (elite troops in the service of the Pasha) is a focal point for the eye. When tourism began on a large scale at the end of the sixties, its rose-coloured dome was hastily painted a neutral white. The Information Office is housed there today.

At the north west end of the harbour promenade there is the *Nautical Museum*, which is well worth a visit (see below). If you go round the promontory along the water's edge in a westerly direction, you come to a small, shady forest with juniper trees and places to sit. Behind this, there are the remains of an old *bastion*, and the Xenia Hotel with its swimming pool. This can also be used by non-residents for c. £1. The Venetian city wall, with what used to be its adjacent ditch, runs inland from here, and there are houses nestling in its shade.

Kastelli Quarter: To the east of the Venetian harbour, on the hill overlooking the modern fishing harbour, there stood the official residence of the Venetian governor of the city (Governor's Palace) and other important official buildings. This important hill was even surrounded by its own wall. Today, everything seems to be higgledy-piggledy up there. Houses and guest houses have been built on the ruins of the fortifications, and there are many areas of rubble between Venetian gateways, the remains of old Roman houses and the empty shells of historic palazzi. The Governor's Palace has disappeared and a barracks has been established in its place.

The foundation walls of four *Minoan Villas* have been excavated on Kanevaro St. They are behind a fence of wire netting directly on the road. The rich yield of finds from them can be seen today in the Archaeological Museum (see below). A total of just under 200 vases was found in one of the houses! You can descend to the arsenals and other historic ruins on the harbour from the eastern end of Kanevaro St.

Also worthy of note is Platia 1821, which is a short distance into the city from the fishing harbour. The large *Church of San Nicolo*, with a minaret for its right bell tower, is in this square; it was used as a mosque during the Turkish occupation.

Venetian ruins on the fishing harbour

Fishing and yacht harbour: The most original part of the harbour, and still hardly "prepared" for tourism. Some of the massive Venetian *arsenale* still stand here to this day, and are used by the fishermen as dry docks, storerooms and workshops where repairs are carried out. It is a nice walk out along the long *mole* with the ruins of a fort and the lighthouse at the end of it. The panorama of the White Mountains at sunset is particularly beautiful from here.

If you go along the water's edge in an easterly direction from the point where the long mole begins, you will come to a break in the former city wall, with massive bastions and huge lumps which have broken off from the wall. This is where the tourist section of the harbour ends. Another wide bay with a fortified quay and a fine view of the eastern area on the outskirts of Chania is spread out in front of you. The inhabitants sit here in front of their doors in the late afternoon, and there is the idyllic atmosphere of a suburb.

Chalepa: An eastern outer suburb of the city, which is crossed when going to the Akrotiri Peninsula. This former diplomatic quarter had its heyday at the end of the last century, when Chania was the capital of the island. Numerous, beautiful classical villas have slumbered here, forgotten and neglected, for many years, but now the people of Chania are beginning to recognise the value of Chalepa as a residential area. There are signs of new life here and there, along with vigorous restoration and investment. It is not by accident that the most stylish hotel and one of the most elegant restaurants in the city are situated in Chalepa.

Chalepa can be reached from the centre via wide El. Venizelou St.

Museums

Archaeological Museum: This is situated in the Venetian Church of San Francesco on Chalidon St., opposite the square with the cathedral. The inconspicuous facade is completely incorporated into the building line of the street and can almost be missed from the outside. All the more rewarding, then, is the rambling vaulted interior of this attractive pillared basilica. There are mostly finds from western Crete on show here, dating from the Neolithic to the Minoan and Greek-Hellenistic periods up to the Roman occupation. The *Minoan pottery* mostly originated from excavations which were carried out in Chania itself in the sixties and seventies. Of especial interest, for example, are the numerous well-preserved *sarcophagi*, some of them containing decaying skeletons. In the background there are classical Greek sculptures and reliefs, and some fine *mosaic floors* decorated with brilliant figures and subjects from antiquity.

The red-figure (showcase 32) and black-figure vases (showcase 33) of the Greek period are especially attractive, as are the Roman glass vases (showcase 38). There is even a lump of the glittering turquoise-green raw material on display.

A focal point in the museum garden is provided by an elegant, cylindrical-shaped Turkish *fountain house*. Next to it is the portal of a Venetian palazzo and the stump of a minaret, from the period during which the church was used as a mosque by the Turks.

• OPENING TIMES: Mon and Wed-Sat 8.00 a.m.-7.00 p.m., Sun 8.00 a.m.-7.00 p.m. Closed on Tuesdays. **Admission** c. £1, students and schoolchildren receive a slight reduction.

Nautical Museum: This is situated at the north west end of the harbour promenade, and can be recognised by the large black-painted anchor at the entrance. Souda, the harbour of Chania, was always a place of considerable strategic importance, and even today the Akrotiri Peninsula is a highly-militarised zone. Hence this martial collection of articles from Greek nautical history.

Right at the entrance, a sixteen-and-a-half-foot long torpedo instils fear into the visitor, and this is followed by models and photos of battleships, torpedo boats and submarines. The old navigational instruments date partly from the period preceding the First World War. You can see a reconstruction of the helm of a ship, ancient machine guns, compasses, telescopes and a ship's propeller . . . One room is dedicated to historic sea battle; for example the Battle of Salamis between the Greeks and the Persians in 480 BC has been reconstructed, using little model ships.

After all this sabre-rattling bellicosity the last room, which contains a wonderful collection of sea shells, provides a pleasant contrast and a thoughtful epilogue. The visit is worthwhile for this room alone! Some really unique examples, ranging from only millimetres in size to those almost 3 feet long have been brought together here. There are also corals, starfish and the preserved skeletons of sea animals.

• OPENING TIMES: Tues-Sun 10.00 a.m.-2.00 p.m. Also on Tues, Thurs, Sat 5.00 p.m.-7.00 p.m. Closed on Mondays. **Admission** £0.50. students/schoolchildren just over half price.

Historical Museum: A villa in the classical style in the New City, at 20, Sfakianakis St. (not far from the elegant square with the over-dimensional Court House). The glorious recent past of Crete is relived here. Martial paintings, weapons, tattered flags and a lot of other exhibits bear witness to the Cretan struggle for freedom against the Turks and up to the Battle of Crete in the Second World War. Such heroic representations of the atrocities are scarcely to be outdone anywhere else today (Example: the flagpole belonging to a Greek division has been shot away, so a soldier offers himself as a living flagpole). In spite of this, and indeed because of it, this is an exhibition of historical value with a lot of interesting details. For example, there is a coffee mill as big as a chest dating from 1866. In addition there is a huge collection of dusty files and documents, in cabinets a good 15 feet high, on the ground floor. This is said to be one of the largest collections in Greece.

• OPENING TIMES: Mon-Sat 8.00 a.m.-1.00 p.m. **Admission** free.

Chania/Bathing and Surrounding Area

There are several sandy beaches only a few miles outside Chania to the west, on the road to Kastelli. They are, of course, mostly crowded because of their immediate proximity to the city, but offer an ideal opportunity to make a quick escape from it.

Not very attractive from the point of view of landscape and quite built-up, with apartments, villas and hotels springing up everywhere. The atmosphere here is largely determined by the presence of the very busy main road to Kastelli.

Leaving the city by the road to Kastelli (see city plan) and roughly at the city boundary, you pass over a river which is dried up in summer. The road branches to the left here to Omalos and the **Samaria Gorge** (signposted). For details see below.

Aptera Beach: Several hundred yards of beach without any amenities and without shade. To the left of it, and separated from it by a rocky promontory, there is another fine sandy beach, at the beginning of which there is a hotel of the same name.

• **Aptera Beach Hotel:** C class, generously-planned bungalow complex directly on the beach. Large restaurant in a very quiet position. Cost c. £17 for a DR with breakfast, and c. £25 for half board. Tel. 0821/22636.

EOT Beach: Situated after the next hill, only a short distance further on in the direction of Kastelli. Fine sand, no shade, and mostly very crowded.

There are two approach roads, the one to the east (the first from the direction of Chania) is signposted EOT; here, a hundred yards from the beach, is the excellent Jetée Restaurant, run by two Irishmen, Vince and John (see Chania/Food), which also has an agreeable bar under a reed awning.

Camping Chania is situated on the other approach road (also signposted). The road forks when it reaches the sea. One branch goes off to the right over the hill towards the EOT beach. The road to the left passes through a little forest to *Ag. Apostolos Beach*, which is surrounded by cliffs, then on to Glaros and Oasis Beach.

• CAMPING CHANIA: a small to medium-sized site, about 2.5 miles east of Chania. The site is quite humdrum in appearance; only low olive trees, hard ground, but with adequate shade. A very positive point in its favour is the friendly atmosphere created by the staff, and the food in the evenings is delicious. The semi-circular bay is only about 2 minutes away on foot, and there are other beaches in the vicinity. Cheaper than Camping Agia Marina — £2 per person, tents £1, cars £0.60. There may not be enough room for larger tent arrangements. Open from April until October. Tel. 0821/31686.

Connections from Chania: buses go from the corner of Kidonias St/Platia 1866 (only a few yards from the large bus station) to Agii Apostoli, Kalamaki and Galatas.

Glaros/Oasis Beach: Directly on the road, a wide white sandy bay with some amenities, such as showers, restaurant, surf board hire, and pedal boats.

Kalamaki: A village on the road shortly after the turn off to Galatas. Not an attractive place, vigorous building activity going on, and the beach is very crowded.

• ACCOMMODATION : There are various possibilities. The Hotel **Panorama** has the nicest position high above the road. There are also numerous apartments and private rooms in the village.

• OTHER INFORMATION: There is a **Minigolf course** on the road to the east of Kalamaki (on the seaward side).

There is a continuous stretch of beach from Kalamaki to Agia Marina. The road runs directly alongside it at the back; there is building activity everywhere, and there are a lot of hotels.

Agia Marina

At first sight, this seems to consist only of holiday houses and hotels. The beach is beautiful, and the camping site is a good headquarters from which to bathe and/or explore Chania. Because of the road, however, there is a lot of commotion and through traffic. The real centre of the village is situated inland from the road and on a hill. Several nice tavernas have established themselves there.

• ACCOMMODATION: **Amalthia Bungalows** is a C class, immaculate complex directly on the beach. All rooms have bathroom and balcony, and there is a shady terrace at the restaurant on the beach. Cost c. £22 for a DR. Often booked out in the high season. Tel. 0821/68542.

Thodorou is a C class hotel right next to Amalthia Bungalows. Smaller, easier to find your way around and more personal atmosphere. Even has a little lawn and some shady trees. Around £14 for a DR. Tel. 0821/68237. Both of these hotels are often fully booked up by package tourists.

— ★ —

• CAMPING AGIA MARINA: a good site about 5 miles to the west of Chania, opposite the rocky little island of Agii Theodori. Medium-sized site with a relatively large amount of shade. Particularly nice is the fact that you can pitch your tent under low fan-like palm trees! There are miles of fine, sandy beach (!) with shallow water, and there are isolated little rock bluffs in the water. The sun umbrellas are even made of reeds. There is a taverna here, but be careful, it is often closed in the low season! Also a Mini Market with a large selection of goods

(chocolate, fruit juices etc.) Very crowded in the high season, otherwise it is a good place for a few days real relaxation. Cost per person £2 (overnight stay without a tent, using only a sleeping bag costs just over £2), large tent £1.50, small tent £1. Cars £1. Open from April to October. Tel. 0821/68555.

Connections from the bus station in Chania: take the bus to Kolimbari (around 25 x daily), last bus at 9.30 p.m. Exact times of the buses on the bus timetable which is available from the bus station.

• FOOD: on the village square at Agia Marina, a little inland from the main through road, there are three good tavernas with a beautiful view out over the neighbouring valley and its stream. Kostas, the friendly proprietor of **The Falcon**, and Manolis in the neighbouring **taverna** both offer a strong local wine and very good food with generous portions, including some more special dishes such as Stifado or various vegetables.

For the other villages on the road to Kastelli (Platanias, Maleme, and Kolimbari) see below page   447.

Akrotiri Peninsula

Lonely monasteries; Namfi base and rockets; Zorba the Greek's mountain

A low, slightly undulating plateau, protected to the extreme north by a steep and incredibly impressive mountain wall.

There is only sparse vegetation on the rust-red ground: little groups of olive trees, vineyards, a handful of trees and a lot of thorny phrygana. Accordingly, the peninsula is thinly populated. In earlier times it was certainly an ideal place of refuge for the monks, and there are all of four monasteries in this lonely area. Unfortunately, there have also been rockets here since the seventies; in spite of great protests on the part of the population, NATO has established an important firing base for cruise missiles here (known everywhere in the area as Namfi: *NATO missile firing base)*.

For all this, Akrotiri still retains its original character, if you keep away from the airport and the military installations on the eastern side. However, people from Chania are increasingly building holiday homes and apartments for rent on the few beaches there.

The most impressive part is without doubt the barren mountain range at the northern end of the peninsula. A little tip here: large parts of the film *Zorba the Greek* were made in the tiny village of Stavros on the extreme north western tip! Even without this "attraction", a visit there is still worthwhile. Other interesting destinations are the Monastery of *Agia Triada*, the ruins of the former Monastery of *Katholiko* in the middle of the lonely mountains, and above it the newer Monastery of *Gouverneto*.

• HOW TO GET THERE/CONNECTIONS: **El. Venizelou St.** is a wide road leading in an easterly direction from the Market Hall in Chania. Following the signposts, it passes through **Chalepa**, the former diplomatic quarter, which still has a trace of atmosphere left to it. The road then goes up the mountain. At the top, the turn-off to the tomb of El. Venizelos soon comes into view.
Buses run around 4 x daily from the Bus Station in Chania to Stavros and the Monastery of Agia Triada.

Tomb of Eleftherios Venizelos: This is a worthwhile little detour. The spacious complex of white alabaster enjoys a wonderful position under bushy Aleppo pines on the mountain slope, the city is spread out deep below it and the view out towards the Rodopou Peninsula to the west is also superb. If there is no tourist bus about to arrive, there is a wonderful quietness about the site. Venizelos is recognised as the most important politician that Crete has produced and even today, 50 years after his death, he is honoured almost as a saint. He played a decisive part in the realisation of the union with Greece in 1913, which had been longed for by the whole of Crete. A better place for his grave than this one, high above the former capital Chania, could not have been found.

To Stavros: Shortly after the turn-off to the Tomb of Venizelos, you should take the road to *Kounoupidiana*, which branches off to the left from the main road. The latter goes further on to the airport, Namfi Base and Sternes; see below for details.

The road forks at Kounoupidiana, and you should bear right here. The turning to Stavros, just under 5 miles away, is directly after the exit from the village.

After a while, the road reaches the sea. This is *Kalathas*, a village which only seems to consist of apartments, holiday villas and bungalows. Very acceptable beach here, c. 200 yards long, but no shade. The beach is quite level, without any shelving underwater. There is a small offshore island opposite, to which you can easily swim. Paddle boats, canoes, deckchairs and sun umbrellas can be hired here.

Stavros

Who has not heard of the film "Zorba the Greek" with Anthony Quinn in the leading role? He is the inimitable personification of this fictional figure-for many he *is* Zorba.

Here, in the unpretentious little village of Stavros, which is at the most only a place where NATO soldiers from the surrounding firing ranges get together out of season, is the **mountain**, on whose slopes Zorba builds a railway with which to transport the precious tree trunks downhill! But the railway line collapses and everything is lost. The grandiose final scene, in which he dances the Syrtaki at the foot of the mountain, surely remains in the memory of every film fan.

But Stavros has still more to offer: a wonderful, almost semi-circular bay, which is almost completely closed off from the sea by a small promontory. There is the atmosphere of a huge bathtub here at the foot of Zorba's mountain; the water is green, the colour of that found in a spring, and there is fine sand, ideal for children. However, Stavros is overcrowded in the season, due to the many day trippers from Chania. When we came here last time at the beginning of October, we had the whole pool to ourselves, apart from a few fishing boats and pleasure craft. There is absolutely no shade there.

The few holiday homes and houses belonging to the fishermen of the village are built on the low hills and dunes, and in a seaward direction the coast is closed off by strange, gouged-out cliffs; there is also quite a long sandy beach with dunes there. Worth a visit out of season, for the complete solitude it offers.

• CONNECTIONS: Buses 4 x daily from and to Chania (Market Hall).

• FOOD: **Mama's Taverna** is situated right on the round bathing cove. It is **the** meeting place both in the evenings and during the day, with its large shady canopy.

• ACCOMMODATION: Very simple rooms in small wooden huts can be rented at **Mama's** - they are directly next to the taverna. Cost c. £9 (closed from October onwards).

Blue Beach: very attractive guest house, right on the stony coastal cliffs, quite a distance outside the village. The name Blue Beach only refers to the colour of the water, however, and a strip of sand a few yards long between the black cliffs does duty as a "beach". Probably worthwhile, because of its quiet, out-of-the-way position. How to get there: take the signposted turning shortly before Stavros and go round the radar station. Next door to Zorbas Apartments.

• OTHER INFORMATION: There are paddle boats, deckchairs and sun umbrellas for hire on the beach at Stavros.

To the Monastery at Agia Triada: Easily reached via the asphalt road from Chania. Keep to the right at the turn-off beyond Kounoupidiana. From Stavros go back to Chorafakia and on over the bad dust track to the monastery.

The last part of the journey through a shady avenue of cypresses is wonderful. Just before the entrance there is a truly gigantic eucalyptus tree; the monks have created a real oasis here in the stony wilderness.

Monastery of Agia Triada

A large and exceedingly harmonious complex, rectangular in shape. Built in the 17th century in Venetian Renaissance style, Agia Triada clings to the first piece of rising ground which forms part of the mountain massif in the background.

A decorative inner courtyard with attractive stairways and balustrades is hidden behind the monumental *external facade*. You can climb up a flight of steps to the *bell tower* over the entrance, and there is a wonderful view of the flat plateau of the Akrotiri Peninsula from here.

The courtyard is dominated by the impressive *monastery church* with its many domes and beautiful reddish-yellow limestone facade in antique style (half-columns and a lot of decoration). Inside, there is a richly-decorated altar wall (*iconostasis*) with sooty black icons and an old choir stool. Of particular note here are the large and beautiful *frescoes* in the whole interior, and these were only finished in 1986. The Last Supper is spread out over the whole width of the front entrance wall.

One of the monks of Agia Triada

The remains of cloisters can be seen in the buildings around the church, and the monks' cells are also situated there. Until 1973, the Monastery of Agia Triada housed a large *priests' seminary*, which served as a training centre for the diocese of Chania. The empty classrooms are in the block behind the church (the Seminary is housed today in the Monastery of Agios Matheos above Chalepa; the road to the airport goes past it).

On the way out you can take a look at the botanical miracle of Agia Triada. On the right hand side of the front of the church (looking at the facade), there is a graft hybrid *orange tree*, which bears four kinds of fruit and foliage - oranges, lemons, mandarines and limes.

• VISITING TIMES: The Monastery of Agia Triada is inhabited today by seven friendly monks, who like to serve their visitors raki in a room next to the entrance. There is an English pamphlet about the monastery for sale (£2), and there are also various photographs and documents on display.
The complex is closed from 2.00 p.m. to 5.00 p.m.

To the Monastery of Gouverneto: The road passes Agia Triada and goes into the mountains. There are 1.25 miles of dust track at the beginning, after which the road is unexpectedly made up. It winds through an ever-narrowing gorge, with steep slopes rising on both sides and trees and bushes clinging to the area in between. A lovely drive.

Monastery of Gouverneto

The Monastery of Gouverneto, with its forbidding walls, is situated in the middle of a stony wilderness under the brilliant sun. This place is practically the end of the world; only a few miles separate the fortress-like monastery from the jagged rocky wall of the peninsula.

Life is not easy on the edge of civilisation for the two elderly monks and their abbot; the loneliness and boredom here are a trial, especially in winter. At least, that is what we were told by *James*, an Englishman who has lived with the monks for several years, helps them with their work and acts as an interpreter between them and foreign tourists. A breath of fresh air had been brought to the monastery by the new *Abbot Ananeas*. An army chaplain for 28 years, he is a friendly person who speaks good English.

One of the main problems in the coming years will be to find new blood for this lonely monastery.

A tour round the monastery: The Monastery of Gouverneto is an island of its own inside the massive walls. Maintenance work is constantly being carried on. For example, the monks repainted everything only a few years ago.

The facade of the *monastery church* in the middle of the courtyard is a source of fascination. There are monsters' heads, which seem to be screaming at you, half-columns, and other decorations which appear alien to the local tradition. Stairways lead up to the *monks' cells* on all sides of the courtyard. At the great festival of the monastery on 7th October (see below) you may be able to have a look inside them. They are furnished in an astonishingly cosy fashion, some even with wood panelling and a heating stove in the corner. Naturally, there are crucifixes on the walls.

The little *monastery museum* (admission just under £0.40) houses a number of icons, some of them several hundred years old. These include the icon of the Virgin Glikofiloussa (which means "of the sweet kisses"), the Patroness of the monastery. There are also valuable bishops' robes on display, of which the oldest was made two hundred years ago and came from Russia. For those who are interested, copies of icons can be bought more cheaply in the museum here than in Chania.

Cave of the Hermit/Monastery of Katholiko: A steep footpath with rocky steps which have been worn smooth leads after a walk of about 30 mins. into a deep ravine, in which the cave of John the Hermit and the ruins of the old monastery of Katholiko are situated. The hermit lived for many years in this cave during the 10th century, and also died there. He was shot by a hunter, who mistook him for a wild animal.

About half way along the path you come to the so-called *Bears' Cave*. This is a dark stalagmite grotto, which is almost black with the soot from candles. There is a small chapel dating to the 16th century carved into the rock at the entrance, and in the middle of it there is a curiously-shaped stalagmite in which, with a little imagination, you can recognise the shape of a bear. A further 20 minutes' steep downhill climb brings you nearer to the bottom of the ravine and the ruins of the *Monastery of Katholiko*. A beautiful place, where the almost vertical rocky walls rise up on the left and right. The sun can hardly penetrate through to here; thus, it is mostly a pleasant, cool place. Just before you get to the bottom, there is the deep *Cave of John the Hermit* to the left of the path. The cave is about 150 yards long and up to 66 feet high, with numerous heavy stalactites hanging from the roof.

Below it, the monastery buildings with their beautiful, almost Gothic architecture are half set into the rock. A large open area invites you to rest here. Katholiko Monastery had to be abandoned in the 16th century because of constant attacks by Saracen pirates: it was rebuilt several hundred feet further up the mountain.

• BATHING: There is a stony bay at the exit from the gorge, which can be reached in about 30 minutes, though with a certain amount of difficulty.

FESTIVAL OF SAINT JOHN

Once a year, on 7th October, there is a festival in remembrance of John the Hermit at the Monastery of Gouverneto. This takes the form of a kind of "open day" at Gouverneto, when whole caravans of vehicles wind their tortuous way up the little mountain road. The monastery is full of people, coffee is drunk everywhere, blankets are spread out for the night, people joke, chat, and pray. In the middle of all this are the monks, attentive to everyone and conscious of their worthy position. Towards evening, the *Bishop of Chania* arrives in his black limousine; he is a dynamic, almost youthful man in his late forties. With inimitable grace, and with gestures that even an actor could not better, he makes his way through the crowd; everyone wants to kiss his hand, which he freely offers to all. Then a service takes place; the little church is bursting at the seams, there is an endless liturgy and constant coming and going. There is no trace of a stiff, Catholic piety; everything is done in a hearty manner, and this naturalness is retained even at moments of the greatest solemnity.

Another highlight of the day is when all the Faithful climb down the steep path to the Cave of John and the ruins of the Monastery of Katholiko below. Rather a trying march, but a real pilgrimage; even ancient grandmothers wend their tortuous way down the path, gasping for breath, and the air is full of religious fervour and the smell of incense. Those who wish to discover something of the beauty of this path should choose another day to come here, as the hectic traffic up and down the path can be something of a trial for the nerves. Long lines of people carrying candles also make their way through the tunnel-like cave of John on 7th October.

Chania/Hinterland

The panorama of the *Lefka Ori*, the White Mountains, dominates from every angle. But the immediate hinterland of Chania is flat, green and fertile; the most extensive area of orange plantations on the island begins here.

This region was fiercely fought over in the *Battle of Crete*. War memorials and the military cemetery of Maleme on the coast between Chania and Kastelli (see page 449) all attest to this fact. Today, there is a Greek army presence in the form of several large garrisons on this vulnerable plain.

Apart from the grandiose Samaria Gorge, certainly the favourite destination for an excursion from Chania, a visit can also be made to *Meskla* and *Therissos*, two attractive but not very spectacular villages on the gently rising slopes of the White Mountains. The latter is the birthplace of the famous Eleftherios Venizelos who, as Prime Minister of Greece, brought about the union of Crete and Greece in 1913.

To Meskla: From the centre of Chania, take the exit road to Kastelli and turn off to Omalos and the Samaria Gorge (signposted) at the river, which is dried up in the summer months. There are long rows of densely-foliaged olive trees on both sides of the road, their fruit still dark green in the summer.

On the right hand side of the road, shortly before *Agia*, there is the whitewashed flat-roofed building of a *detention centre*. It was built shortly before the Second World War and used by the German Wehrmacht as a military prison and detention centre for partisans. Hundreds of Cretans were tortured and shot there.

A few miles further on, at the crossroads to Alikianos, there is a *memorial* to the 118 partisans from the surrounding villages who were shot by the Germans on 1st August 1941. The names and ages of the dead are engraved on all four sides of the memorial (all age groups are represented, from a 15-year-old boy to a grandfather of 70). In the lower part of the memorial the skulls and bones of those killed can be seen in a glass case.

The road was being widened in 1987, as it is used daily by the tourist buses to the Samaria Gorge.

Fournes: An attractive little village among orange trees. The roofs disappear in a mass of greenery. The road forks here; straight on to the Omalos High Plateau (see below), and left up a river valley to Meskla, 3.75 miles away.

Meskla

In a thickly-wooded and hilly river valley, a green oasis with orange trees and a lot of water.

The stream bubbles down from the slopes in several places at the upper end of the village, and is channelled along the main street by means of canals.

The Chapel of *Metamorfosis Sotiros* is situated right at the beginning of the village, above the road on the left hand side. The key is mostly in the door and once you have allowed the frightened bats to flutter past you, you can have a look inside. The single-naved interior consists of an anteroom and a main room. Both are decorated with frescoes, which have weathered to such an extent that their subject-matter is hardly recognisable.

There is another chapel at the end of the village, but the crowning glory is provided by the domes of the *main church* of Meskla (Panagia), which seems almost classical in style. It is a modern concrete building, but extremely impressive in spite of it. Red and green marble dominates the interior, and the walls are brought to life by modern frescoes. The remains of a *mosaic floor* from an Early Christian basilica can be found to the west, in front of the church.

A place to relax. Directly below on the river, which flows noisily through a channel here, there is a quiet kafenion under a huge plane tree with several branches to its trunk.

• ACCOMMODATION/FOOD: **Ta Lefka Ori**, on the main road, an original kafenion, which also serves as a grocery shop and rents out terrible rooms. Even a gaming machine, beloved of the local schoolchildren, has found its way here.

To Therissos: Take the exit road to Kastelli from Chania, but turn off in the direction of PerivoliaPerivolia before you come to the turning for Omalos.

A really beautiful stretch of road through a curving gorge with almost vertical walls and a lot of trees. In particular, the stream is bordered by large, heavy plane trees. The road is damaged just before you come to Therissos. A wonderful view up into the White Mountains from here.

Therissos

A wonderfully peaceful mountain village with a lot of greenery. No vehicle traffic, but bleating goats instead.

At the exit from the village, tucked under a huge plane tree, there is a low and seemingly ancient chapel with two naves. Just before it is the attractive kafenion *O Madares* with a terrace on the stream under thickly-leafed vines and mulberry trees. It seems so homely and comfortable with the little house behind it, that you feel you would like to stay here for a while too.

About 50 yards behind it, and diagonally above it, there is the plain house where *Eleftherios Venizelos* was born. It has been restored and newly-plastered, and the old baking oven still stands in front of the door. This is the birthplace of the man who, as Prime Minister, brought about the union of Crete with the modern Greek state.

From Chania to Sougia

A panoramic road on the flank of the Lefka Ori. Drive along the same road from Chania as described above, until you come to the cross-roads shortly before Alikianos. Then take the branch of the road via

Alikianos and the winding, narrow road via *Skines* into the mountains. The higher it goes, the more lonely it becomes. There is one of the most magnificent all-round views in this part of Crete at the *turn-off to the Omalos High Plateau*. A short distance further on, at *Epanohori*, you can already see the Sea of Libya. Finally, there is a superb descent through the wide valley down to the sea. For details on Sougia see page 481.

Samaria Gorge

The longest gorge in Europe; orchids, wild goats and cypresses; flooded in the early part of the year

A real experience: from a height of just over 4,000 feet in the middle of the White Mountains down to the Sea of Libya!

Out of an almost alpine mountain landscape with thick tree coverage, almost vertically rising rock walls and great towering rocks, the deep cutting winds down towards the refreshing blue of the sea - 11.25 miles of punishment, a marathon march against the clock in order to catch the last boat at Agia Roumeli. Hardly anyone misses the experience of a walk through what is said to be the longest gorge in Europe! Fantastic rumours abound: that it is impossible to walk through the gorge in track shoes, that you have to leave at the crack of dawn in order to reach the sea by the evening, that you have to reckon on at least 2 days from Chania etc.

Some people back down right away because of the gigantic scale of the operation, and prefer to stay on the beach. But there are always more than enough people in search of adventure, who join in the 5-6 hour hike. But there is much more to it than that; it is simply an essential part of any stay on Crete!

And rightly so. The Samaria Gorge surely offers you some of the most magnificent landscapes on Crete, beginning with the grandiose *Omalos Plateau*, situated at the entrance to the gorge, down to the *Sideroporta*, the "Iron Gate"; at this point, what was previously a wide gorge with walls almost 2,000 feet high shrinks to a width of just under 10 feet. A strong-flowing stream runs almost the whole length of the gorge, forming beautiful, clear pools between the rocks or, in the cooler half of the year until well into April, completely flooding the gorge. It is fun to keep crossing what will have become a very modest stream by summer, and you always have the feeling that there is water nearby; wonderful, clear spring water, as superbly refreshing to drink as it would be for bathing (not allowed).

Finally, you sway along on wobbly knees, but full of relief, towards the inviting tavernas in the little hamlet of *Agia Roumeli* at the exit from the gorge. You look at the sun sparkling on the dazzling shingle beach, gaze at the fantastic deep blue of the sea, and are happy that you made the trip.

HISTORY: This inaccessible gorge had an immense significance during the Cretan struggle for freedom from the Turks. It served as a place of retreat and a head-quarters for the rebels and in spite of repeated attempts, could never be taken (more details under Agia Roumeli, see below).

During the Second World War, members of the Greek Government fled through the gorge to the south coast, whence they were evacuated by a British ship to Egypt.

FLORA: Mention must first of all be made of the rich variety of trees here. This includes fine cypresses, pines, plane trees, scots pine, stony oak and Cretan sycamore on the slopes of the gorge. The cypresses were used by the Minoans for the pillars in their palaces, and they were also exported to the Greek mainland in antiquity. The Venetians also helped themselves to the supply of wood. Tree-felling has been prohibited here since the creation of the Samaria Gorge Nature Park.

Otherwise, there is the famous **Diktamos** (Cretan mountain tea), a plant found regularly on Crete and at home here on the steep slopes of the gorge. There are also rare types of orchids, which grow mostly in the side valleys.

FAUNA: There are 51 different species of bird in the White Mountains, of which 28 alone nest in the gorge. In addition 12 types of mammals live free in their natural habitat there. The most well-known of these is the Cretan wild goat, the **Agrimi**, with its wonderful curling horns. It is a species threatened with extinction and under strict protection. It is estimated that there are c. 300 in the gorge and a further 700 living outside. As they graze at night and hide mostly by day, they are hardly ever seen in the wilds (at the very most in the early morning). There are some in pens in the City Park at Chania.

Otherwise there are hares and badgers in large numbers, as well as partridges and eagles. There are also 4 species of reptile and two species of snake in the gorge.

In order to protect this grandiose mountain environment and its unique flora and fauna, the Greek Government declared the area of the Samaria Gorge a *National Park* in 1962. In 1964 they bought up all private ground there, dispossessed the few inhabitants of the village of Samaria and moved them out of the gorge.

In 1980, the Council of Europe awarded Greece a distinction, in recognition of the gorge as *a superbly protected nature reserve of the greatest importance*. This award comes under review every five years and was given to Greece for the second time in 1984.

The Samaria Gorge is one of the great natural wonders of Crete

Connections

A great favourite are the day trips by bus from the north coast. The best point of departure is Chania; the walk through the gorge can be made in one day, including the journey there and back.

It works like this: bus from Chania/bus station to the Omalos High Plateau (c. 1.5 hrs), walk through the gorge to Agia Roumeli (5-6 hrs), boat trip from Agia Roumeli to Chora Sfakion (1.5 hrs) and bus back to Chania (1.5 hrs).

For a number of years now, the Cretan bus company *KTEL* has been offering organised excursions to the Omalos High Plateau from Chania and nearly all the coastal villages, large hotels and camping sites in both the immediate and the more distant vicinity of Chania. You are brought back to Chania from Chora Sfakion in the evening. Advertisements with the addresses where bookings can be made are on display everywhere. The trips are well-organised and much cheaper than those made by booking with a private company (eg hotel, travel agency).

In 1988, some of the places from which these trips could be made were Kastelli, Camping Mithimna (near Kastelli), Kolimbari, Tavronitis, Chandris Hotel (Maleme), Platanias, Agia Marina (according to a hint from one of our readers the tickets were cheaper at the bus stop than at the camping site!), Stalos, Stavros/Kalathas, Kounoupidiana (for the whole of the Akrotiri Peninsula), Vamos, Georgioupolis, Kalives. KTEL are extending this network every year.

• FROM CHANIA: If you are going under your own steam, take the earliest possible bus from **Chania bus station**. Departures at 6.15, 7.30, 8.30, 9.30,10.00, 11.00 a.m. and 4.30, 6.00 p.m. (in 1988). The best plan is to go to the bus station the day before, check the actual departure times and buy your ticket; the seats are quickly all sold in the high season. Because of the great demand, however, several buses leave the bus station at the individual departure times. The day return ticket costs just under £4, which includes the bus trip from Chania to the entrance to the gorge, and the return trip from Chora Sfakion to Chania. Tickets are only obtainable at the counter, not on the bus! Only as many passengers as there are seats will be accepted on each bus, and there is no standing room.

After the walk through the gorge you should take the 4.00 or 5.00 p.m. boat from Agia Roumeli to Chora Sfakion, in order to catch the last bus back to Chania which leaves at 6.30 p.m. We recommend that you buy your boat ticket as soon as you arrive in Agia Roumeli, as they are quickly sold out. The last boats to Chora Sfakion go at 7.00 p.m., and sometimes even at 8.00 p.m. Those who take these later boats can only catch a bus from Chora Sfakion as far as Rethymnon, but this stops in Vrises on the north coast and there you can change onto a bus for Chania. In every case, you will be back in Chania at the latest by 10.00 p.m.

All the times mentioned above were correct in 1988, but they can vary from year to year. **Information sheets**, with greater details on how to make the trip from Chania and walk through the gorge in one day, are available from the Information Offices in Chania, Rethymnon and Iraklion!

Those not wishing to compress the whole tour into one day and/or want to stay on the south coast have more possibilities open to them:

- On the one hand, you can take the afternoon bus from Chania to the entrance to the gorge and spend the night there or in the nearby village of **Omalos** (for details see below under the heading "How to get there"). Then make a very early start next day, complete the walk through the gorge by midday and take a boat in the early afternoon to Chora Sfakion, Paleochora, Souyia or Loutro. The advantage is that the walk through the gorge is much more pleasant in the early morning, before noon, than it is in the heat of midday.
- On the other hand, you can arrive on the early bus from Chania, walk through the gorge and spend the night in **Agia Roumeli**, and then continue the journey at leisure the day after, taking the boat to Chora Sfakion.
- An interesting variation is to walk up through the Samaria Gorge in the **opposite direction**! Start at the sea and come out on the high plain of Omalos, then take the bus to Chania. This is considerably more tiring than the other way, particularly because of the final uphill stretch to the Omalos High Plateau. But it is gaining more and more favour. We met quite a few people coming in the opposite direction, some with all their baggage on their backs.

There are only limited possibilities for making the trip through the gorge if you have your *own car* or *a rented vehicle*. It is not practicable, unless you leave your vehicle on the Omalos Plateau, at the beginning of the gorge, walk the 11.5 miles down to the sea and come back on one of the following days. Another possibility is to let someone drive you to the Omalos Plateau in the morning and have them pick you up at Chora Sfakion in the evening or on the following day.

How to get there

The journey up into the *White Mountains* is itself a wonderful experience. Although the distance from Chania to Omalos is only 25 miles, the bus trip still takes 90 minutes.

In the morning, the bus station in Chania is crammed with people going to the gorge. Unmistakable trade mark: track shoes and plimsolls of all varieties. Hardly anyone dares to go through the gorge in sandals.

If you are going up on the early bus, try to sit on the right; this is the **shady side** of the bus and you will appreciate the fact when you come to higher altitudes, where the sun beats mercilessly down onto the bus.

The route as far as Fournes is described in the chapter Chania/Hinterland on page 426.

At first, the road crosses the largest area of orange plantations in Crete. There are long rows of these thickly-foliaged trees everywhere on the left and right of the road. The fruit is still dark green in the summer.

Two extremely narrow bridges are crossed at Fournes and the road now enters the mountains. At first, there are only gently rounded hills with olive trees planted on them, then the bus winds higher and higher up the slope in long, snake-like curves. The hilly regions are well-wooded and are mainly cultivated in terraces. Wherever it is possible, the areas have been used for the growing of fruit, vines and olives. The road goes ever upwards, until it reaches Lakki.

Lakki: A favourite resting place for those with rented vehicles. The houses are widely scattered over the crest of a hill between thick pine and deciduous forest. The striking, brilliant blue dome of the church is a fine sight.

That it is extremely cold up here in winter can be seen from the large heating stoves in the kafenia; their pipes extend half way through the rooms.

• ACCOMMODATION/FOOD: The original **kafenion** run by Georgios Koutrouli is situated below the church and is built directly onto a stall. The men are mostly sitting on the terrace and playing tavli.
There are rooms for rent in the **Kri-Kri** taverna and the other tavernas opposite.

Once again the road winds upwards. This is where the wild, furrowed rocky slopes of the White Mountains begin, and it is an area almost devoid of vegetation. There are only thistle bushes, with fern and scrub growing between wind-tanned tooth-like rocks, and there are large boulders strewn everywhere. Then more slopes, into which the roots of the mountain juniper claw their way. The stony ridges with their tall conifers seem almost to form an alpine landscape, but one that is wilder, stonier, less accessible. There is a wonderful view back towards the north coast. In recent years, little trees have been planted all along the edge of the road and protected against nibbling goats by wire cages. Then, suddenly and unexpectedly, the Omalos Plateau, flat as a board, opens out in front of you.

The Omalos High Plateau

Round as a plate and at an altitude of 3,924 feet, completely enclosed by mountains. Like the Lassithi High Plateau in eastern Crete, the Omalos Plateau is also completely flooded during the melting of the snows in the early part of every year. Huge clefts in the limestone take care of the drainage of this mass of water.

During the Cretan struggle for freedom from the Turks, the Omalos, and indeed the whole region of the White Mountains, functioned as an area of refuge for the rebels. There are very few permanent inhabitants there today. Apart from the tiny settlement in the middle of the plain at Omalos, only a few shepherds live in the stone huts on the edges during the summer. There are several tracks through the grazing pastures, and the road to Sougia can be reached by one of them.

Cave of Tsanis : Immediately when you cross the edge of the plateau and enter it, there is a deep, dark cavern on the right hand side, next to the road. A slight mouldiness is apparent in the atmosphere when you go a little way into it. This bottomless cavern is the reason why the Omalos High Plateau is not a lake. The tons of water, which flood the whole plateau to a depth of several metres after the snows have melted, drain away into the unexplored limestone base - it is rather like the drain in an over-dimensional bathtub. A British cave exploration team is said to have gone down to a depth of 8,175 feet without finding the bottom.

There are numerous legends associated with this secretive hole in the rock. In the still of the night, at the time of new moon, you are supposed to be able to hear a shepherd playing the lyra there. He was once robbed of his senses by mountain fairies and drawn down into the depths. You can protect yourself from the numerous devils in the mountains (so-called Farangites) by scratching a cross into the ground with a knife and plunging the knife into the middle of it.

Grave and House of Hatzimichalis Yannaris: On a piece of raised ground on the left of the road, shortly before the village of Omalos. This leader of the Cretan resistance (1831-1916) was captured by the Turks several times but always managed to escape, and became an important Cretan politician and member of the island Parliament after the victorious end of the revolution. His whitewashed tomb is in the modest little building next to the house where he lived.

Omalos Village: Up till now only a handful of houses under wide, spreading trees, but an atmosphere of change prevails here and new buildings are springing up. There are 2 tavernas with "Rooms to Rent" signs on the shady through road. In the evenings the few adventurous tourists who are going through the gorge next morning can be seen sitting here.

• ACCOMMODATION/FOOD: simple private rooms for c. £9 in the tavernas in the village. Try the sheeps' yoghurt in the **Omalos** taverna. There is a new, immaculate taverna called **To Exari** at the southern exit from the village.
The restaurant **To Agrimi** is to the west, outside the village, on the track which leads to Sougia. Groups of tourists are often deposited there (signposted at the southern exit to the village).

Kallergi Hut: About 1.25 miles after Omalos on the left hand side, a terrible rubble track leads up in hairpin bends to a hut at a height of 5,493 feet. The approach can only be made with a four-wheel-drive jeep or on foot! In the summer, it is staffed by the *Alpinschule Innsbruck*, which undertakes mountain hikes from there.

Entrance to the gorge: Just under 2 miles from the village of Omalos, the bus arrives at its destination, the entrance to the gorge. Half-way up the slope there is the Xenia Guest House, a simple establishment in which you can take refreshment before setting off. Breakfast is

available, as well as hot meals both at midday and in the evening.
From the balcony, there is a magnificent view of the incredibly steep
wall of *Gingilos* (6,801 feet) and the thickly wooded entrance to the
gorge. The highest peaks in the Lefka Ori rise up to the east, with
Pachnes to the fore (8,021 feet).

A fine wild cypress stands at the entrance to the Samaria Gorge

• ACCOMMODATION: At the time of most recent enquiry in 1989, the **Xenia** was being completely renovated and extended. The total of 7 beds in 3 little rooms will probably increase.
Tel. 0821/93237 (up to the present).
The pitching of tents has been tolerated up till now because of the scarcity of accommodation.

• FOOD: apart from the Xenia there is a **kiosk** and a **mobile snack bar** with drinks, filled rolls, biscuits etc.

• HIKING: Numerous hikes can be undertaken from the southern edge of the Omalos Plateau up to the neighbouring peaks, not only that which leads through the gorge. A signpost giving target destinations and duration of the hikes is to be found behind the Xenia.

The Way Through the Gorge

From the entrance to the exit on the Sea of Libya, the Samaria Gorge is just under 9.6 miles long. The time needed for the hike is 5 - 6 hours (without stops). Closed shoes (track shoes etc) are recommended.

Wandering into the side valleys off the gorge is prohibited, as they are not watched over by forestry officials and are an area of refuge for the wild goats.

• OPENING TIMES: 1st May-31st October, daily 6.00 a.m.-3.00 p.m. After 3.00 p.m. the public are only allowed into the gorge for a distance of 1.25 miles.

Since 1989 an entrance fee of £1 has been payable. The ticket has to be surrendered at the end of the ravine; thus the authorities can both ensure that nobody spends the night in the gorge and that everyone arrives safely at the other end.

• RESCUE SERVICE: (for broken legs etc): The gorge is patrolled along its entire length, and there are donkeys which can be used for transport in Omalos, Agia Roumeli and at various points along the gorge. The nearest helicopter landing pad is on the harbour at Agia Roumeli (helicopter from Chania) and the nearest doctor at the first aid station in Chora Sfakion.

Before starting your hike, you should read the board posted at the entrance to the gorge. The rules which are to be observed are given here in Greek and English. As there are several thousand visitors here daily in the high season, you should definitely keep to them; only thus can the untouched beauty of the Samaria Gorge be preserved. Amongst other things, the following are prohibited:

Overnight stays in the gorge

Making fires (very important, as there is a high risk of forest fires here and hardly any facility for putting them out)

Making noises, loud singing and shouting (because of the danger of rock falls)

Hunting and fishing

Taking dogs with you

Pulling up plants

Bathing

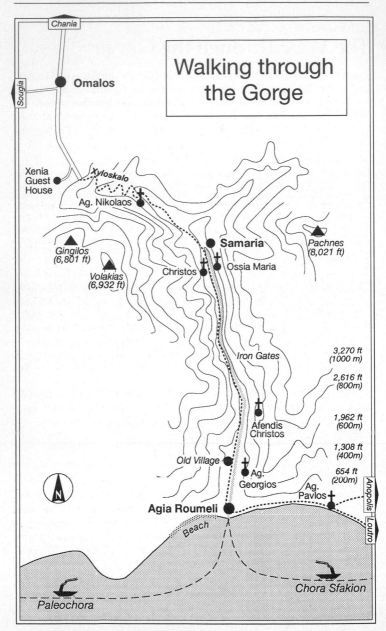

Walking through the Gorge

Chania

Sougia

Omalos

Xenia Guest House

Xyloskalo

Ag. Nikolaos

Gingilos (6,801 ft)

Volakias (6,932 ft)

Samaria

Pachnes (8,021 ft)

Christos

Ossia Maria

Iron Gates

3,270 ft (1000 m)

2,616 ft (800m)

Afendis Christos

1,962 ft (600m)

Old Village

1,308 ft (400m)

Ag. Georgios

654 ft (200m)

Ag. Pavlos

Anopolis

Agia Roumeli

Loutro

N

Beach

Chora Sfakion

Paleochora

A Description of the Route

As if from the edge of a huge plate, you descend the *Xyloskalo* (wooden ladder). This is a stony path with wooden railings, which winds down in narrow hairpin bends 2,616 feet deep into the gorge.

The name of this path is a reminder of the centuries of struggle for freedom. Even in the 17th/18th centuries, the Cretan partisans used large wooden ladders to climb up from the Samaria Gorge to the Omalos Plateau and carry out surprise attacks on the Turks. This steep method of ascent was mainly used by shepherds during the last century; they rammed wooden pegs and tree-trunks into the earth here, and thus made wooden steps. The present path was only constructed at the beginning of our century, but has retained the name of the old one.

Today, you climb slowly down to the floor of the upper part of the gorge by means of large stones and steps that have been marked out for the purpose, hard by the rocky wall between huge knotty cypresses and boulders which are more than man-sized. The gigantic massif of Gingilos rises to a height of nearly 6,600 feet on the right. Even while making the descent you pass several enclosed *springs,* which are ideal places for a few minutes' rest.

At the bottom, at the foot of Gingilos, there is the simple Chapel of *Agios Nikolaos* under towering cypresses. Cement buttresses lend support from the outside, while inside there is a bare wooden iconostasis with pictures of St. Nicholas. The path now continues gently uphill and downhill again over scree; on the way, you cross the stream several times. There is water here even at the height of summer and frequent pools of glass-clear water between the smooth, rounded rocks. Although bathing is officially forbidden, you easily feel tempted here.

The gorge is still wide here, without steep walls, and seems more like a forested park. After about 2.5 hours' walk you can see the abandoned settlement of *Samaria* in a place where the valley broadens out a little; the village has been pushed into a niche below a sheer rock wall.

Samaria

Only a few houses of rough hewn stones, most of them without a roof, but surrounded by shady fig, almond and olive trees. The most favoured place to have a rest in the gorge today: a few benches, a spring, an (often unoccupied) ranger's house and toilet. Years ago, when it was still possible to spend the night in the gorge, Samaria was the traditional place for hikers to stay.

The woodcutters and fishermen who lived in the settlement until 1962 are described as tall and fair-haired; perhaps they are the descendants of Dorians. They had their own laws, far removed from any kind of State authority, and blood feuds are said to have been widespread. When the Greek State made the Samaria Gorge into a

Nature Reserve, the authorities at last had a good pretext for "cleaning up" the "Valley of the Lawless" and removing its inhabitants to Agia Roumeli.

Shortly after the village on the right hand side of the path there is the whitewashed Chapel of *Christos* under an overhanging wall of rock. On the left, on the other side of the stream bed, is the Chapel of *Osia Maria* with several old icons and frescoes. This gave its name to the village and thus to the gorge.

At this point, you have probably covered half of the way, and the most dramatic part of the trek begins. The gorge becomes narrower, the walls get closer together; towering, vertical layers of stone reach up into the sky, overhanging the path in a threatening way, and there are only a few bushes clinging to the outcrops and in the niches. Beneath all this, you feel your way forward through the scree, and only a little sun penetrates here. The path winds down in narrow curves towards the sea, and you have to keep crossing and re-crossing the stream, which becomes a rushing river in the winter. Gigantic boulders are strewn about everywhere, and the walls are over a thousand feet high in places! At last you come to the striking, so-called "*Iron Gates*" (Sideroporta), the narrowest part of the gorge. The rocks get closer together here towards the bottom, with the distance between them at the bottom measuring all of 3 yards!

Round a few more bends, and then there is the official exit from the gorge; you have to hand over your ticket here.

There is a young Cretan selling canned drinks in a **kiosk** here. Prices from just over £1 upwards. The first outpost of civilisation, as it were.

The first derelict houses of the old settlement of Agia Roumeli now come into sight; it was destroyed by the flooding of the river in 1952. A few farmers still live here today. Then on the left of the path there is the beautiful little church of *Agios Georgios*. It stands without protection in the brilliant sun, with a small cemetery around it.

There are still a couple of miles to go through the plain at the end of the gorge (no shade here), until you reach the first houses of the new settlement of Agia Roumeli, directly on the sea.

Agia Roumeli

A village without flair. Unwhitewashed cement buildings, only half-finished, but with a taverna or "rooms to rent" set in amongst them right away. The rise and fall of Agia Roumeli depend on tourism; there is no other source of income there.

On the other hand, the landscape is impressive. It is set in a wide bay with a silvery, but absolutely shadeless shingle beach, and behind it the mighty backdrop of steep rock and scree slopes, with the Turkish fortifications high up on the ridge; an almost romantic sight.

There is hardly a tree or a bush to relieve the unrelenting atmosphere of grey stone and burning sun. The water here seems to be a deep blue, clear and unsullied, that is found nowhere else on Crete.

A most worthwhile sight for all who are interested is the large *photovoltaic solar energy plant* directly on the river. This converts sunlight directly into electric current during the day!

History: There was a city here in antiquity called *Tarra*. It was probably founded by the Dorians, and had its heyday during the Roman period. However, some isolated Minoan finds have been reported. There is practically nothing left to see of Tarra today.

Agia Roumeli was the great centre for timber from the Lefka Ori, and an important centre for shipbuilding during the *Venetian period*. Ruthless exploitation and widespread forest fires led to a permanent destruction of these resources. From the 18th century onwards, Agia Roumeli, just as the whole of the Samaria Gorge, was an important headquarters in the *Cretan resistance struggle* against the Turks. The rebels established one of their largest stores of weapons here. In 1770, the famous resistance leader *Daskaloyannis*, from Anopolis, chose the Samaria Gorge as his headquarters. When the Turks tried to storm the gorge, the partisan leader *Yannis Bonatos* was able to defend the Iron Gates with only 200 men. Even the subsequent attempt by the Turks to enter the gorge from the Omalos Plateau failed, because of the defence of the gorge by local Sfakiot rebels, who knew the lie of the land.

Not even in the 19th century were the Turkish troops able to bring the Samaria Gorge under their control. When they tried to take Agia Roumeli in 1866, they were completely annihilated and had to leave 600 dead behind them. They returned in 1867 with 4,000 men and burned the village to the ground, but the rebels were able to flee unharmed into the gorge.

Finally, when Crete was under the occupation of the German Wehrmacht in 1941, the Greek Government, namely *King George II* and the Prime Minister *Emmanuel Tsouderos*, fled by way of the gorge to Agia Roumeli, whence they were evacuated to Egypt on a British warship.

Boat connections

From May to October, small passenger ferries go several times daily in both directions, via *Loutro* to *Chora Sfakion* and via *Sougia* to *Paleochora*. There are buses waiting in Chora Sfakion for those wishing to return to the north coast.

• DEPARTURE TIMES (as of 1988): Agia Roumeli - Loutro - Chora Sfakion 9.00 a.m., 1.30, 2.30, 4.00, 5.00, 6.00 p.m (also at 7.00 p.m. and 8.00 p.m. in the season). Agia Roumeli - Sougia - Paleochora 4.00, 5.30 p.m.

• DURATION AND COST OF TRIP: c. 1.5 hrs to Chora Sfakion, cost c. £3, c. 2.5 hrs. to Paleochora, cost c. £4.

No matter in which direction you go, a really wonderful trip along the bare, furrowed, sheer cliffs of the south coast awaits you! Here, the rugged foothills of the White Mountains slide directly into a sea of a quite breathtaking blue hue.

Accommodation

There are numerous possibilities, and certainly every other house, especially the tavernas, rents rooms. As the rooms are seldom all occupied, you can negotiate effectively here, especially out of season.

• **Agia Roumeli**: a B class guest house; whitewashed building directly on the beach, a little outside the actual village and ideal for bathers. Quite new and well furnished, all rooms with shower/WC and a small balcony. Restaurant and shady awning, quiet position. Cost c. £14 for a DR without breakfast. There is a shower directly at the hotel for bathers. Tel. 0825/91293.

• **Tara**: a taverna right on the sea, at the place where the boats come in. The rooms are simple, with lino floors, but all have their own shower/WC and balcony. Of course, the nicest rooms are on the front, with a superb view! Cost c. £8-9 for a DR.

• **Zorbas**: one of the newest tavernas in the place, also rooms with sea views. Mrs R. Flügel of the Ida Travel Agency wrote to tell us that the Zorbas has 15 double rooms with shower/WC for c. £9, with breakfast available for a small surcharge. Some rooms have sea views.

• **Samaria**: a taverna diagonally opposite Tara. Rooms with bath c. £9, without £8.

• **Livikon**: our tip. At the back end of the village, just before the steep slope. Absolutely quiet position, very clean and attractively furnished. Inviting passages decorated with posters and pictures. Shady balcony, everything very well-maintained. Cost c. £9 for a DR with bath.

Immediately to the east of the village, where the river enters the sea, there is a little forest of pines where some people **pitch their tents**. There is a stony beach in front of it. There are also occasional tents pitched on the shady little area between the pines and the oleander bushes behind the village, in the direction of the entrance to the gorge.

• FOOD: The best view is to be had from the shady terraces of the restaurants **Tara** and **Zorbas**, 50 yards from the place where the boats come in. The **Kri-Kri** is the first taverna on the way out from the gorge, and a favourite accordingly. Unfortunately, exorbitant prices are sometimes asked here.

• OTHER INFORMATION: there is a **telephone** in the Samaria Restaurant, and a small shop for **provisions**. All of the tavernas will **change money**.

Sightseeing

Solar energy plant: There is no need to emphasize that the production of electricity for the isolated village of Agia Roumeli is of great importance. Earlier, there were numerous private diesel generators in the village, but their use involved a lot of noise and a noticeable pollution of the atmosphere. Thus an *experimental photovoltaic energy plant* was built in 1980/82, to convert sunlight into electrical current during the daytime. It is situated directly on the mouth of the river and can be recognised from its large number of solar reflectors. It construction was financed in equal parts by the Greek Government, the EC, the Varta Battery Company, and the French company Séri Renault. The output is 40 kilowatts (kva), and if necessary there is a 50 kw. diesel generator which can be used. When the solar installation is over-burdened in the evenings during the high season, because of the many guest houses, the diesel generator is brought into use. Both installations cannot be used at the same time. If demand increases further, Agia Roumeli will not be able, in the long run, to avoid dependence on an underwater cable.

Palea Agia Roumeli: About 20 minutes' walk from the harbour brings you to the derelict village of Agia Roumeli, which was abandoned after floods in 1952. Reoccupation of the houses is permitted today, but their ground plan cannot be altered in any way. A wander through the ruins is worthwhile. We found a completely preserved oil mill (in the last but one house going up the river, on the side of the slope right on the path). The grinding and mixing apparatus were worked by a donkey. Down below the oil mill, more towards the river, there are also the remains of a water mill.

Turkish castle: You can climb straight up the steep slope from the harbour to the castle on the rocky ridge in about 45 minutes. The original mule-track has been almost completely covered by landslides and can only be identified in a few places. From its construction, it is easy to see that the castle was not intended for siege purposes; thus the wells are outside the walls, which are themselves low and thin and hardly offer any protection against cannon fire. The place might have been a garrison, which held troops constantly at the ready at this exposed exit from the gorge. The view out over the derelict village, the valley and the new settlement on the sea is superb.

Bathing

Directly to the west of the village and adjoining it there is a curved beach of fine, dark grey pebbles, c. 500 yards long. Apart from the reed awnings at the Agia Roumeli Pension (guest house) there is no shade of any kind here! From around midday onwards, the beach is crowded with people who have hiked through the gorge, but it is deserted when the last boat has left.

A further pebble beach extends to the east from the village and runs for miles along the mountain slopes. Behind it there are some bizarre weathered rocky caves. A place for those seeking solitude.

Hiking from Agia Roumeli

There are no roads to or from Agia Roumeli, and thus no buses! The only connections across country are hiking paths, which are very worthwhile because of the wild landscape. There is complete solitude in places.

Hiking routes:

a) in a northwards direction through the *Samaria Gorge* (for a description see above).

b) eastwards along the coast via *Loutro* to *Chora Sfakion* (c. 6 hrs, see page 491).

c) also to the east, along the coast at the beginning, then later through the mountains via *Ag. Ioannis* and *Aradena* to *Anopolis* or even *Loutro* or *Chora Sfakion* (for a description see below).

> **Note**: The terrain towards Sougia in the west is very inaccessible, steep and dangerous. At least two hikers died of thirst here in recent years, and a third suffered a headlong fall. We advise against making the tour, which takes a good 12 hours anyway.

The mountain way via Ag. Ioannis, Aradena and Anopolis to Chora Sfakion is more tiring, but generally more worthwhile than the purely coastal hike to Loutro. For one thing, it passes through vastly differing landscapes (coast and mountains), and for another it takes you onto very varied types of track (from that along a sandy beach to a path through a high plateau), and in addition there is a very attractive contrast between a completely isolated area (Ag. Ioannis) and the "civilisation" of Anopolis.

Route: Agia Roumeli - Chapel of Agios Pavlos - Agios Ioannis - Aradena - Anopolis - Chora Sfakion.(see sketch map on page 468, **hike no. 5**)

Duration of hike: all in all, you will have to allow for one whole day, if you are carrying luggage; the actual time required to go from Agia Roumeli to Anopolis is only about 6-7 hours, however. It is a further 2.5 hours on to Chora Sfakion.

Description of the route: Going from *Agia Roumeli* in an easterly direction, you cross a river-bed at the exit from the Samaria Gorge. The former is dried-up in summer, but in March/April you mostly have to wade through water which is at least knee-deep. At the beginning you walk on scree, but then continue on along the beach. The path is marked out with blobs of red and yellow paint and follows the telegraph wires. An hour away from Agia Roumeli you reach the *Eligias Gorge*, a place where there are two enormous lumps of rock measuring about 30 x 30 feet in the water.

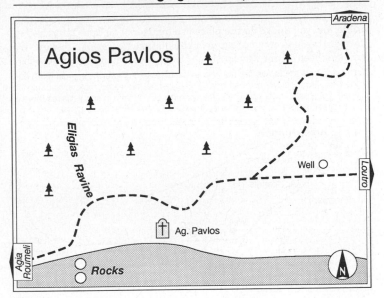

You then climb up through fine sand to a height of about 60 feet above the sea. You can easily walk through the gorge on this sand. On the other side, a well-marked path continues along at this height (partly covered by rock falls). You now come to an extensive forest of pines and will soon be able to see the pretty, stone-built Chapel of **Agios Pavlos**, which is situated below the path. The Apostle Paul is reputed to have landed here on one of his missionary journeys, and converted the first Europeans (Cretans) to Christianity. A swim in the sea near the chapel is very worthwhile; there is a pleasant hot and cold bath effect here, due to cold currents.

A good 1.5 hours from Agia Roumeli and c. 25 mins. to the east of the chapel, there is a fork in the road. Straight on leads along the coast to Loutro (the way is marked and takes about 3 hours; see under Chora Sfakion), while the left-hand fork goes inland and steeply upwards to Ag. Ioannis and Aradena. The markers on the path cannot be missed when coming from the direction of Ag. Roumeli (stones with arrows and large yellow letters). However, when going downhill or from the direction of Loutro, they cannot be seen because they face in a westerly direction.

Climbing up in the direction of Ag. Ioannis, you reach an area of detritus from a ravine. Do not climb up into the ravine, as the route continues at the same height on the other side of it (yellow markers). Another gorge is reached half an hour later and should also be crossed.

About 1 hour from the fork in the road the old paved way becomes visible, and you arrive on the plateau a quarter of an hour later; as yet, however, there is no view out over the plateau by way of a reward. We have now been on our way for three hours since leaving Agia Roumeli.

This stretch from the fork in the road up to the plateau is (by far!) the most tiring part of the hike. From below, you can hardly imagine that the steep rock walls could be climbed; yet a path leads up here in many snake-like curves. In some places there is a magnificent panoramic view out over Agia Roumeli and the Sea of Libya.

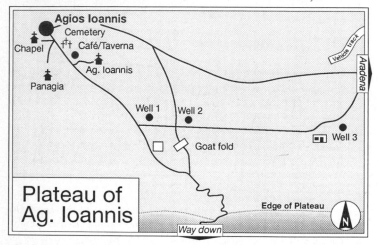

There are many paths marked out on the plateau around Ag. Ioannis (see sketch). At any rate, on reaching the plateau, you should first follow a path marked in reddish-yellow and running in a westerly direction. Soon, you pass a sheep and goat fold; ten minutes later a track branches off to the right at Well 1, and this is the path to follow if you wish to go on in the direction of Aradena. If you want to visit Ag. Ioannis first, you should continue straight on (about three quarters of an hour from the edge of the plateau to the village). You will then pass the Chapel of the Panagia (on the left) and the Chapel of Ag. Ioannis (on the right), and enter the village, which consists of numerous ruins and only a few inhabited houses. Passing the school, you can leave the village in an easterly direction and about three quarters of an hour later reach the place where the path from Well 1/Well 2 is met (this is a little shorter than the path from Ag. Ioannis). On the left hand side you can see a brand new road, still under construction!

The sand and scree track already extended from Anopolis to half way between Aradena and Ag. Ioannis by March 1988. It will have reached Ag. Ioannis by 1990 at the latest, so that this tiny nest off the beaten track will also be easily accessible by car. During the course of roadbuilding, a bridge has been built over a deep gorge at Aradena (see below).

There is a further walk of about half an hour from this meeting point of the two ways until the village of *Aradena* is reached. This is almost completely derelict. What was, until recently, the most difficult part of the track to the east of Aradena (the deep Aradena Gorge), can now be crossed via a new steel bridge with a wooden floor, at a height of c. 260 feet. In earlier times, it was necessary to descend into the gorge and climb up the other side. Anopolis can be reached from Aradena either along the old footpath (c. 1 hour), or via the slightly longer but more comfortable motor road (80 minutes).

Anopolis is a wide, sprawling village without a definite nucleus. You have to pass right through it, and can then walk along the asphalt road, which winds in snake-like curves down to Chora Sfakion (c. 7.5 miles, time needed 2.5 hours). On the way, the view of the sea and Chora Sfakion far below is unique. Another possibility is to climb down to Loutro, directly below Anopolis, in c. 1.5 hours (see under Anopolis for details). Buses also run along the stretch of road from Anopolis to Chora Sfakion; in 1988, however, there was only a bus down at 6.30 a.m. (going on to Chania), and back up at 4.00 p.m.

All further details on Anopolis, Loutro and Chora Sfakion under the individual villages.

From Chania westwards

For beaches in the immediate vicinity of Chania see under Chania: BathIng/Surrounding Area.

The villages of Agia Marina and Platanias have almost fused together along the busy through road. There is intensive building activity here; everywhere "rooms" or "villas to rent" are springing up and bookings have already been taken even though they are only half finished. Parallel to all this and only a few yards from the road, there is a sandy beach miles long. Fine for a short stay, but hardly worth it for longer, because it is totally exposed to the effects of traffic. The building activity stops immediately behind the road and the wild hilly country begins.

Platanias

The new village on the through road is totally exposed to the traffic, but in spite of this, it is where the action takes place. Particularly in the evenings, there is a lot of bustle in the central square with its fountain, when the tourists from the surrounding beach hotels and apartments come to eat here.

On the other hand, the *old centre* of Platanias seems idyllic in its position on the low crest of the hill, overlooking the new houses. If you stroll around the cosy little whitewashed alleys, with their lush vegetation of flowers, convolvulus, figs and grapes, surely some of you will wish to spend some time here. On our first visit, at the beginning of the eighties, we noticed a disproportionately large number of empty ruined houses and areas of rubble. Platanias was on its way to becoming a ghost town. For some years now, this trend has been reversed; Cretans, too, seem to have begun to value the quality of life in Platanias once more.

• CONNECTIONS: The frequent buses from and to Chania, Kastelli and Kolimbari stop here.

• ACCOMMODATION: **Filoxenia**, a B class guest house, is situated in the centre, directly on the road. Very attractive, dining room with warm wood panelling, rooms with balconies, shady. Cost c. £12 for a DR. Tel. 0821/68502.

Platanias, an E class hotel a little further to the east, also on the road. Quite simple, rooms partly overlooking the road and thus rather loud. Cost c. £9 for a DR. Tel. 0821/68397.

— ★ —

• FOOD: **Ta Agrimia**, nice taverna with a terrace above the fountain square. You can also eat well at **Christos**, on the square, although the tables here are right on the roadside.
Milos, at the western end of the village. A former mill has been converted into an appealing restaurant. The large, shady and pleasantly cool terrace/garden is right next to the old millstream. In the evening, a couple of coloured spotlights illuminate an artificial fountain; ducks and geese play on the water. A peacock whiles away his time in captivity in the background. The whole thing is perhaps a little too much aimed at the tastes of middle European tourists, but despite this it is an original place with a lot of atmosphere. The food, however, is not particularly worthy of note. The speciality is rabbit. There is even a bar on the upper terrace. Open daily from 12.00 midday.

• OTHER INFORMATION: The **Post Office** and **OTE public telephone** are housed together in a tiny room about 20 yards from the main square with the fountain.

The road continues to Kolimbari through an area of agricultural plain and hilly land which is not very interesting: a lot of reeds, fruit and vegetable cultivation, vineyards. Continuous shingle and sand beaches border the region on the seaward side.

Maleme

A village on the road; attractive villas with a lot of green, a superhotel. But there is also a fuel dump, a barracks and a military airport. The beach is long and without shade, mainly of sand.
The area around Maleme was bitterly fought for during the landing of the German paratroops and gliders in May 1941. In particular there was the strategically important airstrip, which was subsequently captured. Today, the German military cemetery is situated on what was formerly Hill 107.

• ACCOMMODATION: **Chandris Crete**, A class. A huge complex with every amenity, directly on the beach. A beautiful swimming pool, well-tended lawns, bars and tavernas in the style of Cretan village architecture. Many opportunities here: tennis, minigolf, basket and volleyball, discos, Greek evenings, a precision-planned entertainments and activities programme. Very generously and spaciously planned, some rooms with carpet floors, splendid lobby. Cost in the high season c. £42 for a DR with half board, and in the low season just under £34. Tel. 0281/62221.

Karnezis: E class, on the through road. Relatively comfortable and clean, and also pleasantly cool. Passages with 'rough effect' cement walls. Lift. Cost c. £14-15 for a DR. Tel. 0821/62490.

The Hotel **Mike** and the **Elektra** Guest House are newly-built establishments at the western entrance to the village.

• FOOD: A good taverna is **Zorbas** on the road in the middle of the village.

• OTHER INFORMATION: **Car/Vespa Rentals** at the garage situated at the western exit from the village. There is also a **Pizzeria/Cafeteria** here, with a sea view.

German Military Cemetery

Beautiful position on slightly rising ground in the middle of extended vineyards, on a hillock behind Maleme. There is a wide view out over the sea to the Rodopos Peninsula, and the Monastery of Gonia is visible. The White Mountains are in the background.

4,465 German soldiers from the war years 1941-5 are buried in long rows in this cemetery. The names and dates of two of the dead are engraved on each of the simple gravestones. They are divided into 4 complexes, representing the 4 main areas of conflict: Chania, Rethymnon, Maleme and Iraklion. The names of 400 dead who fell at sea and could not be recovered are listed on the memorial in the middle.

At the entrance there is a register of names of the fallen, all between 20 and 25 years of age, and there is also a visitors' book, in which you can record your impressions. I would like to quote two entries, which are representative of all:

"At the grave of my uncle who, although he so loved his life, lost it near Maleme at the age of 21. What does war bring? Only sacrifices. Let these, like all war graves, be a symbol for peace and friendship among peoples."

"Why?"

• HOW TO GET THERE: Opposite the great edifice of the Chandris Hotel, there is a signposted way leading from the main through road. About 0.9 miles away.

Going further to the west from Maleme you soon cross the massive bridge over the wide bed of the Tavronitis, which is completely dried-up in summer.

Fruits of all kinds can be found in quantity along the main road at Tavronitis

Tavronitis

A quiet rural village, where tourists are only seen at the bus stop. The road branches off here towards Paleochora on the south coast. Particularly noticeable on the long main road are the sumptuous fruit stalls with a huge selection of fruits; you cannot fail to notice that you have now entered a large area of fruit and vegetable cultivation.

On the other hand, there are no traces of the fact that the battle for this village, and especially for the bridge over the Tavronitis, which flows into the sea to the east, was at least as fierce as that for neighbouring Maleme.

The beach below the village is miles long, but consists exclusively of shingle the size of anything from a fist to a man's head, and is not particularly clean. This does, however, prove an advantage. We counted exactly 6 bathers here on a Sunday in August! In spite of this, there are several intact fresh water showers.

• CONNECTIONS: Buses from Chania to Kastelli stop here about 13 x times daily in both directions.
There is a bus 5 x daily from Chania to **Paleochora**, arriving about 30-45 mins. later in Tavronitis. **Bus stop** by the fruit stalls.

• ACCOMMODATION: **Irini**, a guest house with well-kept rooms and a family atmosphere. Mr Kokolakis, the owner, spent long years working in Stuttgart and has given this name to his butcher's shop (on the through road, seaward side). Address: about 750 yards down the approach road to the sea by the side of the "Stuttgart" butcher's shop. There is an astonishing amount of greenery in the front gardens of the houses on this road.

• OTHER INFORMATION: an original **kafenion** with an old, wobbly board floor is situated on the through road, a short distance to the west of the bus stop (telephone with meter available here). There are now one or two simple tavernas on the beach.

Kolimbari

A small fishing and seaside village at the foot of the lonely Rodopou Peninsula. The houses cling to the narrow area of level ground between the sea and the rocky slopes.

They are prepared for tourists; several tavernas and kafenia announce their presence with "breakfast" signs on the village street. Despite this, foreign tourists rarely stray here, certainly because the curved shingle beach is not very prepossessing. By contrast, an interesting place for a visit is the *Orthodox Academy of Crete*. This belongs to the neighbouring Monastery of Gonia (see below).

• CONNECTIONS: The buses from Chania to Kastelli stop on a square on the main road; there are several kafenia and a hotel in the square. The centre of the village is about 500 yards from here, down a shady avenue of trees.
The buses from Chania to Kolimbari go right into the village.

• ACCOMMODATION: **Dimitra**, E class, quiet position, the last house in the village. The steep rocky slope begins right behind it, and the Monastery of Gonia is only a short distance further on. A nice establishment, even if it is a simple one, with a friendly owner. Cost c. £10 for a DR with shower/WC. Tel. 0824/22244.

Rose-Marie, D class, directly on the main through road, on the square where the buses stop. The rooms are nearly all on the road, thus it is quite noisy. However it has an agreeable coffee terrace under fine vine creepers. Cost c. £10 for a DR. Tel. 0824/22220.

There are fine new rooms over the **Lefka** taverna, off a balcony running around it. Further possibilities in the village.

• FOOD: The best and most agreeable restaurant is the **Lefka**, with its shady greenery. Only a short distance from the square with the bus stop on the main road. Good fish dishes.
A nice place to sit is in the kafenia on the cement jetty on the long shingle beach.

Monastery of Gonia: Behind the village on the low coastal cliffs. An undecorative, rectangular building from the outside. The attractive little church with its Byzantine dome and bell tower is in the middle of the paved inner courtyard. The inside of the church is fragrant with incense, and there is a beautiful *iconostasis* (altar wall); some of the most valuable icons produced by Cretan painters are to be seen here. In the long nave, the most impressive painting is that which depicts the Second Coming. Thousands of tiny people are burning in

Hell, with black devils standing guard around them with spears. The Saints are sitting in Heaven and looking on.

The most important festival at the monastery is on *15th August* and is held in honour of the Panagia, to whom the monastery is dedicated.

HISTORY: The Monastery of Gonia is one of the most important monasteries on Crete, even if this is not visible at first glance. It was one of the main centres of resistance in the struggle against Turkish domination and was destroyed several times, but quickly rebuilt again. There are still some Turkish cannon balls embedded in the back wall facing the sea.

In the Second World War, the Monastery of Gonia was also a centre of resistance against the German occupying forces. In spite of that, the Abbot of the monastery at that time agreed, after the war, to keep the bones of fallen German soldiers until they could finally be interred in the Military Cemetery of Maleme in 1965.

VISITING HOURS: The monastery is closed from 1.00 p.m.-3.00 p.m.

Orthodox Academy: The present-day Academy is situated a little to the north of the monastery. It was founded in 1965 by Bishop *Irenaios*, Metropolitan Bishop of the Kissamos district; even today, in spite of his advanced age, he is very active in visiting his congregations (for more information on Irenaios see under Kastelli). The building of the Academy was partly financed from Germany and the Director, theologian and sociologist *Dr. Alexandros Papaderos,* has maintained his contacts from the period of his studies there. The object of the Academy is to give those on holiday the opportunity to deepen their knowledge of Crete. The cultural, social and economic situation on the island is brought home chiefly through the medium of discussion. There are language courses, and in particular leisure courses on icon painting, pottery-making, painting on silk and weaving.

OPEN TO VISITORS: Mon-Fri 10.00 a.m.-1.00 p.m., 5.00 p.m.-8.00 p.m.

▶ **Bathing:** The long shingle beach, which extends eastwards to Maleme and beyond, begins in Kolimbari. There are only low coastal cliffs north of the village.

Peninsula of Rodopou

Mountainous, rugged and forbidding. This is how the peninsula seems from the outside. But inland there is a sea of olive trees, and the main village of Rodopos lives from its luxuriant vineyards.

Communications are practically non-existent on the lonely peninsula. The asphalt road from Kolimbari ends at Afrata. It is possible to continue along dusty tracks, until the asphalt service road to the main village of Rodopos is reached. The rest of this little-populated peninsula is only accessible with difficulty, and there are only paths through the sparse vegetation on the slopes. There is hardly any sandy beach.

A tour of the peninsula: A road leads in winding curves from Kolimbari up into the barren, stony cliffs. After a distance of just under 2 miles it reaches *Afrata*, a wonderfully peaceful farming village with olive trees and a lot of goats. Another 1.25 miles of tolerable track lead to *Astratigos*, and from there straight on until it meets the road to *Rodopos*. This is an attractive village, nestling on a level area between the slopes, with various tavernas and kafenia on the the large square.

THE DEATH OF JOHN THE BAPTIST

The largest religious festival in the diocese takes place on the Rodopou Peninsula on 29th August. The decapitation of John the Baptist is remembered in a day and a night of ascetic vigil. St. John, who lived as a hermit on the banks of the River Jordan, is recognised in the Greek Orthodox Church as the first monk and is the example for all Believers to follow: everyone should pay his respects to St. John at least once in his or her lifetime.

Every year on the morning of 29th August, thousands of people embark on the difficult trek to the chapel dedicated to *Agios Ioannis* in the northern part of the peninsula, a hike lasting a good three hours. They take blankets for the night, as the return journey is made next day. Some people make the whole journey on their knees, so that St. John will hear their prayers, or even because they wish to thank him for granting a request. Others bring quantities of candles, which they place around the chapel. Taking no heed of his age (nearly 80) Bishop Irenaios leads the festivities; this is one of many indications of his robustness and his enormous readiness to join in at all times.

From Kolimbari to Kastelli

A very winding road over the foothills of the Rodopou Peninsula. The mountain and hill landscape is dotted with olive trees, and there are little white village "nests" scattered here and there. Going downhill, there are constant superb panoramic views of the whole Gulf of Kissamos/Kastelli over to the long Peninsula of Gramvousa.

Gulf of Kastelli

Wonderful position between the two long fingers of the Rodopou and Gramvousa Peninsulas. Apart from the little town of Kastelli, the area is very rural and quiet.

The people here live from their olive trees and agricultural activity. Tourism does not yet play a leading role here. It will be another 5-10 years before the newly planned New Road from Chania reaches as far as Kastelli. Building operations have apparently been stopped because of the discovery of the ancient city of Mithimna.

Camping Mithimna, a few miles to the east of Kastelli, is one of the best destinations for campers on Crete. In addition, the region is excellently suited for excursions to the unspoilt west coast.

Kastelli

A small provincial town, easy to find your way around, and with little bustle. Not much to see here, but the place has retained its character.

The actual centre is the main square, where the buses go from. Everything had been turned upside down here in 1988; the pavements had been taken up and water mains were being put in, amongst other things.

There are some nice kafenia on the upper edge of the square. Here too is the main shopping street, with shops, travel agencies, banks and various small tavernas and kafenia. There is an access road from the square down to the beach; the latter is long and spacious, but consists entirely of shingle.

The attractive fishing harbour is several miles to the west of the village, and the ferry and commercial port another 1.25 miles further on from that. Boats from the Peloponnese arrive here several times in the week, and bring a little variety to the life of the town.

Kastelli is the point of departure for excursions to the long sandy beach of Phalassarna, and for excursions to the beach at Elafonisi in the south west of Crete.

Connections

The **boat connections** to and from Kastelli are of eventual interest for those wishing to get to and from Crete. There is a connection 3 x weekly by ferry to the *Peloponnese*, and in 1988 there was a boat 1 x per week to *Santorini*.

Timetable (1988): on Tuesdays via the island of Kythera to Neapolis (Pelop.) and further on via Monemvasia to Piraeus. Wednesdays to Kalamata (Pelop.), Thursdays to Santorini, Fridays via Kythera to Gythion (Pelop.) and further on to Piraeus.

Prices: from and to Neapolis £4 per person, cars £24; Kalamata £9 per person, cars £6 per person, cars £24; Gythion £6 per person, cars £34. Interesting here is the fact that the crossing to Neapolis is almost 40% cheaper than that to Gythion.

Tickets: obtainable at the agency run by E. Xyroukakis (Tel. 0822/22655) on the main square of Kastelli next to the chemist's shop. Information about departure times is also available there.

• **Bus**: about 15 x daily to Chania, 4 x daily to Platanos, 1 x to Phalassarna, 2 x to Sfinari and Kambos (west coast), 2 x to Polirrinia, 1 x to the Monastery of Chrisoskalitissa. Bus station and ticket sales on the main square.

• **Car/motor bike rentals**: on the main road, Anagnostaki Skalidi, eg Hermes Rent a Car.

• **Excursions**: The daily excursion by KTEL buses to the **Samaria Gorge** costs c. £6 from Kastelli, excluding the £3 for the boat trip from Agia Roumeli-Chora Sfakion. Other operators offer the same tour for about £2 more.

There are also daily boat trips to the pirate cove on the **Gramvousa** Peninsula.

— ★ —

• CHANGING MONEY: on Anagnostaki Skalidi, the main road, in the town centre.

• POST OFFICE: on the through road, which runs through Kastelli above the actual centre.

• TELEPHONE: **OTE Office** on the same road, on the square with the garage, where a road leads off to Polirrinia (see below). Mon-Sat 7.30 a.m.-3.10 p.m. Closed on Sundays.

• OTHER INFORMATION: The original **photographic shop** run by Georgios Anifandakis is situated on the main road, a short way from the central Platia. Mr Anifandakis, who provided some of the photos in this book, is a very friendly person and is very happy when people visit his shop.

Accommodation

• **Galini Beach**: a guest house a little outside the village, directly on the long shingle/sand beach. Very quiet situation, spacious, and there are vacancies there even in the high season. Light coloured wooden furniture, tiled/paved floors, all rooms with shower/WC and balcony, large dining room, and friendly staff. Cost c. £12 for a DR. Can be reached from Kastelli by going down the approach road to the sea, then left along the shore promenade to the sports ground. About 15 mins. from the centre on foot.
Tel. 0822/23288.

• **Korakas**: just before the Galini Beach on the shore promenade. A taverna which rents out some rooms on the first floor. These are smaller than those in the Galini Beach, but very nicely appointed; tastefully furnished, modern beds and furniture; only one bathroom for the 4 rooms, but immaculately clean and with a bathtub. Can be noisy, however, because

of the taverna beneath it. Beach right in front of the door. Cost c. £9 for a DR.

• **Mandy Apartments**: at the end of the road to the beach which leads down from the square. A new house, immaculate and stylish. Large rooms with floor tiles and white, rough cement walls. About £14 for a living room/bedroom with balcony and bathroom.

• **Hotel Papadakis**: only a few paces from Mandy Apartments. Very clean and well-furnished rooms with balconies (sea views), and shower/WC. About £14 for a DR.

• There are still more possibilities on the shore promenade and particularly in the centre of town, eg the Hotel **Castron** (C class, on the main square, c. £12 for a DR), or the Hotel **Kissamos** (C class, on the noisy through road; modern, all rooms with shower/toilet and telephone, same price). Reasonably priced private rooms also on the main road, Anagnostaki Skalidi St., among other places.

• If you walk far enough along the shore in an eastwards direction, you could certainly use a sleeping bag on the beach. We also saw tents there.

• READER'S TIP: "Our best accommodation on Crete was at the newly-built apartment complex of **Dimitris Chryssany**, c. 2 miles across the bay to the west of Kastelli. The proprietor is very hospitable, and the furnishings are of the best quality; bedrooms with 2 beds or a double bed, balcony with a sea view, living room with 2 sofas, terrace, bathroom, small kitchen with a refrigerator. Important for us: very clean, quiet, and superbly situated away from any kind of bustle. Tel. 0822/23390 or 22337."

Author's note: In summer, an apartment costs c. £23.

Food

• **Papadaki**: right on the water, at the end of the road leading straight to the beach from the square where the buses stop. Shady awning, fine view of the sea, the interior decorated with fishing nets with all kinds of things hanging in them - shells, starfish, lobsters. Try the fish shish-kebab. Reasonably priced.

• **Makedonia**: diagonally across from Papadaki, providing the competition. Nikos serves at table, his wife cooks. Try the wine from the barrel, otherwise fish is the speciality here.

• **O Stimadoris**: spacious fish restaurant (psarotaverna) half way from Kastelli to the harbour. Unfortunately it is in a rather unfavourable position and has a relatively sober atmosphere about it. Large, cool dining room inside (air conditioning!) completely decorated with equipment and all kinds of implements connected with the sea, and a wide view of the deep blue sea. Large selection of fish dishes, and particularly noticeable here is the fact that they use little oil in cooking.

There are two simple fish tavernas in the little **fishing harbour**. You can sit outside, and there is certainly a lot of atmosphere here in the evenings.

IRENAIOS, BISHOP OF CRETE

Irenaios, who is almost 80 years old, is today one of the most important personalities of the Cretan Orthodox Church. He became Bishop of the Diocese of Kissamos-Kastelli as early as 1958, but in 1972 the Patriarchate of Constantinople named him Metropolitan Archbishop of Western Germany, with his seat in Bonn. Accordingly the Synod of Bishops on Crete wanted to give the vacant seat at Kastelli to someone else, but the community would not go along with this. They "occupied" the official residence of the Metropolitan Archbishop in Bonn and summarily carried off Irenaios back to Crete. The Synod of Bishops and the Patriarchate gave in, and Irenaios became Bishop of the district around Kastelli.

He has achieved much during his long period in office; although the diocese is very poor, there is hardly any unemployment. He has pushed forward the building of schools everywhere in the villages. In answer to the unscrupulous shipping politics carried on by the shipowners in Piraeus, he founded the Cretan shipping company ANEK, using money from members of his diocese. Today, the company belongs to thousands of small shareholders. He also founded the Orthodox Academy at Kolimbari (see under Kolimbari), where Orthodoxy attempts a dialogue with the modern world. Every year, Christians from east and west meet here to exchange views. Such an institution is a very rare occurrence in the Orthodox world.

Kastelli/Surrounding Area and Hinterland

There are several seaside tavernas to the east of Kastelli. They can be reached from the through road by their own service tracks. *Acrogiali*, directly on the beach (signposted from the through road), is worth a visit because of its beautiful position. Fish is mainly served here.

Kaloudiania: The inland route to the sandy beach of Elafonisi begins here. For details see page 460.

Drapanias: A village on the road a few miles to the east of Kastelli; buses from Chania to Kastelli stop there. The beautifully situated Mithymna Camping Site is just under 1 mile below the village, and the approach to it through olive groves and vineyards is signposted. There is a short cut for pedestrians (beginning by the garage a little to the east of the main approach road).

• CAMPING MITHIMNA: A worthwhile destination about 3.75 miles before Kastelli, because of its fine position between the two peninsulas and the nice, personal atmosphere that prevails there. A team of young people run this simple but pleasant site. Friendly Manoussos from Zouvra runs the place together with Michalis; he speaks very good English and can give you a lot of advice and tips about excursions.

The nicest part of the place is behind the washing facilities: an immaculate area of thick lawn, with shady pitches under reed roofs and tamarisks. Everyone meets under the reed roof of the taverna in the evening; the food is palatable, there is good taped music, often live music too (one of the Greeks who frequently comes to the taverna plays the guitar well). There is a small shop, and motor bikes/mopeds for rent. Prices: c. £2 per person, tent slightly less, car £1. Open from April to October. Tel. 0822/31444.

• FOOD: Our tip - try the **Taverna Elisabeth**, at the eastern exit from the village. Very reasonable prices, and a friendly young proprietress.

Bathing/surrounding area: The beach at the camping site and in the whole of the Gulf of Kissamos is quite a mixture of sand and shingle. While the sand predominates near the site, the stones take over at Kastelli. Various things are also washed up, such as roots, seaweed and tar. However there are miles of beach and they are deserted even in the high season. A shower is to be found at the camping site.

A walk along the beach reveals the completely rural nature of the region. Goats, mules and donkeys graze between the fields and plantations, and not far from the camping site there is the estuary of a river with a lot of reeds. The panoramic view is wonderful; the deep blue sea with its white breakers is cradled between the two long peninsulas. Striking mountain peaks beckon to you from the hinterland.

If you continue along the beach to the right of the camping site, you come to the little village of *Nopigia*, about 0.6 miles away. This has been almost abandoned, and there are only a handful of houses which are permanently occupied. Some of the families that spend their holidays here come from Athens. Private rooms can be found here; ask around. At the western entrance to the village, directly at the water's edge, there is a tiny taverna with 3 tables and a lot of peace and quiet.

Polirrinia

The Dorians built a large city on a mountain peak above the modern village of Polirrinia, about 3.75 miles inland from Kastelli. Kissamos (Kastelli) was its harbour.

A detour up here is especially worthwhile in order to take a little stroll through the modern village, and to enjoy the superb view out over the whole gulf from the exposed excavations. There is not much left of the city itself, and the ruins are scattered over a wide area. There are the remains of a Cyclopean wall, the ruins of a temple and burial chambers, and the walls of a later Venetian castle.

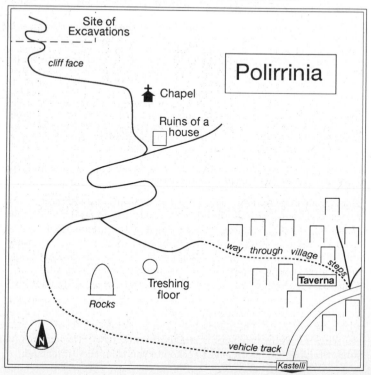

The road to Polirrinia begins in Kastelli, on the through road to the south above the centre of the town. The turn-off is on a three-cornered square with a garage, and is marked by roughly painted blue letters. There is a modern *nunnery*, in which 7 nuns are currently living, a few miles along this road on the left hand side, above Kastelli. (Visiting hours 8.00 a.m.-1.00 p.m., 4.00 p.m.-7.00 p.m.)

A DESCRIPTION OF THE WAY: When you arrive in Polirrinia, the excavations are not very easy to find. If you have come by car, leave your vehicle on the small square with the fountain (just after entering the village). On the left, some steps lead past a kafenion with a beautiful, thickly foliaged terrace, which is a place for a good view. Go a little along here and then keep going diagonally to your left. The path goes between the houses and finally passes a round threshing floor and goes out of the village. Soon it meets a wide track, which comes up from the road. Go along this to the right, turn left by a ruined house and you will pass a chapel and, after about a 30 minute walk, you will come to the thorny terraced slope with the sparse remains of the city.

• CONNECTIONS: There are buses to Polirrinia from Kastelli about 2 x daily.

Peninsula of Gramvousa

Unpopulated and rocky, but there is also the fantastic lagoon and beach in the pirates' bay of Tigani, whose shallow waters shimmer in every shade of turquoise.

A dream of a beach on Gramvousa

There were more visitors here in the past than there are today; the Dorians built a sanctuary on the extreme tip of the peninsula. The ruins of a large castle built by the Venetians lie on the offshore island of *Gramvousa* to the west. Pirates used the above-mentioned bay by the Peninsula of *Tigani* as a headquarters. For a while now, during the season, boat excursions have been arranged from Kastelli.

Pirates' Bay: The hike to this wonderful sandy beach at the Tigani Peninsula on the western side of Gramvousa has always been a real favourite. The point of departure is the little white village of *Kaliviani* at the beginning of the peninsula and in the midst of olive trees. The bus to Platanos stops here, and the way up to the Gramvousa Peninsula leads off the main road in the middle of the village (past the church). The hike takes about 3 hours each way.

The road goes along the east coast of the peninsula past a stranded freighter. You soon get a shock; where previously there have only been a few hikers out and about, workmen are now busy blasting a *road* in the rock! Those concerned with nature preservation are creating a storm of protest against the project, but it is quite well-advanced. In 1988, the road had almost reached the point where the path goes across to the western side of the peninsula over the mountain crest. Thus, one of Crete's last paradises will soon be accessible to drivers of rented cars.

The beach at Tigani consists of fine white coral sand and borders a shallow lagoon. Up till now, there were no facilities there.

From Kastelli to the beach at Elafonisi

The 22 mile long *inland route* from Kastelli to the south-west of Crete leads through what is probably the richest region of forest in Crete. The strong green of the chestnut forests here is wonderfully refreshing, especially in high summer.

Suggestions for day excursions: From Kastelli in the morning, taking the inland route to the beach at Elafonisi, and then late afternoon back along the west coast. This is the time when the sun sinks slowly into the sea.

At *Kaloudiana*, a few miles to the east of Kastelli, there is a turn-off from the coast road which at first leads to *Potamida*. There, about on a level with the church, you can see bizarre eroded cliffs on the left hand side of the road, not unlike the formations to be seen at Cappadocia in Turkey.

The road winds higher into the mountains from *Voulgaro*. Again and again there are wonderful views over the lush green slopes of the valley, with olives, cypresses and various types of deciduous trees. Far ahead you can see a sharply cut ravine.

Topolia, with its narrow, winding main street enjoys a wonderful

The little chapel in the Cave of Agia Sofia

position on the slope between beautiful, tall trees. There is a superb view in every direction just after the entrance to the village; then comes the ravine, mentioned above, with high, steep, rust-brown walls similar to those of the famous Samaria Gorge. After that, the road passes through a small tunnel (one of the two road tunnels in Crete; the other is in eastern Crete near Neapolis). About 300 yards after the exit from the tunnel and on the right hand side of the road, there are steps up to the Cave of Agia Sofia (c. 5 mins.).

Agia Sofia: There is water dripping everywhere, and bizarre chalky-white stalactites form a hall-like grotto here. A tiny chapel is pushed into the entrance of it and a bell, together with a star which is illuminated in the evenings, forms a striking focal point for the eye.

• **Taverna Panorama**: shortly after the cave in a bend in the road. Attractive greenery with bougainvillea and vine creepers. The Dutch especially like to drop in here: "Ned. gesproken". The wife of Emmanuel Motakis is Dutch and serves coffee in remarkable porcelain of the purest Delft blue.

Detour: The little detour via *Vlatos*, *Rogdia* and *Limni* is worthwhile. The road is made up entirely of asphalt, and snakes over the mountain slopes with wide panoramic vistas. The three villages almost disappear in the shimmering green of the towering plane trees, chestnuts, olives and stony oaks. There is at least one kafenion in every village. There is a forestry programme at Vlatos, which is financed by the

Bavarian Ministry of Agriculture. Young trees and forestry experts have been flown in here by German army transport planes; if you like, this is also a kind of reparation. At any rate, the area is certainly a suitable one for the project.

When you get back to the main road again and have a little time to spare, you should drive back to *Elos*, the village of the chestnuts about 0.6 miles away. There are more chestnut trees there than people. It is wonderful to sit in the kafenia in the centre, especially in the shop/taverna/kafenion **Kastanofolia** run by Mr. Kokolakis. A stream flows down here and forms a little pool, on which there are ducks.

From Elos, it is a distance of about 3.25 miles to the turn-off to the Monastery of Chrisoskalitissa on the coast. When you reach the turn-off, please read on page 466 for more details.

The West Coast

Apart from the extreme north and south, it is widely untouched by tourism. There is hardly a single village directly on the sea.

A panoramic asphalt road runs high up along the coast and only becomes a gravel track in part in the last section. The drive is nicest in the evenings, when the sun sinks into the sea. An interesting round trip could be made from Kastelli or the Mithimna camping site.

Platanos: The village lies in front of a moderately high rock wall and is only really important as a place to change buses for Phalassarna and the west coast. The buses to and from Kastelli stop directly at the turn-off to Phalassarna. There is also an original little taverna here, and a grocer's shop. Those who are catering for themselves should stock up here, before they go down to Phalassarna. Careful: the road is not made up at the beginning for a distance of several hundred yards.

• FOOD: **O Zacharias**, one of the last houses on the road to Phalassarna. Zacharias the fisher is a nice person; he offers good fish dishes and sometimes he brings home a fat lobster. He is always warmly recommended by his guests. Also has well-kept rooms with shower/WC for c. £8.

Phalassarna

A wide, curved bay with bizarre sawn-off cliff edges. In front of these is a beach with wonderful soft white sand, just like on the North Sea.

The panoramic view is grandiose when you drive down the winding asphalt road. The inhabitants use the large bay mainly for the hothouse cultivation of tomatoes, cucumbers and even bananas. The

Phalassarna: sand as far as the eye can see

green coverings of these hothouses, on which the sun beats down day after day, cannot be missed.

The strange rocky walls which rise directly behind the beach are a clear proof of the eustatic elevation of the island in the west, whereas in the east, it has sunk into the sea by several feet. The upper edge of the rocks formed the coastline at one time, while the present sandy beach has been formed in the course of centuries through sedimentation. This is why the sea is shallow, and the beach does not shelve. It is wonderful to walk about in the sea, with its soft, sandy floor and superb clear water!

Only a little can be seen of the former ancient harbour-city of *Phalassarna* - today, its supposed remains lie 20 feet above sea level, on the cliffs!

As the fame of Phalassarna is rapidly increasing, more and more campers and motor caravans find their way there. Some of the rucksack tourists have furnished a few of the caves in the black cliff wall as living quarters, others sleep in tents.

● CONNECTIONS: There is a bus directly down to Phalassarna every day from Kastelli. In addition there are 4 other buses from Kastelli to Platanos, the last village before Phalassarna. The beach is c. 3.25 miles from here down the curving panoramic road. Hitch-hiking is easily possible here.

Careful: only the road which runs northwards leads to the beach. The southern branch in the bay leads to a small harbour, from which agricultural products are shipped.

• ACCOMMODATION/FOOD: There are 2 tavernas opposite one another at the end of the road up above the cliff edge.

Sunset: the nearest taverna to the beach. The food offered here is in no way special, but you can enjoy the wonderful sunset over the sea from under the fig tree on the terrace. A favourite rendezvous, and the stout proprietress rents out simple rooms for c. £6. There is a tiny, whitewashed chapel pushed into the rocks down from the cafeteria, and next to it there are several taps providing water for washing, showers etc.

Sundown: the upper taverna. The recently-built Hotel **Falassarna** next door to it is worthy of mention here. Brand new and definitely tasteful, with light-coloured wooden furniture, attractive bathroom, and a super view. About £11-12 for a DR, and there are also two-roomed apartments. Information at the Sundown.

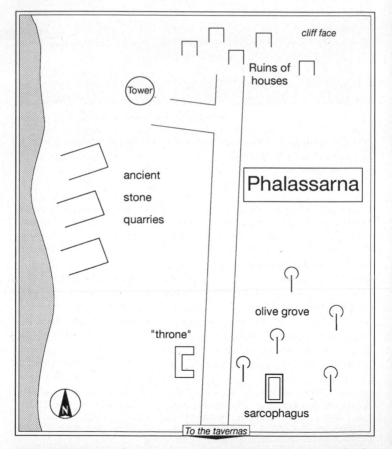

Ancient Phalassarna: Go along the road from the tavernas in a northerly direction. Phalassarna lies at the foot of the rock wall (see sketch), and the foundation walls of houses can be recognised with a little trouble.The most striking point is the round *tower*. You can climb a little over the rocks towards the water from here and will come to some almost rectangular excavations in the rock. Opinions differ as to their nature; although they were identified as harbour basins of the ancient city for a long time, they are now interpreted as quarries. The real harbour basin is thought to lie nearer to the mountain slope (still on that side of the tower) and to have been connected to the sea by a canal.

Going back, you pass a crude "*throne*", directly beside the path. Its function has also not been established. There is a *sarcophagus* in the olive grove on the other side of the path.

A tolerably good asphalt road winds up *from Platanos to Sfinari* and then goes downhill again. The view is stunning. There is also a bus c. 2 x daily from Kastelli via Platanos.

Sfinari

Take care not to run over the chickens asleep in the road. The village up above the long grey shingle beach lies amid a sea of olive trees. The inhabitants are concerned exclusively with farming activity, and there is a complete lack of tourist infrastructure. There are hot-houses, and several streams run over the beach, behind which there are goats grazing.

• ACCOMMODATION: best at **Phidias**, a little below the through road, by the exit to the beach (southern exit from the village). Here, in an informal atmosphere, you can enjoy fish from the charcoal grill. According to a sign, there are rooms for the sensational price of £2 at the house of Antonios **Theodorakis**, at the northern exit from the village.(Of course, they cost more than that!)
Some people pitch their tents on the beach.

Kambos: A village spread out along the road in a deeply-etched valley. Noticeable here is the lush vegetation with chestnut and olive tres. There are rooms for rent.

A wide gravel track runs to the south of Kambos, high above the sea (only asphalt in the villages). Isolated beaches can be seen down below, and to the north of Keramoti a sign invites you to *Free Camping*. But hardly anyone has taken up the offer yet.

From the last stretch of the track before the turn-off there is a wonderful view down over the beach around Elafonisi and over the Monastery of Chrisoskalitissa. In the old garden taverna at *Kefali*, the last village before the turn-off, there are often interesting specialities to try, including delicious yoghurt and home-produced honey. A pleasant place to take a break.

The beach at Elafonisi is certainly a hot tip no longer, but still one of the nicest corners of Crete. Nowadays, there is even a daily bus service there from Kastelli, which is widely used; otherwise the drivers of rented vehicles mainly find their way down there along a track which certainly brings out the perspiration. The shortest way from the north coast is from Kaloudiana along the road from Kastelli-Kolimbari, via Topolia and Elos in an inland cross-country direction. For all the details on this see page 460.

To the Monastery of Chrisoskalitissa/Beach of Elafonisi: The valley above Vathi which leads down to the monastery bears a strong resemblance to the deep Barancos on the island of Gomera in the Canaries. The villages with their red-tiled roofs are situated on step-like terraces.
Beyond the kafenion in *Vathi* there is another memorial to resistance fighters who were executed between 1941 and 1944. The asphalt road ends shortly after *Plokamiana*, but the bumpy track down to the coast presents no problems. At the bottom, the weathered slopes of the valley open out into a hilly shore plain. Be careful; the road forks here. Straight on leads to the quarry at *Stomiou*, and a shingle beach here invites you for a swim after the sweaty journey. The beach at Elafonisi is by far the nicer, even if it is a good 3.75 miles away. Thus you should go left at the fork in the road, and soon the wide scatter of houses around the monastery comes into view.

The Monastery of Chrisoskalitissa

An angular building with a brilliant light-blue roof, on a rock above the sea.

Apart from the church with its striking barrel-vault and some icons, which are hung with numerous votive offerings, there is little to see (but read the box below!) Where once 200 monks are said to have lived a life of work and prayer, there is just one monk and a friendly and nimble nun today. She will gladly open the little museum for you; this contains old icons and various small silver objects.
On 15th August, the feast of the *Ascension of the Virgin,* the inhabitants of the whole region come here for the celebrations.

VISITING TIMES: daily 9.00 a.m.-12.00 p.m., 3.00 p.m.-5.00 p.m.

THE "GOLDEN STEP"

This is the translation of the name Chrisoskalitissa. You see, one of the steps at the monastery is made of pure gold. Only those who have not sinned are able to see it. Please write to me if you can see the golden step.

• CONNECTIONS: In the summer, there is at least one bus daily from Kastelli to the Monastery of Chrisoskalitissa and to the beach at Elafonisi. Arrival and departure at a kafenion above the monastery.

• ACCOMMODATION/FOOD: There are some beds (for rent) in very simply furnished rooms at the monastery. Otherwise there are several kafenia/tavernas around the monastery, which also have rooms for rent.

The dream-destination of all drivers of rented vehicles in western Crete is now not far away. The track winds its tortuous way for a further 3.25 miles over low rust-red hills. Then, after the punishing drive, an almost fantastic vista unexpectedly opens out before your eyes.

The beach at Elafonisi

Crete's south sea island beach; those who have been here enthuse about it. There is a lagoon-like atmosphere between the little offshore islands and the branching coastline. A shallow, light blue sea bay, with soft white, in part reddish sand extending over several miles. Trees provide shade here.

The (un)favourable position far away from the normal routes has prevented the development of tourism on a large scale up to now. Of course, rented cars and motor caravans (careful; don't get stuck in the sand!) find their way here every day, but you can still camp here for weeks without being disturbed and enjoy the peace in the evening. A plea from the heart - please don't deposit litter here, but leave everything as you found it! There are some rubbish containers belonging to the community of Vathi on the beach; they are emptied regularly by those who run the beach tavernas which are accessible from the road.

But the future no longer seems far off here. The well-known politician Mitsotakis from Chania, leader of the Conservative Nea Demokratia Party, has bought up large tracts of land at Elafonisi. Can this be a good thing?

• CONNECTIONS: In summer there is a bus once daily from Kastelli (also stops at Chrisoskalitissa Monastery). There are also boats which bring bathers from Paleochora.

• FOOD: As of late there are several simple tavernas which rely on diesel generators. These establishments cater for the hungry community of campers and drivers of rented cars.

The island of Elafonisi: There is no problem involved in wading over to the island from the beach, as the water is, at the most, around chest deep. On the island there are sand dunes, sand carnations and rough-edged rocks. A little paradise to wander around. A memorial has been erected there to the Australian crew of the "Imperatrice", who lost their lives when it was stranded here in 1907.

There is a very nice hike along the beach at Elafonisi around the south west tip of Crete to **Paleochora** (See there for a description of the route.)

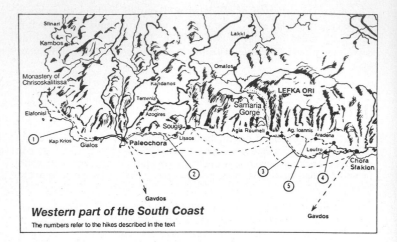

Western part of the South Coast

The numbers refer to the hikes described in the text

The South Coast

The mighty, sheer slopes of the Lefka Ori plunge steeply into the Sea of Libya. They characterise the scenery along the western section of the south coast from Paleochora to Chora Sfakion.

Characteristic of the region are the deep ravines (*farangi*), which run through the White Mountains and open out to the sea. The largest and most famous of these is the *Samaria Gorge*, but there are many more. Numerous rare plants, which only grow here, have been able to flourish on the sheltered steep walls of the ravines. The hidden bathing places and bays at the exits from the ravines are especially favoured by rucksack tourists. But there are sand and shingle beaches tucked everywhere into the niches between the villages, and these can often only be reached on foot.

The approach by road from the north coast does not present any problems; roadways which lead only to some of these little bathing resorts wind up through the high mountains. *Loutro* and *Agia Roumeli,* however, can only be reached by boat or on foot. These ravines, sometimes hundreds of feet deep, are the reason why there is no continuous coast road in this region. Communications are maintained from May to October by little passenger boats. They do not run in winter, however; then, the most that can be arranged is a trip on a fishing boat that is going out.

Apart from the good opportunities for bathing, the region particularly has a lot to offer hikers. Delightful coastal tracks lead to the Monastery of Chrisoskalitissa on the south west tip of Crete and go on almost continuously to Chora Sfakion. Only the stretch from Sougia to Agia Roumeli can be difficult and dangerous. On this stretch alone three people were found dead in 1987; one had suffered a fall, the other two died of thirst.

Finally, you can cross to the offshore island of *Gavdos*, which is the southernmost island in Europe.

• APPROACH FROM THE NORTH COAST: There are roads with regular bus connections running directly to Paleochora, Sougia and Chora Sfakion. Agia Roumeli can be reached on foot from the Omalos High Plateau through the Samaria Gorge (this hike is described above in the chapter on the Samaria Gorge).

• CONNECTIONS: Small **passenger steamers** operate a shuttle service several times daily from May to October between Paleochora, Sougia, Agia Roumeli, Loutro and Chora Sfakion.

• HIKING PATHS: see sketch map. From Paleochora to the Monastery of Chrisoskalitissa **(1)**, from Paleochora to Sougia **(2)**, from Chora Sfakion via Loutro to Agia Roumeli **(3)**, from Anopolis to Loutro **(4)**, and from Agia Roumeli via Aradena to Anopolis **(5)**. (The latter is described in the chapter on the Samaria Gorge/Agia Roumeli. The others are described below.)

From Chania to Paleochora

Superb mountain drive with wide panoramic views of the Lefka Ori.

From the bus station at Chania, buses go along the route about six times daily. At Tavronitis you turn off the coastal road from Chania-Kastelli in a southerly direction; at the beginning, the road is wide and newly-built. It passes through fertile tree and fruit plantations. Only after *Voukoulies* does it begin to go uphill and from *Kakopetro* it winds up in sharp bends into the broken rocky landscape of the *Selinos district,* with its main village of Kandanos.

Kandanos

The main village in the Selinos district. The wooded southern slopes of the Lefka Ori begin here and extend down to the Sea of Libya.

Kandanos is situated in the middle of large olive groves with ancient, knotty trees to the left and right of the road.

The village has achieved a sad fame in Crete, because it was razed to the foundations on 3rd June, 1941 by German troops, as retribution for an attack made by partisans which claimed the lives of 25 German soldiers. Women, children, and even the priest of Kandanos took part in the ambush; one of many examples of how deeply the resistance against the Nazi domination was felt among the population. For this reason Kandanos today consists almost entirely of newly-built houses. In the large *village square* at the exit from the village in the direction of Paleochora there are memorial plaques which recall the tragedy. The destruction of whole villages and the execution of their entire population was, by the way, frequently practised by the German Wehrmacht (see also Anogia in the Ida Mountains).

In the decades following the war, Germans were active in various places in Greece as part of an operation of reconciliation; a modest attempt to atone for crimes committed during the war. They built a *waterworks* in Kandanos. It is situated at the northern exit, immediately beside the road, and also bears a memorial plaque in Greek and German.

• FOOD: The small shady **kafenion** belonging to friendly Mr. Maragakis is situated on the square.

To the south of Kandanos, a road goes down through the thickly forested valley to Paleochora.

Paleochora

Wonderful sandy beach; point of departure for hikes; to Gavdos by boat

An oasis on the sea. Paleochora lies on a peninsula almost completely surrounded by water. The rugged rocky slopes of Sfakia plunge steeply down behind it. A forest of silvery-green olive trees rounds off the picture.

You really could describe the position of Paleochora as beautiful. And beautiful is also an apt description of the miles of sandy beach on the western side of the peninsula.

But Paleochora is **the** tourist centre in the western part of the south coast! What was formerly an absolute centre for rucksack tourists is developing noticeably into a holiday resort, a bustling location for anyone from the "package" type of tourist to the "drop-out" who has made western Crete his/her destination. The overdimensional hotel buildings are still absent and people regularly camp or spread out their sleeping bags on the beach, although this is forbidden. But in the foreseeable future Paleochora will probably become a second Agia Galini.

The village itself is not overwhelmingly attractive. Apart from the little main road, where you can sit pleasantly beneath the shady trees in the tavernas, there is nothing worth seeing. The strict symmetry of the streets and the yellow and white painted houses hardly emit any atmosphere. Building is going on everywhere, and new storeys are being added to the old, low houses, in order to accommodate the herds of tourists.

Perhaps the nicest part is the low plateau on the southern tip of the peninsula. Hardly anything is left of the ruined former castle, but there are fragrant herbs everywhere, and you can have a quiet bird's eye view of the hustle and bustle on the beach . . .

CONNECTIONS

• **Bus**: About 6 x daily from Chania to Paleochora and vice versa. Bus stop at the end of the main road, where a road branches off and runs directly to the west beach.

• **Boat**: Little passenger steamers ply between the coastal villages on the southern coast of the Lefka Ori. The Marina goes daily at 8.30 a.m. from Paleochora to **Sougia** and **Agia Roumeli** (exit from the Samaria Gorge), and so does the Neptune (daily) at 9.00 a.m. (except Mon and Thurs). On Thursday and Sunday there is a boat via Agia Roumeli and Loutro to **Chora Sfakion**. Cost of ticket to Sougia c. £2, to Agia Roumeli £3, and Chora Sfakion £5.

Paleochora is also the most important harbour for excursions to the offshore island of **Gavdos**. The Neptune goes there every Monday and Thursday at 8.00 a.m., tickets c. £4. There is an extra

journey on Saturdays in the high season. The boat returns on the same day at 3.30 p.m. No trips there if the sea is rough! For more details about Gavdos see the chapter/Island of Gavdos, page 493.

Tickets for all journeys are available at the travel agencies in the village or one hour before departure at the Pelican Taverna on the harbour. This is called Pelican because an almost man-sized tame pelican walks around there. He always struts over to the boats when they are about to leave, in the hope of getting a morsel to eat.

• **Taxi**: There are two taxi drivers working in Paleochora who chiefly make the journey to Chania.

• **Car/motor bike rentals**: At the Travel Agency Browns Pelican Travel (see under travel agencies). Cars, motor bikes and bicycles for hire.

— ★ —

• CHANGING MONEY: several banks on the main road.

• POST OFFICE: on the beach road, opposite Elman Apartments.

• TELEPHONE: small **OTE Office** on the main road, open Mon-Fri, 7.30 a.m.-3.10 p.m. Closed Sat/Sun. If it is closed, it is usually possible to make calls from the **kiosk** on the main road. There is normally a large crowd around the kiosk, however.

• TRAVEL AGENCIES: The best source of information is **Brown's Pelican Travel**, which is under British management. There are, however, rumours that it may soon close down. Organised Jeep-Safaris and bus excursions in the area, eg to Elafonisi, the Monastery of Chrisos-kalitissa, the waterfall of Azogires etc. From their advertisements, these would

seem to be really interesting events; if possible only up to 10 people go on each trip, so that the whole thing is not too impersonal. Brown's Pelican Travel also arranges accommodation in Paleochora and on the Island of Gavdos and has vehicles for hire. Address: Ant. Xenaki St., a side alley on the right when you enter Paleochora. Open Mon-Sat 9.00 a.m.-1.30 p.m., 4.30 p.m.-8.30 p.m. Tel. 0823/41125. There is also a branch on the road to the beach.

The Austrian travel agency **Reiseladen** is also on the road to the beach. You can also get friendly information here, and also have rooms arranged, buy boat tickets and hire motor bikes/mopeds. Open Mon-Sat 8.00 a.m.-1.30 p.m., 5.30 p.m.-9.00 pm.

Accommodation

A lot of possibilities, not so many hotels, but any number of private rooms. In spite of this, everything is full in the high season. It would be a pure stroke of luck to find a room then. Rooms can be arranged through both of the travel agencies mentioned above.

• **Elman Apartments**: B class, directly on the long sandy beach. Comfortable apartments (bedroom/living room/bathroom) for c. £20. Tel. 0823/41412.

• **Polydoros**: C class, brand new and one of the best addresses in town at the moment. A few yards west of the main road, on the approach road to the beach. Modern, very appealing hotel with a beautiful inner court (breakfast!) and an agreeable bar. Telephone in all rooms. A little noisier in the evenings because of its central position. About £22 for a DR with bath. Tel. 0823/41150.

• **Eliros**: B class guest house, very elegant, opened a few years ago. Friendly, bright rooms, with wood panelling on the ground floor. Cost between £10-14 for a DR. Address: 6, Daskaloyanni St., to the right of the approach road into the village.

• **Rea**: newly-built, immaculate rooms with bath, some with a balcony, friendly staff. In Ant. Peraki St., near the Eliros. About £13; £9 without a balcony.

• **Oasis**: pleasant house at 4, Ant. Xenaki St., a quiet side alley with shady trees and the fragrance of flowers in the air. Cost c. £8 for a DR. To the west of the main street in the alley in which Brown's Pelican Travel is also situated. Tel. 0823/41328.

• **Paleochora**: E class, simple but clean, with running hot and cold water. Satisfied guests here. Cost c. £9. Address: 15, Kon. Kriari St., parallel to the approach road on the left hand side. Tel. 0823/41225.

• **Livikon**: D class, two storeyed "palazzo" at the entrance to the village. Oldest house in the place, built in 1935. Really nicely dilapidated, scratched furniture, everything a little crooked and wobbly, but perhaps loveable because of this very fact! Partly renovated recently. DR costs £6, three-bedded room £8. Showers on the landings only. Tel. 0823/41250.

• **Pension Lissos**: exactly opposite Livikon. The young proprietor offers new, clean rooms and speaks perfect English. DR costs around £12. Tel. 0823/41266.

— ★ —

• APARTMENTS: numerous possibilities, especially down on the beach. Bookings can be made via Brown's Pelican Travel, for example. A studio (1 room with cooking facilities and bath) costs c. £14, while apartments with living room, bedroom and kitchen cost c. £20 per day. The **Villa Anna** is well-furnished and equipped and is situated a little back from the beach (can be reached by turning off the beach road into the little alley by the school).

— ★ —

• PRIVATE ROOMS: large selection on offer, rooms costing from £7 to just under £10. You generally pay £2 more on the main road!

The **Oriental Bay Restaurant** occupies a quiet position a little away from it all on the eastern side of the peninsula, on a shingle beach on the way to the camping site. However, the disco at the camping site can be heard there. All rooms have balconies, and you can eat in the shady garden in front of the restaurant with the beach before you. Room without private bath c. £7.

One address to be recommended is at 4, Daskaloyanni St., directly in the centre (to the west of the main road). Attractive courtyard, also some three-bedded rooms.

There are freshly renovated rooms for c. £10 in the **Dionysos** Restaurant on the main road.

Neapolis Rooms are down on the beach (next door to the Galaxy Restaurant).

• READERS' TIPS: "**Dictamo** Rooms were recommended to us by other travellers. House no. 14 on the road to the beach, on the right hand side. The rooms face onto

the back courtyard, and are very attractive. Bath/WC. Cost c. £10 . . ."
"**Pension Calypso** on the road to the beach was absolutely super. DR with balcony costs c. £16. Friendly proprietress."

• CAMPING PALEOCHORA: about 20 mins. from the centre. A simple area of bare rock directly on a long shingle beach. Shade offered by low but spreading olive trees. Sanitation in working order, small restaurant with a fine view of the Paleochora peninsula. Cost per person £2, tent £1, car slightly less. Can be

reached from the village by going to the back of the peninsula along the long eastern side (signposted from the centre). Open April to October. Tel. 0823/41225.
The site is not recommended for those who dislike discos; the **disco** here goes on to 3 a.m. But at the same time, it is one of the nicest on Crete.

— ★ —

• LONE CAMPERS: very frequent sight on the long sandy beach, despite the notices which clearly state "camping and nudism forbidden". The favourite place is at the southern end of the sandy beach, where the slope climbs up to the former castle. There are also two showers on the beach here, too. Another favourite location is

among the tamarisks behind the beach. The further north you go, the quieter it is (and there is less chance of being awakened by the police).
There are also some tents pitched over on the other side of the village, on the way to the camping site.

Food

The charm of Paleochora is visibly enhanced in the evenings. Everyone sits in the tavernas on the *main road,* which is then closed to vehicle traffic. Another focus of activity has developed on the eastern side of the peninsula over the last few years, where a kind of *shore promenade* with benches and lighting has been created.

ON THE MAIN ROAD
• **Savvas**: one of the oldest tavernas in the village; **the** village taverna, because it is centrally situated by the town hall (next to the kiosk). Good Greek salad.

• **Dionysos**: the market leader. Recently renovated and a little more expensive.

PROMENADE/EASTERN SIDE
• **Argo**: rather smarter and more expensive; Wiener Schnitzel and Cordon Bleu steaks.

• **Paralia**: favourite place to eat fish.

• **Pelican**: on the harbour front, where the boats to Agia Roumeli and Gavdos cast off. Also traditional good fish dishes.

MISCELLANEOUS
• **Niki**: on the road to the beach. Good pizzas, but a lot of traffic here.

• **Galaxias**: down on the beach, diagonally across from Elman Apartments. Worth a visit at lunchtime; food only lukewarm in the evenings.

• **Stavros**: simple taverna with good food from the charcoal grill. In a side alley to the west of the crossroads, where the buses stop.

• BREAKFAST CAFES: Muesli is available in almost every café. Most of the kafenia are situated around the crossroads where the buses stop. The **Samaria** café bar on the beach road (several houses on from the Interkreta Travel Agency) offers a satisfying "Special Omelette"; friendly service here.

Nightlife

The centre of nightlife is situated around the crossroads where the buses stop during the day. After a cocktail, it is worth your while to make your way to the camping site, which has one of the nicest open-air discotheques in Crete.

• **O Phinikas**: nice café bar with a slim palm tree, at the lower end of the road which leads directly to the beach.

• **Jetée**: on the beach, next to Elman Apartments. This restaurant formerly belonged to the two Irishmen, John and Vince (see Chania) and is now an agreeable cocktail bar, run by friendly Sifis (Joseph). Coloured lights create a cosy atmosphere in the garden where the tamarisk branches hang low towards the ground. Very large selection of cocktails; open evenings from 9.30 p.m.

• **Paleochora Club**: disco on the camping site (see under accommodation). Open air disco with moonlight and sea view. Groups sometimes play here. Drinks from £1.

• **Studio Club**: discotheque on the beach road, opposite Elman Apartments. Air conditioning, long bar and small dance floor. Drinks from £1.

• **Attikon**: open-air cinema behind the beach; turn off the beach road into the little alley by the school (signposted "Cinema").

• **Billiard Hall**: on the road which leads directly to the beach, diagonally across from the Polydoros Hotel.

Sightseeing

The nicest quarter of the village is to the south of the little harbour mole, where the boats to Sougia, Agia Roumeli and Chora Sfakion tie up; that is to say, directly beneath the castle. Fishermen, farmers and chickens live in the little alleys with their whitewashed houses and turquoise blue window shutters. Most of them once lived on the island of Gavdos, until they could no longer scratch out a living from the barren soil of the island.

Selinos Castle: The southern continuation of the main road, past the decorative church and the free-standing bell tower, goes up onto a completely level plateau. There is also a path up the slope from the residential quarter mentioned above.

Selinos Castle was founded by the Venetians in 1282; today, only a couple of windswept tamarisks, a weather station operated by the Civil Aviation Authority and oregano by the bushel can be found within the ruined fortification wall. There is a beautiful view of the village, the coast and the large, new *harbour* which has been built on the foremost tip of the peninsula.

▶ **Bathing:** The long *sandy beach* on the western side of Paleochora is among the best on the south coast. In spite of the bustle, it is never overcrowded because of its length. There are a couple of showers at the beginning of the beach, and surf boards can also be hired.

The long, seldom frequented beach of Anidri can be seen a little further to the east, and can be reached on foot in about one hour. (See also the chapter "Hiking" - from Paleochora to Sougia). Boat excursions go there every day.

There are more little beaches on the road to Gialos (4.75 miles). See Paleochora/Surrounding Area.

Two different worlds meet headlong

Paleochora/Surrounding Area

Gialos: Unattractive sprawling settlement 4 miles west of Paleochora; countless hothouses which are used mostly for the production of cucumbers and tomatoes. An asphalt road runs along the flat coastline with its cliffs, barren rocky scrub and beaches of piled-up shingle. Shortly before Gialos there is a beautiful, soft *beach with sand dunes*, on a landspit with tapering juniper trees which juts far out into the sea. There are private rooms for rent here, too. The asphalt road changes into an extremely dusty track at Gialos, along which the lorries transport the harvest.

Hikers will find an excursion here worthwhile. Gialos is the point of departure for the fine hike over to the beach at Elafonisi and to the Monastery of Chrisoskalitissa.

Anidri: A handful of houses with lush gardens just over 3 miles east from Paleochora. Just 20 people live there today, and there is neither a taverna nor a kafenion. From the camping site, a narrow driveway leads slightly uphill through a ravine, and later through olive groves.

The history of the village is interesting. Anidri was founded by two brothers by the name of Vardoulakis from Chora Sfakion. They had to flee from their home village because of a blood feud. All of the inhabitants of Anidri today are descendants of the two brothers and related to one another.

A short distance below the central gravel square is the church of *Agios Georgios*, where the frescoes have been damaged (reputedly by the Turks, who put out the eyes of the figures in them). Unfortunately, the church is mostly locked, but the key can be acquired in the neighbourhood.

The fine beach of Anidri is a 30-minute walk down a footpath.

Azogires

A worthwhile destination in the vicinity. This quiet mountain village lies to the north east of Paleochora, high up in the mountains between lush green olives, cypresses and pines. (Be careful, though. There are two villages named Azogires near Paleochora!) Water is plentiful there. A walk to the little stream at the back end of the village down below the road is particularly worthwhile. It forms little pools and waterfalls between enormous boulders and tall plane trees; a fine place to refresh yourself.

About 1.25 miles above the village there are the deep caves which were once inhabited by several dozen monks; they served as missionaries in Asia Minor before spending the rest of their lives here. One of the caves contains what are reputed to be their bones. Their leader was St. John who lived as a hermit on the Akrotiri Peninsula (see also there under *Monastery of Gouverneto*).

• HOW TO GET THERE: Go back along the road from Paleochora in the direction of the north coast for about 2 miles. Then take the turn-off to the right - this is not an asphalt road and is steep and bumpy for a distance of about 3.25 miles. The road is soon going to be made up, however, and the taverna proprietors are greatly looking forward to this event.

• ACCOMMODATION/FOOD: The simple **Hotel A** is situated at the back end of the village. There are two tavernas at the entrance to the village. The **Park Café** has a fountain and enjoys the advantage of having a better position. At **Sofia's** you can have a glance into the lovingly arranged interior; photos, paintings and paper money from every country in the world decorate the walls. Sofia will tell you proudly that her son Antonis had five restaurants in Chicago. Today, he is back on Crete and runs the village hotel. The service is good in both tavernas, even if Sofia is very keen on custom. Her omelettes are famous, and there are also thick soups and supposedly chemical-free wine from the barrel.

Another original place is the **Disco River** on the stream mentioned above. A wooden platform has been built over the water, and according to the sign the disco only opens from 10.00 p.m. onwards. But even during the day you can climb down the few steps there and enjoy this relaxing place.

Cave of Agios Ioannis: A driveway leads up to the left in front of the Park Café. The first few yards are very steep, but the rest of the way presents no problems for vehicles, and ends about 1.25 miles on at the food of a rock wall. 50 yards on there is a sign with an arrow, indicating the way to the cave. The path leads to a cleft in the rock and then down to a kind of platform between the huge rock walls. The entrance to the cavern yawns on the right. It is a huge cleft between two walls, which touch at the top and form a cave towards the bottom. You can climb down via three steep and wobbly ladders; extreme care is necessary. It is only for experienced climbers and entirely at your own risk! There is a simple altar on the first platform, but it is not possible to climb further on down without a torch. Light only penetrates weakly down from the opening in the rock high up above.

Paleochora/Hiking

There are many ideal opportunities for hiking, because of the central position of Paleochora in the mountainous south-west corner of Crete.

There are some fine possibilities for hiking along the coast from Paleochora to the beach at *Elafonisi* and the Monastery of *Chrisoskalitissa* (in a westwards direction from Gialos, c. 6.5 hours), and via the ancient site at *Lissos* to the little coastal village of *Sougia* (in an eastwards direction, c. 4.5 hours). Numerous isolated places for bathing can be found along both routes.

Hiking from Paleochora to Elafonisi Beach/Monastery of Chrisoskalitissa

Route: Paleochora - Gialos - Chapel of Agios Ioannis - Elafonisi Beach - Monastery of Chrisoskalitissa (see sketch map on page 468, **hike no. 1**)
Duration of hike: about 5.5 hours from Gialos (just under 5 miles west of Paleochora) to Elafonisi Beach, and 6.5 hours to the Monastery of Chrisoskalitissa.

Description of the route: Point of departure is the sprawling settlement of *Gialos*, just under 5 miles west of Paleochora. An asphalt road leads up to it, and you should try to get there by hitchhiking or by taxi (it is an unfortunate fact that the two local taxi drivers turn up their noses, when asked to go only as far as Gialos).

In Gialos itself, keep a distance of about 200-300 yards from the water and go past the numerous hothouses. You only get nearer to the water when the large shingle bay comes into sight. The path to Elafonisi (marked in red) begins shortly behind this, at the end of a second small bay which adjoins the first (the red markers continue to the end of the path). On the right hand side there is a white villa, the last house before the walls of rock.

The path now climbs steeply for a period of about half an hour, and the sweat finally gets the chance to dry off when you reach a knoll. There is a wonderful view back over the hothouses and Paleochora in the far distance. Shortly beyond the knoll, the path descends to a small cove, overgrown with oleander. Follow the red markers and climb down to the cove. After that, the path ascends once again to a hillock. Half an hour later (80 minutes from Gialos), the Bay of Elafonisi comes into sight. It would be nice simply to row over there in a boat at this minute; however, the markers lead you along the path high up behind the rocky cape (*Cape Krios*) to the Chapel of *Agios loannis*, already easily visible in the distance, which is 1.5 hours away from Gialos. There is a *watering place* nearby, and the path with the markers continues from it. You now climb the mountain ridge and arrive at a rusty fence of wire netting, half an hour on from the chapel; the path goes through an opening in it. Shortly afterwards, you can see Elafonisi once again, and even the Monastery of Chrisoskalitissa. The thinly-marked but easily recognisable way goes further on up the mountain ridge, and reaches a plateau about three quarters of an hour away from Ag. Ioannis. The two domes of a transmitting station can be seen further inland. After a while, the path descends into a gully containing red-brown clay, and then goes uphill again. You now come to the edge of a kind of *precipice,* with the bed of a stream deep below it. The path begins to descend at this point. Care is now necessary: about 3 minutes on from the edge of the precipice, you come to a *place with two paths leading away from it.* The path which leads in the same direction that you have just come from goes downhill to the bed of the stream, and continues on to the village of *Sklavopoula*, which is situated further inland! The path to Elafonisi leads off at a sharp angle to the left, and is hardly recognisable. Both of these paths are actually marked, but the path and markers to Elafonisi are difficult to identify (we erected a pyramid of stones). 15 minutes later you reach the edge of a further precipice, at which the path descends to the *Elafonisi Plain,* which is clearly visible. The markers end at two little goatherds' huts. Several paths cross the plain, but there is no longer any problem involved in getting to the beach, because everything is spread out before you. The hike from Ag. Ioannis to the plain takes about 2.75 hours, that from the beginning of the plain to the beach just under 3/4 hour, and from the beach to the Monastery of Chrisoskalitissa 1 hour, whence there is a bus connection once every day to Kastelli and the north coast.

For information on Elafonisi Beach and the Monastery of Chrisoskalitissa see page 466.

Hiking from Paleochora to Sougia

An ideal introduction to hiking on Crete, because it does not take too long and leads you through diversified terrain. In addition, there are good bus connections both at the point of departure and at the end of the hike.

Route: Paleochora - Cape Flomes - Lissos - Sougia (sketch map page 468, **hike no. 2**)
Duration of hike: a total of just under four and a half hours, provided you are not carrying baggage (Paleochora - Lissos 3 hours, Lissos - Sougia 1.5 hours).

Description of the route: On leaving the centre of Paleochora, you proceed first of all along the eastern side of the peninsula to the *camping site* (15 minutes). From there, a wide motor track runs along the water; on the right hand side there is a shingle beach, while rocks rise up on the left. The motor track comes to an end 30 minutes on from the centre of Paleochora and continues as a footpath (there are coloured markers and stone pyramids). After a walk of 40 minutes, especial care is needed: here, a short way before the end of the bay, there is a clearly recognisable yellow arrow on a stone; this points up to the left and indicates the path to Sougia. When the arrow is followed, continuous yellow markers are soon visible. The path itself is not so easy to make out, as it passes through sharp-edged rocks and scrub. 1.75 hours away from Paleochora you reach a place where the path continues on over rocks, without any vegetation. Erosion is very noticeable here. The path goes uphill for about half an hour shortly after this, and crosses Cape Flomes, which juts out far into the sea and falls away vertically into it. About two and a half hours away from Paleochora you come to a small plateau; there is a fine view of the Lefka Ori and the peninsula of Paleochora with the sea lapping around it. A motor track is now reached, and this divides about 20 minutes later. Neither of the two motor tracks from the crossroads should be followed, but you should continue *straight on* (an arrow made up of stones points in this direction). Now, there is a lot of colour: red, yellow and light green markers indicate the path that leads up to Lissos, a walk of 30 minutes. You will even find a small wooden signpost indicating the direction to Paleochora and Lissos.

LISSOS is a green oasis in a narrow valley which has abundant water. The ruins of an ancient harbour settlement with a famous healing spring and a Sanctuary of Aesklepios have been excavated here. The latter was still in use in the Roman Period.

There are numerous ruins scattered around today, but much is overgrown with scrub and bushes. It is also difficult terrain to negotiate, being largely under cultivation and fenced off. The latter also applies to the Sanctuary of Aesklepios, where a Roman mosaic floor is said to have been discovered (there is a sign here which says "Archaeological Site of Lissos"). Some ruins are visible in the cliffs on the western side of the bay, and these are apparently tombs. The beach of large shingle at Lissos is very polluted with tar.

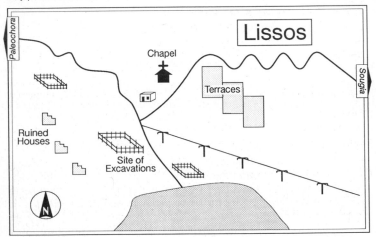

The way to Sougia does not continue along the water, but runs in a northerly direction past a Byzantine *chapel* and a *white house*. (Perhaps this belongs to the custodian of the site?) You only recognise both buildings when you are right in front of them. The path now leads up to several terraces, but cannot be seen very clearly. Pay attention to the markers here: you should come upon a coloured marker or pyramid of stones at least every 5-7 minutes. If not, stand still, have a look around and try to locate them. The path passes hard by the rocks, often under the branches of bushes, and is very narrow (do not walk over the terraces). After climbing for 20 minutes, the path descends again until it reaches a dried-up stream bed with overhanging rock walls in places, a further 20 minutes on. After you have walked down the bed of the stream for yet another 20 minutes, the harbour complex at Sougia will suddenly appear in front of you. The village is about a further 5 minutes' walk from here.

From Paleochora to Sougia

With your own vehicle: There is no direct coastal road in this part of the south coast. You could take the route via Azogires, although it is in bad condition. A better plan, however, is to drive the few miles up to *Kandanos* and then along the fine stretch of road via Temenia (about 17 miles; the turn-off from the main through road is signposted, near the waterworks).

At first the road winds sharply upwards, and there is a fine view of Kandanos and the mountains. The road is still unmade for some miles between *Vamvakades* and *Temenia*, but work has already begun there. Buses also go along this route. The villages along the road have hardly been affected by tourism. *Temenia* lies in a fertile hollow; it has a lemonade factory and there are some rooms to rent there. The road from the north coast to Sougia (details under Chania/Hinterland, see page 440) is met at *Rodoviani*. There is a superb view from here out over the long green valley, where the vegetation is luxuriant in places, in the direction of Sougia.

By boat: A wonderful trip along almost sheer, grey to rust-red walls of rock, especially on the second half of the journey. There are no villages or houses at all, just a rugged wilderness of rocks.

It is clear, from the dark tide marks high above the waterline, that the sea level must have been at least 16-20 feet higher in earlier times. This is an indication that the land level rose in western Crete in the 6th century AD, probably as a result of strong earthquakes.

Sougia

An almost unreal atmosphere here after the turmoil and bustle in Paleohora. A handful of houses, thrust into a wide rocky bay, with a long beach of shingle and grey sand in front of it.

An absolute stillness prevails; there is not even the shrieking of cicadas, just the occasional braying of a donkey in the valley, echoing back several times from the high rock walls.

Although it can be reached by a road from the north coast, Sougia seems almost cut off from the outside world. There are no hotels, but instead almost every house has rooms for rent, and camping freely presents no problem. This latter fact has, of course, not remained a secret, and Sougia has developed into a favourite meeting place for mostly young people, some of whom stay on the beach for weeks or pitch their tents in the shade of a massive carob tree on the terrace-like mountain slope. Accordingly, the relaxing peace and quiet of the daytime is destroyed at night by the inevitable disco, which blasts away until at least 3.00 a.m.

In short, this is a village worth visiting, if you are looking for a little place close to Nature, but in spite of that do not wish to forego contact with people or a little diversionary entertainment . . .

CONNECTIONS

• **Bus**: twice daily 2 x from and to Chania. A beautiful ride along the flanks of the Lefka Ori.

• **Boat**: The two passenger boats Marina and Neptune make the trip to Sougia every morning from Paleochora, and then go on to Agia Roumeli (on Mondays and Thursdays, however, the Neptune goes on to the Island of Gavdos). They make the trip in the opposite direction in the late afternoon. The Neptune leaves for Gavdos every Monday and Thursday at 8.45 a.m. Those wishing to go to Loutro or Chora Sfakion should change at Agia Roumeli. Fare: to Agia Roumeli and Paleochora £2.00 each destination, c. £4 to Gavdos. **Tickets** are available at a kiosk on the beach road or just before departure at the harbour (western end of the bay).

Accommodation

• **Pikilassos**: the only guest house in the village. On the right hand side of the road which leads directly into the village. DR costs c. £9, a three-bedded room £10. Boat trips are offered here, and it is also possible to change money and telephone abroad. Tel. 0823/51242.

• **Zorbas**: a house standing alone on the shore road in the direction of the harbour (next to the church). Suitable for families with children; some rooms are spacious with shower/WC. Self-catering is a possibility here, and there is also a bar and breakfast room. About £9 for a DR.

• **Filoxenia**: taverna at the eastern exit from the village, only a few yards from the beach. Lisa Papaderos rents out these agreeable rooms with a fine view at a price of £7 for a DR.

• **Lissos**: right behind Filoxenia. Modern, well-furnished rooms. Tel. 0823/51341.

• **Paradisos**: only a short way from the latter, on the dried-up river-bed. Friendly establishment with a terrace full of plants. Cost c. £7. Tel. 0825/31359. There are other inviting possibilities here too, eg **Vangelis**.

— ★ —

• INDIVIDUAL CAMPERS: There is no camping site, but camping on the beach is tolerated by the inhabitants. The places to pitch tents under the few tamarisks are quickly taken, but up on the terraces of the slope there are secluded little places under the shady olive and carob trees, between the old stone walls. In addition, there is a super view of the whole bay and the sea! The old settlement of Soyia was reputedly located here 400 years ago.

Food

• **"If you want"**: large self-service restaurant favoured by young people. Food not bad, we even had beef. Music is provided by loudspeakers. Maria, the much-loved proprietress and Stavros with the twirling moustaches also rent out rooms for c. £9.

• **Filoxenia**: old established taverna in the eastern part of the village, a few yards from the beach.

• **Omikron**: right on the beach. At present, Jan from Holland runs this café with the shady reed awning. There are various types of cakes, delicious salads (including a potato, rice and fruit salad), muesli, and all kinds of other things that can scarcely be found in the Greek tavernas. Of course, the lemonade comes from Temenia. Open from morning to evening, and a favourite meeting place.

• **Café Bar Maria**: Elderly Maria has run this place for many years. She now employs helpers. Also has rooms to let.

• **Lotos**: newly opened, on the beach. Breakfast, muesli, cakes, pizzas etc are accompanied by good music.

• **Bla-bla**: diagonally behind the Omikron. Music, breakfast, drinks, a place to sit around in . . .

• **Poliphimos**: in the eastern part of the bay, directly on the beach. You can sit under a reed awning here, gaze out over the glass-clear sea and listen to pure music. Omelettes, fried eggs, fruit salad, freshly-pressed orange juice and other light refreshments are available. The name of the bar refers to the giant Polyphemus, whose cave is nearby to the east. The best thing to do is let Yannis, the owner of the café, tell you the story on the spot.

— ★ —

• **Disco Alabama**: to the east of the village on the dried-up river-bed. **The** meeting place in the evenings, but a disadvantage if you have taken quarters on the eastern edge of Sougia and happen to want to sleep.

▶ **Sightseeing:** The little *church* on the shore road is worth a short visit. It stands on the site of an early Byzantine basilica. Unfortunately the well-preserved and valuable mosaic floor is no longer in situ. A walk of about 30 minutes brings you to the little cruciform-vaulted church of *Agia Irini*, which probably dates from the 12th century. There is also a *spring* under a shady plane tree behind the village, in the rock wall to the west. The best plan is to let someone at Omikron explain the way there to you.

▶ **Bathing:** The beach of large shingle stones is about 0.6 miles long. There is hardly any shade apart from that afforded by a few thin tamarisks, where the campers have settled. There even used to be some fresh water showers here.

Unquestionably the nicest place to bathe is the shingle bay at the east end of the beach. There are little caves and shady spots surrounded by picturesquely weathered rocks and overhanging precipices, where you can get away from it all. As nudism is commonly (but not exclusively!) practised here, the local people of Sougia call this location the *"Bay of Pigs"* . . .

A freshwater stream is said to feed into the bay, hence the rich ungderwater vegetation.

Agia Roumeli: All details on this small village at the exit from the famous Samaria Gorge can be found on page 440.

Loutro

A village of winding alleys with about 15 whitewashed houses and bumpy paths. The whole thing is thrust into a deep bay between the sea and the rock wall, which rises immediately behind it.

Those who wander off the "shore promenade" can suddenly find themselves at one of the little farmsteads and, after a few more yards, at the foot of the low hilly ridge that separates the village from the next bay. You can climb up via a couple of narrow paths, have a look at the ruined castle, go to the tip of the rocky cape, or even hike up to the mountain village of Anopolis; the rocky surroundings of

View from Anopolis down to Loutro

Loutro tempt you to such excursions.

The curious thing here: there is not a single road connecting Loutro to the outside world. The high, sheer cliffs hinder any attempt at building a road, and the tiny village is only reached by boat. In spite of this, there is a lot going on here. Tents are pitched on the cliffs around the village, almost every house has rooms to rent, and the narrow shingle beach in the middle of the village is mostly quite crowded.

All in all, a friendly little place, where it is certainly possible to spend a couple of days.

CONNECTIONS

• **Boat**: Loutro-Chora Sfakion 3-5 x daily, Loutro-Ag. Roumeli likewise. More boats if necessary. In addition, there is a boat at 8.00 a.m. every Saturday from Loutro to Chora Sfakion and on to the Island of Gavdos, from the middle of June to the end of September.

• **On foot**: There is a way downhill from the mountain village of Anopolis (reached by the asphalt road from Chora Sfakion) to Loutro. The walk takes about 1.5 hrs.

• ACCOMMODATION: There is a new hotel called **Porto Loutro** directly on the little shingle beach to the east. Tel. 0825/91227. The tavernas on the shore all have rooms to rent. Prices range from £7-9 according to whether there is a sea view, private shower/WC etc. Those who want absolute quiet can try the last house in the eastern

part of the village. But only take a room with a window on the front.
The rooms at the first restaurant on the quay where the boats moor are very acceptable; small shower/WC, light-coloured wood furniture and lino flooring, balcony and
fine sea view for c. £9. Rooms without a balcony but with a view of the neighbouring
house c. £8. No. 12 is recommended. There is a kind of terrace on top of the house.
Individual camping has been tolerated up till now in various places around Loutro,
including on the rocky cape by the village and on a long sandy beach quite a distance away to the east, in the direction of Chora Sfakion. This beach can be seen
clearly from the boat.
• OTHER INFORMATION: **Money can be changed** at No. 13 on the shore promenade (50 yards from the quay). Small **grocer's shop**, canoes can be hired (c. £1 per
hour). If you wish to rent one for a whole day, you should negotiate the price by bargaining; worthwhile in order to get round into Marble Bay (see below).

Bathing: There are several possibilities. There is a narrow shingle
beach right in the village, with tavernas directly behind it. So everything you need is nearby.
There is a narrow hiking track a little above the coastline through
the rocks, and scree-covered slopes to the large sandy beach between
Loutro and Chora Sfakion. The walk takes about 1 hour.
Some smaller beaches can also be found on the other side of the village,
behind the mountain ridge. They can be reached on foot or by boat.

Loutro/Surrounding Area

The low mountain ridge behind the houses offers itself for walks.
Countless remains of old buildings, low walls and terraces are scattered
around, with single olive trees and the occasional tent between them.
Out in front on the promontory there is the white *Chapel of Sotiros
Christou*, and between the grey-black rocks there are fragrant herb
bushes and patches of rust-red earth. A ruined castle is situated up
on the bluff. Its rounded towers give it the appearance of a true castle
of the Middle Ages, and next to it shaggy sheep with tinkling bells
graze in the shade. Otherwise, there is not a sound to be heard . . .

Finix Bay: It is about half an hour from Loutro to the next bay on the
west side of the mountain ridge. This is said to have been the harbour
of ancient Anopolis. The Hotel/Restaurant Phoenix is superbly
situated here, directly on the sea and by itself in the middle of a rocky
wilderness. Sheep lick salt from the cliffs, and up above there is a
dazzling white church. A place for relaxation. The way there is
signposted from Loutro.

• ACCOMMODATION/FOOD: **Phoenix**, attractive terrace under trees, simple whitewashed rooms with painted concrete floors. Very small cupboards, but new beds.
Narrow balcony towards the sea. Almost idyllic! Cost c. £7 for a DR. Tel. 0825/91257.

• OTHER INFORMATION: There are kayaks for hire; you could reach the mouth of
the Aradena Gorge, among other places, in one of these (see below).

Marble Bay: Going over the next hill you come to a larger rocky bay
with olive trees, a shingle beach and flat rock slabs in the water.

Even in the high season, only a handful of people find their way here. They are mostly rucksack tourists, who have accomplished the sweaty march from Loutro with all their baggage. Nikos lives here from his goat and a couple of hundred olive trees.

• ACCOMMODATION/FOOD: **Niko's Paradise**, everyone gets together in the taverna run by Niko and his mother. He recently built an extension. Rooms cost c. £6.

There is another very fine bathing cove a distance to the west of Marble Bay at the exit from the deep **Aradena Gorge** (c. 80 mins. from Loutro).

Chora Sfakion

Focal point of Samaria tourism; colourful history; Glikanera, the "sweet waters"

An introspective little fishing harbour, surrounded by the rugged coastal mountains of Sfakia.

The peace is abruptly interrupted several times a day, when the over-crowded boats from Agia Roumeli bring exhausted people who have "conquered the Samaria Gorge" to their buses, of which there are often dozens waiting here. Thanks to its convenient position near the Samaria Gorge, Chora Sfakion has almost become a village where you just pass through. Most visitors are in a hurry and only a few of them cast a glance at the village. At first sight, it would seem that there are no opportunities for bathing here.

Those who stay here, however, spend their evening sitting in the taverna passage on the semi-circular bay which contains the harbour, gazing into the gently gurgling water or at the cars which occasionally pass among the tables of the tavernas with only inches to spare. The few steeply-rising alleys are quickly explored, and perhaps you will want to go to bed early, in order to be fresh for the area around Chora Sfakion, for this is what is attractive here. Just three roads lead out of Chora Sfakion, thus the mountains and the coast can only be explored on foot or by boat. It is a walk of between half an hour and one hour to the beaches, and a walk of more than two hours up to the little mountain village of Anopolis, so you should not be out of condition. A highlight, of course, is an excursion to Gavdos. A boat makes this trip to the southernmost island in Europe several times every weekend . . .

View of Chora Sfakion and the barren south coast of Sfakia

FROM DASKALOYANNIS TO THE ALLIES

The little village at the foot of the Lefka Ori has a colourful history. The rough, inaccessible mountains of Sfakia could never be completely taken by the succession of overlords and conquerors of Crete. This is the reason why the Venetians built their massive fortification of Frangokastello only a few miles to the east of Chora Sfakion on the coastal plain.

During the dark period of the Turkish occupation Sfakia was a centre of Cretan resistance. One of the most important leaders here was Yannis Vlachos who, because of his intelligence and prudence, was nicknamed **Daskaloyannis** - Yannis the teacher. He placed all of his not inconsiderable fortune at the disposal of the revolt and had contacts with the Russians, whom he hoped would render assistance against the Turks. But the Turks managed to lure him to Iraklion, under the pretence of an offer of peace negotiations; there, he was skinned alive in front of his own brother, who lost his senses as a result. There is a monument to him in Anopolis, the village of his birth (see Chora Sfakion/Surrounding Area).

During the Second World War, after the German attack on Crete, the last Allied troops went on board ships which had been hastily assembled at Chora Sfakion, and were evacuated to Africa. An inconspicuous memorial on the harbour front recalls this operation today.

CONNECTIONS

• **Bus**: About 4 x daily to Chania, only once daily to Plakias/Agia Galini (in the afternoons, the bus fills quickly!), also once from and to Anopolis (shuttle service - afternoons up, early morning down). The large bus park, where the tourist coaches also wait for those walking through the gorge, is situated at the east end of the harbour promenade.

— ★ —

• **Boat**: Chora Sfakion is the point of convergence for boat traffic on the Sfakia coast. Two companies operate along the stretch to the west. The Sfakia goes c. 3 x daily via Loutro to Agia Roumeli and back, 2 x weekly to Paleochora (stops in Loutro and Agia Roumeli).

The Anendyk Company has four boats (Samaria, Sofia, Ag. Roumeli and Marina) and operates services via Loutro to Agia Roumeli at least 6 x daily. Also once via Loutro, Ag. Roumeli and Sougia over to Paleochora. More departures are added to the timetable if demand is there. Tickets at the kiosk on the harbour.

A boat goes to the island of Gavdos every Friday, Saturday and Sunday at 9.00 a.m. (departs from Loutro at 8.30 a.m.).

Accommodation

• **Xenia**: guest house at the landing place which has a friendly proprietor by the name of Panos. Rooms of varying quality, from very simple, with thin wooden walls where you can hear every noise your neighbour makes, to very acceptable rooms with a nice sea view. Cost between £8-10 for a DR. No private bathrooms. Tel. 0825/91202.

• **Sophia**: friendly place in the alley parallel to and behind the harbour promenade; a lot of rucksack tourists. Spacious rooms with dark-coloured wooden furniture and lino flooring. Very good shower/toilet. Cost c. £9 with a sea view (on the top floor), and £8 without.
Tel. 0825/91259.

— ★ —

• PRIVATE ROOMS: any number of these. The most expensive are at the tavernas on the harbour front, costing between £9-12.

— ★ —

• FOOD: The tavernas are all congregated on the harbour front - we were not able to pick out a favourite here. A walk along the rows of tables is like running the gauntlet; the waiters loudly proclaim the excellence of their fish or "fried chicken" ...

• **Stavris**: a larger building at the western end of the alley parallel to the waterfront. Decent rooms with a view to the west over the coastline and the sea, floor tiles. Cost with private shower/WC just under £10.

• **Panorama**: on the forested hill to the east of the village, directly on the road to Chania and Agia Galini. Fantastic position above a steep-sided rocky bay, and when the sea is rough the wind whistles through the passages just like in a haunted castle. Spacious rooms with own shower/WC, wooden furniture, balcony. Unfortunately the beds are of very bad quality. The taverna on the ground floor is worth a visit and there is a terrace on the edge of the cliff. Cost c. £9-10 for a DR. Tel. 0825/91296.

Those who want to stay right in the centre should walk upwards from the Hotel Stavri; there are several quiet and pleasant possibilities there.

• NIGHTLIFE: **Disko Cobra**, at the eastern end of the harbour promenade, down from the large bus park. Not very much room there and noisy, too. Normally there is not much going on there.

• OTHER INFORMATION: The little **OTE telephone office** and the **Post Office** are at the western end of the alley parallel to and behind the harbour promenade. **Money can be changed** in the same alley at the supermarket and at the Hotel Stavris; stamps can be bought at the Hotel Sophia. Books and newspapers are obtainable in the souvenir shop on the harbour front, and money can also be changed there.

Sightseeing: There are the sparse remains of the walls of a former *fort* on the forested hill to the east of the village. The ascent is worthwhile for the view out over the deep blue sea, the village and the barren, grey-brown mountain ridges.

Down below on the road there is a macabre *monument* with the smashed-in tops of the skulls of Sfakiot resistance fighters.

▶ **Bathing:** There is a semi-circular *shingle beach* directly at the harbour; canoes can be hired there.

A very nice *shingle bay* lies between high rock walls with several shady caves about 20 minutes to the west of the village. It can be reached via the road to Anopolis, from which a path leads down to it.

The highlight, however, is the sand/shingle beach called *Glikanera* (fresh water), a good 800 yards long. It is surrounded by almost vertical steep rock walls and is about an hour to the west of Chora Sfakion on foot. It takes its name from the subterranean springs which bubble up in places from beneath the scree. A small taverna has established itself there during the tourist season, and offers simple meals, cold drinks and breakfast. Camping is permitted on the beach, but shade is in short supply. The beach can be reached via the road to Anopolis; a stony path marked in red leads down at the first sharp bend, when the road goes away from the water towards the slope. The path goes further on to Loutro: see under *Hiking*. For those who find the walk too tiring there is a boat connection from Chora Sfakion 2 x daily in the season.

The rocks in this area have been completely hollowed out above the waterline. It would be a lot of fun to go along here by boat.

From Chora Sfakion to the north coast: this is a grand journey, particularly where the first stretch is concerned. The road winds tortuously up into the barren mountain slopes in unbelievable hairpin bends, and there are constant fine views. Later, the road crosses the *Askifou plateau*. For further details on this route see under Vrises page 394.

There is a wonderful view into the White Mountains from Anopolis

Chora Sfakion/Surrounding Area

Anopolis

Extensive scattered settlement on a plateau high above Chora Sfakion. There is a fantastic view of the White Mountains from between the olive trees, the pastures enclosed by low stone walling and thin vines.

An asphalt road winds up the 7.5 miles from Chora Sfakion in steep curves, and one fantastic panorama follows the other. The journey takes a good two and a half hours on foot but is not really worthwhile because it is asphalt all the way. On the other hand, the hike from Anopolis via Aradena and Agios Ioannis to Agia Roumeli or down to Loutro (see below) is very worthwhile. Anopolis is said to have been an important city in antiquity. Its harbour was reputedly where the Phoenix Restaurant stands today (see Loutro/Phoenix Bay).

There are several tavernas, kafenia and private rooms in the village. At the west end of the village, on the square, there is the *Monument of Daskaloyannis*, the most famous resistance fighter in Sfakia.

• CONNECTIONS: There is a single bus which leaves Chora Sfakion at around 4.00 p.m. It only goes back down from Anopolis in the mornings at around 6.30 a.m. (1988). The best plan is to drive up and walk down.

• ACCOMMODATION/FOOD: The very first house is a **café restaurant**, from the terrace of which there are wonderful views. Amusing proprietor with old photos of his ancestors in the inside room. Two hundred yards on there is the newly-built **Ta Tria Adelphia** which has the best rooms. There are more kafenia on the **village square**, a good 0.6 miles further on.

• HIKING: **From Anopolis to Loutro**. The route to the south begins from the village square with the monument to Daskaloyannis. After leaving the last houses behind you, the way continues up a small hillock (c. 15 mins.) and then descends steeply via a firm but stony mule-track to Loutro. The view of Loutro far below is fantastic! (see sketch map on page 468, **hike no. 4**)

From Anopolis via Aradena to Agia Roumeli: straight on from the square with monument (westwards). This walk is described from the opposite direction under Agia Roumeli.

Chora Sfakion/Hiking

There is a fine coastal hike via Loutro to Agia Roumeli, which lies at the exit from the Samaria Gorge (about 6 hours).

Another interesting hike is from Chora Sfakion via Anopolis, Aradena and Agios Ioannis through the mountains to Agia Roumeli (for a description see under Agia Roumeli).

Coastal Hike from Chora Sfakion to to Agia Roumeli

Route: Chora Sfakion - Agios Stavros - Loutro - Aradena Gorge - Agios Pavlos - Agia Roumeli (see map on page 468, **hike no. 3**).

Duration: a total of 6 hours when lightly loaded (1.75 hours from Chora Sfakion to Loutro, 4.25 hours from Loutro to Agia Roumeli).

Description of the route: The coastal path to Loutro begins just under 30 minutes to the west of Chora Sfakion, at the first hairpin bend in the road to Anopolis. Behind the crash barriers on the side of the road a path (marked in red) leads downhill near to the water. The rock walls towering upwards on the right hand side are almost vertical in places, and on the other side they fall away steeply to the sea. You reach the water 20 minutes later and there is no longer a track, you climb over scree. About 25 minutes after leaving the hairpin bend you come to *Glikanera Beach* (see above under Bathing). The track leads upwards to the right, almost in the form of steps, at the end of the bay. After a short ascent, and about 40 minutes from the asphalt road, you arrive at the Chapel of *Agios Stavros*. The path passes 50 yards to the north of the chapel; soon, Loutro comes into sight and you pass a small bathing cove. At a height of about 120 feet, the way is now marked in red and leads to Loutro, which can be reached in about 1.75 hours from Chora Sfakion. There, you pass through a barred gate and keep left; suddenly you come to Stavros' Taverna by the sea. You have accomplished just under a third of your journey when you arrive in Loutro.

The shortest way over the low ridge of hills to the west, above the houses, begins in the middle of the bay, at the kiosk, where you can buy cigarettes etc. From here, you climb up to the ruins of the castle. When you get to the top, you can soon make out the village of *Livania*, on the mountain to the west. A path follows the 10-kilovolt three-phase power line from the fortress down to *Phoinix Bay* (taverna, hotel - see under Loutro/Surrounding Area). A path leads up from behind the taverna and soon comes to a fence. Go to the right along the fence, until the path divides into two by a tree at the upper right hand corner of the fence. Turn left here (do not go right towards the barred gate; this path leads on into a little ravine). The left hand path leads into the next bay, the so-called *Marble Bay* (taverna/rooms offered by Nikos; see under Loutro/Surrounding Area). Now go along the water's edge until, at the end of the bay, a small flight of steps in the rock leads upwards again (there is a cave at a height of about 60 feet). The path is now marked in yellow; after walking for about 80 minutes from Loutro, you will come to a third bay at the mouth of the steep-walled *Aradena Gorge* (this is crossed by a new bridge, on the way through the mountains via Aradena and Agios Ioannis; see Agia Roumeli/Hiking). This is a very fine bay for bathing.

There is a steep climb lasting about 15 minutes at the end of the bay, for which sureness of foot is essential. From the top, there is a super view over the bay behind and the castle of Loutro. The stretch which follows is not a difficult one, but somewhat monotonous and devoid of shade (red markers). About one and a half hours away from the Aradena Gorge, you will see Agia Roumeli in front of you. You now enter a pine forest, which extends from the slope until just before Agia Roumeli. The path is easily recognised and further marked in red. Occasionally you walk over a carpet of pine needles; there is a sweet pine smell and adequate shade here; a pleasant change. 30 minutes after entering the forest, there is a water cistern (c. 9 feet in diameter, and 3 feet high). 3 minutes later (300 yards on), a path leads off backwards to the right, at a sharp angle, towards Aradena (for a description of the way when approaching from the direction of Agia Roumeli see page 444). When approaching from Loutro, however, the signs indicating the way can hardly be made out. They are on the opposite side of a number of stones, and only visible when approaching from the direction of Agia Roumeli. 20 minutes away from the branching of the paths, the way leads slightly downhill and along over an area of black sand above the *Chapel of Agios Pavlos*. From here, it continues on through sand along the slope (yellow and red markers) and the *Eligias Gorge* is reached after a further 20 minutes' walk. Beyond the gorge, it is advisable to leave the heights and descend to the gravel beach. You will reach the bed of the Samaria River one hour on from the gorge. There is no alternative open to you here, in the early part of the year; you will have to take off your shoes and socks and roll up your trousers, but the cold water does your feet good. Agia Roumeli is reached after about 6 hours of actual hiking.

Island of Gavdos

The southernmost point in Europe (excluding the Canary Islands) is an exceptional white dot on the tourist map. The predominating elements there are the quiet, the wind, and the rocks.

For the most part, Gavdos is a rough skeleton of rock. In particular, the lonely south of the island is completely stony and bare, and the soil has eroded away. However in the interior, especially between the main village of Kastri and Sarakiniko Beach in the north east, there are wild pines, stone pines and other self-sufficient plants growing on the terraced slopes. Good honey is produced using the two types of thyme that grow on Gavdos. The animal world is thinly represented: there are hares, partridges, insects and goats. In the early part of the year and in autumn, Gavdos serves as a resting place for migratory birds during their long flight over the Sea of Libya.

Gavdos is poor. The barren soil can hardly support its inhabitants and most of them have moved over to the "mainland", to Paleochora in particular. Gavdos is said to have been prosperous and fertile in antiquity, with several thousand people living there then. Even in the Middle Ages there were 8,000 inhabitants. Today there are only 50, scattered among the tiny hamlets. Just 1 or 2 families live in some of the "villages". Some of them plant crops for animal feed, and that seems about all that is possible there. There are no asphalt roads, and hardly any vehicles. Electricity is a relatively new phenomenon. (There is a solar installation on Gavdos similar to the one at Agia Roumeli. The one on Gavdos was donated and installed by a company whose headquarters are in Italy).

Gavdos needs tourism, otherwise the island will become a desert. So "yes" to tourism here, but it should be kept under control; our questions were answered with reserve by Yorgo, who owns a piece of ground by the sea. An invasion on a large scale is not desired: the only trump card the island has is its quiet and seclusion. Up till now there has not even been an adequate number of beds for the few strangers who find their way to Gavdos in the summer.The inhabitants are hoping for asphalt roads, more frequent boat connections, and advertising in books, on the television, and on radio.

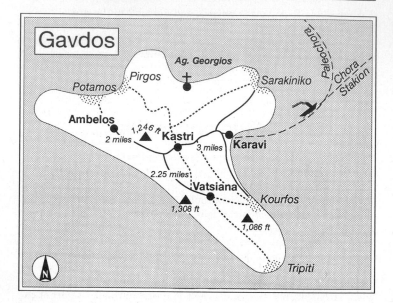

The real hospitality which meets you everywhere is very noticeable. The inhabitants are grateful for any variety in their daily lives. Some of the older inhabitants speak a little German, because German soldiers were stationed here during the last war.

• CONNECTIONS: **Paleochora** and **Chora Sfakion** are the only points of departure for trips to Gavdos (some of the boats stop at Sougia, Agia Roumeli and Loutro, so that it is also possible to cross from there). The duration of the trip depends on the boat used (all types are represented, from a converted fishing boat to a little passenger steamer). Generally however, the trip is quite a bit shorter from Chora Sfakion than from Paleochora.

Departures from Paleochora: once every Monday and Thursday, also Saturdays during the season. Duration of trip 3-4 hours, cost c. £5.
From Chora Sfakion: Fri, Sat and Sun; duration c. 1.5-2.5 hours. Cost c. £4-5.
The boats return on the same afternoon, so that day trips are a possibility. A combination is also possible - eg out from Paleochora on Monday, back to Chora Sfakion on Friday.

IMPORTANT . . .

Crossings to Gavdos are only made from around **the middle of June to the end of September**. In autumn, when the heavy storms set in, Gavdos can only very seldom be reached because of high seas. Choose the summer for a visit, otherwise it may be necessary to stay longer on Gavdos than desired! In emergency you could try to charter a private boat for the return journey.

• TRANSPORT ON GAVDOS: Small tractors with trailers transport the local people and the tourists along the bumpy track from the quay to the main village and to Sarakiniko beach. As of late there are now 3 Volkswagen minibuses on the island. Trips around the island are even offered, if there are enough people interested; about £14 for 10 people. Otherwise transport is by donkey or mule.

— ★ —

• PROVISIONING: The situation is totally dependent upon the deliveries made by boat. The tavernas only offer simple meals and drinks and they often run out of some things and have to wait for the next boat delivery. Readers of the first edition of this book, for example, noted that butter and melons had run out.

There is occasional hoarding.
Water is only supplied by wells, which are scattered around the whole island. **Please be very sparing with this precious commodity!** Electricity is also in short supply, and often the drinks cannot be cooled.

• MEDICAL CARE: a doctor is stationed here during the summer months.

• MAPS: Gavdos is not shown on most of the maps of Crete. The sketch map in this book should be adequate, however. Otherwise Gavdos is shown on the tourist map "Kriti" published by D. & J. Mathioulakis, at a scale of 1:300,000. It can be bought in all souvenir shops and bookshops on Crete. The village of Galana shown on the map does not exist!

Places to go on the island

Gavdos is a good place for hiking, as the inland terrain is only slightly hilly. Only the west consists of steep inaccessible cliffs, and the highest ground on the island is also to be found there (1,300 feet). Otherwise there are several beaches, with *Sarakiniko Beach* of particular note.

In addition there are over 18 churches on Gavdos, most of them unlocked. The finest is *Agios Georgios* (see map). You should definitely put out any candles which have been lit in the churches, as there is no fire brigade on the island! A policeman and a doctor from the mainland are stationed there.

Karavi: The harbour of Gavdos, with two tavernas and some private rooms.

Sarakiniko Beach: Situated in the north east, this is the longest sandy beach on the island, and rises up into high dunes covered with vegetation. You cannot avoid noticing the tar here, together with plastic and other washed-up rubbish. The beach is quite flat underwater, with no shelving, and you can faintly make out the contours of Crete in the far-off haze.

Really primitive camping here; there is a well from which water can be obtained for washing by bucket on a rope; it is not drinking water. Only at the north end of the bay is there a stone cottage, which has two rooms for rent in summer (£4 each; cottage contains beds, but nothing else). It belongs to the sister of one of the taverna owners; she lives in Vatsiana, and her husband is the priest of Gavdos.

There are now nine simple wooden-built tavernas on the beach, in hard competition with each other. One of them is run by a German (sometimes blancmange, muesli, yoghurt with fruit etc. are available). You can no longer expect solitude here, as up to 200 people live in the vicinity of the beach in the summer. They are mostly Germans, and a large number of them are Hippies.

The beach is about 30 minutes on foot from the quay. First take the track leading to the main village of Kastri; this track then divides into two branches.

Kourfos Beach *(Yorgo's Beach)*: A wonderfully lonely beach only a few miles to the south of the quay, with a fine shingle beach and crystal clear water. Behind it stretches wild, primeval terrain, a dried-up river bed, and windswept pines and juniper trees . . . Yorgo, who is actually a builder from Chania, allows people to camp freely. He lives here in the summer with his young wife, child and elderly mother. His little taverna is situated on a hill, high above the sea. Next to it there are a couple of simple rooms which he rents out at c. £6 for a DR. Yorgo's wife does the cooking, while Jorgo catches the fish and takes care of the transport of the guests to and from the boats. Even at the end of August you can spend a couple of days completely alone here; in the high season, by contrast, there can sometimes be up to 40 people in the bay. But it has a large area, so people are not on top of one another. If you follow the course of the river into the hinterland, ten minutes' walk brings you to a spring in the rock wall, where Yorgo's mother does her washing and gets water.

Kastri: The little capital of Gavdos, situated right in the middle of the island. About 5 families are still living there. Kastri can be reached on foot from the quay in about 1 hour. There is a shop, which also functions as a taverna at the same time, where you can hand in letters for posting and make telephone calls. Stelios offers some beds here in dormitory-like accommodation for c. £3 per person. There is also a second kafenion/shop. The little island school is situated on the way to Vatsiana (at the moment it has one teacher and one pupil!), and the main building of the solar power plant, which supplies Kastri with electricity, is also a little outside the village.

Vatsiana: Situated between Kastri and Tripiti; the handful of houses that are inhabited, together with the empty ruins of others, form the southernmost village in Europe. A very poor-looking complex, and only the house belonging to the island priest is painted. You can walk from here to Tripiti in about 1.25 hours.

Tripiti: A shingle beach at the southernmost point of Gavdos and Europe, too. You can have yourself ferried over to the beach by boat or driven to Vatsiana by tractor, and then go the rest of the way on foot.

The steep promontory which borders the beach on the right (as seen from the beach) really is the *very southernmost point in Europe* (this was checked by one of our readers using a compass!). This continues in a northwesterly direction in the form of steep, inaccessible cliffs. The time needed to walk from Sarakiniko Beach to Tripiti is between 3 and 4 hours (you should certainly follow the "road" as far as Vatsiana.

From Chora Sfakion to Plakias

Panoramic road through one of the most beautiful coastal regions of Crete.

After the miles of plain around Frangokastello, behind which the foothills of the Lefka Ori rise in a massive arc, there is a winding road through almost alpine rock massifs. The highlight is the unique bay around Plakias!

• CONNECTIONS: There is only one bus in the afternoon from the bus station in Chora Sfakion to Agia Galini. Change at Selia or Mirthios for Plakias. Be there early, otherwise there will be no room left! Fare to Agia Galini costs c. £4.

Komitades: A village on the road, a few miles to the east of the cross-roads, where the road branches off to the north coast. Half of the village offers petrol from canisters. You should take up the offer if your tank seems rather empty; the next garage is at Plakias.

Frangokastello

A lonely Venetian castle on the sea, visible from afar. In a wide, almost steppe-like plain with fields of vegetables and ankle-high phrygana. Threatening rock massifs tower in the background, and white mountain villages cling to the slopes. There are scattered holiday homes and tavernas along the sea.

Peculiar to the place is the stillness, which is prevalent over the whole landscape. Only a couple of birds are twittering, the wind whistles; it is almost eery.

It is thus hardly surprising that Frangokastello is haunted. In 1828, during the War of Independence against the Turks, *Hatzimichalis Daliannis* defended the fortifications with 385 partisans against a greatly superior Turkish force. The defence was made in spite of urgent warnings from the local people. Frangokastello fell on 17th May. The Cretan resistance fighters lie buried in the coastal sands and every year, in May, they parade slowly past the fortification in the early morning half-light. They are called *Drosoulites,* the "spirits of the dew".

Frangokastello is haunted

For those who do not believe in ghosts, scientists believe that the phenomenon is due to the atmospheric reflection of the Libyan coast opposite, which can only occur in May because of the coincidence of different atmospheric factors.

Whatever the case may be, the beach in front of the castle is especially loved today by the younger generation, who are attracted here not only by the unusual atmosphere, the quiet and the wide landscape, but also by the fact that it is relatively untouched by tourism on a large scale. The disadvantage is the marshy character of the beach region, which is especially attractive to flies that sting (see also reader's tip further on).

There is a much nicer beach a little more to the east.

• CONNECTIONS: Only some of the buses go right down to the beach, which is about 1.25 miles to the south of the through road. Otherwise they stop in the little hamlets of **Patsianos** and **Kapsodasos**. You can walk comfortably from both of these villages to the castle and the sea.

Accommodation

There are simple private rooms to be had in the handful of tavernas below the fort, eg in the taverna directly below it and right on the water's edge, down from the round tower. The rooms in the taverna further to the west by the former mill seemed better to us, as did those in the neighbouring Hotel/Taverna Koral.

• **Kali**: an attractive place to stay, even if it is very simple. Situated a little behind the beach (on the approach road from the castle about 100 yards to the west), about £6 for a DR. Also functions as a café, and is an agreeable place to sit under tamarisks and vines on the terrace. The young owner is very friendly.

• **Petros**: Taverna offering good food on the gravel road which runs up to the road west of the castle. Terrace covered with vines and a very nice proprietor, who also rents out rooms. Diagonally opposite the newly-built **Castello** apartments.

Because of the shortage of rooms and the relatively isolated nature of the region, many rucksack tourists sleep on the beach; apparently this is tolerated.

• READER'S TIP: "The beach at Frangokastello consists of a thin layer of sand over a layer of clay. During the autumn rains, water streams from the clay layer into the sea and you may have to retrieve your tent from a stream. The best thing to do is to camp close by the grassy border of the beach."

Sightseeing: The castle is a massive rectangle in shape with incredibly well-preserved external walls, battlements and watch towers. Of the houses inside, only the foundation walls are left. The inevitable Venetian lion roars down at the beach from over the gateway. The solid intersecting tower in the south-west corner is the best preserved, but unfortunately it is not possible to climb up onto the battlements.

In front of the fort is the lonely monument to the defeated leader Hatzimichalis.

Bathing: Beneath the fort is the delta-shaped beach which is not very extensive and has the disadvantages mentioned above. The beach is very shallow, and does not shelve. It is a favourite destination for excursions (boats from Plakias) and for this reason very crowded.

Almost a natural phenomenon by comparison is the deep bay about 500 yards to the east of the castle, amidst the picturesque steep coast with its vertical walls and boulders that have crashed down from above. Of particular note here are the massive sand dunes which extend upwards from the water to the edge of the precipice, and below there stretches an absolutely deserted, level sandy beach of the finest variety. A fantastic beach!

• OTHER INFORMATION: To cater for the mostly young public, even a disco called **Blue Sky** has now opened here.

The coastal road from Frangokastello goes up into the mountains in the direction of Plakias. The stony slopes are absolutely covered with herb bushes, and bizarre rocks tower upwards on both sides of the road. Beyond *Skaloti* and on through *Argoules* there is a stretch of bumpy dust track a few miles long, though this is getting constantly shorter. Shortly before the Bay of Rodakino there is a wonderful view over as far as the white cliffs of Matala.

Ano Rodakino: A mountain village which still seems largely original in character, with ancient stone houses and a richly-endowed church. Picturesque setting on a plateau above the sea. The inhabitants often wear the traditional island dress.

• ACCOMMODATION: **Sephakakis Rooms**, in the middle of the village on the road. This whitewashed building with a small courtyard and blue painted steps and window shutters would certainly be a most attractive place to stay.

Kato Rodakino: separated from Ano Rodakino by a steep walled ravine, which opens out below and ends at Koraka Beach. The ravine is crossed via some hair-raising sharp bends. An agreeable taverna on the slope side of the road invites you to take a rest.

• ACCOMMODATION: The newly-built **Apollonia** private rooms are not far from the turn-off to Koraka Beach, and there are more rooms at the taverna on the through road, in the direction of the eastern exit from the village.

Koraka Beach: At the western entrance to the village of Kato Rodakino, an asphalt road leads down to a grey sand and shingle beach 1.25 miles away. It is about 400 yards long, shadeless, and without amenities at present. Some bizarre black cliff walls form a separate bay at the eastern end. A driveway leads to more little beaches to the west, and a newly-opened taverna.

The road on to Plakias has been newly constructed and is wider in some places, whereas in others it is narrower and more winding. The scenery changes constantly, varying between desert-like moonscapes which are devoid of human life, sharply-edged boulders and a thin cover of thistle and herb bushes.

The first view of Plakias is grandiose. The rounded grey crests of the *Kedros range* and behind them the *Ida mountains* stretch further into the distance than the eye can see. Deep down below, between wild rocky peaks, there is the circular bay of Plakias with its wide sandy beach. The two rocky *Paximadi Islands* seem to swim out at sea and the outline of Gavdos Island is faintly visible in the haze. The mountain villages of *Selia* and *Mirthios* lie among the olive trees on the long, drawn-out slopes and in the straw-coloured grazing land, as if daubed into the picture by a giant paintbrush. This "composition" is most impressive in the late afternoon, when the sun is sinking and bathes everything in a warm light.

Selia: A grey-white mountain village, crowned by a striking church on a rocky bluff. Narrow main road, some private rooms for rent. The village retains much of its original character.

Kotsifou Gorge: The road forks at the southern exit from the steeply walled ravine. One way goes over to Mirthios, but the main road runs northwards through the gorge into the fertile plain around *Agios* *loannis.* A whole forest opens out here: cypresses, olives, apples, vines, figs and sunflowers.

Via *Agouseliana* with its real "jewel" of a church, the road meets up with the main road, which runs through a wide valley on its way from Rethymnon to Agia Galini (for more information see under Agia Galini).

You often meet the Papás of Plakias playing tavli

Plakias

Worthwhile because of the landscape; miles of sandy beach; good tavernas and dozens of places to stay

Plakias was for many years a hot tip on the southern coast. An enormous, hollowed-out valley, enclosed by steep mountain peaks, a beach of fine sand that you could go crazy over; the village itself only a handful of modest little houses, with two kafenia and a taverna, and two original mountain villages up above on the slope. What more could you want?

Today, Plakias has been discovered; the beach is just as nice as it was before, and so is the archaic mountain landscape in the area. But the place itself almost gives you a fright. Building, investment, calculations: all these are going on in Plakias. The annual flood of tourists has become a dominating factor in the lives of the inhabitants. There is a whole quarter with newly-built hotels and private rooms, the place has more than 20 tavernas, and the stereotyped, half-finished skeletons of buildings point to a "built-up" future. In the space of a few years, Plakias has made the transition from a lonely coastal village, which was a hot tip among rucksack tourists, to a favourite destination for package tourists. The money is rolling in, there is more and more work, and certainly more worry, too.

Thanks to the beauty of the landscape, Plakias continues to be a worthwhile destination for holidaymakers of every hue. It is especially suitable for those who like bathing. Now there is even a sewage disposal plant behind the village.

CONNECTIONS

• **Bus**: From and to **Rethymnon** c. 7 x daily, **Agia Galini** 4 x daily (it is sometimes necessary to change buses in Bale, on the road from Rethymnon to Ag. Galini), **Frangokastello/Chora Sfakion** 1 x. The bus stop is directly in front of the Hotel Livikon at the beginning of the village. The newest timetable is always on display here and you can wait in comfort on the terrace and have some coffee.

• TELEPHONE: At present there is no OTE Office in the village; calls are only possible from hotels or private telephones, and considerable surcharges are levied.

• TRAVEL AGENCIES: **Candia Tours** at

• **Boat**: About 2 x weekly there is a boat from Plakias to Agia Galini, costing c. £4, no return journey possible. Otherwise there are boats several times a week to Preveli Beach and Frangokastello. Information and bookings in the travel agency Candia Tours (see below).

• **Motor bike/moped rentals**: Best from Nikos, the friendly and conscientious proprietor of **Motoplakias** (Panser Rent), directly in the centre on the promenade.

— ★ —

the Lamon Guest House organises excursions, car rentals.

• NEWSPAPERS/MAGAZINES: international selection in the supermarket next to Hotel Livikon.

Accommodation

As almost every house was built with a view to renting out rooms, there is an enormous selection to choose from.

• **Alianthos Beach**: B class, a modern, whitewashed building with rounded arches. Situated before the actual village in the "new quarter" c. 100 yards to the right of the road. Quite immaculate, pleasantly cool and architecturally interesting, with angular passages, small inner courtyard, flowers on the parapets

and balconies. Rooms have well-made wooden furniture, colourful floor paving, comfortable upholstered armchairs. Bathrooms with bathtubs. Cost c. £22 for a DR. Tel. 0832/31227. There is a large swimming pool in front of the house, but there is unfortunately no shade there.

• **Alianthos**: C class; on the approach road to the village, only 100 yards from Alianthos Beach. Old established family hotel, simple but well-kept, passages painted in blue wash with dark brown wood panelling. Rooms have passable furniture, bathroom/showers are rather small, and there are balconies. Large restaurant, and you only have to cross the road for a swim. Cost c. £12. Tel. 0832/31227.

• **Lofos**: C class, in a fine position on a hill. Take the turning next to the Youth Hostel. Friendly atmosphere, and the proprietor and his family speak good English. Cost about £18 for a DR. Tel. 0832/31422.

• **Lamon**: B class guest house on the shore road, a little further than the Alianthos. Large amount of wood used in the interior, large restaurant, terrace. A long tunnel at the back, bare courtyard, rooms of differing quality, with rough whitewashed walls and upholstered chairs. Bathrooms OK. If possible, take a room on the front; large balconies with wooden balustrades. Mention must also be made of the friendly staff, especially Yannis at reception (have a look at the guest book!) Cost. c. £14 without breakfast. Tel. 0832/31279.

• **Livikon**: C class, simple but OK. Light coloured wooden furniture in the rooms, shower partition in the room, balcony. Also on the shore road. Cost. c. £9 for a DR. Tel. 0832/31216.

Private Rooms

Any number of these, both in the newly-built quarter of the village and in the village centre itself. In the new quarter in particular, some of the little white houses are really smart.

• **Christos**: taverna on the little harbour In the middle of the village. Simple accommodation here, but nice because it is directly on the water. Rooms on the upper floor with a balcony running around it. Own shower/WC. DR costs c. £8.

• **Mimosa**: newly-built apartments on the way to the camping site (turn up by the Pizzeria Zorbas). **Thetis Rooms** are also situated here (see reader's tip below).

• The **Villa** on the same path (behind the newly-built apartments) has not as yet been given a name. About 150 yards on the left, a little back from the path. Large

garden with orange and olive trees, and a large balcony on the first floor with a beautiful view over the trees to the sea. About £9 for a DR.

• **Paliakremnos**: a taverna standing alone at the eastern end of the beach, shortly before the rocky cliff wall. About £9 for a DR. Ideal if you like an early morning swim. About 20 minutes to the village on foot.

O Finikas: taverna which also has rooms for rent. Quiet position on a hill on the approach road, about 0.6 miles before the village. Wonderful panoramic view.

— ★ —

• **Readers' tips**: "**Thetis Rooms**, established 1987; on the way to the camping site, c. 100 yards on the left. A new building with steps and balconies, DR c. £10 - bedroom, Shower/WC, small kitchen with refrigerator, small gas cooker and sink."

"**Haus Panorama**, run by Evangelia Baradaki, is situated high above the bay. New and very clean, and use of the kitchen and fridge is permitted. Very friendly owner, and reasonably priced."

— ★ —

• **Youth Hostel**: This has been situated on the approach road, shortly before Plakias, since 1983. Friendly house with small garden, terrace, music, use of refrigerator. Philippo, the proprietor, is a very

nice person but hardly ever seen. Reductions on windsurfing and a free drink in the disco for hostellers. One night's stay costs c. £2. Tel. 0832/31202.

• CAMPING PLAKIAS: A very modest little site, but there is grass and a lot of shade through massive old olive trees. Sanitation awful, often blocked. Facilities: a bar (sometimes open), and a mini-shop at the entrance. The single employee does not take much care of the site. Advantage: personal atmosphere, everyone knows everyone else, and in addition it is dirt cheap. Reached from the shore road either by going through the alley by the Lamion (c. 300 yards, signposted) or turning up by the Pizzeria Zorbas and it is c. 150 yards along on the right.

People also camp freely at the end of the beach, in front of the high rocky cliff (see also under Plakias/surrounding area).

Food

• **Sofia**: the market leader, named after the proprietress, the legendary Sofia. This was already the favourite taverna years ago, when only rucksack tourists came to Plakias. In the meantime the Drimakis family have fully modernised the taverna, greatly increased the seating and have had to employ more waiters to keep control of the crowds. Very good food with a huge menu, in particular with every kind of meat dish, also in clay pots. Not cheap, however.

• **Christos**: the last taverna in the row of restaurants on the waterfront. Directly next to the tiny harbour on a small, projecting tongue of land. It is nice to sit here under the taverna's own trees, and there is mostly less bustle here than at Sofia, for example. Also notably more reasonable, where prices are concerned.

• **Lysseos**: in front of the bridge on the shore road, set at a slightly lower level. New, but despite this it has definitely become a favourite. Excellent Cypriot-Greek food.

• **Zorbas**: Pizzeria right after the bridge. Very good pizzas, but not very cheap.

• **Manoussos**: in the newly-built quarter; small gravel garden with olive trees. Relatively cheap and quiet.

• **Secret Nest**: fish taverna; as the name implies, it is hidden behind the harbour promenade.

• **O Tasomanolis**: to the west of the Christos, round the corner. Away from the bustle. Mostly fish here, too.

NIGHT LIFE

• **Swing Dancing Bar**: two houses after the Sofia Taverna; this is **the** in-place in the evenings (especially out of the high season when the disco is closed). Chic music and clientele. Belongs in fact to the son of the village priest of Plakias, who can sometimes be seen in the bar.

• **Pub House**: around the corner from the Swing Dancing Bar (behind Moped Rentals). Noisy rock music from the sixties and seventies (even Jimmy Hendrix), agreeable little garden in front.

• **Discotheque Meltemi**: a house standing by itself on the beach, and cannot be missed. Guests from the Youth Hostel get a free drink here.

• **Calypso Village**: luxurious large hotel of the A class, to the east of Plakias in the mountains. There are musical evenings at the weekends, with dancing, lyra and laouto; these are especially loved by the Cretans. At the crossroads, where the road from Plakias forks to Mirthios and Lefkogia, an extremely steep track leads down by the garage over a distance of several miles to the hotel.

▶ **Bathing**: The wide shingle/gravel beach is a good 1.25 miles long. The further you go towards the eastern end, the finer and softer the sand, and there are even a few sand dunes. There are mostly a few tents here under the tamarisks on the beach, and behind them a taverna has rooms for rent. The new Plakias Bay Hotel is situated in front of the rocky cliff. There are also surf boards for hire, as Plakias is a wind-trap and a favourite surfing spot in the region.

The beach is bordered at its eastern end by a towering, almost vertical rock wall. The nearer you get to it, the more gigantic it seems. You can walk along a little path at the foot of the wall; it finishes in a dark hole, which goes into the mountain for a distance of about 50 yards. You can walk in without any problem if you have a torch; the hole ends in two apparently artificial excavations in the rock. These might perhaps have been part of a defensive structure dating from the Second World War.

Plakias/Surrounding Area

Suda Beach: This lies to the west of Plakias. In contrast to the east (Damnoni and Ammoudi) this area is very little known. A walk of about 40 minutes brings you to a beautiful gravel beach, which has always been completely deserted until now. A taverna was built there in 1987, and showers were installed. The owner would be very pleased if motor caravans and rucksack tourists were to find their way there in the coming years. This will certainly happen, if the future of Damnoni really develops as I have outlined below.

Damnoni: A few miles to the east of Plakias, and can be reached from the road to Lefkogia (signposted). Wonderful fine gravel beach, about 500 yards of it. There are two tavernas and several showers, and a small stream flows into the sea here. Mainly young people find their way here, and many are established guests who return every year.

• ACCOMMODATION: mostly camping on the beach at Damnoni. **Stavros**, the owner of the beach taverna, allows camping on his property. There is good food in the taverna behind it, called **Akti**, and rooms with shower/toilet can also be had for c. £9. Tourist buses arrive here daily for lunch.

SURROUNDING AREA: two beautiful bays with fine gravel are situated about 10 minutes to the east of Damnoni Beach. In the first one, which is known as the **Bay of Pigs**, the water soon becomes deep (take care with children). The second, the so-called **Mikro Ammoudi Beach**, is a particularly charming place. There is even an underwater passage between the two, super to snorkel through!

> **Info 1988**: Two hotels are being built at Damnoni! Stavros thinks that everything will stay as it is until the end of 1989. Then the hotels will have been completed and those who sleep on the beach may have to look for a new place.

Ammoudi Beach: A short distance to the east from Damnoni, and can also be reached from the road to Lefkogia. A beautiful bay with fine white gravel, a few tamarisks and some showers (most of which are out of order) at the water's edge. Ammoudi Beach is bordered on both sides by jagged-edged cliffs, which are super for climbing. There is also the mouth of a little stream here.

• ACCOMMODATION/FOOD: **Pension Ammoudi**, rather hidden on the left hand side of the approach road to the beach. Pleasant taverna with friendly proprietors, very clean rooms with own shower/WC and balcony. Nice gravel terrace roofed over with reeds behind the house. Cost c. £10 for a DR. About 200 yards to the beach.
There is the occasional tent pitched on the beach.

Mirthios

This attractive mountain village clings to the slope high above Plakias. The narrow stepped alleys, in which you almost feel like an intruder, are a colourful mixture of houses of more recent date and old cottages with their dark and stuffy all-purpose main rooms - bed, cooking niche, chair . . . The Youth Hostel is much-favoured by rucksack tourists, and guests come up here from Plakias especially to eat; there is a fabulous view of the bay from the terrace-like through road, which has been widened.

• CONNECTIONS: **Buses** to Plakias mostly run via Mirthios and stop on the square below the youth hostel.

• ACCOMMODATION: **Rent Lux Rooms**, the sign proudly announces. And it's true, too, in comparison to the accommodation offered at the almost neighbouring Youth Hostel. Clean rooms with good wooden beds and private shower/toilet. Cost c. £9 for a single night, 2 days or more £8. Friendly proprietress.

• MIRTHIOS YOUTH HOSTEL: a favourite meeting point and a colourfully-furnished place to exchange contacts is provided by the hostel leader Steve. There are 48 beds in summer, and 35 in winter (the sexes are not separated). Wonderful panoramic view from the terrace (roof garden), with a reasonably-priced taverna below it. Always something going on here: wine, music, parties. Unfortunately there is only one single warm shower. Tel. 0832/31202.

• FOOD: either at **Giorgio's** taverna below the youth hostel, where you can also sit on the terrace on the road, with a panoramic view; or a few paces further on at the **Antámosi** taverna run by Basiliyannis, with a super view from the balcony.

A walk from Mirthios to Plakias: There are extensive little forests of olive trees between the two villages. The walk takes about 45 minutes.
Go along the road from Giorgio's taverna to the building with the sign "Dairy Cheese Serving Breakfast" (there is a little chapel opposite). This is where the path begins.
Go down the steps to the corner of the building, then straight on (do not take the steps going down on the left), taking the little path alongside the stone wall beside a stream. Crossing over an irrigation canal, you reach a wide field track. Go down this to the left and past three rocks; 10 yards after that, turn right down a small path. After 20 yards you come to two fences; go straight on. Follow this route over a little hill and go past a water hydrant, then there is a short steep stretch and you are once again on a field path. Turn to the right

here, and there is a path leading down on the left 20 yards on. This narrow way brings you past a water pipe and on to a wider road. Follow this to the left as far as a piled-up mound of earth, and here the way leads down through olive trees. Then further on over a kind of stony heath, where there are a lot of herb bushes, eg sage and oregano. Go past the carob tree along the path, into the olive grove and past the bamboo, until you come to the final field path. Follow this to the left as far as an iron gate (on the left hand side), go down to the right by the house after you have walked a further 50 yards, and then past the camping site. You arrive at the bridge in Plakias, just before the actual beginning of the village. We wish all "boy scouts/girl guides" good luck!

Lefkogia

A friendly farming village east of Plakias, the last village before the Monastery of Preveli. The crossroads at the centre entices you to take a rest, with its simple kafenion and the little café bar.

A steep, signposted track leads up to the lonely Skinaria Beach Hotel. Ideal for those who like to spend their holiday in the middle of nature, away from any village.

• **Skinaria Beach Hotel**: C class, about 2 miles from Lefkogia, in a solitary position amid a bizarre cliff landscape. 200 yards in front of it there is a beautiful sandy bay; the hotel is the only building far and wide! 33 very simply furnished rooms with shower/toilet. DR c. £22. Single room (also for two people with convertible beds) for £15. You are paying for the situation and the peace and quiet here, rather than for comfort. There is a small swimming pool. Tel. 0831/23782.

To the Monastery of Preveli

About 0.6 mile east of Lefkogia, an asphalt road (signposted) branches off the main through road.

This leads into the fertile river valley of the Kourtalioti, which is generally known as *Megalopotamos* (the great river). The lush vegetation of beautiful cedars, cypresses, carob and plane trees is a wonderful sight.

About 1.25 miles further on the left hand side of the road there is a *bridge*, which was built in the 19th century on Venetian lines. It spans a wide river which flows quite strongly, even in summer, in a perfectly-formed and elegant arc. The excellently-preserved cobbling on the upper side of the bridge can clearly be seen, and high water marks show the water level when the snows are melting. This is an ideal place to have a rest, with its glass clear water and strong cedars! The road forks here; straight on leads to the Monastery of Preveli, while a gravel track leads off to the left over the stream to the beach at Preveli (see below).

A little later, after a short climb, the grey-black ruins of the Monastery of Kato Preveli (actually called *Moni Mega Potamou,* the Monastery of the Great River) can be seen on the left hand side of the road to the present-day monastery.

Kato Preveli: This rambling settlement is situated in a slightly elevated position on the edge of the fertile river valley. The view of the steep slopes which rise behind it is a very beautiful one.

Kato Preveli was actually only a subsidiary monastery of Preveli Monastery. It was completely burned down at the beginning of the 19th century during the revolt against Turkish domination and has remained abandoned since then. The walls of the buildings and the pointed chimneys are still very well preserved, and the rafters of the upper storey are still in place. Numerous rooms where the monks lived can be recognised inside the ruins, and there are also stalls with hay mangers; the chapel contains the remains of choir stalls and a wooden iconostasis. You can wander at leisure through the complicated terraced buildings, and climb up on the flat roofs to enjoy the view. As can be deduced from the quite modern graffiti on the wall, the ruins were frequently used in earlier years by young travellers as a place to spend the night.

The motor road now goes in a curve away from the river valley and winds up the barren, rust-brown rocky slopes. The deep cutting of the ravine here is a superb feature of the landscape; the Megalopotamos flows along its floor. There are wonderful views far out over the sea, and on clear days you can see as far as Matala and the offshore Paximadi Islands.

The Monastery of Preveli is at the end of the road, 560 feet above sea level.

TIP: The other way to get to the Monastery of Preveli is also extremely attractive to hikers: this involves walking to **Gianiou** (south of Lefkogia) and then on to the monastery, in a one hour walk across the mountain.

Monastery of Preveli

Definitely an attractive monastery, far away from any village in the middle of the rugged rocky landscape.

There are only sparse trees around the monastery; bleak scrub and bare rocky slopes extend down to the sea. A forest fire raged here a few years ago and completely decimated the already sparse vegetation.

A huge door admits you to the airy, spacious monastery complex with its courtyards arranged on terraces, which are bordered towards the slope by farm buildings and the monks' cells. The entrances to the monks' living quarters are especially attractive with their trailing vines and stone benches. The *monastery church* with its two naves is

The Monastery of Preveli was a centre of resistance during the Second World War

situated in the upper courtyard; opposite the main entrance there is the former *guest house* of the monastery, and next to it, under a wide spreading Aleppo pine, there is the little *museum*.

In the 18th and 19th centuries, the Monastery of Preveli was one of the most important centres of resistance against the Turks. It even had a secret assembly room, which could be entered by a door in the back wall of the monastery. This is where the resistance fighters from the mountains met with the monks, who provided them with food and weapons and kept them up to date with the latest news. For this reason, the monastery was razed to the ground and destroyed several times, the last in 1867. During the Second World War too, Preveli served as a secret hiding place for numerous soldiers from Britain, Australia and New Zealand; with the active help of the monks they were able to remain hidden from German troops here until the Allies could evacuate them by submarine from the beach at the mouth of the Megalopotamos. Thus the Germans confiscated the entire possessions of the monastery, especially the animals. Today, there are only 3-4 very elderly monks in residence here.

● VISITING TIMES: daily 8.00 a.m.-1.00 p.m., 5.00 p.m.-7.00 p.m. Long trousers are obligatory. The church and the museum (admission c. £0.50) are only opened by their custodian for a short time, whenever a group of tourists arrives.

A tour of the monastery: The *monastery church* was built in 1836 and restored in 1911. Inside it, there is a beautiful altar wall (*iconostasis*) of cypress wood (which is, by the way, a symbol of eternity because of its durability), the richly carved bishop's chair and pulpit. The large number of little votive offerings (*taximata*) is noticeable; people place these here in the hope that their eye-diseases will be healed. The

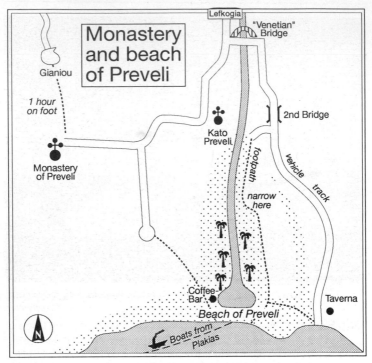

Monastery and beach of Preveli

monastery is especially well-known for this. Here, too, is the most valuable piece in the whole monastery, the *Golden Cross* containing a splinter from the True Cross itself. This is used every year to bless all those with eye diseases, in a ceremony which takes place on 8th May, the date of the greatest festival of the monastery.

The **museum** under the beautiful Aleppo pine (planted in 1890) houses the ecclesiastical treasures of the monastery, including gilded chalices and crosses, richly-embroidered abbots' robes and old icons. On the outside wall there is a small *memorial plaque*, put there on 24th May 1985, on which the Allied military forces express their gratitude to the monks and the surrounding villages for their help in the escapes during the war.

There is an attractive *fountain* in the courtyard below the church, and an old *oil press* in the room next to it, attesting to the agricultural activities of the monastery. Preveli was once one of the richest monasteries in Crete, with the greatest estates and the best agricultural organisation. The monks and their secular assistants produced olive oil, planted fruit trees, vegetables and corn, reared goats and pigs and even kept silkworms.

Palms, fresh water, rapids: you can live on the beach at Preveli

The Beach at Preveli

A crowning conclusion; the beach deep down below at the exit of the river valley is without doubt one of the nicest, if not *the* **nicest place to bathe on the island!**

Those who drive along the road through the barren rocks to the monastery can have no inkling of what they are missing only a few hundred feet below them. An almost subtropical jungle of beautiful date palms, eucalyptus, oleander and many other trees and bushes opens out on both sides of the glass-clear river. This forms a lagoon where it enters the sea, and in front of it is a soft, white sandy beach. The whole thing is surrounded by towering rocky walls, which almost make you dizzy when you look upwards, especially at the back of the valley. Comparisons with "paradise" or the "Garden of Eden" come to mind.

However, you must not expect a heavenly solitude here; the beach at Preveli has been firmly in the hands of rucksack tourists for years. They spend weeks, sometimes months in what is perhaps the most fascinating bay on Crete. Everything necessary for living is to be found here: large quantities of fresh water, shade, contacts. You can pitch your tent under a palm tree, as police checks have not been usual up to the present. A place where it is easy to forget civilisation; instead, you can hear the rushing of the swirling river, try to catch fish, take a walk along the river and see what you can discover, or paint the rocks with brilliant colours and fantastic patterns. "Thank you Crete" is written on one stone, and is certainly intended as a motto. Those who can say this have taken something home with them . . .

• HOW TO GET THERE: There are two possibilities for those with vehicles. The most comfortable of these is to take the road to the Monastery of Preveli and about 0.9 miles before the monastery, turn left up a track (visible over a long distance) over a bare hill plateau above the river valley. This is very bumpy in places, and those who think their vehicles are able to take it can go to the end and leave their cars there (locked!). Otherwise you can park in the hollow before the steep climb, or on the road. At the end of the track (about 500 yards from the road), there is a climb of about 20 mins. down the left of the rocky slope into the bay. A little difficult, but it can certainly be done.

The other motor road goes past the **"Venetian Bridge"** over the Megalopotamos mentioned above, forks to the right immediately after the river and leads in a wide arc across the river valley into the easterly neighbouring bay of the "Palm Beach" as it is sometimes called. There is a taverna in total isolation on this not very prepossessing shingle beach, and as of late there are also reports of rooms for rent. Now you have to climb to the right over the rocks, along the path marked in red. This brings you to the Palm Beach after about 15 mins. If you intend to spend the night here, your vehicle is safer here than at the places mentioned in the first route.

• WALKING: Those who are on foot and want to get to their destination quickly should follow the route just described. It is a walk of about 4.75 miles to the beach from the place where the road to the Monastery of Preveli branches off the through road at Lefkogia. The bus will stop at the crossroads on request. Hitch-hiking is no problem.

The **direct** way on foot across the river valley is only possible with detours, because of one impassable narrow place. For those who have the necessary time, the beach can be reached along the river valley from the "Venetian Bridge" in c. 2.5 hours, by climbing up to the upper edge of the ravine at the narrow point (super view down into the ravine!) and walking from there to the sea, where the descent again poses no problems. However, this route is difficult if you are carrying baggage, as it sometimes goes through areas without a path. Take the vehicle track over the Megalopotamos as described above (turn right after the bridge). After a second cobbled bridge a narrow way branches off to the right into the river valley. You reach the narrow place as already mentioned in about 1.5 hours, and get round it by climbing up to the left.

• FACILITIES: The marked Cretan flair for business has of course reached into the farthest corner of the island. Yorgos, an elderly Cretan, has opened a **café-bar** down on the beach. Every-day, he trudges down the rocky slope with his mules and brings supplies to the little house built of piled-up stones. He offers milk, coffee, bottled water, cola, beer and lemonade, all cooled in water, as there is

of course no electricity or refrigerator. But you can also buy tinned foods, bread and various other provisions, though understandably at a slightly higher price. Places for shopping for Preveli Beach are **Lefkogia** and the tiny village of **Gianiou**, c. 2.5 miles to the north of the Monastery of Preveli (about 1 hour on foot from the monastery in a northerly direction).

• OTHER INFORMATION: The number of rucksack tourists brings of course the usual problems with it. Thus some secluded little places in the shade of a palm tree have been turned into rubbish heaps.

You should beware of **petty thieving**, but above all painstakingly careful with **open fires!** Some of the wonderful palm trees here have already been burnt to the ground in recent years; you can still see their charred remains.

Please do not count on the beach at Preveli staying exactly as I have described it for years to come. Even now the excursion boats from Plakias arrive here almost daily, crowded with day trippers, who then populate the beach. The taverna in the neighbouring bay already signals the approach of organised tourism.

Help us update

We've done our best to make this book as accurate and up-to-date as possible but travel developments are swift and things are always changing. We would greatly appreciate any contributions, suggestions, corrections, improvements or additions you may have for future editions.

Please write us:

Springfield Books Limited c/o Eberhard Fohrer, Norman Road, Denby Dale, Huddersfield HD8 8TH, West Yorkshire, England

Notices